Economics of Cities

Because cities are likely to play an even more predominant role in the global economy in the future than they do at present, it is important to understand how urban centers are created, grow, and function in the process of generating and distributing wealth. This integrated collection of essays exploring the new economic theories concerning cities assembles recent work by a number of the world's leading experts in North America, the United Kingdom and Europe, and Japan. Topics investigated include cities and agglomeration, urban systems, urbanization and growth, and cities and factor markets. The perspectives the editors and contributors offer have strong connections with several branches of modern economics, including industrial organization, public economics, international trade, and endogenous growth and economic development.

Jean-Marie Huriot is Professor of Economics at the Université de Bourgogne (France). He is a recognized authority on urban and spatial economics. Professor Huriot is the author of numerous refereed papers and books in English and French, including *Von Thünen: Economie et espace*, published by Economica (France).

Jacques-François Thisse, a Fellow of the Econometric Society, is Professor of Economics at CORE, Université Catholique de Louvain (Belgium). He has been director of CERAS (France) and a visiting professor at the University of Pennsylvania. The author of nearly 140 papers in refereed journals such as *Econometrica, American Economic Review*, and *Review of Economic Studies*, he is the editor of several books and coauthor of *Discrete Choice Theory of Product Differentiation* (MIT Press).

T0324100

Economics of Cities

THEORETICAL PERSPECTIVES

Edited by

Jean-Marie Huriot
Université de Bourgogne

Jacques-François Thisse
Université Catholique de Louvain

CAMBRIDGE UNIVERSITY PRESS
Cambridge, New York, Melbourne, Madrid, Cape Town, Singapore, São Paulo, Delhi

Cambridge University Press
The Edinburgh Building, Cambridge CB2 8RU, UK

Published in the United States of America by Cambridge University Press, New York

www.cambridge.org
Information on this title: www.cambridge.org/9780521118279

© Jean-Marie Huriot and Jacques-François Thisse 2000

First published 2000
This digitally printed version 2009

A catalogue record for this publication is available from the British Library

Library of Congress Cataloguing in Publication data
Huriot, Jean-Marie, 1945–

Economics of cities : theoretical perspectives / Jean-Marie Huriot, Jacques-François Thisse.

   p. cm.

Includes bibliographical references.

ISBN 0-521-64190-X (hardbound)

1. Cities and towns – Economic aspects. 2. Cities and towns – Growth. 3. Economic
development. 4. Sociology, Urban. I. Thisse, Jacques-François. II. Title.
HT151.H88   1999
330.9173′2 – dc21   98–054608
                                                                CIP

ISBN 978-0-521-64190-6 hardback
ISBN 978-0-521-11827-9 paperback

Contents

Contents

Contributors

Hesham M. Abdel-Rahman
Department of Economics and
  Finance
University of New Orleans
2000 Lakeshore Drive
New Orleans, Louisiana 70148

Catherine Baumont
LATEC, Pôle d'Économie et de
  Gestion
Université de Bourgogne
2, boulevard Gabriel
Dijon F-21000
France

Randy Becker
Center for Economic Studies
Bureau of the Census
4700 Silver Hill Road,
  Rm. 211 WPII
Washington, DC 20233-6300

Jan K. Brueckner
Department of Economics
University of Illinois at
  Urbana-Champaign
1206 South Sixth Street
Champaign, Illinois 61820

Linda Harris Dobkins
Department of Economics
Emory & Henry College
Emory, Virginia 24327

Gilles Duranton
Department of Geography
London School of Economics
Houghton Street
London WC2A 2AE
United Kingdom

Masahisa Fujita
Institute of Economic Research
Kyoto University
Yoshida-Honmachi
Sakyo-ku, Kyoto
606-01 Japan

Thomas Gehrig
Institut zur Erforschung der
  wirtschaftlichen Entwicklung
Albert-Ludwigs-Universität Freiburg
Freiburg D-79085
Germany

Florence Goffette-Nagot
LATEC, Pôle d'Économie et de
    Gestion
Université de Bourgogne
2, boulevard Gabriel
Dijon F-21000
France

Vernon Henderson
Department of Economics
Brown University
Providence, Rhode
    Island 02912

Jean-Marie Huriot
LATEC, Pôle d'Économie et de
    Gestion
Université de Bourgogne
2, boulevard Gabriel
Dijon F-21000
France

Yannis M. Ioannides
Department of Economics
Tufts University
Medford, Massachusetts 02155

Hubert Jayet
MEDEE
Université de Lille 1
Lille
France

Paul Krugman
Department of Economics
Massachusetts Institute of
    Technology
Cambridge, Massachusetts 02139

Jacques-François Thisse
CORE, Université Catholique de
    Louvain
34, voie du Roman Pays
Louvain-la-Neuve B-1348
Belgium

Yves Zenou
CERAS, Ecole Nationale des Ponts
    et Chaussées
28, rue des Saints-Pères
Paris F-75343 cedex 07
France

Introduction

Jean-Marie Huriot and Jacques-François Thisse

Cities began to emerge in several parts of the world after the Neolithic revolution as a consequence of an increase in agricultural surplus. Their very existence may be viewed as a universal phenomenon whose importance was slowly, but regularly, increasing over the centuries before a sudden acceleration in urban growth during the nineteenth century in a small corner of Europe (Bairoch, 1985).

Although the sources of information are dispersed, not always trustworthy, and hardly comparable, the data clearly converge to show the existence of an *urban revolution*. In Europe, the proportion of the population living in cities increased from 10% in 1300 to 12% in 1800 (Bairoch, 1985). It rose to approximately 20% in 1850, 38% in 1900, and 52% in 1950, and it is now close to 75% (Bairoch, 1985; United Nations, 1994). In the United States, the degree of urbanization increased from 5% in 1800 to more than 60% in 1950 and is now near 77%. In Japan, the extent of urbanization was 14–15% in 1800 (Bairoch, 1985) and 50% in 1950, and it is now about 78% (United Nations, 1994). Worldwide, the urban population increased from 30% in 1950 to 45% in 1995 and will exceed 50% in 2005 (United Nations, 1994).

Thus, by the end of the twentieth century, about half of the world's population and three-quarters of Westerners will live in urban areas. The world's urban population currently increases each year by a number equivalent to the population of Spain. Furthermore, concentration in very large cities keeps rising. In 1950, only two cities had populations above 10 million: New York City and Greater London. In 1995, 15 cities belonged to this category. The largest one, Tokyo, with more than 26 million, exceeds the second one, New York, by 10 million. In 2025, 26 mega-cities will exceed 10 million (United Nations, 1994). But such data provide only a very partial description of the urbanization process, as they do not reveal the important changes that have occurred in the *nature* of cities from the time of the city-states of ancient Greece to the metropolises of our time.

Let us briefly examine the main historical changes. The history of cities in the Western world shows a succession of three major types of cities: pre-industrial, industrial, and post-industrial cities. Pre-industrial cities were dominated by the economic power of landowners and the activities of merchants and individual craftsmen. Industrial cities were places of specialized and integrated production in manufacturing, resulting from the Industrial Revolution and the separation between capital owners and workers. Post-industrial cities have resulted from the rise of the service economy and, more recently, from the information revolution. This implies significant changes in the economic nature and composition of cities. At present, economic power and city growth both depend on new tertiary activities such as financial and producer services, research and development, planning, and business administration and, in general, on activities specialized in decision-making and control that are concentrated in cities much more than are manufacturing activities. This necessitates primary roles for education, skilled workers, and information exchanges. From 1920 to 1991, the proportion of the total employment to be found in the sector of producer services increased from 2.8% to 14% in the United States, from 0.8% to 9.6% in Japan, and from 1.6% to 10% in France (Castells, 1996).

Another major dimension of historical change is related to the spatial form of the city and to its separation from the countryside. In medieval Europe, that separation was signaled in two ways: a physical boundary (the walled city) and a legal status (the democratized city). Besides its defensive purpose, the wall was also the symbol of the city's political power. Historians agree that specific legal status was a major criterion for identifying the city, at least until the end of the Middle Ages (Duby, 1980; Bairoch, 1985), if not later on. This clear-cut separation no longer exists. Cities' legal status has been homogenized, except for minor exceptions, in most nations. Urban activities have gradually extended beyond the physical boundaries of the city to create suburbs that are now very much part of the extended economic agglomeration. As a result, the modern city is more dispersed and has fuzzy boundaries. It may also take very different forms ignored in the past, such as the megalopolis, the conurbation, or the urban region.

In addition, beyond the city fringe lies what Mumford (1961) called the *invisible city*, that is, the influence the urban core exerts over consumption, culture, and lifestyles even in the smallest villages because of dramatic advances in transportation and telecommunications. As a result, large cities now dominate modern societies in all areas of culture and human undertaking, whereas traditional towns often served as the nuclei for surrounding tracts of rural activities.

Yet present-day cities may differ from one part of the world to another. Large cities in the Third World differ from large cities in developed countries. On the one hand, they grow at a much faster pace, which possibly may result in a complete reordering of the world's top cities over the next 20 years. On the other hand, they do not have the same production structure and the same economic power at the international level. For example, it is well known that the main centers of financial and business services are London, New York, and Tokyo (Sassen, 1991). It is tempting to add Hong Kong, Singapore, Paris, Frankfurt,

Zurich, Amsterdam, Milan, and Toronto to the list. None of the largest cities of the developing countries appears in this list.

The foregoing suggests some provisional conclusions. First, population alone does not determine the economic significance of a city, which depends much more on the type and organization of economic activities that occur within it. Second, in parallel with the increasing urbanization of human societies, one sees a wide diversity of situations resulting in different urban configurations and systems. It is our contention, however, that beneath this multiplicity lie a few general principles that economic theory may help us to understand.

Cities were at the heart of early economic analyses. One of the first analyses of the emergence and role of cities can be found in the work of Cantillon (1755), who explained the organization of an abstract system of villages, market towns, and cities dominated by a primatial city. According to him, the origin of cities was to be found in the concentration of land ownership that allowed landowners to live at a distance from their estates in places where they "enjoy[ed] agreeable society," as well as in the agglomeration economy related to the landowners' demand, which attracted craftsmen and merchants. That idea is reminiscent of the *preference for variety* used in recent theories of economic agglomeration. Twenty years later, Smith (1776) explained cities on the basis of economic interactions, on the supply side featuring the organization of the division of labor, and on the demand side featuring a market size effect. Here also, that perspective concurs with modern analyses of city formation focusing on the role of intermediate inputs. In these views, the city is both a fundamental form of spatial organization and a key element of economic growth. However, urban economics languished for over a century and became part of mainstream economics only in the 1970s, as Catherine Baumont and Jean-Marie Huriot explain in their retrospective on urban economics in Chapter 2. See Mills (1972), Henderson (1977), and, more recently, Fujita (1989) for the primary texts.

Recently, growing numbers of economists have become interested in studying geographical issues. This increased interest has been fostered by the integration of national economies into trading blocks, such as the European Union and the North American Free Trade Agreement (NAFTA), and by their impact on the development of their corresponding regions and cities. As market integration dissolves economic barriers between nations, national boundaries no longer delineate the most natural unit of analysis. The issue seems important because the continuing growth of trade and especially the development of multinational production systems cast doubt on the relevance of the concept of national economy as the main framework of reference.

More fundamentally, perhaps, trade and exchange tend to develop more and more between large cities, suggesting that interregional and international trade might be replaced by inter-city trade. In this case, the city, more than the nation or the region, is the relevant frame of analysis. Cities must be considered as the main spatial devices allowing for interaction of the highly diversified and specialized economic agents who are at the source of technological and social innovations. In other words, *cities may be viewed as the engines of innovation and growth* in modern economies because they provide the quintessentially urban commodity: information (Jacobs, 1969).

At a very basic level, one may say that the main reason for the existence of cities lies in the presence of indivisibilities in economic and social activities. This was clearly stated as a necessary condition by Koopmans (1957, p. 154): "without recognizing indivisibilities in the human person, in residences, plants, equipment, and in transportation, urban location problems, down to those of the smallest village, cannot be understood."

Even the walled city exhibits increasing returns to scale, because it corresponds to a (local) public good whose supply is governed by size effects: The length of a circular wall is $2\pi r$, whereas the size of the enclosed area is πr^2. The ratio of the circumference to the area falls as r increases, so that a larger number of individuals can be defended at a lower average cost.

From a more general perspective, besides the innovations necessary to generate the agricultural surplus, a fundamental change in social structure was needed for the emergence of cities: *the division of labor into specialized activities*. And, indeed, there seems to be considerable agreement among economists, geographers, and historians to view increasing returns as the most critical factor in the emergence of cities. For example, according to Marshall (1989, p. 25), "apart from considerations related to defense, to royal whim, or to the supposed sacred importance of certain sites, the formation of towns made good economic sense in promoting a level of efficiency in commerce, manufacturing, and administration that would have been impossible to achieve with a completely dispersed population."

Increasing returns appear at the level of specific activities, either public or private, and in the aggregate when cities act as *economic multipliers*. The critical role played by increasing returns in city formation probably explains why this problem has been neglected for so long by mainstream economics, as well as why recent progress in economic theory has made it possible to analyze such problems in a much more relevant and vivid way (Krugman, 1995).

These multipliers can take different forms (see Fujita and Thisse, Chapter 1, this volume). For example, the presence of a large number of firms established within a given city implies a wide variety of locally available products (*varietas delectat*). This effect makes the city more attractive to consumers, so that more of them will choose to settle there. In turn, a larger pool of potential clients will attract more sellers, triggering a snowball effect that can give rise to an economic agglomeration. Similar forces are at work in the labor markets, where firms and workers interact by allowing a finer division of labor. More precisely, increasing returns to scale appear in the aggregate when firms can benefit from using a large array of intermediate products. Finally, informational externalities are likely to be even more crucial, in that they stress the driving forces of circulation of information, accumulation of human capital, and creation of intellectual resources (Lucas, 1988).

All these external effects foster the process of concentration of human activities and, subsequently, specializations in various geographical areas. They also explain why economic agents are prepared to pay high rents in order to live close to the centers of large cities, where these effects are most intense. Contrariwise, external effects such as pollution and crime, as well as high land rents, tend to deter further urban growth and therefore favor dispersion of activities. Among these negative effects, congestion is of fundamental importance insofar as it is intrinsically related to space itself.

What we now see is the emergence of a new economic theory of cities, more closely related to mainstream economics. This book rests on this new theory and may be described as a collective attempt to provide a partial answer to the following fundamental question: *Why do social and economic activities tend to agglomerate in a small number of places?* This new body of theory also deals with some contemporary concrete issues expressed through related questions investigated in this book: What are the main agglomeration or dispersion forces? (See Fujita and Thisse, Chapter 1.) Why do we have cities, and why do they specialize in different activities? (See Abdel-Rahman, Chapter 3; Becker and Henderson, Chapter 4; Fujita and Krugman, Chapter 5; Duranton, Chapter 8.) Why does proximity matter in the era of globalization, and why do cities continue to grow despite the information revolution, which allows for inexpensive interactions over vast distances? (See Fujita and Thisse, Chapter 1.) Why do we observe strong connections between city sizes and their rankings in the urban hierarchy (See Dobkins and Ioannides, Chapter 6.) What are the main reasons explaining the growth of the urban system? (See Duranton, Chapter 8.) What are the dynamics of cities, given that land is not malleable? (See Brueckner, Chapter 7.) How can a monocentric city generate secondary employment centers? (See Zenou, Chapter 10.) What is the empirical relevance of the monocentric paradigm? (See Goffette-Nagot, Chapter 9.) What are the relationships between cities and the emergence of specialized and fragmented labor markets? (See Zenou, Chapter 10; Jayet, Chapter 11.) What will be the impact of globalization on the geography of financial centers? (See Gehrig, Chapter 12.)

In order to try to answer these questions and others, one must consider various explanations and models focusing on different facets of the urban world. Indeed, it would be futile to believe that our need for human interaction could be the sole explanation for the existence of economic spaces corresponding to different stages of development. Furthermore, the variables explaining spatial or regional imbalance within a small country are likely to differ from those explaining economic imbalance between the North and the South. Yet, regardless of the problem under consideration, the creation of cities and economic agglomerations may be viewed as the outcome of a process involving two opposing types of forces, namely, *agglomeration forces* and *dispersion forces*. An economic agglomeration of specific activities is then considered as the result of a complicated balance of particular forces that push and pull consumers, workers, and producers.

The contributors to this book aim to identify some of the primary reasons why particular economic activities become established within cities. Two main approaches seem to emerge from the many recent contributions (see Becker and Henderson, Chapter 4). The first rests on the role of "big agents." In this case, the city is considered as the outcome of a social process involving guilds and city governments, or, nowadays, as the result of policies followed by local governments and land developers. The second approach stresses the role of "many small agents," typically entrepreneurs and workers/consumers, who benefit from the greater division of labor generated by their gathering within a limited area. Both approaches will be discussed in several chapters.

Unlike earlier theories concerning location, the new economic theory of cities developed in this book has strong connections with several branches of modern economics, including industrial organization and public economics, but also the new theories of international trade and of endogenous growth and economic development. This suggests that this field has great potential for further development and that cross-fertilization can be expected. It would be premature to claim that the new economic view of cities has gained complete primacy, but we believe that the recent contributions have been sufficiently rich as to invite economists and social scientists to reconsider the role of cities in economic life and to suggest that cities will be important actors on the economic stage of the future.

References

Bairoch, P. (1985). *De Jéricho à Mexico. Villes et économie dans l'histoire*. Paris: Gallimard. English translation (1988): *Cities and Economic Development: From the Dawn of History to the Present*. University of Chicago Press.

Cantillon, R. (1755). *Essai sur la nature du commerce en général*. London: Fletcher. English translation by H. Higgs, reprinted 1964. New York: A. M. Kelley.

Castells, M. (1996). *The Rise of the Network Society*. Oxford: Blackwell.

Duby, G. (1980). *Histoire de la France urbaine*, vol. 1. Paris: Seuil.

Fujita, M. (1989). *Urban Economic Theory. Land Use and City Size*. Cambridge University Press.

Henderson, J. V. (1977). *Economic Theory and the Cities*. Orlando: Academic Press.

Jacobs, J. (1969). *The Economy of Cities*. New York: Random House.

Koopmans, T. C. (1957). *Three Essays on the State of Economic Science*. New York: McGraw-Hill.

Krugman, P. (1995). *Development, Geography, and Economic Theory*. Cambridge, MA: MIT Press.

Lucas, R. E. (1988). On the mechanics of economic development. *Journal of Monetary Economics* 22:3–22.

Marshall, J. U. (1989). *The Structure of Urban Systems*. University of Toronto Press.

Mills, E. S. (1972). *Urban Economics*. Glenview, IL: Scott, Foresman.

Mumford, L. (1961). *The City in History*. New York: Harcourt Brace Jovanovich.

Sassen, S. (1991). *The Global City: New York, London, Tokyo*. Princeton University Press.

Smith, A. (1776). *An Inquiry into the Nature and Causes of the Wealth of Nations*. London: Straham & Cadell.

United Nations (1994). *World Urbanization Prospects: The 1994 Revision*. New York: United Nations, Population Division.

PART I

Cities and Agglomeration

CHAPTER 1

The Formation of Economic Agglomerations: Old Problems and New Perspectives

Masahisa Fujita and Jacques-François Thisse

1 Introduction

"Nearly half the world's population and three-quarters of all westerners live in cities" (*The Economist*, July 29, 1995). This raw fact can no longer be given lip service and then put aside. We are therefore led to raise the following fundamental question: *Why do economic activities tend to agglomerate in a small number of places (typically cities)?*

More precisely, we want to try to explain why certain economic activities tend to become established in particular places, and we want to examine the resulting geographical organization of the economy. Intuitively, the equilibrium spatial configuration of economic activities can be viewed as the outcome of a process involving two opposing types of forces, that is, *agglomeration* (or centripetal) *forces* and *dispersion* (or centrifugal) *forces*.[1] This view agrees with some very early work in economic geography. For example, in his *Principes de Géographie humaine*, published in 1921, the famous French geographer Vidal de la Blache argued that all societies, rudimentary or developed, face the same dilemma: Individuals must get together in order to benefit from the advantages of the division of labor, but various difficulties restrict the gathering of many individuals. Similarly, Lösch (1940) viewed the economic landscape as the

The authors are grateful to Simon Anderson and Vernon Henderson for helpful discussions during the preparation of this chapter. They also thank Gilles Duranton, Louis-André Gérard-Varet, Yossi Hadar, Jean-Marie Huriot, Yoshitsugu Kanemoto, Xavier Martinez-Giralt, Dominique Peeters, Diego Puga, Tony Smith, and Takatoshi Tabuchi for useful comments. They have also benefited from suggestions and remarks by participants at the trilateral TCER/NBER/CEPR conference on "Economic Agglomeration," the CEPR workshop on "Trade, Location and Technology," the European Summer Symposium in Economic Theory, and seminar audiences at Kyoto University, Université de Bourgogne, and Université Catholique de Louvain. A shorter version of this chapter has been published in the *Journal of Japanese and International Economies*, vol. 10 (1996), pp. 339–78.

[1] The term "agglomeration" is less ambiguous than "concentration," which is used to describe different phenomena. It was introduced in location theory by Weber (1909, ch. 1). Though Weber is known mainly for his work on the location of the firm (Wesolowsky, 1993), his main concern was to explain the formation of industrial clusterings.

outcome of "the interplay of purely economic forces, some working toward concentration and others toward dispersion" (p. 105 of the English translation).

Among the several questions that have been investigated in the literature, the following are central: (1) How are agglomeration and dispersion forces generated? (2) Why do we have cities?[2] (3) Why do various regions and cities specialize in different activities? In order to answer these questions, we must consider a variety of models focusing on different aspects of the economics of cities. Indeed, it would be futile to look for a single model that could explain the economic landscape of economies at different stages of development and in different institutional environments. As mentioned earlier, a model of economic geography must take account of both centripetal and centrifugal forces. The equilibrium spatial configuration of economic activities is then the result of a complicated balance of forces that push and pull consumers and firms until no one can find a better location. As will be seen, the major models that have been developed do reflect such an interplay.

Though convenient at a high level of abstraction, it should be clear that the concept of *economic agglomeration* as used in this chapter refers to a variety of real-world phenomena. For example, one type of agglomeration arises when restaurants, movie theaters, or shops selling similar products are clustered within a single neighborhood of a city. At the other end of the spectrum lies the core–periphery structure corresponding to North–South dualism. For example, Hummels (1995) observed that high-income nations are clustered in small industrial cores in the Northern Hemisphere and that income steadily declines with distance from these cores. Other types of agglomeration can be seen in the existence of strong regional disparities within a given country, in the formation of cities of different sizes, and in the emergence of industrial districts where firms have strong technological and/or informational linkages. This should not come as a surprise, for geographers have long known that scale matters in studying spatial problems. Although we shall consider these different types of spatial clusterings, the main emphasis of this study will be on *city formation*.[3]

In recent years, increasing numbers of economists have become interested in the study of location problems. This is probably best illustrated by the work of Henderson (1988), Lucas (1988), Krugman (1991a,b), and Becker and Murphy (1992), among several others, work that triggered a new flow of interesting contributions in the field. No doubt this increased interest has been fostered by the integration of national economies within trading blocs such as the European

---

[2] This question bears some resemblance to that raised by Coase concerning the reason for firms to exist, because firms are also formed by clusters of individuals performing different tasks. However, if firms can be viewed as composing the nexus of contracts, cities involve more complex systems of relationships.

[3] We do not necessarily consider cities as being monocentric; see Berry (1993) for a critical appraisal of this model.

Union and the North American Free Trade Agreement and their impact on the development of their regions and cities. As market integration increasingly dissolves economic barriers between nations, national boundaries no longer demarcate the most natural units for analysis (economists still tend to suffer from cartographic illusion). Contrary to widespread opinion, this consideration is not new; it was raised by some scholars at the outset of the discussions that were to lead to the European Union (Giersch, 1949). However, the subject remained neglected for a long time, despite the suggestions made by Ohlin (1933, pt. III), who proposed to unify interregional trade theory and location theory. Nowadays the issue seems even more important, for the continuing growth of trade and especially the development of multinational production systems are casting doubt on the relevance of the concept of national economies. As a result, location theory and studies of international trade are increasingly focusing on economic agglomerations, local specializations, and inter-city trade.

Applications of the new theories of growth are also under scrutiny. The role of cities in economic growth since the second half of the nineteenth century has been emphasized by economic historians (e.g., Hohenberg and Lees, 1985, ch. 6 and 7). Indeed, cities and, more generally, economic agglomerations are considered to be the main institutions in which both technological and social innovations are developed through market and non-market interactions. Furthermore, city specializations can change over time, thus creating a geographically diversified pattern of economic development. For all these reasons, it seems reasonable to say that *growth tends to be localized*, a fact that was recognized by the early theorists of development, such as Myrdal (1957) and Hirschman (1958). This observation has been at the core of many recent empirical contributions that have shed new light on the mechanisms of growth (e.g., Glaeser et al., 1992, 1995; Henderson et al., 1995).[4]

In particular, Feldman and Florida (1994) have observed that in the late twentieth century, *innovations have tended to appear in geographic clusters* in areas where firms and universities oriented toward research and development (R&D) have already become established, and such concentrations of specialized resources reinforce a region's capacity to innovate and to grow. Consequently, the connection between growth and geography becomes even stronger when regional specialization in innovative activities is viewed as the outcome of a

---

[4] It is worth noting that pre-classical economists have stressed the role of cities in the process of development. See, e.g., Lepetit (1988, ch. 3) for an overview of the main contributions prior to Adam Smith. In particular, they viewed cities not only as a combination of inputs but also as a "mutiplier" that leads to increasing returns in the aggregate. In accord with modern urban economics (discussed later), pre-classical economists further considered cities as economic agents having the power to make decisions. Not surprisingly, their work is connected to modern theories of growth, thus suggesting that the "new economic geography" and theories of endogenous growth have the same historical roots. There are here several interesting questions that should be explored by historians of economic thought.

combination of specific capabilities and capacities developed in those regions, thus suggesting that the process at work is similar to the one we shall encounter in the formation of agglomerations.

Thus it seems fair to say that the "new economic geography," which can also be termed *geographical economics*, is in many respects more deeply rooted in economic theory than in the traditional theories of location. As we shall see in the course of this study, geographical economics has strong connections with several branches of modern economics, including industrial organization and urban economics, but also with the new theories of international trade and theories of economic growth and development. This suggests that this field has considerable potential for further development and that cross-fertilization can be expected (e.g., Ioannides, 1994; Martin and Ottaviano, 1996; Palivos and Wang, 1996; Walz, 1996). These developments have generated a large flow of empirical studies that have used the modern tools of econometrics, thus leading to more firmly grounded conclusions.

As in any economic field, several lines of research have been and are being explored in geographical economics. The earliest line was initiated by von Thünen (1826), who sought to explain the pattern of agricultural activities surrounding many cities in pre-industrial Germany.[5] More generally, von Thünen's theory has proved to be very useful in studying land use in situations in which economic activities are perfectly divisible (Mills, 1970). In fact, the principles underlying his model are so general that von Thünen can be considered the founder of marginalism (Nerlove and Sadka, 1991). Despite the fact that we now recognize his monumental contributions to economic thought, von Thünen's ideas languished for more than a century without attracting widespread attention. (Note that the same holds for other contributions to location theory, despite the efforts of some scholars to make that literature accessible to a large audience of economists at its very beginning; see, e.g., the survey offered by Krzyzanowski, 1927). Yet, following a suggestion made by Isard (1956, ch. 8), Alonso (1964) succeeded in extending von Thünen's central concept of bid-rent curves to an urban context in which a marketplace was replaced by an employment center (the "central business district"). Since that time, urban economics has advanced rapidly. Furthermore, as observed by Samuelson (1983), the von Thünen model also contains the basic ideas of comparative advantage on which other economists have built the neoclassical theory of international trade. The reason for such a broad range of applications lies in the fact that the model is compatible with the competitive paradigm, because production takes place under constant returns to scale.

However, the von Thünen model has several limitations. Indeed, the following question suggests itself: Why is there a unique city in von Thünen's isolated

---

[5] Note that the von Thünen model has been reformulated in mathematical terms by Launhardt (1885, ch. 30).

state? Or why a unique central business district in most urban economic models? Though such a center may emerge under constant returns when space is heterogeneous (Beckmann and Puu, 1985), this is more likely to occur when increasing returns are at work in the formation of trading places or in the production of some goods; in other words, one must appeal to something that is not in the von Thünen model to understand what is going on.

Conceding the point, Lösch (1940) argued that scale economies in production, as well as in transportation costs, are essential for understanding the formation of economic space. He then proceeded to construct a model of monopolistic competition in the manner of Hotelling and Kaldor as an alternative to von Thünen's model.[6] Lösch's model is still used as a reference in "classical" economic geography, but it differs from the Dixit-Stiglitz model employed in the "new" economic geography discussed later in Section 3.1. In the same spirit, Koopmans (1957, p. 157) made it clear that scale economies are essential in the creation of urban agglomerations: "without recognizing indivisibilities – in the human person, in residences, plants, equipment and in transportation – urban location problems down to the smallest village cannot be understood."

The assumption of nonincreasing returns indeed has dramatic implications for geographical economics that help us understand why so many economists have been tempted to put space aside. Under nonincreasing returns and a uniform distribution of resources, the economy would reduce to a Robinson Crusoe type, where each individual would produce only for his or her own consumption (backyard capitalism). Mills (1972, p. 4) provided a neat description of such a world without cities:

land would be the same everywhere and each acre of land would contain the same number of people and the same mix of productive activities. The crucial point in establishing this result is that constant returns permit each productive activity to be carried on at an arbitrary level without loss of efficiency. Furthermore, all land is equally productive and equilibrium requires that the value of the marginal product, and hence its rent, be the same everywhere. Therefore, in equilibrium, all the inputs and outputs necessary directly and indirectly to meet the demands of consumers can be located in a small area near where consumers live. In that way, each small area can be autarkic and transportation of people and goods can be avoided.

Each location could thus be a base for an autarkic economy, where goods would be produced on an arbitrarily small scale, except possibly (as in the neoclassical theory of international trade) that trade might occur if the geographical distribution of resources was nonuniform. Although pertinent (Courant and Deardoff, 1992; Kim, 1995), an unequal distribution of resources seems insufficient to serve as the only explanation for specialization and trade (Ciccone and Hall, 1996). Furthermore, when capital and labor can move freely, the neoclassical model of trade does not allow for prediction of the sizes of regions

---

[6] See Beckmann (1972) for a modern presentation of this model.

when natural resources are uniformly distributed. Accordingly, nothing can be said about the location of production activities within this model. We can therefore safely conclude that *increasing returns to scale are essential for explaining the geographical distribution of economic activities.*[7] However, when indivisibilities are explicitly introduced, the nonexistence of a competitive equilibrium in a spatial economy is common, as shown by Koopmans and Beckmann (1957) and Starrett (1978).[8]

Furthermore, as noticed by Drèze and Hagen (1978) in a somewhat different context, scale economies in production have another far-reaching implication: The number of marketplaces open at a competitive equilibrium is likely to be suboptimal. Or, to use a different terminology, *spatial markets typically are incomplete*, so that an equilibrium allocation is, in general, not Pareto-optimal. More precisely, there are various levels of Pareto optimality corresponding to different environments, as in club theory (Scotchmer, 1994).

A combined consideration of space and economies of scale has one further implication that turns out to be even more fundamental for economic theory. If production involves increasing returns, a finite economy can accommodate only a finite number of firms that are imperfect competitors. Treading in Hotelling's footsteps, Kaldor (1935) argued that space gives this competition a particular form. Because consumers will buy from the firm with the lowest "full price," defined as the posted price plus the transport cost, each firm competes directly with only a few neighboring firms, regardless of the total number of firms in the industry. The very nature of the process of spatial competition is therefore oligopolistic and should be studied within a framework of interactive decision-making. That was one of the central messages conveyed by Hotelling (1929), but it was ignored until economists became fully aware of the power of game theory for studying competition in modern market economies (see Gabszewicz and Thisse, 1986, for a more detailed discussion). Following the outburst of industrial organization that began in the late 1970s, it became natural to study the implications of space for competition. New tools and concepts are now available to revisit and formalize the questions raised by early location theorists.[9]

[7] This statement, which goes back at least to Lösch (1940, ch. 9), has been rediscovered periodically. For this reason, it can be referred to as the "folk theorem of geographical economics" (see Scotchmer and Thisse, 1992, for a more detailed discussion). In the same vein, planning models of location developed in operations research have also emphasized the trade-off between fixed production costs and transportation costs; see Manne (1964) and Stollsteimer (1963) for early contributions. A recent survey of those models has been presented in Labbé et al. (1995).
[8] The nonexistence of a competitive equilibrium in the presence of indivisibilities is of course related to the possibility of observing duality gaps in integer programming, that is, the primal and the dual take different values at the optimal solution.
[9] Simultaneously, new developments in local public finance have led some to question the relevance of the Samuelsonian paradigm of (pure) public good. There are interesting analogies and contrasts between these two lines of research (Scotchmer and Thisse, 1992).

Conversely, "space" is often used in various economic areas as a label for describing nongeographical characteristics along which economic agents are heterogeneous. In particular, such an approach has been followed in many models of industrial organization.[10]

Despite its factual and policy relevance, the question of why a hierarchical system of cities emerges remains open. In particular, it is a well-established fact that cities tend to be distributed according to some specific relationship relating their size and their rank in the urban system (what is called the rank-size rule). The first attempts to build a spatial theory of the urban hierarchy date back at least to the German geographer Christaller (1933), who pioneered "central place theory," based on the clustering of marketplaces for different economic goods and services.[11] Though the theory proposed by Christaller and developed by Lösch has served as a cornerstone in classical economic geography, as described by Mulligan (1984) in a nice overview, it is fair to say that the microeconomic underpinnings of central place theory are still to be developed. See Henderson (1972) for an early critical, economic evaluation of this theory and Hohenberg and Lees (1985, ch. 2) for an appraisal from the historical perspective.

The topic is difficult because it involves various types of nonconvexities that are even more complex to deal with than are increasing returns in production. For example, a consumer organizes his shopping itinerary so as to minimize the total cost of purchases, including transport costs. This problem is extremely complex: Determining the optimal geographical structure of purchases requires solving a particularly difficult combinatorial problem, and finding an equilibrium becomes very problematic (Bacon, 1984). In the same vein, often there are considerable scale economies in carrying the goods bought by a consumer when shopping. In the extreme, consumers' outlays on transportation can be considered as independent of the quantities purchased. These nonconvexities affect demand functions in complex ways that have not been fully investigated. This is just one example of the many difficulties one encounters in attempting to construct a general spatial model that can account for cities of different sizes trading different commodities. It is therefore no surprise that we still lack such a model, because it is well known that economic theory has serious problems in dealing with nonconvexities. Yet this turns out to be a real embarrassment, because the rank-size rule is one of the most robust statistical relationships known so far in economics (Krugman, 1995, ch. 2).

A major centripetal force can be found in the existence of externalities (later discussion will clarify what we mean by "externality"), in that a geographical

---

[10] Examples include the supply of differentiated products (Ireland, 1987), the various forms of price discrimination (Phlips, 1983), and the competition between political parties (Enelow and Hinich, 1984). Other applications, in particular in labor economics, are possible.

[11] Note that this problem bears some resemblance to that of the firm size distribution studied in the "old" industrial-organization literature.

concentration of economic activities can be viewed as the outcome of a snowball effect.[12] Specifically, more and more agents want to agglomerate because of the various factors that will allow for greater diversity and higher degrees of specialization in the production processes, leading to a wider array of products available for consumption. The setting up of new firms in such regions gives rise to new incentives for workers to migrate there because they can expect better job matching and therefore higher wages. This in turn makes the place more attractive to firms, which may expect to find the types of workers and services they need, as well as new outlets for their products. Hence, both types of agents benefit from being together. This process has been well described by Marshall (1890, 1920, p. 225):

When an industry has thus chosen a location for itself, it is likely to stay there long: so great are the advantages which people following the same skilled trade get from near neighborhood to one another. . . . A localized industry gains a great advantage from the fact that it offers a constant market for skill. . . . Employers are apt to resort to any place where they are likely to find a good choice of workers with the special skill which they require; while men seeking employment naturally go to places where there are many employers who need such skills as theirs and where therefore it is likely [they will] find a good market.

More generally, the "Marshallian externalities" arise because of (1) mass production (the so-called internal economies that are similar to the scale economies mentioned earlier), (2) the formation of a highly specialized labor force and the production of new ideas, both based on the accumulation of human capital and face-to-face communications, (3) the availability of specialized input services, and (4) the existence of modern infrastructures. Not surprisingly, Marshallian externalities provide the engine for economic development in the new growth theories.[13]

Building on Weber (1909, ch. 5), Hoover (1936, ch. 6) has proposed what has become the now-standard classification of agglomeration economies (see also Isard, 1956, ch. 8): *scale economies* within a firm, depending upon the size of the firm's scale of production at one point; *localization economies* for all firms in one industry at one point, depending upon the total output of the industry at that location;[14] *urbanization economies* for all firms in various industries at one

---

[12] This phenomenon is similar to that encountered in studies of network externalities (David and Greenstein, 1990). Besides the network effect, which is an agglomeration force, because consumers always prefer a larger network, it is necessary to identify another effect that plays the role of a dispersion force in order to obtain different networks (Belleflamme, 1998). Note also that the issue of standardization bears some resemblance to that of agglomeration (Arthur, 1994, ch. 2 and 4). Finally, the stratification of a population can be described by a similar cumulative process (Bénabou, 1996a).

[13] They are also at the heart of some early contributions to studies of economic development (see Section 3).

[14] See Chipman (1970) for an early formal analysis of these externalities developed in a nonspatial model.

point, depending on the overall level of activity at that location. Scale economies correspond to Marshallian externalities of type (1); localization economies refer to Marshallian externalities of types (2) and (3); urbanization economies would cover the Marshallian externalities of types (2), (3), and (4), since they typically depend on the presence of public infrastructures and on the agglomeration size (which in turn depends on the division of labor within the city). This classification has been used extensively in empirical studies, as surveyed by Henderson (1988, ch. 5).

The advantages of proximity for production have their counterpart on the consumption side. For example, cities typically are associated with a wide range of products and a large spectrum of public services, so that consumers can reach higher utility levels and therefore will have stronger incentives to migrate toward cities. Furthermore, the propensity to interact with others, the desire of man for man, is a fundamental human attribute, as is the pleasure of discussing and exchanging ideas with others. Distance is an impediment to such interactions, thus making cities the ideal institution for the development of social contacts corresponding to various kinds of externalities (Fischer, 1982, ch. 2 and 3). Along the same line, Akerlof (1997) has argued that the inner city is the basis for the development of social externalities (e.g., conformity and status-seeking) that govern the behaviors of particular groups of agents. For example, social capital arising across individuals living within the same city (or neighborhood) has been explored by Bénabou (1993, 1996a), who has shown its importance for urban development.

Before describing the content of this chapter, we want to clarify the following issue. For many years, the concept of *externality* (also called *external effect*) has been used to describe a great variety of situations. Following Scitovsky (1954), it has been customary to consider two categories: *technological externalities* (such as spillovers) and *pecuniary externalities*. The former deals with the effects of non-market interactions that are realized through processes directly affecting the utility of an individual or the production function of a firm. By contrast, the latter refers to the benefits of economic interactions that take place through the usual market mechanisms via the mediation of prices. For obvious reasons, Marshall was not aware of this distinction, and his externalities turn out to be mixtures of technological and pecuniary externalities. As a consequence, each type of externality may lead to the spatial agglomeration of economic activities.

In order to understand how an agglomeration occurs when Marshallian externalities are present, it is useful to divide human activities into two categories: *production* and *creation*. Roughly speaking, one can say that production encompasses the routine ways of processing or assembling things (such as the preparation of a dinner or the working of an assembly line). For an agglomeration of firms and households to be based on this type of production activity, the presence of pecuniary externalities is crucial.

However, human beings enjoy more pleasure from, and put much value on, creation. Furthermore, in economic life, much of the competitiveness of individuals and firms is due to their creativity. Consequently, as emphasized by Jacobs (1969), economic life is creative in the same way as are the arts and sciences. As pointed out more recently by Lucas (1988, p. 38), personal communication within groups of individuals sharing common interests can be a vital input to creativity: "New York City's garment district, financial district, diamond district, advertising district and many more are as much intellectual centers as is Columbia or New York University." In this respect, it is well known that *face-to-face communication* is most effective for rapid product and process development, where access to information relative to new products and/or production processes turns out to be essential for the competitiveness of firms. For example, Saxenian (1994, p. 33) has emphasized the importance of this factor in the making of Silicon Valley as a center of efficient productive systems:

By all accounts, these informal conversations were pervasive and served as an important source of up-to-date information about competitors, customers, markets, and technologies. Entrepreneurs came to see social relationships and even gossip as a crucial aspect of their business. In an industry characterized by rapid technological change and intense competition, such informal communication was often of more value than more conventional but less timely forums such as industry journals.

Given that different people have different skills (by nature as well as by nurture), the sizes of such groups also give rise to significant scale effects. Furthermore, information and ideas have characteristics of public goods and hence tend to generate spillover effects. In this way, the creative process itself can lead to strong agglomeration tendencies. This agrees with the empirical work of Feldman (1994, p. 2), who observed that "knowledge traverses corridors and streets more easily than continents and oceans." This is especially well illustrated by the findings of Jaffe et al. (1993) in the United States, where approximately 60% of citations come from the primary patent class. Moreover, citations to domestic patents are more likely to be domestic and are more likely to come from the same state and metropolitan statistical areas as the cited patents. Contrary to widespread opinion, information and knowledge are not new locational factors. Economic historians had already stressed their role in the urbanization process that took place during the second phase of the Industrial Revolution (e.g., Hohenberg and Lees, 1985, ch. 6).

Thus, an economic agglomeration is created through both technological and pecuniary externalities, often working together. Recent advances in geographical economics have mainly concentrated on the Chamberlinian models of monopolistic competition developed in industrial organization by Spence (1976) and Dixit and Stiglitz (1977). As will be seen later, this approach allows one to decipher the working of the pecuniary externalities discussed earlier (Krugman, 1991a). Accordingly, the section herein devoted to (technological) externalities will concentrate on production or consumption externalities as they are now defined in modern economic theory (i.e., non-market interactions). These externalities seem to play an increasing role in advanced economies, which are more and more involved in the production and consumption of less tangible goods for which distance matters in a more subtle way than in less advanced economies. This has been observed both in high-tech industries (Saxenian, 1994) and in traditional sectors (Pyke et al., 1990).

The remainder of this chapter will elaborate on many of the issues just mentioned. Because of space constraints, we shall concentrate on the main issues only. They will be organized according to three themes, dealing with *externalities*, *increasing returns*, and *spatial competition*. However, the rates of progress in these three areas have not been the same. In particular, the area of externalities has attracted the most attention, because technological externalities are compatible with the competitive paradigm, and they will be discussed first. In Section 2 we shall limit ourselves to a discussion of technological externalities. Formally, technological externalities are often associated with particular nonconvexities arising in production or consumption. As usual, the assumption of a continuum of firms and of households permits us to retain the assumption of competitive behavior while circumventing the many difficulties encountered when nonconvexities are present. In Section 3 we shall focus on models of monopolistic competition with increasing returns and show how they can serve to illuminate several aspects of the agglomeration process. In this way, pecuniary externalities are formulated as explicit market mechanisms.

One of the most severe limitations of monopolistic competition à la Spence-Dixit-Stiglitz is that price competition is nonstrategic. Yet, as mentioned earlier, spatial competition is inherently strategic because it takes place among the few. Intuitively, one can say that this approach aims at dealing with the "strategic externalities" generated by the proximity of rival firms or suppliers in economic space. Despite the real progress made during the past decade, spatial-competition models are still difficult to manipulate, and much work remains to be done in this area. In Section 4 we shall review what has been accomplished and discuss the corresponding implications for geographical economics. In Section 5 we shall identify a few general principles that seem to emerge from the literature. We shall briefly discuss some other approaches in Section 6 and suggest new lines of research in Section 7.[15]

Before proceeding further, a digression and a final remark are in order. First, there is an interesting analogy between the von Thünen model discussed earlier and the standard growth theory. Both assume constant returns to scale and perfect competition. As in the von Thünen model, where the city cannot be explained within the model, the main reason for growth (i.e., technological

---

[15] The reader is referred to the excellent book of Ponsard (1983) for a historical survey of spatial economic theory.

progress) cannot be explained within the model of exogenous growth. This difficulty has been well summarized by Romer (1992, pp. 85–6):

The paradox. . . . was that the competitive theory that generated the evidence was inconsistent with any explanation of how technological change could arise as the result of the self-interested actions of individual economic actors. By definition, all of national output had to be paid as returns to capital and labor; none remained as possible compensation for technological innovations. . . . The assumption of convexity and perfect competition placed the accumulation of new technologies at the center of the growth process and simultaneously denied the possibility that economic analysis could have anything to say about this process.

Stated differently, explaining city formation in Thünian models is like explaining technological progress in standard growth models. Anticipating the discussion of Section 3, we find it interesting to note that the most common approach to resolving the two difficulties has been the same, namely, use of the model of imperfect competition with increasing returns, by Dixit and Stiglitz, the initial purpose of which was not to deal with growth and geography!

Second, contrary to general belief, location problems have attracted a great deal of attention in various disciplines. In economics alone, the topic has been flourishing since the early 1990s. Thus we have chosen to be selective. As a result, it is fair to say that this survey reflects our idiosyncrasies as much as the state of the art. We extend our apologies to those who have contributed to the field and who feel frustrated by our choice of menu.

2 Externalities

Models involving externalities describe spatial equilibria under the influence of non-market interactions among firms and/or households. Typically, non-market interactions occur in the area of either communication fields or spatial externalities. The former model explicitly encompasses exchanges of information between agents, and the latter involves the concept of accessibility to represent the effects of non-price interactions. As will be shown later, these two types of models often are formally equivalent. Because most models have been developed by urban economists with the aim of explaining the internal spatial structure of cities (or metropolitan areas), we shall concentrate on the agglomeration of various types of economic activities within a city. It should be clear that the same principles apply to the spatial organization of broader areas such as regions or nations.[16]

---

[16] However, they do not necessarily apply to multinational spaces when different national governments are present. Such governments have indeed very specific and powerful instruments, such as money or trade policy, that strongly affect the economic environment in which the agents operate. The study of location problems in the international marketplace is still in its infancy and constitutes a very promising line of research.

The central idea behind the formation of cities has been well summarized by Lucas (1988, p. 39): "What can people be paying Manhattan or downtown Chicago rents *for*, if not for being near other people?" To the best of our knowledge, the first formal model focusing on the role of interaction among individuals as an explanation for cities was due to Beckmann (1976). More precisely, the utility of a household is assumed to depend on the average distance to all other households in the city and on the amount of land bought on the market. In equilibrium, the city exhibits a bell-shaped population density distribution, which is supported by a similarly shaped land rent curve. Focusing on firms instead, Borukhov and Hochman (1977) and O'Hara (1977) studied models of firm location in which interactions between firms generate agglomeration.[17] Those pioneering papers subsequently triggered studies of a large number of models of non-market interactions.

The basic contribution, in that the key variables are independent of the economic system, is due to Papageorgiou and Smith (1983). They considered a trade-off between the need for social contacts, which is negatively affected by distance, and the need for land, which is negatively affected by crowding. Initially the preferences are such that the uniform distribution of individuals over a borderless landscape is an equilibrium. When the propensity to interact with others increases sufficiently, this equilibrium becomes unstable: Any marginal perturbation is sufficient for the population to evolve toward an irregular distribution. In this model, cities are considered the outcome of a social process combining basic human needs that are not (necessarily) expressed through the market.[18] It is probably fair to say that this model captures much of the intuition of early geographers interested in the spatial structure of human settlements. However, it is important to consider less general, abstract formulations and to study models based on explicit economic forms of interactions.

2.1 City Centers or Clusters of Firms

To illustrate more concretely the fundamental mechanism of agglomeration involving both firms and households, we give a brief description of a model developed by Fujita, Imai, and Ogawa. The agglomeration force is *the existence of communications among firms permitting the exchange of information* (e.g., Saxenian, 1994, ch. 2). An important characteristic of information is its

---

[17] Interactions among business firms were first explicitly considered by Solow and Vickrey (1971) in a model dealing with the optimal allocation of land between transportation and business activity.

[18] Another non-market trade-off was recently studied by Lindsey et al. (1995) in which individual preferences involved two terms: the distance to other individuals, and the distance from an ideal location in relation to existing public facilities and geographic amenities available along the real line.

public-good nature: The use of a piece of information by a firm does not reduce the content of that information for other firms. Hence the exchange of information through communication within a set of firms generates externality-like benefits to each of them. Provided that firms own different bits of information, the benefits of communication generally increase as the number of firms rises. Furthermore, because communications typically involve distance-sensitive costs, the benefits are greater if firms locate closer to each other; the quality of the information is also better because the number of intermediates is smaller when firms are gathered (see Banerjee, 1993, for a related application of these ideas). Therefore, all other things being equal, each firm has an incentive to establish itself close to the others, thus fostering the emergence of an agglomeration of firms. On the other hand, the clustering of many firms in a single area increases the average commuting distance for their workers, which in turn increases the wage rate and land rent in the area surrounding the cluster. Such high wages and land rents tend to discourage further agglomeration of firms in the same area. Consequently, the equilibrium distributions of firms and households are determined by the balance between these opposite forces.

To be precise, suppose that in a given location space X there is a continuum of firms (of a given size) that are symmetric with regard to the exchange of information. However, they differ in terms of the information they own, as well as in the goods they produce. Each firm actively engages in communication with other firms. It is assumed that the intensity of communication is measured by the level of contact activity (e.g., the number of face-to-face contacts per unit of time) and that firms are free to choose their optimal levels of contact activity with others. Because firms are symmetric with regard to the process of communication, the optimal level of contact between each pair of them is the same. Communication is costly, because the exchange of information between firms requires some (informal) organization and is time-consuming; it is assumed that firms equally split their communication cost. Each firm also needs some given amounts of land (S_f) and labor (L_f).

Let $f(y)$ be the density of firms at location y, while $R(x)$ and $W(x)$ stand for the land rent and the wage rate at x, respectively. The profit of a firm choosing a location $x \in X$ and a level of contact activity $q(x, y)$ with each firm at location y is given by

$$\Pi[x, q(x, \cdot)] = \int_X \{V[q(x, y)] - c(x, y)q(x, y)\}f(y)\, dy$$
$$- R(x)S_f - W(x)L_f \tag{1.1}$$

where $V(\cdot)$ represents the total contribution of the contact level to the firm's revenue, and $c(\cdot)$ is its corresponding unit cost. Each firm chooses its location

x and its contact field $q(x, y)$ so as to maximize its profit, taking the spatial distribution of firms as given. Because the optimal contact level with any firm at y, denoted $q^*(x, y)$, can be determined independently of the distribution of firms, we can substitute it into (1.1) and rewrite the profit function as follows:

$$\Pi(x) = A(x) - R(x)S_f - W(x)L_f$$

where

$$A(x) \equiv \int_X a(x, y)f(y)dy \equiv \int_X \{V[q^*(x, y)] - c(x, y)q^*(x, y)\}f(y)\,dy$$

(1.2)

is the *aggregate accessibility* of each location $x \in X$, $a(x, y)$ being the *local accessibility*.

Note that $a(x, y)$ can alternatively be interpreted as the *information spillover* experienced by a firm at x from a firm set up at y. Then $A(x)$ will correspond to a *distance-decay function* for information; this function has the nature of a spatial externality. In this case, the amount of information received by a firm is in itself exogenous; however, it still depends on the firm's location relative to the others.

Next, there is a continuum of homogeneous households (of a given size) that seek to locate in the same space. The utility of a household is given by $U(s, z)$, where s represents land consumption, and z the consumption of a composite good. For simplicity, we assume that the land consumption is fixed and is equal to S_h. Furthermore, each household supplies one unit of labor, and the composite good is imported at a constant price normalized to unity. Then, if a household chooses to reside at $x \in X$ and to work at $x_w \in X$, its budget constraint is given by

$$z + R(x)S_h + t_h|x - x_w| = W(x_w)$$

where t_h is the unit commuting cost. Because the lot size is fixed, the objective of a household is to choose a residential location and a working location that will maximize its consumption of the composite good, given by

$$z(x, x_w) = W(x_w) - R(x)S_h - t_h|x - x_w|$$

Finally, in line with mainstream urban economics, it is supposed that land is owned by absentee landlords.

Following the standard approach in land use theory, the equilibrium configuration of firms and households is determined through the interplay of the firms' and households' bid-rent functions of the Alonso type (see Fujita, 1989, ch. 2, for a detailed discussion of this procedure). The *bid-rent function* of a firm is defined as follows:

$$\Phi(x, \pi) = \left[\int_X a(x, y) f(y) \, dy - W(x) L_f - \pi \right] \Big/ S_f$$

which represents the highest price a firm is willing to pay for a unit piece of land at $x \in X$ while earning a profit equal to π.

Similarly, the bid-rent function of a household at $x \in X$ is equal to the highest price per land unit that a household is willing to pay in order to reside at $x \in X$ while enjoying a utility level u:

$$\Psi(x, u) = \max_{x_w}[(W(x_w) - Z(u) - t_h|x - x_w|)/S_h]$$

where $Z(u)$ is the solution to the equation $U(z, S_h) = u$. In this case, $\Psi(x, u)$ is the maximum rent per land unit that a household can bid at location x while enjoying the utility level u.

An equilibrium is reached when all the firms achieve the same maximum profit, and all the households the same maximum utility, while rents and wages clear the land and labor markets. The unknowns are the firm distribution, the household distribution, the land rent function, the wage function, the commuting pattern, the maximum utility level, denoted u^*, and the maximum profit level, denoted π^*. In particular, the equilibrium land rent at x must satisfy the relationship

$$R(x) = \max\{\Phi(x, u^*), \Psi(x, \pi^*), \bar{R}\}$$

where $\bar{R}$ is the opportunity cost of land.

The case of a linear space, $X = (-\infty, \infty)$, has been studied by Fujita, Ogawa, and Imai. They have shown that the properties of the equilibrium configuration crucially depend on the shape of the local accessibility function. Hence, two special cases for this function will now be considered (note that Fujita and Smith, 1990, have shown that these two formulations of the local accessibility function can be derived from explicit benefit functions, thus making them very meaningful examples):

$$a(x, y) = \beta \exp(-\alpha|x - y|) \tag{1.3}$$

and

$$a(x, y) = \beta - \alpha|x - y| \tag{1.4}$$

where α and β are two positive constants, α measuring the intensity of the distance-decay effect. The former corresponds to a *spatially discounted accessibility measure*, and the latter is a *linear accessibility measure*. In the case of a linear accessibility measure, Ogawa and Fujita (1980) and Imai (1982) have

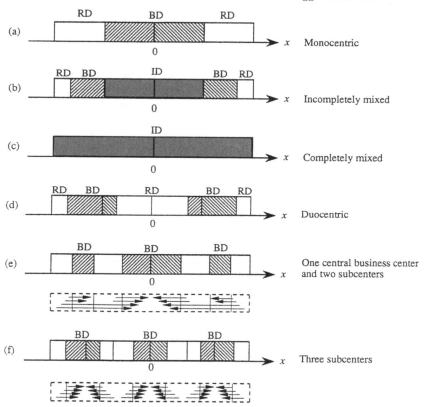

Figure 1.1. Possible equilibrium configurations.

shown that a unique equilibrium configuration exists for each parameter constellation. The equilibrium configuration is *monocentric, incompletely mixed,* or *completely mixed.* These configurations are depicted in diagrams (a)–(c) of Figure 1.1, where RD represents an (exclusive) residential district, BD an (exclusive) business district, and ID an integrated district. The first (second and third, respectively) configuration occurs, not surprisingly, when α/t_h is large (intermediate and small, respectively).[19] Note that one observes a set of equilibrium configurations richer than that assumed in the monocentric city à la

[19] This type of externality was further explored by Kanemoto (1990), who considered the case in which firms can engage in transactions with others. Combining the exchange of intermediate inputs between firms with indivisibilities in their production creates externalities similar to those considered by Fujita-Imai-Ogawa. If τ is the unit transportation cost of the intermediate goods, Kanemoto then shows that the monocentric configuration is an equilibrium when the ratio τ/t_h is large, a condition similar to that stated earlier.

von Thünen. This configuration arises only when α/t_h is large, that is, when information matters much more than transportation and the central business district (CBD) has here a spatial extension.

The case of a spatially discounted accessibility measure leads to more possible cases. Fujita and Ogawa (1982) have shown that in addition to the three configurations just mentioned, several other equilibrium configurations may arise, some including subcenters. Examples are depicted in diagrams (d)–(f) of Figure 1.1, where the arrows denote the commuting directions. Diagram (d) represents a duocentric city, where each business district is segmented into two labor pools associated with the adjacent residential areas. Diagram (e) corresponds to one city with a CBD and two subcenters, and (f) can be viewed either as a system of three cities, each having its own CBD, or as one city with three subcenters. Furthermore, the solution is not necessarily unique: multiple equilibria occur over a wide range of parameter values. Finally, the city may undergo a catastrophic structural transition when parameters take some critical values. These models have been successful in explaining several important features of modern cities, such as the endogenous formation of CBDs and subcenters, as well as the transition from a monocentric city to a polycentric urban configuration (see also Section 3.2).

We offer the conjecture that the difference in results may be explained by the fact that concave accessibility functions can apply only to "relatively" small domains of locations where only one center can arise. On the contrary, convex functions are consistent with wide domains, thus permitting several centers to emerge.

Note, finally, that *the equilibrium configurations in economies with spatially interacting firms (such as those studied in the foregoing) generally are not socially optimal*. This has been shown in various models, such as those of O'Hara (1977), Hamilton (1980), and Tauchen and Witte (1984). The reason for this market failure is that the market does not provide the appropriate signals about the social value of sites, because firms interact all together and choose their locations simultaneously. In other words, the price system does not provide the relevant information about the "mobile" attributes (i.e., the density of firms) of a site. Each firm's location affects the contact fields of all other firms, but the individual firm accounts only for its own benefit in evaluating locations (Koopmans, 1957, p. 154). Hence, everything works as if the (material or immaterial) interaction among firms were at the source of a transactional externality that would prevent the "first welfare theorem" from holding.

2.2 Suburbanization

Thus far, the firm has been considered as a single-unit entity. Consequently, the models discussed earlier are not able to explain a basic trend observed in the spatial organization of large cities, that is, the location of a firm's units in suburban areas. For example, many firms (e.g., banks and insurance companies) have moved some of their activities (such as bookkeeping, planning, and employee training) to the suburbs; similar moves were observed earlier in the case of industrial activities (Hohenberg and Lees, 1985, ch. 6). In this case, a firm typically conducts some of its activities (such as communications with other firms) at the "front office," located in the CBD, and the rest of its activities are carried out at the "back office" set up in the suburbs.

This problem has recently been tackled by Ota and Fujita (1993). Keeping the other assumptions of the Fujita-Imai-Ogawa model unchanged, it is now assumed that each firm consists of a "front unit" and a "back unit." Each front unit is assumed to interact with all other firms' front units for the purpose of business communications, whereas each back unit exchanges information or management services only with its own front unit. Each firm must choose the locations of its front unit and back unit so as to maximize its profit. If a firm sets up its front unit at $x \in X$, and its back unit at $y \in X$, the firm incurs an intra-firm communication cost $\Gamma(x, y)$ that depends only upon the locations x and y. As before, each front unit needs S_f units of land and L_f units of labor; each back unit requires S_b units of land and L_b units of labor. Let $f(x)$ and $b(x)$ denote, respectively, the density of front units and that of back units at $x \in X$.

In this context, the only change from the previous model is in the profit function (1.1). A firm having a front unit at x and back unit at y, and choosing a level of contact activity $q(x, z)$ with the front unit of each other firm at $z \in X$, will have a profit function defined as follows:

$$\Pi[x, y, q(x, \cdot)] = \int_X \{V[q(x, z)] - c(x, z)q(x, z)\} f(z) \, dz$$
$$- R(x)S_f - W(x)L_f - R(y)S_b$$
$$- W(y)L_b - \Gamma(x, y)$$

where the first and second terms represent, respectively, the total benefits and total costs of inter-firm communications, and the last term stands for the intra-firm communication cost. If we define the local accessibility as in (1.2), this function becomes

$$\Pi(x, y) = A(x) - R(x)S_f - W(x)L_f - R(y)S_b - W(y)L_b - \Gamma(x, y)$$

Assuming that the local accessibility measure is linear [see (1.4)] and that the intra-firm communication cost is linear in distance, Ota and Fujita (1993) have shown that no less than 11 different equilibrium configurations are possible, depending on the values of the various parameters. These configurations are the results of two basic effects: (1) As the commuting cost of workers decreases, the segregation of business and residential areas increases. (2) As the intra-firm communication cost gets smaller, back units are separated from front units. The most typical configuration when intra-firm communications costs are low involves agglomeration of the front units at the city center, surrounded by a residential area, with back units being established at the outskirts of the city together with their employees. Hence, advancements in intra-firm communications technologies provide a major impetus for job suburbanization.[20] In other words, recent developments in telecommunications technologies should play a central role in the new spatial organization of production.

Note also that relocation of production plants from industrialized countries to developing countries, where labor is cheaper, can be given a similar explanation, though other factors, more in line with the neoclassical trade theory, are also involved.

3 Increasing Returns

The general principle that lies behind most modern contributions to geographical economics is that *product and/or input differentiation gives rise to agglomeration forces*. This idea has been grafted onto the trade-off between increasing returns and transport costs highlighted in central place theory, in order to generate cumulative processes resulting in the formation of cities and/or industrial clusters. In a sense, this corresponds to a revival of ideas advocated by early development theorists, who used various related concepts, such as the "big push" of Rosenstein-Rodan (1943), the "growth poles" of Perroux (1955), the "circular and cumulative causation" of Myrdal (1957, ch. 2), and the "backward and forward linkages" of Hirschman (1958, ch. 1).[21] Recent additions to this cornucopia include the "dynamic economies of scale" by Kaldor (1985), the "positive feedbacks" by Arthur (1994, ch. 1), and the "complementarities" by Matsuyama (1995).[22]

In this section, our primary objective is to show how simple models of monopolistic competition may capture the agglomeration forces suggested by some of the authors just cited. In particular, we shall see that a major contribution of this approach is to uncover some of the economic mechanisms that underlie the pecuniary externalities evoked in the regional development literature. As

---

[20] See also Tofflemire (1992) for additional developments regarding the impact of new telecommunications technologies on the urban structure.

[21] For further elaboration on this point, see Krugman (1993a).

[22] A comprehensive discussion of monopolistic competition models with differentiated products and increasing returns, as well as their main applications to various economic areas, including interregional economics and growth, can be found in the work of Matsuyama (1995). Among other things, Matsuyama stresses the point that these models are well suited to deal with the circular and cumulative causation processes.

mentioned in Section 1, we retain interpretations based on product variety in consumption and/or intermediate goods that are in line with modern theories of growth and international trade.

Consider a population of homogeneous consumers/workers. Each consumes a homogeneous good together with varieties of a differentiated good. More precisely, when a continuum of varieties of size n is supplied, the utility of a worker is given by a constant-elasticity-of-substitution (CES) type of utility function, with $0 < \rho < 1$:

$$U = z_0^\alpha \left\{ \int_0^n [z(\omega)]^\rho \, d\omega \right\}^{(1-\alpha)/\rho} \tag{1.5}$$

where the preferences between the homogeneous good (z_0) and the differentiated goods [$z(\omega)$] are of the Cobb-Douglas type. When $0 < \rho < 1$, it is well known that ρ measures the degree of substitution between the differentiated varieties, and a low value for ρ means that consumers have a strong preference for variety.[23] More important for our purpose, the utility of each consumer increases with the number n of varieties.[24] To see that, suppose that each variety is sold at the same price p. Let E denote the income the consumer spends on the differentiated good. Then the consumption of each variety is such that $z(\omega) = E/np$ for all $\omega \in [0, n]$. Consequently, the contribution of the differentiated good to the utility (1.5) is measured by the expression

$$D = \left\{ \int_0^n (E/np)^\rho \, d\omega \right\}^{1/\rho} = \frac{E}{p} n^{(1-\rho)/\rho}$$

Plugging this expression into (1.5), it is easily seen that for a given value of E, U strictly increases with the number n of varieties. This effect is stronger, the smaller is ρ (i.e., the more differentiated are the varieties).

Alternatively, as observed by Ethier (1982), the right-hand side (RHS) of (1.5) can be interpreted as the production function of a competitive firm that has constant returns in a homogeneous input (z_0) and a composite of differentiated intermediate goods [$z(\omega)$]. However, this function exhibits increasing returns in the number n of specialized intermediate goods used by this firm, and ρ now expresses its desire for employing a greater variety of intermediate goods in the

---

[23] Alternatively, it can be shown that the CES means that consumers have a positive probability of buying each variety (Anderson et al., 1992, ch. 3). Under this interpretation, it is no longer necessary to assume that each consumer wants to consume all the differentiated goods, regardless of their number.

[24] Since the work of Krugman, we know that preference for variety is a possible cause for international trade. Since Romer, we also know that it is one of the possible causes for the economy to grow.

production of a final good. In other words,

$$x = z_0^\alpha \left\{ \int_0^n [z(\omega)]^\rho \, d\omega \right\}^{(1-\alpha)/\rho} \tag{1.6}$$

can be viewed as the "dual" of the utility model (1.5) in the production sector. The importance of specialized intermediate goods (legal and communications services, non-traded industrial inputs, maintenance and repair services, finance, etc.) for agglomeration and regional development is a well-documented fact (Hansen, 1990).

In both interpretations, because of specialization in production, each differentiated good $z(\omega)$ is produced by a single firm according to the same technology, where the only input is labor. The total amount of labor $L(\omega)$ required to produce the quantity $z(\omega)$ is assumed to be given by

$$L(\omega) = f + az(\omega) \tag{1.7}$$

where f is the fixed labor requirement, and a the marginal labor requirement. Clearly, this technology exhibits increasing returns to scale. These firms choose their mill (f.o.b.) prices and their locations in a *nonstrategic* manner, in the spirit of Chamberlin (Spence, 1976; Dixit and Stiglitz, 1977). In other words, there is free entry, and the number of firms producing the differentiated good/service is very large. Finally, as in the von Thünen model, an iceberg-type transport cost, in which only a fraction of the goods shipped will reach their destination, is assumed (Samuelson, 1983). These assumptions, put together, have a strong implication. Because the impact of a price change on the total consumption of the differentiated good will be negligible (firms are nonstrategic by assumption), a consumer's demand can be shown to be iso-elastic. In consequence, because of the multiplicative structure of the transport cost, the elasticity of an individual demand is the same across locations, thus implying that the elasticity of the aggregate demand is independent of the spatial distribution of consumers. For a firm located at x, the equilibrium price for its product is then unique and is given by

$$p^*(x) = aW(x)/\rho \tag{1.8}$$

where $W(x)$ is the equilibrium wage prevailing at x (an example will be given later). Thus the equilibrium price is equal to the marginal production cost $aW(x)$ times a relative markup given by $1/\rho > 1$, so that equilibrium prices rise with product differentiation.[25] Hence the average cost falls with the total quantity produced, while the marginal cost rises with the local wage.

---

[25] As shown by Anderson et al. (1992, ch. 7), this price is the limit of a Nash price equilibrium when the number of firms becomes arbitrarily large.

Two groups of papers, using variants of the model described earlier, will now be discussed. In the first group, we focus on models of city formation in the case of a linear space, using a partial equilibrium approach. In the second, a two-region economy is considered, and the emphasis is on the emergence of a core–periphery regional structure. Because working with more than two regions (or countries) is known to be complex from the formal point of view, generalizations will consider the polar case of a continuum of locations. In this context, we shall then review some recent extensions dealing with the formation of an urban system in a linear space; this kind of work can be viewed as a start for the construction of a theory of central places. In this group of papers, the approach is in the spirit of general equilibrium.

3.1 City Formation in Linear Space

In the papers of the first group, differentiation in consumption and/or intermediate goods was shown to generate a city endogenously. This idea was developed in a series of contributions published in the late 1980s, including those by Papageorgiou and Thisse (1985), Abdel-Rahman (1988), Fujita (1988; 1989, ch. 8; 1990), Rivera-Batiz (1988), and Abdel-Rahman and Fujita (1990).

Papageorgiou and Thisse (1985) and Fujita (1988) dealt with the following system of centripetal/centrifugal forces: Firms are attracted by places where consumers are numerous, because they will have better access to consumers, but are repulsed by places involving many firms, because competition would be fierce. Households are attracted by places where sellers are numerous, in order to have access to a large variety of goods, but are repulsed by places where households are numerous, because of high land rents. Whereas Papageorgiou and Thisse used reduced forms, Fujita assumed explicit market interactions and obtained reduced forms similar to those supposed by the former authors. In the study by Papageorgiou and Thisse the equilibrium configuration is such that the distributions of firms and of households are bell-shaped when the purchasing pattern of consumers is sufficiently dispersed (i.e., when the products sold by the firms are sufficiently differentiated). In the study by Fujita, two configurations may emerge, depending on the relative numbers of consumers and sellers: If there are relatively more (less) consumers than sellers, then most sellers (consumers) will agglomerate, and most consumers (sellers) will surround them. The equilibrium configurations here explain the formation of a downtown area where people can find large numbers of small stores, restaurants, theaters, and other commercial activities.

On the supply side, it has often been argued that one of the main causes for industrial agglomeration is the availability of specialized local producer services, such as repair and maintenance services, engineering and legal support, transportation and communications services, and financial and advertising services.

Based on this observation, Abdel-Rahman and Fujita (1990) have considered a city with a final-good industry and an intermediate-good industry, where the latter supplies a large variety of specialized services to the former. The production function of a firm belonging to the final-good industry is given by (1.6), where z_0 stands for labor, and $z(\omega)$ represents a specialized service. Finally, the production function of the service firms is as in (1.7).

Abdel-Rahman and Fujita have shown that the aggregate production function of the city is given by (see also Henderson, 1988, ch. 5, for similar expressions)

$$X(N) = AN^{(1-\alpha+\alpha\rho)/\rho} \tag{1.9}$$

where N is the labor force in the city, and A is a constant depending on the parameters of the model. In particular, A rises when the fixed cost f falls, so that the productivity of the final sector is higher when the division of labor in the intermediate sector is finer. Thus, in the aggregate, production in the final sector exhibits increasing returns in the labor force (the exponent of N is larger than unity). In addition, depending on the type of good produced, the parameters of the production function (1.9) are expected to change, so that the degree of increasing returns will vary with the good considered.

This is somewhat surprising, because the underlying individual production functions in the final-good industry show constant returns. The reason lies in the fact that the number of specialized service firms at the free-entry zero-profit equilibrium rises with N, permitting a finer supply of the intermediate good and the emergence in turn of increasing returns at the aggregate level.[26] It would be difficult here not to think of Marshall (1890, 1920, p. 225), who wrote that

the economic use of expensive machinery can sometimes be attained in a very high degree in a district in which there is a large aggregate production of the same kind, even though no individual capital employed in the trade be very large. For subsidiary industries devoting themselves each to one small branch of the process of production, and working it for a great many of their neighbours, are able to keep in constant use machinery of the most highly specialized character, and to make it pay its expense, though its original cost may have been high.

Furthermore, because labor is homogeneous, the equilibrium wage is common to both sectors and is equal to

$$W(N) = AN^{(1-\alpha)(1-\rho)/\rho}$$

which also increases with the labor force. Indeed, having more service firms enhances the productivity of the final sector and hence leads to higher wages

---

[26] This approach is consistent with the idea of Marshallian externalities modeled by Chipman (1970), but here the market interaction leading to these externalities is considered explicitly instead of being assumed through an *ad hoc* specification of an externality affecting cost functions.

in both industries. Nevertheless, increasing N leads to an expansion of the residential area, which in turn yields higher land rents and transport costs. Thus, in equilibrium, the city achieves a finite size.

The following comments are in order. First, the division of labor, expressed here by the diversity of the intermediate sector, is limited by the extent of the market. This is measured by the total population N, which is determined by the trade-off between the (endogenous) presence of increasing returns in the final sector and the workers' commuting costs within the city (Mills, 1967). In turn, the extent of the market is itself limited by the division of labor. Indeed, the latter depends on the degree of increasing returns in the service industry, expressed by the fixed cost f. Accordingly, the division of labor and the extent of the market are interdependent (see Young, 1928, for an early analysis of this idea). Furthermore, because competition is imperfect, the allocation of resources is not optimal within the city. Yet it can be shown that the first-best allocation can be supported as a competitive equilibrium when the total fixed costs are financed by the total differential land rent, a result known as the Henry George theorem (see Wildasin, 1986, for a survey of this theorem).

Note, finally, that the analysis of Abdel-Rahman and Fujita remains incomplete, in that they assumed that both types of firms were located at the CBD. When the final-sector firms are set up at the CBD, it is reasonable to conjecture that the agglomeration of the service firms in the CBD is an equilibrium when the intermediate good is sufficiently differentiated, as in the consumption models discussed earlier.[27]

3.2 The Core–Periphery Structure

The initial objective of the second family of models was to show the possibility of divergence between two regions, whereas the neoclassical model of interregional trade based on constant returns necessarily leads to convergence, either under free trade or under perfect mobility of labor or capital.[28] The prototype model was proposed by Krugman (1991a,b, 1992), and it triggered subsequent studies of trade and growth, such as those by Krugman and Venables (1995a,b,

---

[27] A somewhat related idea, in which different employers face the possibility of uncorrelated shocks, was treated by David and Rosenbloom (1990) in an attempt to describe the dynamics of an industrial district. They showed that paths may converge toward very different equilibrium configurations, depending upon the initial conditions and the parameters of the model.

[28] Michel et al. (1996) have shown that new conclusions emerge when production externalities (as in modern growth theory) and amenities (as in urban economics) are added to the neoclassical model. In the presence of amenities, the skilled workers may receive different earnings in equilibrium, and a core–periphery structure similar to that of Krugman (1991b) may emerge as an equilibrium outcome when production externalities are at work. Such an approach extends the neoclassical model, following the line of research described in Section 2.

1996), Premer and Walz (1994), Englmann and Walz (1995), Kubo (1995), Venables (1996) and Walz (1996), to mention a few.[29]

(a) The basic framework can be described as follows. There are two regions, two sectors, and two types of labor. As in the foregoing, agglomeration may arise because of preference for variety on the consumption side or diversity in intermediate goods on the production side. For the sake of brevity, we deal with the first context only. In (1.5), z_0 stands for a homogeneous agricultural good (A-good) produced under constant returns using one type of labor (A-workers) and sold on a competitive national market (transport costs are zero). The varieties $z(\omega)$ correspond to differentiated industrial goods (I-goods) produced according to (1.7), where $L(\omega)$ is the other type of labor (I-workers), and sold on monopolistically competitive regional markets (transport costs are positive). The A-workers are immobile, and the I-workers are perfectly mobile. Finally, all workers/consumers have a preference for variety expressed by the utility (1.5).

In this model, the immobility of A-workers is a centrifugal force, because they consume both types of goods. The centripetal force is more involved and has a Keynesian feature. It finds its origin in a demand effect generated by a preference for variety. As the number of producers located in a region increases, the number of regional products becomes greater. Then, because firms are mill pricers, the full equilibrium prices will be lower there in comparison with the other region, thus generating a real income effect for the corresponding workers (who are also consumers). That, in turn, will induce workers to migrate toward this region.[30] The resulting increase in the number of consumers ($=$ workers) will create a larger demand for the I-goods in the region, which therefore will lead more firms to locate there. This implies the availability of even more varieties of the differentiated good in the region in question.

This argument is summarized in Figure 1.2, which depicts the circular causation à la Myrdal for the agglomeration of firms and workers through forward linkages (the supply of more varieties of the I-goods will increase the workers' real income) and backward linkages (a greater number of consumers will attract more firms). Therefore, through these linkage effects, scale economies at the individual firm level are transformed into increasing returns at the level of the region as a whole.

Krugman has shown that this mechanism may give rise to a core–periphery pattern in which the entire production of I-goods is concentrated into one region, a regional structure considered by Kaldor (1970) as being more reasonable

---

[29] An earlier analysis that anticipated several aspects of Krugman's work was developed by Faini (1984). Casetti (1980) also developed a simple dynamic analysis that permits the emergence of various equilibria and of catastrophic transitions in a two-region economy. Finally, related ideas also appeared in a simpler framework in an early work by Krugman (1979).

[30] This effect of product variety on consumer migration was first emphasized by Stahl (1983). It is also implicit in the analysis of central places developed by Christaller (1933).

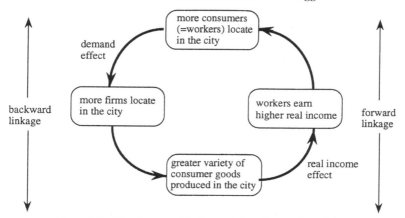

Figure 1.2. Circular causality in spatial agglomeration of firms and workers.

than the convergence between regions, precisely because of the existence of increasing returns. The core–periphery pattern is likely to occur when (1) the transportation rate of the I-goods is low enough,[31] (2) when the I-goods are sufficiently differentiated, or (3) when the share of the industrial sector in the national economy is large enough. Furthermore, because of the existence of multiple equilibria, minor changes in the values of the critical parameters may generate dramatic changes in the equilibrium spatial configuration. This suggests that history (the initial conditions) is important in explaining actual industrial patterns, and circular causation generates a snowball effect that leads manufacturing firms to be locked in within the same region for long time periods (examples include the "industrial belt" in the United States and the "golden triangle" in Europe).[32]

(b) A strong assumption made earlier was that of perfect spatial mobility of the I-workers. If that seems a reasonable approximation for some countries (e.g., the United States), that ceases to be true when we begin studying the economic integration of several countries separated by cultural barriers (as in the case of the European Union). Assuming that all workers are spatially immobile, Venables (1996) has proposed an alternative explanation for the phenomenon of agglomerations, namely, the existence of technological linkages between upstream and

---

[31] In a two-region model with Cournotian firms producing a homogeneous industrial good and no labor migration, Combes (1997) obtained a similar result. This is because price competition is relaxed under Cournot (see Section 4.2), as under product differentiation.

[32] The analogy between cities and technological standards noted earlier has led some authors to believe that the economic activity could well be locked in at suboptimal locations. Since then, empirical studies have shown that the emergence of suboptimal standards is not so frequent (Liebowitz and Margolis, 1994).

downstream industries, which are both assumed to be monopolistically competitive. Using simulations, Venables has shown that reducing transportation costs from high to intermediate will lead to agglomeration of firms, because upstream and downstream firms want to be close to one another in order to reduce the costs of shipping intermediate and final goods. Hence, as in Krugman's work (1991a), there is circular causation. However, the analogy is not complete: Here the uneven demand for labor that follows from the geographical concentration of firms generates regional wage differentials that are no longer sustainable when transportation costs are very low. In this case, dispersion emerges as the equilibrium. We shall return to this question in Section 5.1.

(c) Exploiting the dual model of Ethier, Englmann and Walz (1995) have pursued the line of research initiated by Krugman in order to study growth in a two-region economy. There are two types of labor, the skilled and the unskilled; the former are mobile, and the latter are immobile.[33] There are three sectors: the agricultural sector, using both types of labor; the industrial sector, where the production function is similar to (1.6), but in which the homogeneous input is replaced by the two types of labor; and the R&D sector. Using an endogenous growth device (Grossman and Helpman, 1991, ch. 3), Englmann and Walz suppose that the R&D sector, where only skilled workers are employed and knowledge is accumulated, produces intermediate inputs that are non-traded. Hence, the immobility of the unskilled is a centrifugal force, and the existence of non-traded inputs is a centripetal force. When technological progress is localized,[34] Englmann and Walz show that at the steady state, the production of innovations and of the I-goods will take place in the region with the initial advantage in the number of intermediate, non-traded inputs. The reason for the persistence of leadership lies in the fastest accumulation of knowledge in the region having the initial advantage, and growth is sustained because the marginal productivity of the R&D sector does not decrease to zero. That result provides an explanation for the continuance of a core–periphery structure; it also sheds light on the role of historical accidents that define the initial conditions of the development process.

However, the core–periphery structure is no longer the unavoidable market outcome when knowledge spills over into the other region. More diversified patterns of regional development involving interior solutions arise because the impact of local intermediate inputs is lessened by the transfer of knowledge, which is itself induced by the existence of interregional spillovers. Furthermore, a developed and rich region might well be less ready to adopt a new technology, so that the lagging region might leapfrog the leading region as a reaction to a

---

[33] Though somewhat extreme, this assumption is supported by many empirical studies (Shields and Shields, 1989).

[34] Several empirical studies suggest that knowledge spillovers are strongly localized (Audretsch and Feldman, 1996; Jaffe et al., 1993).

major exogenous change in technology. This would suggest that there is no point of no return (Brezis et al., 1993; Motta et al., 1997). Clearly, regional growth theory is too neglected a topic, and more work is called for.

(d) It is well known that results established for two regions are difficult to extend to the case of an arbitrary number of regions. For this reason, Krugman (1993b) has extended his initial model to a linear spatial economy. Under the three conditions stated earlier, he has shown that the whole industry tends to concentrate into a single city whose location need not be at the center of the segment. Fujita and Krugman (1995) have relaxed the assumption that A-workers are immobile and have allowed for mobility between regions and sectors. Furthermore, the transportation costs of the A-goods have now become positive. They have shown that a single city, surrounded by an agricultural area, arises when varieties are differentiated enough (or when transportation costs are low) and when the population of workers is not too large (Fujita and Krugman, 1995). Indeed, if varieties are close substitutes and/or the population is sufficiently large, an individual producer has an incentive to locate far away from the city and to sell a larger output to local consumers. In this case, there is scope for more than one city. Therefore, the work of Fujita and Krugman provides an endogenous determination of the central city, as in the von Thünen model, but within the context of a completely closed model.

The endogenous determination of several cities has attracted the attention of many scholars, but very few results are thus far available (see, however, the noticeable exception of Henderson, 1974, discussed later). In this respect, a recent contribution by Fujita and Mori (1997) sheds some new light on this classical problem of geographical economics. These authors have shown that as the population in the national economy increases continuously, new cities are created periodically through a catastrophic bifurcation in the existing urban system. As the number of cities increases, the urban system approaches a structure in which cities are more or less equally distant. Specifically, starting from one city, population growth leads to a larger agricultural area. Beyond some threshold, the agglomeration of industrial firms within a single city is no longer an equilibrium. Some I-workers and some firms leave the existing city to form a new city located deep in the agricultural area, together with some A-workers, and new firms are also created. However, the size of the existing agglomeration remains large enough for the other I-workers and firms to stay put. This process keeps going as the population rises. Thus, exactly for the reason suggested by Marshall in the quotation given in the introduction, the locations of the existing cities remain the same, though their sizes may vary with the size of the population. Finally, there is inter-city trade, in addition to trade between cities and rural areas, because the goods produced in the different cities are differentiated and because consumers have a preference for variety. Hence cities do not only trade with their agricultural hinterlands.

(e) However, only one level of city emerges as the outcome of this process. What remains to be investigated is the fundamental question of the formation of an urban hierarchy, that is, the construction of an economic theory of central places. A first step in that direction has been taken by Fujita et al. (1999), who introduced into (1.5) different groups of I-goods, each having different elasticities of substitution and/or transportation rates. They have shown that as the population rises, a (more or less) regular hierarchical central place system reminiscent of Christaller emerges within the economy, in which "higher-order cities" provide larger numbers of groups of I-goods. However, there is two-way trade between cities, because cities specialize in the production of differentiated goods. This leads to a more intricate pattern of trade in which horizontal relationships are superimposed to the pyramidal structure of central place theory. As expected, higher-order cities export more varieties than lower-order cities. However, horizontal relationships between cities of the same order may be more important than trade with lower-order cities, so that the resulting urban hierarchy is more fuzzy than in the Christaller model of central places.

The pattern of specialization and trade stressed by Fujita et al. (1999) seems to fit well the model used by Hohenberg and Lees (1985, ch. 7) to describe the economic landscape that emerged in Europe during the nineteenth century, which combined both the hierarchy of various centers with the existence of networks of cities exchanging specialized goods and services. It also seems to fit the growing "metropolization" of the global economy observed more recently (Sassen, 1991) and to be related to the work of Jacobs (1984, ch. 2), for whom trade between cities of various sizes is the main source of economic development.

(f) That body of work is challenged by Henderson and by Helpman, whose respective models borrow more from standard urban economics. More precisely, they both assume that land is consumed by individuals; on the contrary, cities are supposed to be "punctual" in the Krugman model and subsequent work.

First, Henderson (1974) proposes a different, original approach to the formation of systems of cities. His work is based on Mills (1967), who supposes that the production of a good involves increasing returns [perhaps for the reasons discussed in Section 3.1 that lead to the production function (1.9)] and takes place in the CBD (see Sections 2.1 and 3.1 for possible explanations). Each city then will have a finite size because of commuting costs borne by the workers. Then, assuming a "market for cities," Henderson shows that cities will be created until no opportunity exists for a developer or a local government to build a new one. This corresponds to a free-entry equilibrium in which all cities will be identical. Henderson also shows that cities have an incentive to specialize in the production of traded goods, because combining the production of different goods within a single city will raise commuting costs and land rents. Therefore, if the traded goods involve different degrees of scale economies, which is likely to be the case in view of (1.9), cities will be specialized in the production of different goods they export. That approach explains the existence of an urban system with different types of cities and of inter-city trade involving different goods (see Henderson, 1987, for further developments). Here, also, inter-city trade does not obey the simple principles supposed by Christaller (1933), and cities are specialized in the production of different (instead of differentiated) goods. However, that model does not permit one to predict the locations of cities, nor does it explain the urban hierarchical structure.[35]

In a sense, the Henderson and Fujita-Krugman approaches can be viewed as "dual": Cities have a spatial extension, and in Henderson's approach transportation costs between cities are supposed to be zero; cities have no dimension, but inter-city trade is costly in the Fujita-Krugman approach. In particular, it could be argued that Henderson emphasizes more the role of commuting costs in the formation of cities, whereas Krugman and co-authors retain an approach in which inter-city transport costs are predominant. This distinction might correspond to different stages of development of the urban economy. A first synthesis of the two approaches has been recently provided by Tabuchi (1998). It is discussed in Section 5.1.

Second, Helpman (1998), in a related model, has presented a wider array of results concerning the relationship between the degree of agglomeration and the level of transportation costs (see Krugman and Venables, 1995a, discussed in Section 5.1). Contra Krugman, Helpman's dispersion force lies in the existence of a fixed stock of land to be used for housing, and individuals are all assumed to be mobile. Helpman shows that both regions accommodate industrial firms, even though transportation costs are very low, when the demand for land is high or when products are close substitutes. However, as in the Krugman model, industrial concentration arises provided that the demand for land is low or products are differentiated enough, but now for high transport costs. The difference vis-à-vis Krugman lies in the fact that dispersion is here driven by region-specific supplies (the supply of land) instead of region-specific demands (the demand of agricultural workers). Within Krugman's framework, this amounts to assuming arbitrarily large transport costs for the A-goods, while Krugman supposes that transporting these goods is costless (see Section 5.1).

As mentioned earlier, models based on more diversity or more specialization in the supply of intermediate inputs could be developed. This is true, in particular, for specialized jobs whose existence probably is the main reason for migration (see Becker and Henderson, Chapter 4, this volume, and Hesley

---

[35] A model of inter-city trade in the spirit of those reviewed in Section 3 can be found in the work of Abdel-Rahman and Fujita (1993), whereas Hesley and Strange (1990) study a model along the line considered by Henderson.

and Strange, 1990, for related ideas). More generally, each individual can be considered as a consumer or producer, such that the consumer side likes variety, whereas the producer side specializes in one task in order to enhance productivity. The task may vary with the place of work. In this perspective, Yang and Rice (1994) have studied an interesting model that focuses on the trade-off between economies of specialization and transaction costs; a city then emerges as the outcome of a higher specialization of labor. More work is called for here.

Finally, though all the foregoing models used very specific functional forms and rested on particular market and transport structures, it seems fair to say that they pointed in the right direction. Therefore, they can be viewed as first steps toward the still-missing theories of regional development and of central places. More importantly, combining these various approaches (i.e., preference for variety on the product market, and diversity or specialization on the input markets, especially in the case of differentiated labor) within the same general equilibrium model seems to be an important and challenging task for future research.

Given what we said in the introduction, one of the main limitations of the monopolistic competition models lies in the assumption that firms do not strategically interact (formally this means that we implicitly assume a continuum of firms). This is perhaps because there are many of them in big cities. However, we know from studies of industrial organization that firms often try to restrict entry, thus implying that the zero-profit condition is not an innocuous assumption. In consequence, it is important to deal with oligopolistic rivalry, something that is done in spatial competition. However, as will be seen later, this is not an easy task to accomplish, despite some recent real progress.

4 Spatial Competition

It is now customary to distinguish between two types of models in spatial competition: the shopping and shipping models. Roughly speaking, we have a *shopping model* when firms charge mill prices and their consumers visit the firms and bear the whole transportation costs; in a *shipping model*, firms deliver their products and take advantage of the fact that their customers' locations are observable to price discrimination across locations. The former are rooted in the seminal work of Hotelling (1929), and the latter had their origins in the work of Hoover (1937) and Greenhut and Greenhut (1975). Shopping models seem to be appropriate for studying competition between sellers of consumption goods, whereas shipping models can better describe competition between sellers of industrial goods.[36] As will be seen, strategic interaction is at the heart of these

---

[36] In his study of pricing policies followed by business firms in Japan, the United States, and West Germany, Greenhut (1981) found that about three-quarters of the firms surveyed price-discriminated.

models, and space is the reason for this behavior: competition is localized in shopping models, whereas shipping models involve oligopolistic competition in spatially separated markets. Typically, models of spatial competition assume that the consumer distribution is given. If we introduce a land market and consumer mobility into the Hotelling model, then, as observed by Koopmans (1957, ch. II.9), the locations of firms and consumers become interdependent. Not much has been done in this area thus far, and we have briefly discussed the few existing contributions.

4.1 Shopping Models

Ever since Hotelling, it has generally been accepted that competition for market areas is a centripetal force that leads vendors to congregate, a result known in the literature as the "principle of minimum differentiation." This principle has generated controversy about the inefficiency of free competition, because it suggests that "buyers are confronted everywhere with an excessive sameness" (Hotelling, 1929, p. 54).

The problem of the two ice-cream men provides a neat illustration of this principle. Two merchants selling the same ice cream at the same fixed price compete in terms of location for consumers who are uniformly distributed along a linear segment of length L. Each consumer purchases one unit of the good from the nearer firm. The consumers are thus divided into two segments, with each firm's aggregate demand represented by the length of its market segment. The boundary between the two firms' market areas is given by the location of the marginal consumer who is indifferent between buying from either firm. This boundary is endogenous, because it depends upon the locations selected by the firms. Since the time of Lerner and Singer (1937) it has been well known that the unique Nash equilibrium in pure strategies of this game is given by the location pair

$$x_1^* = x_2^* = L/2$$

regardless of the shape of the transport cost function. Hence, two firms competing for clients will choose to locate together at the market center, minimizing their spatial differentiation. Contrary to widespread opinion, this result is not driven by the existence of boundaries. To see that, consider a continuous distribution over the real line. Then both firms will locate back-to-back at the median of the distribution. It is our belief that several of the results to be presented here can be extended to this framework.

However, things become more complex when (mill) prices are brought into the picture, as in Hotelling's original contribution. Hotelling considered a two-stage game in which the firms first simultaneously chose their locations, and afterward their prices. That decoupling of decisions captures the idea that firms select their locations in anticipation of later competing on price. The boundary between the two firms' markets is now given by the location of the consumer for whom the full prices, defined by the posted prices plus the corresponding transport costs, are equal (transport costs are linear in distance). Because of the continuous dispersion of consumers, a marginal variation in price will change the boundary and each firm's demand by the same order.[37] For each location pair, Hotelling determined what he thought would be the equilibrium prices of the corresponding price subgame. He included these prices, which are functions of the locations, into the firms' profit functions, which then depended only upon locations. These new profit functions were used to study the first-stage location game. As in the foregoing, Hotelling found an equilibrium in which the two firms chose to locate at the market center.

It turns out, however, that Hotelling's analysis was incomplete. When the two firms are sufficiently close, there does not exist an equilibrium in pure strategies for the corresponding price subgame: At least one firm will have an incentive to undercut its rival and to capture the whole market. The study of the location game is accordingly incomplete. Nevertheless, as established by d'Aspremont et al. (1979), if the transport costs are quadratic, rather than linear, a unique price equilibrium exists for any location pair. Reconstructing Hotelling's analysis, those authors then showed that the two firms wish to set up at the endpoints of the market.

This extreme spatial dispersion is the result of a trade-off in which price competition pushes firms away from each other, while competition for market area tends to pull them together. To illustrate how this trade-off works, let Π_1^* be firm 1's profit evaluated at the equilibrium prices $p_i^*(x_1, x_2)$ corresponding to the location pair (x_1, x_2) such that $x_1 < x_2$. Then, because $\partial \Pi_1 / \partial p_1 = 0$, we have

$$d\Pi_1^*/dx_1 = (\partial \Pi_1/\partial p_2)(\partial p_2^*/\partial x_1) + \partial \Pi_1/\partial x_1$$

In general, the terms on the RHS of this expression can be signed as follows. The first one corresponds to the *strategic effect* (the desire to relax price competition) and is expressed by the impact that a change in firm 1's location will have on price competition. Because goods are spatially differentiated, they are substitutes, so that $\partial \Pi_1^*/\partial p_2$ is positive; because goods become closer substitutes when x_1 increases, $\partial p_2^*/\partial x_1$ is negative. Hence the first term is negative. The second term, which corresponds to the *market area effect* uncovered by Hotelling, is positive. Consequently, the impact upon firms' profits of reducing the inter-firm distance is undetermined. However, when firms are close enough,

---

[37] d'Aspremont et al. (1979) have demonstrated that the hypotheses of Hotelling do not guarantee continuity at the global level. For that it is necessary to replace the assumption of linear transport costs by one in which transport costs are increasing and strictly convex in distance.

the first term always dominates the second, so that firms always want to be separated in the geographical space. This implies that the principle of minimum differentiation ceases to hold when firms are allowed to compete in prices (d'Aspremont et al., 1983); one may even observe maximum differentiation. In other words, *price competition is a strong centrifugal force.*

There is no doubt that Hotelling's contribution to economic theory, and in particular to geographical economics, has been fundamental in many respects.[38] Yet, as such, his analysis is unable to explain the currently observed agglomeration of shops selling similar goods. The dispersion of firms turns out to be very sensitive to a particular assumption of the model, namely, that consumers patronize the firm with the lowest full price. Somewhat ironically, when one knows Hotelling's purpose, this corresponds to a very sharp consumer behavior that follows from the fact that firms are supposed to sell identical goods. On the contrary, dramatically different results are obtained when consumers' behavior is smooth enough, for example, because firms sell differentiated products.

The idea that consumers distribute their purchases among several sellers is not new in economic geography and goes back at least to Reilly (1931), who formulated the so-called gravity law of retailing.[39] For a long time, despite their success in empirical studies, gravity models and their extensions, such as the logit, remained somewhat mysterious to economists, because they did not seem to fit the utility-maximization assumption. Psychologists have suggested an alternative model of individual choice that imputes a random term to utility and makes the consumer's decision whether or not to switch firms probabilistic. The use of such models in economics has been pioneered by McFadden (1981) and surveyed by Anderson et al. (1992, ch. 2).

Thus it is now assumed that consumers are influenced by various tangible factors as well as intangible factors at the moment of their decisions, and the relative importance of these factors may change because of external factors. This implies that consumers' purchasing decisions are not based solely on the full prices, but also on firm-specific factors that typically are perceived differently by different consumers. Such behavior means that consumers at the same location will not react in the same way to a firm's unilateral change in its strategy. The presumably wide array of factors influencing consumers' shopping behavior makes it problematic for a firm to predict exactly a consumer's reaction to a reduction in price. In other words, the firm assigns a probability between zero and unity to whether or not a particular consumer on a particular

---

[38] For example, Mueller (1989, p. 180) regarded Hotelling's paper as the pioneering contribution in public choice. The idea to formulate a game on price and locations according to a two-stage procedure was also extremely ingenious and original: it preceded by many years the work of Selten on perfect equilibrium.

[39] The idea of using a gravity model to describe the area of attraction of cities is fairly old. The reader is referred to Sen and Smith (1995, intro.) for a historical overview.

date will respond to a price difference by switching firms. This is modeled by assuming that consumers maximize a random utility rather than a deterministic utility.[40] Firms implicitly sell heterogeneous products, and the random term in the consumer's utility expresses her matching with firms at the time of purchase. An alternative interpretation is that consumers like product variety (see Section 3), so that even if prices do not vary, they will not always purchase from the same firm over time. In both cases, the indirect utility of a consumer at x and buying from firm i can be modeled as follows:

$$V_i(x) = a - p_i - t|x - x_i| + \varepsilon_{ix}, \qquad i = 1, \ldots, n \qquad (1.10)$$

where a is a constant measuring the gross utility of the good, and ε_{ix} is a random variable (with a zero mean) whose realization expresses the matching of product i with a consumer at x. In the special case of the *multinomial logit* (where the random variables ε_{ix} are independently and identically distributed according to the double exponential), the probability that a consumer at x will buy from firm i is given by the following expression derived in the econometrics of discrete choices:[41]

$$P_i(x) = \frac{\exp(-p_i - t|x - x_i|)/\mu}{\sum_{j=1}^{n} \exp(-p_j - t|x - x_j|)/\mu}, \qquad i = 1, \ldots, n \qquad (1.11)$$

where t is the transport rate, and μ is the standard deviation of the variables ε_{ix} (up to a numerical factor). The values of the choice probabilities $P_i(x)$ reflect those of the full prices: the higher the latter, the lower the former. Consequently, the consumer behavior described by (1.11) encapsulates a tendency to buy from the cheapest shops. It is worth noting that the logit and the CES are closely related, in that both models can be derived from the same distribution of consumer tastes; the only difference is that consumers buy one unit of the product in the former, and a number of units inversely related to its price in the latter (Anderson et al., 1992, ch. 3 and 4).

The expected demand to firm i is equal to the integral of the choice probabilities over the market space; it is continuous in prices and locations when μ is strictly positive. However, the continuity of profits does not suffice to restore the existence of an equilibrium. Additional restrictions on the parameters are necessary. As will be seen, these restrictions can be given a simple and intuitive

---

[40] For our purpose, it is worth noting that Anas (1983) has shown that many descriptive gravity- and logit-type models can be derived from the maximization of a random utility.

[41] This formula is well known in classical economic geography, where it is mainly applied to describe the flows of commodities and of individuals. It can be derived from the maximization of an entropy-like utility function (Anderson et al., 1992, ch. 3). In turn, this utility accounts both for the intrinsic utility of the products and for the informational gains generated by a search for the lowest-price firm (Webber, 1979, ch. 2).

interpretation: the relative importance of the transport costs must be small compared with that of the idiosyncratic components of the individual preferences (1.10). Formally, this means that μ/tL must be "large enough," a condition that will be seen to be important for the formation of a clustering of firms.

Let c be the common marginal production cost. In the case of simultaneous choices of prices and locations by firms, the following result holds true: If the choice probabilities are given by (1.11), and if the inequality

$$\mu/tL \geq \frac{1}{2}$$

is satisfied, then the configuration

$$x_i^* = L/2 \quad \text{and} \quad p_i^* = c + n\mu/(n-1), \qquad i = 1, \ldots, n \qquad (1.12)$$

is a Nash equilibrium (de Palma et al., 1985). Therefore, firms will choose to agglomerate at the market center (as Hotelling thought) when their products are differentiated enough and when transportation costs (or market size) are low enough.[42] When firms are gathered at the market center, they constitute a very attractive pole for the consumers, who may find there the best product, as in the study of Fujita and Krugman (1995). However, products must be sufficiently differentiated for the advantage of being agglomerated to dominate the incentive to move away from the cluster and to charge a higher price (see Section 3.1).

When transport costs are low, the benefits of geographical separation are reduced, and prices are lower.[43] Firms will then choose to reconstruct their profit margins by differentiating their products in terms of some nongeographical characteristics, which may be tangible or intangible. Stated differently, product differentiation is substituted for geographical dispersion (this has been shown in a partial equilibrium model of spatial competition by Irmen and Thisse, 1998). In this case, they no longer fear the effects of price competition (the centrifugal force is weakened by the differentiation of products) and strive to be as close as possible to the consumers with whom the matching is the best. Because these consumers are spread all over the market space, they will set up at the market center and therefore minimize their geographical differentiation. This is reminiscent of the market-potential theory developed by Harris (1954) in classical economic geography, according to which firms tend to locate where

---

[42] See Ben-Akiva et al. (1989) and de Fraja and Norman (1993) for similar results when consumers have alternative standard preferences for differentiated products. We may then safely conclude that the existence of an agglomerated equilibrium under sufficient product differentiation is robust against alternative specifications of demand.

[43] This surprising result had already been anticipated by Launhardt (1885, p. 150 of the English translation), for whom "the most effective of all protective tariffs [is] the protection through poor roads."

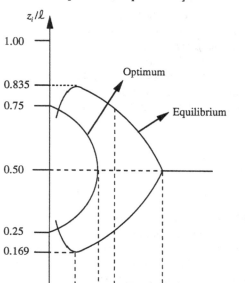

Figure 1.3. Equilibrium and optimal locations under the logit.

they have the "best" access to markets in which they can sell their products. The difference is that here the point of highest "potential" corresponds to a Nash equilibrium. Furthermore, firms will charge a price equal to marginal cost plus an absolute markup that will depend on μ and on the number of firms.[44]

On the contrary, with high transport costs, firms will want to benefit from the advantages of their isolation (i.e., local monopoly power) to earn higher profits, thus confirming the idea of Hotelling (1929, p. 50), for whom "merchants would do well, instead of organizing improvement clubs and booster associations to better the road, to make transportation as difficult as possible."

Consider now the implications of the logit for the *sequential* Hotelling duopoly model. Anderson et al. (1992, ch. 9) have shown the existence and the uniqueness of a price equilibrium for any location pair when μ/tL is large enough. Using this price equilibrium, those authors were then able to study the location game. The following results emerged (they are depicted in Figure 1.3). As μ/tL rises from zero to 0.062, there is no location equilibrium.

---

[44] Observe that the equilibrium price (1.12) bears some resemblance to (1.8). An absolute markup is used here instead of a relative one. This reflects the difference about the nature of individual consumer demands (Anderson et al., 1992, ch. 6). The number of firms also enters the equilibrium price, because we explicitly assume strategic behavior.

For $0.062 \leq \mu/tL < 1.47$ there is a symmetric dispersed equilibrium that initially entails increasing geographical separation of firms. However, when μ/tL goes beyond some threshold (around 0.30), the geographical separation starts to decrease. For $0.76 \leq \mu/tL < 1.47$, an agglomerated equilibrium exists along with the dispersed one; however, the former is unstable, whereas the latter is stable. Finally, for $\mu/tL \geq 1.47$ there is a unique equilibrium that involves central agglomeration.

The intuition behind these results, which is reminiscent of what we saw with the CES, is as follows. An arbitrarily small amount of heterogeneity is not sufficient to restore the existence of equilibrium, because consumers' shopping behavior, though smooth, remains very sharp (i.e., close to the standard 0–1 behavior). When that existence is guaranteed, firms' market areas overlap, thus making price competition so fierce that firms will want to move apart. Beyond some threshold, the product differentiation effect tends to dominate the price competition effect, and firms set up closer to the market center because price competition is relaxed. Finally, for a sufficiently large degree of differentiation, the market-area effect becomes predominant, and an agglomeration of sellers is the market outcome, as in the non-price-competition context. In both the simultaneous and sequential games, the message is the same: agglomeration arises when price competition is weakened enough.[45]

Furthermore, unlike what we observe in the homogeneous-product case, the agglomeration may be socially desirable. The social welfare function includes both product differentiation benefits and transportation costs in an entropy-like function, where μ plays the role of preference for variety. As μ/tL rises from zero to $\frac{1}{2}$, the inter-firm distance decreases from $L/2$ (firms are located at the quartiles) to zero (firms are located at the market center). When μ/tL exceeds $\frac{1}{2}$, it is socially optimal for the duopolists to be located back-to-back; thus, in this model, the market tends to provide excessive geographical dispersion (Anderson et al., 1992, ch. 9). In other words, spatial competition does not necessarily lead to excessive sameness, as Hotelling thought.

Another major approach to explain the clustering of shops is based on *search*. More precisely, Stuart (1979, p. 19) observed that "a seller who does locate as a spatial monopolist might have a hard time *attracting* search-conscious buyers in the first place," so that "a spatial clustering of sellers can result from desires of buyers to search in marketplaces where there are relatively many sellers" (p. 17).

Intuitively, if consumers do not know the characteristics of the products supplied in various places, they can reduce their search costs by visiting the place with the largest number of stores (which may not be the place where they buy). Hence, incomplete information on the consumer side is an agglomeration

---

[45] Another example is provided by price collusion in the context of a repeated price game (Friedman and Thisse, 1993).

force. The conjecture made by Stuart has been proved recently by Fisher and Harrington (1996) and by Schulz and Stahl (1996), building on early attempts by Stahl (1982) and Wolinsky (1983). Those authors suppose that the total demand is variable: Consumers have the same reservation price, but are uniformly distributed along the real line. Thus, if consumers have different tastes and are uncertain about the characteristics of the products on offer, the firms can manipulate the search cost structure by joining an existing market or by establishing a new one. The trade-off faced by a firm is as follows: A firm captures a small market share when setting up in a large market, or obtains the whole market when opening a new one. Because total demand is elastic, a demand externality arises when more firms are located together, because more consumers will benefit from economies of scope in searching (i.e., the extent of the product market is endogenous) and therefore will visit the cluster. Such an externality is obviously a centripetal force.

Though collectively several firms may want to form a new market, it may not pay an individual firm to open a new market in the absence of a coordinating device.[46] Consequently, a new firm entering the market will choose instead to join the incumbents, thus leading to an increase in the agglomeration size. The entry of a new firm creates a positive externality for the existing firms by making total demand larger. Though price competition becomes more fierce, it appears here that firms take advantage of the extensive margin effect to increase their prices in equilibrium.[47]

A related idea has been explored by Gehrig (1998), featuring two differentiated markets located at the endpoints of a linear segment. Unlike Schulz and Stahl, Gehrig supposes that the aggregate demand over the two local markets is fixed. The number of products available in a local market increases with the number of consumers visiting that market, thus reducing the average matching costs. The attractiveness of a market therefore depends on the size of its clientele. Gehrig then shows that in such a setting, an entrant is likely to join one

---

[46] A similar problem of coordination arises when firms are located in an area that is collectively suboptimal but such that no firm finds it profitable to move away unilaterally. As Henderson (1974, 1985) has argued in other contexts, there is a missing agent, e.g., a developer. Building on that idea, Rauch (1993) has shown how a profit-maximizing land developer can coordinate the relocation of firms by discriminating intertemporally over the land market. The same approach could be used for the creation of new markets in space.

[47] In work in progress, Stahl (1995) has developed an alternative shopping model in which transport costs are lump-sum. Indeed, often there are considerable scale economies in carrying the goods bought by a consumer. In the limit, consumers' outlays on transportation can be considered as independent of the purchased quantities (Weinberg, 1985). Therefore, if the utility functions are homothetic, a more distant consumer will have a lower income, and demands will fall in the same proportion. This leads to much simpler aggregate demand functions and allows Stahl to derive new results and to extend those of Schulz and Stahl (1996).

of the existing markets, especially when transportation costs are low.[48] In the same spirit, Stahl and Varaiya (1978) explored the idea that risk-averse firms may choose to congregate, because of the uncertainty associated with the opening of new, separated markets, provided that price competition is not too fierce at the existing markets.

4.2 Shipping Models

Shipping models come from a different tradition that features the analysis of spatial price discrimination in an oligopolistic environment (local markets are segmented, whereas they are tied in shopping models).[49] Indeed, when products are delivered, the locations of the customers are observable to the firms, which are then able to price-discriminate across locations (this corresponds to third-degree price discrimination à la Pigou; see Phlips, 1983, ch. 1).[50] Shipping models were initiated by Hoover (1937) under Bertrand competition and by Greenhut and Greenhut (1975) under Cournot competition.[51] We first consider the latter case, where a firm's strategy is a quantity schedule specifying the amount of output the firm is willing to supply at each location x. In this context, the assumption of local inelastic demand cannot be retained, because any quantity subgame would yield a continuum of equilibria. Consequently, we suppose that each customer has a price-sensitive demand. As usual in Cournot games, we work with the inverse local demand; for simplicity, it is assumed that local demands are linear: $p(x) = 1 - Q(x)$, where $Q(x)$ is the total quantity sold at x, and $p(x)$ is the corresponding market clearing price.

Assuming two firms producing a homogeneous good, each customer is served by both of them if $tL \leq (1-c)/2$. In other words, equilibrium involves market overlapping when shipping costs are low, thus implying that there is market interpenetration (however, at each location the lower-cost firm sells more than its rival). The fundamental difference from the standard Hotelling model is that under Cournot competition, profits do not go to zero when both firms are located together. This is because competition is less fierce than in the Bertrand case.[52] Therefore, as shown by Anderson and Neven (1991), agglomeration at

---

[48] The demand externality provides organizers of markets with some market power, so that the process of opening new markets can in turn be cast within the framework of spatial competition. This line of research has been investigated by Economides and Siow (1988).

[49] Another motivation for studying these models was to explain intra-industry trade, which cannot be accounted for by the neoclassical framework of international trade (Brander, 1981).

[50] This raises the possibility of firms using various spatial price policies. The structure of incentives that lead to the emergence of a particular policy is a difficult issue (Thisse and Vives, 1988).

[51] See Anderson and Thisse (1988) for a detailed comparison of these two discriminating policies.

[52] This is well known in industrial organization; see d'Aspremont et al. (1991) for a unifying framework.

the market center is the unique equilibrium for any given number n of firms when shipping costs are sufficiently low, that is, when $tL \leq (1-c)/n$. Hence, though products are homogeneous, firms choose to agglomerate when transportation costs are low enough. The reason is similar to that discussed in Section 4.1: quantity-setting firms do not fear the effects of price competition, so that the market-area effect is dominant. There is another major difference from the shopping models discussed earlier: firms gain from improvements in transportation means.

However, when t goes beyond some threshold, the center is no longer an equilibrium: firms want to differentiate their locations in order to retain enough customers near the market endpoints. This new effect, called the *market-periphery effect,* corresponds to a centrifugal force. As noticed by Smithies (1941), it is present in any spatial-competition model in which local demands are price-sensitive. When transportation costs are low, this effect is not strong enough to prevent the market-area effect from dominating, thus leading to agglomeration. The opposite holds when transportation costs become higher: the market equilibrium involves gradual dispersion of producers. As in the foregoing, both agglomerated and dispersed equilibria may coexist for some range of t (Gupta et al., 1997).

Assume now that firms compete in price schedules. This means that each firm announces for each location a delivered price at which it is willing to supply the corresponding customers. Then, firms always want to be located far apart when the product sold is homogeneous (Lederer and Hurter, 1986). This is again because price competition is such a strong centripetal force that firms are hurt by geographical proximity. As a result, firms prefer high transportation costs. However, for exactly the reasons discussed in Section 4.1, discriminating duopolists choose to reduce their geographical dispersion when they supply products that are more and more differentiated under the logit (Anderson and de Palma, 1988). Furthermore, the equilibrium configurations tend to be very similar to those depicted in Figure 1.3. Accordingly, though shopping and shipping models have different aims, it seems fair to say that they are governed by the same centrifugal and centripetal forces, thus leading to similar locational patterns under similar conditions. In particular, high transportation costs always constitute a centrifugal force that results in distinct locations.

4.3 Spatial Competition with a Land Market

In all the models of spatial competition discussed earlier, the distribution of consumers is fixed. Ideally, one would like to make it endogenous. So far there have been few attempts to do so because of the complexity of the problem. Because firms have more market power than consumers, it seems reasonable to assume that firms locate first, anticipating the subsequent consumers' locations and demand functions.[53] When products are homogeneous, such a process may reinforce the tendency toward dispersion. Indeed, when firms are dispersed, consumers pay smaller transport costs on average and may also pay lower average land prices, because the supply of attractive lots (those close to firms) is greater. The resulting income effect will increase consumers' demand for private goods and make geographical isolation even more profitable than in the Hotelling model (Fujita and Thisse, 1986).

However, the mere existence of a public facility or of a major transportation node might be enough to attract firms within the same urban area. Indeed, other things remaining the same, transportation costs are reduced for consumers, who then have higher disposable incomes to buy the composite good sold by the firms (Thisse and Wildasin, 1992). In other words, the presence of a preexisting public facility provides an incentive for agglomeration of firms and consumers within an urban area (see Fujita and Mori, 1996, who have studied the formation of port cities using a monopolistic competition model similar to those discussed in Section 3.2).[54] Clearly, more attention should be given to spatial-competition models when consumers are mobile.

In this perspective, a more general model has recently been developed by Berliant and Zenou (1996). They consider a two-stage, general equilibrium framework: Firms first choose their locations strategically (as in Fujita and Thisse, 1986), and prices are determined competitively (as in Anderson and Engers, 1994), an assumption made for technical tractability. Consumers/workers then determine their residences, working places, and consumption bundles, taking the firm locations and the prices of goods as given. There is a continuum of consumers and a finite number of firms that each use an area of land as well as a type of labor. Each firm produces one good and purchases the other goods from other firms. Trade among firms is a surrogate for technological linkages and acts as an agglomeration force. Workers buy all their goods from the firm in which they work, so that firms are in fact factory towns. Firms are said to be "connected" if the union of the areas they use is an interval, that is, they are agglomerated. The transportation cost of a good between connected firms is supposed to be the least possible. If an equilibrium exists, then in the one-dimensional case firms are agglomerated when there are at least

---

[53] This approach to firms' and consumers' locational choices is analogous to the Cournot-Walras model used in general equilibrium with imperfect competition (Bonanno, 1990). In this model, firms select quantities, and prices are then established at the Walrasian equilibrium of the corresponding exchange economy. Hence firms are able to determine the demand functions relating the quantities they supply to the equilibrium market prices. Using these inverse demands, firms choose their outputs at the Cournot equilibrium. In the spatial setting, the locations of firms correspond to outputs, whereas the residential equilibrium, which is influenced by the locations chosen by firms, corresponds to the competitive equilibrium in the Cournot-Walras model.

[54] For example, it is well documented that railway stations have played a major role in the spatial organization of many cities.

two goods. In other words, firms choosing their locations strategically and purchasing goods from one another form a CBD around which consumers/workers are distributed. Showing the existence of an equilibrium turns out to be a hard task is such a setting. Berliant and Zenou use the tools of modern general equilibrium theory to show existence and local uniqueness. This suggests the use of alternative, new techniques to get existence of noncooperative equilibria in spatial-competition models.

5 The New Economic Geography: Some Tentative Conclusions

Though the economic analysis of agglomeration is still in its infancy, a few general principles seem to emerge from the results discussed in the foregoing. They will be briefly considered next, and some possible policy implications will be drawn. The convergence/divergence question will then be analyzed in light of the existing results.

5.1 The Determinants of Economic Agglomerations

It should be clear that the existence of scale economies at the level of firms is a critical factor for explaining the emergence of agglomeration. Indeed, the mere existence of indivisibilities in production makes it profitable for firms to concentrate production in a relatively small number of plants producing for dispersed consumers, so that increasing returns to scale constitute a strong centripetal force. However, we cannot leave the argument at that. Indeed, the geographical extension of markets and the corresponding transportation costs (defined broadly in order to include all the impediments to trade) imply that the entire production generally is not concentrated in one place. In other words, the spatial dispersion of demand is a centrifugal force. Therefore, there is a fundamental trade-off between scale economies and transportation costs in the geographical organization of markets. The market solution is characterized by a more or less dense packing of firms, depending on the firms' strategic behavior and on the spatial price policy they use. For example, under discriminatory pricing, competition is fierce, and markets involve a small number of large firms; under mill pricing, competition is softer, leading to a larger number of smaller firms (Norman and Thisse, 1996). In particular, the fact that the competition policy may affect the fundamental trade-off of a spatial economy has been neglected in the economics of antitrust.

We have also seen that the geographical distribution of economic activities is the outcome of a trade-off involving centripetal and centrifugal forces. One major problem is therefore to evaluate how globalization of the economy will impact these forces. In view of the foregoing developments, it seems that the secular decrease in transportation costs often intensifies the tendency toward agglomeration. Although that decrease might have been seen to suggest that firms would become indifferent about their location, we have seen in various models that low transport costs (or, more generally, trade costs) tend to favor the formation of geographical clusters and to deter the creation of new ones. In other words, footloose activities, by nature independent of the physical geography, mold a new geography of economic agglomerations because of the interplay of centripetal forces that become predominant only when transport costs are low enough. This seems to confirm the work of Kaldor (1970, p. 340), for whom, "as communication between different regions becomes more intensified (with improvements in transport and marketing organisation), the region that is initially more developed industrially may gain from the progressive opening of trade at the expense of the less developed region whose development will be inhibited by it."

There seem to be at least two reasons behind this phenomenon. First, as transportation costs decrease, firms have an incentive to concentrate their production in a smaller number of sites in order to reduce fixed costs, as suggested by the trade-off mentioned earlier. Second, as seen in Section 4.1, low transportation costs make price competition fierce, thus inducing firms to differentiate their products to relax price competition. That, in turn, leads firms to benefit from the advantages of "central locations," where, on average, they are as close as possible to the consumers for whom the matching is best. The counterpart of that result is that product differentiation is a strong force toward agglomeration (see Sections 3.2 and 4.1). Behind this result lies the following fundamental cause: when price competition is relaxed (e.g., price collusion or quantity competition with a homogeneous product), firms no longer fear the devastating effects of price competition, and the various centrifugal forces discussed in this chapter may well be predominant. In other words, even if products are potential substitutes, additional forces make them *complements*. Agglomeration may then emerge as an equilibrium outcome, because competition is overcome by other effects (Markusen, 1983; Matsuyama, 1995; Schulz, 1995; Stahl, 1995).[55] Observe also that similar arguments apply to labor: Wage competition is a centrifugal force, as is price competition, whereas better access to a diversified labor pool for both firms and workers is a centripetal force.[56]

The size of the population is also an important determinant of the urban structure of the economy. In particular, more cities are likely to emerge when the population rises. Indeed, because production is characterized by increasing

---

[55] The role of complementary goods in the making of agglomeration was also discussed by Fujita et al. (1988).

[56] In the context of a Thünian model, a related conclusion was obtained by Nerlove and Sadka (1991), who showed that as the cost of transporting agricultural goods falls, land is cultivated farther and farther from the city, and the labor force working in town increases. However, in accord with von Thünen, industrial firms are supposed to be located within the city.

returns to scale, larger markets allow for the entry of more firms, which can serve as a basis for new clusters and a denser urban pattern. Furthermore, a larger population also permits a better match between consumers/workers and products/job requirements, as well as a wider range of intermediate inputs. In the aggregate, this is reflected by a higher degree of returns to scale on the production side, but also by higher welfare levels on the consumption side. However, this process comes to an end when the addition of a consumer/worker leads to increases in transportation and congestion costs that offset the benefit this individual may derive from variety. Hence, beyond some threshold, firms and consumers/workers have an incentive to form a new city. However, as shown by Fujita (1995), in a hierarchical urban system a population increase can instead boost the growth of the highest-order cities (e.g., think of New York, Paris, and Tokyo, but also of some urban giants in the Third World).

Finally, in several models of geographical economics there is multiplicity of equilibria. This is because agglomeration of economic activities has the nature of a cumulative, self-reinforcing process and because the emergence of a particular site as a major agglomeration does not depend only upon the intrinsic features of the site (e.g., Krugman, 1991a, ch. 1; Arthur, 1994, ch. 4; Matsuyama, 1995; Bénabou, 1996a). In other words, history matters for economic geography in the sense that initial conditions appear to be essential for the selection of a particular equilibrium. This property was anticipated long ago by Myrdal (1957, pp. 26–7) in his analysis of the consequences of the cumulative causation principle: "Within broad limits, the power of attraction of a centre has its origin mainly in the historical accident that something was once started there, and not in a number of other places where it could equally well have been started, and that start met success." In such a context, it is then well known that minor changes in the socioeconomic environment may result in very different geographical configurations, a fact noticed by Casetti in a paper written in 1970, but published in 1980, long before the outburst of the new economic geography. These nonlinearities in the dynamics of locational configurations might well explain why the emergence of new agglomerations is so difficult to predict. However, a rule based on random local interactions has been proposed by Arthur (1994, ch. 4) to select a particular locational equilibrium.

Accordingly, it seems that we have a putty-clay geography: There is *a priori* a great deal of flexibility in the choice of locations, but a strong rigidity of the urban structure once the process of urbanization has started. Those factors, together or in isolation, could explain why, in many countries and at different times, many "planned cities" failed to develop further once governments stopped supporting most of the urban activities before some critical mass was reached (exceptions, involving massive involvement of national governments through huge coordination programs, include Brasilia and Saint Petersburg).

Some equilibria turn out to be socially preferable to others, so that there is scope for regional policy. More precisely, the role of the government here would be to create the conditions for the "best" equilibrium to arise. Yet it is fair to say that our knowledge of the underlying dynamics is far too rudimentary to permit us to make detailed policy recommendations. In addition, even though a spatial structure might well be inefficient, it likely would be difficult to change, because of the lock-in effects associated with existing agglomerations. Another reason for this inertia, related to the work of Krugman (1991c) and Matsuyama (1995), is the formation of self-fulfilling prophecies about the development of some areas. Indeed, it seems reasonable to consider existing cities as focal points that help agents coordinate their spatial decisions. In such a context, reshaping the urban landscape would then require major changes in agents' expectations.

5.2 Convergence versus Divergence

The preliminary results we have reviewed seem to fit well the explanations for the waves of urbanization that occurred in Europe in the twelfth century, as well as the process of urban growth that has taken place since the beginning of the Industrial Revolution in Europe and the United States. An analysis of these various processes at work, as developed by Bairoch (1985) in his economic history of cities, shows the relevance of the approaches surveyed in this chapter.

However, it should be kept in mind that those models are still very simple. In richer models integrating more realistic patterns of migration, new effects might emerge that could more than offset the direct effects identified earlier. For example, Puga (1999) has shown that a drastic decrease in transportation costs may lead to geographic dispersion when the mobility costs of workers between regions are arbitrarily large and the mobility costs between sectors are positive but finite (contra Krugman, 1991a, who assumes prohibitive costs). He also supposes the existence of input/output linkages, as in the work of Venables (1996) and Puga and Venables (1996); otherwise there would be no agglomeration force. In this context, the agglomeration of firms into a single region intensifies competition on the corresponding local labor market. Though firms can attract workers from the agricultural sector, but not from the other region, the latter effect turns out to be a dominant centrifugal force when transportation costs are low enough, because firms are able to supply the other region at low cost while benefiting from low wages.[57]

Mori (1997) has reported comparable results in a continuous model with a land market: firms are willing to locate away from cities because of the lower

---

[57] From a historical perspective, it is worth noting that the trade-off between the place of minimum transportation cost and the place with the lowest labor cost was already at the heart of the Weberian theory of industrial location (Weber, 1909, ch. 4).

wages they pay in the agricultural areas and because the costs of transporting the manufactured goods to the cities are low; workers are willing to leave cities because the costs of agricultural goods are lower and therefore real wages are higher in the rural hinterlands, and manufactured goods are available at prices close to those prevailing in cities. Thus new cities may emerge when the population is large enough, leading to a more dispersed pattern of economic activities, as shown by the emergence of edge cities (Garreau, 1991). Finally, using simulations, Krugman and Venables (1995a) have predicted the collapse of the core–periphery structure and convergence between regions when trade costs are sufficiently low, for reasons similar to those discussed earlier. They have summarized their results as follows (p. 476):

The world economy must achieve a certain critical level of integration before the forces that cause differentiation into core and periphery can take hold; and when differentiation occurs, the rise in core income is partly at peripheral expense. As integration proceeds further, however, the advantages of the core [are eroded], and the resulting rise in peripheral income may be partly at the core's expense.

These preliminary findings suggest that there is no monotonic relationship between the degree of geographical concentration and the level of transportation costs. Very high or very low trade costs would favor the dispersion of economic activities, and agglomeration would emerge for intermediate values of these costs once the spatial mobility of workers was low. In other words, the relationship between trade costs and the degree of geographical concentration of the economy would be U-shaped. However, Puga (1999) has also shown that agglomeration keeps rising even for low transportation costs when the regional mobility of workers is high; in this case, the foregoing relationship is monotonically decreasing, as in Krugman (1991b).

It is worth noting that the foregoing results suppose that wages are freely determined on each local labor market. If wages are determined at the national level (e.g., according to a nationwide bargaining process between employers and unions), there is no wage gap between regions, so that agglomeration is expected to arise for both intermediate and low transportation costs. One may expect a similar conclusion to hold when wages do not adjust downward, as in Keynesian economics, so that regional unemployment may occur.

An alternative line of research has been pioneered by Rosen (1979) to explain persistent regional wage differences. He has taken a broader view by considering the role of regional amenities in the decision to migrate (see Knapp and Graves, 1989, for an overview of studies on migration driven by amenities differentials). In the context of hedonic migration theory, individuals are both suppliers of labor and consumers of regional externalities, and migration is viewed as a mechanism to equalize utilities across locations. Some regional amenities, such as social interaction among individuals (as in Section 2), or the supply of local public goods, depend positively on the total regional population. On the other hand, a growing population is likely to generate a local crowding effect in the form of pollution, criminality, and congested infrastructures that will negatively affect the individuals residing in the region. Thus, there is a trade-off at the consumption level to the extent that regional amenities favor concentration of workers into a single region, and crowding operates as a dispersion effect. Subsequently, Rosen's analysis has been extended by Robak (1982) and Michel et al. (1996), who have added a production side to the framework. The results obtained then suggest that regional wage differentials emerge as the most natural outcome. The system is in equilibrium, however. Indeed, though wages are different (and observable), utilities are equal (but unobservable) across regions.

Furthermore, the assumption of zero transport cost for the A-goods, made thus far, is not as innocuous, as already suggested by Helpman (1998), who assumes prohibitive costs. Indeed, when transport costs for the I-goods are low relative to those for the A-goods, the (relative) price of the A-goods may increase faster than the price of the I-goods, so that real income does not necessarily rise in the agglomeration. This makes the concentration of activities into a single region less attractive for both workers and firms, and the core–periphery structure may become unstable (Calmette and Le Pottier, 1995). Accordingly, though the trade costs for both types of goods have declined since the beginning of the Industrial Revolution, what matters for the regional distribution of economic activities is not only the absolute levels of transport costs but also their relative values. In particular, Kilkenny (1998) has shown that a rise in relative agricultural transport costs widens the gap between urban and rural nominal wages. Cheaper rural labor then attracts industrial firms (see Section 2.2 for related developments), thus fostering rural development.

However, as acknowledged by Krugman (1996a) himself, it should be kept in mind that industrialized countries are becoming more involved in the production of information, and less in that of tangible goods. Hence the agricultural and industrial sectors become less crucial in economic growth. In such a context, it seems reasonable to believe that the agglomeration and dispersion forces at work are different from those emphasized in the core–periphery model discussed earlier.

In the same spirit as the aforementioned papers, Tabuchi (1998) has shown that positive intraregional transport (commuting) costs associated with competition among workers for land consumption also generate a U-shaped relationship (see Brakman et al., 1996, and Krugman, 1996a, for a similar idea cast in different frameworks). As in Henderson's work, this is because a high concentration of workers into a single urban area gives rise to high land rents. That, in turn, fosters the relocation of workers into the peripheral region, leading to more firms in that region. Though still preliminary, this work, together with that of Helpman, as well as Martin and Rogers (1995), may be considered the first attempt to integrate models stemming from different traditions in geographical economics. Such a synthesis is interesting not only from the theoretical viewpoint but also because it provides a unified framework to study the process of city formation in various historical stages characterized by different values of the ratio between interregional transport costs of goods and commuting costs of individuals.

It should also be stressed that the results discussed earlier were derived in the context of models that did not integrate the informational externalities discussed in Section 2 and neglected the phenomenon of learning by doing on local labor markets. They do not capture well the concept of innovation, because horizontal product differentiation is assumed, although vertical product differentiation allows for a better description of product innovation (see Jayet, Chapter 11, this volume). As observed by several authors, a combination of various factors seems to be essential for localized accumulation of knowledge within a region. For example, Feldman and Florida (1994, p. 226) concluded a detailed study of the geography of innovation in the United States by noting that

innovation is no longer the province of the inventor, the risk-taking entrepreneur, the insightful venture capitalist, or the large resource-rich corporation. Innovation instead has its sources in a broader social and spatial structure – a landscape of agglomerated and synergistic social and economic institutions welded into a technological infrastructure for innovation.

It is not clear that the convergence of real wages mentioned earlier would remain the same if all these elements were taken into account. More work is therefore needed to check the robustness of the results discussed here, and empirical studies will be required to evaluate their real-world implications. In any case, it seems fair to say that there are strong tendencies toward agglomeration, but there are also powerful countervailing tendencies toward transnational flows and a spatially global economy. In other words, there is no simple relationship between the economic and the spatial.

A better understanding of the impact of trading costs on the spatial division of labor is indeed very important, for such costs would suggest that "incompletely" integrated markets, which characterize most trading blocks, would favor the polarization of space, whereas full integration would be associated with a large diffusion of economic activities across regions.[58] At this point, it seems worth noting that we might have here an explanation for the much higher regional disparities observed within the European Union (EU) than within federal countries (e.g., Armstrong and Vickerman, 1995). For example, the EU is far less integrated than the United States, and any comparison between the two

[58] It might be worth mentioning that Beckmann (1972) has shown that in a spatial-competition model, a decrease in transportation cost leads to higher prices when the market structure evolves from monopoly to competition. On the other hand, as seen earlier, prices decrease under complete market integration.

entities seems to be at least premature. Note that there is also great dispersion *within* some of the main member states of the EU. The reason, we believe, is that many markets in European countries, especially the labor markets, are more segmented than those in the United States, thus strengthening the tendency toward more dispersion at the EU level. In any case, as pointed out by Armstrong and Vickerman (1995, p. 8), the absence of long time series of harmonized statistics for EU regions makes any comparison rather problematic. This is *a fortiori* true at the international level, where the definition of a region is very heterogeneous. (Does it make sense to compare California and a Greek region, or the city region of Hamburg and the state of Mississippi?) Another difficulty lies in the different criteria used to evaluate the possible convergence between regions (see, e.g., the debate between Quah, 1996, and Sala-i-Martin, 1996, as well as the selective overview provided by de la Fuente, 1997). Instead of using variables borrowed directly from nonspatial growth theories, it seems more reasonable to integrate into the econometric studies the main centripetal and centrifugal factors studied in the new models of geographical economics. Finally, another important aspect to be accounted for is the impact of the *scale* chosen when comparing levels of economic activity between different geographical areas. For example, one may observe convergence at some intermediate level (e.g., nations or regions), whereas intraregional or international disparities keep rising because of the increased polarization of the corresponding areas. It should also be kept in mind that the more detailed the disaggregation, the greater the regional disparities that will emerge. Clearly, what matters for individuals is what is going on where they live and work, but such local data are not available.

In addition, as discussed in Section 2.2, low transportation costs may also favor relocation of activities that do not need to be close to other producers and/or are labor-intensive. Most models in geographical economics suppose a space homogeneous in terms of socioeconomic factors. Still, it is well known that some firms seek to locate in areas where the labor cost is very low because their products can be produced by means of labor-intensive techniques. Under such circumstances, the decrease in transportation costs can be viewed as a dispersion force that fosters convergence across countries. In this perspective, it seems promising to model the firm as a *multi-location agent* and to integrate the possibility of foreign direct investment as a strategy of the firm. Roughly speaking, two polar cases of spatial division of production may be considered. The spatial division of a firm is said to be *horizontal* when the whole production process is carried out in each plant. The trade-offs described earlier between scale economies and transportation costs, as well as the proximity and size of local markets, are likely to govern the horizontal pattern of production activities. Furthermore, each plant may produce specific products that fit the particularities of the local market. On the other hand, the spatial division of a firm is said to be *vertical* when the production process in broken up into different units with the aim of internalizing the comparative advantages of particular sites (see Section 2.2 for an illustration). For example, research and development, as well as management operations, are likely to be conducted at the core of the global economy, whereas production activities may take place in the periphery when production is labor-intensive. Therefore, the way firms organize their activities may induce particular forms of convergence/divergence between various areas in ways that are not captured in the models mentioned earlier, nor in standard models of international trade. One way to explore these issues is to integrate various organizational models of the firm into the theory of firm location (as briefly discussed in the foregoing).

More broadly speaking, there is a strong need to integrate the agglomeration models surveyed in this chapter with neoclassical models of trade based on comparative advantage in order to study the new international division of labor. Some preliminary attempts to deal with the tension between agglomeration and factor price equalization can be found in the work of Matsuyama and Takahashi (1998), Michel et al. (1996), and Puga and Venables (1996).

6 Alternative Approaches and Suggestions for Future Research

There are other domains of geographical economics that also can shed light on the process of agglomeration. Without attempting to be complete, we shall summarize some of the main ideas developed in those various domains in Section 6.1. Some suggestions for further developments of the reviewed models are then proposed in 6.2.

6.1 Alternative and Classical Approaches

One major domain of classical economic geography not yet covered in this survey is the theory of firm location. Since the mid-1970s, substantial progress has been made in this important domain of classical economic geography, as surveyed by Hurter and Martinich (1989, ch. 3). For our purpose, the most relevant approach deals with location issues in networks (see Labbé et al., 1995, for an extensive survey). Formally, this means that the transportation support is represented by a topological graph. Given a finite set of input and output markets situated in the network, it can be shown that a profit-maximizing firm will choose as a location either a market or a node of the network, provided that the transportation cost functions are increasing and concave in distance.[59] This assumption is in accord with empirical evidence; see Hoover (1948, ch. 2) and Isard (1956, ch. 2). Hence, the profit-maximizing location is to be sought

---

[59] The same holds in a setting in which oligopolistic firms compete à la Cournot on markets situated at the vertices of the network (Labbé and Hakimi, 1991). Furthermore, this property also remains valid when the firm aims at internalizing spatial externalities similar to those discussed in Section 2.1 (Thisse and Papageorgiou, 1981).

within a finite subset of the network. Because the network contains a continuum of points, this property of finiteness provides us some useful insights about the impact of transport infrastructure on the geographical organization of production. The candidate points are also characterized by other production activities and/or have a high degree of centrality in the network. Furthermore, when the fixed component of the transportation cost is "large" compared with the variable component,[60] the firm will necessarily choose to set up at a market. In other words, the firm agglomerates with some of its customers/suppliers.[61] For example, a hub is a major transportation node, and Krugman (1993c) has shown that in a model similar to those discussed in Section 3, such a node tends to attract producers. Hence we can safely conclude that the changes in transportation technologies that have been occurring for many decades, reflected in higher fixed costs and lower variable costs with respect to distance, as well as in the more recent development of hub-and-spoke networks, have acted as an additional centripetal force.

As mentioned in the introduction, another major field of classical economic geography is central place theory, the object of which is to explain the spatial distribution of economic activities in a hierarchical system of urban centers. Specifically, different goods, characterized by nested market areas and indexed accordingly by $i = 1, \ldots, n$, are supplied by different firms. The theory then aims to explain that a location where good i is available also accommodates firms supplying all goods of order lower than i. A location where commodities 1 to i are available is called a *central place of order i*. The bulk of the theory has been directed toward identifying geometric conditions under which a superposition of regular structures is possible. However, that literature has focused far too much on geometric considerations (what Krugman, 1995, ch. 2, has called the "Germanic geometry"). Indeed, there are no economic forces that lead firms selling different goods to cluster, so that it is hard to see why central places should emerge. To the best of our knowledge, Eaton and Lipsey (1982) were the first to propose an economic foundation for such clusterings. In their model, the force driving the formation of clusters involving firms selling different goods is the occurrence of *multipurpose shopping* (see Thill and Thomas, 1987, for a survey showing the empirical relevance of such behavior). In other words, consumers can group their purchases of different goods in order to reduce transport costs. This opportunity creates demand externalities that firms exploit by locating with firms selling other goods. Assuming non-price competition, Eaton and Lipsey have identified a set of conditions under which the only equilibria verify the hierarchical principle. Relaxing the given price assumption, Thill (1992) has shown that a firm selling goods of

---

[60] This seems to correspond fairly well to the capitalistic nature of modern transport means.
[61] See Hoover (1948, ch. 3) for an early, but informal, discussion of similar results.

orders 1 and 2 will not locate with a firm selling only a good of order 1, because price competition will be strong enough to push them away. However, because the multiproduct firm is more attractive, its rival will select a location closer than it would in standard spatial competition in which each firm would provide only one good. Finally, using the Eaton-Lipsey framework, Quinzii and Thisse (1990) have proved that the socially optimal configuration of firms always involves the clustering of firms selling goods of orders 1 and 2. It is fair to say, however, that the spatial-competition approach to central places taken in those papers very quickly becomes intractable, so that a need exists for other approaches [see, e.g., Section 3.2(e)].

Finally, a neglected aspect of our survey is that the urban landscape is also shaped by "big" agents, such as local governments, land developers, and major corporations. This has led to a new approach to the study of formation of cities, pioneered by Henderson and co-authors. In this new strand of literature, which shares some features of spatial-competition models, cities are shaped by agents who have market power and behave strategically. Henderson and Slade (1993) have revisited the model of Fujita and Ogawa (1982), assuming now that two developers compete strategically to attract workers and firms in the areas to be developed. The issue faced by a developer is to choose the size of the labor force and to have either a monocentric pattern (the business districts are contiguous) or a duocentric pattern (the business districts are separated). They have shown that for a small change in the opportunity cost of labor, one observes an enormous change from a configuration in which the duopolists locate their business districts together to a configuration in which the business districts are far apart, with their business borders separated by almost half the population of residents. Henderson and Mitra (1996) have taken another approach. They suppose a small number of large developers (typically one) who initiate massive planned private and/or public developments, manipulating the decisions of atomistic agents who reside in the core city. This leads to new urban equilibria; in particular, suburbanization takes the form of "edge cities" whose locations may be chaotic. Finally, Fujita et al. (1997) have shown how the introduction of a large firm in a medium-size city will affect both the land and labor markets, because they are interdependent. The firm can behave strategically and manipulate both markets in order to maximize its profits. It is shown that the creation of jobs within the city may vary drastically according to the location selected by the new firm, thus suggesting that inter-city competition to attract new firms can have very different impacts on the urban economy.[62]

---

[62] A strategic approach to community formation was considered by Henderson and Thisse (1997), who showed that the number of viable communities supplying local public goods and housing will depend on the income range.

6.2 Suggestions for Future Research

One of the main limitations of most models of geographical economics is that the findings seem to depend heavily on strong assumptions made about the economy. In particular, very specific functional forms, like the CES or the logit, are used, both of which imply strong gross substitutability, whereas spatial-competition models posit, instead, that goods are weak gross substitutes. It is reasonable to think that such strong assumptions were needed at an early stage of development of the theory. However, one should now strive for more robust conclusions. For example, it might well be possible to extend the CES model by using the random-utility model of monopolistic competition developed by Anderson et al. (1992, ch. 6) that permits one to retain the idea of symmetry within a much more general framework. See Mirrlees (1995) and Ottaviano and Thisse (1998) for other extensions of the standard basic models. For example, the Cournot model seems to be a sensible alternative, because it allows for both strategic interaction and soft pricing (Combes, 1997). Furthermore, mill pricing is not the most common spatial price policy used by firms (Greenhut, 1981); hence, it should be worthwhile to study how alternative spatial pricing rules could affect the formation of economic agglomerations (Ottaviano and Thisse, 1998).

From a more fundamental viewpoint, it should be worthwhile to study the abstract foundations of the idea of "preference for variety" (Kreps, 1979, might be a good starting point). Similarly, we should explore more systematically how varying the dimension of the commodity space affects the efficiency of production, in order to have a deeper understanding of the gains associated with a greater division of labor. In short, what are the foundations for the ideas that stand behind using the CES as a utility or production function when the number of commodities is variable?

The iceberg approach concentrates on the fact that transportation consumes resources. Yet using an iceberg transport cost function implies that any increase in the mill price is accompanied by a proportional increase in transport cost, which seems both unrealistic and undesirable. It is worth recalling here that there once was a debate in international trade about the iceberg approach versus an explicit modeling of the transport sector, a debate that, strangely enough, has been forgotten. What is important for us is that the two approaches do not lead to the same results, thus casting some doubt on the results derived under the iceberg model (Bottazzi and Ottaviano, 1996). This is especially important for the debate described in Section 5.1 concerning the (possible) interregional convergence.

It is also known that aggregating local demands across locations may lead to demand systems that exhibit undesirable features, such as discontinuities or outward kinks. Still, even if simplifying assumptions probably are unavoidable, more attention should be paid to the aggregation problem over space. In the monopolistic competition models discussed in Section 3, it is not clear what the assumption of nonstrategic interaction implies, and one should try to find a way to relax it. In spatial-competition models (see Section 4), there clearly is a need for more work devoted to endogenous determination of the consumers' locations and the combination of atomistic and non-atomistic markets.

The following topic should also be investigated: Models in which cities are viewed as the outcome of a process involving big interacting agents who plan large sectors of the city economy, as in Henderson, would be more relevant for describing the emergence and growth of American cities, which often were created *ex nihilo*. On the other hand, the self-organizing approach in which cities result from the interactions of many agents, put forward by Krugman, might well better fit what has been observed in Asia and Europe, where few major cities have been created since the beginning of the Industrial Revolution (see, e.g., Eaton and Eckstein, 1997, for a study of the French and Japanese urban structures), but where urban growth has been mainly the outcome of a process involving large numbers of agents over long periods of time. It should also be kept in mind that several pre-industrial Asiatic and European cities were ruled by "big agents," such as guilds, aristocrats, and religious orders (Weber, 1921). However, as suggested by the study of De Long and Shleifer (1993), the economic impact of those agents varied with the nature of the city government. A study in urban history stressing these aspects is needed. Note, finally, that there are new models of urbanization that offer an alternative to the CES-type models, and they should be given more attention (see, e.g., Duranton, Chapter 8, this volume, and Jayet, Chapter 11, this volume).

There are several important questions that remain on the research agenda. First, more work is needed on the emergence of urban hierarchies. Central place theory probably is the main topic in geographical economics, though very few major results are thus far available. There is no doubt that the problem is difficult, but it is too important to be ignored any longer (insightful suggestions for new approaches have been offered by Stahl, 1987). In particular, it would be interesting to pursue a comparison of the self-organization approach advocated by Krugman (1996b) and that developed by Henderson and co-authors. For a recent analysis in that direction, see Becker and Henderson (Chapter 4, this volume), who provide a comparison based on a model of task specialization within firms and cities.

Each approach has its own merits that should be further investigated. In this perspective, there is a new line of research that has emerged in modern economic theory in which agents have a certain probability of meeting that depends on socioeconomic and geographical factors; when the interaction occurs, a transaction may take place between the agents (Kirman, 1995). This type of model might prove useful for studying the emergence of market towns where people meet in order to trade goods or exchange information.[63] It also seems to be in accord with the self-organization approach mentioned earlier, to the extent that agents are small and behavior is nonstrategic.[64] See David et al. (in press) for an application of similar ideas to the problem of the emergence and stability of technological enclaves.

Before proceeding, it is worth noting that economic historians have stressed the roles of two models of urban systems. These systems, as described by Hohenberg and Lees (1985, pp. 4–5), seem to have different potentials for growth and development and should be compared from the economic standpoint, the latter bearing some resemblance to the Henderson (1974) approach:

The first model is based on the role of a city as a central place, supplying its surroundings with special services – economic, administrative, or cultural – that call for concentration at one point in space. A hierarchy of such centers, the higher-level ones serving as central places for central places, [forms] a region around the principal center.... Yet cities are more than the point around which the threads of regional unity are wound. They also link the region with the world beyond, permitting it to reconcile the advantages of specialized activity with the enriching experience of diversity.... In this perspective cities also belong to networks of trade, information, and influence that reach far beyond the borders of a country.

The process of integrating these two models within a unified framework and studying their interaction is probably one of the most important lines of research in geographical economics. Second, the question of regional convergence/divergence has at last received the attention it has long deserved, especially in the empirical literature. However, the models still are too preliminary to allow us to draw strong policy recommendations, and more studies are required. In particular, we do not know much about the circumstances that can allow a region to recover. In the real world, we observe that some regions are successful in their efforts at economic revival, whereas others seem to decline inexorably. It is not always clear why such different evolutions arise.

Third, the potential connections between growth and agglomeration should be explored more systematically. If few people would object to the claim that the pecuniary externalities associated with product variety and input diversity favor both agglomeration and growth, the long-run impact of agglomeration on technological externalities is less clear. Indeed, through the processes of face-to-face communication and information exchange that characterize metropolitan areas, it is not unreasonable to expect a decrease in the diversity of the population.

---

[63] For general equilibrium models of marketplace formation, see Wang (1993), Berliant and Wang (1993), and Berliant and Konishi (1994).

[64] Note that the principles of self-organization were applied in geography some years ago in order to study the dynamics of agglomeration (e.g., Allen and Sanglier, 1979, 1981). However, the microeconomic foundations of the models used often left much to be desired. A more recent approach developed along the same lines can be found in the work of Arthur (1994, ch. 3).

Consequently, if the heterogeneity of the labor force is an engine of growth (Bénabou, 1996b), restrictive immigration policies, such as those implemented in Japan and, to a less extent, in France, might well be damaging to the growth of those economies in the long run. Furthermore, very little attention has been paid in theory to the interaction between innovation activity and regional growth. This is rather surprising, because the localized nature of business and academic research is a well-documented fact (Jaffe et al., 1993; Feldman and Florida, 1994; Audretsch and Feldman, 1996).[65] In this case, we may expect the cost-reducing spillover functions to be convex in distance because their impact is mainly local. Despite the fact that competition on the product market becomes fiercer, firms tend to agglomerate in order to internalize the R&D externalities generated by the others (Long and Soubeyran, 1996; Mai and Peng, 1999). However, agglomeration does not necessarily occur when spillovers are concave in distance. Put in a broader perspective, these results, together with those presented in Sections 2.1 and 3.1, suggest that dispersed (concentrated) contact fields associated with the demand (supply) side favor the emergence of a unique agglomeration.

The role of public capital, emphasized in the endogenous growth literature, has not been studied in the new theories of regional economics. So far we have very few insights about what could well be a "good" infrastructure policy in the context of a spatial economy. See, however, Martin and Rogers (1995) for a first attempt to evaluate the impact of infrastructure on the regional distribution of production in a model similar to those reviewed in Section 3.2. Building transportation infrastructure is often presented as the main remedy to regional imbalance, because accessibility is improved, but this is a policy in search of a theory (see, however, the results presented in Section 5.2). Furthermore, from the empirical point of view, assessing the impact of such infrastructure on regional development remains a difficult task (Gramlich, 1994; Cain, 1997).

Note also that most models of economic agglomeration assume a one-dimensional world. Though acceptable as a first approximation, one should try to go further and construct more general models allowing for a second dimension. This creates unsuspected difficulties in that the metrics proposed in location theory for measuring distance in a two-dimensional space have different mathematical properties. See Erlenkotter (1989) for a discussion of some of the problems raised by the choice of a particular distance function in a spatial-competition model, and see Rushton and Thill (1989) for some preliminary results.

Last, all existing models of geographical economics reviewed in this chapter assume full employment (see Zenou, Chapter 10, this volume, for a survey of the few papers dealing with unemployment in a geographical setting). Even

---

[65] Observe that artistic activities tend to be even more geographically concentrated (Menger, 1993).

during the "golden sixties," some regions experienced persistent unemployment. Nowadays the distribution of unemployment in Europe seems to be fairly uneven across regions, even within a given country, as if increasing regional imbalance was one of the outcomes of slower growth (MacKay, 1995). We have a very poor understanding of these questions, and the appeal to low regional mobility of workers, though relevant in some cases, seems weak as the main explanation for regional unemployment disparities. This important economic and social problem should be given more attention in the future. A possible line of research would be to integrate concepts of labor economics, such as the basic ingredients of matching and search models, into the corpus of geographical economics. In addition, the work of Weitzman (1982), who built his theory of unemployment on increasing returns and monopolistic competition, seems to be worth investigating, because the ingredients of his analysis are the same as those used in the new models of economic geography reviewed in Section 3.

References

Abdel-Rahman, H. (1988). Product differentiation, monopolistic competition and city size. *Regional Science and Urban Economics* 18:69–86.

Abdel-Rahman, H., and Fujita, M. (1990). Product variety, Marshallian externalities, and city sizes. *Journal of Regional Science* 30:165–83.

Abdel-Rahman, H., and Fujita, M. (1993). Specialization and diversification in a system of cities. *Journal of Urban Economics* 33:189–222.

Akerlof, G. A. (1997). Social distance and social decisions. *Econometrica* 65:1005–27.

Allen, P. M., and Sanglier, M. (1979). A dynamic model of growth in a central place system. *Geographical Analysis* 11:256–72.

Allen, P., and Sanglier, M. (1981). A dynamic model of central place system. II. *Geographical Analysis* 13:149–64.

Alonso, W. (1964). *Location and Land Use.* Cambridge, MA: Harvard University Press.

Anas, A. (1983). Discrete choice theory, information theory, and the multinomial logit and gravity models. *Transportation Research B* 17:13–23.

Anderson, S. P., and de Palma, A. (1988). Spatial price discrimination under heterogeneous products. *Review of Economic Studies* 55:573–92.

Anderson, S. P., de Palma, A., and Thisse, J.-F. (1992). *Discrete Choice Theory of Product Differentiation.* Cambridge, MA: MIT Press.

Anderson, S. P., and Engers, M. (1994). Spatial competition with price-taking firms. *Economica* 61:125–36.

Anderson, S. P., and Neven, D. (1991). Cournot competition yields spatial agglomeration. *International Economic Review* 32:793–808.

Anderson, S. P., and Thisse, J.-F. (1988). Price discrimination in spatial competitive markets. *Papers and Proceedings of the European Economic Association* 32:155–64.

Armstrong, H. W., and Vickerman, R. W. (eds.) (1995). *Convergence and Divergence Among European Regions (European Research in Regional Science 5)*. London: Pion.

Arthur, W. B. (1994). *Increasing Returns and Path Dependence in the Economy*. Ann Arbor: University of Michigan Press.

Audretsch, D. B., and Feldman, M. P. (1996). R&D spillovers and the geography of innovation and production. *American Economic Review* 86:630–40.

Bacon, R. W. (1984). *Consumer Spatial Behaviour. A Model of Purchasing Decisions over Space and Time*. Oxford: Clarendon.

Bairoch, P. (1985). *De Jéricho à Mexico. Villes et économie dans l'histoire*. Paris: Gallimard. English translation (1988): *Cities and Economic Development: From the Dawn of History to the Present*. University of Chicago Press.

Banerjee, A. (1993). The economics of rumours. *Review of Economic Studies* 60:309–27.

Becker, G., and Murphy, K. (1992). The division of labor, coordination costs, and knowledge. *Quarterly Journal of Economics* 107:1137–60.

Beckmann, M. J. (1972). Spatial Cournot oligopoly. *Papers and Proceedings of the Regional Science Association* 28:37–47.

Beckmann, M. J. (1976). Spatial equilibrium in the dispersed city. In: Y. Y. Papageorgiou (ed.), *Mathematical Land Use Theory*, pp. 117–25. Lexington, MA: Lexington Books.

Beckmann, M. J., and Puu, T. (1985). *Spatial Economics. Density, Potential and Flow*. Amsterdam: North Holland.

Belleflamme, P. (1998). Adoption of network technologies in oligopolies. *International Journal of Industrial Organization* 16:415–44.

Bénabou, R. (1993). Workings of a city: location, education and production. *Quarterly Journal of Economics* 106:619–52.

Bénabou, R. (1996a). Equity and efficiency in human capital investment: the local connection. *Review of Economic Studies* 63:237–64.

Bénabou, R. (1996b). Heterogeneity, stratification, and growth: macroeconomic implications of community structure and school finance. *American Economic Review* 86:584–609.

Ben-Akiva, M., de Palma, A., and Thisse, J.-F. (1989). Spatial competition with differentiated products. *Regional Science and Urban Economics* 19:5–19.

Berliant, M., and Konishi, H. (1994). The endogenous formation of a city: population agglomeration and marketplaces in a location-specific production economy. Mimeograph, Washington University, St. Louis.

Berliant, M., and Wang, P. (1993). Endogenous formation of a city without agglomerative externalities or market imperfections: market places in a regional economy. *Regional Science and Urban Economics* 23:121–44.

Berliant, M., and Zenou, Y. (1996). Heterogenous labor and agglomeration in general equilibrium. Mimeograph, Washington University, St. Louis.

Berry, B. J. L. (ed.) (1993). *The Multinodal Metropolis*, special issue of *Geographical Analysis* 25(1):1.

Bonanno, G. (1990). General equilibrium theory with imperfect competition. *Journal of Economic Surveys* 4:297–328.

Borukhov, E., and Hochman, O. (1977). Optimum and market equilibrium in a model of a city without a predetermined center. *Environment and Planning A* 9:849–56.

Bottazzi, L., and Ottaviano, G. (1996). Modelling transport costs in international trade: a comparison among alternative approaches. Mimeograph, Boconi University, Milan.

Brakman, S., Garretsen, H., Gigengack, R., van Marrewijk, C., and Wagenvoort, R. (1996). Negative feedbacks in the economy and industrial location. *Journal of Regional Science* 36:631–51.

Brander, J. A. (1981). Intra-industry trade in identical commodities. *Journal of International Economics* 11:1–14.

Brezis, E. S., Krugman, P. R., and Tsiddon, D. (1993). Leapfrogging in international competition: a theory of cycles in national technological leadership. *American Economic Review* 83:1211–19.

Cain, L. P. (1997). Historical perspectives on infrastructure and US economic development. *Regional Science and Urban Economics* 27:117–38.

Calmette, M.-F., and Le Pottier, J. (1995). Localisation des activités: un modèle bisectoriel avec coûts de transport. *Revue Economique* 46:900–9.

Casetti, E. (1980). Equilibrium population partitions between urban and agricultural occupations. *Geographical Analysis* 12:47–54.

Chipman, J. S. (1970). External economies of scale and competitive equilibrium. *Quarterly Journal of Economics* 85:347–85.

Christaller, W. (1933). *Die zentralen Orte in Süddeutschland*. Jena: Gustav Fischer Verlag. English translation 1996: *The Central Places of Southern Germany*. Englewood Cliffs, NJ: Prentice-Hall.

Ciccone, A., and Hall, R. E. (1996). Productivity and the density of economic activity. *American Economic Review* 86:54–70.

Combes, P.-P. (1997). Industrial agglomeration under Cournot competition. *Annales d'Economie et de Statistique* 45:161–82.

Courant, P. N., and Deardoff, A. V. (1992). International trade with lumpy countries. *Journal of Political Economy* 100:198–210.

d'Aspremont, C., Dos Santos Ferreira, R., and Gérard-Varet, L.-A. (1991). Pricing schemes and Cournotian equilibria. *American Economic Review* 81:666–73.

d'Aspremont, C., Gabszewicz, J. J., and Thisse, J.-F. (1979). On Hotelling's stability in competition. *Econometrica* 47:1045–50.

d'Aspremont, C., Gabszewicz, J. J., and Thisse, J.-F. (1983). Product differences and prices. *Economics Letters* 11:19–23.

David, P., Foray, D., and Dalle, J.-M. (in press). Marshallian externalities and the emergence and spatial stability of technological enclaves. *Economics of Innovation and New Technology*.

David, P., and Greenstein, S. (1990). The economics of compatibility and standards: an introduction to recent research. *Economics of Innovation and New Technology* 1:3–42.

David, P., and Rosenbloom, J. L. (1990). Marshallian factor market externalities and the dynamics of industrial localization. *Journal of Urban Economics* 28:349–70.

de Fraja, G., and Norman, G. (1993). Product differentiation, pricing policy and equilibrium. *Journal of Regional Science* 33:343–63.

de la Fuente, A. (1997). The empirics of growth and convergence: a selective survey. *Journal of Economic Dynamics and Control* 21:23–73.

De Long, J. B., and Shleifer, A. (1993). Princes and merchants: European city growth before the Industrial Revolution. *Journal of Law and Economics* 36:671–702.

de Palma, A., Ginsburgh, V., Papageorgiou, Y. Y., and Thisse, J.-F. (1985). The principle of minimum differentiation holds under sufficient heterogeneity. *Econometrica* 53:767–81.

Dixit, A. K., and Stiglitz, J. E. (1977). Monopolistic competition and optimum product diversity. *American Economic Review* 67:297–308.

Drèze, J., and Hagen, K. (1978). Choice of product quality: equilibrium and efficiency. *Econometrica* 48:493–513.

Eaton, B. C., and Lipsey, R. G. (1982). An economic theory of central places. *Economic Journal* 92:56–72.

Eaton, J., and Eckstein, Z. (1997). Cities and growth: theory and evidence from France and Japan. *Regional Science and Urban Economics* 27:443–74.

Economides, N., and Siow, A. (1988). The division of market is limited by the extent of liquidity: spatial competition with externalities. *American Economic Review* 78:108–21.

Enelow, J. M., and Hinich, M. J. (1984). *The Spatial Theory of Voting: An Introduction.* Cambridge University Press.

Englmann, F. C., and Walz, U. (1995). Industrial centers and regional growth in the presence of local inputs. *Journal of Regional Science* 35:3–27.

Erlenkotter, D. (1989). The general optimal area problem. In: F. Louveaux, M. Labbé, and J.-F. Thisse (eds.), *Facility Location Analysis: Theory and Applications,* pp. 45–70. Basel: Baltzer.

Ethier, W. (1982). National and international returns to scale in the modern theory of international trade. *American Economic Review* 72:389–405.

Faini, R. (1984). Increasing returns, non-traded inputs and regional development. *Economic Journal* 94:308–23.

Feldman, M. P. (1994). *The Geography of Innovation.* Dordrecht: Kluwer.

Feldman, M. P., and Florida, R. (1994). The geographic sources of innovation: technological infrastructure and product innovation in the United States. *Annals of the Association of American Geographers* 84:210–19.

Fischer, C. (1982). *To Dwell Among Friends: Personal Networks in Town and City.* University of Chicago Press.

Fisher, J. H., and Harrington, J. E., Jr. (1996). Agglomeration and product diversity. *Rand Journal of Economics* 27:281–309.

Friedman, J. W., and Thisse, J.-F. (1993). Partial collusion fosters minimum product differentiation. *Rand Journal of Economics* 24:631–45.

Fujita, M. (1988). A monopolistic competition model of spatial agglomeration: a differentiated product approach. *Regional Science and Urban Economics* 18:87–124.

Fujita, M. (1989). *Urban Economic Theory. Land Use and City Size.* Cambridge University Press.

Fujita, M. (1990). Spatial interactions and agglomeration in urban economies.

In: M. Chatterji and R. E. Kuenne (eds.), *New Frontiers in Regional Science*, pp. 184–221. London: Macmillan.

Fujita, M. (1995). On the self-organization and evolution of economic geography. *Japanese Economic Review* 47:34–61.

Fujita, M., and Krugman, P. (1995). When is the economy monocentric? von Thünen and Chamberlin Unified. *Regional Science and Urban Economics* 25:505–28.

Fujita, M., Krugman, P., and Mori, T. (1999). On the evolution of hierarchical urban systems. *European Economic Review* 43:209–51.

Fujita, M., and Mori, T. (1996). The role of port in the making of major cities: self-organization and hub-effects. *Journal of Development Economics* 49:93–120.

Fujita, M., and Mori, T. (1997). Structural stability and evolution of urban systems. *Regional Science and Urban Economics* 27:399–442.

Fujita, M., and Ogawa, H. (1982). Multiple equilibria and structural transition of non-monocentric urban configurations. *Regional Science and Urban Economics* 12:161–96.

Fujita, M., Ogawa, H., and Thisse, J.-F. (1988). A spatial competition approach to central place theory: some basic principles. *Journal of Regional Science* 28:477–94.

Fujita, M., and Smith, T. E. (1990). Additive-interaction models of spatial agglomeration. *Journal of Regional Science* 30:51–74.

Fujita, M., and Thisse, J.-F. (1986). Spatial competition with a land market: Hotelling and von Thünen unified. *Review of Economic Studies* 53:819–41.

Fujita, M., Thisse, J.-F., and Zenou, Y. (1997). On the endogenous formation of secondary employment centers in a city. *Journal of Urban Economics* 41:337–57.

Gabszewicz, J. J., and Thisse, J.-F. (1986). Spatial competition and the location of firms. In: J. J. Gabszewicz, J.-F., Thisse, M. Fujita, and U. Schweizer (eds.), *Location Theory*, pp. 1–71 (*Fundamentals of Pure and Applied Economics 5*). Chur: Harwood.

Garreau, J. (1991). *Edge-Cities. Life on the New Frontier*. New York: Doubleday.

Gehrig, T. (1998). Competing exchanges. *European Economic Review* 42:277–310.

Giersch, H. (1949). Economic union between nations and the location of industries. *Review of Economic Studies* 17:87–97.

Glaeser, E., Kallal, H. D., Scheinkman, J. A., and Shleifer, A. (1992). Growth in cities. *Journal of Political Economy* 100:1126–52.

Glaeser, E., Scheinkman, J. A., and Shleifer, A. (1995). Economic growth in a cross-section of cities. *Journal of Monetary Economics* 36:117–43.

Gramlich, E. (1994). Infrastructure investment: a review essay. *Journal of Economic Literature* 32:1176–96.

Greenhut, J., and Greenhut, M. L. (1975). Spatial price discrimination, competition and locational effects. *Economica* 42:401–19.

Greenhut, M. L. (1981). Spatial pricing in the USA, West Germany, and Japan. *Economica* 48:79–86.

Grossman, G., and Helpman, E. (1991). *Innovation and Growth in the World Economy*. Cambridge, MA: MIT Press.

Gupta, B., Pal, D., and Sarkar, J. (1997). Spatial Cournot competition and agglomeration in a model of location choice. *Regional Science and Urban Economics* 27:261–82.

Hamilton, B. W. (1980). Indivisibilities and interplant transportation cost: do they cause market breakdown? *Journal of Urban Economics* 7:31–41.

Hansen, N. (1990). Do producer services induce regional development? *Journal of Regional Science* 30:465–78.

Harris, C. (1954). The market as a factor on the localization of industry in the United States. *Annals of the Association of American Geographers* 64:315–48.

Helpman, E. (1998). The size of regions. In: D. Pines, E. Sadka, and Y. Zilcka (eds.), *Topics in Public Economics*, pp. 33–54. Cambridge University Press.

Henderson, J. V. (1972). Hierarchy models of city size: an economic evaluation. *Journal of Regional Science* 12:435–41.

Henderson, J. V. (1974). The sizes and types of cities. *American Economic Review* 64:640–56.

Henderson, J. V. (1985). The Tiebout model: bring back the entrepreneurs. *Journal of Political Economy* 93:248–64.

Henderson, J. V. (1987). Systems of cities and inter-city trade. In: P. Hansen, M. Labbé, D. Peeters, J.-F. Thisse, and J. V. Henderson (eds.), *Systems of Cities and Facility Location*, pp. 71–119 (*Fundamentals of Pure and Applied Economics* 22). Chur, Switzerland: Harwood.

Henderson, J. V. (1988). *Urban Development. Theory, Fact and Illusion*. Oxford University Press.

Henderson, V., Kuncoro, A., and Turner, M. (1995). Industrial development in cities. *Journal of Political Economy* 103:1066–90.

Henderson, J. V., and Mitra, A. (1996). The new urban landscape: developers and edge cities. *Regional Science and Urban Economics* 26:613–43.

Henderson, J. V., and Slade, E. (1993). Development games in non-monocentric cities. *Journal of Urban Economics* 34:207–29.

Henderson, J. V., and Thisse, J.-F. (1997). On strategic community development. Discussion paper no. 1550, CEPR, London.

Hesley, R., and Strange, W. (1990). Matching and agglomeration economies in a system of cities. *Regional Science and Urban Economics* 20:189–212.

Hirschman, A. O. (1958). *The Strategy of Development*. New Haven, CT: Yale University Press.

Hohenberg, P., and Lees, L. H. (1985). *The Making of Urban Europe (1000–1950)*. Cambridge, MA: Harvard University Press.

Hoover, E. M. (1936). *Location Theory and the Shoe and Leather Industries*. Cambridge, MA: Harvard University Press.

Hoover, E. M. (1937). Spatial price discrimination. *Review of Economic Studies* 4:182–91.

Hoover, E. M. (1948). *The Location of Economic Activity*. New York: McGraw-Hill.

Hotelling, H. (1929). Stability in competition. *Economic Journal* 39:41–57.

Hummels, D. (1995). Global income clustering and trade in intermediate goods. Mimeograph, University of Michigan.

Hurter, A. P., and Martinich, J. S. (1989). *Facility Location and the Theory of Production*. Dordrecht: Kluwer.

Imai, H. (1982). CBD hypothesis and economies of agglomeration. *Journal of Economic Theory* 28:275–99.

Ioannides, Y. M. (1994). Product differentiation and growth in a system of cities. *Regional Science and Urban Economics* 24:461–84.

Ireland, N. J. (1987). *Product Differentiation and Non-Price Competition*. Oxford: Basil Blackwell.

Irmen, A., and Thisse, J.-F. (1998). Competition in multi-characteristics spaces: Hotelling was almost right. *Journal of Economic Theory* 78:76–102.

Isard, W. (1956). *Location and Space Economy*, Cambridge, MA: MIT Press.

Jacobs, J. (1969). *The Economy of Cities*. New York: Random House.

Jacobs, J. (1984). *Cities and the Wealth of Nations*. New York: Random House.

Jaffe, A. B., Trajtenberg, M., and Henderson, R. (1993). Geographic localization of knowledge spillovers as evidenced by patent citations. *Quarterly Journal of Economics* 108:577–98.

Kaldor, N. (1935). Market imperfection and excess capacity. *Economica* 2:35–50.

Kaldor, N. (1970). The case for regional policies. *Scottish Journal of Political Economy* 17:337–48.

Kaldor, N. (1985). *Economics without Equilibrium*. Armonk, NY: M. E. Share.

Kanemoto, Y. (1990). Optimal cities with indivisibilities in production and interactions between firms. *Journal of Urban Economics* 27:46–59.

Kilkenny, M. (1998). Transport costs and rural development. *Journal of Regional Science* 38:293–312.

Kim, S. (1995). Expansion of markets and the geographic distribution of economic activities: the trend in U.S. regional manufacturing structure, 1860–1987. *Quarterly Journal of Economics* 110:881–908.

Kirman, A. P. (1995). Economies with interacting agents. Mimeograph, European University Institute, Florence.

Knapp, T. A., and Graves, P. R. (1989). On the role of amenities in models of migration and regional development. *Journal of Regional Science* 29: 71–87.

Koopmans, T. C. (1957). *Three Essays on the State of Economic Science*. New York: McGraw-Hill.

Koopmans, T. C., and Beckmann, M. J. (1957). Assignment problems and the location of economic activities. *Econometrica* 25:1401–14.

Kreps, D. M. (1979). A representation theorem for "preference for flexibility." *Econometrica* 47:565–77.

Krugman, P. (1979). Increasing returns, monopolistic competition, and international trade. *Journal of International Economics* 9:469–79.

Krugman, P. (1991a). *Geography and Trade*. Cambridge, MA: MIT Press.

Krugman, P. (1991b). Increasing returns and economic geography. *Journal of Political Economy* 99:483–99.

Krugman, P. (1991c). History versus expectations. *Quarterly Journal of Economics* 106:651–67.

Krugman, P. (1992). A dynamic spatial model. Working paper no. 4219, NBER, Cambridge, MA.

Krugman, P. (1993a). Toward a counter-counterrevolution in development theory. In: *Proceedings of the World Bank Annual Conference on Development Economics 1992*, pp. 15–38. Washington: International Bank for Reconstruction and Development World Bank.

Krugman, P. (1993b). First nature, second nature, and metropolitan location. *Journal of Regional Science* 33:129–44.

Krugman, P. (1993c). The hub effects: or, treenes in interregional trade. In: W. J. Ethier, E. Helpman, and P. Neary (eds.), *Theory, Policy and Dynamics in International Trade. Essays in Honor of R. W. Jones*, pp. 29–37. Cambridge University Press.

Krugman, P. (1995). *Development, Geography, and Economic Theory*. Cambridge, MA: MIT Press.

Krugman, P. (1996a). Urban concentration: the role of increasing returns and transport costs. *International Regional Science Review* 19:5–30.

Krugman, P. (1996b). *The Self-organizing Economy*. Oxford: Basil Blackwell.

Krugman, P., and Venables, A. J. (1995a). Globalization and the inequality of nations. *Quarterly Journal of Economics* 110:857–80.

Krugman, P., and Venables, A. J. (1995b). The seamless world: a spatial model of international specialization. Discussion paper no. 1230, CEPR, London.

Krugman, P., and Venables, A. J. (1996). Integration, specialization and adjustment. *Papers and Proceedings of the European Economic Association* 40:959–67.

Krzyzanowski, W. (1927). Review of the literature of the location of industries. *Journal of Political Economy* 35:278–90.

Kubo, Y. (1995). Scale economies, regional externalities, and the possibility of uneven regional development. *Journal of Regional Science* 35:29–42.

Labbé, M., and Hakimi, S. L. (1991). Market and locational equilibrium for two competitors. *Operations Research* 39:749–56.

Labbé, M., Peeters, D., and Thisse, J.-F. (1995). Location on networks. In: M. Ball, T. Magnanti, C. Monma, and G. Nemhauser (eds.), *Handbook of Operations Research and Management Science: Networks*, pp. 551–624. Amsterdam: North Holland.

Launhardt, W. (1885). *Mathematische Begründung der Volkwirtschafslehre*. Leipzig: B. G. Teubner. English translation (1993): *Mathematical Principles of Economics*. Aldershot: Edward Elgar.

Lederer, P. J., and Hurter, A. P. (1986). Competition of firms: discriminatory pricing and location. *Econometrica* 54:623–40.

Lepetit, B. (1988). *Les villes dans la France moderne (1740–1840)*. Paris: Albin Michel.

Lerner, A., and Singer, H. W. (1937). Some notes on duopoly and spatial competition. *Journal of Political Economy* 45:145–86.

Liebowitz, S. J., and Margolis, S. E. (1994). Network externality: an uncommon tragedy. *Journal of Economic Perspectives* 8:133–50.

Lindsey, J. H., Pratt, J. W., and Zeckhauser, R. J. (1995). Equilibrium with agglomeration economies. *Regional Science and Urban Economics* 25:249–60.

Long, N. V., and Soubeyran, A. (1996). R&D spillovers and location choice under Cournot rivalry. Document de travail no. 96A35, GREQAM, Université d'Aix-Marseille II.

Lösch, A. (1940). *Die räumliche Ordnung der Wirtschaft.* Jena: Gustav Fischer Verlag. English translation (1954): *The Economics of Location.* New Haven, CT: Yale University Press.

Lucas, R. E. (1988). On the mechanics of economic development. *Journal of Monetary Economics* 22:3–22.

McFadden, D. (1981). Econometric models of probabilistic choice. In: C. F. Manski and D. McFadden (eds.), *Structural Analysis of Discrete Data with Econometric Applications*, pp. 198–272. Cambridge, MA: MIT Press.

MacKay, R. R. (1995). Non-market forces, the nation state and the European Union. *Papers in Regional Science* 74:209–31.

Mai, C.-C., and Peng, S.-K. (1999). Cooperation vs. competition in spatial models: economics of Silicon Valley. *Regional Science and Urban Economics* 29:463–72.

Manne, A. S. (1964). Plant location under scale economies: decentralization and computation. *Management Science* 11:213–35.

Markusen, J. R. (1983). Factor movements and commodity trade as complements. *Journal of International Economics* 14:341–56.

Marshall, A. (1890). *Principles of Economics.* London: Macmillan (8th edition, 1920).

Martin, P., and Ottaviano, G. I. P. (1996). Growth and agglomeration. Discussion paper no. 1529, CEPR, London.

Martin, P., and Rogers, C. A. (1995). Industrial location and public infrastructure. *Journal of International Economics* 39:335–51.

Matsuyama, K. (1995). Complementarities and cumulative process in models of monopolistic competition. *Journal of Economic Literature* 33:701–29.

Matsuyama, K., and Takahashi, T. (1998). Self-defeating regional concentration. *Review of Economic Studies* 65:211–34.

Menger, P. M. (1993). L'hégémonie parisienne: économie et politique de la gravitation artistique. *Annales ESC* 48:1565–600.

Michel, P., Perrot, A., and Thisse, J.-F. (1996). Interregional equilibrium with heterogeneous labor. *Journal of Population Economics* 9:95–114.

Mills, E. S. (1967). An aggregate model of resource allocation in a metropolitan area. *American Economic Review* 57:197–210.

Mills, E. S. (1970). The efficiency of spatial competition. *Papers and Proceedings of the Regional Science Association* 25:71–82.

Mills, E. S. (1972). *Studies in the Structure of the Urban Economy.* Baltimore: Johns Hopkins University Press.

Mirrlees, J. (1995). Welfare economics and economies of scale. *Japanese Economic Review* 46:38–62.

Mori, T. (1997). A model of megapolis formation: the maturing of city systems. *Journal of Economics* 42:133–57.

Motta, M., Thisse, J.-F., and Cabrales, A. (1997). On the persistence of leadership or leapfrogging in international trade. *International Economic Review* 38:809–24.

Mueller, D. (1989). *Public Choice II. A Revised Version of Public Choice.* Cambridge University Press.

Mulligan, G. (1984). Agglomeration and central place theory: a review of the literature. *International Regional Science Review* 9:1–42.

Myrdal, G. (1957). *Economic Theory and Underdeveloped Regions.* London: Duckworth.

Nerlove, M. L., and Sadka, E. (1991). Von Thünen's model of the dual economy. *Journal of Economics* 54:97–123.

Norman, G., and Thisse, J.-F. (1996). Product variety and welfare under soft and tough pricing regimes. *Economic Journal* 106:76–91.

Ogawa, H., and Fujita, M. (1980). Equilibrium land use patterns in a non-monocentric city. *Journal of Regional Science* 20:455–75.

O'Hara, D. J. (1977). Location of firms within a square central business district. *Journal of Political Economy* 85:1189–207.

Ohlin, B. (1933). *Interregional and International Trade.* Cambridge, MA: Harvard University Press (revised edition, 1968).

Ota, M., and Fujita, M. (1993). Communication technologies and spatial organization of multi-unit firms in metropolitan areas. *Regional Science and Urban Economics* 23:695–729.

Ottaviano, G., and Thisse, J.-F. (1998). Agglomeration and trade revisited. Discussion paper no. 1903, CEPR, London.

Palivos, T., and Wang, P. (1996). Spatial agglomeration and endogenous growth. *Regional Science and Urban Economics* 26:645–69.

Papageorgiou, Y. Y., and Smith, T. R. (1983). Agglomeration as local instability of spatially uniform steady-states. *Econometrica* 51:1109–19.

Papageorgiou, Y. Y., and Thisse, J.-F. (1985). Agglomeration as spatial interdependence between firms and households. *Journal of Economic Theory* 37:19–31.

Perroux, F. (1955). Note sur la notion de pôle de croissance. *Economique appliquée* 7:307–20.

Phlips, L. (1983). *The Economics of Price Discrimination.* Cambridge University Press.

Ponsard, C. (1983). *History of Spatial Economic Theory.* Berlin: Springer-Verlag.

Premer, M., and Walz, U. (1994). Divergent regional development, factor mobility, and nontraded goods. *Regional Science and Urban Economics* 24:707–22.

Puga, D. (1999). The rise and fall of regional inequalities. *European Economic Review* 43:303–34.

Puga, D., and Venables, A. J. (1996). The spread of industry: spatial agglomeration in economic development. *Journal of Japanese and International Economies* 10:440–64.

Pyke, F., Becattini, G., and Sengenberger, W. (1990). *Industrial Districts and Inter-firm Cooperation in Italy.* Geneva: International Institute for Labour Studies.

Quah, D. T. (1996). Empirics for economic growth and convergence. *European Economic Review* 40:1353–75.

Quinzii, M., and Thisse, J.-F. (1990). On the optimality of central places. *Econometrica* 58:1101–19.

Rauch, J. (1993). Does history matter only when it matters little? The case of city-industry location. *Quarterly Journal of Economics* 108:843–67.

Reilly, W. J. (1931). *The Law of Retail Gravitation*. New York: Pilsbury.

Rivera-Batiz, F. (1988). Increasing returns, monopolisitic competition, and agglomeration economies in consumption and production. *Regional Science and Urban Economics* 18:125–53.

Roback, J. (1982). Wages, rents, and the quality of life. *Journal of Political Economy* 90:1257–78.

Romer, P. (1992). Increasing returns and new developments in the theory of growth. In: W. A. Barnett, B. Cornet, C. d'Aspremont, J. J. Gabszewicz, and A. Mas-Colell (eds.), *Equilibrium Theory with Applications*, pp. 83–110. Cambridge University Press.

Rosen, S. (1979). Wage-based indexes of urban quality life. In: P. Mieszkowski and M. Straszheim (eds.), *Current Issues in Urban Economics*, pp. 74–104. Baltimore: Johns Hopkins University Press.

Rosenstein-Rodan, P. N. (1943). Problems of industrialization of eastern and south-eastern Europe. *Economic Journal* 53:202–11.

Rushton, G., and Thill, J.-C. (1989). The effect of distance metric on the degree of spatial competition between firms. *Environment and Planning A* 21:499–507.

Sala-i-Martin, X. X. (1996). Regional cohesion: evidence and theories of regional growth and convergence. *European Economic Review* 40:1325–52.

Samuelson, P. A. (1983). Thünen at two hundred. *Journal of Economic Literature* 21:1468–88.

Sassen, S. (1991). *The Global City: New York, London, Tokyo*. Princeton, NJ: Princeton University Press.

Saxenian, A. (1994). *Regional Advantage: Culture and Competition in Silicon Valley and Route 128*. Cambridge, MA: Harvard University Press.

Schulz, N. (1995). Are markets more competitive if commodities are closer substitutes? *International Economic Review* 36:963–83.

Schulz, N., and Stahl, K. (1996). Do consumers search for the highest price? Equilibrium and monopolistic optimum in differentiated products markets. *Rand Journal of Economics* 27:542–62.

Scitovsky, T. (1954). Two concepts of external economies. *Journal of Political Economy* 62:143–51.

Scotchmer, S. (1994). Public goods and the invisible hand. In: J. Quigley and E. Smolensky (eds.), *Modern Public Finance*, pp. 93–105. Cambridge, MA: Harvard University Press.

Scotchmer, S., and Thisse, J.-F. (1992). Space and competition: a puzzle. *Annals of Regional Science* 26:269–86.

Sen, A., and Smith, T. E. (1995). *Gravity Models of Spatial Interaction Behavior*. Berlin: Springer-Verlag.

Shields, G. M., and Shields, M. P. (1989). The emergence of migration theory and a suggested new direction. *Journal of Economic Surveys* 3:277–304.

Smithies, A. (1941). Optimal location in spatial competition. *Journal of Political Economy* 49:423–39.

Solow, R. M., and Vickrey, W. S. (1971). Land use in a long narrow city. *Journal of Economic Theory* 3:430–47.

Spence, M. (1976). Product selection, fixed costs, and monopolistic competition. *Review of Economic Studies* 43:217–35.

Stahl, K. (1982). Differentiated products, consumer search, and locational oligopoly. *Journal of Industrial Economics* 31:97–114.

Stahl, K. (1983). A note on the microeconomics of migration. *Journal of Urban Economics* 14:318–26.

Stahl, K. (1987). Theories of urban business location. In: E. S. Mills (ed.), *Handbook of Regional and Urban Economics*, vol. 2, pp. 759–820. Amsterdam: North Holland.

Stahl, K. (1995). Towards a microeconomic theory of the retailing sector. Mimeograph, Universität Mannheim.

Stahl, K., and Varaiya, P. (1978). Economies of information: examples in location and land use. *Regional Science and Urban Economics* 8:43–56.

Starrett, D. (1978). Market allocations of location choice in a model with free mobility. *Journal of Economic Theory* 17:21–37.

Stollsteimer, J. F. (1963). A working model for plant numbers and locations. *Journal of Farm Economics* 45:631–45.

Stuart, C. (1979). Search and the spatial organization of trading. In: S. Lipman and J. J. McCall (eds.), *Studies in the Economics of Search*, pp. 17–33. Amsterdam: North Holland.

Tabuchi, T. (1998). Urban agglomeration and dispersion: a synthesis of Alonso and Krugman. *Journal of Urban Economics* 44:333–51.

Tauchen, H., and Witte, A. D. (1984). Socially optimal and equilibrium distributions of office activity: models with exogenous and endogenous contacts. *Journal of Urban Economics* 15:66–86.

Thill, J.-C. (1992). Spatial duopolistic competition with multipurpose and multistop shopping. *Annals of Regional Science* 26:287–304.

Thill, J.-C., and Thomas, I. (1987). Toward conceptualizing trip chaining: a review. *Geographical Analysis* 19:1–17.

Thisse, J.-F., and Papageorgiou, Y. Y. (1981). Reconciliation of transportation costs and amenities as location factors in the theory of the firm. *Geographical Analysis* 13:189–95.

Thisse, J.-F., and Vives, X. (1988). On the strategic choice of spatial price policy. *American Economic Review* 78:122–37.

Thisse, J.-F., and Wildasin, D. (1992). Public facility location and urban spatial structure. *Journal of Public Economics* 48:83–118.

Tofflemire, J. M. (1992). Telecommunication external economies, city size and optimal pricing for telecommunications. *Journal of Regional Science* 32:77–90.

Venables, A. J. (1996). Equilibrium locations of vertically linked industries. *International Economic Review* 37:341–59.

von Thünen, J. H. (1826). *Der isolierte Staat in Beziehung auf Landwirtschaft und Nationalökonomie*. Hamburg: Perthes. English translation (1966): *The Isolated State*. Oxford: Pergamon Press.

Walz, U. (1996). Transport costs, intermediate goods and localized growth. *Regional Science and Urban Economics* 26:671–95.

Wang, P. (1993). Agglomeration in a linear city with heterogeneous households. *Regional Science and Urban Economics* 23:291–306.

Webber, M. J. (1979). *Information Theory and Urban Spatial Structure*. London: Croom Helm.

Weber, A. (1909). *Ueber den Standort der Industrien*. Tübingen: J. C. B. Mohr. English translation (1929): *The Theory of the Location of Industries*. University of Chicago Press.

Weber, M. (1921). *Die Stadt*. Tübingen: J. C. B. Mohr. English translation (1958): *The City*. New York: Free Press.

Weinberg, J. (1985). Bertand oligopoly in a spatial context: the case of quantity independent transportation costs. *Regional Science and Urban Economics* 15:263–75.

Weitzman, M. L. (1982). Increasing returns and the foundations of unemployment theory. *Economic Journal* 92:787–804.

Wesolowsky, G. O. (1993). The Weber problem: history and perspectives. *Location Science* 1:5–23.

Wildasin, D. E. (1986). *Urban Public Finance (Fundamental of Pure and Applied Economics* 10). Chur: Harwood.

Wolinsky, A. (1983). Retail trade concentration due to consumers' imperfect information. *Bell Journal of Economics* 14:275–82.

Yang, X., and Rice, R. (1994). An equilibrium model endogenizing the emergence of a dual structure between the urban and rural sectors. *Journal of Urban Economics* 35:346–68.

Young, A. A. (1928). Increasing returns and economic progress. *Economic Journal* 38:527–42.

CHAPTER 2

Urban Economics in Retrospect: Continuity or Change?

Catherine Baumont and Jean-Marie Huriot

1 Introduction

The history of spatial economic thought shows four major paradigms associated with the pioneering works of von Thünen, Launhardt and Weber, Christaller and Lösch, and finally Hotelling (Ponsard, 1983). The present-day theoretical and empirical relevance of these historical contributions has often been underscored by adjoining the works of other investigators, such as Greenhut (Norman, 1993), and by examining the complementarity of these paradigms (Ponsard, 1983; Fujita and Thisse, 1986; Fujita, Ogawa, and Thisse, 1988). Yet their relevance extends beyond the realm of spatial economics proper, because some theories in international economics and industrial economics have successfully incorporated the ideas of spatial economists (Helpman and Krugman, 1985; Tirole, 1988).

The earliest of these paradigms was that of von Thünen. It was formed more than a century and a half ago to study the spatial arrangement of crop systems around a single central city. It was also at the core of one of the most highly developed parts of spatial economic theory, especially the microeconomics of cities (Fujita, 1989; Papageorgiou, 1990). A direct transposition of the monocentric model of agricultural location to analyses of intra-urban locations led in the 1960s to the emergence of the *new urban economics*. More recently, research into more general assumptions has raised new issues about both the origin and the consequences of multiple centers. Agglomeration economics (Fujita and Thisse, Chapter 1, this volume) has been developed with the aim of explaining both the formation and the structure of cities, within the analytical framework of the *new economic geography* (Krugman, 1991a,b, 1995; Fujita and Krugman, 1995).

However, the present-day relevance of von Thünen's *Isolated State* raises a number of issues: the question of the enduring validity of a method of analysis, but also questions about the originality and the scope of contemporary urban

We thank Pierre-Henri Derycke, Florence Goffette-Nagot, Christian Michelot, Bertrand Schmitt, Jacques Thisse, Bernard Walliser, and a referee for helpful comments.

microeconomic theory. These questions can be answered by detailed analysis and synthesis of new-urban-economics models developed since the works of Alonso (1964) and Muth (1969), and indeed this method of investigation has been used on several occasions (Fujita, 1989). Our approach is different. It consists in studying the pattern of development of the monocentric model from the time of von Thünen (Huriot, 1994) to the current state of the art in urban economics through the concepts of *continuity* and of *change*.

The past two decades have seen an upsurge of interest in the history of economic thought. Blaug (1985) has attributed this to the crisis in economics that arose in the 1970s. Rather than reflecting any weakening of the discipline, the term "crisis" reflects the increasing complexity and rapid development of economics and the coexistence of multiple approaches that sometimes are difficult to compare. In such a context, economists are tempted to look to the past for the sources of contemporary debates in the hope of finding some justification for their own methods of analysis, or of finding fresh insight.

Thus, an examination of the relationships between von Thünen's theory and urban microeconomic theory may reveal only much historical deadwood or even irrelevance, or, on the contrary, it may show how a series of opportune changes have adapted the paradigm to its new subject: contemporary urban life.

By concentrating on the historical and methodological approach, Section 2 characterizes the phenomena of continuity and change that may arise in theoretical thought. Application of these principles to the development of von Thünen's paradigm is detailed in the next two sections: The marks of continuity reflected by the preservation and adaptation of the monocentric model are discussed in Section 3, and the transformation from the agricultural model to the urban model is emphasized in Section 4. Section 5 discusses the primary change leading to the emergence of the new economic geography. In the concluding section we shall look at the prospects for further development of the economics of cities.

2 Patterns of Development of Theoretical Thought

The development of economic theory is too complex to comprehend in its entirety. We can argue only on the basis of a simplified representation to which we apply a method of analysis. This method will consist in appraising the developments of theoretical thought in terms of continuity and change. But these concepts must be used with care, because they have no absolute meaning and can be defined only by convention (Baumont and Huriot, 1996).

Our reasoning will lead us from an examination of the most varied forms of development suggested by combinations of these two phenomena to the question of the relationships among continuity, change, progress, and innovation.

2.1   Continuity and Change: A Necessary Combination

The history of economics, and of science in general, can be analyzed using a narrow combination of processes of continuity and change. Most authors have seen stages of continuity interspersed by periods of more or less intensive change.

Among the classical contributions to general scientific method, Popper's can be interpreted in terms of continuity if we use the degree of falsifiability as the criterion for evaluating theories: a theoretical statement is better if it is more falsifiable (i.e., it is more general because it contains more information and is simpler) and if it resists falsification (i.e., there is a high degree of corroboration). But it may also be described in terms of multiple changes. A theory can never be more than provisionally valid, because even if its degree of corroboration is high, it could possibly be rejected at any time. We may speak of a "permanent revolution" to convey the idea that the history of science is reduced to a series of conjectures and refutations (Popper, 1959; Blaug, 1992).

Kuhn gave further impetus to the idea of scientific revolution, but as a transition from one continuous process to another. He turned it into an exceptional and radical process. His idea of revolution has become a sort of universal reference for the study of changes in the history of science. "Normal science," the practice of research regulated and standardized by a research tradition (the paradigm) accepted by a group of scientists, develops continuously. But a crisis arises when confidence in the foundation on which a paradigm was built collapses, along with the consensus that guaranteed its durability. Revolution occurs whenever another paradigm appears to be more relevant to the scientific community. The transition from one paradigm to another, although revolutionary, is the "usual developmental pattern of mature science" (Kuhn, 1970, p. 12). Such a revolution is a genuine upheaval, because the successive paradigms are entirely different, and their component parts are no longer directly comparable.

In economics, Schumpeter, too, combined the ideas of continuity and change. He emphasized the important role of the "filiation" of ideas,[1] while admitting that there were irregularities, and even highlighting certain forms of scientific revolution.

Accepting that history combines processes of continuity and change raises the question of the nature of those combinations that can lead to the development of science. It seems, rather, that there is an overlap where continuity and change are both necessary and mutually dependent. One could establish a reciprocal relationship of cause and effect between the processes of continuity and change. Often the ground for a change is prepared by ill-adapted continuous

---

[1] The "process by which men's efforts to understand economic phenomena, produce, improve and pull down analytic structures in an unending sequence" (Schumpeter, 1954, p. 6).

development (e.g., in the case of excessive durability of a paradigm sustained by *ad hoc* modifications, or theoretical or empirical degeneration of a research program). Likewise, changes beget periods of scientific emulation during which "consolidating" and "expanding" theories thrive and gradually accumulate as part of the new paradigm (Walliser, 1994).

But so numerous are the nuances that have been introduced to describe the phenomena of continuity and change that one can move imperceptibly from the idea of continuity to that of change. Walliser (1994) has made a distinction between (1) the stages of continuous development of a theory, characterized by a series of "micro-revolutions" (i.e., by processes of generalization, improvement, and mutation), and (2) stages of "macro-revolution" akin to Kuhn's scientific revolutions. Elsewhere, Granger (1995) has drawn a distinction between external and internal discontinuities. The former include the transition in an area of thought from the "protoscientific" to the scientific stage, whereas the sequence of theories within the scientific stage is described using the concept of internal discontinuity.

Finally, there may well be continuity of ideas interrupted by a purely temporal discontinuity. This is the case, as pointed out by Schumpeter in particular, for theories that have been partly or completely forgotten for some time and then reappear, as happened with spatial theory, which is our subject here. This is also the case in most rediscoveries of the works of earlier economists and the borrowings from them to construct "new" theories.

2.2 Progress, Permanence, and Innovation

The question of *progress* is a recurrent theme in the evaluation of theories. Has there been progress in economic knowledge since Adam Smith? Is the new urban economics an advance past von Thünen? *Innovation* (contrasted with *permanence*) is another continuing concern, especially among economists who overuse expressions such as "the new theory of . . . " or "the new economics of . . . " as if to convince themselves that they really have something new (which might be merely an appearance) and to mark a break with the past (which might be considered illusory).

Unfailing Progress? For Kuhn (1970), science and progress were inseparable. Schumpeter considered that economic "analysis," as "tooled knowledge" (Schumpeter, 1954, p. 7), was by nature the framework of scientific progress, by contrast with other aspects of economic "thought" subjected to value judgments and personal preferences.

But what is progress? Once again it is difficult to go beyond intuition and provide any general criterion. Definitions often are no more than statements about the forms of progress.

We sometimes have the impression that progress is most closely related to constant, cumulative development. For example, Carnap (1962) related "progress" to increased confirmability: One theory is better than another when it is more often confirmed by observation. The idea of progress also occurs within a research program in the sense of Lakatos (1970) if the integration of new proposals, which can be used to predict an increasingly vast set of phenomena, does not challenge the hard core of the program. For Kuhn, progress is the natural result of efficiency in the organization of normal research. In each conception, the conditions for scientific progress are directly related to a process of adaptation by regular transformation and accumulation of the explanatory and predictive capabilities of theories.

But things are not quite so simple. On the one hand, there can easily be development without progress, as in some stages of degeneration of a research program or of *ad hoc* modifications of a paradigm, aimed at sustaining it by artificially reducing its degree of falsifiability. On the other hand, the stages of revolutionary change, even when they generate incommensurability, may bring about progress. In Kuhn's interpretation, progress is also a consequence of scientific revolutions. Even if these revolutions result in both losses and gains, they extend the "list of problems solved by science" (Kuhn, 1970, p. 170).

Progress is, however, more difficult to evaluate after a break with the past than as part of continuous development, because progress is more directly visible when there is a constant accumulation of resolved questions. In this way, scientific progress can be compared with the knowledge of a single person learning continuously down the centuries (Pascal, 1954).

By contrast, because a sharp break relates objects that are at least partly incomparable, it implies a sudden change in the accumulation process, which raises problems about evaluating scientific progress. Progress becomes "nonmeasurable," subjective, or relative because it stems from the abandonment of a paradigm that no longer inspires trust in favor of another paradigm that is judged better.

Finally, the idea of progress collapses when, as is commonplace in economics, several paradigms coexist but are opposed in their fundamental principles, their outlooks, and their methods. Of course, there is almost invariably a dominant paradigm, and progress remains meaningful within that paradigm. But as long as quarrels arise between schools, progress can be contested.

Permanence and Innovation. Continuity can perhaps be related to a certain form of historical determinism: It would be possible to know entirely, by a process of recurrence, the state of science at any future time *t* if we could have complete information about the state of knowledge at time zero.

This image illustrates the idea that in continuous evolution like this, nothing really *new* can arise, because any development becomes predictable through knowledge of the initial conditions: It is as if everything were pre-programmed. If everything has already been said, there is permanence in the evolution of discourse: Its transformations are merely appearances maintained by technical improvements and minor arrangements. In this perspective, it would be true to say that today we know no more about economics than did Adam Smith, just as today we know no more about spatial economics than did von Thünen! Innovation, then, can arise only after changes or discontinuities. If economic theory really is a creation, then it must be constructed and must develop through change. Yet steady evolution may give rise to wholesale changes, much as with bifurcations and chaotic behavior in nonlinear systems, in which case determinism is no longer equivalent to predictability.

In this section we have supported the hypothesis that the strengths and weaknesses of economic theories, highlighted by historical and methodological analyses, can be grasped in connection with complex processes of continuity and change. We must now attempt to tease out the lines of continuity and the changes from the time of von Thünen through to contemporary urban microeconomics.

In view of the relative nature of continuity and change, we have opted to assess the style and size of the observed transformations by analyzing semantic changes: Do the theoretical propositions in the models of von Thünen, of the new urban economics, and the new economic geography always have the same content, the same scope, and the same relevance? We therefore put changes in meaning before formal innovations, even if, as we shall be led to show, the former are sometimes largely dependent on the latter.

More specifically, our priority will be to look into the way the spatial organization of activities is worked into economic theory, that is, to look at both how space makes it possible to understand the workings of the economy and the way in which economic theory can account for locations. The basic question is, For what reasons and by what processes is the spatial economic order built up? The monocentric model goes some way toward answering these questions by describing the ordering of agricultural space in the von Thünen model and the ordering of residential space in the new urban economics. It is, however, unable to answer the general question of how economic space forms. The agglomeration theories proposed by urban microeconomics or the new economic geography provide clues as to the direction in which the monocentric model needs to be developed (if not abandoned altogether) in order to respond to the current concerns of spatial economic theory.

We shall endeavor to understand in what way continuity may be a factor promoting excessive durability of a mode of thought, that is, in what way permanence is an obstacle to innovation and the capacity to resolve new problems. We shall also try to understand how change has made it possible to renew analysis. In other words, is the new urban economics in a position to face up to the theoretical challenges raised by the modern city? And to what extent are continuity and change involved?

3 The Monocentric Model: Permanence and Continuity

The modern theory of urban land use is essentially a revival of von Thünen's theory of agricultural land use. Despite its significance as a monumental contribution to scientific thought, von Thünen's theory has languished without attracting the widespread attention of economists for over a century. During that time human settlement grew extensively and outpaced the traditional guidance of urban design. It was the outburst of urban problems since the late 1950's that manifested the urgent need for a systematic theory of urban space and brought back the attention of theorists and economists to von Thünen's theory. (Fujita, 1986, p. 73)

Like Fujita, most scholars in urban economics acknowledge their debt to von Thünen, and von Thünen's *Isolated State* has lent its name to the *Isolated City-State* of Papageorgiou (1990). We shall trace the continuity of this filiation and then seek out its consequences for the theoretical and empirical relevance of urban theory.

3.1 The Marks of Continuity

A straightforward comparative examination of the ways of thinking involved, of the theoretical assumptions and results, shows obvious signs of kinship between the work of von Thünen and the new urban economics. These links warrant application of the name of von Thünen's *paradigm* to all of the theories thus related.

Deductive Models. From von Thünen to the new urban economics the same hypothetico-deductive method prevails. Von Thünen had an intuitive, abstract, and deductive way of thinking. The abstract concept of the *Isolated State* was a prerequisite for his empirical work. Even if each observation stemmed from a general law, "each result is not a general law." Von Thünen argued that the general law must be established by deductive reasoning. The *Isolated State* is not an accurate reflection of a real situation, but a "method of investigation," a "permanent condition" that cannot be observed in the real world (Huriot, 1994). These could easily be the words of an author expounding the new urban economics.

Von Thünen's approach was therefore essentially deductive. He started with abstract assumptions and drew general propositions from them. He explicitly used the method of successive approximations developed later by Pareto. He began by analyzing a simple and ideal situation, eliminating what were judged to be secondary factors, so as to isolate provisionally the effects of the action of a single factor: the cost of transport from the place of production to the market town. Then he made the assumptions more flexible by introducing secondary factors. Similarly, the new urban economics first constructs a "basic model" from a first body of simple but restrictive assumptions, intended to be relaxed and broadened out to encompass different generalizations of the model that will offer a more realistic representation of space. Marks of continuity are to be found in both the first body of core assumptions and in the broader assumptions.

The First Core Assumptions. It is surprising that von Thünen's work, the first part of which was written in 1826, begins with a statement of assumptions that immediately places us in the context of a deductive theoretical model. Consider the opening lines of the *Isolated State*, giving a highly simplified representation of space:

Imagine a very large town, at the center of a fertile plain which is crossed by no navigable river or canal. Throughout the plain the soil is capable of cultivation and of the same fertility. Far from the town, the plain turns into an uncultivated wilderness which cuts off all communication between this state and the outside world.

There are no other towns on the plain. The central town must therefore supply the rural areas with all manufactured products, and in return it will obtain all its provisions from the surrounding countryside.

The mines that provide the State with salt and metals are near the central town which, as it is the only one, we shall in future call simply "the town." (von Thünen, 1826, English translation, 1966, p. 7)

In the new urban economics, the basic assumptions of the urban equilibrium model concerning the *ex ante* representation of space are merely a more concise formulation of the same principles, except that the plain that was to be covered by crops becomes the space to be occupied by urban activities, and the central city becomes the *a priori* city center. Von Thünen's theory can then be transposed by saying that outside the city center, the urban area is homogeneous, displaying circular symmetry around the center, that the city center is the working place for all the individuals whose residential locations are to be determined endogenously, and that the transport system is dense and radial.

The modern theory further explains what goes unsaid by von Thünen, specifying that space is available everywhere at no cost, so that it is as if allocation of land to activities leads to an "instantaneous metropolis," without congestion or neighborhood externalities.

This brief examination shows that there is marked continuity in the spatial assumptions of the two models.

Despite progress in the formulation of the assumption of rationality, it can be said that there is continuity in the overall meaning of the assumption. Von Thünen explicitly assumed that everyone pursued their own interests in a situation of sufficient, if not perfect, information, thus allowing the general interest to be served exactly as Adam Smith supposed. In that context, each farmer sought exclusively to earn the highest net income. That reasoning is substantially of the same type as that directing the behavior of economic agents in the new urban economics. From there we move imperceptibly to the rule for allocating land to the use that will yield the highest land rent, or the highest willingness to pay. In the von Thünen model, as in the new urban economics, nothing is said about the process by which this allocation is made.

More Flexible Assumptions. Greater flexibility of the spatial assumptions was anticipated by the agricultural model of the past century. Although von Thünen addressed the question only in an appendix, it is clear that he saw intuitively how his model would have to be altered to make it more realistic and the consequences that such modifications might have for his results. He constructed a multicentric space by locating a secondary city away from the central city. He broke the circular symmetry by introducing a navigable radial route on which transport costs were lower. He abandoned homogeneous space for areas with different levels of fertility. He even superimposed a micro-spatial concentric structure (around each farm or each village) upon the same type of structure that was described at the macro-spatial level of the *Isolated State*. He thus ended up with a highly refined description of the agricultural space, in a framework capable of reflecting practically all the possible deformations and complications of the basic monocentric design. Unfortunately, the formal instruments available to von Thünen were a long way from being capable of integrating all those factors into a comprehensive formal model.

The main efforts of the new urban economists in the past 25 years have been directed at escaping from the straitjacket of the basic assumptions we have cited. Among the alterations they made, many were derived from von Thünen's thinking. We shall emphasize only the major trends of those works.

With regard to the assumptions about urban space, von Thünen's idea of introducing a second center was used first. The occurrence of several centers, however, raised formal problems that von Thünen could not have suspected, problems that may underlie the changes we shall illustrate in the next section. Alterations were made to the circular-symmetry assumption, and it was shown how the urban circles were deformed in the presence of varying numbers of rapid radial and/or peripheral connections (e.g., with Euclidean distance, Mohring, 1961, and with rectangular distance, Alonso, 1964). It was more difficult to abandon spatial homogeneity in a very formal framework. That was reflected by the fact that factors other than the cost of transport to the center varied with location. Those factors might be wages or the quality of location related to the amenities or characteristics of the social or racial environment.

In the context of such spatial assumptions, what do we wish to do? Mainly, in both models, we seek to explain the spatial behavior of variables such as the price of land and the pattern or the intensity of land use. It follows directly from the assumptions made that the essential explanatory variable is the distance from the center.

Results. In view of the very close similarity between the sets of spatial assumptions, it is perhaps trivial to note that the results from the basic models are also very similar. The continuity of results can nevertheless be illustrated by the law of intensity. Von Thünen's law states that "for production of a given commodity, farming is more intense as one approaches the central city" (Huriot, 1994, p. 221). Likewise, in the basic version of urban residential equilibrium, it can easily be shown that residential density–which is a form of intensity of urban land use–decreases with distance from the center and is a convex function if some further conditions are met by the transport cost function. Land rent decreases from the center to the periphery in the urban model as in the agricultural model. In both cases, the basic assumptions imply that different economic agents take up locations in concentric rings, whether they be producers of different agricultural goods or residents with different income levels.

The durability of the assumptions and the ensuing spatial results accounts for the fact that we refer to both models as monocentric, although they have been implemented a century and a half apart. It may even be claimed that there is sufficient unity in the spatial schemes for them to be placed at either end of the "von Thünen paradigm" (Huriot, 1994).

Inevitable Continuity. Von Thünen and the new urban economists came up with the same solution to a certain theoretical problem from the outset. How is human space formed? How are human activities distributed, concentrated, or dispersed over a given area? To attempt to answer this, geographers and economists use a simplified representation of space that is usually the Euclidean plane, or more generally a set of locations separated by distances.

In the absence of any point of reference capable of attracting activities, it is impossible to construct a significant economic space, that is, a space in which activities can be arranged in any *order*. This is what the *spatial impossibility theorem* states. Under a certain number of assumptions, Starrett (1978) has shown that there is no competitive equilibrium with positive transport costs. A solution is possible only with no transport cost, but it is trivial, as it distributes all activities uniformly through space (i.e., in the greatest disorder), creating "backyard capitalism." As all activities are found equally in all places, it is as if space did not exist. To escape from this impossibility, an agglomeration force must be introduced. The models of von Thünen and of the new urban economics stem from what is certainly the easiest way to generate spatial order: to assume a single center of attraction. By locating certain activities at that center, the locations of others can be deduced from the relationships they have with the former. Von Thünen located all nonagricultural activities in a given market town and sought to deduce the locations of crops from that starting point. New urban economics locates all jobs in a given city center, and the program then consists in locating the households. If transport costs are non-zero, economic agents will seek to be as close as possible to the center. So the assumptions that there is a given city center and that agents need to be close to that center combine to constitute a force for agglomeration. This force is then combined with a dispersion force represented by the exclusive consumption of a certain area of land by each economic agent. Activities are then ordered in concentric rings at varying distances from the center, depending on the way they relate to these two forces.

The idea of monocentric space that underpins this entire line of research refers us back to the first foundations of spatial analysis. During a private talk with W. Isard concerning the idea of "center," he showed us the necessity of having, at a given moment, a single reference point for any spatial action or any specific spatial problem. This is the idea on which the models of von Thünen and the new urban economics are based.

3.2 A Weighty Legacy

In what way can the elements of continuity between von Thünen and the new urban economics form a limit to the explanatory and predictive capacity of the latter? Is this legacy an obstacle to the development of specifically urban models? Is there anything intrinsically restrictive in von Thünen's legacy as used in urban models?

The Implications of the Monocentric Model. The monocentric assumption, as a logical and simple response to the problem of the organization of space, is restrictive by its very simplicity. It is so in two ways, by its nature and by its use.

First of all, positing an *a priori* center supposes that at least some activities or economic agents are located there. Of course, this assumes that the major part of the problem is solved: Because an agglomeration of activities is taken as a starting point, the distribution of activities in space can no longer be explained completely. A *partial equilibrium* is established for a subset of activities whose locations thus determined depend on given locations, but are supposed to have no effect on the given locations. In this way, the new urban economics usually is nothing more than a method for determining residential locations of households, all other things being equal. These households have no point of reference other than the center, meaning in particular that each of them has relationships with only this single place, and therefore that trips are exclusively radial. In fact, some of the spatial assumptions listed earlier are only the logical consequences of this primary assumption. These assumptions are poor representations of the complexity of relationships that are built up inside a city in which each agent is located and acts relative to several places of reference in a multicentric space, and where location of consumers and location of firms interact in a process of simultaneous determination.

Then the monocentric assumption implies that apart from the single center, space is supposed *ex ante* to be completely empty, and the properties of equilibrium are determined *instantaneously* and *statically*. Equilibrium is already a sort of *realized ideal*: ideal because there is no inertia in land use, no constraint limiting the available locations or preventing them from being freely allocated by the land market; realized because the questions are about the properties of this equilibrium and not about the way it is elaborated. Once again the monocentric assumption appears to be the point of departure for properties that are readily open to criticism. The instantaneous formation of a perfectly concentric spatial arrangement around a single point seems as simplistic as it is unrealistic to those who wish to understand the complexity and the rapid development of the contemporary urban phenomenon.

It is usually on the basis of such arguments that some economists reject the new urban economics as inevitably and ultimately unable to account for contemporary urban problems. It is unable, at any rate, to explain the formation of cities (Krugman, 1995, 1996). Nevertheless, although the assumptions of the model seem simplistic, the monocentric model does have greater empirical relevance than might be thought.

Is Space Monocentric? In the nineteenth century, difficulties with transport could explain the relative isolation of certain agricultural regions, their self-sufficiency, and their almost exclusive orientation toward a central city. Thus von Thünen's spatial assumptions – featureless plain, isotropic transport – do not overly belie the reality of northern Germany at that time (Butler, 1980, pp. 75–6).

It may legitimately be doubted that this is quite so relevant nowadays. Transport today is far faster and represents a much smaller proportion of production costs. It is therefore doubtful that this cost is still the main factor in agricultural location. Other factors may become preponderant, such as soil quality and labor costs (Grotewold, 1959) or regional specialization (e.g., Kellerman, 1977, 1981). Progress in transport has allowed diversification of spatial relationships and has complicated their representations. New means of transport structure the network and differentiate the transport area. Combined with the development of mass production, they imply that production is no longer solely for the local market, but now also for a national market or even the world market (Sinclair, 1967).

It is true that if we take an agricultural area at random anywhere in the world, there is a relatively small probability of observing von Thünen circles. But such structures can be found on several spatial scales and in specific instances. We could give an endless list of observations that seem to confirm the presence of concentric spaces on micro-spatial scales (farm and village) and meso-spatial scales (typical von Thünen space of the region around a large city). However, many of these observations are relatively old or concern developing countries, which limits their scope (Huriot, 1994). Attempts at interpreting agricultural structures by the concentric configuration on an international scale are sometimes less than convincing. Thus it seems that globally, von Thünen's model has lost some of its relevance for the agricultural world.

The urban monocentric model provides, at times, an acceptable representation. Some North American cities fit in fairly well with the general pattern that features a strongly marked center. They confirm, in particular, the law of diminishing residential density away from the center, often in the precise form of a negative exponential function (termed Clark's law), as established purely deductively by Muth (1969). We generally find an arrangement whereby households are located in terms of increasing income from the center toward the periphery, as predicted by the new urban economics. Admittedly, European cities conform less readily with these patterns, because they are influenced much more by history and are therefore further removed from the idea of an "instantaneous metropolis." However, the monocentric model overlooks phenomena such as edge cities. It provides a poor account of what happens in polycentric cities (Baumont, 1993), and above all it fails to explain how multiple centers are formed; this is its main shortcoming, which leads to the major change to be described later.

3.3 Troubled Continuity

The continuity that is assumed between the von Thünen model and microeconomic analysis of urban areas is not without a few subtle distinctions that illustrate the irregularities that we presented in Section 2. First, there has not been a continuous temporal process, as von Thünen's work was forgotten for a long time. Next, the modern analysis has not necessarily retained all the characteristics of the initial model, and it has lost some of the richness of von Thünen's analysis along the way. Finally, it is not unique and is in competition with other contenders, whether acknowledged or not.

Time for Oblivion. Von Thünen was more famous in his lifetime for his contribution to agricultural economics than for his spatial theory, which was not fully understood, nor was its scope appreciated before the end of the nineteenth century (Huriot, 1994). The theory of circles was then stated in algebraic form by Launhardt (1885). It was not until 1940 that it was again taken up in its algebraic form and simplified by Lösch (1940), and it was only in the 1960s that applications of von Thünen's model to agriculture began to multiply. Then such applications again became scarce, even though some mathematical reformulations appeared sporadically (e.g., Beckmann, 1972; Samuelson, 1983; Huriot, 1994).

It is obvious that today we would no longer speak of von Thünen, other than as an important but outdated voice in spatial economic thought, if his analysis had not been applied to the issue of urban equilibrium, thus turning the country model into a city model. It should not be forgotten that von Thünen was also one of the first economists to apply marginalist reasoning. It is the transposability of his spatial model to the analysis of cities, probably enhanced by his contributions to marginal reasoning, that makes von Thünen a modern thinker and provides the basis for the continuity we highlighted in the preceding discussion.

Lost Characters. In some respects, the filiation from von Thünen to the new urban economics is conveyed first, and surprisingly *a priori*, by a regression in the wealth of the array of problems and the spatial structure proposed.

For technical reasons of formalization, the range of problems addressed in the new urban economics is more simplistic than von Thünen's. Von Thünen sought to allocate land to composite activities that were systems of closely interdependent production activities, such as different systems for crop rotation, producing grain but also a set of joint products. The new urban economics localizes simple activities around the city center: the production of a determined commodity, or the residences of households presenting clearly identified characters. The new urban economics here runs up against a technical problem of formalization. The needed simplification had been anticipated by Lösch's algebraic formalization of the agricultural model, which has served as a basis for all current presentations of the model.

The spatial structure of urban models is also simpler than that proposed by von Thünen's schema. Recall that von Thünen, even if he did not draw all possible consequences from it, suggested the superposition of a concentric structure around the market town, and a series of concentric structures on a smaller scale resulting from the structuring capability of the farmhouse on the farm. Thus, because daily transport costs on the farm itself were added to the costs of transport to market, the overall pattern of crop location could be locally modified. Contemporary models retain only the main structure around the city center.

Those two aspects of the original model meant that the ring was never an exclusive area of location for one type of land use.

Rival Filiations. The new urban economics has resulted from the combination of the monocentric spatial pattern, with the city as object, and the microeconomic method. But von Thünen was the originator of other filiations.

An explicitly acknowledged line of descent accompanied another rediscovery of von Thünen's model in conjunction with the neo-Ricardian theory of production. Thus a connection is made between von Thünen and Sraffa (1960) by rewriting a Sraffa-type linear production model in the context of a monocentric space. Transport cost to the single market center is introduced into the land rent function attached to each production process. Expenditures on labor and various working-capital outlays appear explicitly in this function, with a profit proportional to capital advances, according to neo-Ricardian economics. Production processes are then located according to von Thünen's criteria of land allocation to the activity that would yield the highest rent. This leads to location of production activities in rings at varying distances from the center, depending on the technical combination used and the extent of the transport costs incurred, but also the relative levels of distribution variables, that is, the wage rate and the profit rate (Scott, 1980; Huriot, 1981, 1987).

A monocentric configuration of space is also found in other approaches, such as that of the Chicago sociological school in the 1920s. It is via a temporal process of "invasion-succession," based on a process of social climbing and migration of most favored social groups from the center outward, that a monocentric social structure of space is formed. This is a long way from the instantaneous allocation process of von Thünen's filiation, and the main explanation does not involve the cost of travel to the center. But the social structure of space is reminiscent of that of urban equilibrium, with the wealthier individuals located on the outskirts. This is a more tenuous and unacknowledged filiation.

The various disturbances affecting the idea of continuity nevertheless conserve the principle. But from von Thünen to the latest developments of urban microeconomics a number of changes have occurred that affect the deep meaning of the analysis.

4 The City Model and the Country Model: Adaptations and Changes

It seems that even if we bear in mind the highly relative and subjective character of the separation between continuity and change, several transformations have been sufficiently far-reaching to be referred to as changes. These affect both the current sense of the analysis and perhaps, above all, its potential for development. They did not necessarily occur suddenly. A vague idea can float about for a long time and yet lead to no tangible consequence. It is at the moment that the idea is brought into focus and is spread that it causes change.

But what kind of change are we speaking of? Major changes, relating to a scientific revolution in Kuhn's sense, are rare. Von Thünen's foundation for the research tradition to which we have given his name was prepared by a number of earlier analyses, such as those of W. Petty, R. Cantillon, and J. Steuart

(Huriot, 1994), but it still remains a true foundation. It may be spoken of in the sense of change that Granger gives to "external discontinuity," which takes us from the protoscientific to the scientific stage, unifying dispersed knowledge into a true paradigm.

From that foundation to the current state of urban microeconomics, we shall first identify a number of changes that entailed consequences at different levels of the theory, such as the object of analysis, the mode of reasoning, and the temporal framework of the theory. These changes appear as what Granger calls "internal discontinuities"; they take the form of Walliser's "micro-revolutions." Recall that our criterion is that of the construction of spatial economics and the mode of handling space. From this point of view, these changes are not substantial breaks, even if some pertain to the transition from a classical to a neoclassical approach, simply because the monocentric model is preserved with its limits.

In the next section, our spatial viewpoint will then lead us to inquire into the consequences of a more profound change concerning spatial assumptions and their effects on the nature of the problem.

4.1 From Country to City

The first and most obvious change was that of the subject matter. This change, for which the works of Beckmann (1957) and Wingo (1961) made way, was effected by the key work of Alonso (1964), who conducted the first complete analysis of the monocentric equilibrium of the city, on the basis of the individual behaviors of optimization and by means of the generalization of von Thünen's concept of rent curves as *bid curves*.

An Announced Change? The change of subject is the result of the development of the historical context of the urban world itself and of the economic and social issues raised. Consider von Thünen's few lines on the internal configuration of cities:

If we want to know the reasons for the disproportionate rise in ground rent with approach to the town centre, we shall find them in labour economies; in the greater general convenience of a central situation; in the time-savings to be made in trade and business: for one and the same law governs ground as well as land rent. (von Thünen, 1826, English translation, 1966, p. 133)

We do not rightly know whether we should deduce that he appears once again as a distant pioneer of the great transposition that came about 150 years later or (perhaps more plausibly) whether the question was unimportant for him.

Marshall (1890) returned more systematically to this question of the internal structure of cities, but without referring to a monocentric or derived model: His location rent was determined generally by the set of advantages provided by a place. Nothing there, either, really foreshadows the change of the 1960s.

The transition from country to city can be accounted for by two factors. On the one hand, we are witnessing urban growth today on a scale that von Thünen probably could never have imagined. We have shifted from a world dominated by agriculture (which profoundly marks the classical analysis) to an urban civilization. On the other hand, we have witnessed at the same time a decrease in the monetary costs of transporting commodities between localities and a relative increase in the cost of travel, in terms of time, for people within cities. These are good reasons for seeking to apply to the city a form of reasoning that attempts to explain the structure of space essentially in terms of the cost of transport to the center.

The Consequences of the Change of Subject. This change is not necessarily related to the internal logic of the development of theories. It does not, therefore, necessarily imply discontinuity of the theoretical approach itself, and it could be judged secondary to our problem. In fact, the entire question is whether or not the change of subject involves a change in reasoning (i.e., the question is that of the urban specificity of the analysis). The connection between the specificity of the subject and the specificity of the reasoning is complex and does not obey any general rule. But it may be thought that the simple transposition of the same reasoning from agricultural space to urban space depends on the implicit assumption that urban space is only a formal category of space, with no marked specificity compared with agricultural space or space in general. Under such circumstances, the discourse on urban space is not fundamentally different from that on any other space. If, on the other hand, we think that urban space is qualitatively different from any other space, we need to know whether a nonspecific method will be able to bring out this specificity or whether we need a revised or completely new method. These questions underlie many of the points raised in this chapter.

The transposition of von Thünen's model directly entails at least one other break concerning the agents involved in the analysis and their relationships with land. A new category of agents necessarily appears: urban residents, considered as land and housing consumers. We are now looking at built land, and this entails a renewal of the problems. On the one hand, we analyze the behavior of farmers using the land directly as a production factor. On the other, we have residents who consume land or housing. We can, of course, introduce the producers of housing, who, like farmers, use land as part of a productive combination. But house builders, unlike farmers, are not themselves located while producing a clearly localized commodity.

Toward Contemporary Urban Issues. The work of Alonso is seminal relative to the change of subject. This change naturally entails extensions of the set of problems. The flexibility of the framework of reasoning in which the new urban economics is developed has made it possible to include in the analysis a whole series of probing questions about contemporary cities and has given rise to a huge literature that could be interpreted in terms of "expansive" works (Walliser, 1994), lending substance to Popper's idea of permanent revolution.

The earliest and most significant advance concerns the treatment of urban externalities. More precisely, different components can be introduced relating to the quality of the environment close to the resident's location. We speak generally of amenities, a concept covering the most varied phenomena: The utility of an agent can be affected by the quality of the air he breathes, by noise, by the residential density of the neighborhood, or by the presence of ethnic or social groups he either seeks out or seeks to avoid. In another category of urban externalities are the effects of traffic congestion, introduced very early on into urban models, and giving rise to calculations of the social costs of congestion. The effects of congested land use refer to amenity externalities. Finally, the spillover effects cover the case in which residents benefit from infrastructures (e.g., transport) without contributing to their funding, because they pay taxes in another district. These different effects are at least as important as travel to the workplace in explaining both individual location and urban equilibrium. The flexibility of the standard microeconomic model of the city allows it to be used outside the city to describe the location behavior of households in peri-urban rural areas on the basis of their trade-off between urban attraction and rural amenities (Goffette-Nagot, Chapter 9, this volume).

A further contemporary problem, although not specifically an urban problem, unemployment, is beginning to be included in new-urban-economics models (Zenou, Chapter 10, this volume), which thus become more akin to models of labor economics, by what Walliser termed a "hybridization" phenomenon (Walliser, 1994).

4.2 Modes of Reasoning

The change in subject has been accompanied by changes in approach and reasoning, but that certainly is not the only cause of these transformations. They are also related to the development of economic reasoning itself and of its mathematical tools, regardless of the specific subject of the city.

Fundamental Choices. Von Thünen was writing at the height of the classical period. Although he is known as the pioneer of the theory of marginal productivity and, more generally, of the marginal revolution, his approach to spatial structure was still, for the most part, connected with classical forms of thinking. Certainly he did not take part in the great classical debates about the distinction between productive work and unproductive work, about the theory of value, or about the logic of overproduction crises. But his thinking was part of classicism in several ways. He was a free-market proponent, which did not prevent him from having progressive and humanistic ideas favorable to the German revolution of 1848, but other, more typically classical authors were socialists, after all. He was, above all, interested in production, in assigning production conditions a decisive place in spatial economic equilibrium. Finally, when seen in contemporary light, he generally considered fixed production techniques as if he were thinking of production functions without substitution between factors, but with joint products in fixed proportions.

In the new urban economics, the vision was reversed from an analysis essentially in terms of production to one emphasizing consumption. It could be considered that this reversal is simply the result of a change in the subject of analysis: country to city. This is not a valid reason, or not a sufficient reason. Even if the new urban economics seeks only to structure residential space, that could easily be done by analyzing the conditions of the production of housing, which neo-Marxists and neo-Ricardians have done in the classical framework. If we leave aside the few models that followed Muth (1969), who integrated housing production in the analysis, land is no longer the main production factor, but rather a consumption good. Favoring consumption and consumers of land or of housing stems, then, from a choice different from the choice of the subject of analysis.

Modeling Techniques. At the same time as we have shifted from predominantly classical to neoclassical thinking, we have adopted the analytical framework of microeconomics and the high degree of mathematical formalization that characterizes its advances.

By using the approach of contemporary microeconomics, the urban economist introduces the question of urban space into the well-worn framework of the hypothetico-deductive studies of equilibrium based on optimizing behavior, a framework that has proved easily adaptable to varied problems and productive in formal theoretical propositions. But to take advantage of this approach, we must force the problem to fit into the analytical framework, thus determining a number of characteristics of the theory. Thus, individual optimization behaviors constitute the source of the entire construction. In a residential model, we first study the properties of equilibrium in a given urban space for an individual or household seeking to maximize a utility function under budgetary constraint, isolating, in particular, spending on land (or housing) and spending on transport. We can then move to the study of city equilibrium, combining all the individual equilibria.

With microeconomics comes mathematics. Von Thünen would not have looked askance at this, for although he did not use mathematics very much, he advocated the use of algebraic reasoning to establish sufficiently general propositions so as to avoid traps of particular cases. Von Thünen's model, like Ricardo's, can be easily mathematized.

Algebra provides us with the necessary tool; for if the nature of the subject allows letters to be substituted for numbers, and if the calculations made with the letters reach the same result as those made with figures, then this result will be generally valid, not merely a local rule. (von Thünen, 1826, English translation, 1966, p. 33)

Alongside the transformation in the vision of economics, we have a transformation that consists in systematizing the analysis by including a problematic in a coherent and productive mode of reasoning. But this may contain reductionism in itself, through its assumptions of methodological individualism and rationality, perhaps also because its generality and neutrality erase all specificity of the problem at hand to make it a special case of optimization under constraint. The mathematical tool itself is considered by some economists to be sufficiently reductionist to be rejected, and with it all the models that draw on it abundantly. It is rather easy to refute this type of attack, even though the reverse position of absolute trust in the power of mathematics is not tenable either.

4.3 The Dynamics of Urban Structures

From von Thünen to much of the new urban economics we are to some extent outside of time. The *Isolated State* is an unreal and timeless "permanent state," a sort of ideal space. The "instantaneous metropolis" of the new urban economics is a static equilibrium that is constructed regardless of history and of the constraints of successive land use and is also timeless and utopian (Baumont and Huriot, 1997). Urban equilibrium, however, readily lends itself to the pseudotemporal game of comparative statics, which is one of the more exciting and more productive aspects of such models. But real time, historical time, is missing.

A further break appears with the transition to dynamic models, in which real time, that of constraints on the succession and nonreversibility of phenomena, is finally present, which substantially changes the meanings of the models in regard to their ability to handle contemporary urban problems. Dynamic models introduce durability of urban constructions and the resulting costs of replacement. These factors are signs of the inertia of land occupation, of which Lösch (1940) had the intuition without drawing the consequences.

In the static model of agricultural location, nothing opposes the achievement of equilibrium: The commodity grown at each place is simply the one that will yield the highest rent. But inertia may arise, as already identified by von Thünen (Huriot, 1994, p. 257). Lösch investigated a particular manifestation of this phenomenon: He supposes that only wheat is grown, and therefore it occupies the land in the center. If potato crops are introduced, it is no longer sufficient that the rent curve for the new commodity overtake that for wheat in the center for the potato to be grown at that place. Tradition may oppose that, and the potato will then be pushed to the outskirts. This suboptimal arrangement will be maintained or not depending on the strength of tradition compared with the dynamism of the economy. This example potentially contains a dynamic theory of land use of which neither Lösch nor his successors perceived all the consequences. Two new features appear relative to the static pattern of crop circles: At any given moment, decisions about land use depend on the allocation of land already in place, and that allocation may be more or less rigid depending on the dynamism of the economy. From there to the inclusion of reallocation costs there is but a step, and the inertia will then vary with the extent of that cost. But those budding ideas went unused until recently. The existence of the idea did nothing to change the theory until there was a shift in the construction of true dynamic models.

The dynamic models that are being developed in the new urban economics take into account the expectations of agents with regard, in particular, to land prices and property rents. Several modes of expectation are possible: perfect, myopic, rational, and adaptive. These models handle issues like discontinuous urban expansions, urban rehabilitation, filtering on the property market, and urbanization in uncertain situations.

The dynamic viewpoint introduces substantial differences as compared with the static model (Fujita, 1986). Urban specificity is related in part to the existence of durable constructions. Accordingly, the cost of adjustment of land use is very high. In a static model, with no reallocation costs, comparison of rents by use of bid curves is sufficient to determine land allocation. With high reallocation costs, the concept of land rent becomes difficult to define. It is land price that must bring about the equilibrium between supply and demand for land in each location, and it is the concept of bid price for land that becomes central. Dynamic models consider a new category of agents: developers who bid for land and make the decisions about changes in land allocation. It is no longer the residential-services market that is at the core of the analysis, but the land market in which such developers operate (see Brueckner, Chapter 7, this volume, for a panorama of the state of the art in dynamic urban models).

At the same time as it renews the analysis, dynamization opens up new gateways. Whenever the question of the development of urban structures is raised, the field of urban microeconomics becomes permeable to other issues developed outside of spatial economics that perhaps, in turn, condition future developments in this branch of spatial economics. Thus, macroeconomic analyses of growth applied to regions use agglomeration economies produced by cities as explanatory factors in growth dynamics (Baumont, 1997).

Even if this approach breaks with the standard static urban model, it has not thus far produced a tidal wave comparable to the one that was to introduce the idea of formation of cities by endogenizing the city center.

5 From the Monocentric City to the Formation of Cities: The New Economic Geography

The archetype of the city in microeconomic theory is the household-location model in an *ex ante* monocentric space. We have shown in particular that there is a shift in the subject of analysis, entailing a modicum of adaptations in the questions raised and also a change in the method of reasoning. However, the most important strand of continuity between this model and that of von Thünen passes through the monocentric assumption and its role in explaining the spatial distributions of people and economic activities. The very idea of a single city center has been much criticized. But the most limiting aspect of the approach is that it does not explain how and where cities form.

5.1 From Exogenous Centrality...

The preoccupation with adhering closely to the real situation of contemporary urban life, of enhancing representations, and of providing more general results has led some authors to fix several centers of attraction in order to define spatial behavior and determine the city structure. This leads to a more satisfactory representation of location behavior, but we still face the same problems of given and unchangeable spatial centers.

What may be considered a genuine weakness of the new urban economics is more the exogeneity of the single center (or of the multiple centers), which makes it impossible to explain its (or their) creation and development.

It should be emphasized that it is impossible to generalize from the basic model to the simultaneous location of all agents without abandoning exogeneity of the economic center. Alonso's attempt to construct a general equilibrium model of location for all types of agents (households, industrial firms, and farmers) in a monocentric space, despite its pioneering role, proved a failure. The model obtained was in fact no more than a juxtaposition of unrelated partial equilibrium models. Each agent, whatever the nature of his functions, was localized relative to a single given center. That supposed that each had a relationship with that center only and that therefore the activities with which he was involved were in the center. Thus, on the one hand, households could not be located in the city unless businesses occupied the city center, and on the other hand, the locations of firms could be determined only if households occupied the center of the urban area. That led to an inconsistency: In the first case, the supply of labor was concentrated, whereas in the second, it was dispersed.

5.2 ... to Endogenous Centrality

The simultaneous location of all agents that form cities must be studied in a space with no preexisting center. Fujita and Ogawa (1982; Ogawa and Fujita, 1980, 1989) termed such a space "nonmonocentric." We are then confronted with a problem of general spatial equilibrium. It is the actual interactions between agents that cause spatial concentrations to emerge at equilibrium. For instance, in different studies Fujita and Ogawa showed under what circumstances interactions between firms lead to concentration in more or less specialized areas. The areas of concentration of firms appear as the economic centers of the city.

This new framework of analysis represents a true change compared with the initial corpus of the new urban economics. This change consists in a transition from study of the internal organization of a city around a given center to analysis of the formation of cities, that is, the birth of the new economic geography.

When we ask the question of the reason for the rise of economic centers, we immediately destroy the monocentric configuration, in which we do not have, by assumption, the means to explain why the center is located where it is or, by extension, why new centers appear in what were previously monocentric urban structures. The monocentric model fails to foresee the breakup of urban spaces (Berry and Kim, 1993).

The key to a general theory of space formation is in the inclusion of indivisibilities and increasing returns and therefore in abandoning the assumption of pure competition, as was suggested by Koopmans (1957) and shown by Starrett (1978), Krugman (1991a, 1995), and Thisse (1992). More concretely, agglomeration economies cause agents to group together because they derive advantages from proximity. There are three main sources of agglomeration economies (Fujita, 1990; Fujita and Thisse, Chapter 1, this volume):

1. non-market interactions, which generate spatial externalities or proximity effects; this is true in particular of social or business interactions and information exchanges requiring personal contacts;
2. monopolistic competition structures in which firms produce differentiated goods and consumers express a preference for variety;
3. strategic externalities that appear because of the geographic proximity of competing firms and refer back to the theory of spatial competition derived from Hotelling's model.

The most simple example of advantage due to proximity relates to the need for social contact between identical individuals. This is a sufficient condition to generate a nonuniform distribution of individuals in a bounded space, with a higher concentration closer to the geometric center (Beckmann, 1976; Borukhov and Hochman, 1977).

More generally, the need for proximity in interactions between firms and households gives rise to an irreversible process of agglomeration. Let us assume that activities are perfectly uniformly distributed in space. This equilibrium is unstable: The slightest disturbance, say from a single agent relocating, will produce spatial heterogeneity that will be amplified by a cumulative process reminiscent of Myrdal's circular causality. This can be illustrated quite simply. Let us assume that there are two categories of economic agents, A and B, linked by a mutual need for proximity. Each A finds it advantageous to be close to many Bs, and vice versa. If any one location brings together more As than other locations, that will be sufficient for Bs to be attracted to it, which will attract new As, and so on. For instance, in the framework of monopolistic competition, consumer preference for variety attracts firms manufacturing differentiated goods, which in turn attract consumers seeking variety.

Spatial externalities can also explain the formation of multiple centers when agglomeration economies give way to agglomeration diseconomies caused by saturation of the monocentric space: The formation of other centers then becomes a more efficient means of organizing urban space. The works of Ogawa and Fujita (1980, 1989; Fujita and Ogawa, 1982) and of Clarke and Wilson (1985) have formalized this type of analysis by showing how the process of interaction among agents, combined with different assumptions about the shape of space and the form of agglomeration economies, can lead to the emergence of various urban structures, perhaps with no center (uniform distribution of activities) or with a single center or several centers. Their models have shown that the different urban structures arise as a result of bifurcation processes, depending on the values allocated to parameters such as transport costs and the rate of substitution between differentiated goods. The cities thus obtained are qualitatively different from each other. (See Fujita and Thisse, Chapter 1, this volume, for a more extensive presentation of agglomeration models.)

At the same time as the monocentric assumption vanishes, other underlying assumptions must be reconsidered. That is the case, for example, for the radial-displacement arrangement. In the nonmonocentric model, any type of movement is possible *ex ante*. But *ex post* the shape of the commuting network will depend on the form of urban equilibrium achieved. However, if we are in a two-dimensional space, the need to consider any type of movement considerably hampers the formal resolution of general urban equilibrium, unless we assume that urban space is symmetrical around its geometric center. Under this condition, Ogawa and Fujita (1989) have demonstrated that the radial pattern of movement is the result of the nonmonocentric model. But assuming circular symmetry amounts to a return to the concentric arrangement of space. That limits the analytical consequences of the change introduced by nonmonocentric models. But this is only the manifestation of a general restriction on the search for general spatial equilibrium.

5.3 The Limits of Endogenization

No theory can explain everything from nothing. It is of the essence of hypo-thetico-deductive reasoning that it is necessarily based on an initial statement. It is therefore impossible to explain the formation of cities without assumptions, both about the activities that are to be localized and about the space from which one starts.

A first set of assumptions deals with the question of why people and activities tend to be concentrated. We encounter the assumption of indivisibility already suggested by Koopmans (1957) and widely illustrated since. We also come upon the economic advantages of proximity grouped under the general heading of agglomeration economies. These advantages appear as a consequence of the interaction of agents. They are generated in the course of the agglomeration process. But the existence of these advantages and their link with proximity must be postulated *a priori* for us to be able to determine an equilibrium exhibiting spatial concentrations.

A second set is required to determine where spatial concentrations will show up. In a uniform, unbounded space, all locations are identical, and the location of an endogenous center is undetermined. To localize the center, we need to be given factors of spatial heterogeneity. We commonly take natural hetero-geneity relative to endowments in natural resources, what Krugman calls the "first-nature causes" (Krugman, 1993), or we emphasize the chance factor of "historical accidents" (Arthur, 1990; Krugman, 1991a).

But even when theory seeks to study the pure effect of space (i.e., by as-suming an equal distribution of natural endowments across locations), it must still introduce a certain form of exogenous spatial heterogeneity to succeed in locating a first agglomeration. This heterogeneity can be achieved simply by the mere existence of a boundary (Papageorgiou and Thisse, 1985). Just compare the one-dimensional space of the segment and the circle: A segment of a straight line, which is bounded by definition, has a geometric center and differentiated locations relative to the point of best access, whereas on a circle or a torus all locations are equivalent until we introduce an exogenous differentiation factor.

5.4 The Scope of the Change

From von Thünen's model to the new urban economics, and then to the new economic geography, we have highlighted a series of adaptations and one major change. From a methodological viewpoint, the new urban economics is much closer to von Thünen than to the recent developments of the new economic geography.

Despite numerous adaptations, the new urban economics still is unable to say anything about the central issue of spatial economics: the formation of economic space. But agglomeration theory, which gives answers to this basic spatial enigma, does not totally dismiss the new urban economics and the monocentric model. Von Thünen's model did not claim to say everything. It set out a clearly delimited problem and replied with considerable elegance for that time. The new urban economics has a clearly stated objective, and it is practically the only theory to achieve such a virtually complete statement of objective: to set out the consequences of the operation of a perfect land market on the structure of a monocentric urban space. Although it is sometimes considered that the new urban economics does not provide a satisfactory explanation of cities, monocentric models are still regularly developed, integrating new aspects of contemporary urban life, such as segregation, congestion, pollution, and unemployment, in a partial equilibrium analysis producing a number of useful results. Above all, we must reckon with the capacity for adaptation found in the new urban economics, which reflects the well-known flexibility of microeconomic theory in general. There is no denying that this capacity is much greater than that of von Thünen's model. But this capacity can be discussed from two viewpoints.

First, it is limited, because, as Krugman says,"economics tends, understandably, to follow the line of least mathematical resistance" (Krugman, 1991a, p. 6). In the case of the monocentric model, traditional assumptions of pure competition and nonincreasing returns can be preserved. Adaptations are limited to secondary assumptions and do not affect the core of the competitive model, because the monocentric assumption makes that unnecessary. But we know that it is impossible to explain the formation of cities while keeping the pure-competition assumption. Consequently, we can think that the weight of continuity is such that it drastically limits the capacity of these models to penetrate the mysteries of urban formation and evolution.

Second, no one can identify the bounds of the propensity of the new urban economics to effectively take up new problems. Like Morishima (1984), we might invoke the law of decreasing returns of mathematized economics or fear that the hypertrophy of formalized microeconomics will develop at the expense of semantics, with the new urban economics producing increasing numbers of theorems that would have steadily decreasing validity.

The new economic geography has a much broader objective, uses a completely new approach, and produces more general and sometimes less directly intuitive results. It deals with the basic questions of spatial heterogeneity, of spatial agglomeration and dispersion. It aims to explain global spatial configurations of cities and city systems in the framework of spatial general equilibrium. It is based on a major change in the microeconomic assumptions and emphasizes the role of increasing returns, monopolistic competition, and spatial externalities. The new economic geography shows how urban configurations emerge in the way emphasized by Schelling in his book *Micromotives and Macrobehavior* (1978).

We feel that we have really managed to shed light on a phenomenon when we show how that phenomenon, the "macrobehavior", emerges from the interaction of decisions by individual families or firms. (Krugman, 1996, p. 15)

The process that leads from micromotives to macrobehavior takes the form of a sort of self-organization (Krugman, 1996), inasmuch as global equilibrium results from interactions between agents and cumulative processes of circular causation. But this has nearly nothing to do with the self-organization models of cities developed by the geographers, which are not based on micromotives.

In this context, the emergence of macro-spatial configurations may be surprising, or counterintuitive, in the sense that it is not entirely predictable from knowledge of the initial assumptions. This is reinforced by the existence of multiple equilibria and the sensitivity of the results to the initial conditions. Finally, these models ascribe an important role to historical time: "History matters," even if often it is only through the initial conditions.

The most noteworthy result from these models is that agglomeration can be encouraged by lower transportation or communication costs and higher differentiation of products. Explanations are given, in particular, as to why economic agents invariably seek proximity despite the development of new possibilities to communicate from a distance (e.g., Gehrig, Chapter 12, this volume).

These results can lead to original statements about questions related to both the past evolution of city systems and the future tendencies toward agglomeration or dispersion. The existence of spatial cumulative processes may lead us to predict strong urban growth, despite the costs of such growth, which occasionally entail predictions of the decline of cities. More specifically, one can predict an increasing polarization of European geographical space as a consequence of the integration policy that makes trade easier (Jayet et al., 1996). Furthermore, insofar as any cumulative process is highly dependent on its initial stage (and therefore on history), such processes lead to the "entrenchment" of locations that regional development policy may find it difficult to counteract.

But the new economic geography also has its weaknesses, which are gradually receding. Let us evoke two of them. First, most agglomeration models are specialized in the sense that each of them focuses on a single process of agglomeration, such as production of differentiated goods, or externalities generated by the existence of local public goods or by information exchanges. Each of these models grasps a facet of urban reality. But the city can be considered as the result of a complex combination of several agglomeration processes, the nature of which is still quite mysterious.

Complexity renders futile any attempt to seek *the* model of agglomeration. In consequence each of a growing number of theoretical studies concentrates on some particular aspect, thereby contributing to the list of known, partially interconnected, reasons for the existence of cities. (Papageorgiou, 1990, p. 33)

Second, the theory of city formation is based on the concepts of agglomeration economies and spatial externalities, which are still, for the most part, black boxes. On this point, some heterodox contributions relative to economies of proximity and local productive systems have had things to say that could be useful to mainstream agglomeration theory. It seems that those approaches are more focused on the upstream aspects of economies of proximity and attempt to explain why these economies can appear, whereas agglomeration theory is rather focused on the downstream aspects and tries to state the spatial consequences of these economies.

6 Conclusion

The emergence of the new economic geography and agglomeration theory has broader consequences in terms of integration of spatial economics in economic theory.

First, the theory of city formation derived from the endogenization of centers operates in a more extended realm relative to the theory of space formation based on the same general principles of general spatial equilibrium, and including theories of interregional equilibrium initiated by Krugman (1991a,b). General mechanisms of agglomeration are somewhat similar at the urban level and at the regional level. Moreover, the regional level for the United States may be close to the international level for Europe (Krugman, 1997). But the main sources of concentration and dispersion may depend on the spatial scale of analysis. For instance, models of city formation include commuting costs and land prices as dispersion forces, whereas regional agglomeration models base dispersion on localized activities like agriculture. It is worth noting the convergence between these two approaches, clearly demonstrated in two contributions (Fujita and Krugman, 1995, Chapter 5, this volume).

Second, the new economic geography somewhat repositions spatial economic theory more centrally in the framework of contemporary economic theory and its most recent advances. Spatial economic thought clearly was kept at the margins of economic theory during the nineteenth century and for most of the twentieth century. Economic-geography models are increasingly being integrated into mainstream economic theory. It must be emphasized that the radical change in assumptions leading to the theory of city formation is an important factor in this integration. It forges new links between spatial theory and other fields of economic theory. Increasing returns, monopolistic competition, and externalities play important roles in the theory of space formation, as in endogenous growth theory, new international trade theory, and industrial economics. This illustrates the role played by a new and increasingly widespread mode of reasoning in the evolution of the questions with which theories can deal, such as city formation for urban economics, uneven growth for growth theories, and strategic behaviors for industrial economics.

Finally, the filiation with von Thünen is no longer as clear as Fujita claimed in 1986 in the quotation given earlier. Current urban microeconomics is turning toward studies of the formation of cities and studies of the creation and transformation of monocentric or multicentric space. They address the question of spatial economics at the grass roots, the formation of a heterogeneous space and the formation of cities.

References

Alonso, W. (1964). *Location and Land Use.* Cambridge, MA: Harvard University Press.

Arthur, W. B. (1990). Silicon Valley locational clusters: When do increasing returns imply monopoly? *Mathematical Social Science* 19:235–51.

Baumont, C. (1993). *Analyse des espaces urbains multicentriques: la localisation résidentielle.* Dijon: LATEC (Bibliothèque d'analyse économique).

Baumont, C. (1997). Croissance endogène des régions et espace. In: F. Celimène and C. Lacour (eds.), *L'intégration régionale des espaces*, pp. 33–61. Paris: Economica.

Baumont, C., and Huriot, J.-M. (1996). De von Thünen à Fujita: continuité ou rupture? Working paper no. 9601, LATEC, Dijon.

Baumont, C., and Huriot, J.-M. (1997). La ville, la raison et le rêve: entre théorie et utopie. *L'espace Géographique* 2:99–117.

Beckmann, M. J. (1957). On the distribution of rent and residential density in cities. Paper presented at the Inter-Departmental Seminar on Mathematical Applications in the Social Sciences, Yale University.

Beckmann, M. J. (1972). Von Thünen revisited: a neoclassical land use model. *Swedish Journal of Economics* 74:1–7.

Beckmann, M. J. (1976). Spatial equilibrium in a dispersed city. In: Y. Y. Papageorgiou (ed.), *Mathematical Land Use Theory*, pp. 117–25. Toronto: Lexington Books.

Berry, B. J. L., and Kim, H.-M. (1993). Challenges to the monocentric model. *Geographical Analysis* 25:1–4.

Blaug, M. (1985). *Economic Theory in Retrospect*, 4th ed. Cambridge University Press.

Blaug, M. (1992). *The Methodology of Economics*, 2nd ed. Cambridge University Press.

Borukhov, E., and Hochman, O. (1977). Optimum and market equilibrium in a model of a city without a predetermined center. *Environment and Planning, A* 9:849–56.

Butler, J. H. (1980). *Economic Geography, Spatial and Environment Aspects of Economic Activity*, New York: Wiley.

Carnap, R. (1962). *Logical Foundations of Probability*. University of Chicago Press.

Clarke, M., and Wilson, A. G. (1985). The analysis of bifurcation phenomena associated with the evolution of urban spatial structures. In: M. Hazewinckel, R. Jurkovich, and J. H. P. Paelinck (eds.), *Bifurcation Analysis: Principles, Applications and Synthesis*, pp. 67–99. Dordrecht: Reidel.

Fujita, M. (1986). Urban land use theory. In: J. J. Gabszewicz, Thisse, J.-F., Fujita, M., and Schweizer, U. (eds.), *Location Theory*, pp. 73–149. Chur, Switzerland: Harwood.

Fujita, M. (1989). *Urban Economic Theory. Land Use and City Size*. Cambridge University Press.

Fujita, M. (1990). Spatial interactions and agglomeration in urban economics. In: M. Chatterji and R. E. Kunne (eds.), *New Frontiers in Regional Science*, pp. 184–221. London: Macmillan.

Fujita, M., and Krugman, P. (1995). When is the economy monocentric? von Thünen and Chamberlin unified. *Regional Science and Urban Economics* 25:505–28.

Fujita, M., and Ogawa, H. (1982). Multiple equilibria and structural transition of nonmonocentric urban configurations. *Regional Science and Urban Economics*. 12:161–96.

Fujita, M., Ogawa, H., and Thisse, J. F. (1988). A spatial competition approach to central place theory: some basic principles. *Journal of Regional Science* 28:477–94.

Fujita, M., and Thisse, J. F. (1986). Spatial competition with a land market: Hotelling and von Thünen unified. *Review of Economic Studies* 53:819–41.

Granger, G. G. (1995). *La science et les sciences*, 2nd ed. Paris: PUF.

Grotewold, A. (1959). Von Thünen in retrospect. *Economic Geography* 35:346–55.

Helpman, E., and Krugman, P. (1985). *Market Structure and Foreign Trade*. Cambridge, MA: MIT Press.

Huriot, J.-M. (1981). Rente foncière et modèle de production. *Environment and Planning, A* 13:1125–49.

Huriot, J.-M. (1987). Land rent, production and land use. *Sistemi Urbani* 2/3:167–92.

Huriot, J.-M. (1994). *Von Thünen: économie et espace*. Paris: Economica.

Jayet, H., Puig, J.-P., and Thisse, J.-F. (1996). Enjeux économiques de l'organisation du territoire. *Revue d'Economie Politique* 106:127–58.

Kellerman, A. (1977). The pertinence of the macro-Thünian analysis. *Economic Geography* 58:255–64.

Kellerman, A. (1981). The pertinence of the macro-Thünian analysis: the case of Israel. *Geographical Research Forum* 4:46–54.

Koopmans, T. C. (1957). *Three Essays on the State of Economic Science*. New York: McGraw-Hill.

Krugman, P. (1991a). *Geography and Trade*, Cambridge, MA: MIT Press.

Krugman, P. (1991b). Increasing returns and economic geography. *Journal of Political Economy* 99:483–99.

Krugman, P. (1993). First nature, second nature and metropolitan location. *Journal of Regional Science* 33:129–44.

Krugman, P. (1995). *Development, Geography, and Economic Theory*. Cambridge, MA: MIT Press.

Krugman, P. (1996). *The Self-Organizing Economy*. London: Blackwell.

Krugman, P. (1997). The rise, decline, and return of geographical concentration. Presented at the Joint International Seminar in International Trade and CEPR Geography Seminar, a CEPR/NBER conference, Paris, 23–25 May.

Kuhn, T. S. (1970). *The Structure of Scientific Revolutions*, 2nd ed. (1st ed., 1962). University of Chicago Press.

Lakatos, I. (1970). Falsification and the Methodology of Scientific Research Programmes. In: I. Lakatos and A. E. Musgrave (eds.), *Criticism and the Growth of Knowledge*, pp. 91–196. Cambridge University Press.

Launhardt, W. (1885). *Mathematische Begrundung der Volkswitschaftslehre*. Leipzig: Teubner. English translation by J. Creedy (1993): *Mathematical Principles of Economics*. Aldershot, UK: Elgar.

Lösch, A. (1940). *Die raumliche Ordnung der Wirtschaft*. Jena: G. Fischer. English translation by W. H. Woglom and W. F. Stolper (1954): *The Economics of Location*. New Haven, CT: Yale University Press.

Marshall, A. (1890). *Principles of Economics*. London: Macmillan (8th ed., 1920). London: Macmillan.

Mohring, H. (1961). Land values and the measurement of highway benefits. *Journal of Political Economy* 69:236–49.

Morishima, M. (1984). The good and bad uses of mathematics. In: P. Wiles and G. Routh (eds.), *Economics in Disarray*. Oxford: Blackwell.

Muth, R. F. (1969). *Cities and Housing*. University of Chicago Press.

Norman, G. (1993). Of shoes and ships and shredded wheat, of cabbages and cars: the contemporary relevance of location theory. In: H. Ohta and J.-F. Thisse (eds.), *Does Economic Space Matter?* New York: St. Martin's Press.

Ogawa, H., and Fujita, M. (1980). Equilibrium land use patterns in a nonmonocentric city. *Journal of Regional Science* 4:455–75.

Ogawa, H., and Fujita, M. (1989). Nonmonocentric urban configuration in a two-dimensional space. *Environment and Planning, A* 21:363–74.

Papageorgiou, Y. Y. (1990). *The Isolated City-State. An Economic Geography of Urban Spatial Structure*. London: Routledge.

Papageorgiou, Y. Y., and Thisse, J.-F. (1985). Agglomeration as spatial interdependence between firms and households. *Journal of Economic Theory* 37:19–31.

Pascal, B. (1954). *Préface sur le traité du vide*. In: *Oeuvres complète*. Paris: Bibliothèque de la Pléiade.

Ponsard, C. (1983). *History of Spatial Economic Theory*. Berlin: Springer-Verlag.

Popper, K. (1959). *The Logic of Scientific Discovery*. London: Hutchinson.

Samuelson, P. A. (1983). Thünen at two hundred. *Journal of Economic Literature* 21:1468–88.

Schumpeter, J. (1954). *History of Economic Analysis*. London: Allen & Unwin.

Scott, A. J. (1980). *The Urban Land Nexus and the State*. London: Pion.

Schelling, T. (1978). *Micromotives and Macrobehavior*. New York: Norton.

Sinclair, R. (1967). Von Thünen and urban sprawl. *Annals of the Association of American Geographers* 57:72–87.

Sraffa, P. (1960). *Production of Commodities by Means of Commodities*. Cambridge University Press.

Starrett, D. (1978). Market allocation of location choice in a model with free mobility. *Journal of Economic Theory* 17:21–37.

Thisse, J. (1992). Espace et concurrence. In: P.-H. Derycke (ed.), *Espace et dynamiques territoriales*, pp. 113–35. Paris: Economica.

Tirole, J. (1988). *The Theory of Industrial Organization*. Cambridge, MA: MIT Press.

von Thünen, J. H. (1826–63). *Der isolierte Staat in Beziehung auf Landwirtschaft und Nationalökonomie*. Vol. I, 1826, Hamburg: Perthes. Vol. II, Section 1, 1850, Rostock: Leopold. Vol. II, Section 2, and Vol. III, posthumous edition by H. Schumacher, 1863, Rostock: Hinstorff. Complete edition by H. Schumacher-Zarchlin, 1875, Wiegandt: Hempel und Parey. Partial English translation in P. Hall (ed.), 1966, *Von Thünen's Isolated State*, Oxford: Pergamon Press.

Walliser, B. (1994). *L'intelligence de l'économie*. Paris: Odile Jacob.

Wingo, L. (1961). *Transportation and Urban Land*. Washington, DC: Resources for the Future.

Urban Systems

Urban Systems

CHAPTER 3

City Systems: General Equilibrium Approaches

Hesham M. Abdel-Rahman

1 Introduction

Cities are complex economic systems. However, casual observation of cities' industrial composition, in developed countries as well as developing countries, leads us to conclude that specialized as well as diversified cities coexist in all urban systems. Furthermore, within a given country, the urban system tends to be dominated by a large metropolis (e.g., Cairo, Mexico City, Tokyo, New York) that has a diversified industrial composition. In addition, diversified cities tend to be larger than specialized cities. On the other hand, inter- and intra-city income disparities seem to be increasing, and those increases are more pronounced in developing countries. An understanding of the forces behind the formation of cities, their industrial composition, and the structure of urban systems is becoming more important over time, for two main reasons: (1) the growing percentages of populations living in urban areas and (2) the impact of cities' industrial composition on city growth. The former has been documented by the United Nations *Human Development Report* (1996), in which it is stated that the percentage of the world population living in urban areas increased from 34% in 1960 to 44% in 1993. Furthermore, the percentage of the population living in urban areas in industrialized countries increased from 61% to 73% over the same period, whereas the increase in developing countries was less pronounced. The latter factor has been shown to have mixed effects on urban growth. Glaeser et al. (1992) reported that diversity of industrial composition in cities stimulates urban growth, but Henderson et al. (1995) stated that only new industries are attracted to diversified cities, whereas mature industries grow faster in specialized cities. The objective of this chapter is to provide a survey of recent theories that have attempted to explain the forces behind the

This research was conducted while the author was visiting the Institute of Economic Research, Kyoto University. The comments of Jean-Marie Huriot, Jacques Thisse, and the participants in a seminar at Doshisha University are appreciated.

existence as well as the structure of city systems.[1] More precisely, we shall address the following questions: *What are the main factors that lead to the formation of cities? When do cities become specialized in production, and when do they become diversified? When do both specialized and diversified cities coexist? What is the role of trade in a system of cities? What determines the number and size of cities of different types in an economy? What are the factors that determine income disparities among different types of households?* These questions are addressed in the context of a simple spatial, general equilibrium model of a closed economy consisting of a system of cities. To simplify the basic model that will be used to investigate these issues, we shall impose some assumptions that will facilitate such a task in a limited space. Thus, we adopt the monocentric city model pioneered by Alonso (1964). In this model, the "central business district" is the only employment center in the city. Models of systems of cities that will be discussed are in the spirit of Mills (1967) and Henderson (1974), who typically considered two types of forces, forces that lead to a concentration of population and economic activities (*agglomeration forces*) and forces that lead to deconcentration (*dispersion forces*). When these forces are balanced at the margin, the equilibrium city size is determined. These types of models do not provide explanations for the spatial distribution of cities. Thus, distance between cities is not taken into consideration, in contrast to the pioneering work of Christaller (1966) and Lösch (1940), in which distance between centers was explicitly modeled.

The agglomeration forces cited in the literature on city systems can be classified into two main categories, depending on whether they influence the *supply side* or *demand side* of the economy. The former includes the various forces that lead to geographical concentration of production activities, such as (1) economies of scale at the firm level, leading to the formation of company towns, (2) economies of localization, which are economies of scale at the level of industries, leading to the formation of a multi-firm specialized city, and (3) economies of urbanization, which are scale economies at the level of the urban area, leading to the formation of a multiproduct, diversified city. This chapter will focus on models that present a microfoundation for these agglomeration forces. Economies of localization result from (1) information externalities stemming from interactions among agents and face-to-face communications that enhance productivity and foster innovation,[2] as shown in Table 3.1,[3] (2) access to a wide range of specialized intermediate inputs, (3) matching

[1] For a review of the literature, see Henderson (1987). Also, for a recent survey of city formation, as well as growth, see Fujita and Thisse (Chapter 1, this volume) and Quigley (1998).

[2] The classification of agglomeration in this chapter is in the spirit of Hoover (1939) and Weber (1929), who introduced the concept. Models of information externalities will not be discussed in this chapter, because it focuses on a microfoundation model of agglomeration.

[3] See Jacobs (1969) for an argument on the impact of interaction on creativity in production.

Table 3.1. *Supply side*

Economies of scale	Mirrlees (1972), Dixit (1973), Kanemoto (1980)
Localization economies	
1. Externalities	Mills (1967), Henderson (1974), Kanemoto (1980)
2. Differentiated intermediate good	Abdel-Rahman and Fujita (1990)
3. Matching in the labor market	Helsley and Strange (1990), Abdel-Rahman and Wang (1995, 1997)
4. Matching of used assets in the capital market	Helsley and Strange (1991)
5. Acquisition of task-specific skills	Becker and Henderson (Chapter 4, this volume)
Urbanization economies	
1. Cross product technological externalities	Abdel-Rahman (1990)
2. Shareable input	Abdel-Rahman (1991, 1996)
3. Economies of scope	Abdel-Rahman and Fujita (1993) , Abdel-Rahman (1994)

in the labor market, which reduces search costs, (4) matching of used assets in the capital market, which enhances the salvage value of assets from failed projects in large cities, and (5) acquisition of task-specific skills, which enhances productivity. Economies of urbanization result from (1) cross-product technological externalities,[4] (2) the use of shared specialized intermediate inputs, and (3) economies of scope in production.

In the latter we find the forces leading to agglomeration of the population, such as (1) the existence of a large variety of goods and services and (2) the

---

[4] This model will not be discussed, for the same reason that has been stated in footnote 2.

Table 3.2. *Demand side*

Local public good	Stiglitz (1977), Kanemoto (1980), Helsley and Strange (1993), Tsukahara (1995), Abdel-Rahman (1998)
Differentiated good	Hobson (1987) and Abdel-Rahman (1988)

provision of various local public goods (Table 3.2). In these models, the only dispersion force stems from the higher commuting costs resulting from the physical expansion of the city (Mills, 1967).

Models of systems of cities can be classified into two main groups: (1) models in which the industrial composition within cities in the system is predetermined and (2) models in which the industrial composition within cities in the system is determined by the model. In the former, the main issues to be addressed are the factors that determine the number of cities within the system and the city size. In the latter, the issues to be addressed are the factors that determine the structure of the system of cities, the factors that determine the cities' industrial composition, and the size and number of each type of city within the system.

Moreover, models of city systems can be further classified into (1) models with identical households, in which all households are assumed to have the same income, and (2) models with multiple types of households, in which households are assumed to have different incomes. The latter are of more interest, because they enable us to address the issue of income inequality and its impact on social welfare.

The organization of this chapter is as follows: Section 2 reviews models that generate specialized or diversified systems of cities with identical households. Section 3 is devoted to models of identical households that generate cities of different types, sizes, and industrial compositions. Section 4 is devoted to the modeling of a system of specialized cities with heterogeneous households. Section 5 offers conclusions and directions for future research.

2 Exogenous Industrial Composition

In this section we review models of a system of cities in which the industrial composition for cities within the system is predetermined. Two types of models will be discussed: (1) models that result in a specialized system of cities with inter-city trade and (2) models that result in a diversified system of cities with no trade. First, we present a simple model of city formation based on preference for variety (Dixit and Stiglitz, 1977) in the consumption of non-traded goods.[5] Then we consider a model of a system of specialized cities in which each city produces a differentiated product, and trade occurs among cities. Finally, we consider the formation of cities as a result of differentiated intermediate inputs (Ethier, 1982). This section focuses on the factors that determine city size, the number of cities, and the type of regulation of monopolistic competitive firms that will lead to a first-best solution.

We first describe the common framework that we use to review the literature. We consider a closed economy consisting of a system of circular cities spreading over a flat, featureless plane. The total population of the economy is given by N. It is assumed that all households are identical, and each is endowed with one unit of labor (this assumption will be relaxed later in Section 4). Each household is free to choose the city in which to reside and work. Two final goods, X and Z, are produced within the system. Cities are formed in this economy by local governments.[6] The local government of each city rents the land for the city at the opportunity cost, which is assumed to be zero. Then the local government sublets the land to households at the market rent. Each city government chooses the population size for the city, n, that will maximize the utility of its residents.

2.1 Household Behavior in a City

Each household in a given city resides at one location and has one job that requires commuting to the central business district (CBD), where all firms are located. As in any monocentric-city model, each location within a city can be characterized by its distance from the CBD. For simplicity, we postulate that each household consumes one unit of land (i.e., demand for land is perfectly inelastic). In addition, all households in the economy are assumed to have identical utility functions of the following Cobb-Douglas form:

$$u = x^\alpha z^{(1-\alpha)} \tag{3.1}$$

where x and z are the quantities of the two goods consumed by a household, and $\alpha \in (0, 1)$.[7] We now specify the budget constraint facing a household residing at a distance r from the CBD in a given city as

$$x(r) + Pz(r) + R(r) + Wtr = Y \tag{3.2}$$

---

[5] See Stahl (1983) for an initial work on the impact of product variety in consumption on migration.
[6] See Becker and Henderson (Chapter 4, this volume) for the large-versus-small-agents mechanism of city formation.
[7] See Fujita (1989, ch. 2) for a partial equilibrium model of a single city with identical household utility and different incomes. For a general equilibrium model with the same specification, see Abdel-Rahman and Wang (1995, 1997) and Abdel-Rahman (1996).

where P is the (relative) price of good z in units of good x, $R(r)$ represents the unit land rent at distance r, W is the wage rate, t is the amount of time required to commute one unit of distance, and Y denotes the household income. Given that each household is endowed with one unit of labor, if a household resides at distance r, its net labor supply is $1 - tr$. On the other hand, one can interpret this as a household working one unit of time and paying an out-of-pocket commuting cost of Wt per unit distance. Both interpretations are consistent with the budget constraint. From the first-order conditions for the maximization of (3.1), subject to (3.2), we obtain the demand for x and z:

$$x(r) = \alpha[Y - Wtr - R(r)] \tag{3.3}$$

$$z(r) = (1 - \alpha)P^{-1}[Y - Wtr - R(r)] \tag{3.4}$$

Substituting (3.3) and (3.4) into (3.1), we derive the indirect utility function for a representative household in a given city as

$$V = \alpha^{\alpha}(1 - \alpha)^{(1-\alpha)}P^{-(1-\alpha)}[Y - Wtr - R(r)] \tag{3.5}$$

For simplicity, public ownership of land is assumed, so that the household income is given by

$$Y = \text{ALR}/n + W \tag{3.6}$$

where ALR is the aggregate land rent in a given city, and n is the size of a representative city in the economy.[8] Recall that each household consumes precisely one unit of land. Thus, the total population of a representative city is given by

$$n = \int_0^b 2\pi r \, dr = \pi b^2 \tag{3.7}$$

where b represents the urban-fringe distance for each city.

Locational equilibrium requires that all workers in a given city achieve the same utility level. Hence, from (3.3) and (3.4), at each $r \leq b$ we derive that $W - Wtr - R(r) = W - Wtb - R(b)$. Recall that, for convenience, we normalize the opportunity cost of land to be zero, so that $R(b) = 0$. Thus, the land rent schedule under locational equilibrium is $R(r) = Wt(b - r)$. Using (3.7) and integrating the foregoing land rent schedule, we can derive the aggregate land rent in each city as

$$\text{ALR} = \int_0^b R(r)2\pi r \, dr = W\mu n^{3/2} \tag{3.8}$$

where $\mu \equiv t/(3\pi^{1/2})$.

---

[8] This assumption will be modified later, on when local governments use ALR to finance the provision of public goods.

Substituting (3.6)–(3.8) into (3.5), we derive the indirect utility function for a representative household in a given city as

$$V = \alpha^\alpha (1 - \alpha)^{(1-\alpha)} P^{-(1-\alpha)} W \left[1 - 2\mu n^{1/2} \right] \tag{3.9}$$

It can be seen from the foregoing equation that V is increasing in household net labor supply, given by the term in square brackets. The foregoing equation is essential in solving for city size. This is because the objective of local government is to maximize the utility of a representative household.

2.2 A Differentiated Non-traded Good in Consumption

Consider the case in which z in (3.1) is a sub-utility function of the constant-elasticity-of-substitution (CES) form given by

$$z = \left(\sum_l^m q_l^\rho \right)^{1/\rho} \tag{3.10}$$

where q_l is the quantity of the variant l of a non-traded differentiated good or service, such as restaurants or movie theaters. According to Hobson (1987) and Abdel-Rahman (1988), the desire of households to consume a variety of non-traded differentiated product is one of the main reasons for the existence of large cities. As $\rho \to 1$, products become close to perfect substitutes, and households derive less utility from product variety. Alternatively, as $\rho \to 0$, products become highly differentiated, and households derive more utility from product variety. The budget constraint facing a household in a given city is given by

$$x(r) + \sum_l^m P_l z_l(r) + R(r) + W tr = Y \tag{3.11}$$

From the maximization of (3.1) and (3.10) subject to (3.11) we derive the household demand for each differentiated service as

$$q_l(r) = \left\{ (1 - \alpha) P_l^{-1} z^{-\rho} [Y - Wtr - R(r)] \right\}^{1/(1-\rho)} \tag{3.12}$$

Substituting (3.3), (3.6), and (3.12) into (3.1), we derive the indirect utility function as

$$V = \alpha^\alpha (1 - \alpha)^{(1-\alpha)} \xi^{-(1-\alpha)} W \left[1 - 2\mu n^{1/2} \right] \tag{3.13}$$

where

$$\xi = \left[\sum_l^m P_l^{-\rho/(1-\rho)} \right]^{-(1-\rho)/\rho} \tag{3.14}$$

Differentiated-Good Production. Each of the differentiated services, q_l, is assumed to be produced by the same production process, where labor is the only input. The amount of labor L_l required for production of q_l is assumed to be given as

$$L_l = f + cq_l \tag{3.15}$$

where $f > 0$ is the fixed labor requirement, and $c > 0$ is the marginal labor requirement. Hence, the average labor requirement is decreasing in the amount of the output, which represents the reason for the formation of a city (i.e., economies of scale at the firm level). Assuming that each firm in the service sector can differentiate its product without cost, at equilibrium it can be seen that each service will be supplied by one firm. Then the profit of the firm is given by

$$P_l q_l - W L_l \tag{3.16}$$

From the profit maximization, we have the following equality between the marginal revenue and the marginal cost:

$$P_l\left(1 - E_l^{-1}\right) = Wc \tag{3.17}$$

where E_l is the price elasticity of demand. Following the Dixit and Stiglitz (1977) model of monopolistic competition, and considering symmetric equilibrium, the elasticity of substitution is given as

$$E = (1 - \rho)^{-1} \tag{3.18}$$

Then the common equilibrium price for each service produced is given as

$$P_q = Wc\rho^{-1} \tag{3.19}$$

This shows that each firm will charge its price at a *markup* over the marginal cost. Thus the resulting equilibrium is not efficient. Given the common output price, each firm will produce the same amount of output, q. From (3.15), (3.19), and the long-run zero-profit condition, we can derive the equilibrium output as

$$q^* = f\rho[c(1 - \rho)]^{-1} \tag{3.20}$$

Manufactured-Good Production. The perfectly competitive low-tech product X is made by labor only, with a simple constant-returns-to-scale technology:

$$X = \lambda L_x \tag{3.21}$$

where L_x and X are respectively the quantity of labor and the quantity of output, and $\lambda > 0$. It is assumed that X is a non-traded good. Thus, each city will produce X as well as $\{q_l\}$. Given (3.21), production efficiency requires that a representative firm in the manufacturing industry hire labor in a given city at a wage given by

$$W_x = \lambda \tag{3.22}$$

Assuming that full employment prevails in each city, the total population of a representative city is given as

$$n = L_x + m L_z \tag{3.23}$$

Because all cities in the economy are identical, the aggregate demand of each city for good X can be derived by integrating (3.3) as

$$\text{AD}_x = \alpha \int_0^b [W - Wtr + (\text{ALR})n^{-1} - R(r)]\,dr \tag{3.24}$$

From (3.6)–(3.8) and (3.22), and by equating the aggregate demand to the aggregate supply, λL_x, we have

$$L_x = \alpha n \big[1 - \alpha \mu n^{1/2} \big] \tag{3.25}$$

From (3.15), (3.20), (3.23), and (3.25) we have

$$m = f^{-1}(1 - \rho)n \big[(1 - \alpha) + \alpha \mu n^{1/2} \big] \tag{3.26}$$

Observe that the number of varieties is increasing with city size. This suggests that the formation of large cities involves a substantial amount of product diversity, and increasing product diversity is a sufficient condition for the formation of larger cities [see also equation (3.27)]. This result is supported by the casual observation that all large cities offer large varieties of goods and services. Cities are formed by local governments. The objective of the local government is to maximize the utility of a representative household by the choice of city size. To determine the city size, we substitute (3.19), (3.22), and (3.26) into (3.13) and obtain

$$V(n) = A \big[(1 - \alpha)n + \alpha \mu n^{3/2} \big]^{(1-\rho)(1-\alpha)/\rho} \big(1 - \mu n^{1/2} \big) \tag{3.27}$$

where

$$A = \alpha^\alpha (1 - \alpha)^{(1-\alpha)} c^{-(1-\alpha)} \rho^{(1-\alpha)} \lambda^\alpha [(1 - \rho)f^{-1}]^{(1-\rho)(1-\alpha)/\rho}$$

Observe that the indirect utility is a function of city size only. It can be shown that this function is strictly concave in n, which shows that product variety in the non-traded differentiated service is sufficient for the formation of cities. The increasing segment of the indirect utility is due to the increase in product variety (i.e., the agglomeration force dominates). On the other hand, the decreasing segment is due to high commuting costs resulting from the physical expansion of the city (i.e., the dispersion force dominates). Maximizing (3.27) with respect to n, we can derive the equilibrium size of a representative city as follows:[9]

$$n^* = \left[\frac{2(1-\alpha)(1-\rho)}{\{\rho + 2(1-\alpha)(1-\rho)\}\mu} \right]^2$$

Observe that city size increases with the degree of preference for variety (i.e., the smaller the parameter ρ, and the smaller the commuting cost t). The intuition behind this result is that the higher the consumer desire for variety, the larger the number of firms, which in turn is positively related to city size by equation (3.26). The equilibrium number of cities is given by N/n^*, because all cities in the economy are identical. We know *that the equilibrium city size and product variety are not first-best optima, because of the average-cost pricing given by (3.19). However, if firms are subsidized to induce them to marginal-cost pricing, and if the local governments use the ALR to subsidize firms in the service sector, then the ALR will be sufficient to cover the fixed cost,* and the *equilibrium will be efficient* (Hobson, 1987; Abdel-Rahman, 1988).

2.3 Differentiated Traded Goods

Henderson and Abdel-Rahman (1991) have used product differentiation to examine the formation of a system of cities in which each city specializes in the production of a differentiated traded good. The purpose is to explain national economies of scope arising from product diversity. In other words, large nations are able to provide a larger variety of goods. In this framework, the reason for the formation of cities in the economy is the presence of economies of scale in the production of each variant, as given by (3.15). Given that a differentiated product is traded at no transportation cost, each city will specialize in the production of one variant and the production of the non-traded good. This is because producing more than one differentiated good in a given city would increase commuting costs without generating any productivity gain.

Production sectors are the same as in the preceding section. However, full employment in each city requires that

$$n - 2\mu n^{3/2} = f + cq + L_x \tag{3.28}$$

Substituting (3.20) and (3.25) into (3.28), we have

$$f(1-\rho)^{-1} = (1-\alpha)\left[n - \mu n^{3/2}\right] \tag{3.29}$$

This defines the equilibrium city size. *Henderson and Abdel-Rahman (1991) have shown that the equilibrium city size is larger than the optimal size, whereas the optimal number of cities is larger than the equilibrium number.*

---

[9] It can be seen that the equilibrium city size is decreasing in ρ, α, and t.

2.4 Differentiated Services in Production

In this section we consider a differentiated-product model as a microfoundation for the black-box approach to external economies of scale that has been used in the city-size model (Henderson, 1987). Thus, we explicitly model the availability of specialized services, such as repair and maintenance services, engineering and legal support, transportation and communication services, and financial and advertising services, that have been suggested as the major causes of external economies of scale. Furthermore, these services constitute a significant share of employment in almost all industrialized countries (see Hansen, 1990, for the U.S. case). Thus, to understand city formation and industrial composition, we have to take into consideration the service sector. The central idea behind the model is that increasing returns to scale and the desire for variety of intermediate inputs are the basic causes of industrial agglomeration and city formation (Abdel-Rahman and Fujita, 1990). The production function for the final good is given by

$$Z = L_z^\beta \left[\left(\sum_l^m q_l^\rho \right)^{1/\rho} \right]^{(1-\beta)} , \qquad \rho, \beta \in (0,1) \tag{3.30}$$

where q_l is the quantity of intermediate input l, and L_z is the quantity of labor used in the production of Z. The problem of the firm is to choose inputs L_z and $\{q_l\}$ so as to maximize its profit, given by

$$\Pi = PZ - WL_z - \sum_{l=1}^m P_l q_l \tag{3.31}$$

From the first-order conditions, we have

$$L_z = \beta PZW^{-1} \tag{3.32}$$

$$q_l = \left[(1-\beta)PZ \left(\sum_{l=1}^m q_l^\rho \right)^{-1} P_l^{-1} \right]^{1/(1-\rho)} \tag{3.33}$$

The behavior in the differentiated service is as presented in the preceding section.

The reason for the formation of cities in this economy is the existence of economies of scale in the production of each intermediate good, and the reason for the concentration is the desire of industry Z to employ a large variety of intermediate services and the fact that such services are non-traded within the urban system. Then, full employment in a given city is

$$n = L_z + L_x + mL_q \tag{3.34}$$

One can derive the number of intermediate services as in (3.20). It can then be shown that the wage prevailing in industry Z is given as

$$W(m) = BPm^{(1-\beta)(1-\rho)/\rho} \tag{3.35}$$

where $B = (1 - \beta)\beta\rho^{(1-\beta)}c^{-(1-\beta)}$. We see that *the wage is an increasing function of the number of variants.*[10] *This implies that the larger the variety of intermediate goods, the higher the productivity of labor in industry* Z. This relationship is supported by empirical evidence (Hansen, 1990). Furthermore, it can be shown with the use of (3.15), (3.19), (3.20), (3.22), (3.25), and (3.34) that city size is an increasing function of the number of intermediate goods, as shown in the preceding model. Consequently, the wage is also an increasing function of city size. This is the reason behind city formation in the presence of product variety in intermediate goods. *It is interesting to note that this model generates a wage equation that is structurally the same as the one assumed in the Marshallian externalities model* (Abdel-Rahman and Fujita, 1990). In other words, the product differentiation model can be used as a microfoundation for Marshallian externalities.

Substituting (3.15), (3.19), (3.20), (3.22), (3.25), (3.32), and (3.35) into (3.13), we derive the indirect utility function as a function of city size as

$$V = \Psi^{(1-\alpha)}\left[1 - \mu n^{1/2}\right]\left[\alpha n + (1-\alpha)\mu n^{3/2}\right]^{(1-\alpha)(1-\rho)(1-\beta)/\rho} \tag{3.36}$$

where $\Psi = \alpha^{\alpha}(1-\alpha)^{(1-\alpha)}\lambda^{\alpha/(1-\alpha)}B[(1-\beta)(1-\rho)f^{-1}]^{(1-\beta)(1-\rho)/\rho}$.

As in the preceding model, the local government maximizes the utility of a representative household by choosing the city size. It can be shown that the foregoing utility function is strictly concave in n, with a unique maximum that represents the equilibrium size for a given city in the economy.[11] The increasing segment of the indirect utility is due to the productivity gain resulting from increasing the range of product variety (i.e., the agglomeration force dominates). On the other hand, the decreasing segment is due to high commuting costs resulting from the physical expansion of the city (i.e., the dispersion force dominates). Here also, the total number of cities will be given as $M = N/n$. *Abdel-Rahman and Fujita (1990) have shown unlike the case of the Marshallian externality model, in which the equilibrium city size is a first-best optimal city size with no subsidy, monopolistic competition requires subsidies to firms in order to achieve the first-best outcome.*

The foregoing model can generate cities of different sizes. For example, *if the economy produces two final goods, each of which uses a different group of non-traded differentiated services, then the economy generates two types of*

---

[10] This equation provides a microfoundation for the existence of localization economies.

[11] The necessary condition for this result is that $\alpha > 0.5$. The intuition for that is that the industry with productivity dependent on the product variety will have a higher expenditure share.

cities, each specializing in the production of one final good and the group of differentiated services used in its production. This will be the case as long as no benefit can result from the location of both industries within the same city. We shall elaborate on this model in Section 3.

On the other hand, if locating two industries within the same city leads to some productivity gain, then we shall end up with a system of diversified cities. This case can occur in the foregoing framework if industry X has the following production function:

$$X = L_x^\gamma \left(\left[\sum_{l=1}^{m} q_l^\rho \right]^{1/\rho} \right)^{(1-\gamma)/\rho} \quad , \qquad \gamma, \rho \in (0,1) \qquad (3.37)$$

Indeed, *if industries X and Z share the use of differentiated services, all cities in the economy will produce both consumption goods as well as the corresponding differentiated intermediate services* (Abdel-Rahman, 1990).

3 Endogenous Industrial Composition

This section reviews models that generate cities of different types, sizes, and industrial compositions. These types of models seek to explain not only the reasons behind the formation of cities of different sizes and industrial compositions but also the reasons behind the coexistence of specialized and diversified cities.[12] Thus, these classes of models enable us to explain the factors behind the structures of different city systems. Three models are reviewed in this section. In the first model, the reason for the formation of specialized cities is economies of scale due to the use of differentiated intermediate services. On the other hand, the reason for the formation of diversified cities is high inter-city transportation costs. In the second model, the reason behind the formation of specialized company towns is scale economies at the firm level resulting from the existence of fixed costs in production. On the other hand, the reason for the formation of diversified company towns is the existence of economies of joint production in the final goods (i.e., economies of scope). Finally, in the third model, the reason for the formation of diversified and multi-firm cities is economies of scope in the non-traded intermediate services.

3.1 Transportation Costs

In this section we discuss models in which the industrial composition within the city system will depend on the parameters of the model. Thus, the model

---

[12] For a partial equilibrium model of specialized and diversified cities with external scale economies, see Abdel-Rahman (1990).

leads to a different equilibrium configuration (i.e., a different city system) under each set of parameter values. The first model, by Abdel-Rahman (1996), uses product variety in the intermediate-goods sector, as introduced in Section 2. The model generates two equilibrium configurations: (1) pure specialization, in which each city specializes in the production of one group of intermediate producer services and one final good, and (2) pure diversification, in which all cities in the economy produce two groups of intermediate producer services and two final goods. In the context of this model, cities specialize in the production of a particular final good. The reason for that is *the desire of the final-good industry to take advantage of productivity gains offered by using a wider variety of non-traded differentiated services* (Abdel-Rahman and Fujita, 1990). On the other hand, the reason for diversification is *the high inter-city transportation cost of the final goods.*

The production functions for X and Z are as given in (3.30) and (3.37), where X uses a group of differentiated services q_{l1}, and Z uses a group of differentiated services q_{l2}. Thus, the production sectors are the same as presented in Section 2. Furthermore, it is assumed that good X is used only for commuting. The utility function is now given by[13]

$$u = z \tag{3.38}$$

where z is the quantity of the only consumption good. We assume Samuelson's iceberg transportation cost for both traded goods. In this context, when one unit of the good is transported from one city to another, regardless of the distance between them, only a given fraction, $\tau < 1$, of this good will arrive. Hence, the transportation cost is an inverse function of τ. The budget constraint for a given household at distance r_d from the CBD in a given diversified city of type d is given by

$$Pz(r_d) + R(r_d) = Y_d - tr_d \tag{3.39}$$

where good X is used only for commuting. The budget constraint for a household at distance r from the CBD in specialized cities of types x and z is given by

$$P\tau_z^{-1}z(r_x) + R(r_x) = Y_x - tr_x \tag{3.40}$$

$$Pz(r_z) + R(r_z) = Y_z - \tau_x^{-1}tr_z \tag{3.41}$$

In a pure specialized equilibrium, we solve for the indirect utilities, with the use of (3.6)–(3.8), for each type of city as

$$V_x = P^{-1}\tau_z\left[\varepsilon_x n_x^{(1-\beta_x)(1-\rho_x)/\rho_x} - 2\mu n_x^{1/2}\right] \tag{3.42}$$

$$V_z = P^{-1}\left[\varepsilon_z P n^{(1-\beta_z)(1-\rho_z)/\rho_z} - 2\tau_x^{-1}\mu n_z^{1/2}\right] \tag{3.43}$$

---

[13] The assumption that good X is not a consumption good is only for analytical convenience and does not affect the result of the model.

where

$$\varepsilon_j = \beta_j^{\beta_j}(1-\beta_j)^{(1-\beta_j)}\rho_j^{(1-\beta_j)}C_j^{-(1-\beta_j)}$$
$$\times f_j^{-(1-\beta_j)(1-\rho_j)/\rho_j}(1-\rho_j)^{(1-\beta_j)(1-\rho_j)/\rho_j}, \quad j = x, z$$

It can be shown that under some regularity conditions, both functions are strictly concave on $\{n \mid V(n) > 0\}$. Given that the number of cities of each type is large, so that local governments behave as price-takers, we solve for the city size that will maximize utility. In equilibrium, utilities must be equalized between cities of types x and z. Thus, from (3.42) and (3.43) we solve for a unique equilibrium utility level for the specialized system. It has been shown that this utility is increasing in τ_z and τ_x (Abdel-Rahman, 1996). In other words, *higher transportation costs lead to lower equilibrium utility*. Thus, there exist different combinations of τ_x and τ_z that can sustain a given equilibrium utility. This result makes intuitive sense, because higher transportation costs imply that fewer resources will be used for consumption goods.

In a pure diversified equilibrium configuration, all cities in the economy will produce both final goods and both groups of intermediate goods. Assuming that full employment will prevail in each city, we have

$$n_d = L_x + L_z + m_z L_{qz} + m_x L_{qx} \tag{3.44}$$

Using the same procedure as in Section 2, we derive the indirect utility as

$$V_d = P^{-1}\left[\varepsilon_d n_d^{3(1-\rho_x)(1-\beta_x)/2[\rho_x+(1-\rho_x)(1-\beta_x)]} - 2\mu n_d^{1/2}\right] \tag{3.45}$$

where

$$\varepsilon_d = \varepsilon_x\left[2\mu(1-\beta_x)(1+\rho_x)f_x^{-1}\right]^{[(1-\beta_x)(1-\rho_x)]/\{[\rho_x+(1-\beta_x)(1-\rho_x)]\}}$$

The foregoing function can be shown to be strictly concave on $\{n \mid V(n) > 0\}$. The local government maximizes utility by choosing city size. With the use of a material balance condition, we solve for the equilibrium price and the equilibrium utility level. Note that the equilibrium utility level, V_d^*, is independent of τ_z and τ_x, because no trade will occur in a diversified system. Thus, the curve in Figure 3.1 represents the locus of points along which V_s^* is held constant, and the utility level is the same whether we have pure specialization or pure diversification.[14] Given any city formation mechanism in which local governments maximize utility, the type of equilibrium configuration that will provide the highest utility will be the one sustainable. As can be seen in Figure 3.1, *high values of τ (i.e., low transportation costs) will lead to pure specialization, and high transportation costs will lead to pure diversified equilibrium*. The intuition behind this result is that a specialized system will be the equilibrium outcome

---

[14] See Abdel-Rahman (1996, p.16) for the derivation of this curve.

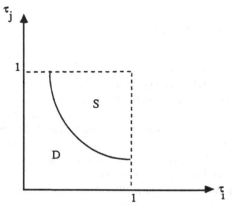

Figure 3.1. Parameter ranges for two equilibrium configurations.

if the benefit from economies of scale (i.e., product differentiation) dominates the loss due to transportation cost. On the other hand, the system will be diversified if the reverse is true. This result can be tested empirically by comparing the industrial compositions of cities in developed countries possessing well-developed inter-city transportation systems with those of cities in developing countries. An alternative approach for testing the result is to compare cities' industrial compositions over time in a given country.

3.2 *Economies of Scope*

Abdel-Rahman and Fujita (1993) have introduced a model that can explain the coexistence of a diversified city and a specialized city based on the concept of economies of scope (Panzar and Willig, 1986).[15] In this framework, the reason for the formation of a diversified city is the benefit of joint production. This benefit is the cost saving that results from the existence of economies of scope, in which the total cost of producing more than one good jointly in one firm/city is less than that of producing them separately. On the other hand, the formation of specialized cities is due to scale economies at the firm level, resulting from the existence of fixed costs of production. Unlike the case for the models presented in the preceding section, cities are formed here by surplus-maximizing developers. The model generates three equilibrium configurations: (1) pure specialization, in which each city specializes in the production of one traded good, (2) pure diversification, in which all cities in the economy produce two goods, and (3) a mixed system, in which specialized and diversified cities

---

[15] See also Goldstein and Gronberg (1984) for a discussion of economies of scope in an urban context.

coexist in the economy. The total labor requirement $L(X, Z)$ for the production of outputs X and Z in a given city is given as

$$\begin{array}{lll} F_x + X^2 & \text{if } X > 0 & \text{and } Z = 0 \\ F_z + Z^2 & \text{if } Z > 0 & \text{and } X = 0 \\ F_d + X^2 + Z^2 & \text{if } X > 0 & \text{and } Z > 0 \end{array} \qquad (3.46)$$

where F represents fixed labor requirements. Hence the average labor requirement is U-shaped, which provides the reason for the formation of a city.

If we assume that the commuting time is the only cost, the total labor supply is given as

$$L^S(n) = n - 2\mu n^{3/2} \qquad (3.47)$$

where the second term on the left-hand side (LHS) of (3.47) represents the amount of labor devoted to commuting. Furthermore, it is assumed that the number of cities in the economy is sufficiently large that developers will behave as utility-takers as well as price-takers. Thus, given the national utility level U and a price vector P, a developer must choose the optimal consumption bundle (x, z) per household by solving the following cost-minimization problem:

$$\min_{x,z} P_x x + P_z z \quad \text{subject to} \quad x^\alpha z^{(1-\alpha)} = U \qquad (3.48)$$

From the foregoing problem we derive the total consumption cost (TC) for a city having population n such that each household achieves the national utility level U as

$$TC(P, U, n) = TUn \qquad (3.49)$$

where $T = \alpha^\alpha (1 - \alpha)^{(1-\alpha)} P^{-(1-\alpha)}$. Therefore, the surplus S from the development of a specialized city of type i, where $i = x, z$, is given by

$$S_i = P_i \left(n - 2n^{3/2} - F_i \right)^{1/2} - TUn \qquad (3.50)$$

where the first term on the LHS of (3.50) represents the total revenue from production, which is obtained from (3.46) and (3.47). The surplus from the development of a diversified city is given by

$$S_d = \left[P_x^2 + P_z^2 \right]^{1/2} \left(n - 2\mu n^{3/2} - F_d \right)^{1/2} - TUn \qquad (3.51)$$

The developer's problem is to maximize the surplus from the city development by choosing the city size. The solutions to the foregoing problem in the cases of specialized and diversified systems are shown in Figures 3.2 and 3.3,

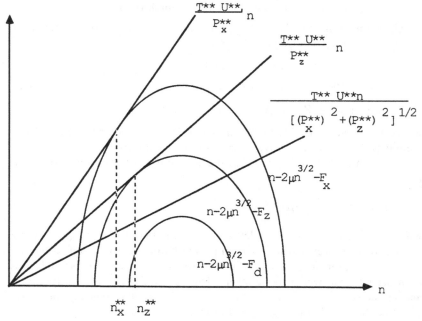

Figure 3.2. Determination of the equilibrium city sizes n_x^{**} and n_z^{**} with pure specialization.

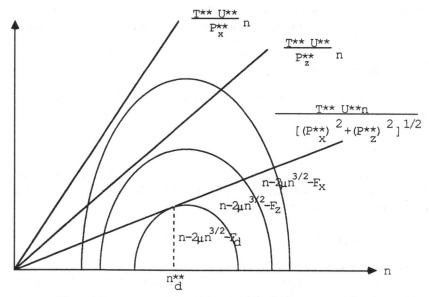

Figure 3.3. Determination of the equilibrium city size n_d^{**} with pure diversification.

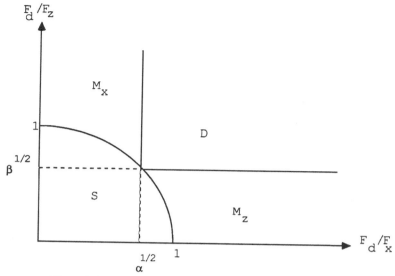

Figure 3.4. Parameter ranges for four equilibrium configurations.

respectively. Figure 3.2 characterizes the equilibrium of a specialized system in which the surplus is zero for both types of specialized cities, and negative for diversified cities. On the other hand, Figure 3.3 characterizes the equilibrium of a diversified system in which the surplus is zero for diversified cities and negative for specialized cities.

Given the foregoing behavior, four equilibrium configurations have been shown to exist, as depicted in Figure 3.4. In pure specialization, S, each city specializes in the production of one good; this equilibrium configuration exists if the fixed costs for specialized cities, F_x and F_z, are relatively small compared with the fixed cost for the diversified city, F_d, so that the ratios $(F_x/F_d, F_z/F_d)$ belong to the set S in Figure 3.4. The intuition behind this result is that forming specialized cities is more economical than forming diversified cities if production in diversified cities has strong diseconomies of scope. Conversely, in order to have pure diversification, the fixed cost F_d must be relatively small compared with F_x and F_z, so that $(F_x/F_d, F_z/F_d)$ is in the set D in Figure 3.4. In other words, production in diversified cities has strong economies of scope. Thus, diversified cities are more economical to form than are specialized cities. Finally, in order to have equilibrium configurations of the mixed-x type (mixed-z type), the fixed cost F_x (F_z) must be relatively small compared with F_d, and F_d must be relatively small compared with F_z (F_x), so that $(F_x/F_d, F_z/F_d)$ is in the set M_x (M_z) in Figure 3.4. *In addition, it has been shown that whenever a specialized city and a diversified city coexist in an economy, the diversified city will be larger than the specialized city.* Furthermore, it has been shown that if commuting costs are zero, then the results of the model coincide with the findings of MacDonald and Slivinski (1987) and Panzar and Willig (1986) in the industrial-organization literature, as well as those of Goldstein and Gronberg (1984), who studied multiproduct cities without space.

Abdel-Rahman (1994) has extended the foregoing model in two respects: first, by introducing a market for intermediate goods (services), which leads to a multi-firm city; second, by examining the impact of economies of scope due to lower variable costs resulting from interaction and coordination between two production processes. As a result, it has been shown that *if the economies of scope are in the form of lower fixed costs* (Abdel-Rahman and Fujita, 1993), *the only possible equilibrium configurations are pure specialization and pure diversification* (contra Abdel-Rahman and Fujita, 1993). *However, if economies of scope are in the form of lower variable costs, mixed systems are also possible.* Therefore, the model generates different equilibrium parameter spaces depending on the form of the economies of scope (i.e., whether economies of scope affect fixed or variable costs, and to what degree).

The model has also been extended by Tsukahara (1995) to explain the joint provision of an essential public good, such as police and fire protection, and an optional public good, such as museums or stadiums. It was assumed that the costs of providing the public goods were the only fixed costs. In that context, *it was shown that if the fixed cost required for provision of the essential public good was large, that resulted in a large city size. Therefore, the per-capita cost of providing the optional public good would be low, and joint provision would lead to higher utility.* On the other hand, if the cost of providing the essential public good was small, that would result in a small city size. Therefore, the per-capita cost of providing the optional public good would be high, and joint provision would not be the equilibrium outcome.

4 Heterogeneous Households and Income Disparities

This section reviews more realistic models of a system of cities in which households are heterogeneous. Thus, it enables us to analyze the factors that determine income inequality, as well as their impact on welfare. These issues are important, given the rise in income disparities since World War II (Fujita and Ishii, 1990). This is done in a core–periphery city system. Skilled labor produces a high-tech good at the core, and unskilled labor produces a low-tech good in the periphery. The wage for the unskilled labor is determined competitively, and the wage for the skilled labor is determined via Nash bargaining. Abdel-Rahman and Wang (1995) have analyzed the factors that determine income disparities in a core–periphery model of a system of cities with a symmetric

Nash wage bargain.[16] In this context, the core region is a large metropolis, and the periphery region consists of a system of identical local cities. The model results in intraregional income inequality. Furthermore, Abdel-Rahman and Wang (1997) have considered a nonsymmetric Nash wage bargaining that results in intraregional as well as interregional income inequalities. In addition, they have considered the impact of income inequality on social welfare. Because the first model is a special case of the second, we shall discuss the second model.

Abdel-Rahman and Wang (1997) have considered an economy populated by a continuum of unskilled workers of mass N and skilled workers of mass M.[17] It is assumed that the economy produces two homogeneous goods. Good X can be produced by skilled or unskilled workers, but good Z can be produced only by skilled workers. Unskilled workers are homogeneous. On the other hand, skilled workers are heterogeneous in their skill characteristics. Their type (T) can be thought of as uniformly distributed on a circle with unit circumference, such that $M(T) = M_0$ for all $T \in [0,1]$. Because the mass of skilled workers can be written as

$$M = \int_0^1 M(T)\,dT = M_0 \tag{3.52}$$

that implies $M(T) = M$ for all $T \in [0, 1]$. The wage for the unskilled workers, W_L, is determined competitively, whereas the wage for skilled workers, W_M, is determined via a Nash wage bargain with the high-tech firms. Figure 3.5 provides a graphic description of the productivity profile over the skill-characteristic space. Each individual firm of type $S \in [0, 1]$ in the high-tech industry has a different skill requirement. In particular, it would be ideal for a firm of type S to employ a worker of skill type $T = S$, because a perfect match generates maximal output per worker, a. Skill matching is generally imperfect: A high-tech firm of type S may need to employ skilled workers of type T at distance $\delta = |T - S|$ away from the ideal skill match. In this case, the corresponding productivity is given by $a - C\delta$, where C measures the productivity loss from a mismatch.

Production of a High-Tech Good. Let D denote the maximal distance of skill mismatch that will be endogenously determined in a Nash outcome. We can

---

[16] See Helsley and Strange (1991) and Becker and Henderson (Chapter 4, this volume) for models of heterogeneous households in a system of identical cities. Also see Abdel-Rahman (1998) for a model of heterogeneous households in a system of two types of specialized cities, with time allocation among leisure, commuting, and work.

[17] For a model in which the skill distribution is determined endogenously, see Abdel-Rahman (1998).

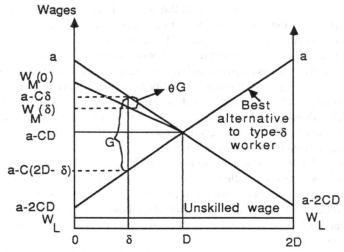

Figure 3.5. Nash wage bargain.

now specify the output of a high-tech firm of type S as

$$Z(S) = 2 \int_{S}^{D+S} (\alpha - C\delta) M \, d\delta - K = 2 \int_{0}^{D} (\alpha - C\delta) M \, d\delta - K$$

(3.53)

where K is the fixed entry cost. The second equality is a result of symmetry. Because each firm employs skilled workers over an interval of measure $2D$, the total number of firms in the high-tech industry will be $m = 1/(2D)$. Under the symmetry assumption, and with the use of equation (3.53), the profit of a type-S firm is given by

$$J(S) = 2 \int_{0}^{D} [(\alpha - C\delta) - W_M(\delta)] M \, d\delta - K$$

(3.54)

Now consider a bargaining situation facing a skilled worker at a characteristic distance away from the most closely adjacent firm. To bargain with the most closely adjacent firm, a worker needs to take the best alternative into account. In principle, the best alternative could be the potential earning from employment in the X sector, or employment by the second most closely adjacent firm, in the Z sector. Assuming that the unskilled wage is sufficiently low, the best alternative employment will be with the second most closely adjacent firm. The surplus of matching between this particular worker and the most closely adjacent firm is therefore the productivity differential between the most productive match, $a - C\delta$, and the best alternative, $a - C(2D - \delta)$, as depicted in Figure 3.5.

When the two productivity schedules intersect, the area of emolument D is determined. The matching surplus is measured by the difference between the two productivity schedules, $G = 2C(D - \delta)$. Thus, if θ denotes the fraction of surplus going to the firm, the wage for the skilled labor is given by

$$W_M(\delta) = a - 2\theta CD - (1 - 2\theta)C\delta \tag{3.55}$$

When $\theta = \frac{1}{2}$, this wage schedule reduces to the uniform wage, as in the study by Abdel-Rahman and Wang (1995), in which within the core, income disparities are absent. Unrestricted entry implies that each firm will earn zero profit in equilibrium, that is, $J(S) = 0$ for all S. Thus, the equilibrium wage is given as

$$W_M(\delta) = a - 2(\theta Ck/M)^{1/2} - (1 - 2\theta)C\delta \tag{3.56}$$

The foregoing equation represents a microfoundation for localization economy. Indeed, any increase in the size of the labor force enhances matching in the labor market and increases productivity and the wage rate.

The production of good X is as presented in Section 2. Thus the wage in this industry is given by

$$W_L = \lambda P \tag{3.57}$$

Cities in this economy are formed in part because of increasing returns in the provision of public infrastructure necessary for the development of a city. It is assumed that the public-infrastructure cost schedules for local cities and the metropolis are respectively FL^ε and FM^ε, where $\varepsilon \in (0, 1)$ and $F > 0$. Without loss of generality, we simply assume that these public infrastructures are produced using the high-tech good Z. Because $\varepsilon < 1$, the per-capita share of the infrastructure cost is decreasing in the size of the city. In addition, it is assumed that the aggregate land rent in a particular city, net of the infrastructure cost, will be shared equally by the city residents in that city. Furthermore, it is assumed that the utility of a given household is given by (3.1) and that the commuting cost t is in terms of good Z. Thus, the indirect utility of a household of type δ residing in the metropolis is given by

$$V_M^*(\delta) = \alpha^\alpha(1 - \alpha)^{(1-\alpha)} P^{-(1-\alpha)}[\alpha - \Lambda - 2(\theta Ck/M)^{1/2} - (1 - 2\theta)C\delta] \tag{3.58}$$

where $\Lambda \equiv 2\mu M^{1/2} + FM^{\varepsilon-1}$. Because households are price-takers, the two-level hierarchical system with only a single metropolis will be guaranteed if the utility of any skilled worker is strictly increasing in the mass of skilled workers. A condition to support this equilibrium is that the marginal benefit from positive matching externalities exceeds the marginal cost of increased transportation costs, net of the marginal benefit from reduction in per-capita city-formation costs.

Local cities are formed by local governments. The local-government problem is to maximize the utility of a representative household, which is given by

$$V_L = \alpha^\alpha (1 - \alpha)^{(1-\alpha)} P^{-(1-\alpha)} \left[\gamma P - 2\mu L^{1/2} - F L^{\varepsilon - 1} \right] \tag{3.59}$$

From the first-order condition we derive the equilibrium city size as

$$L^* = \left\{ \frac{3F(1 - \varepsilon)\pi^{1/2}}{t} \right\}^{2/(3-2\varepsilon)} \tag{3.60}$$

It has been shown that the ALR, as well as a congestion tax, will be used to finance the fixed cost, which gives a modified version of the *Henry George theorem*.[18]

The income-inequality measure that has been used is based on earned income, both within the core and between the core and the periphery region. In particular, within the core, income inequality is specified as

$$I \equiv (1/D^*) \int_0^{D^*} [W_M^*(\delta) - (\alpha - C D^*)] \, d\delta \tag{3.61}$$

where $a - C D^*$ reflects the lowest skilled wage rate when the mismatch reaches the maximal acceptable critical value. On the other hand, the interregional inequality can be measured as

$$Q \equiv (1/D^*) \int_0^{D^*} [W_M^*(\delta) - W_L^*] \, d\delta \tag{3.62}$$

It has been shown that *within the core, income inequality is increasing in the cost of entry, K, or mismatch, C, but decreasing in the bargaining power of a high-tech firm, θ, as well as the mass of skilled workers, M. On the other hand, the interregional income inequality is increasing in the commuting costs, t, or city-formation cost, F, as well as in the mass of unskilled workers, N, and the level of productivity of skilled workers, a.* Thus, the main determinants of geographical income inequalities include (1) traditional economic factors, such as labor productivity and the mass of unskilled labor, (2) spatial factors, consisting of the costs to commute to and from the CBD, and (3) search and matching factors, such as entry and mismatch costs, relative bargaining power, and mass of skilled workers.

To examine the impact of income inequality on the social welfare, Abdel-Rahman and Wang (1997) used a social welfare function that uniformly aggregated all households' utilities achieved in equilibrium. They showed that *a reduction in the cost of entry or a mismatch or increase in the bargaining*

---

[18] See Stiglitz (1977) for this result. Also see Helsley and Strange (1993) for a strategic model of city formation with a public good.

power or mass of skilled workers will reduce within-the-core income inequality and enhance social welfare. Also, a decrease in the cost of commuting or city formation will reduce the interregional income inequality and increase social welfare. Furthermore, a lower level of maximal productivity by the skilled workers or a smaller mass of unskilled workers will decrease the interregional income inequality, but reduce social welfare. Therefore, public policies designed to reverse the observed urbanization trend of widening geographical income inequality may not necessarily improve welfare.

Abdel-Rahman (1998) has presented another approach to modeling income inequality and analyzing its impacts on social welfare. The model is of a two-sector economy consisting of two types of cities, with the number of cities of each type determined endogenously. Cities are formed as a result of investment in public infrastructures. This investment leads to a reduction in commuting cost and consequently to an increase in the time that households can utilize for work and leisure. In the context of the model, the level of investment in public infrastructures is chosen optimally. Thus, the equilibrium solution is also socially optimal. Skilled labor locates in one type of city, and unskilled labor locates in the other type. Wages in both labor markets are determined competitively. Furthermore, the number and size for each type of city are determined endogenously. This model explains the variation in city sizes as a result of differences in how households value time.

Helsley and Strange (1991) have extended the idea of matching and search to the capital market in a nonspatial model. The idea hinges upon the assumption that the salvage value of assets in large cities is higher than in small ones. The reason is that a bank allocates credit to projects that have addresses in a characteristic space, and if the project fails, then the bank repossesses the asset. The second-best use for an immobile and specialized asset is more valuable where the density of possible uses is greater, as it is in large cities.

5 Conclusion

Even with such a large number of contributions to this area of study, several issues have not yet been explored. Furthermore, just as the theory of city systems was developed by adopting from the theory of industrial organization, there is much room for the same kind of development with the theory of endogenous growth. In addition, there is room for cross-fertilization between the city-system theory and trade. This is especially the case given the current economic integration in Europe. It would seem that cities are more logical units for analysis than are countries. The following are just a few of the questions that have not been addressed: What is the impact of infrastructure on city growth?[19] Will

---

[19] See Palivos and Wang (1996) and Black and Henderson (1997) for initial work on endogenous growth and city formation.

cities diversify or specialize over time? How does urban growth affect income inequalities? How will free trade affect income inequalities and social welfare?

First, can local governments affect the formation of different types of cities through the provision of an infrastructure? This question is important to cities and local governments. Furthermore, it is also important from a theoretical point of view, because the provision of an infrastructure has been used as an argument to explain agglomeration economies. However, there is no formal model that

Table 3.3. *General equilibrium of a system of cities*

Exogenous industrial composition	*Identical households*		Henderson (1974), Henderson and Abdel-Rahman (1991)
	Heterogeneous households		Helsley and Strange (1990), Becker and Henderson (Chapter 4, this volume), Abdel-Rahman and Wang (1995, 1997), and Abdel-Rahman (1998)
Endogenous industrial composition	Specialized and diversified	*Identical*	Abdel-Rahman (1996)
		Heterogenous	Abdel-Rahman (1998)
	Specialized, diversified, and mixed	*Identical*	Abdel-Rahman and Fujita (1993), Abdel-Rahman (1994)
		Heterogenous	Vacuum

explains the microfoundation for the impact of infrastructure on productivity. On the other hand, there is vast empirical literature that documents a positive relationship between the level of provision of infrastructure and productivity. Second, how can we explain the coexistence of specialized and diversified city systems with heterogeneous households (as indicated in Table 3.3)? This is actually what we observe in all city systems, either in developed countries or in developing countries. However, there is no model that explains that structure of an urban system. This can be done in a model in which skilled labor is used to produce a high-tech intermediate input, with unskilled labor to produce a final consumption good. Finally, a model involving cross-product technological externalities, a model that would result in the formation of a multiproduct city, has not been explored in a general equilibrium context. This can be done by closing the model proposed by Abdel-Rahman (1990) and by characterizing the conditions under which a purely specialized system, a purely diversified system, and a mixed system will occur in equilibrium.

References

Abdel-Rahman, H. M. (1988). Product differentiation, monopolistic competition and city size. *Regional Science and Urban Economics* 18:69–86.

Abdel-Rahman, H. M. (1990). Agglomeration economies, types, and sizes of cities. *Journal of Urban Economics* 27:25–45.

Abdel-Rahman, H. M. (1991). Shareable inputs, product variety, and city sizes. *Journal of Regional Science* 30:359–74.

Abdel-Rahman, H. M. (1994). Economies of scope in intermediate goods and a system of cities. *Regional Science and Urban Economics* 24:497–524.

Abdel-Rahman, H. M. (1996). When do cities specialize in production? *Regional Science and Urban Economics* 26:1–22.

Abdel-Rahman, H. M. (1998). Income disparity, time allocation and social welfare in a system of cities. *Journal of Regional Science* 38:137–54.

Abdel-Rahman, H. M., and Fujita, M. (1990). Product variety, Marshallian externalities and city sizes. *Journal of Regional Science* 30:165–83.

Abdel-Rahman, H. M., and Fujita, M. (1993). Specialization and diversification in a system of cities. *Journal of Urban Economics* 33:189–222.

Abdel-Rahman, H. M., and Wang, P. (1995). Toward a general equilibrium theory of a core–periphery system of cities. *Regional Science and Urban Economics* 25:529–46.

Abdel-Rahman, H. M., and Wang, P. (1997). Social welfare and income inequality in a system of cities. *Journal of Urban Economics* 41:462–83.

Alonso, W. (1964). *Location and Land Use; Toward a General Theory of Land Rent. Cambridge*, MA: Harvard University Press.

Black, D., and Henderson, J. V. (1997). Urban growth. Mimeograph, Brown University.

Christaller, W. (1966). *The Central Places of Southern Germany.* Englewood Cliffs, NJ: Prentice-Hall.

Dixit, A. (1973). The optimum factory town. *Bell Journal of Economics and Management Science* 4:637–51.

Dixit, A., and Stiglitz, J. E. (1977). Monopolistic competition and optimal product diversity. *American Economic Review* 67:297–308.

Ethier, W. (1982). National and international returns to scale in modern theory of international trade. *American Economic Review* 72:389–405.

Fujita, M. (1988). A monopolistic competition model of spatial agglomeration: a differentiated product approach. *Regional Science and Urban Economics* 18:87–124.

Fujita, M. (1989). *Urban Economic Theory: Land Use and City Size*. Cambridge University Press.

Fujita, M., and Ishii, R. (1990). Global economic restructuring and urbanization processes in East Asia: an overview. Mimeograph, University of Pennsylvania.

Glaeser, E., Kallal, H. D., Scheinkman, J. A., and Shleifer, A. (1992). Growth in cities. *Journal of Political Economy* 36:117–43.

Goldstein, G. S., and Gronberg, T. J. (1984). Economies of scope and economies of agglomeration. *Journal of Urban Economics* 16:63–84.

Hansen, N. (1990). Do producer services induce regional economic development? *Journal of Regional Science* 30:465–76.

Helsley, R. W., and Strange, W. C. (1990). Matching and agglomeration economies in a system of cities. *Regional Science and Urban Economics* 20:189–222.

Helsley, R. W., and Strange, C. (1991). Agglomeration economies and urban capital market. *Journal of Urban Economics* 29:96–112.

Helsley, R. W., and Strange, C. (1993). City formation with commitment. *Regional Science and Urban Economics* 24:373–90.

Henderson, J. V. (1974). Types and sizes of cities. *American Economic Review* 64:640–57.

Henderson, J. V. (1987). System of cities and inter-city trade. In: P. Hansen et al. (eds.), *System of Cities and Facility Location*. New York: Harwood Academic.

Henderson, J. V., and Abdel-Rahman, H. M. (1991). Efficiency through decentralization with product diversity. *Regional Science and Urban Economics* 21:491–510.

Henderson, V., Kuncoro, A., and Turner, M. (1995). Industrial development in cities. *Journal of Political Economy* 103:1066–90.

Hobson, P. (1987). Optimum product variety in urban areas. *Journal of Urban Economics* 22:190–7.

Hoover, E. M. (1939). *Location Theory and the Shoe and Leather Industries*. Cambridge, MA: Harvard University Press.

Jacobs, J. (1969). *The Economy of Cities*. New York: Random House.

Kanemoto, Y. (1980). *Theories of Urban Externalities*. Amsterdam: North Holland.

Kim, S. (1990). Labor specialization and the extent of the market. *Journal of Political Economy* 97:692–705.

Lösch, A. (1940). *Die raumliche Ordnung der Wirtschaft*. Jena: Gustav Fischer Verlag.

MacDonald, G. M., and Slivinski, A. (1987). The simple analytics of competitive equilibrium with multiproduct firms. *American Economic Review* 77:941–53.

Marshall, A. (1890). *Principles of Economics* London: Macmillan (8th ed., 1920).

Mills, E. S. (1967). An aggregative model of resource allocation in metropolitan area. *American Economic Review* 57:197–210.

Mirrlees, J. A. (1972). The optimum town. *Swedish Journal of Economics* 74:114–35.

Palivos, T., and Wang, P. (1996). Toward a new growth theory of spatial agglomeration dynamics. *Regional Science and Urban Economics* 26:645–69.

Panzar, J. C., and Willig, R. D. (1986). Economics of scope. *American Economic Association Papers and Proceedings* 71:268–72.

Quigley, J. (1998). Urban diversity and economic growth. *Journal of Economic Perspectives* 12:127–38.

Rivera-Batiz, F. (1988). Increasing returns, monopolistic competition and agglomeration economies in consumption and production. *Regional Science and Urban Economics* 18:125–53.

Stahl, K. (1983). A note on the microeconomics of migration. *Journal of Urban Economics* 14:318–26.

Stiglitz, J. E. (1977). The theory of local public goods. In: M. S. Feldstein and R. P. Inman (eds.), *The Economics of Public Services*. London: Macmillan.

Tsukahara, K. (1995). Independent and joint provision of optional public services. *Regional Science and Urban Economics* 25:411–25.

United Nation Development Programme (1996). United Nation Human Development Report.

Weber, A. (1929). *Theory of Location of Industries*. University of Chicago Press.

CHAPTER 4

Intra-industry Specialization
and Urban Development

Randy Becker and Vernon Henderson

1 Introduction

Urban economists, regional scientists, and economic geographers continue to struggle with fundamental issues concerning the nature of cities. The first question is why the population of a country will agglomerate into a relatively few small areas on the map, rather than spreading somewhat evenly over the national landscape. For example, what centripetal forces are involved in the fact that well under 5% of the land is subject to intensive human habitation in the United States? Then, given these centripetal forces, what are the centrifugal forces acting to ensure that, in a large industrialized economy, not all of the population will agglomerate into one city? What forces limit city sizes and determine city numbers in an economy? In the formation of new cities and in the determination of the sizes of existing cities, what are the roles of local entrepreneurs, land markets, governments, and institutions designed by governments that affect the operation of markets? Is the presumption by the United Nations (1993) and the World Bank (Renaud, 1981) that cities tend to be oversized correct? Alternatively viewed, under what conditions will cities tend to be of efficient sizes?

Concerning the bases for agglomeration, in 1890 Alfred Marshall wrote that

subsidiary trades grow up in the neighborhood, supplying it with implements and materials, organizing its traffic, and in many ways conducing to the economy of its material ... for subsidiary industries devoting themselves each to one small branch of the process of production, and working it for a great many of their neighbors, are able to keep in constant use machinery of the most highly specialized character. (Marshall, 1890, p. 332)

Nowadays, we identify that statement as reflecting the benefits of local intra-industry specialization in the tasks that firms perform. Great scale permits a high degree of intra-industry specialization by firms, which increases the

The authors acknowledge the helpful comments of Will Strange and also Jim Rauch on an earlier draft of this chapter.

138

local efficiency of industrial production. The modern urban literature contains several microfoundation models of the black-box scale economies discussed by Henderson (1974). These models reflect the three other bases described by Marshall for urban agglomeration: the effects of static information spillovers among firms (Fujita and Ogawa, 1982), the diversity of non-traded intermediate inputs (Abdel-Rahman and Fujita, 1990), and scale economies in the processes of search and matching in local markets (Helsley and Strange, 1990). In this chapter, we provide microfoundations for the fourth basis of agglomeration: specialization within cities.

In modeling specialization, we explicitly consider the role of urban entrepreneurs. Entrepreneurs (supplanting Marshall's specialized machinery) invest time in mastering the different specialized tasks necessary for industry output. This formulation highlights the role that urban entrepreneurs play in city productivity and suggests public policies that individual cities might follow to encourage efficient local entrepreneurship. In addition, exploitation of economies of scale involves joint agglomeration of workers and entrepreneurs, presenting potential conflicts between these different residents as to what policies are best for cities.

In Section 2 of this chapter, in the context of a representative city, we detail the centripetal forces created by the greater opportunities for specialization that are entailed in greater urban scale. Then we turn to the centrifugal forces that limit the size of a modern representative city. We focus on internal limitations to city size (Mills, 1967), rather than on explanations based on the transport costs for cities whose function is primarily to serve agricultural markets (Krugman, 1993).

Given the model of a representative city, in Sections 3–5 we analyze how cities are formed in national land-development markets. There is disagreement in the literature about how to model this process. At one extreme, in the urban literature (Henderson, 1974) and in the literature on urban public finance (Hamilton, 1975), as reviewed by Wildasin (1987), there are "large agents" in national land markets who control or even own entire new cities and who can orchestrate large-scale movements of people. Each large agent controls the land on which one city might potentially be formed, and, as such, it is common to call these large agents "land developers." The term "large agent" is somewhat misleading. Typically, in the literature, when interacting across cities, these large agents always behave as perfect competitors in attracting population; they display no strategic behavior. Only recently has the literature allowed for strategic interaction (e.g., Hoyt, 1991; Henderson and Slade, 1993). In the traditional literature, as in this chapter, large agents are large only in the sense that they each recognize how markets operate *within* their own cities and act upon that knowledge. But they each perceive fixed prices in input and output markets facing their cities.

At the other extreme, in modeling community markets, in the urban literature (Henderson, 1974) and the new-economic-geography literature (Krugman, 1993) large agents do not exist, and cities are formed through "self-organization." Natural agglomerations are based on the locations and migration decisions of atomistic workers milling around on the economy's flat, featureless plane. There are some unresolved issues concerning how to model this self-organization that we shall analyze.

Central to the debate about appropriate modeling choices is a question of fact: Are there large land-development agents present, at least at the time of city formation? There are examples of present-day large cities historically controlled by single companies, such as Vancouver (Canadian Pacific Railways) and Calcutta (the British East India Company), and we know that today a significant fraction of the world's largest corporations are land-development companies. In the modern U.S. economy, Reichman (1976) has described the formation of communities controlled by private residential "governments" or developers. Joel Garreau (1991) has described the widespread existence among "edge cities" of large urban multi-use developments tightly controlled by single agents, and Henderson and Mitra (1996) have more fully documented the widespread existence and size of some of these single-agent developments. However, one main point of this chapter is that the presence of large land developers is not critical to the process of orchestrating large-scale reconfigurations of people. The presence of autonomous local governments operating in urban agglomerations may also do the trick.

In analyzing city formation, we begin in Section 3 with the large-agent case and present some results obtained with our model, synthesizing previous work in the literature, including results on efficient and equilibrium city sizes and the Henry George theorem (Flatters et al., 1974; Stiglitz, 1977). We also address the issue of just how large developers need to be, as raised by Helsley and Strange (1993). For example, do they need to own all the land in a city, or only the business district?

In Section 4, we turn to the case in which large agents of any description are nonexistent in an economy. We present a new, general approach to a self-organizing economy, with an important new proposition. We find that under self-organization, cities will generally be oversized. This suggests that the concerns of the United Nations (1993) and the World Bank (Renaud, 1981) about overconcentration are valid in countries where large land developers either have yet to evolve or, perhaps more critically, are restricted from operating effectively.

In Section 5, we argue that large agents, in the form of land developers, are in fact not essential to the process. Autonomous local governments acting on behalf of self-organizing atomistic agents can restore efficiency to the city-formation process. This suggests that devolution of power to cities and allowance for the free formation of autonomous local governments can substitute for the evolution of free national land-development markets.

2 The Internal Structure of Cities

A model of Adam Smith specialization within firms has been presented by Becker and Murphy (1992). We adapt that work to model specialization among local firms within a given industry. We first present this specification of technology and then turn to specification of the remaining primitives necessary to model a system of cities.

2.1 Technology

There are two types of atomistic agents in the economy: workers and entrepreneurs. Both live in cities, and both are perfectly mobile throughout the economy. Entrepreneurs operate firms and hire and manage workers. Within a firm, the entrepreneur allocates her time across a range of activities, spending time at each activity to master task-specific skills and supervise workers at that task. Each firm spans a range of activities (service production, parts production, purchasing, retailing, assembly, etc.), which, when combined with the activities of other local firms in the same industry, results in a final industry output for the city. Exactly how this occurs will be specified later. For now, looking at any entrepreneur, the more functions or activities a firm undertakes, the more the entrepreneur's time is splintered across different tasks, and the less time she has to spend mastering or supervising any specific task. Therein lies the basis for intra-industry specialization: Each entrepreneur improves task performance and worker efficiency by restricting her establishment's range of activities, but all local firms combined span the range of activities necessary to produce the final industry output. Therein also lies a basic externality: When an entrepreneur enters a city, she captures certain returns to her own firm, and she also provides external benefits to other entrepreneurs by taking on some of their tasks, allowing them to invest more time in improving their productivity at their remaining tasks.

Tasks, functions, and activities are indexed by s, and a firm's *potential* output from task s is denoted by $y(s)$,

$$y(s) = ET(s)^\gamma n(s)^\delta, \qquad 0 < \delta, \ \gamma < 1 \qquad (4.1)$$

where $n(s)$ is the quantity of labor employed at task s, and $\delta < 1$ is necessary to have an equilibrium in the quantity of labor hired at any task. $T(s)$ is the amount of the entrepreneur's time devoted to supervising workers at task s or learning more about task s, and γ represents the productivity of that time. The constraint $\gamma < 1$ ensures that equilibria will be Nash equilibria and will be robust. Later we shall develop restrictions on γ and $\gamma + \delta$ that are necessary for the existence of equilibria.

The entrepreneur must decide how many different tasks her firm will undertake. We present a simple Becker-Murphy version of this, and we outline a more complex version that marries the concepts of specialization and diversity. For the simple version, we assume that the tasks *required* for industry output cover the unit circle and that each firm chooses a set of tasks on the unit circle in which to engage. Without any loss of generality, for purposes of calculation, it is assumed that a firm spans a contiguous set of tasks, or that each entrepreneur covers one uninterrupted segment of the unit circle. Each entrepreneur has one unit of time to devote to all activities, so given a segment of width w and time $T(s)$ devoted to each task, $\int_a^b T(s)\,ds = 1$, where $b - a = w$. Given that the technology is the same for each task, $T(s)$ will be chosen to be the same at each s.[1] Thus, dropping the indicator s, we have an entrepreneur's time constrained by

$$Tw = 1 \tag{4.2}$$

Each city contains an endogenous number of entrepreneurs, m. How do these m firms interact to produce both their own output and industry output? The total output for a firm is given by

$$w \cdot \min_{0 \le s \le 1} \{y(s)\} \tag{4.3}$$

This specification combines two features. The first is the simple Becker-Murphy requirement that for any industry output to result, all tasks on the unit circle must be performed, and the most that a firm can get from one of its own tasks is based on the minimum $y(s)$ at any point on that circle. Given this, any Nash equilibrium among m firms will have (1) all firms choosing the same $y(s)$ and (2) firms spanning the unit circle. In a symmetrical equilibrium, firms will choose equal widths w, so that

$$wm = 1 \tag{4.4}$$

The second feature of this specification concerns the division of industry output by firms. Each firm "sells" its own span of products, w (though the market structure for this is not really specified), and all firms' local outputs are combined costlessly to form the final city output. We assume that the city sells its output in competitive world markets, as a price-taker. However, there is a bargaining problem within any city, because each firm's output is required for any industry output to result, and firms can bargain over the division of output and profits. As detailed later, we assume a symmetrical equilibrium in which there is an equal division of industry sales among firms, dictated by the technology in (4.3), where each firm's contribution is wy.

---

[1] This is a result of the Becker-Murphy technology regardless of the magnitude of γ, and it holds generally for other technologies if $\gamma < 1$.

In summary, *ex post* combining (4.1) and (4.3), firm output is $y = w(ET^\gamma n^\delta)$. Given (4.2) and (4.4), we know $T = w^{-1} = m$, so firm output is

$$y = Em^{\gamma-1}n^\delta \tag{4.5}$$

Industry output then is $Y = my$, or

$$Y = Em^\gamma n^\delta \tag{4.6}$$

Finally, we note that labor's marginal product to the firm at task s in equation (4.1) is

$$\delta y(s)/n(s) \quad \text{if } y(s) \le y(k) \quad \text{for } y(k) = \min_{\substack{0 \le k \le 1 \\ s \ne k}} [y(k)]$$

$$0 \quad \text{otherwise} \tag{4.7}$$

That is, marginal productivity drops to zero once $y(s)$ exceeds the minimum task output elsewhere on the unit circle. In the best Nash equilibrium, y and n are the same across firms, such that at each s, $\delta y(s)/n(s) = p_n$, where p_n is the opportunity wage of labor.

Use of the terms "symmetrical" and "best" as descriptions of the Nash equilibrium we are looking at indicates that with the Leontief technology in (4.3), there is the potential for coordination failure. If, for example, all firms' $n(s)$ values are set so that $\delta y(s)/n(s) > p_n$, that is also a Nash equilibrium, because no firm acting on its own can gain by expanding any $n(s)$. In this chapter we slough off this problem by simply picking the best, symmetrical equilibrium. There are two justifications. First, city developers, as specified later, potentially could and would impose such an outcome. Second, once we move away from the strict Leontief specification, the problem disappears. We footnote a generalization of the technology in (4.3) that combines notions of specialization and Dixit-Stiglitz diversity[2] and eliminates the coordination problem.

---

[2] Assume that final output from the city, Z, is produced with a Dixit-Stiglitz technology, where locally produced intermediate inputs or tasks go into production of Z. That is, $Z = [\int y(s)^\rho \, ds]^{1/\rho}$. Each firm produces a different span of products, indexed by s, of width w. Each product $y(s)$ is sold in monopolistically competitive markets at a price $p(s)$. The production function for $y(s)$ is as in (4.1), and the entrepreneur allocates her time across her tasks so that (4.3) is satisfied. The firm's costs are labor costs and coordination costs, Mw^β. Coordination costs help limit the scope of the products that the firm produces. This formulation thus combines Becker-Murphy and Dixit-Stiglitz technology, in our context with two factors of production. A firm's maximization problem is given as

$$\max \int_0^w p(s)[ET(s)^\gamma n(s)^\delta] \, ds - \int_0^w p_n n(s) \, ds - Mw^\beta \quad \text{s.t.} \quad \int_0^w T(s) \, ds = 1$$

Given internal symmetry, this collapses to $\max_{w,n} pEw^{1-\gamma}n^\delta - wp_n n - Mw^\beta$. With

2.2 *Urban Structure*

The internal spatial structure of our cities is the simplest standard version. All production in a city occurs at a point, defined as the central business district (CBD). Surrounding the CBD in a circle are residences, where each resident lives on a lot of fixed size, 1, and commutes to the CBD (and back) at a cost per unit distance of t (paid in units of city output). Equilibrium in the land market is characterized by a rent gradient, extending from the CBD at zero to the city edge at u_1, where rent at distance u from the city center is $R(u)$. Rents at the city edge (in the best alternative use) are normalized to zero.

An equilibrium in residential markets requires all residents (living on equal-size lots) to spend the same amount on rent plus commuting costs. For any consumer group, all members then have the same amount left over to spend on all other goods, and utility levels are equalized within that consumer group. At the city edge, rent plus commuting costs are tu_1, because $R(u_1) = 0$; elsewhere they are $R(u) + tu$. Equating total rent plus commuting-cost expenditures at the city edge with those amounts elsewhere yields the rent gradient $R(u) = t(u_1 - u)$. From this, we calculate total rents in the city to be $\int_0^{u_1} 2\pi u R(u)\,du$ (given lot sizes of 1, so that each "ring" $2\pi u\,du$ contains that many residents), or $\frac{1}{3}\pi t u_1^3$. Total commuting costs are $\int_0^{u_1} 2\pi u(tu)\,du = \frac{2}{3}\pi t u_1^3$.

Each firm employs nw workers, and because there are m firms, total worker employment is $nwm = n$, given (4.4). City population is thus

$$\text{pop} = n + m \tag{4.8}$$

consisting of all workers and entrepreneurs. Both groups have the same willingness to pay to live closer to the CBD, so they are arbitrarily mixed throughout the city. Given a circular city with lot sizes of 1, $n + m = \pi u_1^2$ or $u_1 = \pi^{-1/2}(n + m)^{1/2}$. We can then write

$$\text{total commuting costs} = B(n + m)^{3/2} \tag{4.9}$$

$$\text{total land rents} = \tfrac{1}{2}B(n + m)^{3/2} \tag{4.10}$$

$$B \equiv \tfrac{2}{3}\pi^{-\frac{1}{2}}t$$

Dixit-Stiglitz symmetry across firms,

$$Z = \left[\int y(s)^\rho\,ds\right]^{1/\rho} = \left[\int_0^{w_1} y(s)^\rho\,ds + \int_{w_1}^{w_2} y(s)^\rho\,ds + \cdots + \int_{w_{m-1}}^{w_m} y(s)^\rho\,ds\right]^{1/\rho}$$
$$= (mw)^{1/\rho}y.$$

Given (4.1) and (4.3), we get $Z = Em^{1/\rho}w^{(1-\rho\gamma)/\rho}n^\delta$ for industry output. Based on this form for Z, one can proceed with a command solution for a city by choosing n, m, and w to maximize net surplus, given total coordination costs $(Mw^\beta m)$, the opportunity costs of workers and entrepreneurs, and commuting costs, as we do later. Unfortunately, unlike the simpler Leontief version, solution of this model requires simulation.

Note that total commuting costs and rents increase (at an increasing rate) as city size $(n + m)$ increases.

3 City Formation with Large Agents

In this section we consider the formation of cities when there are large agents operating in national land markets. We assume these large agents are "large" only locally, controlling their individual cities. Nationally they are small, in that they are perfect competitors in output markets and national labor markets in seeking to attract entrepreneurs and workers to their cities. Mobile workers achieve the same utility across cities, and mobile entrepreneurs are also equally well off. Workers and entrepreneurs will generally have different utilities, and those utility levels are perceived as exogenous by any individual city developer. The agents operating in national land markets are land-development companies, or developers, who operate competitively. We start by outlining a folk-theorem type of entry game under which city formation occurs. Then we turn to the issue of what developers need to own or control to carry out the large-agent role.

By analogy to the industrial-organization problem of determining the equilibrium number of firms in a market, we specify a folk-theorem type of entry game (which avoids the usual integer problem), subject to subgame perfection, that is a refinement of that described by Helsley and Strange (1990). There are $\tilde{S}$ potential development companies in the economy, each in control of all the land at a site where a city potentially could exist. What such "control" entails is part of the analysis to follow. To ensure competition, each company controls only one site. The number of potential sites, $\tilde{S}$, will remain unexhausted. In a staged game, development companies enter in an arbitrary predetermined sequence, although the order of entry has no effect on final city sizes, numbers, or factor returns. Each company has the one-time option (at its stage of the game) to enter or not. If the specified equilibrium described later has S^* ($<\tilde{S}$) cities, the first part of the game will have S^* stages in which S^* companies will choose to enter. After the first S^* stages, each of the S^* companies will offer contracts to workers and entrepreneurs (the details of these contracts will be discussed next). In the penultimate stage, workers and entrepreneurs will simultaneously choose a contract, or city. In the final stage, the internal equilibrium of the city will be played out: Local firms will choose segments of tasks, workers will choose local firms, and workers and entrepreneurs will choose locations within the city.[3] As usual, the game is solved by backward induction to make it consistent with subgame perfection.

What is the objective function, and what are the corresponding contracts offered by developers? We consider two alternatives. The first is a "command"

---

[3] Recall the coordination-failure problem under a pure Leontief technology. The developer can rectify that by specifying firm employment.

specification, where the developer "owns" the city. For each potential city, the locally omnipotent owner hires workers and entrepreneurs in competitive national factor markets, collects urban land rents, and sells the city's output in competitive output markets. Each owner chooses m and n to maximize the profits of her urban operation. Thus, in each potential city, the owner maximizes as follows:

$$\max_{m,n} = Em^{\gamma}n^{\delta} - \bar{V}n - \bar{R}m - B(n+m)^{3/2} \tag{4.11}$$

Equation (4.11) is total city output [see (4.7)], less required net compensation to each worker and entrepreneur in national factor markets of $\bar{V}$ and $\bar{R}$ respectively, less urban commuting costs, from (4.10). The contract the developer offers can be specified as $\{n, m, \bar{V}, \bar{R}\}$.

The second alternative is a more familiar, or perhaps realistic, land-development specification. Land-development companies, which are owned by Arrow-Debreu shareholders, seek to maximize land rents, net of any costs, from each of their cities. Specifically, a company seeking to maximize profits for its shareholders specifies a contract (alluded to in the game just described) of $\{n, m, T_n, T_m\}$, where n and m are the workers and entrepreneurs at its site, and T_n and T_m are any per-person subsidies to workers and entrepreneurs who locate in the development. The company allows firms to freely choose their tasks, workers to freely choose firms, and entrepreneurs and workers to freely choose residential locations. Entrepreneurs pay workers their effective value of marginal product (VMP); entrepreneurs collect residual firm profits; and workers and entrepreneurs pay their own commuting costs and rents. Workers and entrepreneurs, as Arrow-Debreu shareholders, also collect any dividends from development companies in which they hold shares.

A company's problem in any city, therefore, is to

$$\max_{n,m,T_n,T_m} \pi = \tfrac{1}{2}B(n+m)^{3/2} - T_n n - T_m m$$

$$\text{s.t.} \quad T_n + E\delta n^{\delta-1}m^{\gamma} - \tfrac{3}{2}B(n+m)^{1/2} - \bar{V} = 0 \tag{4.12}$$

$$T_m + E(1-\delta)n^{\delta}m^{\gamma-1} - \tfrac{3}{2}B(n+m)^{1/2} - \bar{R} = 0$$

In the objective function, the company collects total local land rents and pays workers and entrepreneurs their required subsidies. The subsidies are set (in the constraints) to ensure that local factor compensation, less per-person rents plus commuting costs, will equal the going compensation rates in national markets (given also perceptually fixed dividend payments from shareholding). We can solve (4.12) directly, or note that by substituting the constraints defining T_n and T_m into the objective function, the optimization problem in (4.12) collapses to that in (4.11).

To develop the characteristics of a solution, we can proceed with either or both optimization problems. From the first-order conditions for (4.11), for example, we get

$$\bar{R} = E\gamma m^{\gamma-1}n^{\delta} - \tfrac{3}{2}B(n+m)^{1/2} \tag{4.13a}$$

$$\bar{V} = E\delta m^{\gamma}n^{\delta-1} - \tfrac{3}{2}B(n+m)^{1/2} \tag{4.13b}$$

In (4.13b), a worker's compensation equals the wage a firm would pay $[E\delta m^{\gamma}n^{\delta-1}$ from (4.6) and (4.7)], less the worker's rent plus commuting costs. That is, a city owner will be able to let firms pay workers competitively and let workers take equilibrium prices in local land markets. For entrepreneurs, as we shall see, the story is different. Their compensation of $E\gamma m^{\gamma-1}n^{\delta}$ differs from the residual return to entrepreneurs from operating firms, which is $E(1-\delta)m^{\gamma-1}n^{\delta}$. How does this work?

Proposition 1. *In an equilibrium, large agents will be induced, through competition in national land markets, to transfer all local urban land rents to local entrepreneurs or businesses.*

To prove Proposition 1, we must solve for equilibrium compensations from (4.11). To do so, we utilize a folk-theorem type of assumption: In a sufficiently large national economy, developers will enter the market for cities until profits in (4.11) exactly equal zero. Substituting (4.13a) and (4.13b) into (4.11) and setting the result equal to zero, we get

$$\tfrac{1}{2}B(m+n)^{3/2} = E(\gamma+\delta-1)m^{\gamma}n^{\delta}. \tag{4.14a}$$

The left-hand side is total local land rents from equation (4.10). The right-hand side is the difference between the total required (noncommuting) compensation of entrepreneurs in the city $(E\gamma m^{\gamma}n^{\delta})$ and their total (residual) compensation from firm operations $[E(1-\delta)m^{\gamma}n^{\delta}]$. Therefore, in city-formation markets, through competition, city owners transfer all urban rents to entrepreneurs as payments for their externality benefits, over and above their private returns to operating firms.

The alternative way to derive this result is to solve the optimization problem in (4.12), where factors earn market returns (VMP for workers and the residual return to entrepreneurs). Here

$$T_n^* = 0$$

$$T_m^* = \tfrac{1}{2}B(m+n)^{3/2}/m \tag{4.14b}$$

All urban land rents are transferred to urban entrepreneurs.

Proposition 1 is a version of the "golden rule" of Flatters et al. (1974), aptly renamed the Henry George theorem by Stiglitz (1977). In equation (4.13), the $E\gamma m^{\gamma-1}n^{\delta}$ paid to entrepreneurs is the value of their *social* marginal product to a city in equation (4.11). Urban rents are used to make up the gap between this social marginal product and competitive compensation. Entrepreneurs generate an externality upon entry to a city, by allowing other entrepreneurs to achieve a greater degree of specialization. To realize an efficient number of entrepreneurs in a city, developers need to subsidize their compensation. This result has clear implications for the local public policy needed to encourage efficient local entrepreneurship.

To determine equilibrium city size, we impose national full employment in a system of symmetrical cities:

$$m = An \tag{4.15}$$

where A is the national ratio of entrepreneurs to workers. We then substitute (4.15) into (4.14a) and solve for the efficient worker population for any city, n^*. From now on, we shall loosely call this n^* the city size. Obviously, the true city size is $n^* + m^*$, or $n^*(1 + A)$.

$$n^* = \{\epsilon 2B^{-1}E(1 + A)^{-3/2}A^\gamma\}^{1/(\frac{1}{2}-\epsilon)} \quad \epsilon \equiv \gamma + \delta - 1 > 0 \tag{4.16}$$

where ϵ is the degree of local economies of scale in production and must be positive for $n^* > 0$.

Proposition 2. *The equilibrium city size increases with either advances in technology [specifically, increases in E in production technology, and decreases in t (in B) in commuting technology] or increases in the degree of scale economies, ϵ.*

The proposition follows from inspection of (4.16), assuming $\epsilon < \frac{1}{2}$ (see Proposition 5). If E, the level of technology in the production function, increases, city size increases. E can increase with investment in human capital and other endogenous growth-generating activities. For example, if E is proportional to levels of human capital accumulation, by time-differentiating (4.16) we get

$$\frac{\dot{n}}{n} = \frac{1}{\frac{1}{2} - \epsilon}\frac{\dot{E}}{E} > 0$$

where $\dot{E} \equiv dE/dt$. In a growth model, with steady-state growth of human capital, so that $\dot{E}/E$ equals a constant, equilibrium city sizes will increase continuously.

Similarly, if t (in B), the unit cost of commuting, falls, city size increases. Since 1890, U.S. cities have faced several changes in commuting technology that have lowered t: intra-urban rail transit, the automobile, and post–World War II development of intra-urban highways. These commuting-cost considerations, as well as advances in production technology, suggest that efficient city sizes increase over time. That is, increasing city sizes are not evidence of urban overconcentration per se. Rather, they are evidence of technological advance.

Proposition 3. *In an equilibrium with a folk-theorem type of entry, large agents will set the populations of cities to be of efficient sizes.*

To verify that the city size in (4.16) is Pareto-efficient, we formulate a planner's problem in which the planner allocates n and m to each city so as to maximize the utility of the representative worker, holding the utility of the representative entrepreneur constant. That yields the same solution as does maximizing per-capita net city output, which equals gross city output minus total commuting expenses, all divided by city population, $n + m$. Then, maximizing $[Em^\gamma n^\delta - B(m + n)^{3/2}]/(m + n)$ subject to $nA - m = 0$ yields equation (4.16).

Proposition 4. *Given the contract $\langle n^*, m^*, T_n^*, T_m^* \rangle$, the equilibrium is characterized by free mobility.*

This proposition is proved in the next section, based on inspection of equations (4.25a) and (4.25b). The proposition means that neither a worker nor an entrepreneur acting individually can gain by moving from one city to another. This means that, while n^* and m^* are parts of the specified contract, no enforcement is needed to maintain their magnitudes.

Proposition 5. *Given $E, B, A > 0, 0 < \delta < 1$, and $0 < \gamma < 1$, necessary and sufficient conditions for the existence of a well-behaved equilibrium with multiple cities of non-infinitesimal size are*

$$0 < \epsilon < \frac{1}{2}$$

$$\gamma \left(\frac{A + 1}{A} \right), \qquad \delta(A + 1) > 3\epsilon$$

For $0 < \epsilon < \frac{1}{2}$, inspection of (4.16) reveals that $\epsilon > 0$ is required for $n^* > 0$. To have urban agglomerations, there must be overall scale economies to employing workers and entrepreneurs. Also in (4.16), we are requiring the exponent $(\frac{1}{2} - \epsilon)^{-1}$ to be positive. Here the particular issue is that the second-order conditions for the social planner's optimization problem require

$$\epsilon < \frac{1}{2} \qquad\qquad\qquad (4.17)$$

If $\epsilon \geq \frac{1}{2}$, the social planner would want to have only one city in the economy. In an equilibrium with multiple cities, if $\epsilon \geq \frac{1}{2}$, any land developer could gain by, say, continuing to pay current factor rewards and doubling city size. Thus an equilibrium in national land markets cannot have multiple cities if $\epsilon \leq \frac{1}{2}$.

The restrictions $\gamma(A+1)/A, \delta(A+1) > 3\epsilon$ follow from requiring net factor returns at n^* to be positive. If net factor returns are not positive, we assume that economic agents have the option of not participating in the game and consuming their endowments. Endowment utility is normalized at zero. The net returns to entrepreneurs obtained by substituting (4.17) into (4.13) are[4]

$$R^* = n^{*\frac{1}{2}} C_1 \{ \gamma (A + 1) - 3A\epsilon \}$$

$$V^* = n^{*\frac{1}{2}} C_1 A \{ \delta (A + 1) - 3\epsilon \}$$

(4.18)

A solution to the model with positive factor returns, therefore, requires

$$\gamma \frac{(A + 1)}{A}, \ \delta(A + 1) > 3\epsilon$$

(4.19)

Proposition 5 thus defines a region of parameter space in which a first-best competitive equilibrium with large agents exists. Figure A4.1 in the Appendix illustrates the region in (δ, γ) space for different values of $A \leq 1$ (i.e., the number of workers exceeds the number of entrepreneurs). One can show that if the restrictions in (4.19) are met, the complete second-order conditions on the maximization problem in (4.11) are satisfied.[5]

Proposition 6. *From a national perspective, given net factor returns in (4.13) and full employment, if n^{**} and $\tilde{n}$ are the city sizes that will individually maximize the returns to workers and entrepreneurs, respectively, and n^* is the efficient city size, then*

   (1) *if either $A \leq 0.5$ or $A > 0.5$ and $\delta(1 + A) < \frac{3}{2}$, then $n^{**} < n^* < \tilde{n}$,*
   (2) *if $A > 0.5$ and $\delta(1 + A) > \frac{3}{2}$, then $\tilde{n} < n^* < n^{**}$, and*
   (3) *if $A > 0.5$ and $\delta(1 + A) = \frac{3}{2}$, then $\tilde{n} = n^* = n^{**}$.*

Conceptually, Proposition 6 is saying that efficient city size n^*, from a national perspective, represents a trade-off of the marginal gains and losses to workers and entrepreneurs of moving city size between n^{**} and $\tilde{n}$. Moreover, in some regions of parameter space, workers would benefit with cities larger than n^*, whereas in others, entrepreneurs would benefit. Neither atomistic workers nor entrepreneurs can perceive these benefits, but they are there.

To prove the proposition, we fix $m = An$ and substitute in for n in equations (4.13). For workers, this gives us $V = E\delta A^\gamma n^\epsilon - \frac{3}{2} B(1 + A)^{1/2} n^{1/2}$. Maximiz-

---

[4] $C_1 = \frac{1}{2} B A^{-1} (1 + A)^{1/2} \epsilon^{-1}$.
[5] The second-order conditions are satisfied if n exceeds a critical value $\hat{n}$. The issue then is whether or not $\hat{n} < n^*$. That condition is met if

$$2\delta\gamma + \delta(1 - \delta)A + \gamma A^{-1} \left[1 - \gamma - \frac{2}{3}(1 + A)^2 \delta \right] > 0$$

By repeated substitutions we can show that this is satisfied if the conditions in (4.19) are satisfied.

ing V with respect to n yields n^{**}, where the utility of workers alone is maximized. The result is

$$n^{**} = n^* \left[\tfrac{2}{3}\delta(1 + A) \right]^{1/(\tfrac{1}{2}-\epsilon)}$$

Thus,

$$n^{**} < n^* \quad \text{if} \quad \begin{cases} A \leq 0.5 \\ A > 0.5 \quad \text{and} \quad \delta(1 + A) < \tfrac{3}{2} \end{cases}$$

$$n^{**} > n^* \quad \text{if } A > 0.5 \quad \text{and} \quad \delta(1 + A) > \tfrac{3}{2}$$

For entrepreneurs, $R = E(1 - \delta)A^{\gamma-1}n^{\epsilon} - \tfrac{3}{2}B(1 + A)^{1/2}n^{1/2} + \tfrac{1}{2}B(1 + A)^{3/2}A^{-1}n^{1/2}$. In this case,

$$\tfrac{dR}{dn} > 0 \; \forall n \quad \text{if } A \leq 0.5$$

$$\tilde{n} = n^*[2(1 - \delta)(1 + A)(2A - 1)^{-1}]^{1/(\tfrac{1}{2}-\epsilon)} \quad \text{if } A > 0.5$$

Thus,

$$\tilde{n} \begin{Bmatrix} > \\ < \end{Bmatrix} n^* \quad \text{if } \delta(1 + A) \begin{Bmatrix} < \\ > \end{Bmatrix} \tfrac{3}{2}, \quad \text{for } A > 0.5$$

Note that R rises indefinitely, or $\tilde{n}$ is "infinite," if $A \leq 0.5$.

The proposition and the discussion suggest three cases of interest, as illustrated in Figure 4.1.

(1) If $A \equiv m/n \leq 0.5$, there are relatively few entrepreneurs (to divide up land rents). R rises indefinitely, and V peaks at $n^{**} < n^*$; n^* then reflects a trade-off between rising R and declining V beyond n^{**}.

(2) For $A > 0.5$, if $\delta(1 + A) < \tfrac{3}{2}$, V peaks at $n^{**} < n^*$, and R peaks at $\tilde{n} > n^*$, so that again workers want smaller cities than do entrepreneurs.

(3) For $A > 0.5$, if $\delta(1 + A) < \tfrac{3}{2}$, there are many entrepreneurs relative to workers, and workers have high shares (δ) of output. V peaks at n^{**}, and R peaks at $\tilde{n} < n^*$. Here, workers want larger cities than do entrepreneurs.

In certain contexts, this difference in desired city sizes could present problems in an economy. For example, if urban entrepreneurs composed a wealthy class of people with great national political influence, if $\tilde{n}$ (their desired size) were greater than n^{**}, and if this class of people recognize the benefits to them alone of forcing equilibrium sizes beyond n^*, urban entrepreneurs would gain nationally by restricting the ability of national land markets to function and generate more cities.

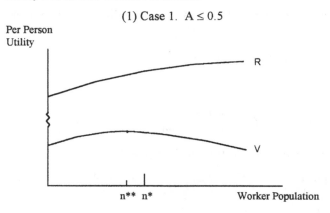

(1) Case 1. A ≤ 0.5

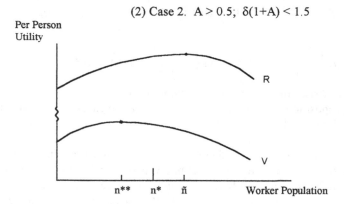

(2) Case 2. A > 0.5; δ(1+A) < 1.5

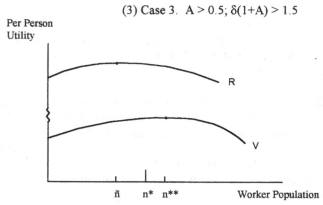

(3) Case 3. A > 0.5; δ(1+A) > 1.5

Figure 4.1. Utility levels for entrepreneurs and workers for m/n fixed at A.

Developer Control

A troublesome issue concerns the developer's access to the income specified in equation (4.11) or (4.12) per se. It looks as though the developer needs to own all urban lands in order to collect the land rent income. That brings into question a developer's ability to assemble such large pieces of land (Helsley and Strange, 1993). This concern is partially misplaced. The specification of the objective function does not require developer ownership of residential land. Suppose, for example, the development company does not own any of the local residential land; it simply controls the commercial district of the city, as in the command-maximization problem in equation (4.11). A requirement in optimizing is that the development company have "access" to local residential land rents, so that it can pay entrepreneurs a lump-sum transfer over and above their residual returns to firm operation. [The developer in equation (4.11) needs to be able also to access firm revenues, through, say, site charges; but then, in practice, all revenues are paid out to factors of production.] In a context of "homeownership," where either city workers and/or entrepreneurs are the owners of local land, accessing these rents is feasible. If workers own the land, the company can redistribute rents to entrepreneurs by imposing a tax on workers in the commercial district and remitting the proceeds to entrepreneurs. If entrepreneurs already own the local land, then no transfers are necessary; the company need only choose n and m. In general, with ownership of local land by local residents and with unconstrained local transfers, the company's optimization problem collapses to that in (4.11) or (4.12), and efficient city sizes can be achieved.

However, if local residential land is owned by absentee owners (rather than city residents), and if developers cannot directly tax residential lands, then there appears to be a problem. Equilibrium city sizes will be smaller than efficient, because the developer will not perceive that he can access sufficient revenues to offer inducements for an efficient number of entrepreneurs to enter the city. Specifically, for example, in equation (4.11), $-B(n+m)^{3/2}$ is now replaced by $-\frac{3}{2}B(n+m)^{3/2}$, because total land rents [in (4.11)] leave the city. Reoptimizing and solving yields

$$n = n^* \left(\frac{2}{3}\right)^{1/(\frac{1}{2}-\epsilon)} \tag{4.20}$$

for n^* defined in (4.16). Given (4.17), $n < n^*$. If $\epsilon = 0.1$, a typical upper-end empirical estimate (e.g., Henderson, 1988), $n = 0.36n^*$. The equilibrium city size, therefore, is just a fraction of the desired size, and there will be 275% more cities than would be efficient. In this context, workers' and entrepreneurs' (net) incomes are approximately 90% of what they would be in an efficient city. However, if the developer (or local residents) owns even half of the land nearest the CBD in a city of equilibrium size (i.e., owns everything within a radius of $0.707u_1$) and collects total rents of $0.396B(n + m)^{3/2}$ in equation (4.11), then $n = 0.78n^*$ for $\epsilon = 0.1$. Incomes then will be nearly 98% of what they would be in an efficient city. The gap will be narrowed even further if the company owns half of the land area needed for an efficient city.[6]

4 Equilibrium City Sizes in the Absence of Large Agents

What happens in a world in which there are no large agents operating in national land markets – no developer forming cities, and no city governments? City formation can occur only through workers and entrepreneurs milling around on the urban landscape, self-organizing, or forming "natural" clusters, given the joint scale economies from agglomerating together. As we shall see, for any region of parameter space where equilibria exist, there will be a "large" interval of feasible equilibrium sizes. Generally, the urban landscape will have inefficiently large cities, and hence too few cities nationally.

To solve for the interval of feasible city sizes, we first note that any equilibrium with cities requires real factor returns to exceed those that would be achievable if factors simply chose to "consume their endowments." This requirement will place an upper bound on city sizes. In any city, workers are paid their VMP from equation (4.7), and they pay rent plus commuting costs. To facilitate comparisons with the large-agent case, we assume that income from urban land is distributed equally among all local entrepreneurs. Thus, entrepreneurs get residual firm income, pay commuting plus rent costs, and receive their share of total local land rent income. Then, in any city, worker utility V and entrepreneur utility R are

$$V = E\delta n^{\delta-1}m^\gamma - \tfrac{3}{2}B(n + m)^{1/2} \tag{4.21}$$

$$R = E(1 - \delta)n^\delta m^{\gamma-1} - \tfrac{3}{2}B(n + m)^{1/2} + \tfrac{1}{2}B(n + m)^{3/2}m^{-1} \tag{4.22}$$

Any equilibrium requires V and R in (4.21) and (4.22) to be each at least non-negative. Otherwise, agents will prefer to consume their endowments, which here is normalized to yield a V or R of zero. In a symmetrical equilibrium across cities, where $m = An$, $V > 0$ and $R > 0$ define two different maximum n-values that the representative city must remain below if it is to maintain

---

[6] In this case, $-B(n + m)^{3/2}$ in equation (4.12) becomes

$$-\tfrac{3}{2}B(n + m)^{3/2} + B\left[\tfrac{3}{4}(n^* + m^*)(n + m)^{1/2} - (0.5)^{3/2}(n^* + m^*)^{3/2}\right]$$

The first term is total commuting costs. The second is total land rents under control of the developer, where n^* and m^* are given by equations (4.16) and (4.15).

positive welfare for residents. These maximal n-values are

$$n_{max}^V = \left[\tfrac{2}{3} B^{-1} A^{\gamma} (1 + A)^{-1/2} E\delta\right]^{1/(\tfrac{1}{2} - \epsilon)} \tag{4.23a}$$

$$n_{max}^R = \left[2 B^{-1} A^{\gamma} (1 + A)^{-1/2} E(1 - \delta)(2A - 1)^{-1}\right]^{1/(\tfrac{1}{2} - \epsilon)}$$

$$\text{for } A > 0.5 \quad (4.23b)$$

n_{max}^R is defined only for $A > 0.5$. For $A \le 0.5$, R rises indefinitely as n rises, for $m = An$ held fixed. The maximum city size in the economy is therefore less than

$$n_{max} = \min\left[n_{max}^V, n_{max}^R\right] \tag{4.24}$$

Note that n_{max} constitutes a size where the agglomeration benefits to at least one factor of production are totally dissipated through having an oversized city. Recall that in an economy with large agents, the worst-case scenario (i.e., local lands owned by absentee owners) implied a 10% loss of income for both entrepreneurs and workers in equilibrium. Here, with self-organization, potentially the losses could approach 100% for both groups.

Nash (Free-Mobility) Equilibria. Any city size below n_{max} is a Nash equilibrium, because, evaluated at $m = An$,

$$\left.\frac{\partial V}{\partial n}\right|_m = -E\delta(1 - \delta)A^{\gamma} n^{\gamma + \delta - 2} - \frac{3}{4} B(1 + A)^{-1/2} n^{-1/2} < 0$$

$$\tag{4.25a}$$

$$\left.\frac{\partial R}{\partial m}\right|_n = -(1 - \delta)E(1 - \gamma)A^{\gamma - 2} n^{\gamma + \delta - 2}$$

$$- \frac{1}{2} B(1 + A)^{-1/2} n^{-1/2} A^{-2}\left(1 + \frac{1}{2}A + A^2\right) < 0 \quad (4.25b)$$

Evaluation of the signs in (4.25) imposes the earlier restrictions that $0 < \delta < 1$ and $0 < \gamma < 1$. Equation (4.25) states that no single agent acting alone can improve her welfare, in a symmetrical equilibrium, by moving to another city. If, given populations n^0 and m^0 in each city, a worker (entrepreneur) leaves city A and goes to city B, then V (R) will rise in city A and fall in city B. This constitutes a proof of Proposition 4.

Robust Equilibria. The simple Nash-equilibrium criterion does not deal with pairwise deviations (say a worker and an entrepreneur deviating together) or other perturbations to equilibria. To arrive at robust equilibria, we revert to traditional notions of local dynamic stability. The simplest criterion is single-market dynamic stability: Assume an economy with a large number of competitive cities, and look at the "partial equilibrium" for any one city. Consider an equilibrium where factor utilities $\bar{V}$ and $\bar{R}$ prevail in national labor markets, and each city has $\bar{n}$ workers and $\bar{m}$ entrepreneurs. Perturb the equilibrium populations in a city. Assume that internal urban markets adjust instantaneously to yield new values of V and R for that city, with national $\bar{V}$ and $\bar{R}$ effectively unchanged (the partial equilibrium assumption). Given the V and R that the city then pays relative to $\bar{V}$ and $\bar{R}$, there will be further factor movements so as to return the economy to the original equilibrium. The dynamic factor-adjustment equations are $dn/ds \equiv \dot{n} = d_n(V - \bar{V})$ and $dm/ds \equiv \dot{m} = d_m(R - \bar{R})$, where s is time, and d_n and d_m are the speeds of migration flows to (from) the city from (to) national markets. Doing a first-order Taylor-series expansion about the equilibrium values, $\bar{n}$ and $\bar{m}$, we have

$$
\begin{bmatrix} \dot{n} \\ \dot{m} \end{bmatrix} = \begin{bmatrix} d_n \partial V(\bar{n}, \bar{m})/\partial n & d_n \partial V(\bar{n}, \bar{m})/\partial m \\ d_m \partial R(\bar{n}, \bar{m})/\partial n & d_m \partial R(\bar{n}, \bar{m})/\partial m \end{bmatrix} \begin{bmatrix} n - \bar{n} \\ m - \bar{m} \end{bmatrix} \quad (4.26)
$$

A necessary and sufficient condition for convergence, for any speeds of adjustment, is that the matrix in (4.26) be "stable," or have negative characteristic roots. For this 2×2 matrix to have negative characteristic roots, its trace must be negative [which it is, by (4.25)], and its determinant must be positive. Evaluating the determinant at $m = An$ results in the condition

$$
n > \left\{ \epsilon 2B^{-1}C(1 + A)^{-3/2}A^{\gamma} \right\}^{1/(\frac{1}{2} - \epsilon)} \quad \text{or} \quad n > n^* \quad (4.27)
$$

where n^* is the efficient city size in equation (4.16).[7] Thus we know that robust city sizes are at least as large as efficient sizes. This analysis leads to Proposition 7.

Proposition 7. *In a self-organizing economy, the equilibrium city size lies between the efficient size, n^*, and n_{max}. The existence of an equilibrium where $n_{max} > n^*$ occurs under the same parametric restrictions as in Proposition 5.*

Equilibrium sizes from (4.27) cannot be less than n^*, and they cannot exceed n_{max}. Existence thus requires

$$
n_{max}^R, n_{max}^V > n^* \quad (4.28)
$$

---

[7] This condition for stability is the same as for a two-city national labor market with workers and entrepreneurs. In this case, the factor-adjustment equations are $\dot{n}_1 = d_n(V_1 - V_2)$ and $\dot{m}_1 = d_m(R_1 - R_2)$. A Taylor-series expansion about, say, V_2 and R_2 results in equations such as

$$
\dot{n}_1 = d_n \left[\frac{\partial V}{\partial n}(n_1 - n_2) + \frac{\partial V}{\partial m}(m_1 - m_2) \right]
$$

Proceeding as before again yields (4.27).

The required conditions for (4.28) are the same as those in (4.19), so the regions of parameter space for existence are the same as those for existence in the large-agent case (see Figure A4.1 in the Appendix).

Given existence, any solution for city size in the interval (n^*, n_{max}) constitutes a robust equilibrium. How large is this interval? To see this, we form the ratio n_{max}/n^*. As noted earlier, n_{max} is defined by n_{max}^V for $A \leq 0.5$ and by (4.24) for $A > 0.5$. Therefore,

$$\frac{n_{max}}{n^*} = \left[\frac{1}{3}\delta\frac{(1+A)}{\epsilon} \right]^{1/(\frac{1}{2}-\epsilon)} \quad \text{for } A \leq 0.5$$

$$= \min\left[\left(\frac{1}{3}\delta\frac{(1+A)}{\epsilon} \right)^{1/(\frac{1}{2}-\epsilon)}, \left(\frac{(1-\delta)(1+A)}{\epsilon(2A-1)} \right)^{1/(\frac{1}{2}-\epsilon)} \right]$$

$$\text{for } A > 0.5 \quad (4.29)$$

In Figures 4.2 and 4.3, we graph this ratio in γ-space, holding A fixed (at 0.1 and 0.3, respectively) and letting δ vary, while imposing the existence restrictions in (4.19). Visual inspection reveals that for the expected values of overall scale economies (an ϵ of, say, 0.08–0.15), n_{max} is many times greater than n^*. Note that $(n_{max}/n^*) \to 1$ as $\gamma + \delta \equiv 1 + \epsilon$ gets "large." For $\epsilon > \frac{1}{2}$, only one city in the economy is desired, so n_{max} and n^* coincide. Note also that n_{max}/n^* gets arbitrarily large as $\epsilon \to 0$ (or $\gamma + \delta \to 1$). Here, $n^* \to 0$ (i.e., no cities are desired), because benefits from agglomerating disappear.

Narrowing the Set of Equilibria. There are various ways in which authors have attempted to narrow the set of potential equilibria, given that equilibrium city sizes can be anywhere in the interval (n^*, n_{max}). The first is to arbitrarily fix the number of cities and assume an interior solution (Westhoff, 1977; Epple and Romer, 1991); that is, divide the national population symmetrically, such that the representative city population is in the interval (n^*, n_{max}). The second is to start with the national population unevenly and (somewhat) arbitrarily spread across a relatively large (fixed) number of urban sites (more than will be finally occupied) and allow migration between sites according to some naive mechanism (such as our "dynamic stability" mechanism). In this case, population agglomerates into a subset of the original sites, with the remainder of the sites being deserted (Krugman, 1993). That is, we generate a specific representative city-size outcome in the interval (n^*, n_{max}) by starting from a specific history (arbitrary initial nonequilibrium allocation).

Another approach to narrowing the set of potential equilibria with no large agents is to naively grow the economy (Henderson, 1974). For example, consider an economy with population growth in n and m such that A remains constant. Starting from any initial equilibrium number of cities, population will grow in each city until the n_{max} bound is hit. Some workers and entrepreneurs will

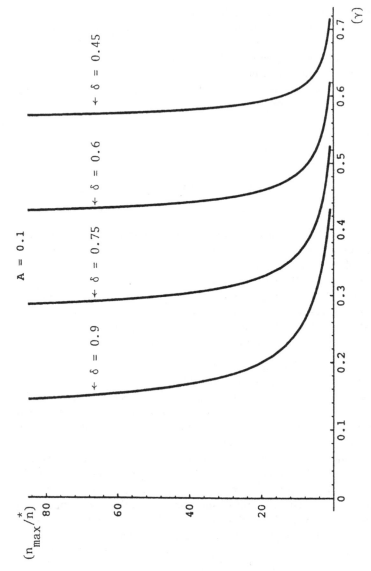

Figure 4.2. (n_{max}/n^*) for $A = 0.1$ and various δ values.

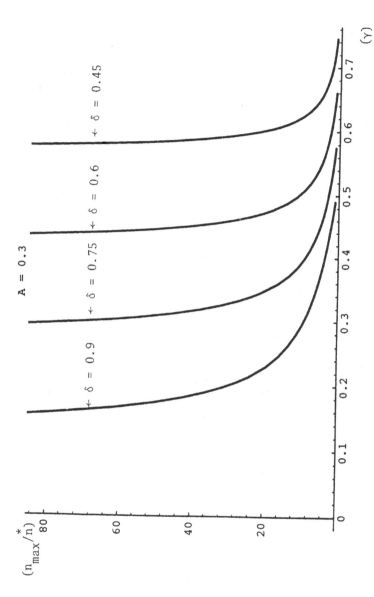

Figure 4.3. (n_{max}/n^*) for $A = 0.3$ and various δ values.

then deviate to form new cities. How many of these tiny new agglomerations will form is not specified, except that in the new instantaneous symmetrical equilibrium the representative city size must again be in the interval (n^*, n_{max}). Population growth then continues until the n_{max} bound is again reached, and some more cities form. This "growth" process of repeatedly hitting a Malthusian upper bound on city size (where worker or entrepreneur utility approaches zero) continues indefinitely. This is a depressing scenario, perhaps according with the sentiments reflected in positions taken by the United Nations!

5 Resolution: Self-organization with Local Governments

The debate over the large-agent solution mechanism versus the self-organization solution mechanism tends to focus on the observability of large agents in the real world. As we discussed earlier, there is ample evidence of large land developers in the United States setting up business districts and residential areas employing/housing thousands of workers. Elsewhere in the world, though large agents may potentially or even actually be widespread, they may lack appropriate institutions and instruments to be effective in allocating resources efficiently. However, the existence and freedom of large land-developing agents may not be the key.

If we think about the problem more closely, large land developers are not essential for the attainment of efficient outcomes. A combination of self-organization and optimizing autonomous city governments will do the trick. We have found that under self-organization, cities will not be less than size n^*, so the tendency is to have too few cities nationally. Optimizing city governments, however, acting to maximize the welfare of the representative worker, will want to restrict city sizes to n^*. Let us see why.

Suppose that local governments control cities, and each acts to maximize the utility of a representative from the majority population. Suppose that workers are the majority $(A < 1)$ and that local lands are owned locally, say by entrepreneurs. The government then seeks to maximize the return to workers, subject to the city's ability to attract entrepreneurs:

$$\max_{n,m,T_m} E\delta n^{\delta-1}m^\gamma - \tfrac{3}{2}B(n+m)^{1/2} - T_m m/n$$

$$\text{s.t.} \quad T_m + E(1-\delta)n^\delta m^{\gamma-1} - \tfrac{3}{2}B(n+m)^{1/2} \qquad (4.30)$$

$$+ \tfrac{1}{2}B(n+m)^{3/2}m^{-1} - \bar{R} = 0$$

In the objective function, the first two terms are wages net of per-worker rents plus commuting costs. $T_m \gtrless 0$ in (4.30) is a transfer payment, where each entrepreneur gets T_m, and each worker $-T_m m/n$. In the constraint, besides collecting T_m and firm profits and paying rents plus commuting costs

$[\frac{3}{2}B(n+m)^{1/2}]$, each entrepreneur also collects a dividend: her share of land rents $[\frac{1}{2}B(n+m)^{3/2}/m]$, which the local government recognizes as endogenous.

Proposition 8. *Autonomous local governments, acting on behalf of the majority local population, will set cities to their efficient sizes n^* and transfer local land rents as subsidies to encourage efficient numbers of local entrepreneurs to locate in each city.*

To prove this, we solve (4.30) and impose national full employment to get efficient sizes. Here, because under self-organization land rents are already assumed to go to entrepreneurs, $T_m^* = 0$. However, the existence of T_m is critical. It functions as a local-government mechanism for entrepreneur–worker transfers, so workers will choose city size n^*, rather than setting n and m to maximize their own returns. Note also, as with development companies, that T_m makes the specification of local residential property rights among local workers and entrepreneurs irrelevant in obtaining the efficient city size in (4.16). Whatever claims exist can be effectively altered by the city government in its choice of T_m^*. Also, reformulating (4.30) so that enterpreneurs are the majority will yield the same outcome.

In the city-formation process, under self-organization, by excluding residents, cities force the formation of new natural clusters whose robust sizes will not be less than n^*. These new agglomerations will also be governed democratically, imposing a limit of n^* residents and forcing the formation of more new cities. With robustness ensuring sizes of at least n^* and city governments imposing a cap of n^* residents, equilibrium city sizes of n^* will emerge, and there will be an efficient number of cities to house the national population. This process assumes that no institutions exist to stop the formation of new natural clusters.

Our requirements for cities to be able to achieve efficient restrictions on city size and composition are that city governments be able to specify population and numbers of businesses and that they can access urban land rents. In the United States that is easy. City governments impose property taxes on land. They restrict their cities' sizes through zoning ordinances and permits governing land use, density, and development. Finally, we note that in economies like that of the United States, spatial form is the product of the three elements of city formation: large agents, local governments, and self-organization. At any point in time, most cities will have been in existence for decades or centuries, with a built-up stock of public infrastructure, private housing, and commercial building capital. In these cities, city governments will work both to compete for national resources and to restrictively zone urban activities and even city size. At the same time, as necessary to satisfy either population growth or interregional population movements, land developers will start new agglomerations or help build up small existing natural clusters of population.

6 Conclusions

Workers and entrepreneurs interact in an urban economy to generate joint economies of scale. Entrepreneurs play a central role in the process by taking advantage of the benefits of intra-industry specialization. They generate an externality, because upon entry into a city they allow other firms in the city to achieve greater degrees of specialization. Efficient outcomes in market economies require subsidization of entrepreneurs, in amounts equal to total urban land rents, a variant of the Henry George theorem.

With large land developers, cities achieve efficient sizes and numbers by implicitly trading off the costs/benefits to workers versus entrepreneurs of increasing city sizes. These developers can take the form of competitive land-development corporations, owned by Arrow-Debreu shareholders. A local development corporation need only control the commercial sector of the city as long as local residents own the local residential land and worker–entrepreneur transfers can be effected. Developers may also be local governments, in a context where all land is owned locally. Again, the pattern of local ownership does not matter as long as the local government can impose transfers between local workers and entrepreneurs. If land is not all owned locally, then the revenue needed to subsidize entrepreneurship is insufficient. If, however, the developer owns, say, the half of the residential land nearest the CBD, equilibrium city sizes will be close to efficient sizes.

In the absence of large agents, we may have self-organization outcomes. There, Nash-equilibrium sizes occur for any city size when both factors earn positive returns. However, robust or "stable" equilibria require city sizes bounded below by the efficient city size and above by the size where the utility of either workers or entrepreneurs goes to zero. Typically, the range of potential equilibrium sizes with self-organization is enormous; the maximum feasible is multifold the minimum. In this case, "history" (accident) generates the actual equilibrium configuration from the feasible range. A particularly depressing result occurs in an economy experiencing ongoing population growth. There, city size is repeatedly bouncing up against the maximal feasible size, a Malthusian urban outcome where the return to one of the factors approaches zero.

However, a combination of self-organization and the presence of local governments that restrict city sizes to maximize the utility of workers can lead to a restoration of efficient city sizes. To the extent that mega-cities are too large in certain countries and land-market operations are restricted, a solution would be to grant autonomy to local governments. National governments would need to allow them to restrict their sizes and set fiscal conditions and to allow new cities (and local governments) to arise freely as self-organizing agents desire.

Appendix

In this Appendix, we define the regions in parameter space for which equilibria exist.

Existence. In Figure A4.1, we graph the regions for existence in (γ, δ) space for various values of A, where γ and δ are entrepreneurs' and workers' shares of total output in equation (4.7), respectively, and A is the national ratio of entrepreneurs to workers. Common to all graphs are the assumptions that $0 < \delta < 1$ and $\gamma + \delta > 1$. These restrictions define some "sides" of the parameter space for existence and eliminate from consideration the area nearest the origin. Another restriction, $\gamma + \delta < \frac{3}{2}$, from (4.17), ensures multiple cities, but is never strictly binding and therefore is not graphed.

In addition to these basic restrictions, city formation requires positive factor returns. By (4.18) and (4.19), this requires

$$\delta(A + 1) - 3(\gamma + \delta - 1) > 0 \tag{a}$$

$$\gamma(A + 1) - 3A(\gamma + \delta - 1) > 0 \tag{b}$$

for $V^* > 0$ and $R^* > 0$, respectively. These restrictions, labeled (a) and (b) in our graphs, complete our definition of the parameter space in which a first-best competitive equilibrium with large agents *and* a robust self-organization equilibrium exist. The shaded areas in the graphs of Figure A4.1 show the regions that satisfy the foregoing restrictions. Each graph features a different value of A, restricting our attention to $A \leq 1.0$, so that the number of entrepreneurs does not exceed the number of workers.

Restriction (a) binds for all values of A. For a particular δ, as γ increases, we eventually hit constraint (a), beyond which worker utility is negative. For a given δ, increasing γ increases economies of scale in production and raises a worker's competitive wage. But it raises her rent plus commuting costs at an even faster rate. Along constraint (a), these costs soak up all of her compensation. Why are entrepreneurs not similarly affected for $A \leq 0.5$? As we shall show later, $dR/dn > 0 \ \forall \ n$ if $A \leq 0.5$. Because entrepreneurs claim local land rents, the increased rent plus commuting costs they face as a result of increased city size are more than offset by the increased compensation from their firms' operations and their landholdings.

Constraint (b) binds only for $A > 0.5$. As A rises beyond 0.5, the implied increase in entrepreneurs means that total local land rents have to be divided up among more people. Then, as city sizes increase, the smaller slices of the total local land-rent pie are not enough to completely offset the increases in

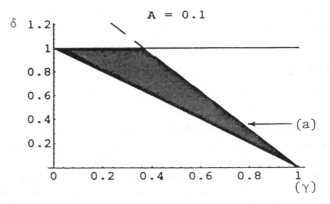

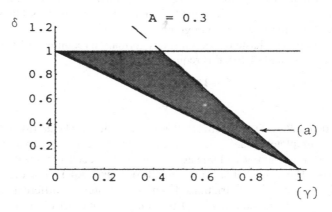

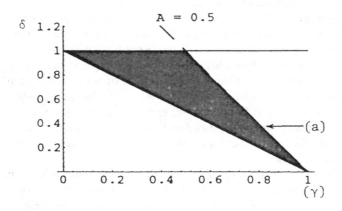

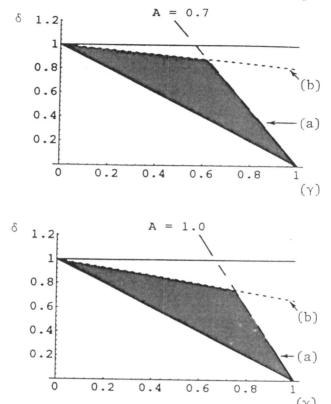

Figure A4.1. Parameter space for existence.

urban costs that come with large cities. For a given δ, there is a certain γ (and a corresponding city size) at which entrepreneur utility R becomes zero. That occurs along constraint (b).

References

Abdel-Rahman, H., and Fujita, M. (1990). Product varieties, Marshallian externalities, and city sizes. *Journal of Regional Science* 2:165–83.

Becker, G., and Murphy, K. (1992). The division of labor, coordination costs, and knowledge. *Quarterly Journal of Economics* 107:1137–60.

Epple, D., and Romer, T. (1991). Mobility and redistribution. *Journal of Political Economy* 99:828–58.

Flatters, F., Henderson, V., and Mieszkowski, P. (1974). Public goods, efficiency, and regional equalization. *Journal of Public Economics* 3:99–112.

Fujita, M., and Ogawa, M. (1982). Multiple equilibria and structural transition of non-monocentric urban configurations. *Regional Science and Urban Economics* 12:161–96.

Garreau, J. (1991). *Edge City*. New York: Doubleday.

Hamilton, W. (1975). Zoning and property taxation in a system of local governments. *Urban Studies* 12:205–11.

Helsley, R. W., and Strange, W. C. (1990). Matching and agglomeration economies in a system of cities. *Regional Science and Urban Economics* 20:189–212.

Helsley, R. W., and Strange, W. C. (1993). City developers and efficiency. Mimeograph, University of British Columbia.

Henderson, J. V. (1974). The sizes and types of cities. *American Economic Review* 64:640–56.

Henderson, J. V. (1988). *Urban Development: Theory, Fact and Illusion*. Oxford University Press.

Henderson, J. V., and Mitra, A. (1996). The new urban landscape: developers and edge cities. *Regional Science and Urban Economics* 26:613–43.

Henderson, J. V., and Slade, E. (1993). The development of non-monocentric cities. *Journal of Urban Economics* 34:207–29.

Hoyt, W. (1991). Competitive jurisdictions, congestion, and the Henry George theorem: When should property be taxed instead of land? *Regional Science and Urban Economics* 21:351–70.

Krugman, P. (1991). Increasing returns and economic geography. *Journal of Political Economy* 99:483–99.

Krugman, P. (1993). On the number and location of cities. *European Economic Review* 37:293–308.

Marshall, A. (1890). *Principles of Economics*. London: Macmillan.

Mills, E. S. (1967). An aggregative model of resource allocation in a metropolitan area. *American Economic Review* 57:197–210.

Reichman, U. (1976). Residential private governments. *University of Chicago Law Review* 43:253–306.

Renaud, B. (1981). *National Urbanization Policy in Developing Countries*. Oxford University Press.

Stiglitz, J. (1977). The theory of local public goods. In: M. S. Feldstein and R. P. Inman (eds.), *The Economics of Public Services*. New York: Macmillan.

United Nations (1993). *World Urbanization Prospects: The 1992 Revision*. New York: United Nations.

Westhoff, F. (1977). Existence of equilibria in economies with a local public good. *Journal of Economic Theory* 14:84–112.

Wildasin, D. (1987). Theoretical analysis of local public economics. In: E. S. Mills (ed.), *Handbook of Regional and Urban Economics*, vol. 2. Amsterdam: North Holland.

CHAPTER 5

A Monopolistic Competition Model of Urban Systems and Trade

Masahisa Fujita and Paul Krugman

1 Introduction

Nearing the twenty-first century, one of the most notable phenomena in world economic geography is the rapid urbanization being experienced by most countries. Today, in most developed countries and many developing countries, more than 70% of people reside in cities (United Nations, 1993). Although in the past, urbanization was almost synonymous with industrialization, the recent progression of so-called deindustrialization has brought about a renewed trend of further urbanization in many countries. As a consequence, today the economic activities of most countries are dominated by cities. Furthermore, cities are becoming more important not only for each national economy but also for the world economy and trade. For example, the trade among developed countries has been increasingly dominated by the exchange of those goods produced in their cities. As another illustration, the world financial market is dominated by several "world cities" such as New York City, London, and Tokyo.

Given the increasing prominence of cities in national and world economies, an obvious question of importance is how to model, in terms of microeconomics, the formation of cities and the resulting trade among cities. In order to investigate this question, one must first note that for the growth of cities in a modern economy, the locational advantages due to "first nature" are becoming increasingly less important in comparison with the self-reinforcing advantages of "second nature" or agglomeration economies. This point is well illustrated in a recent book by the historian William Cronon (1991), who has documented the extraordinary nineteenth-century rise of Chicago as the central city of the American heartland. In fact, this point has been well recognized by economists for a long time. For example, Koopmans (1957, pp. 153–4) has maintained that "as long as indivisibility of commodities is not recognized, these models fail to grasp the essential character of the problems posed by urban conglomerations.

The authors are grateful to Tomoya Mori, Tony Smith, Jacques Thisse, and an anonymous referee for their valuable comments on earlier versions of this chapter.

The manner in which the various activities of a metropolitan area are (or could be) arranged in space has very little relation to mineral deposits or grades of agricultural land. . . . This suggests that without recognizing indivisibilities – in human person, in residences, plants, equipment, and in transportation – urban location problems, down to those of the smallest villages, cannot be understood." Second, we note that cities are different from each other not only in their sizes but also in their functions. In an economy, typically, cities together constitute some form of *hierarchical system*.

What we need, then, is an economic theory that can explain the formation and changes of a hierarchical city system in an economy situated on homogeneous geographical space (having no *a priori* locational differences in terms of first nature). Unfortunately, however, it seems that no microeconomic model yet exists that can generate a hierarchical system of cities in a general equilibrium context of a national (or international) economy. Although countless numbers of articles have been published on "central place theory" since the pioneering work by Christaller (1933), no formal microeconomic model of central place theory seems to have been developed yet.[1] Furthermore, traditional international economic models are, unfortunately, ill-prepared to deal with such questions of urban agglomeration and hierarchical change: They are critically based on the concept of "borders."

Recently, Krugman (1993a) developed a microeconomic model of a spatial economy based on the Chamberlinian monopolistic competition behavior of firms. The model can explain the formation of a metropolis at some specific location in a given continuous geographical space. In this chapter we shall generalize Krugman's model by considering more than one metropolis (or city) and examine its potential capability to yield a variety of urban systems.[2] Since the first version of this chapter was written several years ago, we have done some joint work with Tomoya Mori in which we have proposed an evolutionary approach to examining how the economic landscape changes from one center to several centers, including the emergence of an urban hierarchy (Fujita and Mori, 1997; Fujita et al., 1999). Although the evolutionary approach is useful for choosing a specific path for landscape change, it ignores the rest of the possible configurations. In contrast, in this chapter we examine in detail under what conditions each possible type of configuration can be an equilibrium. The two approaches obviously complement each other, and we believe that

---

[1] Although there have been many attempts to develop formal models in central place theory and city-system theory, they have been either partial or spaceless. For example, Eaton and Lipsey (1982) proposed a partial equilibrium model of shopping centers; in the model of Henderson (1987), no space was explicitly considered.

[2] For specific differences between the Krugman model and our model, see footnote 4. Note also that our model here can be considered as an extension of nonmonocentric urban models (e.g., Ogawa and Fujita, 1980; Fujita and Ogawa, 1982; Fujita, 1988) into a national economic context.

together they provide a basis for valuable future work on the theory of urban systems.

The plan of this chapter is as follows: In Section 2 we present an informal discussion of why monopolistic competition based on product variety in consumption can result in the formation of a system of cities. In Section 3, a formal model is presented. In Sections 4–6 we examine each of the different types of possible equilibrium configurations in detail. It turns out that our model yields a high degree of locational and structural nonuniqueness of equilibria. Hence, in Section 7 we discuss the welfare implications and structural stability of multiple equilibria. Finally, in Section 8 we discuss possible directions for future research.

2 Product Variety and Urban Agglomeration

In this section we discuss informally why monopolistic competition based on product variety in consumption goods can result in the formation of a system of cities. We discuss later, in Section 8, why product variety in intermediate goods can yield a similar result.

Suppose that we have a given population of homogeneous workers. Each worker consumes a homogeneous agricultural good (A-good) together with several groups of manufactured goods (M-goods), where each group of M-goods consists of a large variety of differentiated goods. Because of scale economies in product specialization, each variety of M-goods is supposed to be produced by a single firm (using labor as its sole input) that chooses its f.o.b. price monopolistically (in the sense of Chamberlin). The homogeneous A-good is produced by constant-returns-to-scale technology using labor and land. All workers are assumed to be homogeneous and free to choose their locations. In this context, the mechanism for the formation of a hierarchical system of cities is as follows.

First, let us assume that there is only one group of M-goods (together with the A-good). In this context, if a wide variety of M-goods is produced in a city, those goods can be purchased in the city at lower prices than at more distant places. Thus, given a nominal wage rate, because of the taste for variety, the real income of workers (= consumers) will become higher. That, in turn, will induce more workers (= consumers) to migrate there. Then that increase in the number of consumers (= workers) will create a greater demand for M-goods there, which in turn can support a greater number of specialized firms. (Note that because of scale economies at the individual-firm level, a large number of firms can be supported only when the total demand for M-goods is sufficiently large.) This implies the availability of an even wider variety of M-goods in the city.

Figure 5.1 depicts this circular causality in the spatial agglomeration of firms and workers through a *forward linkage* (where the availability of a greater variety of M-goods increases the real income of workers there) and a *backward*

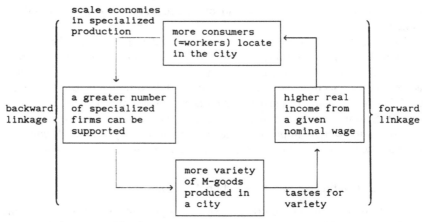

Figure 5.1. Circular causality in spatial agglomeration of firms and workers.

linkage (where a greater number of consumers can support a greater number of specialized firms). In other words, through these forward and backward linkages, scale economies at the individual-firm level are transformed into increasing returns at a city level.

It is, of course, not always necessary for all firms to agglomerate at one location (or city). If the M-goods (in the same group in question) are close substitutes for one another (or transport costs for M-goods are high), then some firms may find that by moving away from the central agglomeration (i.e., the metropolis) and serving primarily farmers in a fringe agricultural area they can earn greater profit. In this case, then, the equilibrium spatial system will contain multiple cities.

Next, let us assume that there are two groups of M-goods, where each group consists of a large number of similar but differentiated goods. Suppose further that goods in the first group are highly differentiated (and hence their price elasticity is low), whereas those in the second group are close substitutes for one another (thus their price elasticity is high). Then, provided that the transport costs for the two groups of M-goods are not too different, it is quite possible that the first group of M-goods will be provided mostly from the central dominant city, and the second group will be provided not only from the dominant city but also from smaller cities. If so, we have a hierarchical system of cities. In this way, by introducing many groups of M-goods, a more complex hierarchical system of cities can be generated.[3]

---

[3] Because of space limitations, we report on the case of a single group of manufactured goods only. Hence the urban systems generated in this study are not truly hierarchical. For a study of hierarchical urban systems with multiple groups of manufactured goods, refer to Fujita et al. (1999).

Note that because we assume that no pair of differentiated goods is perfectly substitutable, the output of any firm will be consumed by every consumer in the economy, provided that the utility function is of a constant-elasticity-of-substitution (CES) type. Therefore, there will be trade between every pair of cities. Thus, the system of cities from our model resembles more that of Pred (1977) than that of Christaller (1933). (Recall that Christaller's system is purely tree-shaped.)

3 A Formal Model of a Spatial Economy

In this section we present a formal model of a spatial economy that represents the foregoing basic ideas in concrete terms. As noted earlier, our model has been developed as an extension of the model of Krugman (1993a).[4]

Consider a long, narrow country in which area is represented by one-dimensional, unbounded location space $X \equiv \mathbb{R}$. The quality of land is homogeneous, and the density of land is equal to 1 everywhere. The country has a continuum of homogeneous workers, with a given size, N. Each worker is endowed with a unit of labor and is free to choose any location and job (i.e., manufacturing work or agricultural work) in the country. The consumers of the country consist of the workers and landlords. All landlords are attached to their land (like weeds) and consume the entire revenue from the land (i.e., land rent) at their locations.

Each consumer consumes a homogeneous agricultural good (A-good) together with a continuum n_1 of differentiated manufactured goods (M-goods). (Here, n_1 is to be determined endogenously.) All consumers have the same utility function, given by

$$U = \alpha_0 \log z_0 + \alpha_1 \log \left[\int_0^{n_1} z_1(\omega)^{\rho_1} \, d\omega \right]^{1/\rho_1} \tag{5.1}$$

where z_0 represents the amount of consumption of the A-good, $z_1(\omega)$ is the consumption (density) of each M-good $\omega \in [0, n_1]$, and α_0, α_1, and ρ_1 are positive constants such that $\alpha_0 + \alpha_1 = 1$ and $0 < \rho_1 < 1$. Note that a smaller ρ_1 means that consumers have a stronger preference for variety in M-goods. Suppose that a consumer has an income Y and faces a set of prices p_0 (for the A-good) and

---

[4] Specifically, the major differences between the two studies are as follows. In the model by Krugman (1993a) there are fixed numbers of two distinct types of workers: agricultural workers and manufacturing workers. Agricultural workers are uniformly distributed over a finite interval of space, with their location being fixed, but manufacturing workers can move freely. In agricultural production, the use of land is not considered explicitly, and thus no land market appears in the model. Furthermore, the formation of only a single metropolis is examined. In this chapter, in contrast, all workers are homogeneous, can move freely, and can work either in agriculture or in manufacturing. In addition, the use of land in agricultural production is explicitly considered, and hence the land market is introduced. Finally, as noted before, this chapter considers more than one city.

$p_1(\omega)$ (for each M-good ω). Then, by choosing the consumption bundle that will maximize (5.1) subject to the budget constraint

$$p_0 z_0 + \int_0^{n_1} p_1(\omega) z_1(\omega) \, d\omega = Y \tag{5.2}$$

the demand functions of the consumer can be obtained as

$$z_0 = (\alpha_0 Y)/p_0 \tag{5.3a}$$

$$z_1(\omega) = \left[\alpha_1 Y / p_1(\omega) \right] \left[p_1(\omega)^{-\gamma_1} \Big/ \int_0^{n_1} p_1(\omega)^{-\gamma_1} \, d\omega \right] \tag{5.3b}$$

for each $\omega \in [0, n_1]$, where $\gamma_1 = \rho_1/(1-\rho_1)$. Note from (5.3b) that the demand for any M-good has the same price elasticity, E_1, given by

$$E_1 = 1/(1 - \rho_1) = 1 + \gamma_1 \tag{5.4}$$

Thus, E_1 increases as ρ_1 (or γ_1) increases. Substitution of (5.3) into (5.1) yields the following indirect utility function:

$$U = (\log Y) \alpha_1^{\alpha_1} p_0(y)^{-\alpha_0} \left(\int_0^{n_1} p_1(\omega)^{-\gamma_1} \, d\omega \right)^{\alpha_1/\gamma_1} \tag{5.5}$$

Next, the A-good is assumed to be produced under constant returns, where each unit of A-good consumes a unit of land and a_0 units of labor. (In this chapter, land is used for A-good production only.) Each M-good is produced with labor only. All M-goods have the same production technology under increasing returns, such that the total labor input, L_1, for production of q_1 of any M-good is given by

$$L_1 = f_1 + a_1 q_1 \tag{5.6}$$

where f_1 is the fixed labor requirement, and a_1 the marginal labor input.

We assume, for simplicity, that the transport cost for each good takes Samuelson's "iceberg" form: If a unit of an M-good is shipped over a distance d, only $e^{-t_1 d}$ units will actually arrive. Because of scale economies in production of M-goods, each variety of M-good is assumed to be produced by a single specialized firm. If a firm locates at $x \in X$ and produces a product, it chooses an f.o.b. price $p_1(x)$ so as to maximize its profit at the Chamberlinian equilibrium. By assumption, then, the (delivered) price $p_1(y \mid x)$ at each location $y \in X$ for any M-good produced at location x is given by

$$p_1(y \mid x) = p_1(x) e^{t_1 |y-x|} \tag{5.7}$$

The unknowns of the model are (1) the price $p_0(y)$ for the A-good at each y, (2) the f.o.b. price $p_1(x)$ for the M-goods produced at each x, (3) the wage rate $W(y)$ at each y, (4) the land rent $R(y)$ at each y, (5) the equilibrium utility level u for workers, (6) the spatial distribution of workers, (7) the spatial distribution of the production of M-goods, and (8) the transport/trade pattern for each good.

A spatial configuration is in equilibrium if all workers achieve the same highest utility, all active firms earn zero profit, and equality of the demand for and supply of each good is attained. It turns out that, depending on the parameters, there can exist a large variety of equilibrium spatial configurations. Furthermore, even under a single set of parameters there can occur a vast array of multiple equilibria.

It is beyond the purpose of this chapter to delineate all possible equilibrium configurations. Rather, we shall study several basic types of equilibrium configurations that together should suggest the rest of the possible equilibrium configurations. Furthermore, for simplicity of analysis, we shall study (spatially) symmetric equilibrium configurations only, leaving study of asymmetric configurations for the future.

Figure 5.2 shows several basic types of possible equilibrium spatial configurations. Suppose that the transport cost for the A-good is much higher than that for the M-goods. Then, as depicted in Figure 5.2(a), no transportation of the A- good will occur, and the production of M-goods will take place everywhere

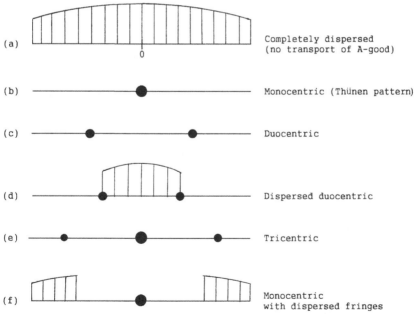

Figure 5.2. Examples of possible equilibrium spatial configurations ($m = 1$).

in the agricultural domain.[5] [In Figure 5.2(a), the height represents the density distribution of M-goods firms, and the horizontal line represents the domain of the land used for agriculture.] In the opposite situation, we have Figure 5.2(b), where all manufacturing takes place at one location (the metropolis). This is the case of the *Isolated State*, by von Thünen (1826). Between the (a) and (b) configurations, a variety of equilibrium spatial configurations is conceivable. For example, Figure 5.2(c) represents the case in which manufacturing takes place in two cities. Note that because each manufacturing firm is specialized in one product, and each consumer consumes every kind of M-goods produced, we have trade of M-goods between the two cities (as well as between the cities and the agricultural area). It is conjectured that when two major cities are located very close together, then the possible equilibrium configuration is not (c), but rather (d), in Figure 5.2, where an *industrial belt* (i.e., a mixed area of manufacturing and agriculture) will emerge between the two cities. Figures 5.2(e) and 5.2(f) show other possible basic types of equilibrium configurations.

In the rest of this chapter we shall focus on the spatial configurations depicted in (b), (c), and (e) of Figure 5.2 and examine in turn the conditions under which each of these configurations emerges as an equilibrium. Then we shall demonstrate the possibility of the structural (as well as locational) nonuniqueness of equilibria.

4 Monocentric Equilibria

First, in this section, we examine under what conditions the monocentric (or Thünen) spatial configuration depicted in Figure 5.3 can be in equilibrium. In the figure, the agricultural area is assumed to extend from $-l$ to l, and the production of all M-goods takes place at the central location, $y = 0$, called the city. In the following, first we determine all unknowns, assuming that all M_1-firms locate in the city. Second, using the potential function, we examine the conditions for the city to be indeed the equilibrium location for all M_1-firms. Finally, we conduct some studies of comparative statics.

4.1 Determination of the Equilibrium

Let the price curve $p_0(y)$ of the A-good be normalized such that $p_0(0) = 1$. Then, because all excess A-good is to be transported to the city, it must hold for all y that

$$p_0(y) = e^{-t_0|y|} \tag{5.8}$$

---

[5] Note that, by assumption, every consumer consumes all types of goods produced in the economy. In this context, if no transportation of the A-good occurs, then there cannot exist a pure agricultural area. This is because in a pure agricultural area there is no other good to be exported from there, and M-goods need to be imported, which is a contradiction. Therefore, if no transportation of the A-good occurs, then the M-goods need to be produced everywhere in the agricultural domain.

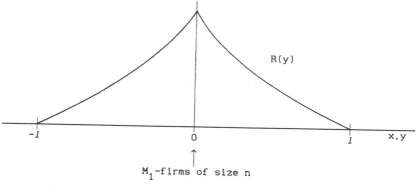

Figure 5.3. A monocentric spatial configuration.

Next, let p_1 be the f.o.b. price for each M_1-good produced at the city. Then, by (5.7), the (delivered) price for each M_1-good at each location is given by

$$p_1(y) = p_1 e^{t_1|y|} \tag{5.9}$$

Further, let n be the number (more precisely, the size) of differentiated M_1-goods produced at the city; by definition, then, n also equals the number of firms producing M_1-goods at the city.

Now, let $W(y)$ be the equilibrium wage rate at each $y \in [-l, l]$. Then, in equilibrium, because all workers must achieve the same utility level, say u, by the indirect utility function (5.5) we have that

$$W(y) = e^u \alpha_0^{-\alpha_0} \alpha_1^{-\alpha_1} n^{-\alpha_1/\gamma_1} p_1^{\alpha_1} e^{(\alpha_1 t_1 - \alpha_0 t_0)|y|} \tag{5.10}$$

and the zero-profit condition for A-good production at each y implies that

$$R(y) = p_0(y) - a_0 W(y) \equiv e^{-t_0|y|} - a_0 W(y) \quad \text{for } y \in [-l, l] \tag{5.11}$$

Because $R(l) = 0$ at the fringe location l, it holds by (5.11) that $e^{-t_0 l} = a_0 W(l)$, which together with (5.10) yields

$$W(y) = a_0^{-1} e^{-\alpha_1(t_0 + t_1)l} e^{(\alpha_1 t_1 - \alpha_0 t_0)|y|} \tag{5.12}$$

Next, because of the optimal pricing by each monopolistically competitive firm at the city, we have the following familiar result:[6]

$$p_1 = a_1 W(0) \rho_1^{-1} \tag{5.13}$$

---

[6] By the assumption of an iceberg transport cost function, it can readily be shown that the price elasticity of the total demand for each firm's output equals the price elasticity of each consumer's demand for that good, given by (5.4). Thus, by the equality of marginal revenue and marginal cost, $p_1(1 - E_1^{-1}) = a_0 W(0)$, we have (5.13).

That is, each firm will charge its f.o.b. price at a markup over the marginal cost $a_1 W(0)$. Substitution of (5.12) into (5.13) yields

$$p_1 = a_1 (a_0 \rho_1)^{-1} e^{-\alpha_1 (t_0 + t_1) l} \tag{5.14}$$

If q is the output of each firm in the city, then its profit equals $p_1 q - W(0)(f_1 + a_1 q) = W(0)\{a_1(\rho_1^{-1} - 1)q - f_1\}$ [by (5.13)] $= W(0)(a_1 \gamma_1^{-1} q - f_1)$. Thus, by the zero-profit condition, we have

$$q = \gamma_1 f_1 / a_1 \tag{5.15}$$

To determine the number of firms, n, in the city, if we let N_A be the number of agricultural workers, and N_M the number of manufacturing workers (in the city), then

$$N_A = 2a_0 l \tag{5.16}$$
$$N_M = n(f_1 + a_1 q) = n f_1 (1 + \gamma_1) \tag{5.17}$$

Hence, by the full-employment condition, $N_A + N_M = N$, we have

$$n = \frac{N - 2a_0 l}{f_1 (1 + \gamma_1)} \tag{5.18}$$

Now, if we know l (the fringe distance of the agricultural area), all unknowns will be determined uniquely by (5.12)–(5.18). The value of l can be determined from the equality of demand for and supply of the A-good, as follows: By (5.3a) the excess supply of the A-good per unit distance at each $y \neq 0$ equals $1 - [\alpha_0 Y(y)/p_0(y)]$ [where $Y(y) \equiv a_0 W(y) + R(y) = p_0(y)$, by (5.11)] $= 1 - \alpha_0 = \alpha_1$. Thus, considering the consumption of the A-good in transportation, the total excess supply of the A-good to the city equals

$$\int_{-l}^{l} \alpha_1 e^{-t_0 |y|} \, dy = 2\alpha_1 t_0^{-1} \left(1 - e^{-t_0 l}\right)$$

and the total demand for the A-good at the city equals $\alpha_0 Y(0)/p_0(0)$ [where $Y(0) = W(0)N_M$ and $p_0(0) = 1$] $= \alpha_0 W(0)N_M = \alpha_0 a_0^{-1}(N - 2a_0 l)e^{-\alpha_1 (t_0 + t_1) l}$ [by (5.12), (5.17), and (5.18)]. Thus, the equality of supply and demand requires that

$$\frac{\alpha_0}{\alpha_1} \left(\frac{N}{2a_0} - l \right) = \frac{1}{t_0} (1 - e^{-t_0 l}) e^{\alpha_1 (t_0 + t_1) l} \tag{5.19}$$

which uniquely determines the equilibrium fringe distance l^*, as demonstrated

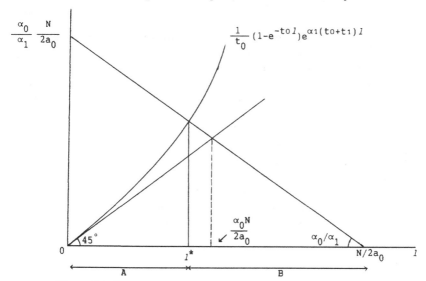

Figure 5.4. Determination of the fringe distance l^* for a monocentric equilibrium.

in Figure 5.4.[7] In the figure, because $N_A = 2a_0 l^*$, we have

$$\frac{A}{A+B} = \frac{N_A}{N} \quad \text{(the share of rural population)}$$

$$\frac{B}{A+B} = \frac{N_M}{N} \quad \text{(the share of urban population)}$$

Substituting l^* into (5.12)–(5.18), all unknowns can be determined. In particular, by (5.10) and (5.18) we have

$$u_1^* = -\alpha_0\alpha_1(t_0 + t_1)l^* + \frac{\alpha_1}{\gamma_1}\log\frac{N - 2a_0l^*}{f_1(1 + \gamma_1)} + \log\alpha_0^{\alpha_0}\alpha_1^{\alpha_1}a_0^{-\alpha_0}a_1^{-\alpha_1}\rho_1^{\alpha_1} \quad (5.20)$$

$$W^*(y) = a_0^{-1}e^{-\alpha_1(t_0+t_1)l^*}e^{(\alpha_1 t_1 - \alpha_0 t_0)|y|} \quad (5.21)$$

---

[7] Note that, in Figure 5.4, if both t_0 and t_1 decrease toward zero, then the curve $t_0^{-1}(1 - e^{t_0 l})e^{\alpha_1(t_0 + t_1)l}$ approaches the 45° line. Hence, if there is no transport cost (i.e., $t_0 = 0 = t_1$), then $l^* = \alpha_0 N/(2a_0)$, and thus $N_A/N = \alpha_0$ and $N_M/N = \alpha_1 (= 1 - \alpha_0)$. Introduction of transport cost makes the agricultural area shrink by substituting M_1-goods for the A-good (to save transport costs for the economy), which in turn makes the rural-population share decrease.

4.2 *The Potential Function and Location Equilibrium for* M_1-*firms*

For the previously determined spatial configuration to be really in equilibrium, we must make sure that (1) no existing M_1-firm can increase its profit by moving away from the city and (2) no new M_1-firm can enter the market. In the present context, however, conditions (1) and (2) are the same. That is, because each firm is of zero measure, neither a change in the location of one existing firm nor an entry by a new firm at any location can alter the present spatial configuration (including all associated price variables) of the economy. Hence, for both (1) and (2), it is sufficient to check that given the present spatial configuration, no (new or existing) M_1-firm can earn a positive profit at any location.

Suppose an M_1-firm locates at $x \in \mathbb{R}$. Then, given the market wage rate $W^*(x)$ at x, the firm will set its f.o.b. price at $a_1 W^*(x)\rho_1^{-1}$ [recall the derivation of (5.13)]. Hence, at each location $y \in \mathbb{R}$, the delivered price $p_1(y\,|\,x)$ of the M_1-good produced by the firm (located at x) is given by

$$p_1(y\,|\,x) = a_1 W^*(x)\rho_1^{-1}e^{t_1|y-x|} \tag{5.22}$$

Using (5.22) as a function of the market wage rate $W^*(x)$ there, the total demand for the firm located at x can be obtained as follows (see the Appendix for the derivation):

$$D_1[x, W^*(x)] = \frac{\alpha_0\gamma_1 f_1}{2a_1}\left(\frac{W^*(0)}{W^*(x)}\right)^{1+\gamma_1}\varphi_1(x) \quad \text{for } x \geq 0 \tag{5.23}$$

where

$$\varphi_1(x) \equiv e^{-\gamma_1 t_1 x}\left\{\frac{2\alpha_1}{\alpha_0} + \frac{t_0}{1-e^{-t_0 l^*}}e^{\gamma_1 t_1 x}\int_{-l^*}^{l^*}e^{-t_0|y|}e^{\gamma_1 t_1(|y|-|y-x|)}\,dy\right\}$$

$$= e^{-\gamma_1 t_1 x}\left\{\frac{1+\alpha_1}{\alpha_0} + \frac{t_0}{2\gamma_1 t_1 - t_0}\frac{e^{(2\gamma_1 t_1 - t_0)x}-1}{1-e^{-t_0 l^*}}\right.$$

$$\left. + \frac{1-e^{-t_0(l^*-x)}}{1-e^{-t_0 l^*}}e^{(2\gamma_1 t_1 - t_0)x}\right\} \tag{5.24}$$

The firm's resulting profit is

$$\pi_1[x, W^*(x)] = a_1 W^*(x)\rho_1^{-1}D_1[x, W^*(x)]$$

$$- W^*(x)\{f_1 + a_1 D_1[x, W^*(x)]\}$$

$$= W^*(x)\{D_1[x, W^*(x)] - \gamma_1 f_1/a_1\} \tag{5.25}$$

which implies that $\pi_1[x, W^*(x)] \gtreqless 0$ as $D_1[x, W^*(x)] \gtreqless \gamma_1 f_1/a_1$. For convenience, we define

$$\Omega_1(x) \equiv \frac{D_1[x, W^*(x)]}{\gamma_1 f_1/a_1} \tag{5.26}$$

Table 5.1. *Possibility of a monocentric equilibrium*

$\alpha_0 t_0 \leq (1 + \rho_1)\alpha_1 t_1$		$\alpha_0 t_0 > (1 + \rho_1)\alpha_1 t_1$
$\alpha_1 \geq \rho_1$	$\alpha_1 < \rho_1$	
		never
always	for small N	

where $\gamma_1 f_1 / a_1$ represents the equilibrium output level (for each existing M_1-firm) determined by the zero-profit condition [recall (5.15)]. By definition, then, it is obvious that

$$\pi_1[x, W^*(x)] \gtreqless 0 \Leftrightarrow \Omega_1(x) \gtreqless 1 \tag{5.27}$$

Following Krugman (1991), we call $\Omega_1(x)$ the (market) potential function for M_1-industry, which represents the relative profitability at each location for M_1-firms.

By (5.23) and (5.26), for $x \geq 0$, we have

$$\begin{aligned}
\Omega_1(x) &= \frac{\alpha_0}{2}\varphi_1(x)e^{(1+\gamma_1)(\alpha_0 t_0 - \alpha_1 t_1)x} \\
&= \frac{\alpha_0}{2}e^{-\tau x}\left\{ \frac{1+\alpha_1}{\alpha_0} + \frac{t_0}{2\gamma_1 t_1 - t_0}\frac{e^{(2\gamma_1 t_1 - t_0)x} - 1}{1 - e^{-t_0 l^*}} \right. \\
&\quad \left. + \frac{1 - e^{-t_0(l^* - x)}}{1 - e^{-t_0 l^*}}e^{(2\gamma_1 t_1 - t_0)x} \right\}
\end{aligned} \tag{5.28}$$

where

$$\tau \equiv (1 + \gamma_1)(\alpha_1 t_1 - \alpha_0 t_0) + \gamma_1 t_1 \tag{5.29}$$

Therefore, we can conclude that for the symmetric monocentric configuration obtained in Section 4.2 to be in equilibrium, it is necessary and sufficient that

$$\Omega_1(x) \leq 1 \quad \text{for } x \geq 0 \tag{5.30}$$

Examining condition (5.30), we can investigate under what conditions the monocentric configuration is in equilibrium. Table 5.1 summarizes the results.[8]

---

[8] For derivation of the results in Table 5.1, refer to Appendix B of Fujita and Krugman (1995).

Because $\Omega_1(0) = 1$ by definition, the monocentric configuration can be in equilibrium only if $\Omega_1(x)$ is not increasing at $x = 0$. By (5.23) and (5.28),

$$\Omega_1'(0) = (1 + \gamma_1) \left\{ \frac{W^{*\prime}(0)}{W^*(0)} + \frac{\varphi_1'(0)}{\varphi_1(0)} (1 + \gamma_1)^{-1} \right\}$$

$$= (1 + \gamma_1) \left\{ \underbrace{(\alpha_0 t_0 - \alpha_1 t_1)}_{\substack{\text{wage pull} \\ \text{toward} \\ \text{the fringe}}} - \underbrace{\rho_1 \alpha_1 t_1}_{\substack{\text{demand pull} \\ \text{of city workers} \\ \text{toward the center}}} \right\} \qquad (5.31)$$

where $\Omega_1'(0) \equiv d\Omega(x)/dx$ at $x = 0$, for example. Hence, if $\alpha_0 t_0 - \alpha_1 t_1 > \rho_1 \alpha_1 t_1$, for example, then when a firm moves a short distance away from the city, the wage rate is decreasing sufficiently fast, while the demand for its product is not decreasing much. In this case, the firm finds it more profitable to move away from the city; hence, as shown in the top row in Table 5.1, the monocentric configuration can never be in equilibrium. This can happen, for example, when the transport cost for the A-good (weighted by expenditure share α_0) is very high in comparison with that for the M_1-goods.

Next, given that $\alpha_0 t_0 \le (1 + \rho_1)\alpha_1 t_1$, the criterion on the second row in Table 5.1 is based on whether or not a firm can become more profitable by moving far away from the city (and by focusing on the local demand by agricultural workers in the periphery).[9] If M_1-goods are highly differentiated from one another, so that $\alpha_1 > \rho_1$, then the price elasticity of each M_1-good is very low. In this case, by moving into the periphery, a firm does not find a great increase in the local demand there, while the demand from the rest of the economy decreases. Rather, each M_1-firm finds it most profitable to locate at the center of the entire demand of the economy (i.e., at the city). Thus, as noted in the table, when $\alpha_1 > \rho_1$, the monocentric pattern is always an equilibrium configuration. Conversely, if M_1-goods are highly substitutable for one another, so that $\alpha_1 < \rho_1$, then given that all other firms stay at the city, a firm that moves into the periphery can capture a large share of local demand there. A large population N implies a large periphery around the city. Thus, when N is large, a large local demand in the periphery makes a firm locating there more profitable than in the city. Therefore, as noted in the table, when $\alpha_1 < \rho_1$, the monocentric configuration can be in equilibrium only if N is relatively small.

Figure 5.5 demonstrates the last conclusion numerically. In this numerical example, except for the population N, all parameters are fixed, such that $\alpha_0 = \alpha_1 = 0.5$, $a_0 = 0.5$, $t_0 = 0.9$, $t_1 = 1$, and $\rho_1 = 0.8$ (i.e., $\gamma_1 = 4$), implying that

---

[9] Note that this criterion (of the second row in Table 5.1) is identical with that of Krugman (1995) for a monocentric equilibrium. For example, the condition $\alpha_1 < \rho_1$ is equivalent to that of equation (25) in the appendix of Krugman (1995).

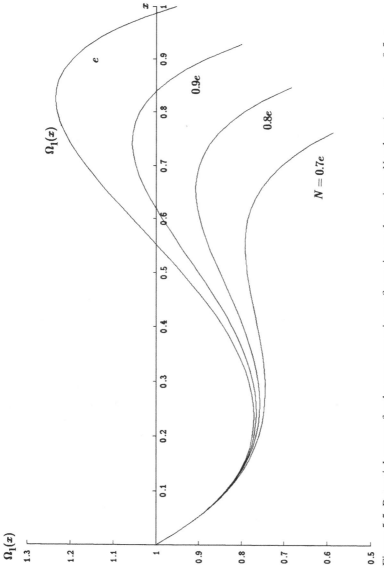

Figure 5.5. Potential curves for the monocentric configuration under various N values ($\alpha_0 = \alpha_1 = 0.5$, $t_0 = 0.9$, $t_1 = 1.0$, $\rho_1 = 0.8$).

Type A

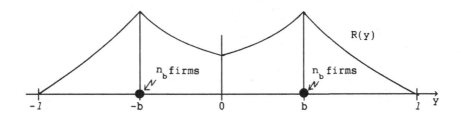

Type B

Figure 5.6. Two types of symmetric duocentric configurations.

$\alpha_0 t_0 < (1 + \rho_1)\alpha_1 t_1$ and $\alpha_1 < \rho_1$.[10] Thus, we have the situation in the middle part of Table 5.1. We can see from Figure 5.5 that as the population N continues to increase from $0.7e$, the potential curve $\Omega_1(x)$ eventually begins to exceed 1 in the periphery. Thus, the monocentric configuration can be in equilibrium only when N is relatively small. When N is sufficiently large, an equilibrium spatial configuration will contain more than one city.[11]

5 Duocentric Equilibria

In this section we examine (symmetric) duocentric spatial configurations. As depicted in Figure 5.6, there are two types of duocentric configurations. In a type-A configuration, the hinterlands of two cities are connected; in a type-B configuration, they are disjoint. We shall study each type in turn.

---

[10] Note that (5.19) and (5.28) do not involve the parameters a_1 and f_1, and hence the potential function $\Omega_1(x)$ is independent of these parameters.

[11] For the comparative statics of the monocentric equilibrium, refer to Fujita and Krugman (1995).

5.1 Type-A Duocentric Configurations

The production of all M_1-goods is assumed to take place in two cities, located at $y = b$ and $y = -b$. The same numbers n_b $(\equiv n_{-b})$ of firms are assumed to operate in the two cities, each firm producing a different variety of M_1-goods. The agricultural land extends continuously from $-l$ to l. Then, normalizing $p_0(b) = p_0(-b) = 1$, the price curve for the A-good (which supports the transportation of excess A-good to the two cities) is given by

$$p_0(y) = e^{-t_0||y|-b|} \tag{5.32}$$

Provided that all firms in the two cities charge the same f.o.b. price p_1, then at each $y \in \mathbb{R}$, the delivered price $p_1(y \mid b)$ [respectively $p_1(y \mid -b)$] for each M_1-good produced in city b [respectively city $-b$] is given by

$$p_1(y \mid b) = p_1 e^{t_1|y-b|} \tag{5.33a}$$

$$p_1(y \mid -b) = p_1 e^{t_1|y+b|} \tag{5.33b}$$

Using these price functions and the indirect utility function (5.5), in a manner similar to (5.10)–(5.18), we can determine all other unknowns as functions of the equilibrium agricultural fringe l^* as follows:[12]

$$u_2^A = -\alpha_0\alpha_1(t_0 + t_1)(l^* - b) + \frac{\alpha_1}{\gamma_1}\log\left(\frac{N - 2a_0l^*}{f_1(1 + \gamma_1)}\frac{1 + e^{-2\gamma_1 t_1 b}}{2}\right)$$
$$+ \log\alpha_0^{\alpha_0}\alpha_1^{\alpha_1}a_0^{-\alpha_0}a_1^{-\alpha_1}\rho_1^{\alpha_1} \tag{5.34}$$

$$W^*(y) = a_0^{-1}e^{-\alpha_1 t_0(l^* - b)}p_0(y)^{\alpha_0}\left\{\frac{e^{-\gamma_1 t_1|l^*-b|} + e^{-\gamma_1 t_1|l^*+b|}}{e^{-\gamma_1 t_1|y-b|} + e^{-\gamma_1 t_1|y+b|}}\right\}^{\alpha_1/\gamma_1} \tag{5.35}$$

$$R^*(y) = e^{-t_0||y|-b|} - a_0 W^*(y) \tag{5.36}$$

$$p_1^* = a_1 W^*(b)\rho_1^{-1} = a_1(a_0\rho_1)^{-1}e^{-\alpha_1(t_0+t_1)(l^*-b)} \tag{5.37}$$

$$q^* = a_1^{-1}\gamma_1 f_1 \tag{5.38}$$

$$n_b^* = \frac{1}{2}\frac{N - 2a_0l^*}{f_1(1 + \gamma_1)} \tag{5.39}$$

$$N_A^* = 2a_0l^* \tag{5.40}$$

$$N_M^* = N - N_A^* = N - 2a_0l^* \tag{5.41}$$

where q^* is the output level for each M_1-firm (in city b and city $-b$).

---

[12] Again, u_2^A emphasizes that it is the equilibrium utility level associated with the duocentric equilibrium of type A.

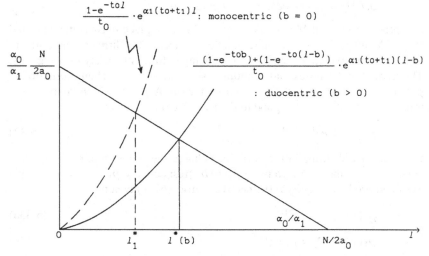

Figure 5.7. Determination of the fringe distance $l^*(b)$ for a type-A duocentric equilibrium.

By the equality of the demand for and supply of the A-good at each city, we can obtain the following relation:

$$\frac{\alpha_0}{\alpha_1}\left(\frac{N}{2a_0} - l\right) = \frac{(1 - e^{-t_0 b}) + \left(1 - e^{-t_0(l-b)}\right)}{t_0} e^{\alpha_1(t_0 + t_1)(l-b)} \quad (5.42)$$

which determines uniquely the equilibrium fringe, $l^* \equiv l^*(b)$, as a function of b. Figure 5.7 explains how to determine $l^*(b)$ for each given b.

Because the right-hand side (RHS) of (5.42) is decreasing in b (provided $b < l$), we can readily see from Figure 5.7 that $l^*(b)$ is increasing in b:

$$\frac{dl^*(b)}{db} > 0 \quad (5.43)$$

Hence, by (5.39)–(5.41), we can see that

$$\frac{dN_A^*}{db} > 0, \qquad \frac{dN_M^*}{db} < 0 \qquad \frac{dn_b^*}{db} < 0 \quad (5.44)$$

That is, as the distance between the two cities increases, the rural population N_A^* increases, and both the total urban population N_M^* and the total number $2n_b^*$ of M_1-firms (i.e., the extent of the variety of M_1-goods in the economy) decrease. The reason is that as the distance between the two cities increases, more agricultural land becomes available between the two cities. That, in turn, gives the urban population greater access to agricultural land. Therefore, a greater amount of the A-good will be produced, substituting for part of the M_1-goods. Consequently, N_A^* will increase, and both N_M^* and $2n_b^*$ will decrease.

In particular, note that when $b = 0$, the duocentric configuration degenerates into a monocentric configuration. Therefore, given the same set of parameters, any duocentric equilibrium (of type A) will have a greater N_A and smaller N_M and n than those of the monocentric equilibrium.

We can readily see by (5.35) that

$$W(b - \varepsilon) < W(b + \varepsilon) \quad \text{for } 0 \leq \varepsilon < b \tag{5.45}$$

and hence, by (5.36),

$$R(b - \varepsilon) > R(b + \varepsilon) \quad \text{for } 0 \leq \varepsilon < b \tag{5.46}$$

That is, given the same distance ε from city b, the wage rate (land rent) on the LHS for city b is lower (higher) than that on the RHS for city b. This is because workers (= consumers) at $b - \varepsilon$ have better access to the M_1-goods produced in city $-b$ than do workers at $b + \varepsilon$ (though they have the same access to the M_1-goods produced in city b). Hence, in achieving the same equilibrium utility u_2^A, workers at $b - \varepsilon$ can be paid lower wages than those at $b + \varepsilon$, which in turn makes the land rent at $b - \varepsilon$ higher than that at $b + \varepsilon$. Therefore, as shown in Figure 5.6, the land rent curve $R(y)$ is asymmetric with respect to city b (and city $-b$).

Note that for the spatial configuration defined by (5.34)–(5.42) to really represent a duocentric equilibrium of type A, two additional conditions need to be satisfied. First, for all the land between the two cities being used for agriculture, as can be seen from Figure 5.6, it must hold that $R(0) \geq 0$. Hence, for a type-A equilibrium, b cannot be too large. To determine the upper limit of b for type A, by substituting $l^*(b)$ for l^* in (5.35) and setting $R^*(0) = 0$ in (5.36), we obtain the following relation:

$$\frac{e^{2\gamma_1(t_0+t_1)b} + e^{\gamma_1 t_0 b}}{2} = e^{\gamma_1(t_0+t_1)l^*(b)} \tag{5.47}$$

Letting $\bar{b}_2$ be the unique solution to the foregoing equation for b, we can conclude that for the type-A configuration defined by (5.34)–(5.42) to be in equilibrium, it is necessary that[13]

$$b \leq \bar{b}_2 \tag{5.48}$$

---

[13] Using (5.42), we can readily see that (5.46) has a unique solution for b. Note that this solution, $\bar{b}_2$, depends on all other parameters of the model. In particular, it can be seen that $\bar{b}_2$ is increasing in N.

Second, we must make sure that no existing firm defects from the city and no new firm enters the economy. To do so, in a manner similar to (5.26), we define the following potential function for the case of a duocentric configuration of type A: For $x \geq 0$,

$$\Omega_2^A(x \mid b) \equiv D_1[x, W^*(x)]/(\gamma_1 f_1/a_1)$$

$$= \alpha_0 e^{(1+\gamma_1)\alpha_0 t_0 |x-b|} \left\{ \frac{e^{-\gamma_1 t_1 |x-b|} + e^{-\gamma_1 t_1 |x+b|}}{1 + e^{-2\gamma_1 t_1 b}} \right\}^{\alpha_1/\rho_1} \varphi_2^A(x \mid b) \tag{5.49}$$

where

$$\varphi_2^A(x \mid b) \equiv \frac{t_0 \displaystyle\int_0^{l^*} \frac{e^{-\gamma_1 t_1 |y+x|} + e^{-\gamma_1 t_1 |y-x|}}{e^{-\gamma_1 t_1 |y+b|} + e^{-\gamma_1 t_1 |y-b|}} e^{-t_0 |y-b|} \, dy}{\left(1 - e^{-t_0 b}\right) + \left(1 - e^{-t_0 (l^*-b)}\right)}$$

$$+ \frac{\alpha_1}{\alpha_0} \frac{e^{-\gamma_1 t_1 |x-b|} + e^{-\gamma_1 t_1 |x+b|}}{1 + e^{-2\gamma_1 t_1 b}} \tag{5.50}$$

Because $\pi_1[x, W^*(x)] \leq 0$ if and only if $\Omega_2^A(x \mid b) \leq 1$, we can conclude that the type-A duocentric configuration defined by (5.34)–(5.42) is in equilibrium if and only if the following condition holds, in addition to (5.48):

$$\Omega_2^A(x \mid b) \leq 1 \quad \text{for } x \geq 0 \tag{5.51}$$

Using (5.48) and (5.51), we can examine when a type-A monocentric configuration emerges as an equilibrium. In particular, note that for $0 < x < b$,

$$\frac{\partial \Omega_2^A(x \mid b)/\partial x}{\Omega_2^A(x \mid b)} = \frac{\partial \log \Omega_2^A(x \mid b)}{\partial x}$$

$$= -(1+\gamma_1)\alpha_0 t_0 + (1+\gamma_1)\alpha_1 t_1 \frac{1 - e^{-\gamma_1 t_1 2x}}{1 + e^{-\gamma_1 t_1 2x}}$$

$$+ \frac{\partial \varphi_2^A(x \mid b)/\partial x}{\varphi_2^A(x \mid b)} \tag{5.52}$$

As b approaches zero, the last two terms of the foregoing equation approach zero. Hence, when b is small,

$$\frac{\partial \Omega_2^A(x \mid b)}{\partial x} \simeq -(1+\gamma_1)\alpha_0 t_0 \quad \text{for } 0 < x < b \tag{5.53}$$

Because $\Omega_2^A(b \mid b) = 1$ by definition, (5.53) implies that when b is small,

$$\Omega_2^A(x \mid b) \simeq 1 + (1+\gamma_1)\alpha_0 t_0 (b - x) > 1 \quad \text{for } 0 \leq x < b \tag{5.54}$$

Therefore, when two cities are very close, a duocentric configuration can never be in equilibrium. In other words, a duocentric configuration can be in equilibrium only when the two cities are sufficiently far apart.[14]

For a numerical example, Figures 5.8 and 5.9 depict potential curves for type-A duocentric configurations under various values of b. [Other parameters are fixed at $\alpha_0 = \alpha_1 = 0.5$, $t_0 = 0.9$, $t_1 = 1$, $\rho_1 = 0.8$ (i.e., $\gamma_1 = 4$), $N = e$.] In the context of this numerical example, we can conclude as follows: (1) When the two cities are very close, type-A duocentric configurations can never be in equilibrium (as suggested before). For example, when $b = 0.1$ (Figure 5.8), the potential curve exceeds 1 both for $x < 0.1$ and in the periphery.[15] (2) As can be seen from Figure 5.9, when b takes values between 0.28 and 0.52, a continuum of type-A duocentric equilibria is possible. (3) Figure 5.9 also suggests that when the two cities are too far apart, type-A duocentric configurations again are not in equilibrium.[16] Therefore, this numerical example suggests that although the locations of two cities in a type-A duocentric equilibria are not unique, they are confined to a relatively small range of b (i.e., the two cities should not be too close or too far apart).

5.2 Type-B Duocentric Configurations

In a type-B duocentric configuration, we assume that there remains vacant land from $y = -r$ to r (Figure 5.6). Then the previous agricultural curve, (5.32), now changes as

$$p_0(y, r) = e^{-t\|y|-b|} \quad \text{for } |y| \geq r \tag{5.55a}$$

$$p_0(y, r) = e^{-t_0(b-r)}e^{t_0(r-|y|)} = e^{-t_0(2r-b)}e^{-t_0|y|} \quad \text{for } |y| \leq r \tag{5.55b}$$

which depends on (an unknown variable) r. Here, it is assumed that if some workers reside in the area between $-r$ and r, the A-good for their consumption will be transported from the nearest agricultural location, r or $-r$. There are no changes in the price curves for M_1-goods, (5.33a) and (5.33b). Therefore, substituting $p_0(y, r)$ for $p_0(y)$ in (5.34)–(5.41), we can determine all other unknowns

---

[14] Intuitively, this is because when two cities are very close, then for an M_1-firm located between the two cities the total demand from the two cities is almost constant regardless of its location. By (5.32), however, the A-good price is almost linearly decreasing from $y = b$ toward $y = 0$, and hence the wage rate also is almost linearly decreasing in the same direction. Therefore, from the cost consideration, the firm finds $y = 0$ to be a more attractive location than either city.

[15] The reason for $\Omega_2(x \mid b)$ being greater than 1 in the central area was explained in footnote 14. When b is small, the potential curve $\Omega_2(x \mid b)$ also exceeds 1 in the far periphery, because there is a large local demand there.

[16] This is because when the two cities are too far apart, an M_1-firm that moves to the center (i.e., near $y = 0$) can tap a large local demand there.

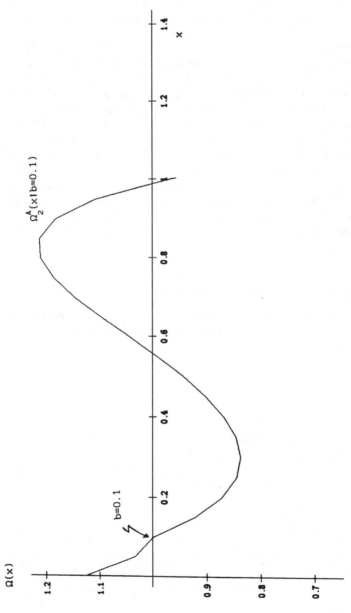

Figure 5.8. The potential curve for a duocentric configuration with $b = 0.1$ ($\alpha_0 = \alpha_1 = 0.5$, $a_0 = 0.5$, $t_0 = 0.9$, $t_1 = 1.0$, $\rho_1 = 0.8$, $N = e$).

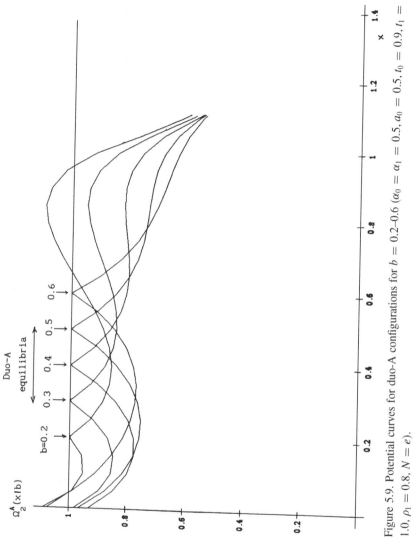

Figure 5.9. Potential curves for duo-A configurations for $b = 0.2$–0.6 ($\alpha_0 = \alpha_1 = 0.5$, $a_0 = 0.5$, $t_0 = 0.9$, $t_1 = 1.0$, $\rho_1 = 0.8$, $N = e$).

as functions of the equilibrium agricultural fringes, r^* and l^*, as follows:

$$u_2^B = -\alpha_0\alpha_1(t_0 + t_1)(l^* - b) + \frac{\alpha_1}{\gamma_1} \log\left(\frac{N - 2a_0(l^* - r^*)}{f_1(1 + \gamma_1)} \frac{1 + e^{-2\gamma_1 t_1 b}}{2}\right)$$
$$+ \log \alpha_0^{\alpha_0}\alpha_1^{\alpha_1}a_0^{-\alpha_0}a_1^{-\alpha_1}\rho_1^{\alpha_1} \tag{5.56}$$

$$W^*(y) = a_0^{-1}e^{-\alpha_1 t_0(l^* - b)}p_0(y, r)^{\alpha_0}\left\{\frac{e^{-\gamma_1 t_1|l^* - b|} + e^{-\gamma_1 t_1|l^* + b|}}{e^{-\gamma_1 t_1|y - b|} + e^{-\gamma_1 t_1|y + b|}}\right\}^{\alpha_1/\gamma_1} \tag{5.57}$$

Each of (5.36)–(5.41) remains the same, but in each of (5.39)–(5.41) l^* needs to be replaced by $l^* - b$.[17]

To determine l^* and r^*, first, by the condition $R(r) = 0 = R(l)$, we can obtain the following relation:

$$e^{-\gamma_1 t_0(l-b)}\left\{e^{-\gamma_1 t_1(l-b)} + e^{-\gamma_1 t_1(l+b)}\right\} = e^{-\gamma_1 t_0(b-r)}\left\{e^{-\gamma_1 t_1(b-r)} + e^{-\gamma_1 t_1(r+b)}\right\} \tag{5.58}$$

Next, by the equality of the demand for and supply of the A-good at each city, the following relation can be obtained:

$$\frac{\alpha_0}{\alpha_1}\left(\frac{N}{2a_0} - l\right) = \frac{\left(1 - e^{-t_0(b-r)}\right) + \left(1 - e^{-t_0(l-b)}\right)}{t_0}e^{\alpha_1(t_0 + t_1)(l-b)} \tag{5.59}$$

Solving (5.58) and (5.59) for r and l, we can determine the equilibrium values of r^* and l^*.

Given r^* and l^*, the potential function for the type-B duocentric configuration can be derived as follows:[18]

$$\Omega_2^B(x \mid b) = \alpha_0 e^{(1+\gamma_1)\alpha_0 t_0|x-b|}\left\{\frac{e^{-\gamma_1 t_1|x-b|} + e^{-\gamma_1 t_1|x+b|}}{1 + e^{-2\gamma_1 t_1 b}}\right\}^{\alpha_1/\rho_1} \varphi_2^B(x \mid b)$$
$$\text{for } x \geq r \quad (5.60a)$$

$$\Omega_2^B(x \mid b) = \alpha_0 e^{(1+\gamma_1)\alpha_0 t_0(2r^* - b - x)}\left\{\frac{e^{-\gamma_1 t_1|x-b|} + e^{-\gamma_1 t_1|x+b|}}{1 + e^{-2\gamma_1 t_1 b}}\right\}^{\alpha_1/\rho_1} \varphi_2^B(x \mid b)$$
$$\text{for } 0 \leq x \leq r \quad (5.60b)$$

---

[17] In these equations, of course, the actual value of l^* will be different from the previous one.

[18] Note that (5.60a) has the same form as (5.49), and (5.61) is different from (5.50) only in that the integral starts from $y = r^*$ instead of $y = 0$.

where

$$
\varphi_2^B(x \mid b) \equiv \frac{t_0 \int_{r^*}^{l^*} \dfrac{e^{-\gamma_1 t_1 |y+x|} + e^{-\gamma_1 t_1 |y-x|}}{e^{-\gamma_1 t_1 |y+b|} + e^{-\gamma_1 t_1 |y-b|}} e^{-t_0 |y-b|} \, dy}{\left(1 - e^{-t_0 b}\right) + \left(1 - e^{-t_0 (l^* - b)}\right)}
$$
$$
+ \frac{\alpha_1}{\alpha_0} \frac{e^{-\gamma_1 t_1 |x-b|} + e^{-\gamma_1 t_1 |x+b|}}{1 + e^{-2\gamma_1 t_1 b}} \tag{5.61}
$$

Therefore, the spatial configuration defined by (5.56)–(5.59) and (5.36)–(5.41) is a type-B duocentric equilibrium if and only if $r^* \geq 0$ and

$$
\Omega_2^B(x \mid b) \leq 1 \quad \text{for all } x \geq 0 \tag{5.62}
$$

Suppose that we have two different spatial configurations of type B: One corresponds to a city-location parameter b, and the other corresponds to b'. Then it can readily be shown that

$$
b < b' \Rightarrow \Omega_2^B(b - \varepsilon \mid b) > \Omega_2^B(b' - \varepsilon \mid b') \quad \text{for all } \varepsilon > -b', \varepsilon \neq 0 \tag{5.63}
$$

Because $\Omega_2^B(b \mid b) \equiv 1 \equiv \Omega_2^B(b' \mid b')$, (5.63) implies that

$$
\Omega_2^B(x \mid b) \leq 1 \quad \text{for all } x \geq 0 \Rightarrow \Omega_2^B(x \mid b') \leq 1 \quad \text{for all } x \geq 0 \tag{5.64}
$$

Therefore, we can conclude that given a city-location parameter b, if the corresponding type-B duocentric configuration is in equilibrium, then it is in equilibrium for any $b' > b$. Figure 5.10 presents a numerical example demonstrating that conclusion. We see that for any given $b \geq 0.65$, the associated potential curve never exceeds 1. Therefore (when other parameters are fixed at $\alpha_0 = \alpha_1 = 0.5, t_0 = 0.9, t_1 = 1.0, \rho_1 = 0.8$, and $N = e$), there exists a continuum of type-B duocentric equilibria.

5.3 Comparison of Type-A and Type-B Duocentric Equilibria and Monocentric Equilibria

On the horizontal axis of Figure 5.10, the range of b in which a duocentric configuration can be in equilibrium is indicated (this range was transferred from Figure 5.9). We can see from Figure 5.10 that under the same set of parameters (noted in the legends for Figures 5.9 and 5.10), there exists a continuum of duo-A equilibria, as well as a continuum of duo-B equilibria. It is therefore, interesting to compare the equilibrium utility levels associated with these equilibria. Figure 5.11 presents the result: The duo-A equilibrium utility level continues to increase as the two cities become farther apart. This means that

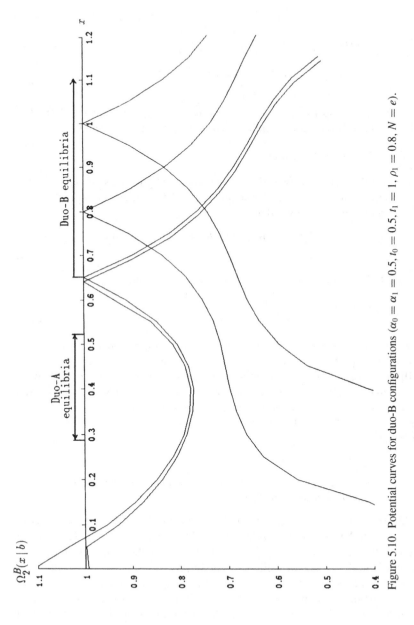

Figure 5.10. Potential curves for duo-B configurations ($\alpha_0 = \alpha_1 = 0.5$, $t_0 = 0.5$, $t_1 = 1$, $\rho_1 = 0.8$, $N = e$).

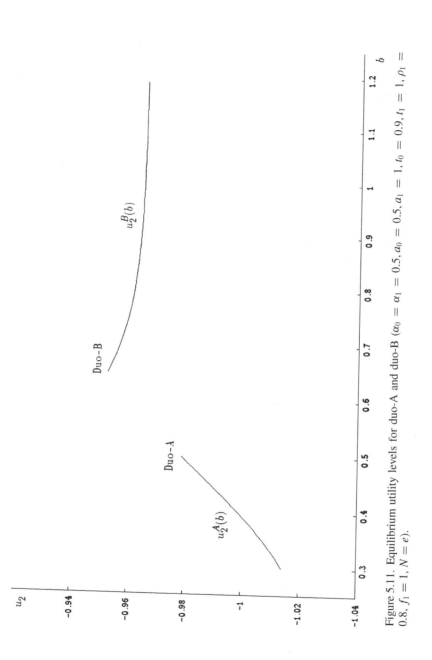

Figure 5.11. Equilibrium utility levels for duo-A and duo-B ($\alpha_0 = \alpha_1 = 0.5, a_0 = 0.5, a_1 = 1, t_0 = 0.9, t_1 = 1, \rho_1 = 0.8, f_1 = 1, N = e$).

the positive effect of increasing the agricultural land between the two cities continues to overwhelm the negative effect of increasing distance (between the two cities) on the trading of M-goods (produced in the two cities) in the economy.

Among all duo-B equilibria, the equilibrium utility level is highest when the two cities are the closest. This is not surprising, because when vacant land exists between the two cities, there is no benefit from further increasing the vacant land there, and the trading of M-goods between the two "separated states" becomes more difficult as they move farther apart.

Next, recall that in the numerical example of Figure 5.5, when $N = e$, the monocentric configuration is not in equilibrium, whereas Figures 5.9 and 5.10 show that under the same set of parameters there is a continuum of both type-A and type-B duocentric equilibria. This suggests that given a monocentric equilibrium, if the population N continues to increase, then the spatial configuration may eventually switch to duocentric.

Finally, although the existence of a duocentric equilibrium does not always assure the existence (or nonexistence) of a monocentric equilibrium, we can infer the existence of a continuum of duocentric equilibria from the existence of a monocentric equilibrium. That is, suppose that given a set of parameters (including population N), the monocentric configuration is in equilibrium. Then, by Table 5.1, it must be that $\alpha_0 t_0 \leq (1 + \rho_1)\alpha_1 t_1$. In this situation (regardless of whether $\alpha_1 \geq \rho_1$ or $\alpha_1 < \rho_1$), if N changes to any smaller number while all other parameters remain the same, the monocentric configuration continues to be in equilibrium. This implies that for any sufficiently large b, the corresponding duo-B configuration must be an equilibrium. This is because when the two cities are sufficiently far apart (e.g., $b \simeq \infty$), then the duo-B configuration consists of two "almost-isolated" states, each having population $N/2$. Because each "completely isolated" state having population $N/2$ is ensured to be in equilibrium, a system of two almost-isolated states will also be in equilibrium. And, as noted earlier, the existence of one duo-B equilibrium implies the existence of a continuum of duo-B equilibria (with different values of b).

6 Tricentric Equilibria

As shown in Figure 5.12, there are three types of (symmetric) tricentric spatial configurations. In a tri-A configuration (top), the excess A-good will always be transported inwardly. For this to happen, the two "side cities" must be relatively small in comparison with the central city. Hence, they can be interpreted as satellite cities of the central metropolis. In contrast, in a tri-B configuration (middle), each city has its own agricultural hinterland. Thus, the economy consists of a system of three regions, each having its own core city. Finally, a

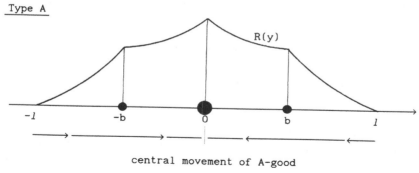

central movement of A-good

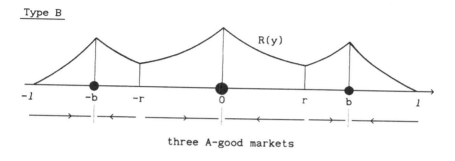

three A-good markets

three A-good markets

Figure 5.12. Three types of tricentric configurations.

tri-C configuration (bottom) consists of three semi-isolated states. Note, however, that because the M-goods produced in any one city will be exported to two other states, the three states are actually not isolated economically. Because tri-C configurations can be interpreted as special cases of tri-B configurations, in the following we shall focus on tri-A and tri-B configurations.

6.1 Tri-A Configurations

Suppose that n_0 varieties of M-goods will be produced in the central city (c-city) at $y = 0$, and n_b ($\equiv n_{-b}$) varieties in each satellite city (s-city), located respectively at $y = b$ and $y = -b$. Normalizing $p_0(0) \equiv 1$, the A-good price curve (supporting the central movement of the A-good) is given by

$$p_0(y) = e^{-t_0|y|} \tag{5.65}$$

which is the same as (5.8). Let p_{10} be the f.o.b price for each M_1-good produced in the c-city, and $p_{1b}(\equiv p_{1-b})$ that for each M_1-good produced in the two s-cities. Then, at each $y \in \mathbb{R}$, the delivered price for each M_1-good produced in the three cities (i.e., the c-city and the s-city at $y = b$, and the s-city at $y = -b$) is given by

$$p_1(y \mid 0) = p_{10}e^{t_1|y|} \tag{5.66a}$$

$$p_1(y \mid b) = p_{1b}e^{t_1|y-b|} \tag{5.66b}$$

$$p_1(y \mid -b) = p_{1b}e^{t_1|y+b|} \tag{5.66c}$$

On the basis of these price curves, we can, as before, obtain the following system of equations:

$$u_3^A = -\alpha_0\alpha_1(t_0 + t_1)l + \frac{\alpha_1}{\gamma_1}\log n_0 + \log \alpha_0^{\alpha_0}\alpha_1^{\alpha_1}a_0^{-\alpha_0}a_1^{-\alpha_1}\rho_1^{\alpha_1}$$

$$+ \frac{\alpha_0\alpha_1}{\gamma_1}\log\{1 + B(e^{\gamma_1 t_1 b} + e^{-\gamma_1 t_1 b})\} + \frac{\alpha_1^2}{\gamma_1}\log(1 + 2Be^{-\gamma_1 t_1 b}) \tag{5.67}$$

$$W(y) = a_0^{-1}e^{-\alpha_1(t_0+t_1)l}p_0(y)^{\alpha_0}e^{\alpha_1 t_1|y|}$$

$$\times \left\{ \frac{1 + B(e^{\gamma_1 t_1 b} + e^{-\gamma_1 t_1 b})}{1 + B\left(e^{-\gamma_1 t_1|y-b|} + e^{-\gamma_1 t_1|y+b|}\right)e^{\gamma_1 t_1|y|}} \right\}^{\alpha_1/\gamma_1} \tag{5.68}$$

$$R(y) = p_0(y) - a_0 W(y) \tag{5.69}$$

$$p_{10} = a_1 W(0)\rho_1^{-1}$$

$$= a_1(a_0\rho_1)^{-1}e^{-\alpha_1(t_0+t_1)l}\left\{ \frac{1 + B(e^{\gamma_1 t_1 b} + e^{-\gamma_1 t_1 b})}{1 + 2Be^{-\gamma_1 t_1 b}} \right\}^{\alpha_1/\gamma_1} \tag{5.70}$$

$$p_{1b} = a_1 W(b)\rho_1^{-1} = a_1(a_0\rho_1)^{-1}e^{-\alpha_1(t_0+t_1)l}e^{(\alpha_1 t_1 - \alpha_0 t_0)b} \tag{5.71}$$

$$q = a_1^{-1}\gamma_1 f_1 \tag{5.72}$$

$$N_A = 2a_0 l \tag{5.73}$$

$$N_M = N - N_A = N - 2a_0 l \tag{5.74}$$

where

$$B \equiv \frac{n_b}{n_0} \left(\frac{p_{10}}{p_{1b}} \right)^{\gamma_1} \tag{5.75}$$

The foregoing system of equations contains three unknowns, n_0, n_b, and l, that can be determined by the following there conditions. First, by the full-employment condition for the economy, we have that

$$n_0 + 2n_b = \frac{N - 2a_0 l}{f_1(1 + \gamma_1)} \tag{5.76}$$

Second, by the equality of the demand for and supply of the A-good at the c-city, and using (5.70) and (5.71), it follows that

$$n_{10} p_{10} + 2n_b p_{1b} = \frac{2\alpha_1 a_1 (1 - e^{-t_0 l})}{\alpha_0 t_0 f_1 (1 + \gamma_1) \rho_1} \tag{5.77}$$

Finally, the equality of the supply of and demand for the M_1-goods produced in the c-city means that

$$\frac{\gamma_1 f_1}{a_1} = \frac{\alpha_1 \rho_1}{a_1} \frac{(1 + \gamma_1) f_1}{1 + 2Be^{-\gamma_1 t_1 b}} + \frac{\alpha_1 \rho_1}{a_1} \frac{n_b p_{1b}}{n_0 p_{10}} \frac{2(1 + \gamma_1) f_1}{1 + B(e^{\gamma_1 t_1 b} + e^{-\gamma_1 t_1 b})}$$
$$+ \frac{\alpha_1}{n_0 p_{10}} \int_{-l}^{l} \frac{e^{-\gamma_1 t_1 |y|} p_0(y)}{e^{-\gamma_1 t_1 |y|} + B\left(e^{-\gamma_1 t_1 |y-b|} + e^{-\gamma_1 t_1 |y+b|}\right)} \, dy \tag{5.78}$$

Unfortunately, however, we cannot obtain closed-form solutions for the unknowns n_0, n_b, and l. Therefore, we must rely on a computer to get exact solutions.

For the spatial configuration determined by (5.67)–(5.78) to really represent a tori-A equilibrium, two additional conditions need to be satisfied. First, by the assumption of an inward movement of the excess A-good, the demand for the A-good by the s-city at b should not exceed the total excess supply of the A-good (net of transport consumption) from the area between b and l, which means that

$$\frac{\alpha_0}{a_0} f_1 (1 + \gamma_1) n_b e^{-\alpha_1 (t_0 + t_1)(l - b)} \leq \frac{\alpha_0}{t_0} \left\{ 1 - e^{-t_0 (l - b)} \right\} \tag{5.79}$$

Second, as usual, we obtain the potential function associated with the foregoing tri-A configuration, which is given by

$$\Omega_3^A (x \mid b) = \alpha_1 \left(\frac{W(0)}{W(b)} \right)^{1 + \gamma_1} \varphi_3^A (x \mid b) \tag{5.80}$$

where

$$\varphi_3^A(x \mid b) = \frac{e^{-\gamma_1 t_1 |x|}}{1 + 2Be^{-\gamma_1 t_1 b}} + \frac{n_b W(b)}{n_0 W(0)} \frac{\left(e^{-\gamma_1 t_1 |b-x|} + e^{-\gamma_1 t_1 |b+x|}\right) e^{\gamma_1 t_1 b}}{1 + B\left(e^{\gamma_1 t_1 b} + e^{-\gamma_1 t_1 b}\right)}$$

$$+ \frac{1}{f_1(1 + \gamma_1) n_0 W(0)}$$

$$\times \int_{-l^*}^{l^*} \frac{e^{-\gamma_1 t_1 |y-x|} p_0(y)}{e^{-\gamma_1 t_1 |y|} + B\left(e^{-\gamma_1 t_1 |y-b|} + e^{-\gamma_1 t_1 |y+b|}\right)} \, dy \tag{5.81}$$

To prevent any firm from leaving any city, it must hold that

$$\Omega_3^A(x \mid b) \le 1 \quad \text{for } x \ge 0 \tag{5.82}$$

Figure 5.13 presents a numerical example for tri-A equilibria. Under the fixed set of parameters noted in the legend for Figure 5.13, it turns out that there exists an upper limit $\bar{b} \simeq 0.8$ such that for each $b \in (0, \bar{b}]$ there always exists a unique tri-A equilibrium. Figure 5.13 depicts potential curves associated with several values of b in this equilibrium range. In the limit of b approaching zero, by definition, the tri-A equilibrium configuration becomes the monocentric equilibrium. On the other hand, if $b > \bar{b}$, then the associated tri-A configuration cannot be in equilibrium, because condition (5.79) would be violated if $b > \bar{b}$ (i.e., the area of agricultural land between $y = b$ and $y = l^*$ would be too small to support the s-city at b). Note that the equilibrium range of b is quite large.

Figure 5.14 demonstrates how the city size ratio, n_{1b}/n_{10}, changes with b. Note that because all firms employ the same number of workers, this ratio is identical with the ratio of the number of workers in an s-city to that in the c-city. As can be seen from the figure, the size of each s-city is always less than half that of the c-city. The reason is as follows. By definition of a tri-A configuration, the A-good price is highest at the c-city. Then for the workers in the c-city to achieve the same utility level as those workers in an s-city, the economies of scale in the consumption of M-goods must be greater in the c-city than in an an s-city. This means that a greater variety of M-goods must be produced in the c-city than in an s-city, and hence the c-city will have a larger population. Because the A-good price ratio, $p_0(0)/p_0(b) \equiv e^{t_0 b}$, keeps increasing in b, for the foregoing reason the city size ratio, $n_{1b}(b)/n_{10}(b)$, must be decreasing in b, as demonstrated in Figure 5.14.[19]

---

[19] Actually, in Figure 5.14, the city size ratio starts increasing slightly from $b \simeq 0.7$. The reason is as follows. As can be seen in Figure 5.13, the potential curve for the monocentric configuration [i.e., $\Omega_3^A(x \mid b = 0)$] is rapidly decreasing beyond $x \simeq 0.7$. Given this situation, in order to transform the monocentric equilibrium to a tri-A equilibrium by creating an s-city at $x > 0.7$, the s-city needs a relatively large population in order to generate agglomeration economies of sufficient size there.

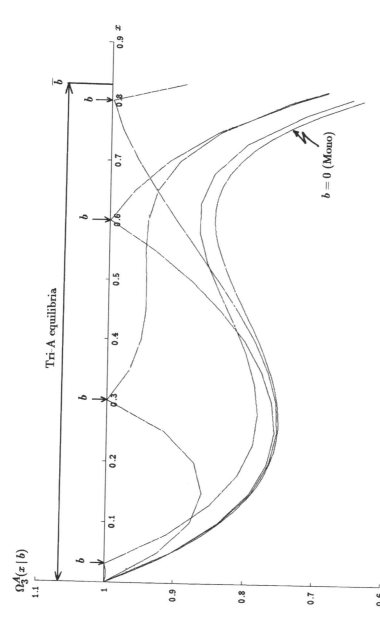

Figure 5.13. Potential curves for tri-A configurations ($\alpha_0 = \alpha_1 = 0.5$, $a_0 = 0.5$, $a_1 = 1$, $t_0 = 0.9$, $t_1 = 1$, $\rho_1 = 0.8$, $N = 0.75e$).

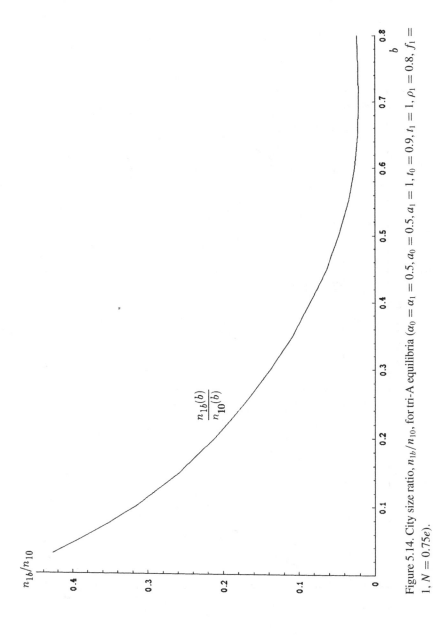

Figure 5.14. City size ratio, n_{1b}/n_{10}, for tri-A equilibria ($\alpha_0 = \alpha_1 = 0.5$, $a_0 = 0.5$, $a_1 = 1$, $t_0 = 0.9$, $t_1 = 1$, $\rho_1 = 0.8$, $f_1 = 1$, $N = 0.75e$).

Figure 5.15 explains how the equilibrium utility level changes with b. As b continues to increase from zero, the equilibrium utility level first decreases for $b < 0.2$. This is because when the two s-cities are close to the c-city, the positive effect of introducing more agricultural land between the two s-cities is relatively small in comparison with the negative effect of increasing the distances among the three cities on the trading of M-goods. For the converse reason, if b exceeds about 0.2, then the equilibrium utility level starts increasing. Therefore, in the context of this numerical example, we can conclude that the equilibrium utility level associated with a tri-A configuration is highest when the two satellite cities are farthest from the metropolis.

6.2 Tri-B Configurations

Now we turn to the tri-B configuration depicted in the middle of Figure 5.12. Let $p(y, r)$ be the associated price function for the A-good. Then, normalizing $p(b, r) = p(-b, r) = 1$, in order to support the transportation of excess A-good as indicated in the figure, it must hold that

$$p_0(y, r) = e^{t_0(2r-b)} e^{-t_0|y|} \quad \text{for } |y| \le r \tag{5.83a}$$

$$p_0(y, r) = e^{-t_0||y|-b|} \quad \text{for } |y| \ge r \tag{5.83b}$$

As before, the price functions for M_1-goods are given by (5.66a)–(5.66c). Because the only change from the previous tri-A case is in the A-good price function, the previous system of equations, (5.67)–(5.75), changes only slightly, as follows:

$$u_3^B = -\alpha_0\alpha_1(t_0 + t_1)(l - b) + \frac{\alpha_1}{\gamma_1}\log n_0 + \log \alpha_0^{\alpha_0}\alpha_1^{\alpha_1}a_0^{-\alpha_0}a_1^{-\alpha_1}\rho_1^{\alpha_1}$$

$$+ \frac{\alpha_0\alpha_1}{\gamma_1}\log\{1 + B(e^{\gamma_1 t_1 b} + e^{-\gamma_1 t_1 b})\} + \frac{\alpha_1^2}{\gamma_1}\log(1 + 2Be^{-\gamma_1 t_1 b}) \tag{5.84}$$

$$W(y) = a_0^{-1}e^{-\alpha_1(t_0+t_1)l}p_0(y, r)^{\alpha_0}e^{\alpha_1 t_1 |y|}$$

$$\times \left\{\frac{1 + B(e^{\gamma_1 t_1 b} + e^{-\gamma_1 t_1 b})}{1 + B\left(e^{-\gamma_1 t_1 |y-b|} + e^{-\gamma_1 t_1 |y+b|}\right)e^{\gamma_1 t_1 |y|}}\right\}^{\alpha_1/\gamma_1} \tag{5.85}$$

$$R(y) = p_0(y, r) - a_0 W(y) \tag{5.86}$$

and each of (5.70)–(5.75) remains the same.

To determine the remaining four unknowns, n_0, n_b, r, and l, first, by the full-employment condition of the economy, we obtain the same relation, (5.76). Second, by the equality of the demand for and supply of the A-good in the central

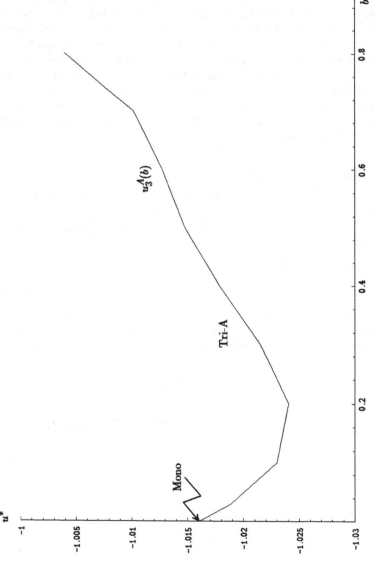

Figure 5.15. Equilibrium utility levels for tri-A configurations ($\alpha_0 = \alpha_1 = 0.5$, $a_0 = 0.5$, $a_1 = 1$, $t_0 = 0.9$, $t_1 = 1$, $\rho_1 = 0.8$, $f_1 = 1$, $N = 0.75e$).

city and in the city at $y = b$, we can obtain the following relations:

$$n_0 = \frac{2\alpha_1 a_1}{\alpha_0 f_1 (1 + \alpha_1)\rho_1 t_0}(1 - e^{-t_0 r})e^{t_0(2r-b)}p_{10}^{-1} \tag{5.87}$$

$$n_b = \frac{\alpha_1 a_1}{\alpha_0 f_1 (1 + \gamma_1)\rho_1 t_0}(2 - e^{-t_0(b-r)} - e^{-t_0(l-r)})p_{1b}^{-1} \tag{5.88}$$

Finally, replacing $p_0(y, r)$ by $p_0(y)$ in (5.78), the zero-excess-demand condition for the M-good produced in the central city is given by

$$\frac{\gamma_1 f_1}{a_1} = \frac{\alpha_1 \rho_1}{a_1}\frac{(1+\gamma_1)f_1}{1 + 2Be^{-\gamma_1 t_1 b}} + \frac{\alpha_1 \rho_1}{a_1}\frac{n_b p_{1b}}{n_0 p_{10}}\frac{2(1+\gamma_1)f_1}{1 + B(e^{\gamma_1 t_1 b} + e^{-\gamma_1 t_1 b})}$$

$$+ \frac{\alpha_1}{n_0 p_{10}}\int_{-l}^{l}\frac{e^{-\gamma_1 t_1 |y|}p_0(y, r)}{e^{-\gamma_1 t_1 |y|} + B(e^{-\gamma_1 t_1 |y-b|} + e^{-\gamma_1 t_1 |y+b|})}\,dy \tag{5.89}$$

For this tri-B configuration to really be in equilibrium, then, as usual, two additional conditions need to be satisfied. First, for no vacant land to be left between $-l$ and l, it must hold that

$$R(r) \equiv p_0(y, r) - a_0 W(r) \geq 0 \tag{5.90}$$

Second, replacing $p_0(y)$ by $p_0(y, r)$ in (5.81), let us define the potential function associated with the tri-B configuration as follows:

$$\Omega_3^B(x \mid b) = \alpha_1 \left(\frac{W(0)}{W(b)}\right)^{1+\gamma_1}\varphi_3^B(x \mid b) \tag{5.91}$$

where

$$\varphi_3^B(x \mid b) = \frac{e^{-\gamma_1 t_1 |x|}}{1 + 2Be^{-\gamma_1 t_1 b}} + \frac{n_b W(b)}{n_0 W(0)}\frac{(e^{-\gamma_1 t_1 |b-x|} + e^{-\gamma_1 t_1 |b+x|})e^{\gamma_1 t_1 b}}{1 + B(e^{\gamma_1 t_1 b} + e^{-\gamma_1 t_1 b})}$$

$$+ \frac{1}{f_1(1+\gamma_1)n_0 W(0)}$$

$$\times \int_{-l^*}^{l^*}\frac{e^{-\gamma_1 t_1 |y-x|}p_0(y, r)}{e^{-\gamma_1 t_1 |y|} + B(e^{-\gamma_1 t_1 |y-b|} + e^{-\gamma_1 t_1 |y+b|})}\,dy \tag{5.92}$$

Then, to prevent any firm from leaving any city, it must hold that

$$\Omega_3^B(x \mid b) \leq 1 \quad \text{for } x \geq 0 \tag{5.93}$$

Figure 5.16 presents a numerical example for tri-B equilibria. Under the set of parameters noted, a tri-B configuration is in equilibrium when b is between $\underline{b} \simeq 0.66$ and $\bar{b} \simeq 0.96$. If $b < \underline{b}$, then the excess demand for the M-goods produced in the central city becomes negative, and hence the configuration is not in equilibrium. If $b > \underline{b}$, then the land rent $R(r)$ at the boundary between the A-good markets of two cities becomes negative, and again the configuration

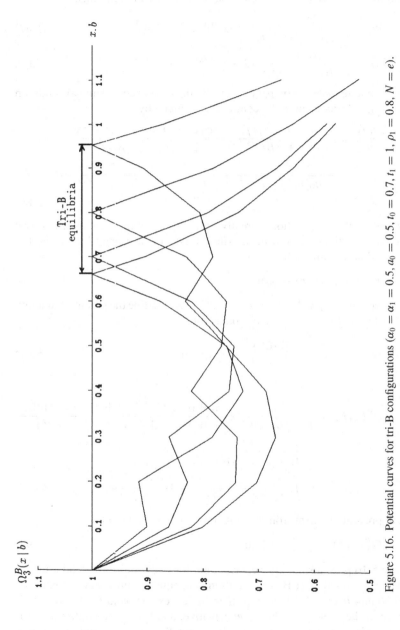

Figure 5.16. Potential curves for tri-B configurations ($\alpha_0 = \alpha_1 = 0.5$, $a_0 = 0.5$, $t_0 = 0.7$, $t_1 = 1$, $\rho_1 = 0.8$, $N = e$).

is not in equilibrium. (Note that each potential curve is kinked upward at r.) Therefore, for a tri-B to be in equilibrium, the two s-cities must be sufficiently far from the central city, but not too far. Note that in this numerical example we have $t_0 = 0.7$, whereas in all the previous examples we have $t_0 = 0.9$. This is because when $t_0 = 0.9$, then whether population N is larger or smaller than e, a tri-B configuration will never be in equilibrium (provided the other parameters are fixed at the same values as before). This suggests that a tri-B configuration can be in equilibrium only when the A-good transport cost, t_0, is sufficiently small.

Next, Figure 5.17 shows how the city size ratio, n_{1b}/n_{10}, changes with b, and Figure 5.18 shows the equilibrium land rent curve associated with each b. We can see from Figure 5.17 that the city size ratio is very sensitive to b, decreasing from $n_{1b}/n_{10} \simeq 2.4$ to 0.5 when b increases from 0.66 to 0.96. Accordingly, as can be seen from Figure 5.18, the land rent curve also is very sensitive to parameter b.

Finally, Figure 5.19 shows that the equilibrium utility level u_3^B increases monotonically in b. This is because a type-B configuration can be in equilibrium only when b is sufficiently large. Furthermore, when b is near its lower limit (≈ 0.66), the relative size of the c-city (in comparison with that of s-cities) is quite small (Figure 5.17), implying that the c-city plays little role in the supply of M-goods. Such a configuration obviously is not efficient for the supply of M-goods. This inefficiency in the supply of M-goods can be mitigated by moving s-cities away from the c-city, because the relative size of the c-city increases rapidly as b increases (Figure 5.17), resulting in enhancement of the equilibrium utility level of workers.

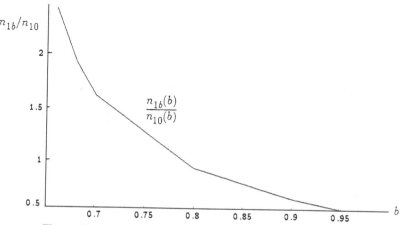

Figure 5.17. City size ratio, n_{1b}/n_{10}, for tri-B equilibria ($\alpha_0 = \alpha_1 = 0.5$, $a_0 = 0.5$, $a_1 = 1$, $t_0 = 0.7$, $t_1 = 1$, $\rho_1 = 0.8$, $f_1 = 1$, $N = e$).

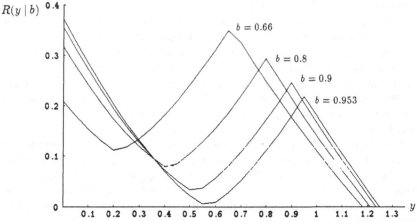

Figure 5.18. Land rent curves for tri-B equilibria ($\alpha_0 = \alpha_1 = 0.5$, $a_0 = 0.5$, $t_0 = 0.7$, $t_1 = 1$, $\rho_1 = 0.8$, $N = e$).

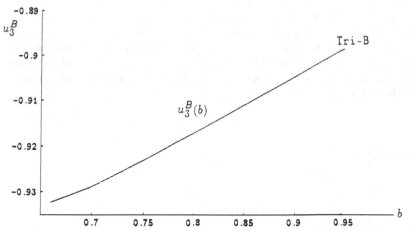

Figure 5.19. Equilibrium utility levels for tri-B configurations ($\alpha_0 = \alpha_1 = 0.5$, $a_0 = 0.5$, $a_1 = 1$, $t_0 = 0.7$, $t_1 = 1$, $\rho_1 = 0.8$, $f_1 = 1$, $N = e$).

7 Welfare Comparison and Structural Stability of Multiple Equilibria

As the results in the previous sections suggest, our model yields a high degree of locational and structural nonuniqueness of equilibria. For example, let us consider the set of parameters

$$\alpha_0 = \alpha_1 = 0.5, \, a_0 = 0.5, \, a_1 = 1, \, t_0 = 0.9, \, t_1 = 1,$$
$$\rho_1 = 0.8, \, f_1 = 1, \, N = 0.75e \qquad (5.94)$$

which were used most frequently in the earlier sections. Then, as indicated in Figure 5.20, under this set of parameters, the following configurations are simultaneously in equilibrium:[20]

(1) the monocentric configuration,
(2) the tri-A configuration for each value of $b \in (0, 0.8]$,[21]
(3) the duo-A configuration for each value of $b \in [0.35, 0.4]$, and
(4) the duo-B configuration for each value of $b \geq 5.2$.

Recall that in the case of a tri-A equilibrium, the parameter b represents the distance of a satellite city from the central metropolis; but in the cases of duo-A and duo-B equilibria, b represents half of the distance between the two cities. Taking this parameter b in the horizontal axis, Figure 5.20 shows equilibrium utility curves associated with the four types of equilibrium configurations. We can see from this figure that duocentric equilibria (both type A and type B) always yield higher equilibrium utility levels than do the monocentric equilibrium and the tri-A equilibria. The reason is that, given $\rho_1 = 0.8$, the monocentric equilibrium achieves the highest equilibrium utility when N equals $\hat{N} \simeq 0.6$. The actual value of $N = 0.75e = 2.039$ in (5.94), however, is more than three times $\hat{N}$. In other words, in the context of Figure 5.20, the metropolis of the monocentric equilibrium is far overcrowded. Therefore, by dividing the manufacturing production between two cities sufficiently far apart, the equilibrium utility can be increased. In particular, as indicated in Figure 5.20, the equilibrium utility level is highest for the duo-B equilibrium with the minimum $b \simeq 0.52$.

Remember that in our spatial economy there are two types of consumers: workers and landlords. Hence, for a welfare comparison of multiple equilibria, in addition to u^* ($\equiv$ the equilibrium utility of workers) we must also take into account the welfare of landlords. As an aggregate welfare measure for landlords, it is natural to consider the total real land rent (TRLR), defined by

$$\text{TRLR} \equiv \int_{-l}^{l} \frac{R(y)}{W(y)} \, dy \qquad (5.95)$$

---

[20] Although we have confirmed the four types of equilibrium configurations indicated in Figure 5.20, they do not necessarily exhaust the possible equilibrium configurations [under the set of parameters given by (5.94)]. We suspect, in particular, that the dispersed duocentric configuration depicted in Figure 5.2(d) might also be in equilibrium (for small values of b). Identification of all possible equilibrium configurations, however, must be left for the future.

[21] We can show that a tri-A configuration and a tri-B configuration cannot be in equilibrium simultaneously. Hence, because tri-A is in equilibrium under the parameter set (5.94), tri-B cannot be in equilibrium.

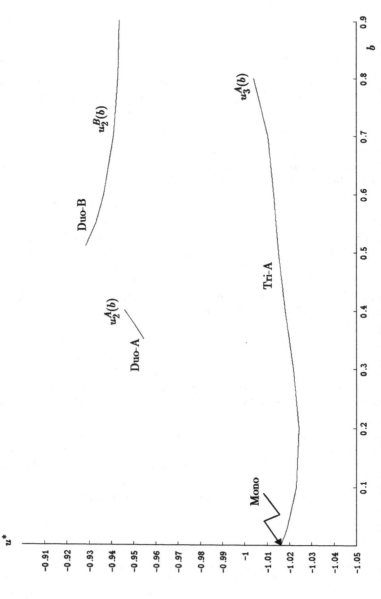

Figure 5.20. Equilibrium utility levels associated with the four types of urban systems ($\alpha_0 = \alpha_1 = 0.5$, $a_0 = 0.5$, $a_1 = 1$, $t_0 = 0.9$, $t_1 = 1$, $\rho_1 = 0.8$, $f_1 = 1$, $N = 0.75e$).

which is the sum of land rents normalized by the equilibrium wage rate at each location.[22] Figure 5.21 shows the TRLR curves associated with the four types of equilibrium configurations.

In comparing Figures 5.20 and 5.21, it is interesting to observe that the relative positions of the three curves and their shapes are almost completely opposite in the two figures. This is because of the following two facts. First, as noted before, the metropolis of the monocentric equilibrium is greatly overcrowded, and hence the equilibrium utility can be increased if the workers are dispersed into two or three cities sufficiently far apart. Second, when all manufacturing workers are concentrated in a smaller number of cities, and when these cities are close to each other, the A-good must be transported over a longer distance on average; hence, by the nature of the land rent curve, TRLR becomes greater. In consequence, u^* curves and TRLR curves exhibit opposite trends.

Observe that each income $W(y)$ at location y yields an equilibrium utility of u^* for a worker there. Therefore, TRLR, defined by (5.95), corresponds to TRLR units of equilibrium utility. Therefore, it is natural to define the overall social welfare (SW) of the economy by

$$SW \equiv Nu^* + TRLR \tag{5.96}$$

Figure 5.22 shows the SW curves for the four types of equilibrium configurations. We can see that Figure 5.22 is qualitatively almost the same as Figure 5.20. This is because, in the present context, $TRLR/Nu^*$ is about 0.2, and hence TRLR is dominated by Nu^*. The unique essential difference between the two figures is that in Figure 5.20 the highest u^* is achieved by the duo-B configuration with the minimum b, but in Figure 5.22 the highest SW is achieved by the duo-A configuration with the maximum b. Therefore, in the present context, we can conclude that among all equilibrium configurations, the duo-A configuration with the maximum b is socially optimal.

Next we shall examine the stability of the equilibria obtained. The stability analysis is important for two reasons. First, because unstable equilibria are rarely observed in the real world, the stability analysis helps to narrow the range of observable equilibria. Second, as illustrated later, the dynamic relationships among equilibria provide useful information on regional development strategies.

Following Krugman (1993b), we consider the following dynamic adjustment process in our spatial economy. Take any time $t \in \mathbb{R}$, and suppose that the production of M-goods takes place in J cities, $j = 1, 2, \ldots, J$, where each city j locates at x_j. Let $N_j(t)$ be the population of each city j (i.e., the number

---

[22] For the present numerical example, it turns out that the values for TRLR are not much different from those for the simple sum of total land rents (TLR), i.e., $TLR \equiv \int_{-l}^{l} R(y)\,dy$. Hence, the following discussion is not affected whether we use TRLR or TLR as the welfare measure of landlords.

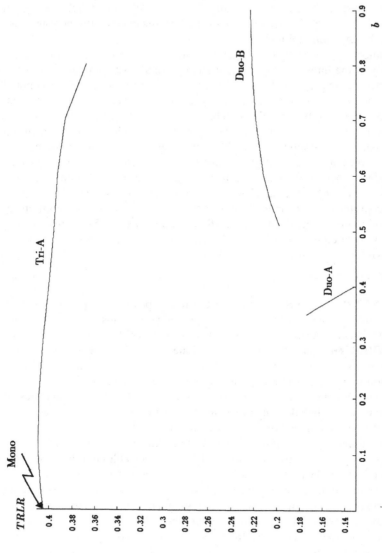

Figure 5.21. Total real land rents associated with the four types of equilibrium urban systems ($\alpha_0 = \alpha_1 = 0.5$, $a_0 = 0.5$, $a_1 = 1$, $t_0 = 0.9$, $t_1 = 1$, $\rho_1 = 0.8$, $f_1 = 1$, $N = 0.75e$).

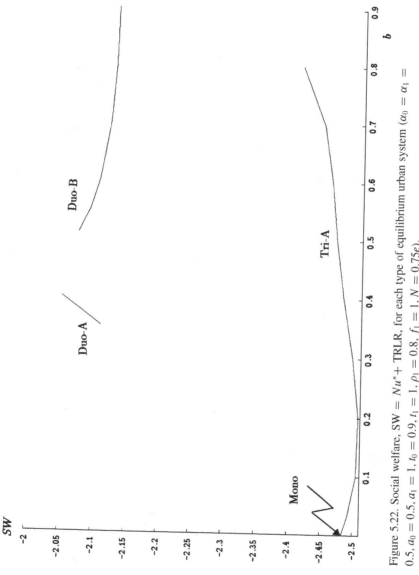

Figure 5.22. Social welfare, SW $= Nu^* +$ TRLR, for each type of equilibrium urban system ($\alpha_0 = \alpha_1 = 0.5, a_0 = 0.5, a_1 = 1, t_0 = 0.9, t_1 = 1, \rho_1 = 0.8, f_1 = 1, N = 0.75e$).

of workers in city j) at time t. Then, given the fixed total number of workers in the economy as N, the number of agricultural workers (A-workers) at time t is given by $N_A(t) = N - \sum_j N_j(t)$. Here we assume that at each given moment of time t, the population of each city is fixed, and hence $N_A(t)$ is also fixed. We assume, however, that at time t all A-workers are free to choose their locations, but they remain A-workers. Given this population distribution, $N_j(t), j = 1, 2, \ldots, J$, and A, we solve the model for $U_j(t)$ (together with all other unknowns), where $U_j(t)$ is the equilibrium utility level for workers in city j, or that for A-workers if $j = A$. Then, for each pair of $j, k = 1, 2, \ldots, J$ and A, the rate of migration from k to j is assumed to be given by $\sigma N_j(t)[U_j(t) - U_k(t)]N_k(t)$. That is, workers move away from a low-utility city (or A-job) toward a high-utility city (or A-job). Hence, for each $j = 1, 2, \ldots, J$ and A, the net change in population at time t is given by

$$\dot{N}_j(t) = \sum_k \sigma N_j(t)[U_j(t) - U_k(t)]N_k(t)$$

or, because $\sum_k N_j(t) = N$, by setting $\bar{U}(t) \equiv \sum_k N_k(t)U_k(t)/N$ we have that

$$\dot{N}_j(t) = \sigma N_j(t)[U_j(t) - \bar{U}(t)]N \tag{5.97}$$

Using this dynamic model, we can examine the stability of each (static) equilibrium.

We use the same set of parameters given by (5.94). Then, it turns out that among the four types of equilibrium configurations (indicated in Figure 5.20), all tri-A equilibria are (locally) unstable, whereas the rest of the equilibrium configurations (i.e., monocentric, duo-A, and duo-B for each b) are (locally) stable. The stability of monocentric, duo-A, and duo-B equilibria is based on the fact that the total population of the economy $N = 0.75e$ is more than three times $\hat{N}(\simeq 0.6)$, under which the monocentric equilibrium achieves the highest equilibrium utility. On the other hand, the instability of tri-A equilibria is not surprising if we recall that the s-city of any tri-A equilibrium is very small in comparison with the central metropolis (and hence the system is basically unstable).

The instability of tri-A equilibria provides a linkage between our model and the "big-push" or "growth-pole" models of economic development advocated by early development theorists such as Rosenstein-Rodan (1943), Perroux (1955), Myrdal (1957), and Hirschman (1958). That is, suppose that at present the spatial configuration of the economy is monocentric and that the planner of the economy intends to develop cities in the hinterland of the unique metropolis. What minimum sizes for these new cities will lead to their self-sustained growth? Let us consider the case of two new cities to be created. Then, in the context of this section, Figure 5.14 provides the answer. That is, let us fix any $\underline{b} \leq 0.8$ in Figure 5.14; then the value $n_{1b}(b)/n_{10}(b)$ provides the minimum size necessary for each s-city (in comparison with the size of the central city) to have self-sustained growth. In particular, the necessary size for each s-city is minimum when each is created at a distance $b \simeq 0.7$ in Figure 5.14.[23] More generally, the unstable equilibrium configurations of our model provide information on the threshold sizes necessary for new cities to attain self-sustained growth.

8 Conclusion

In this chapter, we have presented a microeconomic model of urban systems based on monopolistic competition behavior of firms producing differentiated consumption goods. Our analysis of this model, however, is still preliminary, and a great deal of work remains to be done. In particular, we must thoroughly examine the case of multiple groups of manufactured goods.

In our model, the basic force for spatial agglomeration is generated through product variety in consumption goods. A similar model of spatial agglomeration can be developed by introducing product variety in intermediate goods. For example, suppose that a homogeneous M-good is produced (by M-firms) using labor and a variety of differentiated (producer) services. Because of scale economies in product specialization, each service is assumed to be supplied monopolistically by a single S-firm. In this context, we can reinterpret Figure 5.1 as follows. If a city produces a wide variety of services, then those services can be purchased at lower prices there (assuming f.o.b. pricing by S-firms). Thus, because of complementarity among those services, the productivity of M-firms is high in the city. That, in turn, will induce more M-firms to agglomerate there. That increase in the number of M-firms will create a greater demand for services there, which in turn can support a greater number of specialized S-firms. In turn, that implies an even greater variety of services in the city. Thus, as before, this process involves circular causality in the spatial agglomeration of M-firms and S-firms (as well as their workers). Such an agglomeration force due to product variety in producer services can partly explain, for example, a concentration of high-technology firms (e.g., Silicon Valley) or business firms (e.g., New York).[24]

Another interesting direction for model extension is to consider multilocational firms. That is, suppose that each firm consists of multiple units (e.g., HQs, R&D units, and manufacturing plants) that can be located separately. Then, because different units will experience different agglomeration forces (e.g., availability of business services and convenience of face-to-face communication for HQs, availability of engineers for R&D units, and accessibility to

---

[23] Because our stability analysis is local, it shows only that if a newly created tri-A configuration is such that $n_{1b}(b)/n_{10}(b)$ is above the curve in Figure 5.14, then these s-cities will achieve self-sustained growth. In order to know to what new (stable) equilibrium configuration this original tri-A configuration will eventually lead, we must conduct a global dynamical analysis of the economy, which is left for the future.

[24] For spatial-agglomeration models based on product variety in intermediate goods, see, for example, Helpman and Krugman (1985, ch. 11), Fujita (1990), and Hamaguchi and Fujita (1997).

consumers for manufacturing plants), we will be able to develop a richer class of spatial models.[25] Eventually, by introducing into such basic models various realistic features (such as political restrictions, natural geographic features, and historical and cultural elements), we will be able to develop a realistic regional model that will be useful in studying the future economic geography of a nation or group of nations.

Appendix: Derivation of (5.23)

Because of the iceberg transport assumption, in order to deliver one unit of an M_1-good from the firm at x to consumers at y, $e^{t_1|y-x|}$ units of the good should be dispatched by the firm. Hence, setting $Y = (N - 2a_0l)W^*(0)$ in equation (5.3b), the total demand for the product (of the firm at x) by the consumers at $y = 0$ is given by

$$
Z(0) \equiv \frac{\alpha_1(N - 2a_0l)W^*(0)}{p_1(0\,|\,x)} \frac{p_1(0\,|\,x)^{-\gamma_1}}{np_1(0\,|\,0)^{-\gamma_1}} e^{t_1|x|}
$$
$$
= \frac{\alpha_1\gamma_1 f_1}{a_1}\left(\frac{W^*(0)}{W^*(x)}\right)^{1+\gamma_1} e^{-\gamma_1 t_1 x} \tag{A5.1}
$$

using (5.18), (5.19), and (5.22). Next, at each $y \neq 0$, the total income (for A-workers and landlords) per unit of distance at y equals $p_0(y) = e^{-t_0|y|}$. Hence, setting $Y = e^{-t_0|y|}$ in (5.3b) for $y \neq 0$, the total demand (including transport consumption) for the product (of the firm at x) by all A-workers and landlords can be obtained as

$$
\int_{-l^*}^{l^*} \frac{\alpha_1 e^{-t_0|y|}}{p_1(y\,|\,x)} \frac{p_1(y\,|\,x)^{-\gamma_1}}{np_1(y\,|\,0)^{-\gamma_1}} e^{t_1|y-x|}\, dy = \frac{\alpha_0\gamma_1 f_1}{2a_1}\left(\frac{W^*(0)}{W^*(x)}\right)^{1+\gamma_1} \frac{t_0}{1 - e^{-t_0 l^*}} e^{-\gamma_1 t_1 x}
$$
$$
\times \int_{-l^*}^{l^*} e^{-t_0|y|} e^{\gamma_1 t_1(|y|-|y-x|)}\, dy \tag{A5.2}
$$

using (5.18) and (5.22). Hence, the total demand, $D_1[x, W^*(x)]$ for the product of the firm at x is given by

$$
D_1[x, W^*(x)] = \frac{\alpha_0\gamma_1 f_1}{2a_1}\left(\frac{W^*(0)}{W^*(x)}\right)^{1+\gamma_1} e^{-\gamma_1|x|}
$$
$$
\times \left\{\frac{2a_1}{\alpha_0} + \frac{t_0}{1 - e^{-t_0 l^*}} e^{\gamma_1 t_1|x|} \int_{-l^*}^{l^*} e^{-t_0|y|} e^{\gamma_1 t_1(|y|-|y-x|)} dy\right\} \tag{A5.3}
$$

which leads to (5.23).

---

[25] For spatial economic models with multi-unit firms, see, for example, Helpman and Krugman (1985, ch. 13) and Ota and Fujita (1993).

References

Christaller, W. (1933). *Die zentralen Orte in Süddeutschland*. Jena: Gustav Fischer Verlag. Translated by C. W. Baskin (1966): *Central Places in Southern Germany*. Englewood Cliffs, NJ: Prentice-Hall.

Cronon, W. (1991). *Nature's Metropolis: Chicago and the Great West*. New York: Norton.

Eaton, B. C., and Lipsey, R. G. (1982). An economic theory of central places. *Economic Journal* 92:56–72.

Fujita, M. (1988). A monopolistic competition model of spatial agglomeration: differentiated product approach. *Regional Science and Urban Economics* 18:87–124.

Fujita, M. (1990). Spatial interactions and agglomeration in urban economics. In: M. Chatterji and R. E. Kunne (eds.), *New Frontiers in Regional Sciences*. London: Macmillan.

Fujita, M., and Krugman, P. (1995). When is the economy monocentric? von Thünen and Chamberlin unified. *Regional Science and Urban Economics* 25:505–28.

Fujita, M., Krugman, P., and Mori, T. (1999). On the evolution of hierarchical urban systems. *European Economic Review* 43:209–51.

Fujita, M., and Mori, T. (1997). Structural stability and evolution of urban systems. *Regional Science and Urban Economics* 27:399–442.

Fujita, M., and Ogawa, H. (1982). Multiple equilibria and structural transition of nonmonocentric urban configurations. *Regional Science and Urban Economics* 12:161–96.

Hamaguchi, N., and Fujita, M. (1997). Producer services and the spatial structure of an economy. Discussion paper no. A-6, Center for the Study of Complex Economic Systems, Institute of Economic Research, Kyoto University, Kyoto.

Helpman, E., and Krugman, P. (1985). *Market Structure and Foreign Trade*. Cambridge, MA: MIT Press.

Henderson, J. V. (1987). Systems of cities and inter-city trade. In: P. Hansen et al. (eds.), *Systems of Cities and Facility Location*, pp. 71–119. Chur, Switzerland: Harwood.

Hirschman, A. (1958). *The Strategy of Economic Development*. New Haven, CT: Yale University Press.

Koopmans, T. C. (1957). *Three Essays on the State of Economic Science*. New York: McGraw-Hill.

Krugman, P. (1991). *Geography and Trade*. Cambridge, MA: MIT Press.

Krugman, P. (1993a). First nature, second nature, and metropolitan location. *Journal of Regional Science* 34:129–44.

Krugman, P. (1993b). On the number and location of cities. *European Economic Review* 37:293–8.

Krugman, P. (1995). *Development, Geography, and Economic Theory*. Cambridge, MA: MIT Press.

Myrdal, G. (1957). *Economic Theory and Underdeveloped Regions*. London: Duckworth.

Ogawa, H., and Fujita, M. (1980). Equilibrium land use patterns in a non-monocentric city. *Journal of Regional Science* 20:455–75.

Ota, M., and Fujita, M. (1993). Communication technologies and spatial organization of multi-unit firms in metropolitan areas. *Regional Science and Urban Economics* 23:695–729.

Perroux, F. (1955). Note sur la notion de pôle de croissance. *Economique appliquée* 7:307–20.

Pred, A. R. (1966). *The Spatial Dynamics of US Urban-Industrial Growth.* Cambridge, MA: MIT Press.

Pred, A. R. (1977). *City-Systems in Advanced economies.* London: Hutchison.

Rosenstein-Rodan, P. (1943). Problems of industrialization of eastern and southeastern Europe. *Economic Journal* June–September.

United Nations (1993). *World Urbanization Prospects: The 1992 Revision.* New York: United Nations.

von Thünen, J. H. (1826). *Der isolierte Staat in Beziehung auf Landwrirtschaft und Nationalökonomie.* Hamburg.

CHAPTER 6

Dynamic Evolution of the Size Distribution of U.S. Cities

Linda Harris Dobkins and Yannis M. Ioannides

1 Introduction

Empirical study of trends in city size distributions has engaged economists since the beginning of this century. It has attracted renewed attention recently, in part for the following two reasons: First, the cumulative effects of important contributions to the literature on the new urban economics (Fujita and Thisse, Chapter 1, this volume) have increased the need for new empirical work. Second, the topic appeals to those enamored of the "universality" of power laws (Gell-Mann, 1994).

The distribution of city sizes in an economy may be an indicator of important elements of the economy's structure. It may be characterized by complex dynamic behavior. Important contributions to the literature on city size distributions are found in the work of J. Vernon Henderson, who has studied the determinants of city size through an integration of international trade theory with urban economics. As summarized by Henderson (1974, 1987, 1988), that fundamental approach has led to a model of optimum city size that balances the benefits of larger city size with its costs in terms of disamenities. Several of the implications of these theories have been tested, especially by Henderson himself. To the best of our knowledge, however, Henderson's theories and other theories we shall discuss here have never been tested directly, that is, in terms of data for an entire system of cities. Such an endeavor is timely in view of

Special thanks go to Jacques Thisse for numerous analytical and editorial comments and suggestions. We also thank Kristin Butcher, Anna M. Hardman, Vernon Henderson, Gib Metcalf, Charles Michalopoulos, Will Strange, Aris Spanos, Konrad Stahl, participants at the CEPR workshop on "Location and Regional Convergence/Divergence," Louvain-la-Neuve, October 26, 1996, and members of workshops at Boston College, Brown, Harvard, and Tufts for their helpful comments. We thank Hyungtaik Ahn for his GVC program, Kimon L. H. Ioannides for his help with the graphics, and James Fitzsimmons for his suggestions with the data. The usual caveats apply.

We gratefully acknowledge research support from the National Science Foundation (grants SES9211913 and SBR9618639), the MacArthur Foundation, and Tufts University.

the enormous attention that city sizes have been attracting in the literature on economic geography, regional economics, and urban economics.

Some of the most recent interest in empirical assessments has been prompted by Eaton and Eckstein (1997), who have used data from France and Japan and have found urban systems in those two countries to have remained unchanged over many years. That is, those systems are characterized by parallel growth: Although their cities have grown in size, the city size distributions have not changed significantly over many years. Those countries were chosen for study by Eaton and Eckstein in part because the numbers of cities have remained the same during the time periods studied, from 1876 in France and from 1925 in Japan. They have pursued their empirical work using a model that treats human capital as city-specific.

The work of Eaton and Eckstein is a major contribution to our understanding of urban systems, in part because they have looked at the question from a perspective different from that used in the urban economics literature. However, any observer will naturally wonder what will happen to city size distributions in an economy that experiences extension of its land area and the emergence of new cities. We shall use a new data set that tracks U.S. cities and their metropolitan areas from 1900 to 1990. Beginning from 112 cities in 1900, we have 334 in 1990, using contemporaneous definitions of metropolitan areas, as described in Section 4. Many of the cities involved in our data set had been in existence for many years prior to the time they passed the appropriate threshold of population to become cities. Other cities have actually come into being rather suddenly, the latest one in 1944, and have quickly grown large enough to be included. As one might expect, an examination of the patterns of growth rates for these metropolitan areas yields results that contrast with those of Eaton and Eckstein. We find that the U.S. urban system is characterized by divergent growth, if spatial evolution is ignored, and convergent growth, if it is not. In order to examine this property of the data further, we shall look at the data in more detail (and nonparametrically) by constructing transition matrices to track the movement of each city in a distribution relative to the others.

In Section 2 we review the significant literature on city size distributions from early in the twentieth century to the present. In Section 3 we propose a model of city size distributions within the national economy. Our model emphasizes human capital: Each city within the economy is assumed to contribute to the production of national output by means of specialized labor. In the simplest possible version of the model, demand for national output drives the evolution of cities in the economy. The model is aimed at explaining the endogenous emergence of cities and important stylized facts associated with such emergence, namely, that earnings are positively related to city size, which is generally regarded as an important piece of evidence linking productivity and city size. Section 6 compares the results from different strands of research. We look at city size distributions first nonparametrically and then through a set of regressions that reflect the complexity of the changing systems, with results as noted earlier. We also find significant associations between city size and earnings and between city size and schooling.

2 Historical Perspective on City Size Distributions

Some economists, as well as geographers and other social scientists, have found it useful to invoke the *rank-size rule*, an alleged statistical regularity that is an outgrowth of application of the Pareto distribution to city size data. Stated in its various forms, the rank-size rule – city size multiplied by its rank in its system equals a constant – has been debated, calculated, and dismissed several times over since its first mention (that we can find) by Auerbach (1913). Unlike scientists in some other fields, economists are skeptical about the use of universal constants and power laws[1] in the field of economics.

Singer (1936) suggested that city sizes follow a Pareto distribution (his *courbe des populations*, paralleling Pareto's *courbe des revenues*) (Pareto, 1906). If city sizes follow a Pareto distribution, then the characteristic exponent α in effect expresses the degree of concentration of population in the cities in a system. Proponents of the rank-size rule assert that this coefficient is equal to 1. Strictly speaking, if the Pareto exponent is equal to 1, then the size distribution possesses no finite moments. In that case, the rank-size rule may hold on its own, but it is not associated with an interesting distribution function. Whether or not the critical coefficient α is actually 1, whether or not the α coefficient equal to 1 is the true test of the rank-size rule, and whether or not a Pareto distribution is at all an appropriate measure of city size distributions are all questions addressed in the literature. The higher the threshold city size, the higher will be the estimated Pareto exponent. Madden (1956) provided an interesting nonparametric analysis of urban growth in the United States. He emphasized stability features in the distribution of growth rates and their evolution over time, where he noted that great dispersion coexisted with considerable intertemporal variation for individual cities. We continue that line of inquiry by performing rank-size regressions with our data set. We look, however, at standard metropolitan areas (SMAs), what Singer would have called "conurbations."

---

[1] There are several writers, including Auerbach (1913), who have seen the rank-size rule as part of an overall scheme of things. Lotka (1925) noted the rule as he sought similarity in the "laws" of various disciplines, including economics and physics. Zipf (1949) made the rule an example of his overriding "principle of least effort" in the conduct of human behavior. See also Beckmann (1958). For the latest in this history of fascination with the rank-size rule, see Gell-Mann (1994) and Krugman (1993, 1994, 1996). Krugman has suggested that the rank-size rule may be evidence of complexity theory at work and has linked the "self-organization properties" of complex systems to the statistical regularity implied by the rank-size rule. Krugman's papers fit within the larger explanation of the relationship between increasing returns and path dependence. See also Arthur (1994).

The question of city size distribution also underlies the study by Eaton and Eckstein (1997), who have used empirical transition matrices, but have asked the same question: How have city size distributions changed over long historical periods? Using nonparametric data from France for 1876 to 1990, and from Japan for 1925 to 1985, they have found evidence of "parallel" growth; that is, city size distributions in those countries have remained almost the same over time.

As noted earlier, Eaton and Eckstein's selection of France and Japan was motivated by their roughly stable geographical boundaries and the consistent availability of data. In contrast to such old countries as France and Japan, the United States has grown by continually expanding its land area into a well-defined hinterland. New regions and cities have been brought into the U.S. urban system during the nineteenth and twentieth centuries, older regions have grown and declined, and the spatial distribution of economic activity has undergone some remarkable changes. In Europe, almost no new cities have been created during the twentieth century. The economic forces at work may well be the same as in other economies. However, to the extent that "history matters," the U.S. urban system has developed under initial conditions quite different from those for other countries. It is for this reason, too, that a fresh approach to the U.S. case is of particular interest. Our choice of the time span for this study, the entire twentieth century, should allow us, in principle, to address some of these phenomena. In contrast, Crihfield and Panggabean (1995) have used data for U.S. metropolitan areas for 1960–1982. The peculiarities of cities and their openness would seem natural subjects for study during the current revival of empirical growth theories.

3 Theoretical Models

The dynamics of city size distributions when cities of different sizes and types coexist still are not well understood. Several seminal studies by Henderson (1974, 1983, 1987, 1988) rest on the notion that cities differ because of the varying demands for their products, either as final goods or as intermediate goods. However, growth in a Henderson-type system of cities would consist in the economy giving birth to an increasing number of cities, with the number of each city type growing at the rate of growth of the national population (Henderson and Ioannides, 1981). A drawback of that approach that is not mitigated by the study reported in this chapter is that national space is ignored.[2]

---

[2] This is also true of Ioannides (1994), where the Dixit-Stiglitz-Ethier-Krugman monopolistic competition model is employed to motivate the existence of many city types. Even though that model is symmetric, it is straightforward to see that a model of asymmetric preferences would produce different city types, but not very different dynamics. A later study by Ioannides (1997b) mitigated that. See also Fujita and Thisse (Chapter 1, this volume) for a comprehensive review of monopolistic competition models of urban structure.

When that is brought into consideration, the location of new cities matters, as we shall later discuss further. Eaton and Eckstein (1997) also worked with the assumption that the price of non-urban land use remained constant over time, or at least was exogenous as far as urban growth was concerned, and thus they excluded national space considerations as well.

The dynamics of city growth in the model of Eaton and Eckstein (1997) are assumed to depend critically on knowledge flows across a given number of cities. Each individual's learning productivity depends on a linear combination of the average levels of human capital. The assumption of a nationwide capital market is a second source of the dependence of each city's growth on the growth of all others. Equilibrium city sizes depend critically on the condition that at a steady state, residents of cities will have no incentive to migrate. At one extreme, human capital is general; at the other, it is perfectly city-specific. The model of Eaton and Eckstein shows that the general case in which human capital is partly city-specific implies lower and upper bounds on city size distributions. These bounds share some common determinants, including, in particular, the levels of human capital in the various cities at a steady state, which are, of course, endogenous.

Models of the Henderson genre, on the other hand, feature a theory of city size distribution that directly reflects preferences. For similar reasons, such a theory implies that all determinants are highly interdependent.

The Henderson model explains that the types of goods produced in cities help determine the sizes of those cities; if the types of goods currently in vogue change, then urban concentrations are expected to change. Thus city-specific factors combine with aggregate factors to determine the distribution of city sizes. Abdel-Rahman and Fujita (1993) have shown that diversified and specialized cities can coexist in a system, with the diversified cities being larger. If industrial structures change to favor smaller, more specialized cities, there will be less concentration in large cities, *ceteris paribus*. If industrial structures remain the same over time, we might see a parallel growth pattern, as in the Eaton and Eckstein model. And if industrial structures change to favor larger cities, or if demand conditions change to favor the larger, more diversified cities, we might well see increasing concentration.

3.1 The Model

We propose a model that is aimed at explaining a number of very important stylized facts, such as that urbanization is closely associated with economic growth and that earnings are positively related to city size, which is generally regarded as important evidence linking productivity and city size. Our model emphasizes human capital: Each city within the economy is assumed to contribute to the production of national output by means of specialized labor. In the simplest possible version of the model, demand for national output drives the evolution of cities in the economy. Localization and other spatial factors have not been explicitly brought into the analysis here.

Let there be I_t different cities at time t. Let P_{it} denote the size (in terms of possibly different though not equivalent measures, such as population, or employment, or labor force) of city i at time t, and assume that data are available for cities $i = 1, \ldots, I_t$ and time periods $t = 1, \ldots, T$. Let $P_{Ut}, t = 1, \ldots, T$, be the total urban population, $P_{Ut} = \sum_{i=1}^{I_t} P_{it}$, and $\bar{P}_{Ut} = P_{Ut}/I_t$ the mean city size at time t. We shall suppress the time subscript when no confusion arises. The distribution of city sizes offers a way to study, in approximate terms, the density distribution of economic activity over space when its actual geographical features can be safely ignored. If we think of the distribution of economic activity as a mathematical surface over physical space, urban areas can be identified with regions where a certain threshold is exceeded.

City i uses raw labor P_i with capital and land to produce *skilled labor* of type i. The quantity of skilled labor of type i is denoted by X_i, and its price by W_{X_i}. We neglect, in this chapter, the urban use of land.[3] We assume that city i's demand for capital is independent of its size and is equal to κ. This assumption is justified at equilibrium, as we shall see, where city size depends entirely on the parameters of the technology with which skilled labor is produced in the city.[4] The terms r_L and r_K denote the rental rates for land and capital, respectively.

National output is produced by using as inputs the quantities of specialized labor produced by the economy's set of cities, $\{X_1, X_2, \ldots, X_I\}$, along with land, L, and capital, K:

$$Y = G(\{X_1, X_2, \ldots, X_I\}, L, K) \tag{6.1}$$

National production takes place according to constant returns to scale in terms of all inputs. National land, on the right-hand side (RHS) of (6.1), represents constraints that the major features of national geography represent for national production, whereas capital stands for producible means of production. For example, doubling of the land input would require that all convenient sites for port facilities, and so forth, also be doubled. We assume the following form

---

[3] It would be consistent with some historically observed patterns of urbanization during economic growth to ignore initially the impact of population growth on the demand for land and/or the demand for capital. However, at some point a stage will be reached at which national production will compete with the needs of urban production, which will initiate a qualitatively new phase in national economic growth (Ioannides, 1997b).

[4] Because each city in our analysis is assumed to have a homogeneous labor force, the level of schooling represents the total effect, and thus subsumes the impact on an individual's productivity of the average level of schooling in the community of his residence (Rauch, 1993). Rauch (1993) found that cities with higher levels of human capital had higher wages and higher land rents. He found that each additional year of SMSA average education could be expected to raise total factor productivity by 2.8%.

for $G(\cdot)$:

$$Y = G_0 \left[\sum_{i=1}^{I} X_i^\chi \right]^{\alpha/\chi} L^\beta K^\gamma \tag{6.2}$$

where $0 < \chi < 1$, $\alpha + \beta + \gamma = 1$, and $\alpha, \beta, \gamma > 0$. The larger is χ, the greater the substitutability among different kinds of skilled labor in national production. The aggregate production function (6.2) is invoked to represent the use of specialized labor inputs $\{X_1, X_2, \ldots, X_I\}$ by a large number of different firms in the economy in order to produce a final good that may be consumed or invested.

Derived demands for land, capital, and the specialized labor inputs are determined in perfectly competitive conditions. Let R_L, R_K, R_Y, and W_{X_i} denote the prices (rental rates) for land and capital, the price of national output, and the price of specialized input i. The derived demands for X_i, $i = 1, \ldots, I$, readily follow:

$$X_i = \bar{G}_0 \frac{1}{R_Y^{(\beta+\gamma)/\alpha} R_L^{-\beta/\alpha} R_K^{-\gamma/\alpha}} \left(\frac{W_{X_i}}{R_Y^{1/\alpha} R_L^{-\beta/\alpha} R_K^{-\gamma/\alpha}} \right)^{-1/(1-\chi)} Y \tag{6.3}$$

where $\bar{G}_0$ is a function of parameters. The derived demands for L and K are given by $L = \bar{\beta}(R_Y/R_L)Y$ and $K = \bar{\gamma}(R_Y/R_K)Y$, where $\bar{\beta}$ and $\bar{\gamma}$ are functions of parameters.

City i is assumed to be host to the sole producer of specialized labor of type i, who takes the demand function, from (6.3), as given and decides on its price. This modeling choice readily leads to a determinate solution for the range I of the types of specialized labor, that is, the number of cities in our framework (Ioannides, 1994). We assume that production of specialized labor by city i occurs under increasing returns to scale, in the style of Dixit and Stiglitz (1977).

Specifically, let the labor-requirements function for city i's production be denoted by

$$P_i = \Pi + cX_i \tag{6.4}$$

where Π and c denote, respectively, the fixed and average variable costs of city i's production. Optimal pricing assumes the average wage rate, W_i, at which labor is hired as given, implying the familiar constants-markup formula $W_{X_i} = (1/\chi)cW_i$. Free entry, in turn, leads to zero profit for all firms producing differentiated inputs. This implies $X_i = [\chi/(1-\chi)](\Pi/c)$, which along with the labor-requirements function (6.4) yields

$$P_i = \frac{1}{1-\chi} \Pi \tag{6.5}$$

3.2 General Equilibrium

With overall symmetry, the prices of all intermediate inputs are equal. At equilibrium, the price of national output must be equal to its marginal cost: $R_Y = g_0 R_L^\beta R_K^\gamma (\sum_{i=1}^I W_{X_i}^{-\chi/(1-\chi)})^{-[(1-\chi)/\chi]\alpha}$, where g_0 is a function of parameters. It is convenient to normalize by choosing national output as the numeraire, $R_Y = 1$, which yields a relationship among the three unknown prices R_L, R_K, and W. Equilibrium conditions for land and capital yield two additional equations: $R_L = \bar\beta Y/L$; $R_K = \bar\gamma Y/[\bar K - \kappa(1-\chi)(N/I)]$, where κ denotes city i's demand for capital, which has been assumed to be inelastic. National output is given by

$$Y = y_0 \frac{W^{\beta+\gamma}}{R_L^\beta R_K^\gamma} c^{\beta+\gamma} \Pi I^{\beta+\gamma+\alpha/\chi} \tag{6.6}$$

Equilibrium in the national labor market requires

$$I \frac{1}{1-\chi} \Pi = N \tag{6.7}$$

where N denotes the national labor force. Condition (6.7) determines the equilibrium number of cities I. The model is closed by specifying the demand for national output, which in turn determines the only remaining unknown, namely, the equilibrium wage rate W.

The model may be solved as follows:

$$Y = \upsilon L^\beta \left(K - \kappa(1-\chi)\frac{N}{\Pi} \right)^\gamma N^{\alpha/\chi} \Pi^{\alpha(1-1/\chi)} \tag{6.8}$$

$$W = \omega \frac{1}{c} L^\beta \left(K - \kappa(1-\chi)\frac{N}{\Pi} \right)^\gamma N^{\alpha/\chi-1} \Pi^{\alpha(1-1/\chi)} \tag{6.9}$$

$$R_L = \bar r_L L^{\beta-1} \left(K - \kappa(1-\chi)\frac{N}{\Pi} \right)^\gamma N^{\alpha/\chi} \Pi^{\alpha(1-1/\chi)} \tag{6.10}$$

$$R_K = \bar r_K L^\beta \left(\bar K - \kappa\frac{N}{\Pi} \right)^{\gamma-1} N^{\alpha/\chi} \Pi^{\alpha(1-1/\chi)} \tag{6.11}$$

where $\upsilon, \omega, \bar r_L$, and $\bar r_K$ denote functions of parameters. These expressions for equilibrium output and factor prices reveal the impact of increasing returns. Not surprisingly, output and the rental rates for land and capital increase with the size of the national labor force, provided we ignore the increased demands for land and capital caused by such a change. But so does the wage rate, provided that $\alpha > \chi$, namely, that the higher the share of specialized labor in national output, the higher the substitutability among different kinds of specialized labor, which would be consistent with generation of increasing returns in the manner suggested by this model. In that case, an increase in the national labor force increases national output more than proportionately. We also note that output and factor prices are all decreasing functions of Π, the fixed costs in the production of specialized labor inputs.

Two remarks are in order. First, the positive association between total population and the wage rate reflects directly the impact of increasing returns in the production of skilled labor. In contrast, the modern urban economics literature in the Henderson genre has indicated a positive association by endowing city production with Marshallian external effects: City size confers advantages to city production that are external to each firm and internal to the city economy. Second, it would be appropriate to interpret cities here as the smallest urban centers that are consistent with exploitation of the advantage of increasing returns. This smallest city size can be identified with what Krugman (1996) calls "lumps." The appearance of increasing returns here is not getting something out of nothing. The maintenance of lumps requires resources, which cuts into the amounts of land and capital available for national production.

3.3 Dynamics

Equation (6.7) implies that when the labor force grows, the number of cities also grows, unless perhaps the capacity of each city grows through an increase in fixed costs Π. This could be accommodated if we were to assume that although Π is a fixed cost relative to the production of a specialized input, it could be decreased by means of capital investment and use of land, under decreasing returns to scale.

The dynamic evolution of the economy can be described once we have elaborated on the capital accumulation process. We invoke, for simplicity, a simple neoclassical descriptive (Solow) growth setting in which the economy saves a constant fraction s, $0 < s < 1$, of aggregate national output. Savings, sY_t, are invested in capital used in national production. The law of motion for our model of an urbanized economy readily follows from (6.8): $K_{t+1} = s\upsilon L^{\beta}[K_t - \kappa(1-\chi)\frac{N_t}{\Pi}]^{\gamma} N_t^{\alpha/\chi} \Pi^{\alpha(1-1/\chi)}$, where υ_u denotes a function of parameters. We see that sufficiently strong increasing returns (i.e., $\alpha > \chi$) would make up for the fixity of land in national production. The law of motion, when transformed to intensive form, becomes

$$k_{t+1} = s\frac{\upsilon}{1+\eta}L^{\beta}\left(k_t - \frac{\kappa(1-\chi)}{\Pi}\right)^{\gamma} N_t^{(\alpha/\chi)-(\alpha+\beta)} \Pi^{\alpha(1-1/\chi)} \quad (6.12)$$

where k_t denotes the national capital–labor ratio, $k_t \equiv K_t/N_t$.

At a cost of $\kappa(1-\chi)/\Pi$ per capita, the economy avails itself of growth according to (6.12), which reflects, in effect, an endogenous source of technological change, $N_t^{(\alpha/\chi)-(\alpha+\beta)}$. Provided that $\alpha/\chi > 1 - \gamma$, then the more important is capital in aggregate production, the more likely it is that a given degree of substitutability among specialized labor inputs will cause increasing returns sufficiently strong to overcome the decreasing returns caused by the fixity of land.

We draw a contrast with economic growth in a non-urbanized economy, in which case the counterpart of (6.12) is

$$k_{t+1} = s \frac{\upsilon_n}{1 + \eta} L^\beta k_t^\gamma N_t^{-\beta} \tag{6.13}$$

where υ_n is a function of parameters. It is well known that if a productive factor is available in fixed supply and no exogenous source of technological change is present, standard neoclassical growth with a constant-returns-to-scale aggregate production function admits no steady state. Aggregate output grows at a rate less than that of population. An economy growing along these lines will find it advantageous to urbanize as soon as it is feasible, in order to avoid further decreases in per-capita income.[5] We note that the capital cost of urban production merely delays the onset of urbanization.

It would be consistent with the spirit of this approach if we were to assume that sites could cluster and coalesce into larger metropolitan areas, as long as that process did not affect the technology of production within each city. However, because we have not addressed spatial aspects, it is impossible to say anything about where new cities will be located. Therefore, even though cities in this model are identical, they may cluster and form metropolitan areas of different sizes.

In the presence of population growth, the model of the urbanized economy will be associated with unceasing growth, in spite of the absence of exogenous technological change. Unless Π_0 changes, the number of identical cities will grow in proportion to population.

We shall briefly consider the implications of our theory for the case in which a nation increases its land area. As noted earlier, this is clearly the case for the United States, as the U.S. urban system has expanded into formerly under-developed areas, especially early in the twentieth century. From (6.12) we have that if the land area were to increase at the same rate as the labor supply, and urban production required no land, then the intensity of increasing returns, the exponent of N_t, would increase to $\alpha(1/\chi - 1)$. If urban production did require land, then it would be appropriate to assume that such requirements would increase less than proportionately to population and would in part be offset by

---

[5] This will occur at the smallest value of t for which

$$\upsilon_u L^\beta \left(s \upsilon_n L^\beta K_t^\gamma N_t^\alpha - \kappa(1 - \chi) \frac{N_{t+1}}{\Pi} \right)^\gamma N_{t+1}^{\alpha/\chi} \Pi^{\alpha(1-1/\chi)} \geq \upsilon_n L^\beta \left(s \upsilon_n L^\beta K_t^\gamma N_t^\alpha \right)^\gamma N_{t+1}^\alpha$$

It can be shown that if the effective increasing returns are sufficiently strong, then a transition to the urbanized phase is feasible in finite time.

the use of capital. In other words, such assumptions would reflect the fact that greater use of capital allows higher population densities.

3.4 Different Types of Cities

In the model just described, it is assumed that the cities in the economy are of the same type and size. We know, however, that economies are made up of cities of different types (Henderson, 1974, 1987, 1988) and sizes. It would be straightforward to assume a nonsymmetrical constant-elasticity-of-substitution (CES) aggregator on the RHS of (6.2). In a growing economy, the number of cities will grow, but there are at least two drawbacks to such a formulation: First, there will, in principle, be only one city of each type (unless the CES aggregator is defined to be of the mixed continuous-discrete type). Second, the properties of the CES aggregator assumed will determine entirely the characteristics of the urban system.

In an effort to put greater distance between assumptions and conclusions, we propose a model that takes advantage of increasing returns in a "vertical" (i.e., hierarchical) sense. The intuition here is to emulate the manner in which the productivity of raw labor is enhanced when it is transformed into varieties of differentiated skilled labor that are used as inputs by a higher-level production process. Let the subscript zero denote variables and parameters associated with the production process described earlier. I_{0_t} denotes the number of lumps, minimum-size cities, at equilibrium. We assume that level-0 output, whose quantity Y_{0_t} is given by (6.8), can be used as capital input along with land and differentiated products via a constant-returns-to-scale production process, just as before, to produce output Y_{1_t} (and so on at level 2, etc). If we assume that the corresponding fixed costs for producing specialized labor inputs satisfy $\Pi_0 < \Pi_1 < \Pi_2 < \ldots$, then we can analyze the relative magnitudes of the numbers $I_{0_t}, I_{1_t}, I_{2_t}, \ldots$ of the varieties of differentiated outputs required at each ascending level of the hierarchy.

We assume that the output at the highest existing level is used for consumption and investment; all other outputs are used as intermediate products. The number of levels in the hierarchy evolves endogenously, so that the highest-level output is used for final consumption and for investment as the capital used by the level-0 process. That is, output at level n requires I_{n_t} differentiated products and occurs according to

$$Y_{n_t} = \upsilon_n \left(L_{n_t}\right)^\beta \left(Y_{n-1_t} - \kappa(1-\chi)\frac{1}{\Pi_n}N_{n_t}\right)^\gamma N_{n_t}^{\alpha/\chi} \Pi_n^{\alpha(1-1/\chi)}, \qquad n \geq 1$$

$$\tag{6.14}$$

$$Y_{0_t} = \upsilon_0 \left(L_{0_t}\right)^\beta \left(K_t - \kappa(1-\chi)\frac{1}{\Pi_0}N_{0_t}\right)^\gamma N_{0_t}^{\alpha/\chi} \Pi_0^{\alpha(1-1/\chi)} \tag{6.15}$$

where $L_{0_t}, \ldots, L_{n_t}$ denote land allocated to level-0, $\ldots$, level-n production, respectively. $N_{0_t}, \ldots, N_{n_t}$ denote raw labor used to produce the differentiated skilled labor used in level-0, $\ldots$, level-n production, respectively. K_t denotes capital used in level-0 production. Finally, capital accumulation evolves according to

$$K_{t+1} = sY_{n_t} \tag{6.16}$$

By substituting back from the corresponding production function for Y_{n-1_t} and by working iteratively backward, we get an expression that contains the quantities of land and raw labor used at each level of the hierarchy. Thus, for a hierarchy with level 0 and level 1, we have

$$Y_{1_t} = \upsilon_1 \left(L_{1_t} \right)^\beta \left[\upsilon_0 \left(L_{0_t} \right)^\beta \left(K_t - \kappa \frac{1-\chi}{\Pi_0} N_{0_t} \right)^\gamma N_{0_t}^{\alpha/\chi} \Pi_0^{\alpha(1-1/\chi)} \right.$$
$$\left. - \kappa \frac{1-\chi}{\Pi_1} N_{1_t} \right]^\gamma \left(L_{0_t} \right)^{\gamma\beta} N_{1_t}^{\alpha/\chi} \Pi_1^{\alpha(1-1/\chi)} \tag{6.17}$$

and $K_{t+1} = sY_{1_t}$.

A key question that our framework must address is the number of levels of the hierarchy. We take up this question under the simplifying assumption that the capital requirements for city production are not very large, $\kappa \approx 0$. This assumption is reasonable if we recall that capital requirements by cities were much smaller back at the time the urbanization process started than they are for a metropolis today, especially in the Third World. In the process, we shall examine how our hierarchical setting improves upon the identical-cities case. First, note that competition for land implies that $L_{0_t} = [\gamma/(1+\gamma)]L$ and $L_{1_t} = [1/(1+\gamma)]L$. Competition for raw labor determines the allocation of N_t to different city types: $N_{0_t} = [\gamma/(1+\gamma)]N_t$; $N_{1_t} = [1/(1+\gamma)]N_t$. We now note that an effect of hierarchical production is effectively to increase the elasticities for both total land and total raw labor in the production of the final good used for consumption and investment. That is, these elasticities with respect to land and labor, respectively, are $\beta(1+\gamma)$ and $(\alpha/\chi)(1+\gamma)$. We also note that employment is higher the higher the level in the hierarchy. As a result, the hierarchical organization of urban production strengthens the increasing returns to scale that urban production with one city type makes possible in the first place. In fact, the greater the number of levels in the hierarchy, the stronger this effect. In the limit as $n \to \infty$, the elasticity of raw labor in the production of final output tends to $(\alpha/\chi)[1/(1-\gamma)]$, the elasticity of land tends to $\beta[1/(1-\gamma)]$, and the elasticity of capital used by the level-0 production tends to zero faster the smaller is γ. Consequently, $\beta[1/(1-\gamma)]+(\alpha/\chi)[1/(1-\gamma)] > 1$, and therefore the increasing returns generated by the hierarchical model persist in the limit. It is this strengthening of increasing returns that explains why the economy will be better off if an additional level is added to the hierarchy.

Turning now to the model's implications for city size distributions, we note that the numbers of cities of type 0 and type 1 are, respectively, $I_{0_t} = [(1 - \chi)/\Pi_0]N_{0_t}$ and $I_{1_t} = [(1 - \chi)/\Pi_1]N_{1_t}$. These imply the frequency distribution

$$f_{0_t} = \frac{\gamma/\Pi_0}{\gamma/\Pi_0 + 1/\Pi_1}, \qquad f_{1_t} = \frac{1/\Pi_1}{\gamma/\Pi_0 + 1/\Pi_1} \qquad (6.18)$$

and the total number of cities is

$$I_t = (1 - \chi)\frac{\gamma/\Pi_0 + 1/\Pi_1}{1 + \gamma}N_t \qquad (6.19)$$

We note that the relative proportion of larger cities will decrease with city size if $\gamma > \Pi_{i-1}/\Pi_i$, $i = 1, \ldots, n$.

In sum, our model delivers an explanation for different city types within a hierarchical framework with an endogenous number of levels. This is significant in the context of the literature,[6] as the distributions of city sizes continue to attract a lot of attention. The extraordinary performance of power laws in describing the size distributions of cities has not been satisfactorily explained, in spite of recent attempts, notably by Krugman (1996), but also by Gabaix (1999).[7] Our emphasis has been on developing a model based on explicit economic models. It is for these reasons that further research in this area is warranted.

The fact that a hierarchical model yields a more complex set of outcomes should not be surprising in view of the fact that it involves more complex interactions. In general, cities interact because of their geographical proximity and also because of economic proximity. For example, the Boston area and Silicon Valley (and other high-tech-industry areas), like New York and Los Angeles (in the world of entertainment), may be geographically apart, but economically are quite close. Our hierarchical model imposes strong restrictions on the patterns of economic interaction. These restrictions should be relaxed in future work.[8]

We can imagine a variety of empirical exercises that would allow us to investigate the conclusions of our model. The limited availability of data on cities, both over time and in city-specific detail, imposes constraints on such tests, even in the context of our newly constructed data set. The theory we have developed can be summarized in terms of a sequence of evolving distributions of city sizes $\{f_{0_t}, f_{1_t}, \ldots, f_{n_t}\}$, which will be referred to as f_t for short. We

[6] See Matsuyama (1995) for a hierarchical model with an exogenous number of levels.
[7] Gabaix (1999) has emphasized the emergence of power laws for city size distributions as an outcome of the statistical properties of city growth rates.
[8] We have taken up spatial interaction elsewhere (Dobkins and Ioannides, 1998).

note that whereas it is a drawback of our theory that city sizes are proportional to exogenous parameters, $\Pi_0, \Pi_1, \ldots$, their frequencies are endogenous.

4 Data

Cities pose special definitional problems for data.[9] We define cities as geographical areas in which there is great concentration (density) of economic activity. Density of economic activity is not, of course, unambiguously defined; it could be in terms of value added, employment, population, and so forth. City boundaries can change, and changes in transportation technology and investment have altered the effective economic boundaries of metropolitan areas.

U.S. cities are defined by the Office of Management and Budget (OMB) based on data provided by the U.S. Bureau of the Census. The OMB moved to the standard metropolitan area (SMA) concept in 1950, to standard metropolitan statistical areas (SMSAs) after 1959, and, in 1983, to the classifications of metropolitan statistical area (MSA), primary metropolitan statistical area (PMSA), and consolidated metropolitan statistical area (CMSA).

Most data available prior to 1950 are for "city proper" sizes, reflecting legal city boundaries. Such data are still available, but they cannot reflect the very real fact of suburban integration. Cities do not, in a real economic sense, necessarily coincide with their legal boundaries, and metropolitan-area data reflect this fact. Bogue (1953) used the 1950 SMA definitions to *reconstruct* what the populations would have been in those areas in each of the decennial years from 1900 to 1990. Most of the metropolitan-area data identify city units by counties. (In New England, metropolitan-area definitions may involve parts of counties.) The most cumbersome issue involves these changing definitions within the metropolitan-area structure.

This state of affairs suggests three approaches that might be appropriate for assembling "consistent" data. First, it would be appropriate, for some purposes, to have populations for past years calculated under a consistent set of rules, such as the 1990 standards of the OMB. A second way of generating consistent data would be to use the areas as defined at the time of the appropriate census; that is, use the 1960 definitions for 1960, 1970 definitions for 1970 data, and so forth. That would require returning to original data sources for those years. A third way to generate the data would be to pick a *geographical* area that defines a metropolitan area and use it consistently. For example, we might use the counties that defined a metropolitan area in 1960, and then assign those counties to the city for each year from 1960 forward. That was essentially

---

[9] Technically, a metropolitan area must contain either a city of at least 50,000 or an urbanized area of at least 50,000 and a total metropolitan population of 100,000 (75,000 in New England). See U.S. Bureau of the Census (1992).

what Bogue did in 1953. The issue here is to make this method fit Bogue's work, because the only source we have for the 1900–1940 data is Bogue. In other words, we do not want a pronounced jump in the data between 1950 and preceding years, nor between 1960 and succeeding years. Because of the latter consideration, we opt for the second method.

A major problem that arises in using each year's data in contemporaneous definition is in the span between the most recent censuses, from 1980 to 1990. Because the Bureau of the Census redefined SMSAs as MSAs and CMSAs in 1983, the 18 large metropolitan areas that are now CMSAs would seem to have experienced enormous jumps in size. Therefore, we have reassembled the 1990 data to fit the 1980 definitions (by county). We consequently have metropolitan-area data from 1900 to 1990. The 1900–1940 data have been constructed using the 1950 definitions of SMAs according to Bogue. The 1950–1980 data are consistent with the SMSA definitions in those years. The 1990 data have been reconstructed using the 1980 definitions. We believe that this method, though not perfect, is the most consistent way to construct urban-area sizes. For more details on the data, see Dobkins and Ioannides (1996).

This method highlights a critical issue: the number of metropolitan areas in each census year. If we adhere to a rough definition of metropolitan areas as having populations of more than 50,000 people, then we see a change in the number of cities each year. For 1900, there are 112 urban areas that qualify; that grows to 334 for 1990. We believe that the number of new, "entering" cities, as defined for each decade, is a key feature of the U.S. urban system, especially in its spatial aspects, with many entrants appearing in newly developed geographical areas. In the remainder of this study we shall refer interchangeably to cities and metropolitan areas, as defined here. Our task and method therefore contrast with those of Eaton and Eckstein; the premise for their study was an assertion that the numbers of cities in Japan and France had remained the same over the time periods involved. Of course, this broadened approach is not costless.

We measure "schooling" on the basis of the number of students enrolled in school as a percentage of the population 15–20 years of age. Data unavailability has forced us to accept minor variations in the base cohorts in certain years. See Dobkins and Ioannides (1996) for further details.

We measure wages in terms of the mean wages in the cities proper, which are available for the years 1900–1930. In 1940, the Census Bureau reported details on the frequency in the entire income distribution, up to a maximum of $5,000. For 1950 and 1960, median incomes were reported by SMSAs and smaller cities. Since 1970, median earnings have been reported separately for male and female workers. We have averaged those two numbers for each of the decennial years since then. We have used the national consumer price index (CPI) (1967 = 100) to deflate them. It would have been more appropriate to have used city-specific deflators. Such information has been available only for recent years, when the CPI-U and other cost-of-living figures have been reported for selected metropolitan areas; see the *Statistical Abstract of the United States*, 1994, no. 749. Local indices show greater variability than the national index, but their long-term trends are similar. Our perusal of these numbers suggests strong correlations between city size and real earnings (and personal income) if nominal amounts are deflated by the city-specific index for those areas for which data are readily available.

5 Empirics of the Evolution of City Size Distributions

Because city sizes are the outcomes of economic processes associated with interactions of thoroughly open economic entities, one would expect such interactions to be important. When all cities in an economy are sampled, their sizes exhibit extensive variations simultaneously in both the cross-section dimension (i.e., across i for given t) and the time-series dimension (i.e., across t for given i). In most econometric time-series settings, one studies the dynamics of a vector of random variables whose dimension is fairly small and fixed. Time-series analysis aims at understanding the dynamic behavior of such a vector and the patterns of interactions among its components. Time-series techniques utilize time averaging and other curve-fitting techniques, but do not involve averaging across the components of a vector. Cross-section and panel-data analyses involve investigation of the behavior of the average (or representative) member of each cross section and the deviation of each individual observation from the average across all cross-section units.

As Quah (1993) has forcefully argued, typical cross-section and panel-data techniques do not allow inferences about patterns in the intertemporal evolution of the entire cross-section *distribution*. They do not allow us to consider the impact over time of one part of the distribution upon another (i.e., the effects of the development of large cities, as a group, on smaller cities). Making such inferences requires that one model directly the full dynamics of the entire distribution of cities. In contrast, typical panel-data analyses involve efficient and consistent estimations of models in which the error consists in components reflecting individual effects (random or fixed), time effects, and purely random factors. The evolution of urbanization and suburbanization may affect individual cities so drastically as to render conventional methods of accounting for attrition totally inappropriate. As smaller urban units fuse to create larger ones,[10] and given the small number of time-series observations, nonparametric

---

[10] Such a process has been aptly described by Simon (1955) and Krugman (1996). Similar phenomena have been addressed by the literature on economies with interacting agents. See Ioannides (1997a).

or semiparametric distributional approaches, such as the one proposed here, will be the only appropriate tools. In fact, these techniques are appropriate when the sample of interest is the entire distribution, and individual observations are used to recover information about the entire distribution.

We can further elaborate the process of evolution of systems of cities by considering alternative scenarios that articulate the spatial context. Consider first a situation in which cities of uniform size are uniformly spread over space. The appearance of new cities that are randomly scattered over space is not likely to alter the pattern of uniformity. To the extent that geographical proximity leads invariably to agglomeration, this setting implies creation of larger cities of uniform size. Consider, alternatively, cities of uniform size scattered over space, but in a way that exhibits clustering. The appearance of additional cities of uniform size will make it more likely that ever larger cities will be created through agglomeration of existing cities. The availability of data is severely restricted in both the time and cross-section dimensions: There are only 10 cross sections, one for each of the 10 census years since 1900, with 112 metropolitan areas in 1900, and 334 in 1990.

The paucity of the data naturally leads us toward the techniques used by Quah (1993) and Eaton and Eckstein (1997). That is, one can construct from population data a vector of fairly low dimension indicating the frequency of cities in each of a number of suitably defined intervals (cells).[11] Let f_t denote the frequency (density) distribution of P_{it} at time t. Eaton and Eckstein have assumed that f_t evolves according to a first-order autoregression that applies to the entire distribution function (rather than to scalars or vectors of numbers):

$$f_{t+1} = M f_t \tag{6.20}$$

where M is a matrix of parameters. If the f_t are restricted to be measures defined over a discrete set, then M in (6.20) is a Markov transition matrix.[12]

---

[11] All those studies used six cells, defined relative to the mean. Quah (1993) defined the endpoints within each distribution as the mean in the respective period times $(0, 0.25, 0.50, 1, 2, \infty)$; Eaton and Eckstein defined them as the mean times $(0, 0.30, 0.50, 0.75, 1, 2, 20)$.

[12] More generally, instead of (6.20), we have

$$\forall A \in \mathbb{R}: \quad F_t(A) = \int_A M(x, A) F_{t-1}(dx), \quad \text{where } M: R \times \mathbb{R} \to [0, 1]$$

maps the Cartesian product of the real line R with its Borel sets $\mathbb{R}$ to the unit interval. Then M will be a mixed discrete-continuous analogue of a transition probability matrix. There is a fairly well developed literature on the invariant distributions of such generalized Markov chains (Futia, 1982; Quah, 1993). Arthur (1994, pp. 33–48, 185–201) has provided additional insight. That is, in a nonlinear version of (6.22), Arthur has shown that only stable fixed points of M^* can serve as limit points of f. This fact is particularly interesting within the urban model, because city size often is not uniquely determined, and, of course, not all solutions are stable.

The absence of a random disturbance allows us to iterate (6.20) forward to get

$$f_{t+s} = (M \cdot M \cdot \ldots \cdot M) f_t = M^s f_t \tag{6.21}$$

We can characterize the long-run distribution of city sizes by taking the limit of (6.21) for $s \to \infty$. Divergent, convergent, or parallel growth can be ascertained by the properties of $f_\infty \equiv \lim_{t \to \infty} f_t$. If a limit distribution f_∞ exists, then according to the Perron-Frobenius theorem it is given by the eigenvector corresponding to the unique unitary eigenvalue of M, the nonzero solution of $[M - I] f_\infty = 0]$, where $0]$ denotes a column vector of zeros.

Parallel growth is understood to occur if f_∞ tends to a limit with nonzero probability over the entire support. Convergent growth will occur if f_∞ is a mass point, and divergent growth if f_∞ is a polarized or segmented distribution. Equation (6.20) can be generalized to allow for a stochastic disturbance, U_t,

$$f_{t+1} = M^*(f_t, \varepsilon_{t+1}) \tag{6.22}$$

where M^* is an operator that maps (f_t, ε_{t+1}) to a probability measure. The random-growth model of Simon (1955) can be considered as a special case of processes consistent with specification (6.22).

Quah (1993) has used (6.22) with data for the growth of countries and has conditioned his nonparametric estimation on a number of "exogenous" variables. The transition dynamics are obtained for ordinary-least-squares (OLS) residuals of pooled cross-section and time-series observations, with no individual effects being allowed for in those regressions. Individual effects, Quah has argued, would remove, and thus leave unexplained, the very object of analysis, the relative growth rates of nations. Eaton and Eckstein (1997) did not allow for any conditioning and computed the long-run average transition probabilities. They estimated M by computing the average $M_{i,i+1}$ for all periods in the sample.

We adapt equation (6.22) in order to allow for new cities to enter according to a frequency distribution ε_t. If the number of entrants between t and $t + 1$ is I_t^n, $I_{t+1} = I_t + I_t^n$, then

$$f_{t+1} = \frac{I_t}{I_{t+1}} M_t f_t + \frac{I_t^n}{I_{t+1}} \varepsilon_t \tag{6.23}$$

If M_t and $\iota_t \equiv I_t^n / I_{t+1}$ are time-invariant, then equation (6.23) is amenable to the standard treatment. Letting M and ι be the respective time-invariant values, we can iterate equation (6.23) backward to get

$$f_t = (1 - \iota)^t M^t f_0 + \sum_{\tau=0}^{t} [(1 - \iota) M]^{t-\tau} \iota \varepsilon_\tau \tag{6.24}$$

where f_0 denotes the initial distribution of city sizes.

In general, if there are few or no entrants, $\iota \approx 0$, the homogeneous solution, dominates: The invariant (ergodic) distribution is a useful measure of the state of the urban system in the long run. If, on the other hand, ι is non-negligible, then the particular solution cannot be ignored. In fact, in that case, the magnitude of the largest eigenvalue of $(1 - \iota)M$ is $(1 - \iota)$, and the impact of the initial conditions will be less important the higher is ι, the number of new cities that have entered over the past decade as a proportion of the new total number of cities.

Our approach can be adapted to accommodate a number of different possibilities. One would be Simon's model of "random urban growth" (Simon, 1955),[13] which implies as its stationary solution a law, approximated by a family of skew distributions of the form $f(p; a, b, \beta) = (a/p^\beta)b^p$. This prediction is, in principle, testable. Alternatively, other models, including the hierarchical model we sketched in Section 3.3, also imply laws that can be written as first-order autoregressions like (6.22).

In our data, the values of ι_t are as follows: $\iota_{1910} = .194$, $\iota_{1920} = .067$; $\iota_{1930} = .051$, $\iota_{1940} = .019$, $\iota_{1950} = .012$, $\iota_{1960} = .229$, $\iota_{1970} = .136$, $\iota_{1980} = .245$, and $\iota_{1990} = .036$. These numbers suggest a nonstationary series, and the intertemporal variations in ι_t are interesting and worthy of special analysis. We note that in the absence of a theory for entry of new cities, there is rather limited scope for a purely statistical analysis based on such a small number of time-series observations. There is much greater scope when the microeconomic aspects of the data are exploited. Elsewhere we have pursued further the entry of new cities (Dobkins and Ioannides, 1998).

The stochastic specification of equation (6.23) is, in general, very complicated, especially when M_t can be time-varying. For example, forces that cause urban growth and decline may operate quite differently at the upper level of the distribution than at the lower level, and their patterns may change over time. The distribution of new entrants has most of its mass at the lower end, which to a large extent reflects the nature of our data. Even if M_t is not time-varying, it could be associated with an invariant distribution that could reflect very different properties. The city-formation process, when applied to cities of different types, may imply multiplicity of equilibria, some of which may be stable, and others unstable. As we noted earlier (see also Arthur et al., in Arthur, 1994), only stable equilibria survive in the long run. In view of this great complexity, in the remainder of this chapter we shall eschew a full analysis of the determinants of M and concentrate instead on an approximate treatment of certain key aspects of the dynamic evolution of city size distributions.

---

[13] Briefly, Simon's model considers that a new city, a "lump," may either, with probability ϖ, locate on its own or, with probability $1 - \varpi$, attach itself to a "clump," an existing agglomeration. The probability that a lump will join an existing agglomeration is assumed to be proportional to the clump's size (measured in lumps).

6 Results

6.1 The Rank-Size Rule Revisited

We begin our assessment of the determinants of city size distributions by first returning to the methods of Singer (1936).[14] A random variable p is said to be Pareto-distributed with parameters p_0 and ς if it has a density function given by $f(p; p_0, \varsigma) \equiv (\varsigma/p_0)(p_0/p)^{\varsigma+1}$, with support $[p_0, +\infty)$ and $\varsigma > 0$. The mean exists and is given by $E(p) = [\varsigma/(\varsigma - 1)]p_0$ if $\varsigma > 1$; the variance exists and is given by $\text{Var}(p) = \{\varsigma/[(\varsigma - 1)^2(\varsigma - 2)]\}p_0^2$ if $\varsigma > 2$ (Spanos, 1989, pp. 339–40). The corresponding cumulative distribution function is given by $F(p; p_0, \varsigma) = 1 - (p/p_0)^{-\varsigma}$, and the countercumulative probability function by $1 - F(p; p_0, \varsigma) \equiv (p/p_0)^{-\varsigma}$, which, by taking logarithms of both sides, yields $\ln[1 - F(p; p_0, \varsigma)] = \varsigma \ln p_0 - \varsigma \ln p$.

When we apply the Pareto law with data and hold constant the parameter p_0 (in effect, the size that defines a metropolitan area), then we expect that as $E(p)$ increases over time, the estimated ς will decrease. Consequently, this rather mechanically produced decrease in the estimated parameter ς, for economies where metropolitan-area populations increase over time, should not be interpreted as evidence against (or for) power laws.

We estimate the parameters of a Pareto distribution for each cross section of cities in the 10 census years in our sample. The estimation is based on two versions of the equation

$$\ln[1 - F_{it}] = A_t - \varsigma_t \ln p_{it} + \epsilon_{it}, \qquad i = 1, \ldots, I_t; t = 1, \ldots, T \quad (6.25)$$

where $[1 - F_{it}]$ is the empirical countercumulative distribution of X_{it}, the proportion of cities with populations greater than or equal to X_{it} at time t, and ϵ_{it} is a random variable that is identically normally distributed across I for every t. We allow for A_t and ς_t possibly to be time-varying parameters. This is, of course, a more general version of the equation used in the rank-size-rule literature, and it implies, as a special case, ς_t equal to unity.[15] Finally, we note

---

[14] Recently, geographers have become somewhat disenchanted with the Pareto law and its infinite upper tail and have estimated constrained Pareto distributions with a finite upper bound. See Roehner (1995).

[15] The usual treatment of this relationship in the rank-size literature is simply to define y_{it} to be the rank of the city size P_{it}, or, alternatively expressed, the *number* of cities whose sizes are greater than or equal to P_{it}. As explained earlier, we define y_{it} to be the *proportion* of cities whose sizes are greater than or equal to P_{it}, because we derive our equation (6.25) from the countercumulative probability function of the Pareto distribution. Our formulation, in comparison with the standard formulation, will leave the critical ς_t coefficient unchanged; however, our A_t differs. Alperovich (1984) insisted that A_t should be the logarithm of the size of the largest city if the strict rank-size rule is to hold. However, our A_t is the logarithm of a city's size minus the logarithm of the number of cities in the sample. The A_t values are reported along with the ς_t coefficients in Table 6.1.

Table 6.1. *Estimates of the Pareto distribution for city sizes*

1	2	3	4	5	6	7	8
Year	Obs	Constant	Minimum	ς (s.e.)	R^2	ς (s.e.)	ς (s.e)
1900	112	11.419	91,035	1.044 (0.010)	0.990	.953 (.107)	1.212 (.170)
1910	139	11.106	66,569	1.014 (0.009)	0.989	.919 (.093)	1.120 (.149)
1920	149	11.214	74,161	1.010 (0.009)	0.990	.799 (.088)	1.108 (.143)
1930	157	11.075	64,537	0.985 (0.010)	0.983	.709 (.084)	1.082 (.136)
1940	160	11.263	77,886	0.995 (0.011)	0.982	.677 (.085)	1.131 (.136)
1950	162	11.523	101,013	0.999 (0.012)	0.978	.589 (.084)	1.154 (.138)
1960	210	11.278	79,063	0.977 (0.011)	0.974	.579 (.072)	1.106 (.121)
1970	243	10.986	59,042	0.949 (0.012)	0.963	.558 (.065)	1.096 (.112)
1980	322	11.378	87,378	0.985 (0.010)	0.970	.576 (.058)	1.048 (.098)
1990	334	11.977	159,054	0.949 (0.010)	0.964	.556 (.055)	.993 (.095)

Note: This table gives the number of cities available for each year, the mean size, and the estimated parameters using three methods: the pseudo-Pareto distribution, according to equation (6.25), in columns 3–6; the true Pareto distribution, holding p_0 constant and equal to 10.81978 (corresponding to 50,000), column 7; and the true Pareto distribution using the upper half of the sample, column 8.

Source: 1900–1950: Bogue (1953); 1960–1990: U.S. Bureau of the Census publications.

that when ϵ_{it} is assumed to be normally distributed, estimations according to (6.25) are associated with a pseudo-Pareto distribution. Our estimation results are reported in columns 3–6 of Table 6.1.

We have also estimated this equation by means of a semiparametric method using generalized cross-validation (GCV) (Härdle, 1990, p. 61). For brevity, only the results for 1990 are juxtaposed graphically in Figure 6.1, where the actual data are indicated with circles, the GVC kernel estimate is indicated by squares connected with a curve, and the OLS fitted line is according to equation (6.25). Not surprisingly, the GVC kernel estimate clearly fits the data much better than OLS. Its shape is largely concave and thus in sharp contrast to the convexity of the Pareto countercumulative.

Estimation of a true Pareto distribution is also possible, except that p_0 must be set externally. In our data, there is the obvious choice, namely, $p_0 = 50,000$. Its consequence for the maximum-likelihood estimate of ς is straightforward, as the latter is available in closed form: $\hat{\varsigma}_t = N_t / \sum_i \ln(p_{it}/p_0)$. The larger is p_0, the larger is $\hat{\varsigma}_t$, as a larger exponent is necessary for convergence.

The results reported in Table 6.1 show that the estimated ς_t values are generally lower for the true Pareto distribution, in which case they vary from 0.953

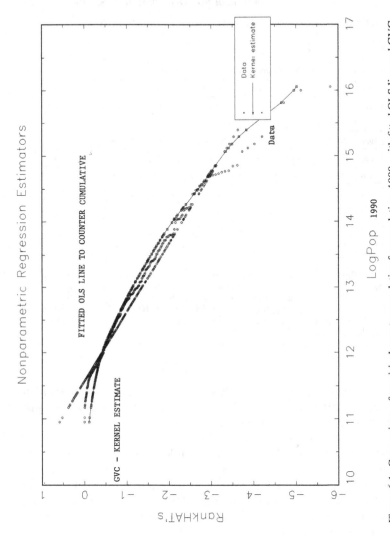

Figure 6.1. Comparison of empirical countercumulative for population, 1990, with fitted OLS line and GVC kernel estimate.

to 0.556, in 1900 and 1990 respectively, than for the pseudo-Pareto, in which case they vary from 1.044 to 0.993. Column 8 reports results for the true Pareto distribution applied to the upper half of the sample, which vary from 1.212 to 0.993. They are higher than when the entire sample is used, and all but one, the one for 1990, lie a bit above 1, thus confirming findings from the previous literature, including, most recently, Krugman (1996).

These results imply an increasing concentration in the upper tail over time, which is to say that more cities are getting larger relative to an increasing mean. The values of the constant reflect the changing proportion of "rank" to the number of cities over time. The estimated ς values offer indications of a subtle change in the U.S. urban structure. Chow tests suggest that each year's ς coefficient significantly differs from the succeeding year's coefficient at the .01 level, except for the period 1950 to 1960 (presumably because of the large increase in the number of cities). Obviously, there are significant differences over longer time periods as well, including 1950 to 1990, 1960 to 1990, 1900 to 1930, and 1900 to 1990.

The jump from 1900 to 1910 may reflect heavy foreign immigration during the first decade of the century. The stagnation of the 1930s is suggested in the table, as is the resurgence of economic activity in the 1950s. One of the most obvious movements is the much-touted counterurbanization of the 1970s.[16] A more subtle reflection may be the move from manufacturing to service industries in U.S. cities, a trend that began in the 1950s and accelerated in the 1960s.

We see that the estimated ς values are much smaller when we use the entire sample than when we use only the upper tail. This is not surprising, given that the sample mean is increasing and the estimates depend on setting x_0 externally and holding it equal to 50,000. Still, the results cast additional doubt upon the relevance of the Pareto distribution as a stylized fact for city size distributions when applied to the entire distribution. We have performed one additional estimation, that by means of the truncated Pareto distribution, as proposed by Roehner (1995), where the largest city in a sample is used to truncate the distribution. As expected, the estimate tracks (but is larger than) that of the true Pareto distribution applied to the entire sample.

All in all, we conclude that the estimate of the Pareto exponent is clearly close to 1, but does not exceed 1. Having said that, we note that the fact that the 1990 estimate is below 1 should raise doubts about the validity of the strict rank-size rule. Our juxtaposition of the OLS and kernel estimates also contributes to our reservations.

---

[16] Mills and Lubuele (1995) examined population (and employment) growth among the *quartiles* of the U.S. city size distribution. They found that the most rapid growth during the 1970s was in the third and fourth quartiles; in the 1980s, the fastest growth occurred in the top three quartiles.

6.2 Empirical Transition Matrices

By coding the position of each city relative to the others within a distribution, we are able to see whether specific cities move up or down in the distribution over time. Though not well known, De Vries (1984, ch. 7) appears to be the originator of this device in the study of urbanization. We have constructed transition matrices, presented in Appendix 6.2, in which each cell gives the proportion of cities that start in a given quantile (column) in a particular year (representing 1900 in the first matrix) and move to a particular quantile (row) in the next year (representing 1910 in the next census). Entries in the diagonal indicate that cities stay in the same category as in the previous time period. Our categories are defined for deciles. (An alternative is to use intervals based on 0.30, 0.50, 0.75, 1.00, 2.00, and 20.00 times the contemporaneous mean, Appendix 6.1. This facilitates comparison with the data of Eaton and Eckstein. Although not included in this chapter, such matrices give results very similar to those shown in Appendix 6.2.)

Both sets of empirical transition matrices suggest that concentration at the upper end of the distribution becomes more pronounced over time: The diagonal entries are higher for higher percentiles. Another observation is that most movements are to nearby cells, with very few big jumps. In interpreting these findings, one must bear in mind that the mean is changing over time.

We have averaged these decennial movements to get an average transition matrix for comparison with the Eaton and Eckstein results. It is presented in Appendix 6.1. As we might expect for the U.S. data, there is somewhat more movement off the diagonal than for the French and Japanese data. Most of that movement is toward greater concentration in the time period from 1900 to 1990.

We have also computed, but do not report here, the invariant distribution that is associated with the average transition matrix [see matrix M in (6.20)] for 1900 to 1990. The result confirms an increasing concentration at the upper end of the distribution of city sizes. This is in great contrast to the computed invariant distributions reported by Eaton and Eckstein (1997) for France and Japan. So it is not just an upward trend in the mean city size, but an overall, and sharp, tendency of the city size distribution that we see.

We note that the stationary distribution, associated with the average computed transition matrix for 1900–1990 (Appendix 6.1), contains most of its mass at the upper portion of its support. However, at any point in time, the actual distribution contains the influence of the newly entering cities, most of which (but not all) enter via the lower end of the support.

However, these transition matrices have limitations. They do not pick up the full effect of "entering" cities, and they do not offer us any more insight into why such changes might occur. Undoubtedly there are other variables that might

Table 6.2. *Descriptive statistics: decennial data, 1900–1990*

1	2	3	4	5	6	7	8	9	10
Year	U.S. Pop. (000)	Mean Size	Median Size	GNP billion $	Interest rate (%)	Manuf. %	Education %	Agric. land value	Earnings $
1900	75,995	259952	121830	71.2	5.95	36	27.8	81.58	1770
1910	91,972	286861	121900	107.5	3.82	36.1	27.6	134.62	1939
1920	105,711	338954	144130	135.9	-.50	39	25.4	105.98	1875
1930	122,775	411641	167140	184.8	6.39	32.5	38.3	98.32	2542
1940	131,669	432911	181490	229.2	1.76	33.9	44.4	72.20	1983
1950	150,697	526422	234720	354.9	7.45	33.7	53.9	81.01	2827
1960	179,323	534936	238340	497.0	1.35	31	63.2	107.07	4108
1970	203,302	574628	259919	747.6	5.12	27.4	74.2	139.65	4763
1980	226,542	526997	232000	963.0	7.97	22.4	70.0	271.29	3520
1990	248,710	577359	243000	1277.8	5.71	17.4	81.1	154.54	3842

Note: All figures are taken from *Historical Statistics of the United States from Colonial Times to 1970,* vols. 1 and 2, and *Statistical Abstract of the United States, 1993.* Columns 5, 6, and 9: GNP, interest rates, and land values adjusted by the implicit price deflator constructed from the foregoing sources (1958 = 100). Column 7: "Manuf." indicates manufacturing employment as a percentage of the total employment for each year. Column 8: Mean percentage of the cohort 15–20 years of age across all cities. Column 10. Mean real annual earnings, by city proper or metropolitan area, in dollars, deflated by the consumer price index (1967=100).

impact on city size distributions. Collection of these data is often constrained either by the number of cities involved or by the time range. In order to give a sense of the change over the century, Table 6.2 presents descriptive statistics for decennial years for the total U.S. population, the mean and median city sizes, the real gross national product, the real interest rate, the percentage of total employment in manufacturing, the average real value of agricultural land and buildings, education, and earnings. Unfortunately, the availability of only 10 years of time-series data prevents us from examining the impact of factors that vary only with time.

6.3 Dynamics of City Population

We now discuss the dynamics of city populations and growth rates. Understanding the possible explanations for changing city sizes may shed some additional light on our question of evolving distributions. Our regression

Table 6.3. *Descriptive statistics: metropolitan areas,
1900–1990: 1990 observations*

Variable	Mean	Std. Dev.	Skewness	Kurtosis	Min	Max
Population (000)	479.5	1001.5	6.6	58.8	50.7	9,372.0
Log(Population)	12.4028	0.9895	1.0	4.1	10.8343	16.374
Growth Rate (%)	10.58	41.99				
New England	.0879	.2833	2.9	9.5	0.00	1.00
Mid Atlantic	0.1276	0.3338	2.2	6.0	0.00	1.00
South Atlantic	0.1673	0.3734	1.8	4.2	0.00	1.00
East North Central	0.2030	0.4023	1.5	3.2	0.00	1.00
East South Central	0.0663	0.2489	3.5	13.1	0.00	1.00
West North Central	0.0910	0.2876	2.8	9.1	0.00	1.00
West South Central	0.1221	0.3275	2.3	6.3	0.00	1.00
Mountain	0.0462	0.2100	4.3	19.7	0.00	1.00
Pacific	0.0884	0.2840	2.9	9.4	0.00	1.00
Education (%)	57.1085	20.9284	-0.4	1.8	11.80	92.73
Real Wage ($)	3197.92	1132.37	0.2	2.3	1020.00	7311.00

equation is

$$\ln P_{it} = a_i + a_t + b \ln P_{i-1,t} + \epsilon_{it}, \qquad i = 1, \dots, I_t,$$

$$I_t = 1, \dots, 334; t = 1910, \dots, 1990 \quad (6.26)$$

where P_{it} is the population of city i at time t, the random variable ϵ_{it} is independently, identically normally distributed for all i and t, the a_t's are time effects reflecting the total effect of time-varying variables, and the a_i's are individual effects. Our setting suggests that fixed effects are more appropriate, although an assumption of random effects may occasionally be convenient.

We account for the possibility of regional effects by coding each city in the sample according to the nine census regions: New England, Middle Atlantic, South Atlantic, East North Central, East South Central, West North Central, West South Central, Mountain, and Pacific. Figure 6.2 is a map indicating the boundaries of the nine regions and the number of cities located in each. Table 6.3 reports the descriptive statistics for all variables used in our regressions. The results of our regressions according to equation (6.26) are reported in columns 1–3 of Table 6.4. The results suggest strong individual effects, in the form of either random or fixed effects.

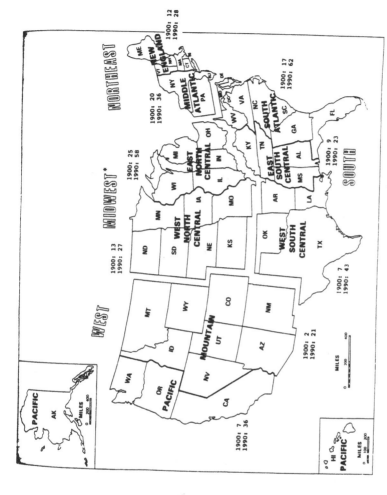

Figure 6.2. Map of United States: states and census regions, with numbers of metropolitan areas, 1900 and 1990. The numbers of cities in our sample in each region are given for 1900 and 1990.
Note: The Midwest Region was designated as the North Central Region until June 1984.
Source: U.S. Department of Commerce, Economics and Statistics Administration, Bureau of the Census.

Table 6.4. *Dynamics of city population and earnings*

	1	2	3	4	5	6
VARIABLE	b (t)	b (t)	b (t)	b (t)	b (t)	b (t)
Constant	.372 (6.75)		.052 (.970)	2.294 (11.51)	5.19 (54.85)	4.56 (71.36)
$\text{Log}P_{t-1}$	.984 (221.2)	.888 (127.5)	.998 (237.4)	-.202 (6.61)		
New England			-.036 (2.00)			.112 (3.34)
Middle Atlantic			-.028 (1.71)			.007 (.21)
South Atlantic			.010 (6.37)			-.025 (.86)
East North Central			.019 (1.29)			.083 (2.85)
East South Central			.057 (2.95)			-.054 (1.5)
West South Central			.119 (7.14)			-.300 (.98)
Mountain			.163 (7.31)			.055 (1.48)
Pacific			.187 (10.20)			.048 (1.49)
LogEducation_t					.398 (27.6)	.492 (49.3)
$\text{Log}P_t$				-.177 (10.98)	.1107 (20.9)	.1158 (22.57)
Observations	1657	1657	1657	1656	1990	1990
LLF	512.4	1101.6	748.0	316.5		905.3
χ^2 p		.0000		.0000		
R^2	.9673	.980	.974	.9597	.464	.824
F		254.6	3819	95.6		564.7

Note: Column 1, OLS regression, logarithm of city population; column 2, OLS regression with fixed effects, logarithm of city population; column 3, GLS regression with random effects and time dummies, logarithm of city population; column 4, GLS regression with fixed effects and time effects, 10-year first difference of logarithm of city population; column 5, GLS regression with random effects and period effects, logarithm of average city annual earnings; column 6, GLS regression with random effects and time dummies, logarithm of average city annual earnings; t-statistics in parentheses.

The estimated coefficient of the lagged value of the dependent variable is very significant and is close to 1, but less than 1, especially when fixed effects are assumed. Inclusion of time dummies is very significant, but does not alter this picture substantially. As for the regional dummy variables, we see highly significant, positive impacts for cities being located in the South Atlantic, East and West South Central, and Pacific regions (in reference to the West North Central region).

The proximity of the estimate of the coefficient of the lagged value of the dependent variable is suggestive of a unit root. Whereas unit roots have attracted particular interest in the macroeconometric time-series literature, several authors, including notably Quah (1994), have drawn attention to special aspects of unit-root inference in data structures resembling random fields, that is,

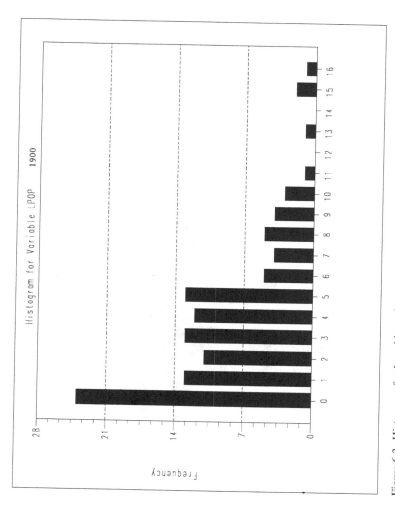

Figure 6.3. Histogram for logarithm of population, 1900. Data based on Census Bureau reports as explained in text.

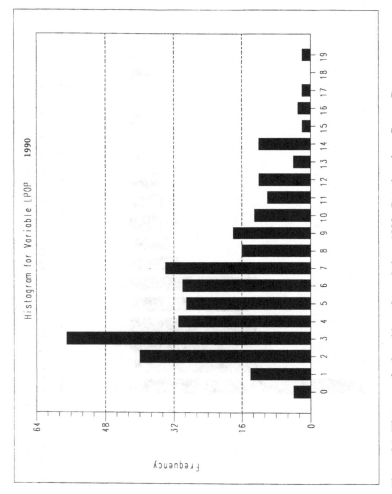

Figure 6.4. Histogram for logarithm of population, 1990. Data based on Census Bureau reports as explained in text.

where the cross-section and time dimensions are comparable.[17] However, in our case, $T = 10$, clearly an order of magnitude smaller than I_t, which ranges from 112 to 334, making those methods inapplicable. We instead ran a number of OLS and panel regressions in which we "imposed" a unit root by restricting the coefficient of the lagged value of the dependent variable to 1. Those restrictions are rejected comfortably in terms of the likelihood-ratio test at the 1% level of significance.

Several authors have used regressions along the lines of (6.26) to test for divergent versus convergent growth across national economies. Column 4 of Table 6.4 reports estimation results for the growth rate of city population, defined as $\ln P_{t+1} - \ln P_t$, as a function of the logarithm of contemporaneous population and of individual effects. Here the contemporaneous city population is treated as predetermined. The availability of only 10 time periods makes it difficult to perform the battery of tests necessary to determine convergence or divergence; $\ln P_t$ has a negative and significant coefficient. We have also worked with the growth rate using the standard definition instead of its logarithmic approximation and have obtained similar results.

6.4 Urban Labor Productivity and City Size

An indirect test of our theoretical model has been provided by regressing labor productivity, measured by earnings, against human capital, measured by education, and city size. The results are reported in columns 5 and 6 of Table 6.4, where we have controlled for individual and time effects and for regional effects. They suggest an important and highly significant effect of city size on earnings. A 10% increase in population is associated with a 1% increase in productivity. The presence of education is also highly significant and is in agreement with a fair amount of recent research, such as that by Ciccone and Hall (1996), Glaeser et al. (1995), and Rauch (1993). As our estimated exponent for the Pareto tail decreases over time, our results imply that urbanization is associated with increasing inequality of earned incomes.

7 Conclusions

This chapter has examined the implications for the theory of city size distribution of increasing returns to scale leading to monopolistic competition. It has proposed a rudimentary model of an urban hierarchy in which the tendency

---

[17] Quah (1994) found that the distribution of the unit-regression-coefficient estimator was neither (unbiased) normal at rate $O_p(N^{-\frac{1}{2}})$, as one might expect from standard panel-data analysis, nor standard Dickey-Fuller at rate $O_p(^{-1})$, as one might expect from standard time-series analysis. Instead, the estimator is consistent and asymptotically normal, but with a nonvanishing bias in the asymptotic distribution.

of monopolistic competition models to generate increasing returns associated with product diversity is reinforced when the productivity of labor is augmented by having successive, vertically arranged sets of sectors produce increasingly skilled labor. Some broad implications of the model have been tested by means of a new data set.

Our data set has been constructed to reflect the changing definitions of SMSAs from 1900 to 1990. Though no ideal data set for cities exists, we feel fairly confident that the one we have constructed anew reflects the changing numbers of cities, the changing city sizes, and the changing distribution. Our methods have been designed to reflect the complexities of our panel of observations, which have varied across both time and cities.

We have addressed in this chapter the city size distributions in the United States in the twentieth century and the determinants of those distributions. The estimated Pareto distributions indicate small but significant movement toward increasing inequality, based on a declining exponent for the Pareto tail and increasing means.

We have studied in a nonparametric manner the transitions in the size distributions over each of the past 10 decades for the United States. In contrast to Eaton and Eckstein's findings for France and Japan, we have found increasing concentration toward the upper end of the distribution for the United States over time, in spite of considerable entry of new cities. When we have regressed the populations of metropolitan areas against their own lagged values, as well as variables reflecting individual and regional effects, the results have suggested that lagged "own population" has a significant coefficient that is close to 1, but less than 1. Growth-rate regressions also suggest convergent growth.

Undoubtedly there are other variables that might be influential. We would like to be able to say something about commuting costs, because standard urban theory suggests that the changing technology of commuting has contributed to urban spread. We shall continue to search for a broader set of measurable factors that might have an impact. Nevertheless, we believe that we have prescribed a method and described results that shed light on the shifting distribution of city sizes in the United States to date and its implications for earnings inequality. Our work in progress on spatial interaction is also promising.

Appendix 6.1: Average Transition Matrix, U.S. Cities, 1900–90

The cells in this matrix are identified by the upper endpoints of the categories, as explained in the text; that is, 0.3, 0.5, 0.75, 1, 2, and 20 times the mean. The entries in the cells are the averages over nine matrices that define decade-to-decade changes. See Appendix 6.2 for the decade-by-decade matrices. The "total cities" column and row give the actual distributions for 1900 (summing to 112) and 1990 (summing to 322).

1990/1900	0.3	0.5	0.75	1	2	20	Total cities
0.3	79.84	6.90	0.41	0	0	0	110
0.5	19.79	66.36	9.07	0	0	0	64
0.75	0.37	25.66	62.54	7.62	2.53	0	51
1	0	1.09	21.48	53.47	4.48	0	23
2	0	0	6.49	38.91	79.23	.85	38
20	0	0	0	0	13.76	98.76	36
Total cities	24	31	15	14	15	13	322/112
Stationary distribution	0.15	0.38	1.00	1.27	8.03	89.17	

Appendix 6.2: Transition Matrices, by Deciles, Decade by Decade

Each cell in these matrices represents the number of cities in the respective category in year $t+1$ (rows) compared with year t (columns), and the associated frequency. For example, in the first matrix, the proportion of cities belonging to the smallest category in 1900 that moved to the next category (between the 10th and 20th percentiles) in 1910 was 58.33%; 7 cities did so. As explained in the text, these matrices do not show the entry of new cities. The first matrix picks up only the 112 cities that meet our criteria for 1900.

Linda Harris Dobkins and Yannis M. Ioannides

TRANSITIONS: 112 cities; 1900 to 1910

1910/1900	0.10	0.20	0.30	0.40	0.50	0.60	0.70	0.80	0.90	1.00	Total	Enter 1910
0.10	0	0	0	0	0	0	0	0	0	0	0	14
	0.00	0.00	0.00	0.00	0.00	0.00	0.00	0.00	0.00	0.00	0.00	
0.20	7	1	0	0	0	0	0	0	0	0	8	6
	58.33	9.09	0.00	0.00	0.00	0.00	0.00	0.00	0.00	0.00	7.14	
0.30	3	3	3	0	0	0	0	0	0	0	9	5
	25.00	27.27	27.27	0.00	0.00	0.00	0.00	0.00	0.00	0.00	8.04	
0. 40	0	5	5	2	0	0	0	0	0	0	12	2
	0.00	45.45	45.45	18.18	0.00	0.00	0.00	0.00	0.00	0.00	10.71	
0. 50	1	0	0	0	0	2	1	3	4	3	14	0
	8.33	0.00	0.00	0.00	0.00	16.67	9.09	27.27	36.36	27.27	12.50	
0.60	0	1	0	5	6	2	0	0	0	0	14	0
	0.00	9.09	0.00	45.45	54.55	16.67	0.00	0.00	0.00	0.00	12.50	
0.70	0	0	0	0	1	6	7	0	0	0	14	0
	0.00	0.00	0.00	0.00	9.09	50.00	63.64	0.00	0.00	0.00	12.50	
0.80	0	0	0	0	1	2	4	7	0	0	14	0
	0.00	0.00	0.00	0.00	9.09	16.67	36.36	63.64	0.00	0.00	12.50	
0.90	0	0	0	0	0	1	0	4	9	0	14	0
	0.00	0.00	0.00	0.00	0.00	8.33	0.00	36.36	81.82	0.00	12.50	
1.00	0	0	0	0	0	0	0	0	2	11	13	0
	0.00	0.00	0.00	0.00	0.00	0.00	0.00	0.00	18.18	100.00	11.61	
Total	12	11	11	11	11	12	11	11	11	11	112	27
	10.71	9.82	9.82	9.82	9.82	10.71	9.82	9.82	9.82	9.82	100.00	

TRANSITIONS: 139 cities; 1910 to 1920

1920/1910	0.10	0.20	0.30	0.40	0.50	0.60	0.70	0.80	0.90	1.00	Total	Enter 1920
0.10	6	3	1	0	0	0	0	0	0	0	10	5
	42.86	21.43	7.14	0.00	0.00	0.00	0.00	0.00	0.00	0.00	7.19	
0.20	6	5	1	0	0	0	0	0	0	0	12	3
	42.86	35.71	7.14	0.00	0.00	0.00	0.00	0.00	0.00	0.00	8.63	
0.30	1	4	8	1	0	0	0	0	0	0	14	1
	7.14	28.57	57.14	7.14	0.00	0.00	0.00	0.00	0.00	0.00	10.07	
0.40	1	0	2	9	2	0	0	0	0	0	14	1
	7.14	0.00	14.29	64.29	14.29	0.00	0.00	0.00	0.00	0.00	10.07	
0.50	0	2	2	4	5	2	0	0	0	0	15	0
	0.00	14.29	14.29	28.57	35.71	14.29	0.00	0.00	0.00	0.00	10.79	
0.60	0	0	0	0	4	10	1	0	0	0	15	0
	0.00	0.00	0.00	0.00	28.57	71.43	7.14	0.00	0.00	0.00	10.79	
0.70	0	0	0	0	2	2	10	1	0	0	15	0
	0.00	0.00	0.00	0.00	14.29	14.29	71.43	7.14	0.00	0.00	10.79	
0.80	0	0	0	0	1	0	3	10	1	0	15	0
	0.00	0.00	0.00	0.00	7.14	0.00	21.43	71.43	7.14	0.00	10.79	
0.90	0	0	0	0	0	0	0	3	12	0	15	0
	0.00	0.00	0.00	0.00	0.00	0.00	0.00	21.43	85.71	0.00	10.79	
1.00	0	0	0	0	0	0	0	0	1	13	14	0
	0.00	0.00	0.00	0.00	0.00	0.00	0.00	0.00	7.14	100.00	10.07	
Total	14	14	14	14	14	14	14	14	14	13	139	10
	10.07	10.07	10.07	10.07	10.07	10.07	10.07	10.07	10.07	9.35	100.00	

TRANSITIONS: 149 cities; 1920 to 1930

1930/1920	0.10	0.20	0.30	0.40	0.50	0.60	0.70	0.80	0.90	1.00	Total	Enter 1930
0.10	9	0	0	0	0	0	0	0	0	0	9	7
	60.00	0.00	0.00	0.00	0.00	0.00	0.00	0.00	0.00	0.00	6.04	
0.20	6	8	1	1	0	0	0	0	0	0	16	0
	40.00	53.33	6.67	6.67	0.00	0.00	0.00	0.00	0.00	0.00	10.74	
0.30	0	3	7	6	0	0	0	0	0	0	16	0
	0.00	20.00	46.67	40.00	0.00	0.00	0.00	0.00	0.00	0.00	10.74	
0.40	0	4	5	4	2	0	0	0	0	0	15	0
	0.00	26.67	33.33	26.67	13.33	0.00	0.00	0.00	0.00	0.00	10.07	
0.50	0	0	2	3	8	2	0	0	0	0	15	1
	0.00	0.00	13.33	20.00	53.33	13.33	0.00	0.00	0.00	0.00	10.07	
0.60	0	0	0	1	3	11	1	0	0	0	16	0
	0.00	0.00	0.00	6.67	20.00	73.33	6.67	0.00	0.00	0.00	10.74	
0.70	0	0	0	0	2	2	9	2	0	0	15	0
	0.00	0.00	0.00	0.00	13.33	13.33	60.00	13.33	0.00	0.00	10.07	
0.80	0	0	0	0	0	0	5	9	2	0	16	0
	0.00	0.00	0.00	0.00	0.00	0.00	33.33	60.00	13.33	0.00	10.74	
0.90	0	0	0	0	0	0	0	4	12	0	16	0
	0.00	0.00	0.00	0.00	0.00	0.00	0.00	26.67	80.00	0.00	10.74	
1.00	0	0	0	0	0	0	0	0	1	14	15	0
	0.00	0.00	0.00	0.00	0.00	0.00	0.00	0.00	6.67	100.00	10.07	
Total	15	15	15	15	15	15	15	15	15	14	149	8
	10.07	10.07	10.07	10.07	10.07	10.07	10.07	10.07	10.07	9.40	100.00	

TRANSITIONS: 157 cities; 1930 to 1940

1940/1930	0.10	0.20	0.30	0.40	0.50	0.60	0.70	0.80	0.90	1.00	Total	Enter 1940
0.10	12	1	0	0	0	0	0	0	0	0	13	3
	75.00	6.25	0.00	0.00	0.00	0.00	0.00	0.00	0.00	0.00	8.28	
0.20	4	9	3	0	0	0	0	0	0	0	16	0
	25.00	56.25	18.75	0.00	0.00	0.00	0.00	0.00	0.00	0.00	10.19	
0.30	0	5	9	2	0	0	0	0	0	0	16	0
	0.00	31.25	56.25	13.33	0.00	0.00	0.00	0.00	0.00	0.00	10.19	
0.40	0	1	4	8	3	0	0	0	0	0	16	0
	0.00	0.64	2.55	5.10	1.91	10.19 0.00	0.00	0.00	0.00	0.00	10.19	
0.50	0	0	0	5	9	2	0	0	0	0	16	0
	0.00	0.00	0.00	33.33	56.25	12.50	0.00	0.00	0.00	0.00	10.19	
0.60	0	0	0	0	3	12	1	0	0	0	16	0
	0.00	0.00	0.00	0.00	18.75	75.00	6.67	0.00	0.00	0.00	10.19	
0.70	0	0	0	0	1	2	13	0	0	0	16	0
	0.00	0.00	0.00	0.00	6.25	12.50	86.67	0.00	0.00	0.00	10.19	
0.80	0	0	0	0	0	0	1	14	1	0	16	0
	0.00	0.00	0.00	0.00	0.00	0.00	6.67	87.50	6.25	0.00	10.19	
0.90	0	0	0	0	0	0	0	2	14	0	16	0
	0.00	0.00	0.00	0.00	0.00	0.00	0.00	12.50	87.50	0.00	10.19	
1.00	0	0	0	0	0	0	0	0	1	15	16	0
	0.00	0.00	0.00	0.00	0.00	0.00	0.00	0.00	6.25	100.00	10.19	
Total	16	16	16	15	16	16	15	16	16	15	157	3
	10.19	10.19	10.19	9.55	10.19	10.19	9.55	10.19	10.19	9.55	100.00	

Linda Harris Dobkins and Yannis M. Ioannides

TRANSITIONS: 160 cities; 1940 to 1950

1950/1940	0.10	0.20	0.30	0.40	0.50	0.60	0.70	0.80	0.90	1.00	Total	Enter 1950
0.10	12	3	0	0	0	0	0	0	0	0	15	2
	75.00	18.75	0.00	0.00	0.00	0.00	0.00	0.00	0.00	0.00	9.38	
0.20	3	10	3	0	0	0	0	0	0	0	16	0
	18.75	62.50	18.75	0.00	0.00	0.00	0.00	0.00	0.00	0.00	10.00	
0.30	1	1	11	3	0	0	0	0	0	0	16	0
	6.25	6.25	68.75	18.75	0.00	0.00	0.00	0.00	0.00	0.00	10.00	
0.40	0	2	2	8	4	0	0	0	0	0	16	0
	0.00	12.50	12.50	50.00	25.00	0.00	0.00	0.00	0.00	0.00	10.00	
0.50	0	0	0	5	8	3	0	0	0	0	16	0
	0.00	0.00	0.00	31.25	50.00	18.75	0.00	0.00	0.00	0.00	10.00	
0.60	0	0	0	0	3	10	3	1	0	0	17	0
	0.00	0.00	0.00	0.00	18.75	62.50	18.75	6.25	0.00	0.00	10.63	
0.70	0	0	0	0	1	3	9	3	0	0	16	0
	0.00	0.00	0.00	0.00	6.25	18.75	56.25	18.75	0.00	0.00	10.00	
0.80	0	0	0	0	0	0	3	10	3	0	16	0
	0.00	0.00	0.00	0.00	0.00	0.00	18.75	62.50	18.75	0.00	10.00	
0.90	0	0	0	0	0	0	1	2	13	0	16	0
	0.00	0.00	0.00	0.00	0.00	0.00	6.25	12.50	81.25	0.00	10.00	
1.00	0	0	0	0	0	0	0	0	0	16	16	0
	0.00	0.00	0.00	0.00	0.00	0.00	0.00	0.00	0.00	100.00	10.00	
Total	16	16	16	16	16	16	16	16	16	16	160	2
	10.00	10.00	10.00	10.00	10.00	10.00	10.00	10.00	10.00	10.00	100.00	

TRANSITIONS: 162 cities; 1950 to 1960

1960/1950	0.10	0.20	0.30	0.40	0.50	0.60	0.70	0.80	0.90	1.00	Total	Enter 1960
0.10	5	0	1	1	0	0	0	0	0	0	7	14
	29.41	0.00	6.25	6.25	0.00	0.00	0.00	0.00	0.00	0.00	4.32	
0.20	9	4	0	1	0	0	0	0	0	0	14	7
	52.94	25.00	0.00	6.25	0.00	0.00	0.00	0.00	0.00	0.00	8.64	
0.30	3	7	2	0	1	0	1	0	0	0	14	7
	17.65	43.75	12.50	0.00	6.25	0.00	6.25	0.00	0.00	0.00	8.64	
0.40	0	4	7	0	0	0	0	0	0	0	11	10
	0.00	25.00	43.75	0.00	0.00	0.00	0.00	0.00	0.00	0.00	6.79	
0.50	0	0	4	12	0	1	1	0	0	0	18	3
	0.00	0.00	25.00	75.00	0.00	5.88	6.25	0.00	0.00	0.00	11.11	
0.60	0	0	2	1	11	4	2	0	0	0	20	1
	0.00	0.00	12.50	6.25	68.75	23.53	12.50	0.00	0.00	0.00	12.35	
0.70	0	1	0	1	4	7	3	2	2	0	20	1
	0.00	6.25	0.00	6.25	25.00	41.18	18.75	12.50	12.50	0.00	12.35	
0.80	0	0	0	0	0	4	7	7	1	0	19	2
	0.00	0.00	0.00	0.00	0.00	23.53	43.75	43.75	6.25	0.00	11.73	
0.90	0	0	0	0	0	1	2	7	10	0	20	1
	0.00	0.00	0.00	0.00	0.00	5.88	12.50	43.75	62.50	0.00	12.35	
1.00	0	0	0	0	0	0	0	0	3	16	19	2
	0.00	0.00	0.00	0.00	0.00	0.00	0.00	0.00	18.75	100.00	11.73	
Total	17	16	16	16	16	17	16	16	16	16	162	48
	10.49	9.88	9.88	9.88	9.88 10.49	9.88	9.88	9.88	9.88	100.00		

TRANSITIONS: 210 cities; 1960 to 1970

1970/1960	0.10	0.20	0.30	0.40	0.50	0.60	0.70	0.80	0.90	1.00	Total	Enter 1970
0.10	15	0	0	0	0	0	0	0	0	0	15	10
	71.43	0.00	0.00	0.00	0.00	0.00	0.00	0.00	0.00	0.00	7.14	
0.20	5	11	0	0	0	0	0	0	0	0	16	8
	23.81	52.38	0.00	0.00	0.00	0.00	0.00	0.00	0.00	0.00	7.62	
0.30	0	6	12	2	0	0	0	0	0	0	20	4
	0.00	28.57	57.14	9.52	0.00	0.00	0.00	0.00	0.00	0.00	9.52	
0.40	1	3	7	9	1	0	0	0	0	0	21	4
	4.76	14.29	33.33	42.86	4.76	0.00	0.00	0.00	0.00	0.00	10.00	
0.50	0	1	1	8	9	2	0	0	0	0	21	3
	0.00	4.76	4.76	38.10	42.86	9.52	0.00	0.00	0.00	0.00	10.00	
0.60	0	0	1	2	10	10	0	0	0	0	23	1
	0.00	0.00	4.76	9.52	47.62	47.62	0.00	0.00	0.00	0.00	10.95	
0.70	0	0	0	0	1	9	13	0	0	0	23	2
	0.00	0.00	0.00	0.00	4.76	42.86	61.90	0.00	0.00	0.00	10.95	
0.80	0	0	0	0	0	0	8	15	1	0	24	0
	0.00	0.00	0.00	0.00	0.00	0.00	38.10	71.43	4.76	0.00	11.43	
0.90	0	0	0	0	0	0	0	6	18	0	24	0
	0.00	0.00	0.00	0.00	0.00	0.00	0.00	28.57	85.71	0.00	11.43	
1.00	0	0	0	0	0	0	0	0	2	21	23	1
	0.00	0.00	0.00	0.00	0.00	0.00	0.00	0.00	9.52	100.00	10.95	
Total	21	21	21	21	21	21	21	21	21	21	210	33
	10.00	10.00	10.00	10.00	10.00	10.00	10.00	10.00	10.00	10.00	100.00	

TRANSITIONS: 243 cities; 1970 to 1980

1980/1970	0.10	0.20	0.30	0.40	0.50	0.60	0.70	0.80	0.90	1.00	Total	Enter 1980
0.10	18	0	0	0	0	0	0	0	0	0	18	16
	7.41	0.00	0.00	0.00	0.00	0.00	0.00	0.00	0.00	0.00	7.41	
0.20	5	6	0	0	0	0	0	0	0	0	11	21
	71.43	25.00	0.00	0.00	0.00	0.00	0.00	0.00	0.00	0.00	4.53	
0.30	1	10	8	0	0	0	0	0	0	0	19	13
	14.29	41.67	33.33	0.00	0.00	0.00	0.00	0.00	0.00	0.00	7.82	
0.40	1	7	6	5	0	0	0	0	0	0	19	12
	14.29	29.17	25.00	20.00	0.00	0.00	0.00	0.00	0.00	0.00	7.82	
0.50	0	1	10	11	3	0	0	0	0	0	25	7
	0.00	4.17	41.67	44.00	12.50	0.00	0.00	0.00	0.00	0.00	10.29	
0.60	0	0	0	7	14	7	0	0	0	0	28	5
	0.00	0.00	0.00	28.00	58.33	29.17	0.00	0.00	0.00	0.00	11.52	
0.70	0	0	0	2	7	12	10	0	0	0	31	1
	0.00	0.00	0.00	8.00	29.17	50.00	40.00	0.00	0.00	0.00	11.52	
0.80	0	0	0	0	0	5	14	10	0	1	30	2
	0.00	0.00	0.00	0.00	0.00	20.83	56.00	41.67	0.00	4.17	12.35	
0.90	0	0	0	0	0	0	1	14	16	0	31	1
	0.00	0.00	0.00	0.00	0.00	0.00	4.00	58.33	66.67	0.00	12.76	
1.00	0	0	0	0	0	0	0	0	8	23	31	1
	0.00	0.00	0.00	0.00	0.00	0.00	0.00	0.00	33.33	95.83	12.76	
Total	25	24	24	25	24	24	25	24	24	24	243	79
	10.29	9.88	9.88	10.29	9.88	9.88	10.29	9.88	9.88	9.88	100.00	

TRANSITIONS: 322 cities; 1980 to 1990

1990/1980	0.10	0.20	0.30	0.40	0.50	0.60	0.70	0.80	0.90	1.00	Total	Enter 1990
0.10	28	3	0	0	0	0	0	0	0	0	31	4
	82.35	9.38	0.00	0.00	0.00	0.00	0.00	0.00	0.00	0.00	9.63	
0.20	4	16	11	0	1	0	0	0	0	0	32	1
	11.76	50.00	34.38	0.00	3.13	0.00	0.00	0.00	0.00	0.00	9.94	
0.30	2	10	12	4	3	0	0	0	0	0	31	3
	5.88	31.25	37.50	12.90	9.38	0.00	0.00	0.00	0.00	0.00	9.63	
0.40	0	2	8	12	7	0	0	0	0	0	29	3
	0.00	6.25	25.00	38.71	21.88	0.00	0.00	0.00	0.00	0.00	9.01	
0.50	0	1	1	15	12	3	1	0	0	0	33	0
	0.00	3.13	3.13	48.39	37.50	9.09	3.13	0.00	0.00	0.00	10.25	
0.60	0	0	0	0	8	20	5	0	0	0	33	1
	0.00	0.00	0.00	0.00	25.00	60.61	15.63	0.00	0.00	0.00	10.25	
0.70	0	0	0	0	1	10	20	2	0	0	33	0
	0.00	0.00	0.00	0.00	3.13	30.30	62.50	6.25	0.00	0.00	10.25	
0.80	0	0	0	0	0	0	6	24	4	0	34	0
	0.00	0.00	0.00	0.00	0.00	0.00	18.75	75.00	12.50	0.00	10.25	
0.90	0	0	0	0	0	0	0	6	26	1	33	0
	0.00	0.00	0.00	0.00	0.00	0.00	0.00	18.75	81.25	3.13	10.25	
1.00	0	0	0	0	0	0	0	0	2	31	33	0
	0.00	0.00	0.00	0.00	0.00	0.00	0.00	0.00	6.25	96.88	10.25	
Total	34	32	32	31	32	33	32	32	32	32	322	12
	10 56	9.94	9.94	9.63	9.94	10.25	9.94	9.94	9.94	9.94	100.00	

References

Abdel-Rahman, H., and Fujita, M. (1993). Specialization and diversification in a system of cities. *Journal of Urban Economics* 33:189–222.

Alperovich, G. (1984). The size distribution of cities: on the empirical validity of the rank-size rule. *Journal of Urban Economics* 16:232–9.

Arthur, W. B. (1994). *Increasing Returns and Path Dependence in the Economy*. Ann Arbor: University of Michigan Press.

Auerbach, F. (1913). Das Gesetz der Bevölkerungskonzentration. *Petermanns Geographische Mitteilungen* 59:74–6.

Beckmann, M. J. (1958). City hierarchies and the distribution of city size. *Economic Development and Cultural Change* 6:243–8.

Bogue, D. J. (1953). *Population Growth in Standard Metropolitan Areas 1900–1950*. Oxford, OH: Scripps Foundation in Research in Population Problems.

Ciccone, A., and Hall, R. E. (1996). Productivity and the density of economic activity. *American Economic Review* 86:54–70.

Crihfield, J. B., and Panggabean, M. P. H. (1995). Growth and convergence in U.S. cities. *Journal of Urban Economics* 37:138–65.

De Vries, J. (1984). *European Urbanization, 1500–1800.* Cambridge, MA: Harvard University Press.

Dixit, A., and Stiglitz, J. E. (1977). Monopolistic competition and optimum product diversity. *American Economic Review* 67:297–308.

Dobkins, L. H., and Ioannides, Y. M. (1996). Documentation of the Dobkins-Ioannides data on U.S. metro areas. Mimeograph, Department of Economics, Emory & Henry College, Emory, VA.

Dobkins, L. H., and Ioannides, Y. M. (1998). Spatial interactions among U.S. cities. Presented at the Econometric Society meetings, Chicago, January 1998.

Eaton, J., and Eckstein, Z. (1997). Cities and growth: theory and evidence from France and Japan. *Regional Science and Urban Economics* 27:443–74.

Futia, K. (1982). Invariant distributions and the limiting behavior of Markovian economic models. *Econometrica* 50:377–408.

Gabaix, X. (1999). Zipf's law for cities: an explanation. *Quarterly Journal of Economics.*

Gell-Mann, M. (1994). *The Quark and the Jaguar.* New York: Freeman.

Glaeser, E. L., Scheinkman, J. A., and Shleifer, A. (1995). Economic growth in a cross-section of cities. *Journal of Monetary Economics* 36:117–43.

Härdle, W. (1990). *Applied Nonparametric Regression.* Cambridge University Press.

Henderson, J. V. (1974). The types and size of cities. *American Economic Review* 64:640–56.

Henderson, J. V. (1983). Industrial bases and city size. *American Economic Review* 73:164–8.

Henderson, J. V. (1987). Systems of cities and inter-city trade. In: P. Hansen et al. (eds.), *Systems of Cities and Facility Location.* Chur, Switzerland: Harwood.

Henderson, J. V. (1988). *Urban Development: Theory, Fact and Illusion.* Oxford University Press.

Henderson, J. V., and Ioannides, Y. M. (1981). Aspects of growth in a system of cities. *Journal of Urban Economics* 10:117–39.

Ioannides, Y. M. (1994). Product differentiation and economic growth in a system of cities. *Regional Science and Urban Economics* 24:461–84.

Ioannides, Y. M. (1997a). The evolution of trading structures. In: W. B. Arthur, S. N. Durlauf, and D. A. Lane (eds.), *The Economy as an Evolving Complex System II,* pp. 129–67. Reading, MA: Addison-Wesley.

Ioannides, Y. M. (1997b). Inequality and space. Mimeography, Department of Economics, Tufts University.

Krugman, P. (1993). On the number and location of cities. *European Economic Review* 37:293–308.

Krugman, P. (1994).Complex landscapes in economic geography. *American Economic Review, Papers and Proceedings* 84:412–16.

Krugman, P. (1996). *The Self-organizing Economy.* Oxford: Blackwell.

Lotka, A. (1925). *Elements of Physical Biology.* Baltimore: Williams & Wilkins.

Madden, C. H. (1956). On some indications of stability in the growth of cities in the United States. *Economic Development and Cultural Change* 4:236–52.

Matsuyama, K. (1995). Complementarities and cumulative processes. *Journal of Economic Literature* 33:701–29.

Mills, E. S., and Lubuele, L. S. (1995). Projecting growth of metropolitan areas. *Journal of Urban Economics* 37:344–60.

Pareto, V. (1906). *Cours d'economie politique.* Geneva: Libraire Droz.

Quah, D. (1993). Empirical cross-section dynamics and economic growth. *European Economic Review* 37:426–34.

Quah, D. (1994). Exploiting cross-section variation for unit root inference in dynamic data. *Economics Letters* 44:9–19.

Rauch, J. E. (1993). Productivity gains from geographic concentration of human capital: evidence from the cities. *Journal of Urban Economics* 34:380–400.

Roehner, B. M. (1995). Evolution of urban systems in the Pareto plane. *Journal of Regional Science* 35:277-300.

Simon, H. (1955).On a class of skew distribution functions. *Biometrika* 44:425–40. Reprinted (1957) in *Models of Man: Social and Rational. Mathematical Essays on Rational Human Behavior in a Social Setting.* New York: Wiley.

Singer, H. W. (1936).The "Courbes des populations": a parallel to Pareto's law. *Economic Journal* 46:254–63.

Spanos, A. (1989). *Statistical Foundations of Econometric Modeling.* Cambridge University Press.

U.S. Bureau of the Census (1992). *1990 Census of Housing.* CH-1-48, July, Washington, DC.

U.S. Bureau of the Census (1994). *Statistical Abstract of the United States.* Washington, DC.

Zipf, G. K. (1949). *Human Behavior and the Principle of Least Effort.* Reading, MA: Addison-Wesley.

Urbanization and Growth

CHAPTER 7

Urban Growth Models with Durable Housing: An Overview

Jan K. Brueckner

1 Introduction

Our understanding of the economics of urban land use took a great leap forward with the development of the static model of a monocentric city. The pioneering contributions in this area were made by Alonso (1964), Mills (1967), and Muth (1969), with important later elaboration provided by Wheaton (1974). The key insight in the monocentric model is that the price of housing varies with accessibility to the central business district (CBD). Consumers residing far from the CBD are compensated for their long commutes with cheap housing, while consumers living at central locations pay a premium for space, canceling the advantage of low commuting costs. Substitution in response to this price variation generates a distinct pattern of housing consumption: Dwellings are small near the CBD, and large at suburban locations far from the CBD. The decline over distance in the price of housing also affects the decisions of housing developers, who combine capital and land to produce dwelling space. For developer profits to be uniform throughout the city, land rent must fall as distance to the CBD increases, mirroring the decline in the unit price of housing. Falling land rents in turn affect the developer's optimal input mix, with capital-to-land ratios declining as distance to the CBD increases. Buildings are then tall near the CBD and short in the suburbs, and with dwelling sizes increasing over distance, it follows that population density declines moving away from the CBD. Density drops abruptly to zero at the edge of the city, where urban land rent dips below the land rent in agriculture.

The element of time is deemphasized in the static model, and this is permissible because of the implicit assumption that housing capital is malleable. This assumption allows the city to be rebuilt every period as underlying conditions change, which means that the city's spatial structure can be predicted at any point in time without regard to its past history. Because the model has been

I thank Jean-Marie Huriot and Alex Anas for helpful comments. Any errors or shortcomings in this chapter, however, are my responsibility.

successful in explaining the broad features of existing cities, this suppression of history is justified. However, the model fails to predict some aspects of urban form on a more detailed level, and this failure is connected to its ahistorical character.

The predictions of the static model that are most troublesome concern the pattern of land-use intensity and sequencing of land development. In the first case, the model predicts that building heights decline smoothly with distance to the CBD. However, real-world cities often exhibit dramatic variation in heights over short distances, with tall and short buildings often located adjacent to one another. Even when building heights vary smoothly, the height contour may exhibit upward-sloping ranges, in contrast to the predictions of the static model. These anomalies sometimes can be explained by an appeal to history, which reveals different construction dates for the buildings in question. Tall and short buildings located in close proximity may have vastly different ages; suburban buildings that loom higher than CBD structures may be much newer. Thus, building-height patterns that appear anomalous from the perspective of the static model may be natural outcomes if the model is enlarged to include a role for history.

In addition, the sequencing of land development in real-world cities sometimes violates the predictions of the static model. In particular, the model cannot explain leapfrog development, where close-in locations are left vacant as the city grows. Because land use can be continuously adjusted, there is no benefit in the static model from postponing development of prime land near the CBD. However, when capital is durable, early development of prime land may leave a legacy that the developer will regret later in the city's evolution. Postponement of development at central locations (and hence leapfrogging) may then be desirable.

Recognizing the deficiencies of the static model, urban economists have expended a large amount of research effort since the mid-1970s in developing models where housing capital is durable rather than malleable. Unlike in the static model, durability of housing makes continual redevelopment of the city uneconomical, and this means that the city's spatial structure at a given point in time depends on its past history. The purpose of this chapter is to provide a self-contained exposition of the major elements of the durable-housing literature, providing a useful reference for students and researchers.[1]

The chapter begins in Section 2 by reviewing the static model, which provides a benchmark against which subsequent models are judged. To emphasize its key feature, the static framework is referred to as the "malleable-housing" model.

---

[1] For earlier surveys, see Wheaton (1983) and Miyao (1987). Wheaton's paper focuses mainly on his own work, while discussion of durable-housing models represents only a small part of Miyao's survey, which focuses on other types of dynamic models.

The subsequent discussion of durable-housing models is divided into two parts. Section 3 considers models where housing development is irreversible, while Section 4 considers models where redevelopment may occur. Irreversibility means that initial land-use decisions are irrevocable, with the structure frozen in place forever in its initial configuration. With redevelopment, the structure can be replaced periodically in response to changes in the market environment.

Section 3 begins with a discussion of the Anas (1978) model, where developers make irreversible land-use decisions with myopic foresight. The discussion then turns to the simplest perfect-foresight model, as exposited by Capozza and Helsley (1989). In the model, land-use intensity is fixed, and the developer's only decision is when to convert land from agricultural use to urban use. With this background, the focus then shifts to a more complex perfect-foresight model where the developer chooses both the conversion date and land-use intensity. The original analysis of such a model is due to Fujita (1982) and Wheaton (1982a), but the discussion follows the later treatment of Turnbull (1988a,b).

Section 4, on redevelopment, begins with a discussion of the perfect-foresight model of Brueckner (1981a), where dwelling deterioration provides the impetus for redevelopment. Relaxing the model's stationary-state assumption, which precludes urban growth, the discussion then considers two models that generate spatial growth along with cycles of redevelopment. The first is the model of Brueckner (1980a), which follows Anas (1978) in assuming myopic foresight, while the second is the perfect-foresight model of Braid (1990).

Section 5 returns to the simplest irreversibility model and asks how uncertainty in the evolution of urban rents affects the process of urban growth. The discussion follows Capozza and Helsley (1990). Section 6 discusses several empirical studies that attempt to test the predictions of the durable-housing models. The studies, which embody a variety of different approaches, are by Harrison and Kain (1974), Brueckner (1986), Yacovissi and Kern (1995), and Rosenthal and Helsley (1994). It should be noted that the literature contains many additional studies beyond those explicitly discussed in this chapter. These are cited at various points in the discussion.

It is useful to stress that the purpose of this chapter is to contrast the predictions of the durable-housing models with those of the malleable-housing (static) model, while simultaneously exposing the logic of the durable-housing approach. Therefore, in line with the foregoing discussion, the analysis focuses mainly on (1) the predicted spatial pattern of land-use intensity within the city and (2) the predicted sequencing of land development, contrasting the results with those of the malleable-housing model. A technical point also worth emphasizing is that the analysis uses the open-city framework, where utility evolves exogenously over time, generating an endogenous time path of population. As explained by Braid (1990), closed-city results are available by simply "inverting" the open-city solution, making this approach acceptably general.[2]

2 The Malleable-Housing (Static) Model

In presenting the malleable-housing model, the discussion follows the exposition of Brueckner (1987), which is modified to include a time index. To begin, let $y(t)$ denote income earned at the CBD at time t. Letting $k(t)$ denote commuting cost per mile at time t, and x denote distance to the CBD, commuting cost at t from distance x equals $k(t)x$. Disposable income then equals $y(t) - k(t)x$.

Consumer preferences are represented by the strictly quasi-concave utility function $U(c, q)$, where c is consumption of a numeraire non-housing good, and q is consumption of housing, measured in square feet of floor space. The utility level in the outside economy evolves over time according to the exogenous function $u(t)$, and free mobility of consumers ensures that utility in the city follows the same path. Therefore, $U(c, q) = u(t)$ must hold, and inverting yields $c = c[q, u(t)]$, which gives the level of non-housing consumption that affords utility $u(t)$ when housing consumption equals q. The function c satisfies $c_q = -U_q/U_c < 0$, $c_{qq} > 0$, and $c_u > 0$, where subscripts denote partial derivatives. Since, after paying rent, the consumer must have $c[q, u(t)]$ left to spend on the non-housing good if he is to reach utility $u(t)$, it follows that the rent payment for a dwelling of size q at location x is given by $R(t, q, x) \equiv y(t) - k(t)x - c[q, u(t)]$. The function R satisfies $R_x = -k(t) < 0$, $R_q = U_q/U_c > 0$, and $R_{qq} < 0$. A key assumption is that y, k, and u vary over time in a way that ensures $R_t > 0$, so that the rent payment rises over time. This requires that disposable income $y(t) - k(t)x$ rise sufficiently rapidly relative to utility.[3]

Housing floor space is produced with capital and land according to a strictly concave, constant-returns production function. The intensive form of the production function is written $h(S)$, where S is capital per unit of land, referred to as structural density, and h satisfies $h' > 0$ and $h'' < 0$. Since capital is malleable, the developer rents rather than purchases his capital input. For simplicity, the purchase price of capital in terms of the non-housing good is assumed to be constant over time. Choice of units then allows the purchase price to be set at unity, implying that the rental price equals the interest rate, denoted i.

---

[2] To see the argument, observe that for each time path of utility in the open city, the model generates a time path for the urban population. To reverse this process, start with an arbitrary time path of population. Then, using the class of open-city solutions, the corresponding utility path can be found, along with the evolution of land use for the city.

[3] More generally, the rate of change of $y(t) - k(t)x$ (which may be negative) must be sufficiently large relative to the rate of change of $u(t)$.

At each point in time, the housing developer chooses dwelling size q and structural density S to maximize profit. Because capital is malleable, both choice variables can be adjusted as their optimal values change over time. The developer's objective function is gross profit per unit of land, which equals $R(t, q, x)h(S)/q - iS$, or rent minus capital cost per unit of land. Note that the first term in this expression is rent per dwelling (R) times dwellings per acre (h/q), which is computed by dividing floor space per acre (h) by floor space per dwelling (q). Alternatively, the first term equals rent per square foot (R/q) times square feet per acre (h).

It is clear that under the latter interpretation, profit maximization requires choosing q to maximize rent per square foot, so that the first-order condition $R_q = R/q$ is satisfied. Let $q(t, x)$ denote the maximizing value of q, and let $p(t, x) \equiv R[t, q(t, x), x]/q(t, x)$ denote the maximal rent per square foot. Recalling $R_q = U_q/U_c$, the first-order condition then says $U_q/U_c = p(t, x)$, indicating that the marginal rate of substitution is set equal to the rental price per unit of housing.

With q determined as above, S is then chosen to maximize $p(t, x)h(S) - iS$, satisfying the first-order condition $p(t, x)h'(S) = i$. The solution gives structural density as a function of t and x, $S(t, x)$. Population density, which equals dwellings per unit of land, is then equal to $D(t, x) \equiv h[S(t, x)]/q(t, x)$. Finally, urban land rent, denoted $r(t, x)$, is equal to gross profit per unit of land, with $r(t, x) \equiv p(t, x)h[S(t, x)] - iS(t, x)$.

By the envelope theorem, the derivatives of the housing rent function $p(t, x)$ are given by $p_t = R_t/q > 0$ and $p_x = R_x/q < 0$. Again using the envelope theorem, the derivatives of the land rent function $r(t, x)$ are given by $r_t = p_t h > 0$ and $r_x = p_x h < 0$. Differentiating the first-order condition for S, the derivatives of structural density $S(t, x)$ are $S_t = -p_t h'/ph'' > 0$ and $S_x = -p_x h'/ph'' < 0$. The derivatives of $q(t, x)$ are found by differentiating $R_q = p(t, x)$, which yields $q_t = (p_t - R_{qt})/R_{qq}$ and $q_x = p_x/R_{qq} > 0$. To sign q_t, observe that $R_{qt} = [\partial(U_q/U_c)/\partial u(t)]u'(t)$, which has the sign of $u'(t)$ when q is normal (the marginal rate of substitution then rises with utility, holding q fixed). As a result, q_t is ambiguous in sign when $u'(t) > 0$, but negative when $u'(t) < 0$.

Thus, housing rent p, land rent r, and structural density S are decreasing in distance x and rising over time, while dwelling size q is increasing in distance but could either rise or fall over time. While population density $D = h/q$ is therefore decreasing in distance, the ambiguity of q_t means that density could rise or fall over time. The effects of CBD accessibility on the levels of p, r, S, q, and D are well known from Muth (1969) and many subsequent studies.

Development of the land is justified only if the returns are greater than those in agricultural use. The developer thus compares the urban land rent at time t to the agricultural rent, given by $r_A(t)$, developing the land if the urban rent is larger. The boundary of the city is then located where the two rents are equal, with the boundary distance $\bar{x}(t)$ satisfying the equality $r(t, \bar{x}) = r_A(t)$. Differentiation yields $\bar{x}'(t) = (r_A' - r_t)/r_x$, and since urban rent is assumed to grow faster than agricultural rent, $r_A' - r_t < 0$ holds, and $\bar{x}'(t)$ is positive, implying that the city grows spatially over time (recall $r_x < 0$). Given $\bar{x}(t)$, the time path of the city's population can be computed. Population at time t is equal to $N(t) \equiv \int_0^{\bar{x}(t)} \theta(x) D(x, t) \, dx$, where $\theta(x) \, dx$ gives the amount of residential land at distance x from the CBD.

For future reference, let the values of S and q at the urban boundary at time t be denoted $\bar{S}(t)$ and $\bar{q}(t)$. These quantities are given by $\bar{S}(t) \equiv S[t, \bar{x}(t)]$ and $\bar{q}(t) \equiv q[t, \bar{x}(t)]$. Differentiating $\bar{S}(t)$ yields

$$\bar{S}'(t) = S_t + S_x \bar{x}' = -\frac{h'}{ph''}(p_t + p_x \bar{x}') = -\frac{h'}{ph''h} r_A' \qquad (7.1)$$

where the last equality comes from substituting $(r_A' - r_t)/r_x = (r_A' - p_t h)/p_x h$ in place of $\bar{x}'$. Equation (7.1) shows that $\bar{S}'(t) > (<) \, 0$ as $r_A'(t) > (<) \, 0$, indicating that agricultural rent and structural density at the boundary move together over time. This conclusion makes sense because structural density varies in step with the level of urban land rent, which equals r_A at the boundary. An analogous calculation shows that $\bar{q}'(t)$ has the same sign as $R_{qt} - r_A'/h$. Therefore, $\bar{q}'(t)$ may be either positive or negative, with its sign depending on time paths of agricultural rent and utility.

For present purposes, the most important properties of the malleable city are the spatial patterns of S, q, and D, which satisfy $S_x < 0, q_x > 0$, and $D_x < 0$, and the fact that urban growth occurs outward from the CBD, without leapfrogging. The following discussion shows that durable-housing models generate cities that need not share these properties.

3 Durable-Housing Models with Irreversible Development

3.1 Irreversible Development with Myopic Foresight

The Anas (1978) model of irreversible development is a natural starting point for the discussion of models of this type.[4] As in all models with irreversibility, structures in the Anas model cannot be torn down and replaced once they are built. This is an extreme assumption, but it is justified by the fact that buildings in real-world cities exhibit great longevity. Irreversibility is also made plausible by the auxiliary assumption that buildings do not deteriorate over time, which removes part of the incentive for redevelopment.[5]

---

[4] Anas's model differs slightly from the one presented here. Earlier durable-housing papers were written by Evans (1975), Muth (1975), Fisch (1977), and Ohls and Pines (1975).

[5] Note that even in the absence of deterioration, intertemporal changes in housing prices can create an incentive for redevelopment.

With buildings lasting forever instead of being redeveloped every period, the developer's expectations regarding future revenue are critical in his choice of structural characteristics. The Anas model assumes that these expectations embody myopic foresight: future dwelling rent is expected to remain the same as current rent. The developer must calculate the expected present value (EPV) of revenue to make his land-use decisions, and under myopic foresight the EPV of revenue per acre for a building constructed at time t at distance x is given by

$$\int_t^\infty \frac{R(t, q, x)}{q} h(S) e^{-i(\tau-t)} \, d\tau \tag{7.2}$$

The key feature of (7.2) is that expected rent at each future date τ is equal to rent at the current date t, $R(t, x, q)$.

The EPV of gross profit per acre is given by (7.2) minus the cost of capital per unit of land, which is now purchased instead of rented. Performing the integration in (7.2), the profit expression is then given by

$$\frac{R(t, q, x)}{iq} h(S) - S \tag{7.3}$$

Except for the presence of the multiplicative factor $1/i$, (7.3) is the same as the gross profit expression in the malleable-housing case. One implication of this fact is that city's spatial growth is the same in the malleable and durable cases. To see this, observe that land is developed wherever urban land value $v(t, x)$, which equals the maximized value of (7.3), exceeds the value of agricultural land, which equals $r_A(t)/i$ under myopic foresight. The distance to the boundary of the durable city then satisfies $v(t, x) = r_A(t)/i$. But since this equation reduces to $r(t, x) = r_A(t)$, given $v(t, x) = r(t, x)/i$, the boundary distance equals $\bar{x}(t)$, the malleable-city value. It follows that land in a given location is initially developed at the same date in the durable and malleable cities. This date is found by inverting the function $\bar{x}(t)$ to get $T(x)$, which gives the (common) development date for land at distance x.

Because the profit expressions are proportional in the malleable and durable cases, identical structures are built when the land in a given location is first developed. As time passes, however, the land undergoes continual redevelopment in the malleable city, while land use is frozen in the durable city. Therefore, the building in a given location in the durable city is the same as the *original structure* built at that location in the malleable city. Since this original structure was located at the city's boundary when it was built, its characteristics can be evaluated using the functions $\bar{S}(\cdot)$ and $\bar{q}(\cdot)$, which apply to buildings at the malleable-city boundary. Thus, structural density at distance x in the durable city is $S(x) = \bar{S}[T(x)]$, which gives the S value of the original building at x in the malleable city (i.e., the boundary value of S at the date when the city's boundary was located at x). Similarly, dwelling size at distance x in the durable city is given by $q(x) = \bar{q}[T(x)]$.

The spatial behavior of S in the durable city is found by differentiating $\bar{S}[T(x)]$, which yields

$$S'(x) = \bar{S}'[T(x)]T'(x) > (<) 0 \quad \text{as } r'_A[T(x)] > (<) 0 \tag{7.4}$$

where (7.1) is used. Thus, structural density increases with distance if agricultural rent is rising over time, and decreases with distance otherwise. The first spatial pattern is, of course, dramatically different from that of the static model, where structural density declines with x, reflecting the effects of accessibility. In the durable city, S instead reflects the level of agricultural rent at the time of development. Since the sign of $\bar{q}'(t)$ is ambiguous from Section 2, it follows that $q'(x) = \bar{q}'[T(x)]T'(x)$ may take either sign, so that dwelling size may rise or fall with distance in the durable city. The same conclusion then applies to population density, given by $h\{\bar{S}[T(x)]\}/\bar{q}[T(x)]$.

This discussion shows that while the sequencing of land development is the same in the malleable-city and Anas models (i.e., no leapfrogging), the various measures of land-use intensity behave differently in the two models. In contrast to the malleable city, structural and population density may rise with distance, while dwelling size may fall. The patterns that emerge depend on the time path of agricultural rent, as well as the time path of utility, which partly governs the intertemporal behavior of dwelling size.

3.2 Irreversible Development with Perfect Foresight

The myopic developer looks only at current conditions in deciding whether or not to develop a parcel of land and choosing structural characteristics. Under perfect foresight, the developer correctly anticipates the future evolution of both urban and agricultural rents in making his decisions. In choosing a development plan for land at a given location, his goal is to maximize the present value (PV) of gross profit per acre. Letting T denote the date when the land is converted from agricultural to urban use, the PV of gross profit per acre at time 0 for land at distance x is given by

$$\int_0^T r_A(\tau)e^{-i\tau}\,d\tau + \int_T^\infty \frac{R(\tau, q, x)}{q}h(S)e^{-i\tau}\,d\tau - Se^{-iT} \tag{7.5}$$

Note that the first term gives the PV of agricultural rent prior to conversion and that the expected rent following conversion follows the actual rent path, rather than equaling initial rent [in contrast to (7.2)].

While the objective function in (7.5) has three choice variables (S, q, and T), the literature's analysis of this optimization problem typically assumes that one or more of these variables is fixed. The simplest model, which is exposited by

Capozza and Helsley (1989), assumes that $q = h(S) = 1$, so that both dwelling size and floor space per acre are equal to unity. S is then equal to $h^{-1}(1) \equiv B$, so that the last two terms in (7.5) become $\int_T^\infty R(\tau, 1, x)e^{-i\tau} d\tau - Be^{-iT}$. Differentiating the modified (7.5), the first-order condition for the remaining choice variable T is

$$R(T, 1, x) - iB = r_A(T) \tag{7.6}$$

while the second-order condition requires $R_t > r_A'$.

Since the left-hand side of (7.6) represents urban land rent (housing rent per acre minus annualized development cost), the equation has the same form as the boundary equations for the malleable-housing and Anas models. The difference is that, as written, the equation determines $T(x)$, the development date for land at x, instead of the urban boundary distance. Differentiating, $T'(x)$ is equal to $R_x/(r_A' - R_t)$. Since $R_t > r_A'$ must hold, it follows that more distant land is developed later, implying that the city grows outward over time. Inverting the function $T(x)$ then gives $\bar{x}(t)$, the boundary distance at date t, with $\bar{x}'(t) > 0$. Because outward growth rules out leapfrogging, the sequencing of development is the same as in the malleable-housing model.[6]

Fujita (1982) and Wheaton (1982a) add complexity to the developer's problem by allowing structural characteristics to be chosen along with T. Subsequent work by Turnbull (1988a,b) provides a simpler and clearer treatment of this type of model, following the formulation of Fujita (1982). Under his approach, $h(S)$ is once again set equal to unity, while T and q are choice variables. The developer's objective function is then

$$\int_0^T r_A(\tau)e^{-i\tau} d\tau + \int_T^\infty \frac{R(\tau, q, x)}{q} e^{-i\tau} d\tau - Be^{-iT} \equiv \hat{z}(T, q, x) \tag{7.7}$$

The first-order conditions for T and q are

$$z_T \equiv r_A(T) - \frac{R(T, q, x)}{q} + iB = 0 \tag{7.8}$$

$$z_q \equiv \frac{1}{q} \int_T^\infty \left[R_q(\tau, q, x) - \frac{R(\tau, q, x)}{q} \right] e^{-i(\tau - T)} d\tau = 0 \tag{7.9}$$

where $z_T = \hat{z}_T e^{iT}$ and $z_q = \hat{z}_q e^{iT}$. The second-order conditions, which require

---

[6] One noteworthy implication of this simple model concerns the value of undeveloped land around the city. As seen earlier, the value of agricultural land at time t with myopic expectations is equal to $r_A(t)/i$. With perfect foresight, land value is equal to the maximized value of (7.5), and this value is close to $r_A(t)/i$ only when x is large [making $T(x)$ near infinity]. Differentiation of the modified version of (7.5) using the envelope theorem shows that as x declines, value rises above $r_A(t)/i$, reflecting the impending conversion of the land to urban use. Therefore, the model generates a price gradient for undeveloped land that mimics the gradient for urban land.

$z_{TT} < 0$, $z_{qq} < 0$, and $J \equiv z_{TT}z_{qq} - z_{qT}^2 > 0$, are assumed to hold. Note that $z_{TT} < 0$ requires $R_t/q > r_A'$.

Equations (7.8) and (7.9) determine $T(x)$ and $q(x)$, the conversion date and dwelling size at a given x. As will become clear, an important feature of the model is that the function $T(\cdot)$ need not be monotonic, which introduces the possibility that development occurs simultaneously at different locations [in this case, $T(\cdot)$ takes the same value at different x's]. To simplify the discussion, it is helpful to suppress this possibility until later, intially considering only those situations where T is monotonic.

Bearing this in mind, the derivatives $T'(x)$ and $q'(x)$ are computed by total differentiation of (7.8) and (7.9). This yields

$$T'(x) = (z_{qT}z_{qx} - z_{Tx}z_{qq})/J \tag{7.10}$$

$$q'(x) = (z_{qT}z_{Tx} - z_{qx}z_{TT})/J \tag{7.11}$$

To sign these expressions, note that $z_{Tx} = -R_x/q > 0$ and $z_{qx} = -\int_T^\infty (R_x/q^2)$ $e^{-i(\tau-T)}\, d\tau > 0$ (the last equality uses $R_{qx} = 0$). Recalling the second-order conditions, the last terms in the numerators of (7.10) and (7.11) are then negative. The overall signs of the expressions thus depend on the sign of

$$z_{qT} = -\frac{1}{q}\left[R_q(T, q, x) - \frac{R(T, q, x)}{q}\right] \tag{7.12}$$

which is easily seen to be ambiguous.[7]

If $z_{qT} \geq 0$ holds at a given x, then both (7.10) and (7.11) are positive, indicating that the conversion date and dwelling size are (locally) increasing in x. If z_{qT} is positive at all x, then $T' > 0$ holds at all locations along with $q' > 0$. This implies that more distant locations are developed later, and hence that spatial growth occurs outward from the CBD. The absence of leapfrogging, together with the increase of dwelling size over distance, means that the city's spatial structure resembles the malleable case.[8]

In the alternative situation where $z_{qT} < 0$, both (7.10) and (7.11) are ambiguous in sign. This ambiguity means that $T'(x) < 0$ may hold, indicating that the conversion date is locally decreasing in x. If T' is negative for all x, the sequencing of development is radically different than in the malleable model. This inequality means that *more central* locations are developed

---

[7] To see this, recall that $R_{qq} < 0$, and suppose that $R(T, 0, x)$ equals zero, so that the function passes through the origin in (R, q) space. Because R is concave, the slope of the tangent (R_q) is then less than the slope of the chord connecting the function to the origin (R/q), and $z_{qT} > 0$. While the same conclusion holds if the R function passes above the origin, the sign of (7.12) is ambiguous if the function passes below the origin. Since any of these cases may be relevant, the sign of z_{qT} is therefore ambiguous.

[8] Of course, structural density is fixed in the present case, unlike in the malleable model. However, if S were fixed in the malleable case, q would still be increasing in x.

later, which implies that the city experiences "outside-in" development, a striking example of the leapfrog pattern. In other words, locations far from the CBD are developed first, and the interior vacant land is gradually converted to urban use as time passes. Wheaton (1982a) provides numerical examples of outside-in development, showing that it is a natural outcome in such a model.

This unusual development sequence is accompanied by a conventional pattern of land-use intensity. Turnbull (1988b) shows that $q'(x) > 0$ must hold when $T'(x) < 0$, which implies that dwelling sizes in a city experiencing outside-in development actually increase with x, as in the malleable case. In order to generate an unconventional pattern for q, $z_{qT} < 0$ must hold along with $T' > 0$. The sign of q' is ambiguous in this case, introducing the possibility that dwelling sizes decline with distance even though spatial growth resembles that of the malleable city.

To explore cases where $T(\cdot)$ is nonmonotonic, allowing simultaneous development at several locations, it is helpful to reinterpret (7.8) and (7.9). Observe that when T is fixed, these equations determine the x values undergoing development at that date, along with the q values at these locations. The solutions can be represented graphically by recognizing that each equation generates a locus in (x, q) space, with the intersections of the two loci giving the solution values.

Total differentiation shows that the slope $\partial q / \partial x$ of the z_q locus equals $-z_{qx}/z_{qq} > 0$, while the slope of the z_T locus equals $-z_{Tx}/z_{qT}$, which is ambiguous in sign. However, Turnbull (1988a) shows that as q increases, z_{qT} can change sign at most once, in which case the sign moves from negative to positive. This implies that the slope expression also changes sign at most once as q increases, in which case the sign moves from positive to negative. These conclusions are illustrated in Figure 7.1, which shows the upward-sloping z_q locus along with a backward-bending z_T locus. The three intersections indicate that three locations are undergoing development at the given T, with the x values given by the horizontal coordinates of the intersection points.

The local pattern of development is different at each intersection point in the figure. At location A, the negative slope of the z_T locus means that $z_{qT} > 0$ holds, implying $T' > 0$ and $q' > 0$. Thus, subsequent development in the neighborhood of A occurs *farther* from the CBD (at x values to the right of A in the diagram) and involves larger dwellings. By contrast, since the z_T locus is upward-sloping at location C, $z_{qT} < 0$ holds. In addition, since the z_q locus is steeper than the z_T locus at C, it follows that $z_{qT} z_{qx} - z_{Tx} z_{qq} < 0$ holds, where the foregoing slope formulas are used. Using (7.10), this implies $T' < 0$ and thus $q' > 0$. Therefore, subsequent development in the neighborhood of C occurs *closer* to the CBD (at locations inside C) and involves smaller dwellings. The same argument shows that subsequent development near location B occurs

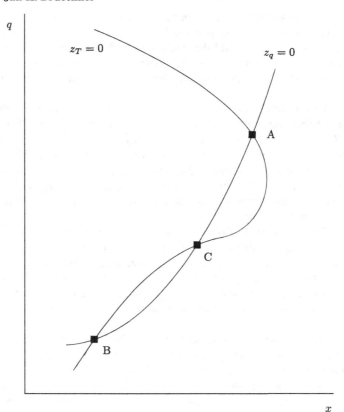

Figure 7.1. Development at multiple locations.

farther from the CBD and involves either smaller or larger dwellings. These patterns indicate that the areas inside of B and between A and C are already developed at the given date. The area between B and C experiences "infill" development as time progresses, while the outer edge of the city expands from location A.

Other examples can be generated using different assumptions on the positions and slopes of the two loci. Note that the first monotonic case considered earlier has only a single intersection for each value of T, at a point like A. The second case also has a single intersection at each T, at a point like C. See Turnbull (1988a,b) for further discussion.

This discussion shows that a perfect-foresight model with irreversible development is capable of generating a striking departure from the land-use patterns of the malleable city. The model can generate leapfrog development as well as unconventional dwelling-size patterns. These results may help explain land-use features that are inexplicable under the standard approach.[9]

4 Durable-Housing Models with Redevelopment

Rather than assuming that development is irreversible, suppose instead that developers are able to replace buildings periodically in response to changing conditions. In reality, a major reason for redevelopment is quality deterioration due to aging. Deterioration puts downward pressure on rents as consumers require compensation for poorer space, and this provides an incentive to replace the structure via redevelopment.[10] Even in the absence of deterioration, redevelopment may be desirable. For example, the developer may wish to increase land-use intensity in response to rising prices. Together, these effects make periodic redevelopment attractive from the developer's point of view.

4.1 Redevelopment in a Stationary State

To formalize the notion of quality deterioration, it is necessary to draw a distinction between dwelling floor space and housing services. Accordingly, suppose that when a dwelling of size q has reached age a, its service level is equal to $f(a)q$. The function $f(\cdot)$ is positive and satisfies $f' < 0$, indicating that services decline with age, as well as $f(0) = 1$, indicating that a square foot of new floor space generates one unit of services.

At time τ, rent for a dwelling built at time t in location x is equal to $R[\tau, f(\tau - t)q, x]$. As noted earlier, the decline of f over time puts downward pressure on rent, which interacts with the pure time effect (represented by R's first argument) in determining the rent path. The first redevelopment model to be considered, that of Brueckner (1981a), suppresses the pure time effect by assuming that the economy is in a stationary state. This means that income y, commuting cost k, and utility u are all constant over time. Under this assumption, the time argument disappears from the rent function, which can be rewritten as $R[f(\tau - t)q, x]$. Dwelling rent then falls continuously as

---

[9] Braid (1988) solves the general optimization problem in (7.5) assuming Cobb-Douglas utility and housing production functions and exponential growth of the exogenous variables. His solution is characterized by outward expansion of the city. The spatial pattern of structural characteristics depends on the growth rates of the exogenous variables. For other perfect-foresight models with irreversible development, see Arnott and Lewis (1978), Arnott (1980), Fujita (1976), and Mills (1981) (the latter model generates leapfrog development).

[10] Maintenance is another response to quality deterioration that may weaken the impetus for redevelopment. The optimal time path of maintenance in aging structures is analyzed by Arnott et al. (1983, 1986). An alternative approach is to assume that land use can be changed over time subject to adjustment costs. Such a model, which falls between the irreversible-development and redevelopment cases, is analyzed by Hochman and Pines (1980, 1982).

time progresses, with the τ derivative given by $f'q R_q < 0$. Rent can eventually become negative, at which point occupation of the dwelling ceases, but this possibility can be ignored because redevelopment will already have occurred (as discussed later).

Using this formulation, consider the PV of gross profit per acre from a structure built at distance x at time t and torn down at time $t + L$. Assuming that the developer has perfect foresight and that demolition costs are zero, this PV as of time t equals

$$\int_t^{t+L} \frac{R[f(\tau - t)q, x]}{q} h(S) e^{-i(\tau-t)} \, d\tau - S \tag{7.13}$$

Note that the integrand equals rent per dwelling at τ times dwellings per acre. Making a change of variable, (7.13) equals

$$\int_0^L \frac{R[f(w)q, x]}{q} h(S) e^{-iw} \, dw - S \equiv \pi(L, S, q, x) \tag{7.14}$$

Because of the stationary state, (7.14) depends only on the building's life span L and not on its construction date t.

The crucial aspect of the redevelopment process is that buildings are replaced when torn down. As of time 0, the PV of gross profit from the sequence of buildings constructed at location x is

$$\pi(L_1, S_1, q_1, x) + e^{-iL_1}\pi(L_2, S_2, q_2, x) + e^{-i(L_1+L_2)}\pi(L_3, S_3, q_3, x) + \cdots \tag{7.15}$$

where the subscripts index buildings in the sequence. The developer must choose the characteristics of each building, but this task is simplified because stationarity of the optimization problem implies that all buildings are identical (Brueckner, 1981a). Thus, (7.15) reduces to $\pi(L, S, q, x)(1 + e^{-iL} + e^{-2iL} + \cdots)$, or

$$\frac{\pi(L, S, q, x)}{1 - e^{-iL}} \tag{7.16}$$

The first-order condition for L is

$$\frac{\pi i e^{-iL}}{1 - e^{-iL}} = \pi_L \equiv R[f(L)q, x][h(S)/q]e^{-iL} \tag{7.17}$$

which indicates that the developer balances the gains from lengthening the life span L (represented by π_L) against the loss from postponement of redevelopment (the first term). Observe that since π must be positive at the optimum, (7.17) shows that a building is replaced when its rent is still positive, as noted earlier.

The dwelling size q is chosen to maximize the present value of rent per square foot over the life of the dwelling, equal to $\int_0^L \{R[f(\tau)q, x]/q\}e^{-i\tau}d\tau$. By analyzing the first-order condition $\pi_q = 0$, it is easily seen that this requires choosing q to be larger than the value that maximizes $R(q, x)/q$, rent per square foot in the new dwelling. If q were instead chosen in this fashion, rent per unit of housing services (R/fq) would decline monotonically as the dwelling aged, an outcome the developer avoids by choosing a larger q. The first-order condition for S, which requires $\pi_S = 0$, generates an equation similar to those in the previous models.

The value of urban land at a particular x is equal to the maximized value of (7.16). Since π_x is negative given $R_x < 0$, it follows from the envelope theorem that land value is decreasing in x. Given that value is constant over time in the stationary state, it follows that the urban land area is fixed, with development extending out to the distance $\bar{x}$ where urban and agricultural land values are equal (the latter value is also constant over time).

Within this fixed land area, buildings are redeveloped periodically according to the foregoing solutions. To explore the spatial aspect of this process, note that the first-order conditions give the choice variables as functions of x: $L(x)$, $S(x)$, $q(x)$. In general, the derivatives of these functions are ambiguous. This means that the development cycle's period, given by L, can vary spatially and that structural characteristics can exhibit unconventional spatial patterns. However, if the utility and housing production functions are Cobb-Douglas and f is negative exponential, then simple patterns emerge. In this case, $L'(x) \equiv 0$ holds, indicating that the redevelopment cycle has the same period in all locations. Thus, the entire city is simultaneously redeveloped in periodic fashion. Moreover, $S'(x) < 0$ and $q'(x) > 0$ hold for all x, indicating that structural density and dwelling size are respectively decreasing and increasing functions of distance. Therefore, aside from its periodic redevelopment, the city resembles a malleable city in a stationary state. See Brueckner (1981a) for further discussion.[11]

4.2 Redevelopment with Myopic Foresight

Although the previous discussion exposes the economics of the redevelopment problem, the absence of urban growth limits the usefulness of the model. Generating growth, however, means dropping the stationary-state assumption, and once this is done, the objective function does not exhibit the convenient stationarity of (7.15). Instead of collapsing into a simple expression like (7.16), the

---

[11] Brueckner and von Rabenau (1981) analyze a different perfect-foresight model where a one-time increase in the price of housing provides the impetus for a single episode of redevelopment (dwelling deterioration is absent). In addition, Sasaki (1990) develops a model similar to that of Brueckner (1981a).

objective function then retains an infinite number of choice variables, making the solution problematic.

In response to this difficulty, Brueckner (1980a) replaces the assumption of perfect foresight with myopic foresight. The developer's decisions are then based on contemporaneous information, avoiding the need for an expression like (7.15). There are several aspects to the developer's myopia. First, in constructing a new building, the developer acts as if he will operate it forever, even though he will later choose to redevelop. Second, while the developer recognizes that housing services decline over time, he expects the price per unit of services to remain constant at the initial level. Therefore, the EPV of gross profit per acre for a building constructed at time t in location x is

$$\int_t^\infty \frac{R(t, q, x)}{q} f(\tau - t) h(S) e^{-i(\tau-t)} d\tau - S \tag{7.18}$$

Note that the t argument reappears in R, reflecting the absence of a stationary state, and that housing services per acre shrink according to the function f. Observe also that if the developer were not myopic with respect to the price per unit of housing services, the actual price $R[\tau, f(\tau - t)q, x]/f(\tau - t)q$ at each τ would replace the R/q term in (7.18).

The developer chooses q to maximize the price per unit of services $R(t, q, x)/q$ for the new dwelling, which is expected to persist forever. Because this problem is the same as in the malleable-city model, the maximizing q [denoted $\tilde{q}(t, x)$] satisfies $\tilde{q}(t, x) = q(t, x)$. Note that the t argument of $\tilde{q}(t, x)$ represents the construction date of the dwelling, which will diverge from the current time as the dwelling ages. R/q is then equal to $p(t, x)$, so that S is chosen to maximize $p(t, x)h(S) \int_t^\infty f(\tau - t) e^{-(\tau-t)} d\tau - S$, with the solution denoted $\tilde{S}(t, x)$ (this gives structural density conditional on construction date and location). Urban land value at time t and location x, again denoted $v(t, x)$, is equal to the maximized value of this expression. The boundary of the city at time t is located where $v(t, x)$ equals $r_A(t)/i$, agricultural land value under myopia.

At each date, the developer considers whether or not to tear down the building and sell the land. He computes the EPV of revenue from continued operation of the building as before. In particular, he assumes that if not torn down, the building will be operated forever and that the current price per unit of housing services will persist. EPV of revenue per acre at time w for a building constructed at t is then

$$\int_w^\infty \frac{R[w, f(w - t)\tilde{q}(t, x), x]}{f(w - t)\tilde{q}(t, x)} f(\tau - t) h[\tilde{S}(t, x)] e^{-(\tau-w)} d\tau \tag{7.19}$$

Note that the ratio involving R is the price per unit of housing services in the dwelling at time w, which is expected to persist forever. The developer tears down the building and sells the land at the date w when land value $v(w, x)$ equals (7.19).

Assuming Cobb-Douglas utility and production functions, a negative exponential form for f, and exponential time paths for y, k, and u, a simple conclusion emerges. Specifically, the life span of a building (the demolition date minus the construction date) is a constant, independent of the building's location and construction date. Given this result, it is easy to generate examples that illuminate the interaction between spatial growth and redevelopment, focusing on the behavior of structural density. The examples make use of the fact that structural density is an increasing function of a building's construction date when $p_t > 0$ (i.e., $\tilde{S}_t > 0$), along with $\tilde{S}_x < 0$.[12]

With this background, consider a simple example where time is measured in discrete years and distance is measured in discrete "blocks" from the CBD. Suppose that the paths of urban and agricultural land values lead the city to grow outward by one block each year, starting at the CBD at time zero. Moreover, suppose that the constant life span of buildings is three years, so that a building built at $t = 0$ is replaced at $t = 3$. Table 7.1 shows the age pattern of buildings at three dates, $t = 2, 3, 8$, and the upper panel of Figure 7.2 illustrates the age pattern for $t = 8$. Observe that at $t = 2$, first-generation buildings occupy blocks 0, 1, and 2. Then, at $t = 3$, the buildings in block 0 reach the end of their life span and are replaced with second-generation structures. Because the city has expanded, first-generation buildings then occupy blocks 1–3. This growth pattern continues, and by $t = 8$ the interaction of spatial growth and redevelopment has generated a sawtooth pattern of building ages, as shown in Figure 7.2.

Now consider the spatial pattern of structural density, which represents building height. Because $\tilde{S}$ is increasing in t, it follows that buildings constructed later in time are taller, while buildings constructed farther from the CBD are shorter given $\tilde{S}_x < 0$. Given these facts, consider the pattern of building heights at $t = 8$, focusing initially on blocks 0, 1, and 2. Buildings in block 1 were built later than those in block 0, and this tends to make them taller. However, block 1 is farther from the CBD, and this tends to make its buildings shorter than those in block 0. While the net effect is ambiguous, suppose that the age effect dominates the distance effect, so that buildings in block 1 are taller than those in block 0, as shown in the middle panel of Figure 7.2. Since buildings in block 2 were built later than those in block 1, the same principles apply, and buildings there are taller than in block 1. By contrast, in moving from block 2 to block 3, the age and distance effects work in the same direction. The reason is that buildings in block 3 were built *earlier* than those in block 2 (they are two years old instead of brand-new), and this tends to make them shorter. Since the distance effect reinforces this tendency, building heights decline sharply moving from block 2 to block 3. These patterns are repeated in blocks 3 through 8, generating a cyclical pattern of building heights.

---

[12] Because q_t can take either sign in the static model, it follows that $\tilde{q}_t$ is ambiguous in sign, indicating that dwelling size may be an increasing or decreasing function of the construction date. The same conclusion applies to population density.

Table 7.1. *Age contours*

t = 2		t = 3		t = 8	
Block	Age	Block	Age	Block	Age
0	2	0	0	0	2
1	1	1	2	1	1
2	0	2	1	2	0
		3	0	3	2
				4	1
				5	0
				6	2
				7	1
				8	0

Other patterns are possible. For example, if the age effect is weak, with $\tilde{S}$ increasing slowly over time, then the distance effect will dominate within the block ranges 0–2, 3–5, and 6–8, leading to downward-sloping building-height contours over these ranges. As before, heights will drop sharply between these ranges. Yet another pattern emerges if $p_t < 0$ holds, in which case $\tilde{S}_t < 0$. Assuming that spatial growth still occurs (which requires rapidly declining agricultural rents), the outcome is shown in the bottom panel of Figure 7.2. The distance and age effects now work in the same direction in the block ranges 0–2, 3–5, and 6–8, implying that building heights decline over these ranges. The discontinuous age increase across blocks 2 and 3 now implies a *jump* in building heights, which is repeated across blocks 5 and 6.

These examples show that the interaction between redevelopment and spatial growth generates irregular building-height patterns that contrast sharply with the smooth contours of the malleable city. Nevertheless, the two patterns are consistent on a more fundamental level. To see this, observe that for buildings constructed at the same date, the model implies that the less central structures are shorter. This can be seen in Figure 7.2, where, holding age constant, height falls as the block number increases. Since the age pattern repeats itself over distance, this fact means that the overall trend of building heights is downward, as seen in the figure. Therefore, while the durability of housing generates irregular local height contours, the global height pattern looks very much like that of the malleable-housing model. In other words, the model can explain discontinuities in building heights, showing that they emerge from age discontinuities like those at blocks 2–3 and 5–6, but it does not supplant the broader insights afforded by the standard approach.[13]

---

[13] In a related paper, Brueckner (1980b) analyzes myopic redevelopment in the presence of two income groups. Vousden (1980) and Wheaton (1982b) present different redevelopment models, also assuming myopic foresight.

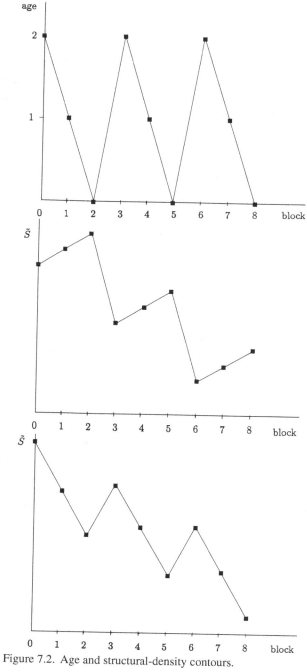

Figure 7.2. Age and structural-density contours.

4.3 Redevelopment with Growth and Perfect Foresight

As noted earlier, the redevelopment problem with perfect foresight is hard to solve in a nonstationary economy. Nevertheless, a recent and incomplete paper by Braid (1990) sketches a solution to this problem based on specific functional forms. To better understand the nature of the problem, return to (7.13) and observe that nonstationarity means that the time argument reappears in R. The π function then includes the construction date of the building, being written $\pi(t, L, S, q, x)$. Because of nonstationarity, the conversion date from agricultural to urban use must also be considered. Letting t_i denote the development date for the ith building in the sequence, the objective function is now written

$$\int_0^{t_1} r_A(\tau) e^{-i\tau} d\tau + e^{-it_1} \pi(t_1, t_2 - t_1, S_1, q_1, x)$$
$$+ e^{-it_2} \pi(t_2, t_3 - t_2, S_2, q_2, x) + e^{-it_3} \pi(t_3, t_4 - t_3, S_3, q_3, x) + \cdots$$
$$(7.20)$$

Note that the $t_{i+1} - t_i$ terms inside the π functions are equal to L_i, the life span of the ith building.

Braid shows that this problem can be solved under the functional form assumptions used in Section 4.2. He shows that $S_i(x)$ is given by $F_i x^d$, where F_i is a constant and d can take either sign depending on parameter values. In addition, $t_i(x) = G_i + (1/b) \ln(x)$, where G_i and b are positive constants. Note that this solution gives the development date for the ith-generation structure built at location x. Inverting the solution yields $M_i(t)$, which gives the distance to the inner edge of the area occupied by ith-generation buildings at time t. The inversion yields $M_i(t) = E_i e^{bt}$, which implies that ith-generation buildings occupy the area from $x = E_i e^{bt}$ to $x = E_{i+1} e^{bt}$ at date t ($E_{i+1} > E_i$).

As in the myopic-foresight model, the area occupied by ith-generation buildings moves outward over time (recall Table 7.1). Also, referring to the above S_i solution, the S contours within each generation's area can be upward- or downward-sloping over distance, while exhibiting discontinuities across areas, just as in Figure 7.2. Therefore, the qualitative implications of Braid's perfect-foresight solution are similar to those of the myopic-foresight model. The behavior of developers in the former model is, of course, more sophisticated and internally consistent.[14]

5 Irreversible Development under Uncertainty

The perfect-foresight models considered up to this point assume that housing developers have complete knowledge of the future evolution of prices in the

---

[14] Amin and Capozza (1993) also analyze a non-stationary-state redevelopment model with perfect foresight, reaching more limited conclusions.

urban economy. However, even when developers have a sophisticated under-standing of the economy's structure, it is unrealistic to assume they can predict the direction of future random shocks that may influence prices. A more re-alistic framework portrays developers as recognizing the uncertainty of future prices and taking it into account in their decisions.

In models with irreversible development, the issue raised by price uncertainty is straightforward. To see it, suppose that urban rents evolve in a random fashion over time. Then, if the developer converts land from agricultural to urban use when current urban rent looks attractive relative to agricultural rent, he may regret this (irreversible) decision later if urban rents fall. Such regret can never arise in the certainty case because rent surprises are ruled out.

Capozza and Helsley (1990) explore this issue in their seminal treatment of irreversible development with rent uncertainty. They adopt the simple model of Section 3.2, where the developer's only choice is the conversion date T, and assume that consumer income evolves randomly over time. With utility follow-ing a deterministic path, this makes the path of housing rents uncertain. The random housing-rent function, which is analogous to $R(t, 1, x)$ from Section 2, is given by

$$\tilde{R}(t, x) = a - kx + gt + \sigma \Omega(t) \tag{7.21}$$

where $\Omega(t)$ is Brownian motion with drift 0 and variance 1, and k is the constant commuting cost parameter. Equation (7.21) shows that rents drift upward over time at rate $g > 0$, with their variance at any time given by σ^2.

Using results from the theory of stochastic processes, Capozza and Helsley compute the "hurdle rent" above which $\tilde{R}$ must rise in order for development to occur. Using this hurdle rent, the conversion date T for land at location x satisfies

$$\tilde{R}(T, x) - iB = r_A(T) + \frac{i - \alpha g}{\alpha i} \tag{7.22}$$

where

$$\alpha = \frac{(g^2 + 2\sigma^2 i)^{1/2} - g}{\sigma^2} > 0 \tag{7.23}$$

Since it can be shown that $i > \alpha g$, the last term in (7.22) is positive. Comparing the equation to (7.6), the conversion condition under certainty, it follows that urban land rent ($\tilde{R} - iB$) must *exceed*, rather than equal, agricultural rent in order for development to occur. Moreover, the required difference is increasing in σ^2, the housing-rent variance. Thus, the possibility of a post-conversion drop in urban land rent makes the developer reluctant to undertake conversion, relative to the certainty case. To convert the land, he requires an urban-rent premium above agricultural rent, which lessens the chance of later regretting his conversion decision. This premium is larger the greater is the uncertainty in the evolution of urban rents.

The existence of the rent premium affects the spatial growth of the city. Solving (7.22) for $\bar{x}$ yields (after replacing T with t)

$$\bar{x}(t) = k^{-1}[a + gt + \sigma\Omega(t) - r_A(t) - iB - (i - \alpha g)/\alpha i)] \qquad (7.24)$$

Since $\Omega(t)$ is random, $\bar{x}(t)$ is itself a random variable. However, given that $\Omega(t)$ has zero expectation, the expected value of $\bar{x}(t)$ is equal to the remaining terms in (7.24). Since the last term, which equals the rent premium from (7.22), is increasing in σ^2, it follows that the *expected value of $\bar{x}(t)$ falls as rent uncertainty rises*. Thus, the developer's greater reluctance to convert land in a more uncertain environment leads to a city that, on average, is spatially smaller at each date.

Using methods similar to those of Capozza and Helsley, Williams (1996) analyzes redevelopment in an uncertain environment, in effect solving the stochastic version of the problem discussed by Braid (1990). However, Williams's analysis is carried out in a nonspatial setting, so that its implications for the process of urban growth are not explored. O'Flaherty (1993) studies redevelopment in a different stochastic environment, where the random component of rents takes only two values (indicating "good" times or "bad" times).[15]

6 Empirical Studies

A number of papers offer empirical tests of the durable-housing models. The earliest, which predates all theoretical work, is the well-known study of Harrison and Kain (1974). These authors test the proposition that the spatial pattern of population density in a city reflects the timing and density of original development, as in the irreversible-development models discussed in Section 3. They start by assuming that the share of single-family housing in a city's new construction can serve as a proxy for population density in the new development. Using an estimate of this relationship, along with the trend of the single-family share in new construction, they then predict the density of incremental development in a city over past decades. The incremental spatial growth of the city can then be inferred from the actual path of population, yielding a set of density-distance pairs. These can be used to estimate a pseudo-population-density function, and the main conclusion of the paper is that these functions resemble those estimated with actual density data. Harrison and Kain view this finding as support for their hypothesis that current densities reflect the nature of original development.[16]

---

[15] For related work, see Capozza and Li (1994) (this paper also contains references to additional related papers by Capozza and various coauthors).

[16] Cooke and Hamilton (1984) develop a related simulation model.

Brueckner (1986) also studies population densities, but focuses on the implications of the redevelopment analysis of Section 4. The key observation is that the population-density contour predicted by the models of Brueckner (1980a) and Braid (1990) exhibits the same kind of discontinuities as the pattern of building heights, shown in Figure 7.2. This suggests that the standard practice of estimating continuous density functions may mask significant underlying irregularity. Therefore, as an indirect test of the redevelopment models, Brueckner (1986) estimates population-density functions using a switching-regression approach, which allows for discontinuities. Visual inspection of the estimated functions reveals striking discontinuities in the density contours for many cities, as would be expected if the redevelopment models are accurate.[17]

While this approach involves regressing density on distance alone, in expectation of a pattern like that in Figure 7.2, Yacovissi and Kern (1995) include additional right-hand variables measuring the age distribution of buildings at each distance. Recalling from Figure 7.2 that building heights (as well as population densities) decline smoothly with distance *holding age fixed*, there is no need to use a switching framework in such a regression. In other words, the theory suggests that a standard regression of density on distance and building age is appropriate. As expected, Yacovissi and Kern's results show a negative effect for distance, and the coefficients on the age-distribution variables indicate how the density of development changes over time. The results reveal that post-1950 development densities are lower than pre-1950 densities, a finding that matches the assumption used in the bottom panel of Figure 7.2. While highlighting the lessons of the theoretical literature, Yacovissi and Kern's study also provides a cleaner test of Harrison and Kain's original hypothesis that current densities are influenced by initial development.

In comparison with the foregoing studies, Rosenthal and Helsley (1994) offer a more direct test of the durable-housing theories by investigating the forces that lead to redevelopment of individual parcels. The key element of their study is a variable measuring the profit differential from redevelopment. This variable equals the PV of profit from optimal redevelopment of a parcel of land minus the PV of profit from continuation of the current land use. In Brueckner (1980a) and related models, an increase in this profit differential raises the likelihood of redevelopment [in Section 4.2, the differential equals $v(w, x)$ minus (7.19)].

---

[17] Brueckner (1981b) uses the same approach to estimate building-age contours over distance, looking for evidence of discontinuities. Recognizing that estimation of smooth density contours may be improper, McMillen (1994) uses a nonparametric approach to estimate contours that closely track the actual pattern of densities. In a different vein, Brueckner (1982) tests the predictions of Brueckner and von Rabenau (1981) by looking for a connection between redevelopment of central-city buildings (as measured by age) and rapid population growth in a cross section of cities.

Using a data set on real-estate transactions along with information about post-sale redevelopment, Rosenthal and Helsley regress a binary redevelopment indicator on the profit-differential variable. The estimated probit coefficient is positive and statistically significant, confirming the theoretical prediction.

The challenge in carrying out such a test is construction of the profit-differential variable itself, and Rosenthal and Helsley adopt an ingenious method for doing so. They assume that the sale price of a parcel not subsequently re-developed is equal to the PV of profit in the current use. Similarly, ignoring demolition costs, they assume that the sale price of a subsequently redeveloped parcel is equal to the PV of profit from optimal redevelopment. Two regressions are then carried out. The first relates the selling price of a nonredeveloped parcel to the characteristics of the existing building. The second relates the selling price of a redeveloped parcel to characteristics of the raw land (mainly location). Using the coefficients from the first regression, profit in the current use can be predicted for *each parcel*, regardless of its actual fate. Similarly, the second regression predicts profit from optimal redevelopment for each parcel, regardless of its fate. Subtraction then yields the profit-differential variable, which is used in the probit regression mentioned earlier. These separate regressions are corrected for selectivity bias, which makes the overall procedure more complex than described here. Munneke (1995) replicates this study using data on commercial and industrial property in Chicago.

It is interesting to note that the results of such studies can be used to make out-of-sample predictions as to which locations in a city are ripe for redevelopment. Using data on property characteristics in a given location along with the regression estimates, the profit-differential variable for a parcel can be computed. Substitution into the estimated probit equation then yields the probability of redevelopment.

7 Conclusion

This chapter has provided a self-contained survey of the literature on urban growth with durable housing. The discussion has exposed the logic of a series of durable-housing models developed since the late 1970s, while showing how the models help explain land-use features that appear anomalous from the perspective of the static model. In particular, the chapter explains how durable-housing models can generate upward-sloping and even discontinuous building-height contours, which resemble those sometimes observed in real cities. In addition, the discussion shows that the puzzling phenomenon of leapfrog development, which leaves vacant land inside the city boundary, is a natural outcome when development is irreversible. These theoretical contributions reflect scientific progress in urban economics, with new theories developed to give insight into unexplained phenomena.

The key feature of durable-housing models is the interaction of time and location. Unlike in the malleable-housing model, the characteristics of land use for a given parcel cannot be inferred simply by observing its distance from the CBD. Instead, the date at which the parcel was (last) developed provides crucial information. While this principle would be obvious to any real-estate professional, demonstrating it formally is a key contribution of the research described in this chapter. As part of this demonstration, the various models show that the time–location interaction can generate a fascinating array of possible land-use patterns.

Given the past research effort, theoretical work on durable-housing models appears largely complete. The state of the empirical literature is less advanced, however. Aside from the study of Rosenthal and Helsley (1994), there has been little exploration of land-use dynamics using disaggregated, parcel-level data. Since redevelopment is likely to become more widespread as cities age, closer study of this process is worthwhile. There is much to be learned from empirical research on land-use dynamics, and it deserves high priority on the agenda of urban economics.

References

Alonso, W. (1964). *Location and Land Use*. Cambridge, MA: Harvard University Press.

Amin, K., and Capozza, D. R. (1993). Sequential development. *Journal of Urban Economics* 34:142–58.

Anas, A. (1978). Dynamics of urban residential growth. *Journal of Urban Economics* 5:66–87.

Arnott, R. J. (1980). A simple urban growth model with durable housing. *Regional Science and Urban Economics* 10:53–76.

Arnott, R. J., Davidson, R., and Pines, D. (1983). Housing quality, maintenance and rehabilitation. *Review of Economic Studies* 50:467–94.

Arnott, R. J., Davidson, R., and Pines, D. (1986). Spatial aspects of housing quality, density, and maintenance. *Journal of Urban Economics* 19:190–217.

Arnott, R. J., and Lewis, F. D. (1978). The transition of land to urban use. *Journal of Political Economy* 87:161–9.

Braid, R. M. (1988). Uniform spatial growth with perfect foresight and durable housing. *Journal of Urban Economics* 23:41–59.

Braid, R. M. (1990). Spatial growth and redevelopment with perfect foresight and durable housing. Unpublished paper, Wayne State University.

Brueckner, J. K. (1980a). A vintage model of urban growth. *Journal of Urban Economics* 8:389–402.

Brueckner, J. K. (1980b). Residential succession and land-use dynamics in a vintage model of urban housing. *Regional Science and Urban Economics* 10:225–40.

Brueckner, J. K. (1981a). A dynamic model of housing production. *Journal of Urban Economics* 10:1–14.

Brueckner, J. K. (1981b). Testing a vintage model of urban growth. *Journal of Regional Science* 21:23–35.

Brueckner, J. K. (1982). Building ages and urban growth. *Regional Science and Urban Economics* 12:197–210.

Brueckner, J. K. (1986). A switching regression analysis of urban population densities. *Journal of Urban Economics* 19:174–89.

Brueckner, J. K. (1987). The structure of urban equilibria: a unified treatment of the Muth-Mills model. In: E. S. Mills (ed.), *Handbook of Regional and Urban Economics*, vol. 2, pp. 821–45. Amsterdam: North Holland.

Brueckner, J. K., and von Rabenau, B. (1981). Dynamics of land-use for a closed city. *Regional Science and Urban Economics* 11:1–17.

Capozza, D. R., and Helsley, R. W. (1989). The fundamentals of land prices and urban growth. *Journal of Urban Economics* 26:295–306.

Capozza, D. R., and Helsley, R. W. (1990). The stochastic city. *Journal of Urban Economics* 28:187–203.

Capozza, D. R., and Li, Y. (1994). The intensity and timing of investment: the case of land. *American Economic Review* 84:889–904.

Cooke, T. W., and Hamilton, B. W. (1984). Evolution of urban housing stocks: a model applied to Baltimore and Houston. *Journal of Urban Economics* 16:317–38.

Evans, A. W. (1975). Rent and housing in the theory of urban growth. *Journal of Regional Science* 15:113–25.

Fisch, O. (1977). Dynamics of the housing market. *Journal of Urban Economics* 4:428–77.

Fujita, M. (1976). Spatial patterns of urban growth: optimum and market. *Journal of Urban Economics* 3:209–41.

Fujita, M. (1982). Spatial patterns of residential development. *Journal of Urban Economics* 12:22–52.

Harrison, D., Jr., and Kain, J. F. (1974). Cumulative urban growth and urban density functions. *Journal of Urban Economics* 1:61–98.

Hochman, O., and Pines, D. (1980). Costs of adjustment and demolition costs in residential construction, and their effects on urban growth. *Journal of Urban Economics* 7:2–19.

Hochman, O., and Pines, D. (1982). Costs of adjustment and the spatial pattern of a growing open city. *Econometrica* 50:1371–91.

McMillen, D. P. (1994). Vintage growth and population density: an empirical investigation. *Journal of Urban Economics* 36:333–52.

Mills, D. E. (1981). Growth, speculation and sprawl in a monocentric city. *Journal of Urban Economics* 10:201–26.

Mills, E. S. (1967). An aggregative model of resource allocation in a metropolitan area. *American Economic Review* 57:197–210.

Miyao, T. (1987). Dynamic urban models. In: E. S. Mills (ed.), *Handbook of Regional and Urban Economics*, vol. 2, pp. 821–45. Amsterdam: North Holland.

Munneke, H. J. (1995). Redevelopment decisions for commercial and industrial properties. *Journal of Urban Economics* 39:229–53.

Muth, R. F. (1969). *Cities and Housing*. University of Chicago Press.

Muth, R. F. (1975). A vintage model of the housing stock. *Papers and Proceedings of the Regional Science Association* 30:141–56.

O'Flaherty, B. (1993). Abandoned buildings: a stochastic analysis. *Journal of Urban Economics* 34:43–74.

Ohls, J. C., and Pines, D. (1975). Continuous urban development and economic efficiency. *Land Economics* 51:224–34.

Rosenthal, S. S., and Helsley, R. W. (1994). Redevelopment and the urban land price gradient. *Journal of Urban Economics* 35:182–200.

Sasaki, K. (1990). An alternative version of a vintage model of an urban housing market. *Journal of Urban Economics* 28:125–39.

Turnbull, G. K. (1988a). The effects of local taxes and public services on residential development patterns. *Journal of Regional Science* 28:541–62.

Turnbull, G. K. (1988b). Residential development in an open city. *Regional Science and Urban Economics* 18:307–20.

Vousden, N. (1980). An open-city model with nonmalleable housing. *Journal of Urban Economics* 7:248–77.

Wheaton, W. C. (1974). A comparative static analysis of urban spatial structure. *Journal of Economic Theory* 9:223–37.

Wheaton, W. C. (1982a). Urban residential growth under perfect foresight. *Journal of Urban Economics* 12:1–21.

Wheaton, W. C. (1982b). Urban spatial development with durable but replaceable capital. *Journal of Urban Economics* 12:53–67.

Wheaton, W. C. (1983). Theories of urban growth and metropolitan spatial development. In: J. V. Henderson (ed.), *Research in Urban Economics*, vol. 3, pp. 3–36. Greenwich, CT: JAI Press.

Williams, J. T. (1996). Redevelopment of real assets. Unpublished manuscript.

Yacovissi, W., and Kern, C. R. (1995). Location and history as determinants of urban residential density. *Journal of Urban Economics* 38:207–20.

CHAPTER 8

Urbanization, Urban Structure, and Growth

Gilles Duranton

1 Introduction

Starting from an economy using a traditional and rural technology, how does an urban network develop? What are the links between urbanization and growth? It seems clear that growth induces urbanization (Moomaw and Shatter, 1996), because larger markets imply a greater division of labor and a shift from agricultural and rural activities to industrial technologies for which the benefits of agglomeration are more important. On the contrary, are there some effects of the urban structure on growth? The evidence here is largely anecdotal, but one can see that most of the developed countries are characterized by high urbanization rates, balanced urban networks, and sustained growth, whereas the less well developed countries are characterized by low urbanization rates, higher rates of urban primacy (Rosen and Resnick, 1980), and sluggish growth. How do those facts relate to one another?

Building on the framework developed by Henderson (1974), in this chapter we study the dynamics of urbanization and growth, starting from a rural economy. Specifically, we consider the links among urbanization, the urban structure, and growth, and we allow each phenomenon to interact with the others. As the population grows, a first (monopoly) city may be developed. Then, for a larger population, new cities may be built. As long as their number remains small, the effects of strategic interactions (city rivalry) are likely to be important. Their implications are described, and we also explore the asymptotic case of a very large population. In particular, for production functions with decreasing marginal costs at the city level, if one city is created in a small economy, then for a large population a balanced urban network will emerge. This emergence will be gradual and will follow population growth. Institutional differences

I thank Roger Guesnerie, Hubert Jayet, Joël Maurice, participants at the conference "Enjeux et Procédures de la Décentralisation" (Marseilles, 16–17 June 1994), and especially Diego Puga and Jacques Thisse for their comments and suggestions. Financial support from the French Ministry for Research and Technology is gratefully acknowledged. Of course, all remaining errors are mine.

(i.e., centralized or decentralized management of cities) between economies or differing fertility rates will have a level impact on production. However, for production functions with nondecreasing marginal costs at the city level, it is possible to have large economies with very small numbers of cities (even possibly a large unique metropolis) and no growth. But it is also possible, with the same assumptions, to have a network of cities, the competition among which is the engine of growth. We show in our analysis that the emergence of one particular configuration can be caused by different political institutions or fertility rates.

We shall argue that the findings from our model may be relevant to an understanding of the differences in urban patterns and economic performance between less well developed countries and developed countries. Indeed, the configuration with high primacy and no growth can be induced by high fertility rates and/or centralized management of the cities. Our patterns of urbanization are thus consistent with the historical stylized facts given by Bairoch (1988). According to him, European countries have experienced a balanced path of urbanization following technological progress in the agricultural sector, whereas in developing countries, "excessive" urbanization is the result of rapid population growth. Our results concerning competition between cities are reminiscent of the processes described by Braudel (1984). The findings of Ades and Glaeser (1995) provide empirical support for our assumptions, as they emphasize the detrimental effects of urban primacy on growth, whereas Henderson (1988) has highlighted the positive role of federalized systems of government in the generation of a "balanced" urban landscape. A short review of the literature on urbanization and development has been provided by Moomaw and Shatter (1996).

From the theoretical perspective, our work relates first to the literature on cities and growth. For production functions concave in capital, our model extends that of Henderson and Ioannides (1981), because we consider global dynamics in a context in which the number of cities can be small. In our analysis, we also consider the development of new cities, whereas it is usually assumed that the number of cities is fixed. For production functions that allow for growth, the models of Palivos and Wang (1996) and Ioannides (1994) can be viewed as spatial versions of those by Lucas (1988) and Romer (1990), respectively. This type of analysis clearly can enrich standard growth models and yield some important insights concerning the spatial distribution of human capital and research-and-development (R&D) facilities. In those papers, the cities (not the urban network) were assumed to influence the growth process, because accumulation could take place only when people agglomerated. Black and Henderson (1999) went one step further and considered the impact of growth on equilibrium city sizes. In our work, growth remains urban-based, but we focus specifically on the impact of the urban structure on the growth process. The city not only is the place wherein growth occurs, as in the previous literature (e.g., growth is driven by some sort of accumulation, and that accumulation is favored in cities), but also is the engine of growth itself (depending on how cities interact, growth may or may not take place).

This chapter also complements prior work on the development of urban networks and the dynamics of urbanization. Fujita and Krugman (Chapter 5, this volume) analyze polycentric urban networks. In the same framework, Fujita et al. (1999) considered the development of new cities in an economy with a growing population.[1] Puga (1998) has looked at the patterns of urbanization in relation to transport costs. What is added here is a focus on capital accumulation. In our model, we take the institutions and the fertility rate as exogenous. Then the urbanization process, the urban structure, and the growth rate of production are derived.

After describing the assumptions of our model (Section 2) and characterizing the urban patterns obtained with a benevolent social planner (Section 3), we look at the case of a monopolistic urban structure (Section 4) and an imperfectly competitive structure (Section 5), as well as the limiting case of a large number of cities (Section 6). Then we analyze more closely capital accumulation for a concave production function (Section 7) and a convex function (Section 8). Some concluding remarks end the chapter.

2 The Model

2.1 Population and Space

Let us consider a model of overlapping generations of individuals who live for two periods. In their first period, they are young and work, whereas in their second period, they are old and retired. Each generation is composed of a mass N_t of persons. The economy starts in period 0 with a cohort of N_0 young agents. It is also assumed that in period 0, population size and the initial endowments are low enough so that no city can be developed. The exogenous evolution of the population is given by

$$N_t = (1 + n)N_{t-1} \tag{8.1}$$

Two goods are consumed in our economy: a composite good and land. The composite good is used as the numéraire. Each member of the generation born in period t consumes, both in period t and in period $t + 1$, one parcel of land and some quantity of the composite good. All individuals have the same

---

[1] The focus of the previous literature on urban dynamics was somewhat different; see Miyao (1987).

preferences[2] and abilities (they differ only in their respective locations):

$$U(z_{1,t}, z_{2,t+1}) = \ln(z_{1,t}) + b \ln(z_{2,t+1}) \tag{8.2}$$

Space is given by the real line. Each parcel of land is of size 1.[3] Urban workers must commute on a regular basis, and this is costly to them. Migration costs, on the contrary, are assumed to be negligible when spread over a lifetime. Land rent is shared equally among people within a given city. This assumption of local public ownership is crucial for the efficiency results, but it does not qualitatively alter the other results (see Duranton, 1995, ch. 4, for more developments on this issue). As long as there is no competition to occupy any specific location, the land rent is equal to the agricultural land rent. Without loss of generality, agricultural land rent is taken to be zero, because the agricultural sector is not explicitly present in the model.

2.2 Production

Two different technologies are available for production of the composite good. The traditional technology (craftsmanship) yields a net income of $\omega_t = B$ units of the composite good per unit of labor. There exists also an urban technology. It is freely available, and its returns are A per unit of labor. We suppose $A > B$. Labor supply is inelastic and normalized to 1 for each youngster.

In order to set up a city, a fixed amount k of capital is required (this assumption will be relaxed later).[4] One unit of capital can be obtained by the transformation of one unit of the composite good. Capital depreciates completely after one period, so that it can be viewed as a fixed cost of production. Alternatively, it is possible to interpret this fixed cost as the cost to provide a public good (urban infrastructure) necessary for the production. Unlike housing, productive

[2] For tractability reasons, a specific functional form is given for the utility function. The constant consumption of space allows us to ignore precise micromodeling of cities and yields a linear bid-rent curve. Note that these simplifying assumptions concerning the consumption of land are frequent in this literature (Henderson, 1988). In general, the results carry on for more general utility specifications (see Fujita, 1989, for discussion).

[3] This variable is normalized because it is redundant with the transport costs. An increase in the density of population is equivalent to a decrease in transport costs. So urban density and the evolution of transport costs are exogenously given in the model. This assumption of constant urban density makes sense in Europe. According to Duby (1981, vol. 3), urban densities in medieval Europe were not so different from those in contemporary Europe. Agricultural densities have increased and then decreased significantly following technological progress. That aspect, however, is not treated here (see Duranton, 1998, for an analysis focusing on that problem).

[4] Usually an urban externality is assumed, be it a pure externality (e.g., Henderson, 1988) or a pecuniary one (e.g., Puga, 1998), to explain the gap between increasing returns at the city level and constant returns at the individual level. Here, we assume the presence of a large actor able to internalize the urban externality. These large actors have always existed: guilds, city council, or land developers. Another argument is that intra-city collusion probably is easier than inter-city collusion. Consequently, the analysis is conducted at the level of this large actor.

activities do not use space and are located in a central business district (CBD). Each CBD is thus a point on the real line. In period t, city j employs $i_{j,t}$ workers, and the total employment in all m cities is

$$I_t = \sum_{j=1}^{j=m} i_{j,t} \tag{8.3}$$

with, of course, $I_t \leq N_t$. We define $l_{j,t}$, the net labor available for city j in period t.[5] We assume that the locations of consumers are not observable, so that the net wage cannot be used as a control variable.[6] We also have $w_{j,t}$, the wage of workers in city j in period t, and $Al_{j,t}$ is the amount of composite good available at the end of the period. The net production of city j is then given by

$$y_{j,t} = Al_{j,t} - k \tag{8.4}$$

Total production in the economy is

$$Y_t = \sum_{i=1}^{m} y_{i,t} + B(N_t - I_t) \tag{8.5}$$

At the beginning of period t, each youngster decides either to go to work in a city (if any) or to become a craftsman, using the traditional technology. At the end of the period, he receives his income, for which he decides an allocation between savings and consumption. At the beginning of the following period, these savings can be stored unproductively or invested to finance the development of a city. Cities are run by private developers whose profits are distributed to savers. The profit is

$$\pi_t = Al_t - w_t l_t - k \tag{8.6}$$

Of course, the profit of a developer must be positive for the old consumers to invest in the development of her city. In that case, each saver gets his initial investment plus his share of profits at the end of the period. If the expected profits are negative, savings can be stored unproductively at no cost (or, equivalently, invested in an alternative technology whose return is normalized to 1).[7]

Note that urbanization is financed here through a savings mechanism motivated by life-cycle considerations. Similar results could be obtained with precautionary savings, which would be historically more meaningful (e.g., instance, people could work for two periods, but their labor supply in the second

---

[5] These commuting costs, as they reduce the labor supply, will explain the difference between total employment i and net labor l.

[6] Otherwise, each consumer would have an incentive to pretend that he lived very far away and to use his spare time to work on his own with the traditional technology. Direct spatial discrimination is thus impossible.

[7] Introducing an explicit alternative technology would not change the qualitative content of the results.

period would be random). The other caveat is that the financing of urbanization is provided by a representative agent. If taken literally, this assumption is difficult to accept in regard to the urbanization of Europe. However, concerning the end of the Middle Ages, as well as the Industrial Revolution, historians put the emphasis on the emergence of a new entrepreneurial class larger than the traditional wealthy aristocracy (Mokyr, 1976; Braudel, 1984). Moreover, if capital is taken in a broad sense, one can note that a large fraction of the investment was made by an important proportion of the population through the development of education.

2.3 Transport and Land Rent

Under the traditional technology, the workplace coincides with the accommodation. In a city, each worker must devote part of his time to commuting.[8] Because of these transport costs, workers compete to locate as close as possible to the CBD. At the spatial equilibrium, the CBD is, of course, located at the center of the city, in the middle of the segment $i_{j,t}$. Consequently, within city j,

$$\text{transport needs} = \int_0^{i_{j,t}} 2\|X - x\| \, dx = i_{j,t}^2/2 \tag{8.7}$$

where X is the location of the CBD. Transport costs reduce the labor supply of the workers. If we note a the speed of transport,

$$\text{time devoted to commuting in city } j = \frac{i_{j,t}^2}{2a} \Rightarrow \frac{i_{j,t}^2}{2a} + l_{j,t} \le i_{j,t} \tag{8.8}$$

Competition among workers to locate as close as possible to the CBD, if any, gives birth to differential land rents. Because the old individuals do not work anymore, and because there is no urban amenity, they move outside the cities to avoid payment of land rent. The spatial equilibrium is such that the utility level is the same everywhere. For any worker located in x, the land rent $r(x)$ is then such that the net income is the same for all inhabitants of the city:[9]

$$r(x) + 2\left\|\frac{i_t}{2} - x\right\| \frac{w_t}{a} = \text{constant } \forall x \in [0, i_t] \tag{8.9}$$

That is, because of the assumption of constant land consumption, then everywhere in i_t the sum of land rent and commuting costs is constant. Note that the worker located on the outskirts of the city pays no land rent. Hence the sum of land rent and transport costs is $i_t w_t/a$. The spatial equilibrium then implies

---

[8] We could have used a more general specification for the transport using some other goods as inputs, but the results would have been the same.

[9] Subscripts are ignored whenever their absence does not create any ambiguity.

that the net income ω_t for each worker is $\omega_t = w_t(1 - i_t/a) + D_t$, where D_t is the land dividend. Finally, the capital available in the economy in $t + 1$ is

$$K_{t+1} = \int_{I_t} S_t(x)\,dx \qquad (8.10)$$

where $S_t(x)$ is the amount of savings accumulated by a youngster located at x in period t. We can now solve the consumption program for everyone:

$$\max U(z_{1,t}, z_{2,t+1}) \quad \text{s.t.} \quad \omega_t = z_{1,t} + S_t \quad \text{and} \quad S_t \frac{\pi_{t+1} + K_{t+1}}{K_{t+1}} = z_{2,t+1} \qquad (8.11)$$

with $\omega_t = w_t(1 - i_t/a) + D_t$ for industrial and urban workers, and $\omega_t = B$ for craftsmen. We get

$$z_{1,t} = \frac{\omega_t}{1 + b} \quad \text{and} \quad z_{2,t+1} = bz_{1,t} \frac{\pi_{t+1} + K_{t+1}}{K_{t+1}} \qquad (8.12)$$

3 The First-Best Optimum

Before analyzing any decentralized solution, we derive, as a benchmark, the urban system developed by a benevolent social planner. However, the problem of the social optimum is not trivial in an overlapping-generations framework. For instance, imagine (1) a given path for which the first generation gets a high level of consumption, and all subsequent generations get a very low level of consumption, and (2) a second path for which the first generation consumes slightly less, but all other generations consume much more. These two dynamic allocations cannot be Pareto-ranked. To make things simple, we measure total social welfare as the intertemporal sum of the welfare measures for all generations (utilitarian criterion). The rate of time preference used by the social planner, b_s, can be different from b. The social planner's objective is then

$$\max_{M_t, Z_{1,t}, Z_{2,t}} \sum_{t=0}^{+\infty} \int b_s^t \{\delta_1(x) \ln[z_{1,t}(x)] + \delta_2(x) \ln[z_{2,t}(x)]\}\,dx \qquad (8.13)$$

$$\text{s.t.} \quad Y_t + M_t k \geq M_{t+1} k + \int b_s^t \{\delta_1(x) \ln[z_{1,t}(x)] + \delta_2(x) \ln[z_{2,t}(x)]\}\,dx$$

where M_t is the positive number of cities in the economy at t. We have $\delta_1(x) = 1$ [respectively $\delta_2(x) = 1$] if x is inhabited by a young [respectively old] individual, and $\delta_1(x) = 0$ [respectively $\delta_2(x) = 0$] otherwise. The quantity of the composite good available at the end of the period is equal to the gross production $Y_t + M_t k$. We assume $b_s(1 + n) < 1$; otherwise the social optimum would not be defined. Production is described by

$$Y_t = AI_t\left(1 - \frac{I_t}{2aM_t}\right) + B(N_t - I_t) - M_t k \qquad (8.14)$$

Conceptually, we face here a classical maximization program performed by a social planner. However, our problem is not standard, because the optimization is not over $\Re$ (which would have enabled us to solve the program using some known methods), but over a series of integers, which do not appear under the form $X_{n+1} - X_n$. Despite this, some results can be obtained.

Proposition 1. *With a central planner,* $k \leq \pi(i^*)/(1 - b_s)$ *is a necessary condition of urbanization, where* i^* *is the size that maximizes the production of a given city.*

Proof. See Appendix A. ∎

This result states that no city will be developed by a central planner if the net present value of the surplus due to urbanization is inferior to the fixed cost of urbanization. To understand this first result, consider some extreme cases. For instance, if b_s is zero, it is straightforward that no city will be set up, because the future is neglected, and all production is consumed at each period. On the contrary, if b_s is close to 1, it might be worth investing for higher production in the future if the urban technology is sufficiently productive. If urbanization takes place, then it is characterized by the following proposition.

Proposition 2. *With a central planner, the intensity of urban development is increasing in* b_s. *When* t *tends toward* $+\infty$ *and when cities are developed, the population of each city will be larger than* $i^{**} = \sqrt{2ak/A}$ *(the production-maximizing size for the whole economy without savings constraint) and smaller than* $i^* = a(1 - B/A)$. *When the planner cares only for the welfare of the limit generation, the city size will be* $i^{**} = \sqrt{2ak/A}$, *and we have* $z_1 = A(1 - i^{**}/a)/(1 + b_s)$ *and* $z_2 = Ab_s(1 - i^{**}/a)/(1 + b_s)$.

Proof. See Appendix B. ∎

Of course, the way in which utilities are aggregated is crucial, and, in particular, the rate of time preference used by the planner is fundamental.[10] If the planner is interested only in the welfare of the limit generation, then the city size will be such that it will maximize total production at each period. However, if there is a high rate of time preference, the planner may prefer to invest less for the purpose of allowing the present generations to consume more. In this case,

---

[10] However, the question is, Why can the government favor some generations at the expense of others? A natural (but arguable) objective is that the planner should try to maximize the welfare of the limit generation. In this case, note that production is eventually maximized at each period.

society will invest less, and this may imply fewer cities of larger size. And thus production will not be maximized in the future, because of insufficient capital accumulation. We now turn to the situation in which the development of cities is not led by a benevolent central planner.

4 The Monopoly

In this section, the cities are developed by a monopolist who can build as many cities as she likes. The effects of competition are analyzed in the next two sections. The justification for this monopoly (or, properly speaking, monopsony) is that there can be a "natural" monopoly when the population is small (in particular, if there is only one city). A second possible justification is that the urban system can be controlled by vested interest; see De Long and Shleifer (1993) and Ades and Glaeser (1995) for some examples. Finally, the development of cities can also be centralized, with a central authority subject to a public-choice behavior, thus trying to maximize total profits.

Proposition 3. *The conditions (SS):* $N_{t-1} \geq k(1 + b)/Bb$ *and (PP):* $N_t \geq k/[A(1 - i_t/2a) - B]$ *are necessary and sufficient for the development of a first city. Moreover, there exists a finite optimal population* $i^* = a(1 - B/A)$ *for the first city.*

Proof. The developer's problem is

$$
\max_{i_t, w_t} \pi_t = A i_t \left(1 - \frac{i_t}{2a} \right) - w_t i_t \left(1 - \frac{i_t}{2a} \right) - k
$$

$$
\text{s.t.} \quad w_t \left(1 - \frac{i_t}{a} \right) + D_t \geq B, \quad i_t \leq N_t, \quad K_t \geq k
$$

(8.15)

It implies $\omega_t = w_t(1 - i_t/2a) = B$. Furthermore, we face the following urbanization conditions:

- *The savings-sufficiency condition.* A city can be developed only if $K_t \geq k$. Using (8.10) and (8.12), we get

$$
\text{(SS):} \quad N_{t-1} \geq \frac{k(1 + b)}{Bb}
$$

- *The positive-profits condition.* For a city to be viable, we need $\pi_t > 0$. With $\omega_t = B$ and $A \geq w_t \geq B$, we get

$$
\text{(PP):} \quad N_t \geq \frac{k}{A(1 - i_t/2a) - B}
$$

Moreover, when the population constraint is not binding, we find the profit-maximizing size with one city to be $i^* = a(1 - B/A)$.   ∎

For some values of the parameters, the conditions (SS) and (PP) cannot be met. For instance, one can think of high commuting costs, poorly productive industrial technologies, highly productive traditional technologies, or high fixed costs. Depending on the value of the parameters, one of the two constraints can be binding longer than the other. When both can be satisfied, the dynamic behavior of the economy is the following: At first, the economy is populated only by craftsmen using the traditional technology. When the foregoing conditions are satisfied, a first city is developed. Its size i_t may grow as the population expands. However, this city size is bounded, because the remotest workers bear steadily increasing transport costs as the population grows. The monopolist then has a most profitable size i^* for her first city. The reason is very simple: Transport costs reduce the accessibility of the CBD, so that the marginal productivity tends to zero as people live farther away [recall that the labor supply is multiplied by $(1 - i_t/2a)$]. Consequently, the marginal product of labor decreases. When $N_t > i^*$, the monopolist stops hiring new workers and realizes a profit of $\pi(i^*)$.

In any case, urbanization is sudden, and this is not specific to our minimal capital requirement, because the result holds with a more general specification, as will be shown in our final section. *A small increase in population is enough to trigger this structural change* (see Papageorgiou, 1980, for more developments on this stylized fact). Note that population growth plays a fundamental role in explaining urbanization. Current theories of growth also often rely on demographic factors as providing a primary engine for evolution (Kremer, 1993; Goodfriend and McDermott, 1995).

The role of the parameter B is ambiguous. On the one hand, if the returns of the traditional activity are high, the savings constraint is less binding (a higher income induces higher savings). On the other hand, it has an adverse effect on the profit constraint. The higher the productivity of the traditional activity, the higher the wages that must be paid by the monopolist. The effect of a high B on the (PP) condition can be such that it can prevent urbanization for good. This result is in line with the findings of Corden and Neary (1982) and, more recently, Matsuyama (1991). It has also been confirmed by Goodfriend and McDermott (1995), for whom industrialization can occur only when the population pressure brings the traditional technology into the region of decreasing returns.

If the population keeps growing, it might become profitable for the monopolist to develop a second city (we still assume that no potential entrant threatens her). We now define $F(m) = \min \sum_{j=1}^{m} i_j/m$, which means that $m F(m)$ is the minimal population of the economy for which the monopolist will develop m cities.

Proposition 4. *The sequence $(F(m))$ is increasing and converges toward $i^{**} = \sqrt{2ak/A}$ if the savings constraint is not binding. The size i^{**} will maximize total production in a large economy. If the constraint is binding at i^{**}, and if cities are developed, the series $(F(m))$ is constant.*

Proof. See Appendix C.   ∎

If the number of cities is small, the monopolist maximizes her profit by dividing the fixed cost between many workers. As the number of cities increases, maximizing total profit becomes equivalent to maximizing the production per worker. From a static point of view, the monopoly is efficient when savings are not binding (see Proposition 2), because the labor supply is inelastic.

5 Imperfect Competition

In this section, we study the effects of imperfect competition among cities. All our assumptions remain the same except that we allow here for competing cities. We assume that there are many (potential) developers, who can build cities and compete to attract workers. Given our previous assumptions, the timing is as follows:

1. Entry decisions of the developers and allocation of savings: Various mechanisms can be considered to allocate savings. We simply suppose that developers enter sequentially into the market. As long as opportunities for profit exist, some new developers will enter. The developers cannot commit to a given rate of return. Each saver allocates his savings independently of the others.
2. The developers make their location decisions.
3. They set their wages.
4. The young generation makes its occupational choices. Those who decide to go into a city also choose which city and select a location within that city.

The same sequence of decisions is repeated at the next period, with a larger population and other players. The equilibrium concept we use here is the perfect Nash equilibrium. We place three natural restrictions on that equilibrium:

- It must be symmetric, because cities are anonymous.
- Equilibrium profits must be positive.
- The savings constraint must be satisfied.

Before any further analysis, note that there is no locational attribute in the model. So we can assume that cities are nonoverlapping, because it is straightforward that if they overlap, each developer increases her profit by locating her CBD farther away from the neighboring CBDs (to decrease total transport costs) and thus increases her profits. Our main result in this section is as follows.

Proposition 5. *The duopoly equilibrium is unique and is such that*

- *if $F(1) \geq F(0)$, then the duopoly exists as soon as $N_t \geq 2F(1)$;*

- if $F(2) \geq F(0) \geq F(1)$, then the duopoly appears for a population N_t such that $2F(0) \geq N_t \geq 2F(1)$;
- if $F(0) \geq F(2)$, then the monopolist develops a second city for $N_t = 2F(2)$, and the duopoly appears later for an economy whose population is inferior to $2F(0)$.

Proof. See Appendix D. ∎

Thus, there is a unique duopoly equilibrium (for some given locations with nonoverlapping cities) when the population is above a given threshold. Two different kinds of equilibria are in fact possible. If $2F(0) < N_t < 2F(2)$, the wage is determined by a competitive process. Developers bid to attract workers to their cities. The wage is then higher than in the monopoly case. The second type of duopoly occurs for larger economies. The wage is no longer determined by a competitive process. Each player is acting as a local monopolist. The final implication of our proposition is that competition induces faster urbanization than does the multiple-city monopoly (because there is still the opportunity for the incumbent monopolist to develop a second city).

6 Perfect Competition

We now consider very large economies. We look for the asymptotic properties of the model when the population becomes high. We find the following:

Proposition 6. *The competitive asymptotic equilibrium exists, is unique, and maximizes asymptotic production (city size is i^{**}) as well as the welfare of the limit generation. Moreover, the Henry George theorem applies.*[11]

Proof. See Appendix E. ∎

This result is standard in a competitive nonspatial framework, but more surprising in a spatial framework. The first reason for this efficiency result is that there are some urban developers who are able to control the sizes of cities. Competition between self-interested agents leads to greater efficiency because it induces them to maximize their own-city surplus (remember that the land rent is redistributed within the city) in the absence of any economy-wide externality. The second reason is because of the dynamic general equilibrium structure. Competition between developers induces not only static efficiency but also better dynamic efficiency than does a monopoly. The idea is that the monopolist makes substantial profits that are not reinjected into the economy, whereas competition leads to higher wages and thus higher savings and higher investments. It is now possible to derive some comparative-statics results.

---

[11] That is, the total differential land rent is equal to the fixed costs.

1. Concerning the returns from the traditional technology, there is a threshold, as with the development of the first city. If the condition $A(1 - i^{**}/a) \geq B$ is satisfied, cities can be developed. Otherwise, if B is above this threshold, urbanization will not occur. Below the threshold, a higher productivity of the traditional technology will induce a slower development of cities, but the same asymptotic landscape for a very large population.

2. Speed of transport: $\partial w(i^{**})/\partial a \geq 0$ and $\partial i^{**}/\partial a \geq 0$. Lower transport costs induce larger cities. This benefits the workers, who receive higher wages because of higher average productivity. At the aggregate level, if there is a constant population, then lower transport costs will reduce the number of cities, and that may induce "catastrophes" in some areas. By "catastrophe" we mean the death of a city and the emigration of its labor force toward other cities. Empirically, the decline of transport costs for commuting as well as for the shipping of goods is a well-established stylized fact; see Bairoch (1988), Hugill (1993), and Mokyr (1990) for more details. According to Hugill (1993, ch. 5), a slight decline in average commuting costs and increases in physical area by a factor of 5 or even 10 over the past century are not uncommon for many cities in the Western world. Historically, such a reduction in the number of cities may have been avoided because of the significant increase of the size of the overall population. (Note that this is different from the popular explanation, for which the causality runs directly from an increase in population to larger cities.) Empirically, this fact is consistent with the regressions of Moomaw and Shatter (1996).

3. Fixed cost: $\partial w(i^{**})/\partial k \leq 0$ and $\partial i^{**}/\partial k \geq 0$. A higher fixed cost must be divided across more workers, so that the size of the cities increases. This larger size reduces efficiency and then lowers wages.

4. Industrial productivity: $\partial w(i^{**})/\partial A \geq 0$ and $\partial i^{**}/\partial A \leq 0$. Higher industrial productivity makes commuting costs relatively more expensive and hence pushes toward smaller cities. Given the zero-profit condition, this benefits the workers. At the aggregate level, the number of cities increases. This effect is opposed to the effects of lower transport costs. *Because technological progress induces both higher industrial productivity and lower transport costs, the overall effects on the size and number of cities are ambiguous.* A real catastrophe is likely to arise after an exogenous asymmetric shock, such as the removal of trade barriers. The latter can be interpreted as a shock to transport costs without an immediate increase in industrial productivity.

7 Bounded Endogenous Capital Accumulation

The production function used in the benchmark model is quite restrictive. We propose here a more general specification:

$$Y_{i,t} = AK_{i,t}^{x} l_{i,t} - K_{i,t}, \qquad \text{with } x < 1 \tag{8.16}$$

This specification enables us to consider endogenous capital accumulation in each city. As for the development of a first city, the constraint on savings disappears, and we are left with only one condition on profits. After straight-forward transformations, this condition can be written

(PP'): $[AK^x(1 - i/2a) - B]i \geq K,$ with $K \leq \dfrac{bB}{(1 + b)(1 + n)} N$

Analysis of (PP') shows that despite the flexibility of capital, the development of a first city is sudden. For a larger population, analysis of the dynamic behavior of the economy with a monopolist is reduced to the problem of construction of city $m + 1$ when m cities are already present. However, it is now more complicated than in Section 4, because the arbitrage equation [the analogue of (A8.13) in Appendix C] must take into account not only the allocation of labor but also the allocation of capital across cities. It is nonetheless possible to analyze the asymptotic behavior of the model for a very large population. Assume that the monopolist develops m cities with s savers for each (s denotes the "savings area," whereas i is the city size; of course, we need $s \geq i$). Her profit is equal to $m\pi$. Maximizing this quantity is equivalent to maximizing the same quantity divided by the total population ms, that is, the rate of profit π/s. Because in the preceding period the net income of each youngster (worker or craftsman) was B, the quantity of disposable capital for a city with a savings area s is

$$Q = s\frac{Bb}{(1 + b)(1 + n)} \tag{8.17}$$

After replacements in the profit function, we can write

$$\frac{\pi}{s} = AQ^x\frac{i}{s}\left(1 - \frac{i}{2a}\right) - \frac{Q}{s} - \frac{Bi}{s} \tag{8.18}$$

The first-order condition for s is

$$s(i) = \left[(1 - x)AB^{x-1}\left(1 - \frac{i}{2a}\right)\right]^{-1/x}\left(\frac{(1 + b)(1 + n)}{b}\right), \quad \text{with } s(i) \geq i \tag{8.19}$$

The first-order condition with respect to i is

$$i(s) = a\left(1 - \frac{B}{AQ^x}\right) \tag{8.20}$$

After simplifications, we find the solution to be

$$s = \frac{1}{B}(1 - x)^{-1/2x}\left(\frac{(1 + b)(1 + n)}{b}\right)^{(1+x)/2x} \quad \text{and}$$

$$i = a\left(1 - \frac{Bb\sqrt{1 - x}}{A(1 + b)(1 + n)}\right)^{(1-x)/2} \tag{8.21}$$

where $N_t \geq s \geq i$. These solutions are positive only if x and A are sufficiently large. Equation (8.21) shows that i increases in x, whereas i/s decreases in x for x sufficiently close to 1. So the monopolist will restrict the number of cities she develops when x is close to 1. She will do so because returns at the city level will be higher because of more slowly decreasing returns. In other words, it is worth restricting the number of cities and not using some of the labor force in order to develop fewer cities with a high quantity of capital for each.

If competition is made possible when $x < 1$, all the results obtained in Sections 5 and 6 still hold. Our assumptions about the competitive process imply that in equilibrium, capital is allocated equally across cities. Then one simply needs to replace $A K_{i,t}^x$ by A', and $K_{i,t}$ by k'. The results are the same given A' and k'. Moreover, the quantity of accumulated capital in the economy is bounded. This standard result is easy to prove. Because of the existence of decreasing returns, for $K_{i,t}$ arbitrarily large the production is inferior to $K_{i,t}$, whatever its feasible population. Because this capital fully depreciates, net production should decrease over time and reach its steady state. The steady state is then such that the level of accumulated capital in each city ($Q_t = K_t/m$) is constant over time. In particular, if urbanization takes place, straightforward calculations yield that city size and incomes asymptotically are

$$ i^{**}(Q) = \sqrt{\frac{2a Q^{1-x}}{A}} \quad \text{and} \quad \omega = A - \sqrt{\frac{2A Q^{1-x}}{a}} \tag{8.22} $$

From here, we find that the steady-state accumulated capital per city Q_∞ in the economy is the unique positive solution of

$$ \frac{Q_\infty(1+b)(1+n)}{b} + 2Q_\infty^{1-x} - \sqrt{2aA Q_\infty^{1-x}} = 0 \tag{8.23} $$

The analysis most closely related to this one is that by Henderson and Ioannides (1981). The first difference is that here we allow not only for perfect competition but also for imperfect competition, whereas they considered only the perfectly competitive case. The second difference is that we consider an overlapping-generations economy, instead of infinitely lived agents. This enables us to analyze some more complicated dynamics in which the number of cities can change over time. In this neoclassical growth framework, for the economy to produce more with a constant population, we need an exogenous increase in the total factor productivity A. The underlying assumption behind this is that the growth process is exogenous to the system of cities and is independent of geography. In the next section, on the contrary, we take the view that geography and cities play crucial roles in the growth process.

8 Unbounded Endogenous Capital Accumulation

We focus now on the case for which $Y_{i,t} = A K_{i,t} l_{i,t} - K_{i,t}$. Under some conditions, this enables us to get sustained growth over time. However, consider the following.

Proposition 7. *For linear returns to the reproducible factor, the monopolist will develop only one city. The monopoly is the market structure that maximizes static production. Dynamically, it implies convergence toward a steady state with no growth.*

Proof. For any population i of cities ($i < a$) and any quantity K of savings, the total production with one city, $Y(1)$, is superior to what is obtained with two cities, $Y(2)$:

$$Y(2) = 2 \left[A \frac{K}{2} i \left(1 - \frac{i}{2a} \right) - \frac{K}{2} \right],$$

$$Y(1) = A K i \left(1 - \frac{i}{2a} \right) - K + Bi \Rightarrow Y(1) \geq Y(2) \tag{8.24}$$

The same argument holds for profit if we denote $\Pi(1)$ the profit obtained with one city and $\Pi(2)$ the profit obtained with two cities. We find

$$\Pi(1) = A K i \left(1 - \frac{i}{2a} \right) - K - Bi \quad \text{and}$$

$$\Pi(2) = 2 \left[A \frac{K}{2} i \left(1 - \frac{i}{2a} \right) - \frac{K}{2} - Bi \right] \tag{8.25}$$

This implies immediately that $\Pi(1) - \Pi(2) = Bi > 0$. So the last expression states that it is possible to realize a higher profit with one city instead of two. The asymptotic population of the unique city is

$$i^*(K) = a \left(1 - \frac{B}{AK} \right) \xrightarrow[K \to +\infty]{} a \tag{8.26}$$

Then it is straightforward that $\omega_t = B$, because the monopolist puts people at their reservation level. So capital per capita does not increase. ∎

Even for production functions homogeneous of degree 1 in the reproducible factor, the economy converges toward a no-growth steady state. We can contrast this result with what can be obtained in a competitive framework.

Proposition 8. *For linear returns to capital in the city production function, competition in a large economy induces the existence of many cities. Furthermore, these cities enjoy perpetual growth.*

Proof. The stages 1, 2, 3, and 4 are solved as in Section 6. At stage 1, all m developers receive the same amount of capital, that is, $Q_t = K_t/m$. For m very large, we find the wage to be $w_t = AQ_t(1 - 2i_t/a)/(1 - i_t/a)$. The zero-profit condition then implies $i = \sqrt{2a/A}$. Of course, we need the zero-profit condition to able to be satisfied; that is,

$$(PP''): \quad [AQ(1 - i/2a) - B]i \geq Q$$

Then we observe that

$$\frac{K_{t+1}}{K_t} = \frac{\sqrt{2a}A - \sqrt{aA}}{\sqrt{aA} - \sqrt{2}} \frac{b}{1+b} \tag{8.27}$$

∎

In the competitive case, the economy experiences endogenous growth, with unbounded capital accumulation and a finite growth rate (if $K_{t+1}/K_t \geq 1+n$). In the previous sections, the difference between monopolistic and competitive market structures was one of level (competition led to a better steady state). Here, the difference is one of nature: Monopoly leads to stagnation, whereas inter-city competition fuels economic growth. The intuitions of Propositions 7 and 8 are quite easy to understand. The monopolist puts all workers at their reservation wage (i.e., the returns of the traditional sector, B). As a consequence, net wages do not increase, and neither do savings, capital, and production. On the contrary, *competition allows redistribution of the gains generated by increasing returns, redistributed through higher wages. Then the savings of the generation born in t are higher than the savings of the generation born in t − 1, so that the accumulated capital in t + 1 exceeds the capital in t.* From this result, higher production, higher wages, and still higher savings in $t + 2$ are obtained. Consequently, *if the rate of time preference and the demographic pressure are not too strong, production per capita steadily grows.* Note that the growth rate depends negatively on the transport costs.

There are thus dynamic gains from competition between cities. On the contrary, as stated by Proposition 7, production is maximized at each period (or statically) by developing only one city. The intuition of this result is rather simple. Because the production function exhibits increasing returns to scale, there is no reason for the "first welfare theorem" to hold. Here, the increasing returns are so strong that the monopoly is optimal in the short run (if, of course, the population size is large enough and the fixed cost is low enough). Despite increasing returns, competition is possible because of the impossibility of coordination among savers (just as in any standard general equilibrium framework, where savers prefer their firms to be monopolists in their sector).

Despite the fact that there are significant differences in how Lucas (1988) and Romer (1990) and all subsequent papers in this literature view the issue, steady growth typically is given by the assumption of linear returns for capital (so that the marginal productivity of capital is nondecreasing). In an overlapping-generations framework, such as that here, if the share of wages multiplied by the propensity to save is greater than 1, capital will increase over time. *The urban structure affects the growth rate because it determines the share of wages in production.*

Growth is characterized here by continual increases in the quantity produced through "learning by doing." Bairoch (1991) has confirmed that, historically, "science then played almost no part in the technological development associated with the beginning of industrialization." Growth is not the result of the consumers' will, nor is it sought by the developers. *It is then just a by-product of competition.* In the historical literature, competition among cities is not always regarded as a factor for growth. The reason is that the Industrial Revolution saw the emergence of many new urban centers, because of constraints related to raw materials (Bairoch, 1988). These centers probably competed with one another to attract workers. But in the beginning, the competition was not so intense, because some new cities were replacing the old ones and because agricultural wages had been falling (thus releasing competition through lower reservation wages). Within our model, the first industrial cities are local monopolists. This may be the reason why real wages during the Industrial Revolution did not increase immediately, but only after 1820 or 1840 in England.

Furthermore, competition among cities was at the heart of the growth process before the Industrial Revolution. The fact has been documented by Braudel (1984). He described a world of European cities fighting for leadership, and he attributed the rise of Europe (material superiority leading to military domination) to that competition. In his description, competition was exacerbated because of a monopoly rent for the leader (holding a pivotal role in the funneling of internationally traded goods). Successively, Venice, Genoa, Amsterdam, London, and New York held that key role and derived important economic advantages from it. Among geographers, that fact has also been asserted by Marshall (1989).

It is now possible to contrast our results with those from the sparse literature dealing with cities and endogenous growth. In particular, Lucas (1988) raised the idea that cities were the places where human capital was accumulated. Formal versions of that argument were proposed by Palivos and Wang (1996) and Black and Henderson (1999) using a CBD in which human-capital externalities operated. Another analysis was that by Ioannides (1994), using an R&D-based model of endogenous growth. All those arguments analyzed a growth process that took place within the city, whereas we propose the hypothesis of development driven by the interaction between cities, that is, by the urban structure.

More importantly, our last result offers an explanation concerning the existence of urban giants. Ades and Glaeser (1995), in an empirical study, stressed the importance of political factors. Their explanation was that nonbenevolent dictatorship favored overagglomeration because of distortionary taxation. In another econometric analysis, Henderson (1988) found that a federalized system of government was correlated with a low Herfindahl-Hirschman index of urban concentration. So "competitive" Western countries may have many urban centers of limited size, whereas "noncompetitive" Third World countries have only very large primate cities (Mexico City, Lagos, Jakarta, Manila) with stagnant production. This is consistent with the cross-section results of Moomaw and Shatter (1996). They showed that poverty is associated with a high degree of primacy and low rates of urbanization. This is also consistent with the work of Ades and Glaeser (1995) who showed the detrimental effects of high degrees of urban primacy. This also replicates the evidence of Rosen and Resnick (1980) concerning the high degree of primacy in poor countries. Note, finally, that a low intensity of competition can result not only from political factors but also from strong demographic pressure. Starting from a competitive urban structure, it is possible to end up with local monopolies if population increases faster than production.

So concerning urban primacy, our argument is an alternative to that of Krugman and Livas Elizondo (1996), which is related to protectionism. They would interpret barriers to trade as higher inter-city transport costs for the manufactured goods. These higher transport costs, in their model, are favoring higher urban concentrations. Puga (1998) has explained urban primacy in a dynamic framework. If urbanization takes place in a world of high transport costs, it leads to a balanced landscape with many cities. On the contrary, if urbanization takes place when transport costs are lower, urban primacy may occur.

9 Conclusion

This chapter has examined the urbanization patterns in an economy with a growing population and has analyzed the links between urban structure and growth. As population expands, an urban network emerges. We have examined several constraints that limit the urbanization process. First of all, urbanization is capital-intensive (in the simplest version of the model, a fixed cost must be incurred, but the interpretation of this fixed cost can be more general and encompass all urban amenities). Second, urbanization must be profitable. Apart from the costs of urban amenities, urbanization also induces commuting costs. This must be balanced by higher returns from the urban technologies for urbanization to occur.

When the city production function allows for unbounded growth, we can see striking differences between urban networks with competing cities and urban networks in which cities are in a position of local monopoly on the labor market. In this second case, cities are larger, and there may even be only one metropolis. This latter configuration can be induced by some specific institutional features (like a self-interested dictatorship or any kind of control by vested interests) or can be the result of surplus labor. In the short run, this single-metropolis configuration is efficient for maximizing production. However, because most of the surplus is not reinvested, the single metropolis acts as a brake on development and makes it impossible to sustain growth in the long run. On the contrary, competitive urban systems yield self-sustained growth.

Appendix A

The concavity of the utility function implies that, optimally, all members of a given generation should receive equal quantities of goods (equal treatment within each generation). Thus,

$$\max_{M_t} \sum_{t=0}^{+\infty} b_s^t [N_t \ln(z_{2,t}) + N_{t-1} \ln(z_{2,t})] \tag{A8.1}$$

$$\text{s.t.} \quad Y_t + M_t k \geq M_{t+1}k + N_t z_{1,t} + N_{t-1} z_{2,t}$$

Optimal distribution of consumption between the generations present in t yields

$$z_{1,t} = z_{2,t} = \frac{Y_t + M_t k - M_{t+1}k}{(2+n)N_t/(1+n)} \tag{A8.2}$$

The social program can then be written again:

$$\max_{M_t} \sum_{t=0}^{+\infty} [(1+n)b_s]^t \ln \left[\frac{Y_t + M_t k - M_{t+1}k}{(2+n)N_t/(1+n)} \right] \tag{A8.3}$$

By a straightforward concavity argument, the cities have the same population numbers and have their CBDs located at their centers. The occupational choice for the young agents is solved by $I_t = \min(M_t i^*; N_t)$, with $i^* = a(1 - B/A)$. If the population size i of one city exceeds i^*, the marginal worker located in $i/2$ has production equal to $(1 - i/2a) < (1 - i^*/2a) = B$. His being a craftsman is then socially profitable. In this Appendix A only, and without loss of generality, the creation of the first city is taken to be the origin of time. Independently of any further construction, the development of a first city will not improve social welfare if and only if

$$\sum_{t=0}^{t=T} b_s^t N_t \ln \left[\frac{BN_t}{(2+n)N_t/(1+n)} \right] \geq N_0 \ln \left[\frac{BN_0 - k}{(2+n)N_t/(1+n)} \right]$$

$$+ \sum_{t=0}^{t=T} b_s^t N_t \ln \left[\frac{BN_t + \pi(i^*)}{(2+n)N_t/(1+n)} \right]$$

$$\forall (T, N_0) \in (N, R^+) \tag{A8.4}$$

We assume $\pi = \pi(i^*)$ (and this implies that we need t such that $I_t > i^*$). This is without loss of generality, because if the city is not profitable in the most favorable case, it will never be profitable. The preceding expression can be transformed into

$$
\ln\left[\frac{BN_0 - k}{BN_0}\right] + \sum_{t=0}^{t=T}[b_s(1+n)]^t \ln\left[\frac{BN_t + \pi(i^*)}{BN_t}\right] \leq 0 \, \forall \, N_0 \text{ and } T
$$

(A8.5)

Suppose now that the planner has built m cities. We take the current period as the origin of time. The construction of a new city will not improve the social welfare if and only if

$$
\sum_{t=0}^{t=T} b_s^t N_t \ln\left[\frac{BN_t + m\pi(i^*)}{(2+n)N_t/(1+n)}\right] \geq N_0 \ln\left[\frac{BN_t + m\pi(i^*) - k}{(2+n)N_t/(1+n)}\right]
$$

$$
+ \sum_{t=0}^{t=T} b_s^t N_t \ln\left[\frac{BN_t + (m+1)\pi(i^*)}{(2+n)N_t/(1+n)}\right]
$$

(A8.4′)

From this we get

$$
\ln\left[\frac{BN_0 + m\pi(i^*) - k}{BN_0 + m\pi(i^*)}\right] + N_0 \ln\left[\frac{BN_0 + m\pi(i^*) - k}{(2+n)N_t/(1+n)}\right] \leq 0 \, \forall \, N_0 \text{ and } T
$$

(A8.5′)

This expression is equivalent to (A8.5), because it is possible to set $N_0' = BN_0 + m\pi(i^*)$. Then if the construction of a first city does not improve the social welfare, no subsequent construction will improve it either. This proves that the social optimum is such that the number of cities either is zero or becomes arbitrarily large as the population grows. A direct implication of this is that (A8.5) is a necessary and sufficient condition for nonurbanization. We define

$$
f(T, N_0) = \ln\left(1 + \frac{-k}{BN_0}\right) + \sum_{t=0}^{t=T}[b_s(1+n)]^t \ln\left(1 + \frac{\pi(i^*)}{BN_t}\right)
$$

(A8.6)

Note that $f(\cdot)$ is increasing in T. Then if (A8.5) is satisfied for T arbitrarily large, it is satisfied for all T, and we can set $T = +\infty$. The derivation of $f(\cdot)$ with respect to population yields

$$
\frac{\partial f}{\partial N_0} = \frac{-k}{BN_0^2}\left(1 + \frac{-k}{BN_0}\right)^{-1}
$$

$$
- \sum_{t=0}^{t=\infty}[b_s(1+n)]^t \frac{\pi(i^*)}{BN_t^2}\left(1 + \frac{\pi(i^*)}{BN_t}\right)^{-1}
$$

$$
\geq \frac{1}{BN_0^2}\left(k - \sum_{t=0}^{t=\infty} b_s^t \pi(i^*)\right)
$$

(A8.7)

Consequently, if $k \geq \pi(i^*)/(1 - b_s)$, $f(\cdot)$ is increasing in N_0. And for N_0 very large, it is possible to approximate $f(\cdot)$ by

$$f(N_0) = \frac{1}{BN_0}\left(-k + \frac{\pi(i^*)}{1 - b_s}\right) + O(1/N_0) \tag{A8.8}$$

Hence, for all $k \geq \pi(i^*)/(1 - b_s)$, urbanization is not socially profitable. ∎

Appendix B

We consider two economies, 1 and 2, whose rates of time preference vary: $b_1 > b_2$ (economy 2 discounts the future more heavily than does economy 1). Suppose there exists t such that $M_1(t) + 1 = M_2(t) = M_2(t - 1) + 1$ and $T > t$ such that $M_1(T + 1) = M_1(T - 1) + 1 = M_2(T)$. This corresponds to a situation in which it is optimal for economy 2 to build a new city in t, whereas economy 1 will build it later (if T does not exist as defined earlier, the proof can be carried out with T being the period in which economy 1 develops yet another city). Intuitively, this can be interpreted in terms of economy 1 catching up with economy 2. Optimality of the construction in t implies that $\forall \underline{M}_2(i) < M_2(t)$, for $i = t - 1, \ldots, T - 1$, and $\underline{M}_2(T) < M_2(T)$,

$$U[M_2(t - 1); M_2(t - 1) + 1]$$

$$+ \sum_{i=t}^{i=T}[b_2(1 + n)]^i U[M_2(t); M_2(t + 1)]$$

$$\geq \sum_{i=t-1}^{i=T} [b_2(1 + n)]^i U[\underline{M}_2(i); \underline{M}_2(i + 1)] \tag{A8.9}$$

In particular, it is true for $\underline{M}_2(i) = M_2(t)$. From this, we get

$$\sum_{i=t-1}^{i=T} b_2^i S_i - \text{constant} > 0 \tag{A8.10}$$

The variable S_i is positive for $i > i^{**} = \sqrt{2ak/A}$, where i^{**} is the size that maximizes production asymptotically (for $i < i^{**}$, see later). The constant can be interpreted as the shadow construction cost of a new city for the generation that must pay for it. Because $b_1 > b_2$, if (A8.10) is satisfied, it implies that this inequality is also satisfied for b_1. This contradicts the optimality of $M_1(t)$, because economy 1 can improve its welfare by following the strategy of economy 2. Furthermore, the employment i^{**} corresponds to the maximum production by unit of distance. If the employment is smaller than i^{**}, one can improve present production and future production by increasing the size of each city (better short-run efficiency). Then, for a same rate of time preference, the social planner will develop factories at the same rate or at a slower rate than the private monopolist. Conversely, if the size is superior to i^*, one can improve production by reducing the labor force. Besides, if $i^{**} > i^*$, that means that the development of cities is not profitable.

When we restrict our analysis to the welfare of the "limit" generation toward which the economy converges, note, first, that a limit social optimum must maximize production at each period. The argument is straightforward. Whatever the distribution of income, it is always possible to improve a situation with a higher income. Consequently, each city has a population equal to i^{**}. We define $R(W)$, the total income (given the savings) for the two periods. Of course, we impose the condition that the youngster of the next generation will receive the same income at the next period. We denote by W the first-period income. To find the optimal intertemporal distribution, we observe that

$$R(W) = A(1 - i^{**}/a)(1 + n) - nW(1 - i^{**}/2a) \qquad \text{(A8.11)}$$

After a straightforward utility maximization, we get the following result. To maximize the welfare of the asymptotic generations, the central planner should develop cities of population i^{**} and let people consume

$$z_{1,t} = A(1 - i^{**}/a)/(1 + b) \quad \text{and} \quad z_{2,t} = \frac{bA}{1 + b}bA(1 - i^{**}/a)/(1 + b)$$

$$\text{(A8.12)}$$

∎

Appendix C

The monopolist will develop a new city when it becomes profitable. Consequently, $F(m)$, the minimal population of a new city when $m - 1$ cities have already been developed, is such that the profit with m cities is equal to the profit with $m - 1$ cities:

$$m\pi[F(m)] = (m - 1)\pi\left(\frac{mF(m)}{m - 1}\right) \qquad \text{(A8.13)}$$

subject to $mF(m)/(m - 1) \leq i^*$ [if this condition is not satisfied, it will be possible to build a similar argument by replacing $mF(m)/(m - 1)$ by i^*]. Developing (A8.13) yields, after simplifications,

$$F(m) = \sqrt{\frac{2ak(m - 1)}{Am}} \qquad \text{(A8.14)}$$

It is straightforward that $F(m)$ is increasing in m. The convergence is immediate, because

$$i^{**} = \lim_{m \to +\infty} F(m) = \sqrt{2ak/A} \qquad \text{(A8.15)}$$

If the savings constraint is binding for i^{**} [i.e., $F(1) > i^{**}$], urbanization takes place in the following way. When savings are sufficient, a first city of population $F(1)$ is developed. As long as N_t does not exceed $2F(1)$, no other development is possible. If the population keeps growing, a new city will become profitable, because one can check that $2\pi[F(1)] \geq \pi[F(1)]$. Then we have $F(1) = F(2)$. Recursively, $F(m)$ is stationary. For all intermediate cases in which the savings constraint is binding, but with $F(1) < i^{**}$, it is immediate that $F(m)$ is stationary and then increasing. Finally, it is straightforward that the population i^{**} enables asymptotic maximization of both production and profit.   ∎

Appendix D

The last stage of the game is the spatial equilibrium. We have i_h and i_j, the respective sizes of the two cities. The spatial equilibrium is such that workers are indifferent between the cities, that is, $\omega_h = \omega_j$. This is equivalent to $(1 - i_h/2a)w_h = (1 - i_j/2a)w_j$. Because we have $i_h + i_j = I_t = N_t$, as long as $N_t < 2i^*$ we can write, for stage 3,

$$i_h(w_h) = \frac{2a}{w_h + w_j}\left[w_h - w_j\left(1 - \frac{I}{2a}\right)\right] \qquad (A8.16)$$

This expression can be plugged into the profit function. The first-order condition (necessary and sufficient) is

$$\frac{\partial \pi_h}{\partial w_h} = 0 \iff w_h = \frac{w_j[w_j(1 - I/2a) + A(3 - I/a)]}{w_j(3 - I/a) + A} \qquad (A8.17)$$

There is a symmetric condition for developer j. The unique nonzero solution to this system is $w_h = w_j = A(1 - I/2a)$. The equilibrium wage W_t must also satisfy (SS). Hence,

$$W_t = \max\left[A\left(1 - \frac{I_t}{2a}\right), \frac{4aB}{4a - I_t}\right] \quad \text{for } I_t \leq 2a\left(1 - \frac{B}{A}\right) \qquad (A8.18)$$

This equilibrium wage solves stage 3 of our game. Stage 2, the location decision, and stage 1, the allocation of savings, are trivially solved (i.e., all developers locate sufficiently far apart and receive the same amount of capital, larger than K). We define $F(0) < i^{**}$, the population of the economy for which the players start to behave as local monopolies.

$$A\left(1 - \frac{F(0)}{a}\right) = \frac{2aB}{2a - F(0)} \iff F(0) = \frac{a}{2}\left(3 - \sqrt{1 + \frac{8B}{A}}\right) \qquad (A8.19)$$

To know when a duopoly will arise, three cases must be distinguished:

- $F(2) \geq F(1) \geq F(0)$. A duopoly will appear for a population $N_t = 2F(1)$. For a population below $2F(1)$, it is not possible to build two cities, whereas for a population above $2F(1)$, both cities will be profitable. Each developer is then a local monopolist in that situation.
- $F(2) \geq F(0) \geq F(1)$. A duopoly will appear for a population between $2F(1)$ and $2F(0)$, because profits are negative for $N_t = 2F(1)$, and positive for $N_t = 2F(0)$.
- $F(0) \geq F(2) \geq F(1)$. The duopoly arises when the monopolist builds a second city. Three sub-cases must be distinguished. The first case is the one for which the savings constraint is not binding at $F(2)$ and where $F(2) < i^*$. For the second case, the savings constraint is still satisfied, but $F(2) > i^*$. For the third case, the savings constraint is binding longer than the profit constraint. We observe different values of $F(2)$ for each sub-case.
- If $2\sqrt{ak/A} \leq a(1 - B/A)$ and (SS) is satisfied, then $F(2) = \sqrt{ak/A}$. In order to compute the profit for the new entrant when $I_t = 2F(2)$, it suffices to use the equilibrium wage in a duopoly. It is injected into the profit function for each player, and it is possible to check that $\pi[F(2)] = kF(2)/a < 0$. Then a duopoly is impossible for $N_t < 2F(2)$. The profit for each player is increasing with size (for $N_t < 2i^{**}$). Given that the profit for each player is positive for $N_t = 2F(0)$, the entry of the second developer will take place for a population of the economy between $2F(2)$ and $2F(0)$, that is, after the construction of a second city by the first developer.
- If $2\sqrt{ak/A} > a(1 - B/A)$ and (SS) is satisfied, then $F(2) = a(1 - B/A) - \sqrt{1.5a^2(1 - B/A)^2 - ak/A}$. We can again verify that $\pi[F(2)] < 0$ and $\pi[F(0)] \geq 0$; then the duopoly emerges for an economy whose population is between $2F(2)$ and $2F(0)$, that is, after the construction of a second city by the first developer.
- If (PP) is satisfied before (SS), then $F(2) = k(1 + b)(1 + n)/Bb$. In that case, $\pi[F(2)]$ can be either positive or negative. Then for some values of the parameters, the duopoly will appear for $N_t = 2F(2)$, because of the constraint on savings. Otherwise, it will appear for $N_t > 2F(2)$. Consequently, the duopoly is "dominated," because the first developer will build a second city before the entry of a second competitor. ∎

Appendix E

Again, the spatial equilibrium is given by the indifference of the marginal worker between city h and any other city. So stage 4 is solved by $\omega_h = \omega_j \Leftrightarrow (1 - i_h/2a)w_h = (1 - i_j/2a)w_j$, with $h \neq j$. Assuming for the moment that the savings constraint is not binding, developer h maximizes her profit with respect to her wage, taking the behaviors of all developers and consumers as given. Furthermore, we have $i_h + \sum_{h \neq j} i_j = I_t = N_t$, the population of the economy at t. Given the symmetry of the equilibrium, all $m - 1$ competing cities are similar. After replacements,

$$i_h(w_h) = \frac{2a}{w_h + w_j/(m-1)} \left[w_h - \left(1 - \frac{I}{2a(m-1)}\right) w_j \right]$$

$$(A8.20)$$

This expression gives the city size depending on the wage. Next, profit is maximized with respect to wages. The first-order condition (necessary and sufficient) is

$$\frac{\partial \pi_h}{\partial w_h} = 0 \Rightarrow w_h$$

$$= \frac{w_j \left[A \left(2 + \frac{1}{m-1} - \frac{I}{a(m-1)}\right) + \frac{w_j}{m-1}\left(1 - \frac{I}{2a(m-1)}\right) \right]}{A + \left(1 + \frac{2}{m-1} - \frac{I}{2a(m-1)}\right) w_j}$$

$$(A8.21)$$

The symmetric equilibrium wage is

$$w = \frac{A\left(1 + \frac{1}{m-1} - \frac{I}{a(m-1)}\right) + \frac{1}{m-1}\left(1 - \frac{I}{2a(m-1)}\right)}{1 + \frac{2}{m-1} - \frac{I}{2a(m-1)}}$$

$$(A8.22)$$

This is the outcome of stage 3. One can easily check that for $m = 2$, we obtain condition (A8.17) again. For m very large, we find $w_\infty = A(1 - i_\infty/a)/(1 - i_\infty/2a)$. Free entry of developers drives profit to zero:

$$\pi(w_\infty) = 0 \Leftrightarrow i_\infty = \sqrt{2ak/A} = i^{**} \qquad (A8.23)$$

The welfare result is immediate from the expression of w_∞, i_∞, and Proposition 2. Note that eventually, the Henry George theorem applies, because the total differential land rent is equal to k. If the savings constraint is not satisfied, all competitors will have positive profits, and a straightforward calculation shows that in that case, investment is more important than with a multiple-city monopoly.   ∎

References

Ades, A., and Glaeser, E. (1995). Trade and circuses: explaining urban giants. *Quarterly Journal of Economics* 110:195–228.

316   **Gilles Duranton**

Bairoch, P. (1988). *Cities and Economic Development.* University of Chicago Press.
Bairoch, P. (1991). The city and technological innovation. In: P. Higonnet et al. (eds.), *Favorites of Fortune,* pp. 159–76, Cambridge, MA: Harvard University Press.
Black, D., and Henderson, V. (1999). Urban growth. *Journal of Political Economy* 107:252–84.
Braudel, F. (1984). *Capitalism and Material Life, 1400–1800.* London: Fontana Collins.
Corden, M., and Neary, P. (1982). "Booming sector and deindustrialization in a small open economy. *Economic Journal* 92:825–44.
De Long, B., and Shleifer, A. (1993). Princes and merchants: European city growth before the industrial revolution. *Journal of Law and Economics* 36:671–702.
Duby, G. (1981). *Histoire de la France Urbaine,* 5 vols. Paris: Le Seuil.
Duranton, G. (1995). *Economie Géographique, Urbanisation et Développement.* Ph.D. dissertation, EHESS, Paris.
Duranton, G. (1998). Labor specialization, transport costs and city size. *Journal of Regional Science* 38:553–74.
Fujita, M. (1989). *Urban Economic Theory, Land Use and City Size.* Cambridge University Press.
Fujita, M., Krugman, P., and Mori, T. (1999). On the evolution of hierarchical urban systems. *European Economic Review* 43:209–51.
Goodfriend, M., and McDermott, J. (1995). Early development. *American Economic Review* 85:116–33.
Henderson, J.-V. (1974). The sizes and types of cities. *American Economic Review* 64:640–56.
Henderson, J.-V. (1988). *Urban Development, Theory, Facts and Illusions,* Oxford University Press.
Henderson, J.-V., and Ioannides, Y. (1981). Aspects of growth in a system of cities. *Journal of Urban Economics* 10:117–139.
Hugill, P. (1993). *World Trade since 1431.* Baltimore: Johns Hopkins University Press.
Ioannides, Y. (1994). Product differentiation and economic growth in a system of cities. *Regional Science and Urban Economics* 24:461–84.
Kremer, M. (1993). Population growth and technological change: one million B.C. to 1990. *Quarterly Journal of Economics* 108:681–716.
Krugman, P., and Livas Elizondo, R. (1996). Trade policy and Third World metropolis. *Journal of Development Economics* 49:137–50.
Lucas, R. (1988). On the mechanics of economic development. *Journal of Monetary Economics* 22:3–42.
Marshall, J. (1989). *The Structure of Urban Systems.* University of Toronto Press.
Matsuyama, K. (1991). Increasing returns, industrialization, and indeterminacy of equilibrium. *Quarterly Journal of Economics* 106:617–50.
Miyao, T. (1987). Long-run urban growth with agglomeration economies. *Environment and Planning A* 19:1083–92.
Mokyr, J. (1976). *Industrialization in the Low Countries, 1795–1850.* New Haven, CT: Yale University Press.
Mokyr, J. (1990). *Lever of Riches.* Oxford University Press.
Moomaw, R., and Shatter, A. (1996). Urbanization and economic development: a bias

toward large cities. *Journal of Urban Economics* 40:13–37.

Palivos, T., and Wang P. (1996). Spatial agglomeration and endogenous growth. *Regional Science and Urban Economics* 26:645–69.

Papageorgiou, Y. (1980). On sudden urban growth. *Environment and Planning A* 12:1035–50.

Puga, D. (1998). Urbanisation patterns: European vs less developed countries. *Journal of Regional Science* 38:231–52.

Romer, P. (1990). Endogenous technical change. *Journal of Political Economy* 98:S71–S102.

Rosen, K., and Resnick, M. (1980). The size distribution of cities: an examination of the Pareto law and primacy. *Journal of Urban Economics* 8:165–86.

CHAPTER 9

Urban Spread Beyond the City Edge

Florence Goffette-Nagot

1 Introduction

It has been reported that urban systems in developed countries have experienced a trend toward concentration in their largest cities (Dobkins and Ioannides, Chapter 6, this volume). At the same time, an opposite tendency has been observed during recent decades, that is, a dispersion of population through the expansion of cities into their surrounding rural areas (Mills, 1972; Champion, 1992). This urban spread involves households, as indicated by a flattening of population density curves. But it also involves employment, either through a continuous sprawl of jobs over the urban area or through the emergence of secondary centers and the so-called edge cities (Garreau, 1991; Henderson and Mitra, 1997).

It is important to distinguish two different patterns of urban dispersion. On the one hand, there is a movement, which can be referred to as *decentralization*, that consists in a shift of population and human activities from the urban center to the periphery. This is, for instance, the well-known suburbanization movement seen in the United States. On the other hand, there is a tendency toward *deconcentration*, which consists in small urban areas growing faster than the large ones, in terms of population as well as employment (Carlino, 1985; Suarez-Villa, 1988). Whereas the phenomenon of decentralization is widely accepted, deconcentration is more controversial, because it seems to contradict the observed growth of the largest cities.

This chapter focuses on decentralization, namely, the enlargement of urban areas with decreasing population densities, compatible with the trend toward concentration at the level of metropolitan areas.[1] The second movement

This study was conducted during a visit at CORE (Université Catholique de Louvain-la-Neuve). The author thanks Mark Henry, Jean-Marie Huriot, Bertrand Schmitt, and Jacques-François Thisse for helpful comments, as well as PIR-Villes and CNRS for financial support.

[1] See Parr and Jones (1983) for a description of the plausible interrelationships between the city size distribution and population densities within the urban area, especially the fact that increasing concentration at the inter-urban level leads to a decentralization at the intra-urban level.

implies a deconcentrating pattern of employment, based on firms changing their decision criteria regarding their locations. Thus, an analysis of deconcentration necessitates a focus on the role of the differentials of agglomeration economies between urban areas depending on their sizes, and it requires a theoretical framework different from that necessary to analyze decentralization. Moreover, in the case of France, employment deconcentration remains a rather minor phenomenon, thus allowing us to concentrate on population dispersion within metropolitan areas.

Population decentralization was first reported in the United States, where it is referred to as suburbanization (Mills, 1972). It appeared later in Europe (e.g., during the 1970s in France). Moreover, in the French case, decentralization does not seem to have slowed down so far (Hilal et al., 1995). In France, population spread takes the form of demographic growth in rural "communes,"[2] which are sufficiently far away from the cities for these areas not to be reached by the advance of city boundaries, thus allowing us to speak of noncontiguity. We shall call this form of urban spread "exurbanization" (*périurbanisation* in French) because it generates a wave of construction of detached houses in exurban areas; that is, new homes are built beyond city boundaries and contiguous built-up land areas. The strong relationships in terms of commuting between such growing rural peripheries and the urban core show that this growth can be considered a new form of urbanization, although the areas where it takes place are still considered rural, because of the dominating agricultural and natural land uses.

An understanding of this phenomenon will be useful for both theoretical and policy purposes. From a theoretical point of view, economic geography deals with the formation of systems of cities and the factors that explain the sizes of cities. At the same time, there remains a need for explanations of the internal configurations of cities and particularly of urban spread, which was the original goal of urban economics, as developed by Alonso (1964) and Muth (1969).[3] An internal urban configuration depends on firms' and households' interactions in the city and can change following changes in urban size and the evolution of agglomeration economies. At the same time, because of its durability, the urban configuration will largely determine future transport costs, land rents, congestion, and finally the rise of agglomeration economies. In other words, urban spread is a consequence of concentration in the largest cities, and in turn it will determine future concentration levels. To that extent, comprehension of urban dispersion, in the form of suburbanization or exurbanization, is useful in order to explain the evolution of a system of cities and the level of development

---

[2] The commune is the smallest administrative entity in France. There are about 36,500 communes in France. In 1990, 30,600 communes had fewer than 2,000 inhabitants.

[3] Anas et al. (1998) have provided a comprehensive survey of the question of urban spatial structure.

of agglomeration economies. From a policy point of view, it is important to understand the determinants of this movement for regional planning. Indeed, exurbanization raises concerns about public services for communes hit by a sudden surge in their population. Moreover, it seems that exurbanization may also be advantageous for the economic development of such communes by creating population-serving jobs.

The aim of this chapter is twofold. First, we want to see if urban spread can be accounted for by the analytical properties of the monocentric model of urban economics and some of its extensions. Second, we estimate an empirical residential model based on French data for the 1980s in order to test the empirical relevance of the principles of urban economics beyond the city edge. Furthermore, we shall see that exurbanization raises some new questions about the conceptual definition of urban areas.

The next section presents a brief survey concerning the different ways in which urban economists seek to explain population dispersion. Section 3 deals with empirical work on urban spread. Section 4 describes the empirical model. Estimation results are reported in Section 5. In Section 6, conclusions are drawn as to the relevance of urban economics for understanding exurbanization and the changing nature of cities.

2   Urban Economics and Urban Spread

2.1   The Static Monocentric Model

The main objective of monocentric urban models, pioneered by Alonso (1964) and Muth (1969), is to explain the spatial structure of cities and, among other facts, the suburbanization of population (see Fujita, 1989, for a comprehensive presentation). Recall that in such models the city is assumed to be a uniform space with a single center, referred to as the central business district (CBD), surrounded by a dense radial transportation network. All employment occurs at the CBD. Households are located so as to maximize utility under their budget constraint. They incur a commuting cost dependent on their distance from the center, and they compete for land use. This standard model provides a set of results consistent with the most striking features of urban structure. In particular, it can be used to explain the decrease in urban land rents with increasing distance away from the center.

Analytical properties concerning residential location relate population dispersion to three main factors. First, provided that the income elasticity of demand for housing is higher than the income elasticity of the marginal commuting cost, then distance from the center will increase with income level – a result that can be interpreted as a preference for "privacy" as against "community" (Papageorgiou, 1990, ch. 9). Second, an increase in household size with a fixed number of working members will increase housing consumption and lead to residential locations farther away from the CBD (an increase in housing consumption due to specific preferences will have the same effect). Third, improvements in the means of transportation that reduce monetary costs or transport time will contribute to a flattening of land rents and population densities.

Hence, population dispersion in the United States and in European countries can be related to increased housing consumption due to growth in net income, as well as to decreased commuting costs due to the spread of automobile use, encouraged by improved road facilities. In particular, one can think that the adoption of automobile transport by low-income households reduces their total transport cost, thus flattening both their individual bid–rent curves and the global land rent curve.[4] Unemployment (which reduces expected incomes), increasing congestion, and a decrease in the average household size due to general demographic trends can explain the slowing down of the suburbanization rate observed during the 1970s in the United States.

2.2 Dynamic Monocentric Models

Although the traditional monocentric model gives quite consistent results regarding the general features of urban structure, it is obvious that some facts remain unaccounted for by the static model. Besides the addition of specific assumptions about space attributes, another way of improving the consistency of the monocentric model would be to take into account housing durability, as in dynamic models. Those models consider spatial variations in densities as a consequence of housing durability and specific patterns of land development ensuing from land developers' foresight. Two of their major results differ from those of the static model. First, densities do not necessarily decrease continuously with distance from the center. Second, leapfrog land development can occur, leaving some undeveloped plots inside the urban area (Brueckner, Chapter 7, this volume).

Noncontiguity between the successive residential zones in exurban areas is a strong feature of urban sprawl that distinguishes these areas from cities. Thus, dynamic models provide some explanation for this particular distribution of residential locations. Indeed, irreversible land development by developers with perfect foresight can be seen as one reason for the existence of free land inside urban areas and for residential development beyond the city edge. But although this mechanism can work to explain the existence of "gaps" in the built-up area, which will later be filled in, it seems to be insufficient to explain the development of the most remote exurban areas. Hence, other factors should be considered. For example, the existence of nonmonotonicity in amenity levels or preferences for low densities may play important roles.

---

[4] For a more detailed discussion of mode choice and residential location, see DeSalvo and Huq (1996).

Nevertheless, models that incorporate durable housing allow for estimations of residential densities that can account for both the decrease in density due to the high land prices at locations nearer the center and the decrease in density ensuing from changes over time in exogenous factors, such as income and transport costs. Accordingly, they are useful for understanding the temporal pattern of exurban development.

2.3 Models with Employment Decentralization

In order to achieve a better fit with urban decentralization, urban models have been developed that permit the location of jobs outside the CBD. These models either allow firms to be interspersed with households or assume the existence of secondary employment centers. In both cases, job dispersion can be exogenous (Yinger, 1992) or endogenous (Fujita et al., 1997). Such phenomena increase the population spread, because less concentration of employment is likely to induce greater dispersion of the population.

The forces governing employment dispersion are related to transport costs and labor costs. For instance, Hartwick and Hartwick (1974) have shown that integrated patterns of firms and households ensue from high commuting costs relative to transport costs for output. Fujita and Ogawa (1982) have derived integrated configurations when commuting costs are sufficiently high compared with transactions costs between firms. Transport costs can also explain the development of employment subcenters, as in the study by Helsley and Sullivan (1991), where subcenter growth ensues from the fact that diseconomies in transportation dominate external scale economies in the city center, beyond a certain size of the CBD. Spatial differentiation of labor costs in the city has been taken into account by Fujita et al. (1997) in a model explaining the endogenous formation of secondary employment centers. In this model, a firm that is sufficiently large as to have market power enters the labor market of a city. It competes with other firms in both the labor market and the land market. The commuting costs for its workers give this firm an incentive to locate outside the CBD, because avoidance of such costs will allow the firm to pay lower wages outside the CBD.

Finally, forces driving employment dispersion induce population spread, as do factors that affect residential location itself. Also, population dispersion is a source of employment location outside the city center, because it provides market areas for population-serving firms and a dispersed labor pool as well.

3 Empirical Evidence of Urban Spread

Theoretical models seem to have followed the changing form of urban spread. Whereas the first models dealt with contiguous urban development, considering employment as concentrated in the CBD, recent models have been developed to account for leapfrog urban development, employment deconcentration, and emergence of secondary centers. All these phenomena have been studied in empirical research.

3.1 Dispersion of Population

Many empirical studies have been concerned with urban population dispersion, usually providing descriptions of urban spatial structure, its determinants, and its evolution. Such studies generally have dealt with American cities (exceptions include Zheng, 1991, for the Tokyo metropolitan area and Tabourin, 1995, for Lyon, in France).

In American cities, studies of the density gradients for urban populations have shown a continuous path of population dispersion (starting before World War II), apparent through a flattening of population density curves, a decline in central densities, and a shift over time in the density peaks (related to the existence of a crater of population density at the center) farther out from the CBD (Clark, 1951; McDonald, 1989). The highest decentralization rates occurred during the 1950s and 1960s and were followed by a general slowing down during the 1970s (Macauley, 1985), although not as strong as expected.

Further work has related the dispersion trends to different determinants. As discussed in Section 2, the standard monocentric model suggests that increases in income and decreases in commuting costs should explain population spread in metropolitan areas. These standard factors perform well. For instance, Margo (1992) attributed 43% of the postwar suburbanization to income increases. Zheng (1991) found that within the Tokyo metropolitan area, variations in automobile registration rates and in personal incomes could explain the variations in population densities over time. The evolution of population density gradients has also been driven by government policies concerning mortgage guarantees, highway networks, and crime (Carlino, 1985).

Besides these factors, one can assume that differences in local attributes can also help explain population suburbanization. Thus, proponents of the idea of "white flight" consider suburbanization in the United States to be the consequence of characteristics of the center, namely, a high percentage of African-Americans in the urban population, high rates of poverty, and high crime rates. Such factors generate disamenities and thus an incentive for households to locate in suburban areas. For instance, in a simultaneous model of population and employment densities, Carlino and Mills (1987) have shown that once the negative effects of low incomes, racial composition, and high taxes in the center have been taken into account, central-city counties appear to be more attractive than suburban counties. Nevertheless, Mills (1992), in a model measuring both population and employment suburbanization in metropolitan areas, has concluded that the percentage of blacks in the population, the crime rate, and the median income per capita play only small roles in explaining population dispersion. Thus, there is still controversy about the relative effects of differences in urban and suburban land prices and the amenity differential between urban and suburban locations as determinants of suburbanization (Boarnet, 1994).

Another promising line of research is provided by empirical dynamic models of urban densities, such as the model of Yacovissi and Kern (1995). Their regressions of population density in zones of the Baltimore metropolitan region in 1980 include both a density decline with distance due to long-run equilibrium conditions (standard monocentric model) and a density decline due to the timing of development (dynamic model of land development). Their findings show that the contemporaneous decline of densities with distance from the center results from both a flattening of the density curve over time (especially during the 1950s and 1960s) and the usual density gradient explained by static models, the latter remaining the most important factor in the explanation.

Finally, the pattern of urban spread seems to be quite general among developed countries, but as Mills (1992) has noted, most of the studies trying to measure the determinants of such decentralization have concerned U.S. cities. Therefore, there is a need for such studies in European countries to see if similar patterns exist.

3.2 Decentralization of Employment

Macauley (1985) provided a rather comprehensive study of suburbanization in which he measured both population and employment gradients for 18 standard metropolitan statistical areas (SMSAs) in the United States, distinguishing also between different employment sectors. He observed a continuing pattern of employment decentralization. However, employment gradients steepened in some cases, whereas employment decentralization rates, like those for population, were lower during the 1970s than earlier. Carlino (1985) explained the employment growth in adjacent nonmetropolitan counties partly on the basis of employment decentralization due to enlargement of the field of agglomeration forces.

Employment decentralization either can be determined by local attributes or can be a consequence of population suburbanization. Actually, there is debate as to whether jobs follow people or people follow jobs. Evidence at the intrametropolitan level appears to support the idea of suburbanization of population preceding job decentralization. The dispersion of employment then permits another outward leap farther from the urban center, even into nonmetropolitan adjacent counties (Carlino, 1985; Carlino and Mills, 1987; Henry et al., 1997). Furthermore, employment decentralizes to the suburbs and centralizes within the suburbs, giving birth to secondary employment centers (Helsley and Sullivan, 1991). Finally, population-serving jobs, rather than manufacturing jobs, are the forms of new exurban employment (Macauley, 1985).

4 An Empirical Residential Model for French Exurban Areas

Using the general framework of urban decentralization described in Sections 2 and 3, we present a model that allows us to deal with population dispersion in France during the 1980s. The question is as follows: What are the determinants of residential behavior that encourage urban workers to settle down in a rural district? It should first be pointed out that the choice of a location is closely related to the other factors of residential choice: Locations in exurban areas in France mainly involve families that become homeowners for the first time and generally purchase new detached houses. A complete study of exurbanization would therefore require an analysis of the choice of housing type and tenure. However, we concentrate here on the spatial aspect only and therefore on the factors standing behind the choice of a specific location.

A monocentric residential model in which the employment center is the city itself is used in order to estimate residential behavior in French exurban areas between 1984 and 1988. This type of model was originally designed to analyze cities. In particular, the monocentric model assumes a clear split between agricultural and residential land uses and considers the frontier between these two uses as being the city edge. This split obviously does not exist anymore, neither in American suburban areas nor in French exurban areas. Thus, it is sometimes suggested that the U.S. Census concept of metropolitan statistical area (MSA) does not really fit the concept of urban areas as described by urban economics, whereas "census urbanized areas" within MSAs better correspond to this concept (Brueckner and Fansler, 1983; Macauley, 1985; Mills, 1990). However, most empirical studies dealing with the structure of urban areas have used MSAs that may have included agricultural and natural land uses, without addressing the question of the relevance of urban economics for their purposes. Because exurban areas are characterized by noncontiguity between different residential areas, we suggest that the specific nature of those spaces calls for a number of specific assumptions to supplement those of the standard urban model.

4.1 Adapting the Urban Monocentric Model to Exurban Areas

In agricultural-location models built along von Thünen lines (Huriot, 1994), as well as in urban economic models used to investigate the competition between residence and agriculture on the fringe of the city, there is a strict separation between urban and agricultural activities. Therefore, the use of such models would seem inappropriate for studying exurban areas.

However, in these areas, residential use almost invariably drives out agriculture. This can be explained in terms of the determinants of agricultural and residential land rents. Agricultural activity (barring some exceptions) no longer seeks proximity to the city, and agricultural land rent, instead of depending on distance to the city, as in the von Thünen model, is largely explained by the productivity of the different production systems. Agricultural land rent can then be considered as exogenous and fixed, compared with the urban system. By contrast, land rent for residential purposes is largely determined by distance to the city and is much higher in and near the city than is agricultural land rent. Consequently, in areas extending out to a large distance from the city, agricultural land rent is lower than residential land rent.

Accordingly, as in the standard monocentric urban model, we assume the existence, at any point, of a fixed and exogenous agricultural land rent representing the opportunity cost of land. Residential choices are made in this space relative to a city center where jobs are concentrated, and they are made in the presence of a competing activity that is not related to the city itself. These observations justify analyzing exurban areas along the lines developed for the city in the standard monocentric model. Therefore, application of the monocentric model in order to explain residential location in exurban areas must first involve a change in scale. The zone to be analyzed far exceeds the city's boundaries. Jobs are no longer located in the city center alone, but may be spread throughout the city. The city replaces the CBD, with the *exurban zone* corresponding to the residential ring of the standard urban model. In other words, we explicitly take into account the spatial deconcentration of jobs within the city.

The fact that exurban areas are not solely residential implies the introduction of other elements into our application of urban economics. First, the differences in building densities between urban and exurban locations must necessarily be considered. Second, we have to make the necessary assumptions to account for spatial heterogeneity between cities and rural areas. Spatial heterogeneity can be introduced into a monocentric model in several ways. Space attributes can be represented by a vector of characteristics, or by only one characteristic, or by two indices representing natural amenities, on the one hand, and the urban characteristics of the environment (public services, retailing, and the like), on the other hand, or by only one of these two indices (Fujita, 1989).

We choose to differentiate rural and urban areas without positing *a priori* assumptions about any household preference for city or country. We therefore assume the existence of two types of location attributes that are exogenous, one type decreasing continuously with distance from the center, and the other type increasing continuously: The former includes the location of local services, such as public services and retail shops, and the latter comprises natural amenities. Each type is represented by a synthetic index that enters the utility function. We thus make assumptions about the spatial distributions of these two types of attributes, assumptions that are tested empirically when estimating the model.

This choice means that the model is kept flexible with regard to the overall effect of distance on household utility. Distance from the city produces a loss of utility, *ceteris paribus*, because of one's remoteness from the urban facilities; but it also yields gains, because of one's remoteness from the city's negative externalities and because of the decrease in residential density and the increase in natural amenities. The purpose of this option is to try to investigate *a priori* whether an exurban location choice is solely the outcome of a price effect of housing in rural communes or whether the attraction of natural amenities also exerts an influence.

To sum up, exurban areas exhibit rural characteristics. That is, they differ from those areas usually analyzed in urban economics because of the presence of agricultural activities and low building densities. But they also exhibit some urban characteristics, insofar as they include an active population working in the employment center, which is indeed the definition of a city in standard urban economics. We assume that even if there is noncontiguity in residential development between urban and exurban areas, such a discontinuity does not invalidate the use of an urban monocentric model for analyzing exurbanization, and the inclusion of factors to account for the differences in local attributes between the two types of spaces is sufficient to conduct the analysis.

4.2 A Simultaneous-Equations Model for Residential Location

The main assumptions of the urban monocentric model are therefore maintained. As usual, we assume a space structured by an employment center, which is no longer the CBD, but rather the entire city. Land is everywhere available for residential use. Households locate relative to the center at distances that may be zero (i.e., a location inside the city) or may be strictly positive (i.e., a location in a rural commune).[5] They incur transport costs dependent on those distances, knowing that a radial transport network links all locations directly to the center. Space is assumed to be heterogeneous; that is, there are two types of location attributes, each of which has a positive marginal utility, one type diminishing and the other increasing with distance from the center.

There is no preference for proximity to the center, but distance from the center entails the presence of certain attributes in the immediate dwelling environment (natural amenities and local services). Distance is also supposed to influence location choice through travel time. The usual assumption in most monocentric models is that distance gives rise to a travel–time cost that can be included in the household's budget constraint. Another option is to introduce leisure time into the utility function as a decreasing function of distance from the center. This option seems preferable, in that evaluating the opportunity cost of travel time by the marginal wage or a fraction of it (which is the usual solution in monocentric models) seems unwarranted in the real world. Indeed, the rigidity of work time

---

[5] Hence we neglect transport costs within the city.

in fact prevents people from arbitrating between traveling or working longer (Goffette-Nagot, 1994).

However, these two assumptions about location attributes and leisure time do not exhaust the influence of distance on residential choice. There is also a strong link between distance from the center and the characteristics of the housing supply. The spatial variation in building density (flats in the center, and detached houses on the periphery) can be explained in the standard monocentric model as the outcome of housing producers' behavior (Muth, 1969). The choice of residential location is therefore not independent of the choice of a certain housing type. For detached houses themselves, the composition of the housing in terms of floor space and adjoining land can vary widely. Accordingly, two housing components are included in the model, namely, floor space and adjoining land, with the price of the floor space being constant across locations, whereas the price of adjoining land will vary with distance.

A Stone-Geary utility function is used (Phlips, 1983). The variables include the quantity of a composite good, the floor space, the land adjoining the house, leisure time, and the commune levels of local services and natural amenities. The budget constraint includes the corresponding expenditures, knowing that the housing price is composed of both the price of the "bare" floor space (i.e., regardless of any quality effect) and the price of land (including the land adjoining the house and the ground area occupied by the building).

Maximization of the consumer utility function under the budget constraint is as follows:

$$\max U = c_1 \ln(X - a_1) + c_2 \ln(H - a_2) + c_3 \ln T + c_4 \ln \ell(D)$$
$$+ c_{5_1} \ln Z_1(D) + c_{5_2} \ln Z_2(D) \tag{9.1}$$

under the constraint

$$Y \geq p_x X + p_s \left(T + \frac{H}{\omega} \right) + p_h H + n p_t D \tag{9.2}$$

Here, Y is income; X is the composite good of price p_x, and a_1 is the corresponding vital minimum; H is the "bare" floor space at price p_h and vital minimum a_2; ω is the coefficient providing H/ω, the land area of the building; T is the consumption of adjoining land; p_s is the unit land price, depending on the distance from the center and the quantities of attributes; D is the distance from the center; $\ell(D)$ is leisure time, a linearly decreasing function of distance, such that $\ell(D) = \ell_0 - \beta D$; $Z_1(D)$ is the local service index, depending on distance from the center; $Z_2(D)$ is the natural-amenity index, depending on distance from the center; p_t is the unit transport cost; n is the number of trips made during the period corresponding to income Y.

The Stone-Geary utility function leads to a linear expenditure system. In our case, the expenditure on each consumed good is a linear function of net income, that is, income minus transport cost. Summing these equations and replacing net income gives a relationship among transport cost, income, and the spending on the different goods. Finally, because transport cost is assumed to be proportional to distance to the center, we obtain the following equilibrium location equation:

$$D = A1 + BY + C\left(\frac{p_s}{\omega} + p_h\right) + D1 p_s T + D2\left(\frac{p_s}{\omega} + p_h\right)H$$
$$+ F1Z_1T + F2Z_2T \tag{9.3}$$

Equation (9.3) relates distance of location to income, land and floor–space prices, spending on land and floor space, and rents paid for the local attributes. It is further assumed that land rent and location attributes are related to distance from the center. That is why estimating this equation alone would introduce a simultaneity bias. Therefore, this equation describing the demand side and two equations concerning the spatial distribution of location attributes, (9.6), that is, the supply side, and a land price equation describing the market equilibrium, (9.7), are included in a simultaneous-equations model.

The land price is assumed to be the sum of a location rent (in the form of a negative exponential of distance from the center, which is a traditional result of monocentric urban models) and of rents generated by the location attributes. It is written

$$p_s = p_0 e^{-\alpha D} + p_1 Z_1(D) + p_2 Z_2(D) \tag{9.4}$$

where p_0 is the price of land at $D = 0$ (i.e., in the city), with p_1 and p_2 being the implicit prices of local services and natural amenities, respectively.

The local attributes are further assumed to be dependent on the population of the residential commune (this population is introduced in quadratic form), following the traditional observation that commune facilities increase with the population of the commune, and assuming that the level of natural amenities decreases when population density rises. Moreover, we suppose that the population of the employment center has the same kind of effect on the local attributes. The system to be estimated is

$$D = A1 + BY + C\left(\frac{p_s}{\omega} + p_h\right) + D1 p_s T + D2\left(\frac{p_s}{\omega} + p_h\right)H$$
$$+ F1Z_1T + F2Z_2T + u_1 \tag{9.5}$$
$$\forall i \in (1; 2), \quad Z_i = A2_i + G_i D + H_i \text{POPCOM} + I_i \text{POPUUZ}$$
$$+ J_i(\text{POPCOM})^2 + u_2 \tag{9.6}$$
$$p_s = A3 + (\text{POPCZ})^{P_0} e^{-AD} + P1Z_1 + P2Z_2 + u_3 \tag{9.7}$$

with the same notations as before, POPCZ being the population of the central commune of the employment center, POPUUZ that of its urban unit, and POPCOM that of the residential commune of the household, and $A1$, B, C, $D1$, $D2$, $F1$, $F2$, $A2_i$, G_i, H_i, I_i, J_i, $A3$, P_0, A, $P1$, and $P2$ being the parameters to be estimated.

5 Estimations for French Exurban Areas

The purpose of the formalization set out in Section 4 is to estimate, at the level of exurban areas, a model of residential location and spatial configuration derived from urban economics. This means considering an area and a working population in accordance with these assumptions.

5.1 Data

We use individual data concerning households located in the French "Zones de Peuplement Industriel et Urbain" (ZPIUs), as defined by INSEE (French National Institute for Statistics) in 1990. The ZPIUs, which cover areas including urban and rural communes,[6] are defined based on commuting patterns. They are indicative of *labor-market areas*. We select only the ZPIUs whose main city has more than 20,000 people. This main city contains the majority of jobs and can be considered as the employment center of the exurban area (Goffette-Nagot and Schmitt, 1998). We thus have a delineation of exurban rings. Residential locations are defined by their distances from the center city. They range from suburbs to the most remote rural communes included in the ZPIU. The mean distance from the center in our sample is 11 km.

Individual data are from the 1988 INSEE housing survey, which for each household in the survey provides information on the members, activity, income, dwelling characteristics, and location of residence commune. In order to get households whose situations still correspond to their location decisions, the total sample in our analysis consists of homeowner households that have moved into their new detached houses within the past four years. Moreover, in order to have only households for which the distance to the city matters, that is, which made their location decisions relative to the city center, we select households for which at least one member works in the city considered as the employment center. This choice affects neither the local attributes, which are the same regardless of the household considered, nor the land-market equilibrium equation, because there is no reason that these households would pay a price different from the others.

---

[6] An urban commune, as defined by INSEE, is a commune having a population agglomeration of more than 2,000 people.

Distance to the employment center is calculated as the crow flies from the residence commune.[7] The different prices cited are in 1988 French francs. Income is the 1988 current annual income; purchase prices (of land and floor space) are converted into annual costs as fractions of the purchase cost.[8] The price of the floor space is an implicit price obtained by prior estimations of a hedonic price equation used to separate out the price of the "bare" floor space from the total dwelling price. It is therefore the same variable for all individuals, with the term $(p_s/\omega) + p_h$ becoming p_s/ω in the estimation.[9] Local services and natural amenities are measured using data from the 1988 INSEE communal inventory (a survey on communes' main characteristics and facilities). These measures are provided by two synthetic indices varying from 0 to 1, constructed at the commune level, that are weighted sums of indices of the presence/absence of the different items (e.g., the presence in the district of an elementary school, a cloth shop, and a post office gives an index of 0.13, the maximum index being 1). The local service index includes food and cloth shops, doctors, hospitals, post offices, banks, public transport networks, schools, and some cultural, leisure, and sports facilities. The natural-amenity index includes tourist attractions, lakes, hiking paths, and the share of the commune surface in forest.

The system is estimated for several subsets of the total sample, differing by the size of the employment center or by social category. We detail here the results concerning one of the subsamples, results that can be supplemented by information from estimations on other subsamples (Goffette-Nagot, 1996). We use the three-stage least-squares method. The system is nonlinear; thus the potential instruments are the exogenous variables, their squares, and their cross-products. Among this set, we choose variables so that we have no collinearity between the instruments.

5.2 Results

First, in all the estimations, the natural-amenity equation performed poorly. Hence, we dropped the natural-amenity equation and estimated a three-equations system. The results in Table 9.1 relate to the subsample of households that each bought a building plot and had a house built on it, excluding households of the Paris ZPIU. The first, hardly surprising, observation is that the facility level for communes increases with their size, even if this effect seems to be attenuated

---

[7] Measured on the basis of the file of Lambert's coordinates (Institut Géographique National).

[8] The prices are measured as 9.5% of the purchase outlay, including use spendings (insurance, upkeep) and financial expenses (mortgage interests and opportunity cost of homeowner contribution).

[9] This should be interpreted as representing the effect of the land price. The ω coefficient slightly reduces its variance (the coefficient is more important where the price is higher); but the weak variability of the ω term leads to only a small underevaluation of the role of land price.

Table 9.1. *Estimated coefficients for the three-equations system*

	Ordinary least squares		Three-stage least squares	
Distance from residential commune to employment center, equation (9.5)				
Constant	11.8	**(8.10)**	13.4	**(8.23)**
Income	-2.16 (10^{-6})	(-0.30)	-15.7 (10^{-6})	(-1.87)
Land price	-0.12	**(-3.53)**	-0.27	**(-5.54)**
Outlay on adjoining land	0.10 (10^{-3})	(1.75)	0.48 (10^{-3})	**(5.00)**
Outlay on floor space	-22.2 (10^{-6})	(-0.47)	-59.9 (10^{-6})	(-1.10)
Rent for local services	-3.35 (10^{-3})	**(-4.20)**	-3.61 (10^{-3})	**(-3.80)**
Rent for amenities	3.04 (10^{-3})	**(3.11)**	1.07 (10^{-3})	(1.01)
Root-mean-square error	6.07		6.60	
Local services index, equation (9.6)				
Constant	0.61	**(22.73)**	0.75	**(12.90)**
Distance	-8.09 (10^{-3})	**(-3.71)**	-24.1 (10^{-3})	**(-4.12)**
District population (1000 inhab.)	10.1 (10^{-3})	**(10.50)**	9.24 (10^{-3})	**(5.82)**
ZPIU center city pop. (1000 inhab.)	0.20 (10^{-3})	**(5.03)**	0.25 (10^{-3})	**(4.40)**
Square of district pop. (1000 inhab.)	-40.4 (10^{-6})	**(-9.06)**	-38.9 (10^{-6})	**(-6.04)**
Root-mean-square error	0.174		0.197	
Land price in French francs/m², equation (9.7)				
Constant	2.06	(0.64)	-3.49	(-0.77)
Pop. of ZPIU center district (P_0)	0.63	**(23.68)**	0.65	**(18.53)**
Distance (-A)	-65.5 (10^{-3})	**(4.47)**	-85.7 (10^{-3})	**(4.51)**
Facility index	10.4	**(2.61)**	17.9	**(2.70)**
Natural-amenity index	0.37	(0.09)	2.13	(0.55)
Root-mean-square error	13.81		14.07	

Population: households that bought a lot and built a house, except people working in Paris ZPIU (observation number, 249); *t* statistics are given in parentheses; *t* statistics reaching the 5% level of significance are in bold print.

for the largest cities by the negative parameter of the quadratic term. A more interesting result is the influence of the city on the level of facilities in its surrounding rural communes. The farther one goes from the employment center, the fewer facilities exurban communes have. In addition, at equal distances from the center, these communes are better endowed when their employment centers are large.

Supplementary estimations were performed for two subsamples of ZPIUs with medium-size centers (from 20,000 inhabitants up to 170,000 inhabitants) and large centers (more than 170,000 inhabitants). The findings show that the aforementioned structuring is less marked around the medium-size employment centers. Cities influence the level of local service facilities less than proportionally to their sizes, but over greater distances as size increases. The assumption can be made that exurbanization in large ZPIUs (where it is more intense and has spread further from the center) has made it possible to develop, or at least maintain, a certain number of local services in rural communes. This purportedly has already shaped exurban areas and differentiated them from other types of rural areas. That, in turn, will influence later exurbanization.

Estimation of the land rent equation also shows this structuring of exurban areas by employment centers. The negative-exponential form is significant, with a land rent gradient of 8.6% per kilometer [coefficient A in equation (9.7) and Table 9.1]. The estimated value in the city (i.e., at zero distance) is proportional to a term on the order of the square root of central-district population [coefficient P_0 in equation (9.7) and Table 9.1]. The level of facilities also affects land values, whereas natural amenities do not seem to do so [coefficients P_1 and P_2, equation (9.7)].

In the residential location equation (9.5), the negative coefficients of land rent and income (the latter being significant at the 7% level) can be construed as showing a preference for accessibility to the center relative to the consumption of land. This means, in the context of our assumptions, a preference for leisure (which decreases with distance from the center), as there is no direct measure of utility associated with accessibility. The land price parameter in the location equation stands for the effect on location choice of an increase in the land rent curve as a whole. It can be demonstrated that the negative sign of the parameter indicates that households will reduce their consumption of land rather than diminish their consumption of accessibility (Goffette-Nagot, 1994). The idea is as follows: An increase in land rent has a price effect that reduces the consumption of land and therefore induces people to locate nearer the center. At the same time, it has an income effect, that is, the households reduce their consumption of accessibility, thus locating farther away from the center. The negative coefficient shows that these two effects result in a move closer to the center, which means that the reduction in distance due to the price effect is greater than the increase following the net-income effect.

In addition, there is a specific income effect on location choice that works in the same direction. In our sample, the negative effect of income on the location distance is thought to be a consequence of the greater net income elasticity of the demand for accessibility compared with the net income elasticity of the demand for space. These two results tend to show that, overall, exurban households move out less far when they have high incomes, and exurbanization movements result from a demand for space that households try to satisfy at a lower price by moving away from the center, even if that means sacrificing part of the attraction of centrality if their resources are inadequate. On the contrary, suburbanization in the United States is the result of high-income families locating far away from the center in order to consume more land, the land net-income elasticity being higher than the accessibility net-income elasticity.

Other determinants are involved in the choice of a distance from the city. It is observed that the demands for adjoining land and for local services also exert the expected effects on location: Greater demand for adjoining land induces remoteness from the employment center, whereas the effect of demand for local services is the reverse.

The results of additional estimations, for two subsamples comprising households of clerical and manual workers, on the one hand, and households of intermediate, executive, and intellectual professionals, business directors, and liberal professionals, on the other hand, suggest a nonmonotonic relationship between income and location distance. Whereas a positive variation in income causes a move nearer to the center for households in the wealthier social categories, the same variation in income has the opposite effect on location choices for households in more modest social categories.

Because local attributes have already been introduced, this income effect is not due to the spatial distribution of amenities. But it seems to be the consequence of the existence of a threshold in housing consumption. That is, households with medium incomes apparently consume more floor space, and then less accessibility than lower-income families. But high-income households increase their housing consumption very little compared with medium-income families. They rather favor reduced traveling time and locate nearer to the center.[10] This result is consistent with an analytical result derived by Fujita for households whose only income is from wages and which have positive pecuniary transport costs and wage elasticity of lot size lower than unity (Fujita, 1989, ch. 2). Nevertheless, it contradicts the positive monotonic relationship between income and location most often observed in American cities (e.g., Margo, 1992). Faced with similar observations, Brueckner et al. (1999) have argued that amenities must explain such differences, believing that the occurrence of different behaviors (such as different valuations of leisure time) between countries is highly implausible. That would mean, in our case, that the index accounting for local services would be incomplete, which is possible. In particular, such factors as cultural facilities and historical characteristics have not been taken into account. Differences in transport networks could also be included to explain those differences. We think, however, that other factors such as lifestyles and preferences should also be taken into account in order to explain these differences (Jayet, Chapter 11, this volume).

---

[10] The distribution of house floor spaces supports this view.

6 Concluding Remarks

6.1 The Determinants of Exurbanization in France

A residential monocentric model has been built in order to analyze exurbanization in France during the 1980s. Exurban areas differ from the cities usually considered in urban economics inasmuch as they include residential, natural, and agricultural land uses. In order to take these features into account, local attributes have been included in the household utility function, as well as leisure time, in order to account for transport time. These assumptions have involved the estimation of a simultaneous-equations system dealing with the structure of exurban areas in terms of attribute and land rent distributions.

The trade-off between decreasing housing costs and rising transport costs is fundamental to explaining suburbanization in the United States and exurbanization in France. In addition to this traditional explanation, the model shows the roles of local services and the demand for adjoining land in the household-location choice. Moreover, a nonmonotonic relationship between income and distance from the center has been observed, contrasting with the usual positive relationship observed in American cities. In French cities, there seems to be an attraction for the center, which may be explainable, in view of our assumptions, by the utility of leisure time. But it may also be the case that the centers of French cities are attractive for their cultural and historical aspects. Further research is needed in order to better understand the differences in income distributions with distance around American and French cities.

A point worth noting is that the movement toward deconcentration of population around cities in France is closely related to the housing consumption of specific households. The mean characteristics of the sample show that the households concerned here are at a medium stage in the life cycle. This means a period when the birth of children and the accumulation of wealth give rise to increased demands for housing and, for those with adequate resources, the first purchase of housing. It seems that it is the ensuing surge in housing spending that induces the shift in household equilibrium location. Thus, the development of exurbanization in France since the beginning of the 1970s can be related to increased homeownership by ever-younger households of increasingly modest social categories, a movement that has been thoroughly described in France (Taffin, 1985). Both the reduction in transport costs and the homeownership subsidies that favor rural areas can be seen as determinants of the French exurbanization movement.

6.2 Relevance of Urban Economics Beyond the City Edge

All the estimated coefficients of our model support the idea that exurban areas are affected, in terms of land rents and levels of local services, by the employment center, far beyond the strict urban boundaries as defined on the basis of built-up areas. The existence of such effects and the estimates for the location equation (results are significant, and their signs consistent with expectations) confirm the relevance of using a monocentric urban model to analyze residential location in exurban areas. It could even be claimed that exurban areas are nowadays closer to the monocentric structure of urban models than are the cities. This could be explained, on the one hand, by the ease with which agricultural uses are outbid by housing in such areas and, on the other hand, by the speed of exurban development. It follows, then, that exurban areas are closer to a situation of instantaneous equilibrium than is the city, which is subject to more rigidities in land uses. It is then similar to a situation where the entire city is rebuilt at each period, which is what is considered in monocentric urban models.

Thus, exurbanization in France seems to correspond to a specific urbanization process in areas that should be considered as rural because of their low population densities and the predominant use of land for farming and forestry. These areas, however, are part of the urbanized landscape, inasmuch as they are commuter areas. It is this feature that justifies their analysis by monocentric urban models, even though they have characteristics quite different from those of cities.

6.3 Nature of City and Definition

Our findings question the conventional wisdom regarding the nature of cities. As discussed in Section 4, the statistical areas that best fit the concept of cities analyzed in urban economics are the urbanized areas in the United States and the *Unités Urbaines* in France. These entities are characterized by a minimum density or a certain compactness. On the contrary, the dispersed residential areas surrounding the cities are different from this traditional concept of city, because suburbanization or exurbanization involves noncontiguity between successive residential areas.[11]

However, exurban areas fit the definition of city from the residential point of view, which is that of the standard monocentric model. One could, in fact, define different kinds of space. A city can still be defined on the basis of continuous use of land by firms and residences. But beyond the city's edge exists another kind of space, that is, suburban or exurban areas that undergo an urbanization process. These spaces form urbanized areas that fit the assumptions of the monocentric residential model, that is, the existence of commuting flows toward the center. This new urbanization process has been recognized for many years in the United States through the use of MSAs. Analysis of MSAs by urban economic models is common in the United States. But it is only recently that "urban areas" (*Aires*

---

[11] Although it is obvious that the definition of noncontiguity depends on an arbitrary threshold.

Urbaines in French), including rural communes in their traditional definition, have been defined in France to account for urban sprawl (Le Jeannic, 1996). Beyond these urbanized areas begin rural areas that are only slightly linked to the city, and their economic development rests on a different basis than that for exurban areas (Schmitt, 1999).

6.4 Possible Extensions

This analysis raises some new questions. First of all, there are differences between American suburbs and French exurban areas that deserve further analysis. We have already mentioned that the income–distance relationships are different in the two countries. Moreover, there exists a clear break in the residential land use between the urban boundaries and the exurban areas in France, where exurbanization develops at a distance from the urban boundary, either in a diffuse manner or as housing estates around villages. On the contrary, suburban land development in American cities seems to be more diffuse. Two reasons could be examined in order to explain this difference. First, there may be behavioral differences between the United States and France concerning the valuation of the housing environment and particularly the neighborhood density. For instance, American suburban migration seems to be associated with greater consumption of land adjoining each house. Second, differences in prior spatial configurations could also be relevant. Indeed, historical circumstances have generated a developed network of villages around French cities that can be thought of as generating externalities in the form of additional facilities. These externalities attract households, thus causing the exurban residential development to concentrate into a few places, instead of in a diffuse manner. In order to explore this point, it would be necessary to account for the discontinuity in spatial attributes, such as densities and public services (e.g., public transport network).

The analysis of residential development in exurban zones also suggests further observations about the distribution of population and activities between cities and rural areas. In estimating the land price equation (9.7), we noticed that the size of the city center influences land values throughout the exurban area. Accordingly, land competition within the city itself, which causes land prices to rise at the same time as the population, seems to have repercussions beyond the urban boundary. This influence of the size of the city center helps to explain why the exurbanization rings are more widely spread when the employment center is larger: The higher the price in the center, the greater the location distance resulting from trade-offs among transport cost, housing cost, and location attributes. For instance, in France, cities of more than 200,000 people have exurban areas whose radii range from 20 to 40 km; the radii for exurban rings around cities with 50,000 to 100,000 inhabitants range from 15 to 20 km (Hilal et al., 1995). Finally, distances from the city are such that the exurbanization rings cover large parts of France's rural areas. In 1990, 38%

of the rural communes were under the influence of a city of 20,000 or more inhabitants.

Furthermore, the influence of cities on exurban rural areas, via residential locations, has consequences for the development of jobs in such areas. Some jobs seem to be induced by population growth. These are population-serving activities, such as shops and household services (Hilal et al., 1995). This observation is reminiscent of the earlier observation that local services increase with the proximity to and the size of the city center.

In conclusion, three lines of further work are suggested. First, whereas the model presented here deals with residential location only, a broader model is needed to analyze spatial configurations, namely, population and employment density gradients and the emergence of secondary centers in exurban areas. To this end, following the lines of economic geography, it will be necessary to take into account externalities that encourage people to locate arround preexisting villages, as well as agglomeration economies that link firms with each other and with households (Goffette-Nagot and Schmitt, 1999). Second, one also could develop a dynamic model explaining how population growth in exurban areas is followed by increases in local service facilities and then in land rents, which in turn influence later exurban development. Our comparison has been restricted to the United States and France. Clearly, there is a need for international comparisons in land-use patterns. Is France (or Europe) the exception or the rule?

References

Alonso, W. (1964). *Location and Land Use*. Cambridge, MA: Harvard University Press.

Anas, A., Arnott, R., and Small, K. A. (1998). Urban spatial structure. *Journal of Economic Literature* 36:1426–64.

Boarnet, M. G. (1994). An empirical model of intrametropolitan population and employment growth. *Papers in Regional Science* 73:135–52.

Brueckner, J. K., and Fansler, D. A. (1983). The economics of urban sprawl: theory and evidence on the spatial size of cities. *Review of Economics and Statistics* 65:479–82.

Brueckner, J., Thisse, J.-F., and Zenou, Y. (1999), Why is central Paris rich and downtown Detroit poor? An amenity-based theory. *European Economic Review* 43:91–107.

Carlino, G. A. (1985). Declining productivity and the growth of rural regions: a test of alternative explanations. *Journal of Urban Economics* 18:11–27.

Carlino, G. A., and Mills, E. S. (1987). The determinants of county growth. *Journal of Regional Science* 27:39–54.

Champion, A. G. (1992). Urban and regional demographic trends in the developed world. *Urban Studies* 29:461–82.

Clark, C. (1951). Urban population densities. *Journal of the Royal Statistical Society A* 114:490–6.

DeSalvo, J. S., and Huq, M. (1996). Income, residential location and mode choice. *Journal of Urban Economics* 40:84–99.

Fujita, M. (1989). *Urban Economic Theory.* Cambridge University Press.

Fujita, M., and Ogawa, H. (1982). Multiple equilibria and structural transition of monocentric urban configuration. *Regional Science and Urban Economics* 12:161–96.

Fujita, M., Thisse, J.-F., and Zenou Y. (1997). On the endogenous formation of secondary employment centers in a city. *Journal of Urban Economics* 41:337–57.

Garreau, J. (1991). *Edge City. Life on the New Frontier.* New York: Doubleday.

Goffette-Nagot, F. (1994). Analyse microéconomique de la périurbanisation: un modèle de localisation résidentielle. Doctoral dissertation, Université de Bourgogne, Dijon.

Goffette-Nagot, F. (1996). Choix résidentiel et diffusion périurbaine. *Revue d'économie régionale et urbaine* 2:229–46.

Goffette-Nagot, F., and Schmitt, B. (1999). Agglomeration economies and spatial configurations in rural areas. *Environment and Planning A* 31:1239–57.

Hartwick, P. G., and Hartwick, J. M. (1974). Efficient resource allocation in a multinucleated city with intermediate goods. *Quarterly Journal of Economics* 88:340–53.

Helsley, R. W., and Sullivan, A. M. (1991). Urban subcenter formation. *Regional Science and Urban Economics* 21:225–75.

Henderson, V., and Mitra, A. (1997). The new urban landscape: developers and edge cities. *Regional Science and Urban Economics* 26:613–43.

Henry, M., Barkley, D., and Bao, S. (1997). The hinterland's stake in metropolitan growth: evidence from selected southern regions. *Journal of Regional Science* 37:479–501.

Hilal, M., Piguet, V., and Schmitt, B. (1995). Communes rurales et petites villes dans la hiérarchie urbaine. *Economie et statistique* 282:21–36.

Huriot, J. M. (1994). *Von Thünen: économie et espace.* Paris: Economica.

Le Jeannic, T. (1996). Une nouvelle approche territoriale de la ville. *Economie et statistique* 294–5:24–45.

Macauley, M. K. (1985). Estimation and recent behavior of urban population and employment density gradients. *Journal of Urban Economics* 18:251–60.

McDonald, J. F. (1989). Econometric studies of urban population density: a survey. *Journal of Urban Economics* 26:361–85.

Margo, R. A. (1992). Explaining the postwar suburbanization of Population in the United States: the role of income. *Journal of Urban Economics* 31:301–10.

Mills, E. S. (1972). *Studies in the Structure of the Urban Economy.* Baltimore: Johns Hopkins University Press.

Mills, E. (1990). Do metropolitan areas mean anything ? A research note. *Journal of Regional Science* 30:415–19.

Mills, E. S. (1992). The measurement and determinants of suburbanization. *Journal of Urban Economics* 32:377–87.

Muth, R. (1969). *Cities and Housing.* University of Chicago Press.

Papageorgiou, Y. Y. (1990). *The Isolated City State.* London: Routledge.

Parr, J. B., and Jones, C. (1983). City size distributions and urban density functions: some interrelationships. *Journal of Regional Science* 23:283–307.

Phlips, L. (1983). *Applied Consumption Analysis.* Amsterdam: North Holland.

Schmitt, B. (1999). Economic geography and contemporary rural dynamics: an empirical test on some French regions. *Regional Studies* 33.

Suarez-Villa, L. (1988). Metropolitan evolution, sectoral economic change, and the city size distribution. *Urban Studies* 25:1–20.

Tabourin, E. (1995). Les formes de l'étalement urbain. In: *Les Annales de la Recherche Urbaine (numéro spécial "Densités et espacement")*, pp. 33–42. Paris: CNRS/PIR-Villes.

Taffin, C. (1985). Accession à la propriété et "rurbanisation." *Economie et statistique* 175:55–67.

Yacovissi, W., and Kern, C. R. (1995). Location and history as determinants of urban residential density. *Journal of Urban Economics* 38:207–20.

Yinger, J. (1992). City and suburb: urban models with more than one employment center. *Journal of Urban Economics* 31:181–205.

Zheng, X. P. (1991). Metropolitan spatial structure and its determinants: a case-study of Tokyo. *Urban Studies* 28:87–104.

PART IV

Cities and Factor Markets

CHAPTER 10

Unemployment in Cities

Yves Zenou

1 Introduction

It is commonly observed in the countries of the Organization for Economic Cooperation and Development (OECD) that unemployment is unevenly distributed among cities and that it has increased considerably during the past 20 years. The incidence of unemployment varies between the regions of a country (Isserman et al., 1986; Gordon, 1987; Blanchflower and Oswald, 1994), between cities of different sizes and functions (Marston, 1985; Hasluck, 1987), between the inner and outer areas of cities, and between urban and rural areas. Its increasing incidence has led to renewed interest in the spatial dimension of unemployment.

In this chapter, the focus is on intra-urban unemployment. Table 10.1 shows that in large U.S. cities the unemployment rates are higher in the city centers than in the suburbs. This is largely because U.S. city centers are generally characterized by ghettos and poverty. The European situation is more complex and is not uniform (Table 10.2). One might think that these differences between the United States and Europe are mainly due to the fact that their cities have had different histories (Brueckner et al., 1999a). However, Brussels is a surprising case, as it has followed the same pattern as U.S. cities, with a substantial part of its historical center having been demolished and replaced by office buildings (the so-called Brusselization phenomenon). The cases of London and Paris are more complex. At first glance, unemployment appears higher in inner-city locations than in suburban locations. In fact, the inner–outer dichotomy is too crude, and the reality is more complex. For example, in Paris, where the city center is clearly richer than the suburbs (Table 10.3), important differences exist between various districts and various suburbs. Table 10.4 shows that rich districts (with high land prices) have low unemployment rates, whereas the poor districts have high rates. This is also true for the suburbs, where some are

I would like to thank Richard Arnott and Jacques Thisse for valuable comments.

Table 10.1. *Unemployment rates in large U.S. MSAs*

	Central-City (%)	Suburbs (%)	All (%)
New York MSA, NY	8.2	4.5	7.6
Los Angeles PMSA, CA	8.9	7.2	7.9
Chicago PMSA, IL	6.7	4.4	5.1
Houston PMSA, TX	7.0	4.5	5.7
Philadelphia PMSA, PA	7.6	5.2	5.9
San Diego MSA, CA	6.5	6.3	6.4
Dallas PMSA, TX	5.9	3.9	4.6
Phoenix MSA, AZ	3.8	3.3	3.5
Detroit PMSA, MI	10.0	4.0	5.0
San Antonio MSA, TX	5.0	3.2	4.4

Note: PMSA, primary metropolitan statistical areas; MSA, metropolitan statistical area.
Source: Local-area unemployment statistics, annual average for 1995, U.S. Bureau of the Census.

Table 10.2. *Unemployment rates in large European agglomerations*

	Central-City (%)	Suburbs (%)	All (%)
Paris Agglomeration (Ile de France)	12.2	9.6	10.5
Extended Brussels	13.3	5.4	10.6
Greater London	9.6	5.5	7.0

Source: Paris, INSEE, 1995; Brussels, census of population, 1991; London, census of population, 1991.

rich (e.g., Hauts de Seine), and others very poor (e.g., Seine Saint Denis, with a high concentration of immigrants). Paris is a city with several centers, and the center–suburbs dichotomy is too shallow to explain its reality. The same argument applies to London. Another possible explanatory factor is that the local governments are heavily invested in central-city infrastructure in Paris and London, and less so in Brussels and in U.S. cities (Ades and Glaeser, 1995). Such a policy tends to attract rich people to places where tax resources

Table 10.3. *Incomes within the Parisian agglomeration*

	Central-City (FF)	Suburbs (FF)	All (FF)
Paris Agglomeration (Ile de France)	124,000	106,000	112,000

Source: INSEE, 1990.

Table 10.4. *Unemployment rates and land prices within the Parisian agglomeration*

	Unemployment rate (%)	Land Price (FF per m^2)
1st to 4th District	11.61	19,690
5th District	8.24	22,213
6th District	7.64	24,159
7th District	7.91	26,238
8th District	8.49	23,579
9th District	11.53	15,846
10th District	13.63	13,484
11th District	13.51	15,143
12th District	9.48	16,194
13th District	12.64	16,376
14th District	9.07	19,005
15th District	7.71	19,747
16th District	8.25	24,613
17th District	10.52	17,967
18th District	15.84	13,989
19th District	14.88	13,286
20th District	13.76	14,110
Seine et Marne	9.1	
Yvelines	8.0	
Essonne	8.5	
Hauts de Seine	9.6	
Seine St. Denis	14.3	
Val de Marne	10.3	
Val d'Oise	10.4	

Source: INSEE, 1995, and Blondel and Marchand (1997).

are heavily invested in developing the capital city; then the unemployed workers who cannot afford to live in expensive central areas will move to other areas, generally outside of Paris or London.

Despite all this evidence, very few theoretical attempts have been made to explain urban unemployment and intra-urban differences. The aim of this chapter is to review the theoretical studies that have dealt explicitly with urban unemployment. In order to do this, we shall seek to answer two questions: Where do the unemployed locate in a city? What are the causes of urban unemployment?

The location of the unemployed workers in a city is a crucial issue that has not received much attention from urban economists. Instead, urban economists have concentrated their research on the locations of rich households and poor households. The main finding of Hartwick, Schweizer, and Varaiya (1976) is that rich workers tend to locate farther away from the central business district (CBD), whereas poor workers tend to reside in the vicinity of the city center. The main assumptions of that model are that workers are identical in all respects except their incomes, that land is a normal good, and that time costs are not included in commuting costs. The explanation for their finding is that it is necessary for the poor to live near their workplaces in order to economize on transport costs, whereas the rich have a high income elasticity for space. If, for example, one introduces time costs, then the equilibrium urban configuration will crucially depend on the magnitude of the wage elasticity of marginal transport cost versus the wage elasticity of lot size (Fujita, 1989, ch. 2). The question that arises is, Can we apply this model to the locations of unemployed and employed workers? Obviously this gives a very narrow, unrealistic view of the unemployed. Therefore, in Zenou and Smith (1995), which is the first paper to explicitly introduce the location of the unemployed workers with an endogenous level of urban unemployment, the two categories of workers have been differentiated on the basis of their transport costs. Indeed, in the standard model, workers go to the CBD to work and to buy goods, but transport costs cannot be the same for the unemployed and the employed, because the former go to the CBD only to buy goods, whereas the latter commute to the CBD to shop and to work. If we assume that the two kinds of workers consume the same amount of space, it is easy to show in a monocentric-city framework that, at the urban equilibrium, the unemployed will reside at the outskirts of the city, because the employed workers, who have higher commuting costs, will bid them away. However, this is true only in a model in which unemployed workers do not search for jobs and are not interviewed for jobs. By contrast, if the probability of getting a job is inversely related to distance (because as the distance from the CBD increases, the intensity of the job search decreases, and the probability of job matching is lower), the equilibrium location for the unemployed will crucially depend on the trade-off between transport costs and search costs: The unemployed want to be as close as possible to the CBD in order to increase their probability of getting a job, as do the employed, who bear higher commuting costs. Observe that the equilibrium location will depend on the shape of the search-intensity function, because the slope of the bid-rent curve for the unemployed will depend only on this function and on the linear transport cost. If this function is linear with distance, then there will be only two possible configurations: Either the unemployed will be close to the CBD, or they will be farther away from the CBD. If this function is now decreasing, and if it is a (sufficiently) convex function of the distance to the CBD, the unemployed will locate in the vicinity of the CBD and at the outskirts of the city, whereas the employed will reside in between those two areas. If it is concave, then we will have the reverse result. Within this framework, we are able to discuss the problem of urban segregation and to see why ghettos form in different places in a city. In particular, it can be shown that urban segregation can be due to racial prejudice from landlords, employers, or white residents. So far, we have assumed that the city is monocentric. What happens if the city has two centers, the CBD and a secondary employment center (SEC) located at the city edge? We can show that if the types of jobs are different between the CBD and the SEC, the unemployed will locate in the middle of the city in between the employed workers. By using different assumptions, we can have several other urban configurations in which the locations of the unemployed are quite different.

What are the causes of urban unemployment? The first answer that we suggest begins with the supposition that there is a moral-hazard problem for the workers within each firm: Each worker is tempted to shirk whenever he has the opportunity to do so. Because that can be costly, the firm will set a self-enforcing contract by paying its workers an efficiency wage that will induce them not to shirk and to stay in the city. This (efficiency) wage will be greater than the market-clearing wage, and thus, because all firms will behave the same way, there will be a durable level of (involuntary) unemployment in the city. Here the introduction of space increases the efficiency wage and thus the level of unemployment. Of course, all other theories of wage rigidities (such as the other microfoundations of the efficiency-wage theory or the bargain wage) can be applied here, and the results will be similar, though not depending on the same parameters. Another possible way of explaining urban unemployment is to assume that there is a demand shock that reduces price or demand, and that leads to an involuntary type of unemployment. What is interesting is to study the consequences of this shock on the spatial behavior of workers. There is another type of urban unemployment that is due to frictions in the labor market. If we assume that unemployed workers search for jobs and that the search is costly, then even if firms pay the market-clearing wage there still will be a durable level of unemployment in the city, because there is a stochastic rationing that cannot be eliminated by price adjustments. Finally, we consider the so-called spatial-mismatch unemployment that was first pointed out by Kain (1968). It has been observed in the United States that when a firm decides to locate at the outskirts of its city, it leaves a segment of its workforce behind, essentially its African-American workers. Why? The most common explanation is that landlords refuse to rent to blacks, outside of ghettos, because of racial prejudice. Thus, when a firm relocates in the suburbs, its black workers have long commuting trips to work. In this situation, some black workers will prefer to be unemployed until they can find work closer to their residences. This is what is called spatial-mismatch unemployment.

This chapter is organized as follows: Section 2 presents the notation for the basic model that will be used throughout. We shall, in particular, define the model with full employment and the model with the risk of unemployment. In Section 3 we shall try to show what the locations will be for unemployed and employed workers in a monocentric city and a polycentric city. We shall, in particular, deal with the critical issue of why the locations of the unemployed are different in European and American cities. This will lead us to an examination of the problem of ghettos and urban segregation. A second primary question that we shall try to answer concerns the causes of urban unemployment. We shall treat this issue in Section 4, proposing four main factors: efficiency wage, demand shock, job search and job matching, and spatial mismatch. Finally, Section 5 discusses conclusions.

2 The Full-Employment Case and the Risk of Unemployment

In this section, we develop a benchmark model in which there is full employment. We then go on to study workers' location decisions when they face unemployment risk. In both cases, all workers are employed today, and thus we do not model the locations of the unemployed workers in the city.

2.1 The Full-Employment Case

We use a simple framework in order to illustrate this basic model; for a more extensive description of this model, see Brueckner (1987) or Fujita (1989). There is a finite number of firms located in the CBD and a continuum of workers, whose mass is L, residing outside the CBD. The city is linear and closed, and all the land is owned by absentee landlords. The utility of each worker is $U(h, \sigma)$, where h and σ are respectively the housing consumption and the composite-good consumption, the latter being taken as the numéraire. This function is assumed to be well-behaved, that is, continuous, twice differentiable, increasing in each argument, and concave. The budget constraint reads $w = \sigma + hR(x) + T(x)$, where w is the current wage, $R(x)$ is the land rent at a distance x from the CBD, and $T(x)$ is the monetary commuting cost at a distance x from the CBD. By using the budget constraint, we can rewrite the utility function; thus, each worker solves the following program:

$$\max_{h} U[h, w - hR(x) - T(x)] \tag{2.1}$$

First- and second-order conditions give a unique $h^* = h[w - T(x), R(x)]$. The indirect utility function is

$$V[w - T(x), R(x)] = U[h^*, w - h^*R(x) - T(x)] \equiv u \tag{2.2}$$

where u is the equilibrium utility level in the city. The bid rent, which is the maximum rent per unit of land that a worker who resides at a distance x from the CBD can pay in order to achieve a utility level u, is therefore

$$\Psi(x, u) = V^{-1}[w - T(x), R(x)] \tag{2.3}$$

The city equilibrium is defined as follows.

Definition 2.1. *In a monocentric linear city, an urban equilibrium with full employment is a vector* $[u, x_f, R(x)]$ *such that*

$$R(x) = \begin{cases} \max[\Psi(x, u), 0] & \text{for } x \leq x_f \\ 0 & \text{for } x > x_f \end{cases} \tag{2.4}$$

$$\Psi(x_f, u) = 0 \tag{2.5}$$

$$\int_0^{x_f} \frac{1}{h(x, u)} \, dx = L \tag{2.6}$$

where x_f is the city fringe.

Equation (2.4) means that the land is offered to the highest bids in the city. In equation (2.5), the bid rent at the city fringe is equal to agricultural rent (normalized to zero for simplicity). Equation (2.6) is the population constraint condition. By solving the two equations (2.5) and (2.6), we obtain the equilibrium values for the two unknowns u^* and x_f^* as functions of the two exogenous variables w and $T(x)$.

We shall now describe the labor market. All workers residing outside the CBD earn the same wage, and each supplies inelastically one unit of labor. All firms, whose number is M, are located in the CBD. Each of them chooses its labor demand l to maximize its profit, the wage w being determined in a competitive way. The profit is

$$\Pi = pf(l) - wl \tag{2.7}$$

where p is the price of the output, and $f(l)$ is the production function, which is well-behaved, with $f'(l) > 0$ and $f''(l) < 0$. The first-order condition is

$$\frac{w}{p} = f'(l) \tag{2.8}$$

Because all firms are identical, $L = Ml$. Hence, if we now introduce the aggregate production function, F, defined for all L by $F(L) = Mf(L/M)$, and observe that by definition $F'(L) = Mf'(L/M)(1/M) = f'(l)$, it follows that in equilibrium, the profit-maximization condition (2.8) must have the equivalent aggregate form:

$$\frac{w}{p} = F'(L) \tag{2.9}$$

This equation states that the real wage is equal to the marginal productivity of labor. Equation (2.9) defines the labor demand (L) curve. By using the properties of $F(\cdot)$, it is easily shown that

$$\frac{\partial L}{\partial w} < 0 \tag{2.10}$$

That is, the labor demand curve is downward-sloping in the $(L - w)$ space. Because the labor supply is perfectly inelastic in the same space, there exists a unique labor-market equilibrium with full employment $(N = L^*)$.

2.2 The Risk of Unemployment[1]

We now assume that employed workers face unemployment uncertainty. There is indeed an exogenous probability δ that the job will be destroyed and that the worker will lose his job. Therefore, each worker maximizes the following expected utility:[2]

$$\max_{h}\{\delta U[h, w_0 - hR(x) - T_0(x)] + (1 - \delta)U[h, w_1 - hR(x) - T_1(x)]\} \tag{2.11}$$

where w_i $(i = 0, 1)$ is the wage for a worker of type i (with $w_1 \geq w_0$, w_0 being the unemployment benefit). Observe that we assume that unemployed and employed workers have the same preferences, but not the same commuting costs. Employed workers go to the CBD more often than do unemployed workers, because employed workers both shop and work there, so that $T_1(x) > T_0(x) \,\forall\, x$. Observe also that (2.11) means that we are studying the *delayed-uncertainty model* (Drèze and Modigliani, 1972), in which workers make all their decisions

---

[1] This section is based on studies by DeSalvo and Eeckhoudt (1982) and Zenou and Eeckhoudt (1997).

[2] For notational simplicity, group 0 refers to the unemployed workers, and group 1 to the employed workers. We therefore index all variables with a subscript $i = 0, 1$ when referring to these workers.

ex ante (i.e., before the risk is known). So here workers are deciding to-day their housing consumption, their bid rent, and consequently where to live before knowing their future employment status. If a worker becomes unemployed, he will not change his location and his housing consumption $(h_0 = h_1 = h)$, but will reduce his composite-good consumption, $\sigma_0 = w_0 - hR(x) - T_0(x)$. We assume that w_0 is large enough to cover spatial fees if the worker is unemployed. First- and second-order conditions give a unique $h^* = h[w_1 - T_1(x), w_0 - T_0(x), \delta, R(x)]$. The indirect utility function can therefore be written as

$$V[w_1 - T_1(x), w_0 - T_0(x), \delta, R(x)]$$
$$= \delta U[h^*, w_0 - h^*R(x) - T_0(x)]$$
$$+ (1 - \delta)U[h^*, w_1 - h^*R(x) - T_1(x)] \equiv u_d \qquad (2.12)$$

where u_d is the equilibrium utility level under delayed uncertainty. The employed worker's bid rent is thus

$$\Psi_d(x, u_d) = V^{-1}[w_0 - T_0(x), w_1 - T_1(x), \delta, R(x)] \qquad (2.13)$$

We easily obtain

$$\frac{\partial \Psi_d(x, u_d)}{\partial \delta} < 0 \qquad (2.14)$$

which means that when unemployment uncertainty increases, employed workers will submit lower bid rents. In this model, there is very little flexibility for workers, because they have to decide everything before the risk is known. There is another way to study decision in the presence of unemployment risk that allows more flexibility: the so-called *timeless-uncertainty model* (Drèze and Modigliani, 1972). In this case, workers decide *ex ante* (before the risk is known) their bid rents and their locations in the city, but adjust *ex post* (when their new employment status is known with certainty) their housing consumption and composite-good consumption. For example, young people will buy a parcel of land today and decide on the size of their house when they know their employment status. In this context, each worker solves the following problem:

$$\delta \max_{h_0}\{U[h_0, w_0 - h_0R(x) - T_0(x)]\}$$
$$+ (1 - \delta)\max_{h_1}\{U[h_1, w_1 - h_1R(x) - T_1(x)]\} \qquad (2.15)$$

Observe that, according to the state of nature, each worker will choose a different housing consumption. Indeed, first- and second-order conditions give a unique $h_0^* = h_0[w_0 - T_0(x), R(x)]$ and a unique $h_1^* = h_1[w_1 - T_1(x), R(x)]$, and neither depends on the probability δ. The indirect utility function can therefore be written as

$$V[w_0 - T_0(x), w_1 - T_1(x), \delta, R(x)]$$
$$= \delta\{U[h_0^*, w_0 - h_0^* R(x) - T_0(x)]\}$$
$$+ (1 - \delta)\{U[h_1^*, w_1 - h_1^* R(x) - T_1(x)]\} \equiv u_t \qquad (2.16)$$

where u_t is the equilibrium utility level under timeless uncertainty. The employed worker's bid rent is thus

$$\Psi_t(x, u_t) = V^{-1}[w_0 - T_0(x), w_1 - T_1(x), \delta, R(x)] \qquad (2.17)$$

It is again easy to show that

$$\frac{\partial \Psi_t(x, u_t)}{\partial \delta} < 0 \qquad (2.18)$$

We are now able to compare three models: decision under certainty (Section 2.1), decision under delayed uncertainty, and decision under timeless uncertainty.

Proposition 2.1. *A worker residing at a distance $\bar{x}$ from the CBD and enjoying a utility level $\bar{u}$ proposes the following bid rents:*

$$\Psi(\bar{x}, \bar{u}) < \Psi_t(\bar{x}, \bar{u}) < \Psi_d(\bar{x}, \bar{u}) \qquad (2.19)$$

This proposition says that workers tend to offer higher bid rents when they have more flexibility in their decisions. We can now calculate the city equilibrium by using Definition 2.1 for each model. Zenou and Eeckhoudt (1997) have shown that, at the city equilibrium, an increase in δ or L will raise the equilibrium utility level, whereas an increse in w_1 or w_0 will decrease it in the delayed-risk model. In the other model, the effects are more ambiguous. In particular, it is possible that in the timeless-risk model increasing the unemployment benefit may be welfare-reducing because of the flexibility it allows.

This model can be extended to incorporate urban segregation (Gannon and Zenou, 1997). If some workers experience discrimination on the basis of their appearance (color, race), their probability of finding jobs is lower than the probability for nondiscriminated workers. This affects their bid-rent curves, which become steeper, and thus their locations: Discriminate workers tend to be segregated around the CBD and to have little chance of leaving the "ghetto." It is the discrimination in the labor market that affects the urban equilibrium by segregating some workers around the CBD.

3 Where Do the Unemployed Workers Reside in the City?

We now explicitly introduce the locations of unemployed and employed workers in the city. Throughout this section, we assume that there is an exogenous wage w_1 that is greater than the market-clearing wage and leads to a durable level of unemployment. We shall develop distinct models that generate different urban equilibrium configurations. In particular, we shall explain the locations of the unemployed in the vicinity of the city center and at the outskirts of the city. We shall also develop more complicated urban patterns in the context of a monocentric city and a polycentric city, with the unemployed being able to reside in different locations in the city. This section is mainly devoted to the land market. In the next section, we shall study the interaction between the labor market and the land market and its policy implications.

As in the preceding section, there is a continuum of workers of both types, employed and unemployed, whose masses are respectively L_1 and U, with $N = L_1 + U$. Each worker can live anywhere outside the city center and is endowed with one unit of labor. There are no relocation costs. All the land is owned by absentee landlords. The density of land at each point is constant and is equal to 1. Moreover, the total population of workers residing in the city is fixed, whereas their utility level is endogenous, which implies that we are in the context of a closed-city model (Fujita, 1989).

3.1 A Static Model without Search

In this section we assume that workers do not search for jobs and do not go to interviews. There is only an exogenous probability of finding a job. It is a very simple model that will explain the urban equilibrium configuration through the differences in commuting costs and/or housing consumption.

3.1.1 A Monocentric-City Framework with Fixed Housing Consumption.[3] We

develop a simple model that explains the location of the unemployed at the outskirts of the city.

Assumption 3.1. *The city is monocentric, with a CBD, where all the firms are located.*

Assumption 3.2. *The land consumption for each worker is fixed and is normalized to 1 (i.e., $h_0 = h_1 = 1$). Moreover, $U(1, \sigma_i) = U(\sigma_i) = \sigma_i = w_i - T_i(x) - R(x) = u_i$, where u_i is the equilibrium utility level for a type-i worker, $i = 0, 1$.*

These instantaneous utilities are in fact net revenues or indirect utilities. At the urban equilibrium, all workers of the same type will have the same utility level, and the bid rent for a type-i worker (i.e., the maximum land rent a type-i worker can pay in order to reach a utility level u_i at a distance x from the CBD) is

$$\Psi_i(x, u_0) = w_i - T_i(x) - u_i, \qquad i = 0, 1 \tag{3.1}$$

---

[3] This section is based on Zenou and Smith (1995).

Assumption 3.3. *The unemployed workers go to the CBD only to shop, whereas the employed go to the CBD to shop and to work. At a distance x from the CBD, the total commuting cost for the former is $T_0(x) = \alpha_s tx$ ($\alpha_s t > 0$ is the fraction of the commuting cost devoted to shopping), whereas for the latter it is $T_1(x) = (\alpha_s + \alpha_1)tx$ ($\alpha_1 t > 0$ is the fraction of the commuting cost devoted to working).*

We can therefore rewrite the bid-rent functions (3.1) as follows:

$$\Psi_1(x, u_1) = w_1 - (\alpha_s + \alpha_1)tx - u_1 \tag{3.2}$$

$$\Psi_0(x, u_0) = w_0 - \alpha_s tx - u_0 \tag{3.3}$$

and their slopes are respectively

$$\frac{\partial \Psi_1(x, u_1)}{\partial x} = -(\alpha_s + \alpha_1)t < 0 \tag{3.4}$$

$$\frac{\partial \Psi_0(x, u_0)}{\partial x} = -\alpha_s t < 0 \tag{3.5}$$

with

$$\left| \frac{\partial \Psi_1(x, u_1)}{\partial x} \right| > \left| \frac{\partial \Psi_0(x, u_0)}{\partial x} \right|$$

Therefore, the employed reside close to the CBD, whereas the unemployed locate at the outskirts of the city. The intuition behind this result is quite simple. Because the employed bear higher commuting costs, they outbid the unemployed at the periphery of the city. We refer to this equilibrium as urban equilibrium A. Let us focus on the equilibrium conditions.

Definition 3.1. *In a monocentric linear city, the urban equilibrium A, in which the unemployed reside at the outskirts of the city, and the employed live in the vicinity of the CBD, is a vector $[u_0, u_1, x_b, x_f, R(x)]$ such that*

$$R(x) = \begin{cases} \max[\Psi_0(x, u_0), \Psi_1(x, u_1), 0] & \text{for } x \leq x_f \\ 0 & \text{for } x > x_f \end{cases} \tag{3.6}$$

$$\Psi_0(x_b, u_0) = \Psi_1(x_b, u_1) \tag{3.7}$$

$$\Psi_0(x_f, u_0) = 0 \tag{3.8}$$

$$\int_0^{x_b} dx = x_b = L \tag{3.9}$$

$$\int_{x_b}^{x_f} dx = x_f - x_b = N - L = U \tag{3.10}$$

where x_b is the border between the employed and the unemployed, and x_f is the city fringe.

Equation (3.6) means that the land is offered to the highest bids in the city. Equations (3.7) and (3.8) show that the bid rents are equal at the border, x_b, and that at the city fringe, x_f, the unemployed worker's bid rent is equal to the agricultural bid rent normalized to zero for simplicity. Equations (3.9) and (3.10) are the population constraint conditions.

By solving these equations, we obtain the following equilibrium utility levels (closed city):

$$u_0^* = w_0 - \alpha_s t N \tag{3.11}$$

$$u_1^* = w_1 - \alpha_s t N - \alpha_1 t L \tag{3.12}$$

Proposition 3.1. *Under Assumptions 3.1, 3.2, and 3.3, the unemployed will reside at the outskirts of the city, whereas the employed will locate in the vicinity of the CBD.*

Once again, this proposition highlights the fact that in the vicinity of the CBD, employed workers outbid the unemployed because the commuting cost for the employed is higher and they thus have a strong preference for the city center. It follows that if a worker loses his job, he can no longer afford a central location and must relocate at the periphery of the city. Here, becoming unemployed implies a change in residence.

3.1.2 A Monocentric City Framework with Endogenous Housing Consumption. We relax Assumptions 3.2 and 3.3.

Assumption 3.4. *The commuting costs for the employed and the unemployed are identical:* $T_0(x) = T_1(x) = tx$.

Assumption 3.5. *Land is a normal good.*

The utility function for a worker of type i is now assumed to be

$$U(h_i, \sigma_i) = \tfrac{1}{2} \log h_i + \tfrac{1}{2} \log \sigma_i, \qquad i = 0, 1 \tag{3.13}$$

Using the budget constraint, this utility can be rewritten as

$$U(h_i, \sigma_i) = \tfrac{1}{2} \log h_i + \tfrac{1}{2} \log[w_i - tx - h_i R(x)], \qquad i = 0, 1 \tag{3.14}$$

The first-order condition with respect to h_i yields

$$h_i^* = \frac{w_i - tx}{2R(x)}$$

The indirect utility function is

$$V = U(h_i^*, \sigma_i^*) = \log \left[\frac{w_i - tx}{2\sqrt{R(x)}} \right] = u_i$$

and the bid rents are therefore

$$\Psi_0(x, u_0) = \tfrac{1}{4}(w_0 - tx)^2 e^{-2u_0} \tag{3.15}$$

$$\Psi_1(x, u_1) = \tfrac{1}{4}(w_1 - tx)^2 e^{-2u_1} \tag{3.16}$$

and their slopes are

$$\frac{\partial \Psi_0(x, u_0)}{\partial x} = -\frac{1}{2} t (w_0 - tx) e^{-2u_0} < 0 \tag{3.17}$$

$$\frac{\partial \Psi_1(x, u_1)}{\partial x} = -\frac{1}{2} t (w_1 - tx) e^{-2u_1} < 0 \tag{3.18}$$

with

$$\left| \frac{\partial \Psi_0(x, u_1)}{\partial x} \right| > \left| \frac{\partial \Psi_1(x, u_0)}{\partial x} \right|$$

We get this result because the employed are richer than the unemployed, $w_1 > w_0$. And because, by Assumption 3.5, land is a normal good, the employed want to consume more land, and thus they seek to locate where the land is cheaper (i.e., at the outskirts of the city). We have here a second type of equilibrium labeled urban equilibrium B. Its definition is as follows.

Definition 3.2. *In a monocentric linear city, the urban equilibrium B, in which the unemployed reside in the vicinity of the CBD, and the employed live at the outskirts of the city, is a vector $[u_0, u_1, x_b, x_f, R(x)]$ such that*

$$R(x) = \begin{cases} \max[\Psi_0(x, u_0), \Psi_1(x, u_1), 0] & \text{for } x \leq x_f \\ 0 & \text{for } x > x_f \end{cases} \tag{3.19}$$

$$\Psi_0(x_b, u_0) = \Psi_1(x_b, u_1) \tag{3.20}$$

$$\Psi_1(x_f, u_0) = 0 \tag{3.21}$$

$$\int_0^{x_b} \frac{1}{h_0(x, u_0)} \, dx = L \tag{3.22}$$

$$\int_{x_b}^{x_f} \frac{1}{h_1(x, u_0)} \, dx = U \tag{3.23}$$

By solving these equations, we obtain the equilibrium values for u_0^*, u_1^*, x_b^*, and x_f^* as functions of the parameters.

Proposition 3.2. *Under Assumptions 3.1, 3.4, and 3.5, the employed will reside at the outskirts of the city, whereas the unemployed will live in the vicinity of the CBD.*

3.1.3. A Polycentric-City Framework.[4]

Thus far we have only a very crude explanation for the locations of workers in a city. We now introduce a polycentric city. We use the model of Section 3.1.1, and we study the optimal location for a new center in the city. For that (and only for this section), we introduce three types of workers: the unemployed workers; workers in the primary sector, where jobs pay well and are stable; workers in the secondary sector, where pay is low and jobs are short-term. All workers are *ex ante* identical, but *ex post* they are allocated to the different employment groups: unemployed, group 0; employed in the primary sector, group 1; employed in the secondary sector, group 2 (with $w_1 > w_2 > w_0$).

Assumption 3.6. *There are two employment centers, the CBD and the SEC, located at x_2.*

The primary sector, where all the good jobs are concentrated, is assumed to be in the CBD, and the secondary sector, with the bad jobs, is located in the SEC (Secondary Employment Center). This captures the idea that in cities in general, manufacturing jobs (say large, assembly-line production plants) are located outside of the city, whereas better-paid jobs belonging to the service sector are in the city center. The allocation of workers is exogenous. We focus here only on the locations of all workers in the city.

Assumption 3.7. *All workers shop at the CBD, but some work at the CBD, and some at the SEC. The total commuting costs for CBD and SEC workers are respectively $T_1(x) = (\alpha_s + \alpha_1) tx$ and $T_2(x) = \alpha_s tx + \alpha_1 t|x - x_2|$. The total commuting cost for the unemployed is $T_0(x) = \alpha_s tx$.*

The utility functions for type-0 and type-1 workers are, as before, given by Assumption 3.2, whereas that for a type-2 worker is

$$u_2 = w_2 - \alpha_s tx - \alpha_1 t|x - x_2| - R(x) \tag{3.24}$$

depending on whether the worker resides to the right or to the left of the location of the SEC, x_2. His bid rent is therefore given by

$$\Psi_2(x, u_2) = w_2 - \alpha_s tx - \alpha_1 t|x - x_2| - u_2 \tag{3.25}$$

At equilibrium, the slope of the SEC worker's bid-rent function for all locations in the city is $(\alpha_1 - \alpha_s)t > 0$ for all $x < x_2$, and $-(\alpha_e + \alpha_s)t < 0$

---

[4] This section is based on Smith and Zenou (1997).

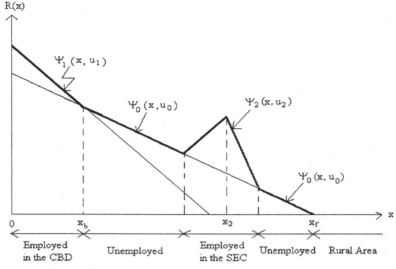

Figure 10.1. Urban equilibrium with a subcenter.

for all $x > x_2$. The SEC firm must decide where to settle in the city. Because the locations occupied by the SEC must form a connected interval containing x_2, and because type-1 workers are located in the vicinity of the CBD (i.e., $x_2 < L_1 + L_2/2$), three different locations for the SEC firm are possible, corresponding to three different urban configurations:[5]

- If $L_1 + L_2/2 \leq x_2 \leq \underline{x}_2$, the SEC firm will be located inside the city and can be considered as a subcenter (Figure 10.1). In this case, type-1 workers will reside in the vicinity of the CBD, whereas the unemployed will be located in between type-1 and type-2 workers and at the outskirts of the city.
- If $\underline{x}_2 \leq x_2 \leq \bar{x}_2$, the SEC firm will be located at the edge of the city (Figure 10.2). In this urban equilibrium, the unemployed will be located in between type-1 and type-2 workers.
- If $x_2 > \bar{x}_2$, the SEC firm will be located outside of the city in the suburbs (Figure 10.3). The unemployed will be all together, close to type-1 workers, whereas type-2 workers will be surrounded by agricultural land.

It is easily verified that

$$\underline{x}_2 = N - \frac{L_2}{2} \quad \text{and} \quad \bar{x}_2 = N - \left(\frac{\alpha_1 - \alpha_s}{2}\right) L_2 \tag{3.26}$$

[5] We exclude a fourth configuration in which the SEC firm will bid away workers of type 1 and

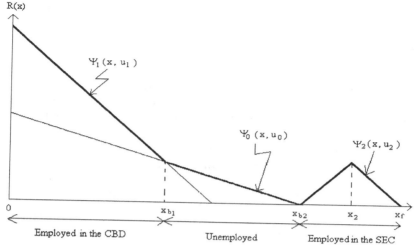

Figure 10.2. Urban equilibrium C with an edge city.

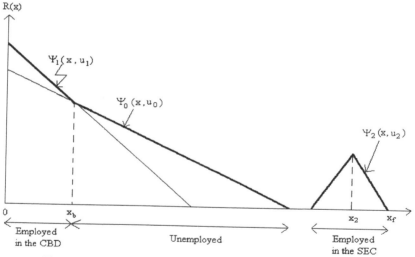

Figure 10.3. Urban equilibrium with a suburb.

Assumption 3.8. *The SEC firm pays a land price, but does not consume space. Moreover, it has (low) interaction costs with CBD firms that vary with x.*

It can be shown (Smith and Zenou, 1997) that the optimal location for the SEC

locate in the vicinity of the CBD.

(i.e., the one that will maximize its profit) is at the edge of the city (Figure 10.2); that is,

$$x_2^* = \bar{x}_2 = N - \left(\frac{\alpha_1 - \alpha_s}{2}\right) L_2 \tag{3.27}$$

This result is due to the fact that the SEC firm wants to be as far as possible from the CBD, in order to pay a low land price. That constitutes a repulsion force between the SEC firm and the CBD. However, the SEC firm is assumed to interact with the CBD firms (face-to-face communications, city-center services), and that constitutes an attraction force between the SEC firm and the CBD. The equilibrium location is the one that will balance the two forces, and the SEC firm optimally will locate at the edge of the city if the interaction force is not too large, $0 < \varepsilon < \alpha_s t$ (where ε is the interaction cost per unit of distance).

Definition 3.3. *In a nonmonocentric linear city, the urban equilibrium C (Figure 10.2), in which the CBD-employed workers reside in the vicinity of the CBD, the SEC-employed workers live around the SEC at the outskirts of the city, and the unemployed are located in between the two employed groups, is a vector* $(u_0, u_1, u_2, x_{b_1}, x_{b_2}, x_f)$ *such that*

$$\Psi_1\left(x_{b_1}, u_1\right) = \Psi_0\left(x_{b_1}, u_0\right) \tag{3.28}$$

$$\Psi_2\left(x_{b_2}, u_2\right) = \Psi_0\left(x_{b_2}, u_0\right) \tag{3.29}$$

$$\Psi_2(x_f, u_2) = 0 \tag{3.30}$$

$$x_{b_1} = L_1 \tag{3.31}$$

$$x_{b_2} - x_{b_1} = U \tag{3.32}$$

$$x_f - x_{b_2} = L_2 \tag{3.33}$$

where $L_1 + L_2 = L$.

By solving these equations, we obtain

$$u_0^* = w_0 - \alpha_s t (N - L_2) \tag{3.34}$$

$$u_1^* = w_1 - \alpha_s t (N - L_2) - t L_1 \tag{3.35}$$

$$u_2^* = w_2 - \alpha_s t (N - L_2) - \left(\frac{\alpha_s + \alpha_1}{2}\right) t L_2 \tag{3.36}$$

Proposition 3.3. *Under Assumptions 3.2, 3.6, 3.7, and 3.8, there is a polycentric city with a CBD and an SEC located at the edge of the city. In this urban configuration, the employed will locate in the vicinity of the CBD as well as at the outskirts of the city. The unemployed will reside in between the two groups of employed workers.*

The locations for all workers in the city can be explained primarily by the optimal location for the SEC in the city. If, for example, there were no interaction costs, the SEC would locate in the suburbs, and we would have a different urban configuration, in which the SEC would be surrounded by agricultural land. In that case, the urban equilibrium would not be unique. A greater change would be seen if the interaction costs were very large, $\varepsilon > \alpha_s t$. In that case (i.e., the SEC would be considered as a subcenter), the unemployed would be spread out in the city, surrounding the SEC. In other words, the existence of local labor markets is contingent on the location of the SEC. If the SEC locates in the suburbs, there will be two separated local labor markets, one in the CBD, and one in the SEC, that will not interact with each other. If the SEC sets up inside the city (edge city or subcenter), there still will be two local labor markets, but they will be highly connected.

3.2 A Dynamic Approach with Job Search[6]

Thus far, we have assumed that workers do not search for jobs: There is a random drawing for jobs that affords all unemployed workers in the city equal chances. It is a strong assumption, and we relax it in this section. Instead, we assume that the probability of obtaining a job depends on a worker's search intensity, which in turn is affected by the worker's location. This captures the fact that workers, and especially low-skill workers, rely heavily on informal channels and networks to get jobs. Using data from the youth cohort in a national longitudinal survey in the United States, Holzer (1989) found that among the 16–23-year-old workers who reported job acceptance, 66% used informal search channels, 11% used state agencies, and 10% used newspaper advertisements. Such reliance on these informal methods of job search suggests that information on the available job opportunities may decay rapidly with distance from one's place of residence (Ihlanfeldt and Sjöquist, 1990; Zax and Kain, 1996; Ihlanfeldt, 1997; Rogers, 1997). Therefore, we assume throughout this section that the distance between residence and workplace has a negative influence on a worker's search effectiveness and thus the probability of finding a job. The farther away workers live from the CBD, the poorer their information on job opportunities, and thus the lower the probability of getting a job.

In order to model the job-search process, we consider a dynamic model, in the sense that agents (workers and firms) take into account all the possible events in their lifetimes when they make decisions. Throughout this section, in order to have neat and intuitive results, we shall focus on a monocentric city with two types of workers: the unemployed (group 0) and the employed (group 1). In this section, Assumptions 3.1 and 3.2 remain valid.

---

[6] This section is based on Wasmer and Zenou (1999).

3.2.1. A First Model with Exogenous Search Intensity. We assume that each worker lives indefinitely and that his employment status at various times can be either employed or unemployed. The changes in employment status are governed by a Poisson process, so that the intertemporal utility functions for the employed, I_1, and the unemployed, I_0, are respectively equal to[7]

$$r I_1 = w_1 - T_1(x) - R(x) + \delta \left[\left(\max_{x'} I_0(x') \right) - I_1(x) \right] \qquad (3.37)$$

$$r I_0 = w_0 - T_0(x) - R(x) + a \left[\left(\max_{x'} I_1(x') \right) - I_0(x) \right] \qquad (3.38)$$

where a is the probability per unit of time of acquiring a job while in the unemployment pool (i.e., the job-acquisition rate), δ is the probability per unit of time that a worker will be separated from his job, and r is the discount rate. Let us interpret (3.37). When a worker is employed today, he resides in x, and his net income is $w_1 - T_1(x) - R(x)$. Then there is a probability δ that he will lose his job, after which he will optimally relocate at x' and suffer a reduction in his income of $I_0(x') - I_1(x)$. We assume that when a worker changes his employment status he automatically changes his residence and that the relocation cost is zero. The interpretation of (3.38) is similar. In equilibrium, all workers of the same type will enjoy the same level of utility (i.e., $r I_0 = r \bar{I}_0$ and $r I_1 = r \bar{I}_1$), both of which are determined by the urban equilibrium.

Assumption 3.9. *The unemployed workers go to the CBD to shop and for job interviews, whereas the employed go to the CBD to work and to shop. At a distance x from the CBD, the total commuting cost for the former is $T_0(x) = (\alpha_s + \alpha_0)tx$ ($\alpha_0 t > 0$ is the fraction of the commuting cost devoted to interviews), whereas for the latter it is $T_1(x) = (\alpha_s + \alpha_1)tx$.*

Assumption 3.10a. *The probability of obtaining a job is a decreasing function of the distance to the CBD [i.e., $a'(x) < 0$].*

As discussed earlier, Assumption 3.10a introduces a negative correlation between the job-acquisition rate and the unemployed workers' locations. This captures the fact that space is an obstacle in the search for job opportunities. By using Assumptions 3.9 and 3.10a, (3.37) and (3.38), we can write bid rents as follows:

$$\Psi_1(x, \bar{I}_1, \bar{I}_0) = w_1 - (\alpha_s + \alpha_1)\, tx + \delta(\bar{I}_0 - \bar{I}_1) - r \bar{I}_1 \qquad (3.39)$$

$$\Psi_0(x, \bar{I}_1, \bar{I}_0) = w_0 - (\alpha_s + \alpha_1)\, tx + a(x)(\bar{I}_1 - \bar{I}_0) - r \bar{I}_0 \qquad (3.40)$$

It is interesting to observe that bid rents depend on intertemporal utilities for the employed as well as the unemployed. When each worker sets his bid

---

[7] Equations (3.37) and (3.38) are easily derived from the correspondent Bellman equations provided that the transversality conditions are met.

rent, he maximizes his intertemporal utility and thus takes into account all the possible changes in his employment status. In the previous static cases with no job search, each type of worker took into account only his current utility when bidding for land rents. The slopes of the bid-rent curves are

$$\frac{\partial \Psi_1(x, \bar{I}_1, \bar{I}_0)}{\partial x} = -(\alpha_s + \alpha_1)t < 0 \tag{3.41}$$

$$\frac{\partial \Psi_0(x, \bar{I}_1, \bar{I}_0)}{\partial x} = -(\alpha_s + \alpha_0)t + a'(x)(\bar{I}_1 - \bar{I}_0) < 0 \tag{3.42}$$

According to (3.41) and (3.42), the equilibrium urban configuration depends on the following trade-off: On the one hand, unemployed workers want to be close to the CBD, because they can save on (marginal) transportation costs and because the closer they are to the CBD, the greater will be the probability of finding a job. On the other hand, employed workers also want to reside in the vicinity of the CBD because they want to save on commuting costs. The equilibrium urban configuration will depend on the relative magnitudes of these two slopes.

Assumption 3.10b. *The probability of finding a job is a linear function of distance:*

$$a(x) = b - dx \tag{3.43}$$

This assumption means that the job search involves fixed costs, b, such as buying newspapers, postage for application forms, and other miscellaneous *variable* costs. The slope of the unemployed worker's bid-rent curve can be rewritten as

$$\frac{\partial \Psi_0(x, \bar{I}_1, \bar{I}_0)}{\partial x} = -(\alpha_s + \alpha_0)t - d(\bar{I}_1 - \bar{I}_0) < 0 \tag{3.44}$$

There are two possible urban equilibria, as described by Definitions 3.1 and 3.2 (referred to as urban equilibria A and B). In the first one, in which the unemployed reside at the outskirts of the city, we obtain the following equilibrium values by using Definition 3.1 and (3.39) and (3.40):

$$\bar{I}_1 - \bar{I}_0 = \frac{w_1 - w_0 - (\alpha_1 - \alpha_0)tL}{r + \delta + a(L)} \tag{3.45}$$

In urban equilibrium B, where the unemployed reside in the vicinity of the CBD, we obtain the following equilibrium values by using Definition 3.2 and (3.39) and (3.40):

$$\bar{I}_1 - \bar{I}_0 = \frac{w_1 - w_0 - (\alpha_1 - \alpha_0)tU}{r + \delta + a(U)} \tag{3.46}$$

Proposition 3.4. *Under Assumptions 3.1, 3.2, 3.9, and 3.10b, the unemployed workers will reside at the outskirts of the city (urban equilibrium A) if*

$$w_1 - w_0 < \left(\frac{1+b}{d}\right)(\alpha_1 - \alpha_0)t \tag{3.47}$$

whereas they will locate in the vicinity of the CBD (urban equilibrium B) if

$$w_1 - w_0 > \left(\frac{1+b}{d}\right)(\alpha_1 - \alpha_0)t \tag{3.48}$$

This proposition is quite intuitive. If the difference in commuting costs for the employed and the unemployed is greater than the marginal gain in utility from getting a job, then the unemployed will reside at the outskirts of the city. In the reverse case, the unemployed will reside in the vicinity of the CBD. Thus, contrary to the previous cases, there is not just one possible urban equilibrium, but two possible equilibria, and the "selection" of equilibria will depend crucially on the labor-market equilibrium through the wage determination. This will be investigated in Section 4.4.

3.2.2. A Direct Extension of the Exogenous-Search-Intensity Approach. With the same type of framework, we can explain more complicated urban configurations. In particular, the two following definitions propose other urban equilibria.

Definition 3.4. *In a monocentric city, the urban equilibrium D (Figure 10.4), in which the unemployed reside both in the vicinity of the CBD and at the outskirts of the city, with the employed located in between the two groups of the unemployed, is a vector $(\bar{I}_1, \bar{I}_0, x_{b_1}, x_{b_2}, x_f)$ such that*

$$\Psi_1\left(x_{b_1}, \bar{I}_1, \bar{I}_0\right) = \Psi_0\left(x_{b_1}, \bar{I}_1, \bar{I}_0\right) \tag{3.49}$$

$$\Psi_1\left(x_{b_2}, \bar{I}_1, \bar{I}_0\right) = \Psi_0\left(x_{b_2}, \bar{I}_1, \bar{I}_0\right) \tag{3.50}$$

$$\Psi_1(x_f, \bar{I}_1, \bar{I}_0) = 0 \tag{3.51}$$

$$x_{b_1} = U_1 \tag{3.52}$$

$$x_{b_2} - x_{b_1} = L \tag{3.53}$$

$$x_f - x_{b_2} = U_2 \tag{3.54}$$

where $U_1 + U_2 = U$.

Definition 3.5. *In a monocentric city, the urban equilibrium E (Figure 10.5), in which the employed reside both in the vicinity of the CBD and at the outskirts of the city, with the unemployed located in between the two groups of the employed, is a vector $(\bar{I}_1, \bar{I}_0, x_{b_1}, x_{b_2}, x_f)$ such that*

$$\Psi_1\left(x_{b_1}, \bar{I}_1, \bar{I}_0\right) = \Psi_0\left(x_{b_1}, \bar{I}_1, \bar{I}_0\right) \tag{3.55}$$

$$\Psi_1\left(x_{b_2}, \bar{I}_1, \bar{I}_0\right) = \Psi_0\left(x_{b_2}, \bar{I}_1, \bar{I}_0\right) \tag{3.56}$$

$$\Psi_1(x_f, \bar{I}_1, \bar{I}_0) = 0 \tag{3.57}$$

$$x_{b_1} = L_1 \tag{3.58}$$

$$x_{b_2} - x_{b_1} = U \tag{3.59}$$

$$x_f - x_{b_2} = L_2 \tag{3.60}$$

where $L_1 + L_2 = L$.

We again use the job-search model of the previous section, but we relax Assumptions 3.10a and 3.10b. Instead, we have the following.

Assumption 3.11a. *The probability of obtaining a job* (a) *is a decreasing and convex function of the distance to the CBD* [*i.e.,* $a'(x) < 0$ *and* $a''(x) > 0$].

Contrary to Assumption 3.10a or 3.10b, this assumption means that for residential locations close to the CBD, the variation of a is quite important, whereas it is less so for locations farther away. In this case, the slopes of the bid-rent curves are as before, but

$$\frac{\partial \Psi_1^2(x, \bar{I}_1, \bar{I}_0)}{\partial x^2} = 0 \tag{3.61}$$

$$\frac{\partial \Psi_0^2(x, \bar{I}_1, \bar{I}_0)}{\partial x^2} = a''(x)(\bar{I}_1 - \bar{I}_0) > 0 \tag{3.62}$$

In this context, three different urban configurations can emerge. As before, urban equilibria A and B can occur, depending on the slope of $\Psi_1(\cdot)$ (which is a line) relative to the slope of $\Psi_0(\cdot)$, but there can also be an urban equilibrium D, as defined earlier.

Proposition 3.5. *Under Assumptions 3.1, 3.2, 3.9, and 3.11a, we can have the following equilibrium urban configurations:*

- *If* $\Psi_1(0) < \Psi_0(0)$ *and if* $\Psi_0(x_f) < \Psi_1(x_f) \equiv 0$, *then the unemployed will reside in the vicinity of the CBD, and the employed at the periphery of the city (urban equilibrium B).*
- *If* $\Psi_0(0) < \Psi_1(0)$ *and if* $\Psi_1(x_f) < \Psi_0(x_f) \equiv 0$, *then the unemployed will locate at the outskirts of the city, and the employed close to the CBD (urban equilibrium A).*
- *If* $\underline{\Delta} < \Psi_1(0) < \Psi_0(0)$ *and if* $\Psi_1(x_f) < \Psi_0(x_f) \equiv 0$,[8] *where* $\underline{\Delta}$ *is the intercept of the line that is parallel to* $\Psi_1(\cdot)$ *and tangent to* $\Psi_0(\cdot)$, *then the unemployed will reside both in the vicinity of the CBD and at the outskirts of the city, with the employed located in between the two groups of the unemployed (urban equilibrium D, Figure 10.4).*

---

[8] One might have imposed $\Psi_u(\cdot)$ to satisfy the Inada conditions, i.e., $\lim_{x \to 0} \partial \Psi_u / \partial x = +\infty$ and $\lim_{x \to +\infty} \partial \Psi_u / \partial x = 0$; but because we want $\Psi_u(x_f) = 0$, that is not possible.

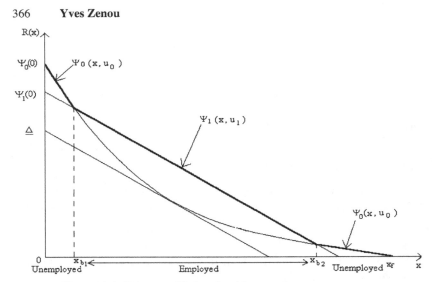

Figure 10.4. Urban equilibrium D with unemployment.

Let us study other types of equilibria by changing Assumption 3.11a.

Assumption 3.11b. *The probability of obtaining a job (a) is a decreasing and concave function of the distance to the CBD [i.e., $a'(x) < 0$ and $a''(x) < 0$].*

With this assumption, workers who locate far away from the CBD are much more penalized than under the other assumptions about $a(x)$. This assumption implies that the unemployed worker's bid-rent curve is decreasing and concave.

Proposition 3.6. *Under Assumptions 3.1, 3.2, 3.9, and 3.11b we can have the following equilibrium urban configurations:*

- *If $\Psi_1(0) < \Psi_0(0)$ and if $\Psi_0(x_f) < \Psi_1(x_f) \equiv 0$, then the unemployed will reside in the vicinity of the CBD, and the employed at the periphery of the city (urban equilibrium B).*
- *If $\Psi_0(0) < \Psi_1(0)$ and if $\Psi_1(x_f) < \Psi_0(x_f) \equiv 0$, then the unemployed will locate at the outskirts of the city, and the employed close to the CBD (urban equilibrium A).*
- *If $\Psi_0(0) < \Psi_1(0) < \bar{\Delta}$ and if $\Psi_0(x_f) < \Psi_1(x_f) \equiv 0$, where $\bar{\Delta}$ is the intercept of the line that is parallel to $\Psi_1(\cdot)$ and tangent to $\Psi_0(\cdot)$, then the employed will reside both in the vicinity of the CBD and at the outskirts of the city, with the unemployed located in between the two groups of the employed (urban equilibrium E, Figure 10.5).*

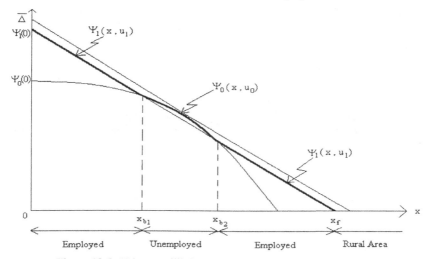

Figure 10.5. Urban equilibrium E with unemployment.

So in the context of an exogenous-search-intensity framework we can always obtain urban equilibria A and B under sufficient conditions. However, the possibility of a third equilibrium will depend on the assumptions regarding the shape of $a(x)$. If workers who locate far away from the CBD are greatly penalized [when $a(x)$ is convex], then the third equilibrium will be the one with the unemployed locating in the middle of the city in between the two groups of employed workers. This can easily be understood: No unemployed worker will want to live very far away from the CBD, because that would greatly diminish his chances of getting a job. If location far away from the CBD is not penalized [when $a(x)$ is concave], then the third equilibrium will be such that the unemployed will reside both close to and far away from the CBD.

3.2.3. An Endogenous-Search-Intensity Model. Thus far, we have seen that the assumptions about $a(x)$ are crucial for the analysis of urban equilibrium configurations. In this section, we make no assumptions about the relationship between a and x, but rather derive it endogenously. In search theory, efficiency is seen primarily as a function of the effort of workers, rather than as a function of the locations of workers. We can modify the model in this direction to get slightly more complicated results, which nevertheless are easy to understand, given that the intuitions of the model are exactly the same.

Assumption 3.12. *The search portion of the commuting cost is an increasing and convex (or linear) function of the effort level e devoted to job search [i.e., $\alpha'_0(e) > 0$ and $\alpha''_0(e) \geq 0$].*

Assumption 3.13. *The probability of finding a job is an increasing and concave (or linear) function of the effort level devoted to job search [i.e., $a'(e) > 0$ and $a''(e) \leq 0$].*

In other words, the more time a worker spends on job search, the larger his search cost, but the greater the probability of getting a job. However, at the margin, the commuting cost increases, but the probability of finding a job decreases (decreasing returns to scale). The unemployed worker located at a distance x from the CBD chooses e^* that will maximize his intertemporal utility (3.38). The first-order condition yields

$$a'(e^*)(\bar{I}_1 - \bar{I}_0) = \alpha'_0(e^*) \, tx \tag{3.63}$$

The interpretation is straightforward. The left-hand side (LHS) of (3.63) is the marginal probability generated by one more interview times the surplus of a worker when he leaves unemployment, and the RHS of (3.63) is the marginal commuting cost of searching for a job. Of course, they are the same when $e = e^*$. By totally differentiating (3.63), we obtain

$$\frac{\partial e^*}{\partial x} = \frac{\alpha'_0(e^*)t}{a''(e^*)(\bar{I}_1 - \bar{I}_0) - \alpha''_0(e^*) \, tx} < 0$$

and thus

$$\frac{\partial a}{\partial x} = \frac{\partial a}{\partial e} \frac{\partial e}{\partial x} < 0 \tag{3.64}$$

The bid-rent curve for the employed worker and its slope are still the same and are given by

$$\Psi_1(x, \bar{I}_1, \bar{I}_0) = w - (\alpha_s + \alpha_1) \, tx + \delta(\bar{I}_0 - \bar{I}_1) - \bar{I}_1$$

$$\frac{\partial \Psi_1(x, u_0, u_1)}{\partial x} = -(\alpha_s + \alpha_1)t < 0 \tag{3.65}$$

and the bid-rent curve for the unemployed worker is now

$$\Psi_0(x, \bar{I}_1, \bar{I}_0) = b - \{\alpha_s + \alpha_0[e^*(x)]\} \, tx + a[e^*(x)](\bar{I}_1 - \bar{I}_0) - \bar{I}_0 \tag{3.66}$$

and by the envelope theorem, the slope of the unemployed worker's bid-rent curve is

$$\frac{\partial \Psi_0(x, \bar{I}_1, \bar{I}_0)}{\partial x} = -\{\alpha_s + \alpha_0[e^*(x)]\}t < 0 \tag{3.67}$$

$$\frac{\partial^2 \Psi_0(x, \bar{I}_1, \bar{I}_0)}{\partial x^2} = -\left(\frac{\partial \alpha_0}{\partial e^*} \frac{\partial e^*}{\partial x} \right) t > 0 \tag{3.68}$$

It follows that the unemployed worker's bid-rent curve is decreasing and convex with the distance to the CBD. As in the previous section, different configurations can emerge. However, only Proposition 3.5 is valid.

4 What Are the Causes of Urban Unemployment?

We now focus on the labor-market equilibrium. In order to simplify the exposition, we consider only linear bid rents for both unemployed and employed workers, such that only two equilibrium urban configurations can emerge: The unemployed either reside in the vicinity of the CBD or reside at the outskirts of the city. For that, throughout this section we shall use different assumptions for the commuting cost and for the probability of getting a job.

4.1 Urban Unemployment Due to Efficiency Wage[9]

We assume that the representative firm cannot perfectly monitor (c is assumed to be the monitoring cost) its workers because there is some moral hazard regarding their effort levels. When the firm hires a worker, it does not know his behavior: He can either shirk ($\phi = 0$, where ϕ is the level of effort) and contribute to zero production or not shirk ($\phi > 0$) and contribute to a ϕ level of output. Let us denote the efficiency wage by w_e. The instantaneous utility functions for a non-shirker (NS) and a shirker (S) are written respectively

$$u_1^{NS} = w_e - \phi - (\alpha_s + \alpha_1)tx - R(x) \tag{4.1}$$

$$u_1^{S} = w_e - (\alpha_s + \alpha_1)tx - R(x) \tag{4.2}$$

For the unemployed, the utility function is still given by

$$u_0 = b - \alpha_s tx - R(x) \tag{4.3}$$

In this section, urban equilibrium A prevails; that is, the employed reside close to the CBD, and the unemployed live at the outskirts of the city. In this context, the equilibrium utility levels are

$$u_1^{NS*} = w_e - \phi - \alpha_s tN - \alpha_1 tL \tag{4.4}$$

$$u_0^* = w_0 - \alpha_s tN \tag{4.5}$$

Observe that at equilibrium, nobody will shirk, because all workers will be paid the efficiency wage. That is why we have just the (non-shirker) employed

---

[9] This section is based on Zenou and Smith (1995).

and the unemployed. We can, however, define (out of equilibrium) the utility of a shirker as

$$u_1^{S*} = w_e - \alpha_s t N - \alpha_1 t L \tag{4.6}$$

Let us now calculate the efficiency wage. In order to avoid the moral-hazard problem, the firm will set a contract such that the worker will never shirk. Because the firm controls a fraction of workers, it must set a contract such that the intertemporal utility for a non-shirker will be greater than or equal to the intertemporal utility for a shirker. Assuming that changes in employment status are governed by a time-homogeneous Markov process with two states, 0 and 1, these intertemporal utilities are

$$I_1^{NS} = \int_0^\infty \left[P_t^{NS}(1, 1) u_1^{NS*} + P_t^{NS}(1, 0) u_0^* \right] \exp(-rt) \, dt \tag{4.7}$$

$$I_1^S = \int_0^\infty \left[P_t^S(1, 1) u_1^{S*} + P_t^S(1, 0) u_0^* \right] \exp(-rt) \, dt \tag{4.8}$$

where $P_t^{NS}(i, j)$ and $P_t^S(i, j)$ are the transition probabilities from state i to state $j (i = 0, 1, j = 0, 1)$ for the non-shirkers and the shirkers, respectively. The firm must therefore set an efficiency wage such that

$$I_1^{NS} \geq I_1^S \tag{4.9}$$

which is the non-shirking condition (NSC). This condition is equivalent to

$$w_e \geq w_0 + \phi + \frac{\phi}{c}(a + \delta + r) + \alpha_1 t L \tag{4.10}$$

At equilibrium there is no reason to pay a higher wage, and the efficiency wage is

$$w_e = w_0 + \phi + \alpha_1 t L + \frac{\phi}{c}(a + \delta + r) \tag{4.11}$$

The labor-market equilibrium is now described. Each firm solves the following problem:

$$\max_L \Pi = [pF(L) - wL] \quad \text{s.t} \quad w \geq w_e \tag{4.12}$$

The solution of (4.12) is unique if $F'(0) > 1/p(b + \phi/q)$. It is equal to

$$w_e = F'(L)$$

which is the labor demand.

We can now close the model by the following condition on flows:

$$a(N - L) = \delta L \tag{4.13}$$

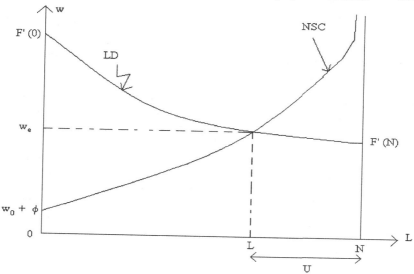

Figure 10.6. Labor-market equilibrium under urban efficiency wage.

stating that in the steady state the flow into the unemployment pool will be equal to the flow out. The efficiency wage can be rewritten as

$$w_e = \{w_0 + \phi\} + \{\alpha_1 t L\} + \left\{ \frac{\phi}{c} \left(\frac{\delta N}{N - L} + r \right) \right\} \qquad (4.14)$$

The interpretation of (4.14) is quite intuitive. Three terms compose this efficiency wage, each of them being in curly brackets. The first one, $w_0 + \phi$, is the *base wage level*, namely, the wage level required in order to induce any worker to leave welfare and expend effort in working. The second one, $\alpha_1 t L$, is the *space cost differential* between employment and unemployment (i.e., the monetary compensation to workers to induce them to leave welfare and work in the presence of these spatial costs). The last term is the *wage surplus* that must be paid to induce effort in the presence of imperfect monitoring by firms. When unemployment is zero, $L = N$, this wage surplus goes to infinity, meaning that unemployment is not compatible with efficiency wages.

The labor equilibrium can now be described (Figure 10.6). The NSC curve plays the role of a supply curve, and because it never cuts the (inelastic) supply curve, there will always be unemployment at an equilibrium. This means that when $L = N$, $a = +\infty$, so any shirking worker would immediately be rehired. Knowing this, workers will choose to shirk. In other words, the efficiency wage is not compatible with full employment: Unemployment serves as a "worker discipline device." The unemployment is involuntary, because the unemployed workers are ready to work for a lower wage in order to get jobs, but firms will never accept that offer because the NSC will not be respected and all workers will shirk. Therefore, it is the presence of high and sticky wages that create (involuntary) unemployment.

Proposition 4.1. *Urban unemployment is due to the fact that the efficiency wage is too high and is downward by rigid. In a spatial context, the efficiency wage has two roles: to deter shirking and to compensate workers for spatial costs.*

Observe that in this model there are some interactions between the labor market and the land market. On one hand, the efficiency-wage policy of urban firms depends on urban costs, such as commuting costs [see (4.11)]. Indeed, if, for example, t or α increases, then the efficiency wage must rise because of its "compensation" component. On the other hand, workers' bid rents will depend strongly on the labor-market equilibrium. If, for instance, L decreases, then the efficiency wage will be lower (the opportunity cost of losing a job is greater), and the capacity to pay for land will decrease. As a consequence, the new urban equilibrium implies a smaller city size.

4.2 Urban Unemployment Due to Demand Shock

In this section, we shall focus on a Keynesian type of unemployment, where the main cause of unemployment is a demand shock that negatively affects the output and thus the profit of firms (i.e., the revenue of the firm is random). For that, we assume that prices are volatile, so that the profit function is

$$\tilde{\Pi} = \tilde{p} f(l) - wl \tag{4.15}$$

where $\tilde{p}$, the price of the output, is described by a random variable whose mean is chosen to be 1, without loss of generality, and its variance is σ^2. For analytical simplicity, we assume that risk-averse firms have a mean-variance utility function given by

$$P = E(\tilde{\Pi}) - \frac{\varphi}{2} \operatorname{Var}(\tilde{\Pi}) \tag{4.16}$$

where $\operatorname{Var}(\cdot)$ is the variance, where φ is a measure of firms' risk aversion (the higher is φ, the greater is the degree of risk aversion), and where $\tilde{\Pi}$ is defined by (4.15). Observe that when firms are risk-neutral (i.e., $\varphi = 0$) there is no uncertainty, because $E(\tilde{\Pi}) = \Pi = f(l) - wl$ (in this case, the price of the output is taken as the numéraire). We can therefore rewrite (4.16) as

$$P = f(l) - wl - \frac{\varphi}{2}\sigma^2 [f(l)]^2$$

The firm chooses l that will maximize P. The first-order conditions are

$$f'(l) - w - \varphi\sigma^2 f(l) f'(l) = 0 \tag{4.17}$$

As we saw in Section 2, $F'(L) = f'(l)$. It follows that at equilibrium the profit-maximization condition (4.17) has the equivalent aggregate form:

$$w = F'(L)[1 - \varphi\sigma^2 F(L)] \tag{4.18}$$

This equation states that the wage is equal to the marginal productivity of labor (which includes the price volatility of the output). Equation (4.18) defines the labor demand (L) curve. By using the properties of $F(\cdot)$, it is easy to show that

$$\frac{\partial L}{\partial w} < 0, \qquad \frac{\partial L}{\partial \sigma^2} < 0, \qquad \frac{\partial L}{\partial \varphi} < 0 \tag{4.19}$$

The equilibrium level of employment, L^*, is the value of the labor demand corresponding to the wage, w^*. It is defined by

$$w^* = F'(L^*)[1 - \varphi\sigma^2 F(L^*)] \tag{4.20}$$

This equilibrium (w^*, L^*) is depicted in Figure 10.7, where N is the exogenous labor force ($N = L + U$, where U is the level of unemployment in the economy). Observe that if there is no uncertainty ($\varphi = 0$), firms will demand more labor, and the level of employment will be higher: $L_c^* > L^*$, where L_c^* is the

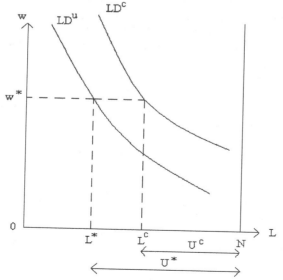

Figure 10.7. Labor-market equilibrium under demand shock.

equilibrium employment when there is no uncertainty on price [it is defined by equation (4.18), with $\varphi = 0$]. Thus, when prices become volatile, firms will transfer their risk onto the labor demand. This leads to an unemployment level U^* that can be interpreted as Keynesian unemployment. Observe also that according to (4.19), the larger is σ^2 or φ, the larger is the unemployment level U^*.

We can summarize our results by the following proposition.

Proposition 4.2. *Urban unemployment is due solely to the fact that prices are volatile. The larger the price volatility and/or the greater the degree of firms' risk aversion, the higher the level of unemployment in the economy.*

Here again there are some interactions between land and labor markets. In particular, it can be shown that the characteristics of the labor market (such as σ^2 or φ) affect urban equilibrium utilities, bid rents, city size, and x_b, the border between the employed and the unemployed. For example, when product demand becomes very volatile, then x_b increases.

4.3 Urban Unemployment Due to Both Efficiency Wage and Demand Shocks: A Dual Labor-Market Approach[10]

We have seen two types of urban unemployment. The first is due to demand shock, and the second to the efficiency-wage manpower strategy of firms. It seems natural to think that the latter is not responsible for a large part of the global urban unemployment, whereas the former certainly bears more responsibility. We shall now propose a model that illustrates this idea. There are three periods. In the first period, we have exactly the model of Section 4.1, where urban equilibrium A prevails. There is an SEC firm that wants to enter into the city. It proposes menial jobs, so that no monitoring is required, and thus no efficiency wage. It can hire only the unemployed workers, because the type-1 workers are better off working in the CBD firms. This SEC firm will pay the minimum wage $\bar{w}_2 < w_e$ imposed by the government, because it has no interest in paying a higher wage.

In the first period, the SEC firm cannot enter the city because the level of unemployment due only to the efficiency wage is too low: There are not enough unemployed workers to meet its needs, and if it should enter, its profit would be negative. In the second period, there is a demand shock (such as the one in Section 4.2), so that the price of demand becomes uncertain, and CBD firms hire fewer workers. Now the level of unemployment is high, and because of that, the SEC firm can now enter. So in the third period in enters. Where does

---

[10] This section is based on Smith and Zenou (1999).

it locate? We have answered this question in Section 3.1.3, and we have shown that it will locate exactly at the edge of the city [i.e., $\bar{x}_2 = N - (\alpha_1 - \alpha_s)L_2/2$]. When it enters, it hires exactly $\bar{L}_2$ workers, which corresponds to

$$\bar{w}_2 = F'\bar{L}_2$$

However, its entry reduces the global level of urban unemployment, and CBD firms must increase their efficiency wage in order to meet the NSC. What is the new efficiency wage? We know already the equilibrium utilities for all workers in the city [see (4.4), (4.5), and (4.6) in Section 4.1]. The intertemporal utilities for a non-shirker and a shirker are

$$I_1^{NS} = \int_0^{+\infty} \left[P_t^{NS}(1, 1)u_0^* + P_t^{NS}(1, 1)u_1^{NS*} + P_t^{NS}(1, 2)u_2^* \right] \exp(-rt)\, dt$$

$$(4.21)$$

$$I_1^S = \int_0^{+\infty} \left[P_t^S(1, 1)u_0^* + P_t^S(1, 1)u_1^{S*} + P_t^S(1, 2)u_2^* \right] \exp(-rt)\, dt \qquad (4.22)$$

Once again, the efficiency wage is such that $I_1^{NS} \geq I_1^S$. By solving this inequality, we obtain the following efficiency wage:

$$w_e = \{\Theta w_0 + (1 - \Theta)[\bar{w}_2 - (\alpha_s + \alpha_1)tL_2/2] + \phi\}$$

$$+ \{tL_1\} + \left\{ \frac{\phi}{c}(a + \delta + r) \right\} \qquad (4.23)$$

with

$$\Theta = \frac{a + \delta + r}{a + \mu + \delta + r} < 1$$

where μ is the secondary-sector job-acquisition rate. There are now two steady-state conditions on flows:

$$a(N - L_1) = \delta L_1 \qquad (4.24)$$

$$\mu(N - L_1 - L_2) = \delta \frac{L_2 N}{N - L_1} \qquad (4.25)$$

Using (4.24) and (4.25), the efficiency wage can be rewritten

$$w_e = \{\Theta w_0 + (1 - \Theta)[\bar{w}_2 - (\alpha_s + \alpha_1)tL_2/2] + \phi\}$$

$$+ \{tL_1\} + \left\{ \frac{\phi}{c}\left(\frac{\delta N}{N - L_1} + r \right) \right\} \qquad (4.26)$$

where Θ is equal now to

$$\Theta = \frac{[r(N - L_1) + \delta N](N - L_1 - L_2)}{\delta N L_2 + [r(N - L_1) + \delta N](N - L_1 - L_2)}$$

and we have a new value for the efficiency wage. As in the one-sector efficiency-wage model, the efficiency wage (4.26) is composed of three parts. The first term in curly bracket on the RHS of (4.26) is the *effort cost*. It is composed of the *composite opportunity wage*, $\Theta w_0 + (1 - \Theta)[\bar{w}_2 - (\alpha_s + \alpha_1)t L_2/2]$, which is a convex combination of the unemployment benefit w_0, the net wage in sector 2, $\bar{w}_2 - (\alpha_s + \alpha_1)t L_2/2$, and the effort required in sector 1. This composite opportunity wage is in fact an expected discounted wage for CBD workers (i.e., the expected wage that they can earn if they lose their CBD jobs). The second term in curly bracket on the RHS of (4.26) corresponds to the *space cost differential* between sector 1 and the unemployment sector (i.e., the monetary compensation to induce individuals to leave welfare in the presence of these spatial costs). Last, the third term in curly bracket on the RHS of (4.26) is the *wage surplus* for sector 1, which represents the portion of wages directly attributable to the prevention of shirking behavior. It is easily checked that when $L_2 = 0$, this efficiency wage (4.26) becomes equal to the one-sector efficiency wage (4.11). Thus, it is a generalization of (4.11), and it is readily verified that the efficiency wage (4.26) is greater than (4.11), because $\Theta w_0 + (1 - \Theta)[\bar{w}_2 - (\alpha_s + \alpha_1)t L_2/2] > w_0$.

Proposition 4.3. *Urban unemployment occurs because wages are too high (in both the primary and secondary sectors) and the product price is too low.*

In this model, primary CBD firms set efficiency wages in order to deter shirking and to compensate their workers for urban costs. By doing so, they take into account the different opportunities for their workers when they become unemployed: The laid-off workers can either join the unemployment pool or find jobs with SEC firms. Consequently, land-market characteristics (such as t, α_s, α_1) affect the labor-market equilibrium through the efficiency-wage policy. On the other hand, the labor market also affects the urban equilibrium through ϕ, w_0, $\bar{w}_2$, c, and so forth. However, the more important effect here is through the demand shock. Indeed, if the demand shock is small, then the SEC firm will not enter, and we go back to the model of Section 4.1 with urban equilibrium A. If the demand shock is sufficiently large, then different equilibrium urban configurations can emerge, as shown in Figures 10.4–10.6. Therefore, depending on the magnitude of the demand shock, the unemployed workers can reside either in the vicinity of the CBD or close to the city fringe.

4.4 Urban Unemployment Due to Frictions in the Labor Market[11]

In this section we shall use the job-search model of Section 3.2.1 for the locations of workers in the city, but we shall model the labor market explicitly. In particular, we shall more precisely determine $a(x)$, the probability of finding a job. Observe that some other studies (Jayet, 1990a,b; Simpson, 1992) have tried to put together job search and urban economics, but their formalizations of the urban space were very crude (e.g., they did not explicitly consider the location of the unemployed workers in the city), and therefore we shall not consider them here. In our model, the main cause of urban unemployment is that the allocation of resources is time-consuming and involves *frictions* in the labor market, because workers and firms do not find or accept new jobs and fill vacancies instantly. There are mismatches among unemployed workers, firms, and vacancies because of the skill requirements of the jobs, the preferences of people, and/or the geographic locations of workers and firms (see Holzer, 1989, for empirical evidence).

Firms are all (*ex ante*) identical, as are all workers. A firm is a unit of production that can either be filled by a worker whose production is y units of output or remain unfilled and thus unproductive. In order to find a worker, a firm posts notice of a vacancy that can be filled according to a random Poisson process. Similarly, workers who are looking for jobs will find them according to a random Poisson process. In this context, the number of unemployed workers U and the number of vacancies V are both determined at a given period of time. Moreover, there are numerous contacts between the two sides of the market that we assume to be determined by the following *matching function*:

$$z(\bar{s}U, V) \tag{4.27}$$

where $\bar{s}$ is the average efficiency of search conducted by the unemployed workers. We assume that $z(\cdot)$ is increasing in both its arguments, is concave, and is homogeneous of degree 1 (or, equivalently, has constant returns to scale). Therefore, (4.27) is the well-behaved matching function that gives the number of jobs being carried out at any moment of time as a function of the number of "efficient units" of searching workers and the number of firms looking for workers (Pissarides, 1990). By using the property of constant returns to scale of (4.27), the probability for a vacancy to be filled is

$$q(\theta) \equiv z\left(\frac{1}{\theta}, 1\right) \tag{4.28}$$

where $\theta = V/U\bar{s}$ is a measure of labor-market tightness in efficiency units.

---

[11] This section is based on Wasmer and Zenou (1999).

Similarly, for a worker i with efficiency s_i, the probability of making contact with a vacancy is

$$\theta q(\theta) s_i(x) = a(x) \tag{4.29}$$

Therefore, workers' endogenous choices of locations will be strongly influenced by the search process and by the labor-market conditions. At each period, there is also a probability δ that a match will be destroyed. All these transition probabilities describe a Poisson process.

As we saw in Section 3.2.1, two urban equilibria can occur. Either the unemployed will reside close to the CBD, or they will locate in the suburbs. By using the two definitions, we easily obtain the following results. In urban equilibrium B (in which the unemployed reside in the vicinity of the CBD), we obtain

$$\bar{I}_{1_B} - \bar{I}_{0_B} = \frac{w_B - w_0 - (\alpha_1 - \alpha_0)t U_B}{r + \delta + a(U_B)} \tag{4.30}$$

and the average efficiency level is

$$\bar{s}_B = b - d\bar{x}_B = b - d\frac{U_B}{2} \tag{4.31}$$

In urban equilibrium A (in which the unemployed locate in the suburbs), we have

$$\bar{I}_{1_A} - \bar{I}_{0_A} = \frac{w_A - w_0 - (\alpha_1 - \alpha_0)t(1 - U_A)}{r + \delta + a(1 - U_A)} \tag{4.32}$$

$$\bar{s}_A = b - d\bar{x}_A = b - d\left(1 - \frac{U_A}{2}\right) \tag{4.33}$$

It is easily checked that $\bar{s}_B > \bar{s}_A$. This means that, on average, unemployed workers are more efficient when they reside closer to the employment center. This highlights the fact that informal information networks are more effective for workers residing closer to jobs.

Definition 4.1. *A steady-state labor-market equilibrium is a triple* (w, θ, U) *such that given the matching technology defined by (4.27), all agents (workers and firms) will maximize their respective objective functions.*

We assume that the wage in the economy is exogenous and is equal to $w_A = w_B = \bar{w}$. Let us determine the free-entry condition and the labor demand.

We denote by I_J and I_V the intertemporal profit for a job and for a vacancy, respectively. If γ is the search cost for the firm per unit of time, and y is the product of the match, then I_F and I_V are written as

$$r I_F = y - \bar{w} + \delta(I_V - I_F) \tag{4.34}$$

$$r I_V = -\gamma + q(\theta)(I_F - I_V) \tag{4.35}$$

Firms post notice of vacancies up to a point where

$$I_V = 0 \qquad (4.36)$$

which is a free-entry condition. This can be rewritten as

$$I_F = \frac{\gamma}{q(\theta)} = \frac{y - \bar{w}}{r + \delta} \qquad (4.37)$$

In other words, the value of a job is equal to the expected search cost (i.e., the cost per unit of time times the average duration of search for the firm). Notice that this value is increasing in $\bar{s}$, the average search efficiency determined by the urban equilibrium. From the free-entry condition (4.36), we have a decreasing relationship between labor-market tightness and wages:

$$\bar{w} = y - (r + \delta) \frac{\gamma}{q(\theta)} \qquad (4.38)$$

Note that this labor demand curve is independent of the type of urban equilibrium. That is because, independently of workers' locations, firms post notice of vacancies up to $I_V = 0$. The L^d curve (4.38) is independent of x_b and is downward-sloping in the plane (θ, w). Because the wage is independent of the urban equilibrium, we have a unique $\theta^* = \theta_1 = \theta_2$. This means that, depending on the values of θ^*, only one urban equilibrium will prevail.

Proposition 4.4. *There is a unique urban equilibrium. If $\theta^* q(\theta^*) > \bar{m}$ (respectively $< \bar{m}$), equilibrium B (respectively equilibrium A) will prevail, where*

$$\bar{m} = \frac{(\alpha_1 - \alpha_0)t(r + \delta)}{d(\bar{w} - w_0) - (\alpha_1 - \alpha_0)tb} > 0 \qquad (4.39)$$

The intuition of this proposition is straightforward. When the probability of obtaining a job is very high, the unemployed will locate close to the employment center, whereas in the other case they will reside at the outskirts of the city.

As stated earlier, equation (4.38) determines a unique θ^* that gives a unique relationship between V and U. We can now close the model by the following steady-state condition on the flows:

$$\theta q(\theta) \bar{s}_k U_k = (1 - U_k)\delta, \qquad k = A, B$$

which is equivalent to

$$U_k = \frac{\delta}{\delta + \theta q(\theta) \bar{s}_k}, \qquad k = A, B \qquad (4.40)$$

This equation can be mapped in the plane (U_k, V_k); it corresponds to the *Beveridge curve* $U V_k$ (Figure 10.8).

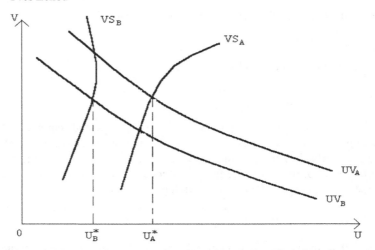

Figure 10.8. The Beveridge curve and labor-market equilibrium under search.

Proposition 4.5. *When the wage is exogenously determined, there exists a unique and stable labor-market equilibrium characterized by*

$$\theta^* = \theta_A = \theta_B, \qquad U_A^* > U_B^*, \qquad \bar{s}_B^* > \bar{s}_A^* \qquad (4.41)$$

The following comments are in order. Obviously there are "bad" and "good" urban equilibria. Indeed, in urban equilibrium B, in which all unemployed workers are close to the employment center, for the same level of labor tightness the level of unemployment is lower and the average search efficiency is higher, compared with urban equilibrium A. This means that in the latter equilibrium, workers, on average, tend to stay unemployed for longer periods than in equilibrium B. An intuitive interpretation is that "segregated" cities (i.e., cities in which unemployed workers are far away from the employment center) are less efficient than "integrated" cities. This leads to interesting predictions about government policy. Indeed, the (local) government should try to impose equilibrium B. How is this possible? In view of Proposition 4.5, the following policies suggest themselves. If the government can control $\bar{w}$ (e.g., if it is a minimum wage), then, other things being equal, the government should increase $\bar{w}$ and decrease the level of unemployment benefits. That would lead to a more "integrated" city, because the unemployed would be induced to reside in the vicinity of the employment center. Another interesting policy suggestion is that the government should subsidize the commuting cost t. It is commonly observed in American cities that the main problem in gaining access to employment is the commuting cost. A lot of "segregated" cities (e.g., Los Angeles, CA; Detroit, MI; and St. Louis, MO) have very poor public transportation systems, and thus access to employment is made difficult. Our model shows that subsidizing commuting costs (e.g., by building an efficient transportation system) will change the shape of a city and reduce its level of unemployment. The local government can also help job-seekers by reducing their fixed search cost b and by increasing their variable search cost d – both policies that would induce job-seekers to be closer to employment centers.

This analysis can be extended by relaxing the exogenous wage assumption. Instead, the wage can become endogenous through Nash bargaining. There will therefore be the two following wages (Wasmer and Zenou, 1999):

$$w_A = (1 - \beta)[w_0 + (\alpha_1 - \alpha_0)t L_A] + \beta[y + s(L_A)\theta_A \gamma] \qquad (4.42)$$

for urban equilibrium A, and

$$w_B = (1 - \beta)[w_0 + (\alpha_1 - \alpha_0)t U_B] + \beta[y + s(U_B)\theta_B \gamma] \qquad (4.43)$$

for urban equilibrium B. Here, $0 < \beta < 1$ is a measure of labor's bargaining strength. These interpretations bear some resemblance to the efficiency-wage interpretations. Each bargained wage is composed of three terms. The first, w_0, is the *base wage level*, the minimum wage to be paid in order to induce workers to leave welfare. The second, $(\alpha_1 - \alpha_0)t L_A$, is the *space cost differential* between employment and unemployment (i.e., what must be added to induce individuals to leave welfare in the presence of these spatial costs). These two elements are weighted by β, the workers' bargaining power. The third term, $y + s(L_A)\theta_A \gamma$, constitutes the *wage surplus* that must be paid to induce work in the presence of frictions in the labor market. Indeed, $s(x)\theta_k \gamma = a(x)\gamma/q(\theta_k)$, where $\gamma/q(\theta_k)$ is the expected search cost. Therefore, this third term is equal to y, the productive value of the match plus the probability of finding a job times the expected search cost associated with it.

The introduction of endogenous wage-setting complicates the analysis and makes the comparison of the two urban equilibria more difficult because of the different externalities associated with the two wages. However, it can be shown that a unique urban equilibrium and a unique labor-market equilibrium exist.

The important feature of this model is that the interactions between land and labor markets are more pronounced than in the other models presented earlier. Indeed, all of the variables in the labor market, such as labor-market tightness, the unemployment and vacancy levels, the separation rate, and the wage, determine which urban equilibrium will prevail, A or B. According to the values of these parameters, the unemployed can reside either close to the city center or in the suburbs. On the other hand, the urban equilibrium affects the labor-market equilibrium. In particular, the aggregate efficiency, $\bar{s}_k$, and the level of unemployment both depend on the type of urban equilibrium (see Proposition 4.5). We see here that there are important feedbacks between the markets and that each market is strongly affected by the other.

4.5 Urban Unemployment Due to Spatial Mismatch[12]

As discussed in the introduction, Kain (1968) has proposed the *spatial-mismatch hypothesis* to explain the high rates of poverty and unemployment among black inner-city residents. Residing in segregated areas distant from and poorly connected to major centers of employment growth, blacks were said to face strong geographic barriers to finding and keeping well-paid jobs, because firms and thus jobs tended to be located at the outskirts of cities (see Garreau, 1991, for an explanation of these *edge cities*). In this context, blacks are forced to stay in the ghetto in the city center and are therefore far away from jobs because of discrimination in the housing market in suburbs. For example, Zax and Kain (1996) have shown that the suburbanization of employment tends to reduce opportunities for blacks and increase black unemployment. Indeed, when a firm decides to relocate to the periphery of its city, housing discrimination usually forces some blacks to quit their jobs rather than follow their employer. If one compares the situations before and after the relocations of firms, one can observe that the hiring rate for blacks and the number of applications by blacks will both have decreased because of the geographic distance between their residences and their new workplaces. In other words, that study points out the fact that for a given level of labor discrimination, the main problem is access to employment: The farther away the unemployed are located, the higher the unemployment level. That observation has been empirically verified. In particular, one of the main conclusions of Holzer (1991), who has reviewed 20 years of empirical studies on the spatial-mismatch hypothesis, is that blacks in central-city areas have less access to employment than do blacks in the suburbs.

Despite a lot of empirical studies, surprisingly few theoretical attempts have been made to model the spatial-mismatch hypothesis. To the best of our knowledge, the first paper to model the spatial-mismatch hypothesis was by Brueckner and Martin (1997). Because they did not explicitly introduce unemployment in their model, we do not consider their approach here. The same applies to Arnott (1998). We shall therefore discuss the paper by Coulson et al. (1997), who modeled the spatial-mismatch hypothesis under search unemployment (similar to the case in the previous section). However, in contrast with our treatment of all other models discussed in this chapter, we do not model explicitly the intra-urban locations of workers, but rather their mobility between two job centers, the CBD and the SEC.

Assumption 4.1. *The city consists of two zones: a CBD and an SEC, indexed by i, j = C, S, respectively.*

---

[12] This section is based on Coulson et al. (1997).

There is a continuum of workers who reside at the two locations $i = C, S$ and who inelastically supply one unit of labor, and there is a continuum of firms that provide vacancies at the two locations $j = C, S$. In order to generate the spatial mismatch, the following assumptions are needed.

Assumption 4.2. *The fixed entry cost is greater in the CBD than in the SEC (i.e., $\gamma_C > \gamma_S$).*

Assumption 4.3. *Workers are heterogeneous in their comparative advantage in effective commuting or in their disutility of transportation. This is indexed by $\lambda \in [0, 1]$. It is distributed uniformly in $[0, 1]$; that is, the density function $g(\cdot)$ is such that $g(\lambda) = 1$. The commuting cost for a worker residing at i and working at j is denoted by $t^{ij} > 0$, with $t^{ii} = 0$.*

Assumption 4.4. *The effective contact rate at which a worker at i locates a vacancy at j is a^{ij}, with $a^{iC} = a_C e^i$ and $a^{iS} = a_S(1 - e^i)$, where $e^i \in [0, 1]$ [respectively $(1 - e^i)$] denotes the search activity of a representative worker residing at location i locating a job at the CBD [respectively the SEC], $i = C, S$.*

These three assumptions are crucial for deriving the results. Assumption 4.2 is needed to generate an asymmetry between the CBD and the SEC in favor of the latter. It is important to observe that within each center, firms are identical in all respects, and between centers the only difference between firms is the fixed entry cost. Assumption 4.3 creates heterogeneity between workers. It is moreover assumed (for simplicity) that it is costless to commute within a center, but costly to commute from one center to another. Assumption 4.4 reflects the presence of search frictions with endogenous search effort (as in Section 3.2.3). As in the preceding section, the expected values for the (intertemporal) utility functions of the employed and the unemployed located at i and working or searching at j are respectively

$$r I_e^{ij} = w^{ij} - t^{ij} + \delta \left[\max_{e^i} \left\{ I_u^i(e^i) \right\} - I_e^i \right] \tag{4.44}$$

$$r I_u^{ij} = w_0 + a^{ij} \left[I_e^{ij} - I_u^{ij} \right] \tag{4.45}$$

and the expected profits for a vacancy at location j filled by a worker residing at i and for an unfilled vacancy at location j are respectively

$$r I_F^{ij} = y^i - w^{ij} + \delta \left(I_V^i - I_F^{ij} \right) \tag{4.46}$$

$$r I_V^j = \eta^j \left[Q^j I_F^{1j} + (1 - Q^j) I_F^{2j} - I_V^j \right] \tag{4.47}$$

where $Q^j = U^{1j}/(U^{1j} + U^{2j})$ measures the fraction of workers from the CBD searching for jobs at location j. Whereas (4.44)–(4.46) are standard and similar to those in the preceding section, equation (4.47) deserves special attention.

Indeed, in this equation, the terms Q^j and $(1 - Q^j)$ appear because vacancies can be filled by workers from either location, so that the surplus I_F can vary with the location of the worker. Wages are determined by a symmetric Nash bargain between firms and workers. In the bargaining solution, it is assumed that firms do not discriminate among workers according to their residences. In this context, wages are based upon the expected flow rate of the matching, $a^{ej} = Q^j a^{1j} + (1 - Q^j)a^{2j}$, and therefore are equal to

$$w^j = \left[\frac{r + \delta + a^{ej}}{2(r + \delta) + a^{ej}} \right] (y^j - rI_V^j) \tag{4.48}$$

As in the preceding section, there are numerous contacts between the unemployed and the vacancies that we assume to be determined by a well-behaved *matching function*. However, whereas in (4.27) the matching process took place between firms in the CBD and workers living in the city outside the CBD, the matching now takes place within each center and between the centers:

$$z(U^j, V^j), \qquad j = C, S \tag{4.49}$$

where U^j is the total measure of workers searching in $j = C, S$, and V^j is the measure of job vacancies at location $j = C, S$. We normalize the total population to unity, so that we have

$$E^j + U^j = 1, \qquad j = C, S \tag{4.50}$$

where E^j is the total measure of individuals working in $j = C, S$. Under constant returns to scale, the matching function (4.49) can be rewritten

$$\eta^j = x \left(\frac{\eta^j}{a^{ej}}, 1 \right) \tag{4.51}$$

where η^j corresponds to the flow probability that a firm at location $j = C, S$ will locate a searching worker. Comparing with the preceding section, η^j corresponds to $q(\theta)$, and a^{ej} to $\theta q(\theta)s_i$. So the two matching functions are similar, except for the fact that in (4.50) there are two centers to search, whereas in (4.27) there is only one job center. The steady-state condition for flows (inflows equal outflows) is

$$\delta E^j = a^{ej} U^j \tag{4.52}$$

which, by using (4.51), can be rewritten as

$$U^j = \frac{\delta}{\delta + a^{ej}} \tag{4.53}$$

Consider an equilibrium in which the wage is greater in the SEC than in the CBD. Therefore, because workers are heterogeneous in their search, the ones with greater λ being more able than the others (Assumption 4.3), it is natural to think that high-ability workers will search for employment at the SEC. We assume that there is a critical value $\tilde{\lambda}^i$ such that workers of type $\lambda \in [0, \tilde{\lambda}^i]$ will optimally search for jobs at the CBD, and workers of type $\lambda \in [\tilde{\lambda}^i, 1]$ will optimally search for jobs at the SEC. In this case, and by using (4.53), the mass of workers residing at i and searching for jobs at j is equal to

$$U^j = \frac{\delta \tilde{\lambda}^i}{\delta + a^{ej}} \tag{4.54}$$

This means that the distribution of unemployed workers can be partitioned into stayers and movers. In this context, the definition of the (steady-state) labor-market equilibrium is similar to Definition 4.1, and it can be shown that there exists an equilibrium in which none of the unemployed workers in the SEC will search for jobs at the CBD (Coulson et al., 1997). We have the following proposition.

Proposition 4.6. *The labor-market equilibrium is characterized by*

- *a higher rate of unemployment for central-city residents than for suburban residents,*
- *a higher rate of job vacancies for suburban firms, and*
- *the possibility of reverse commuting, with higher wages earned in the suburbs.*

As can be seen from this proposition, at equilibrium the city has the features associated with the spatial-mismatch hypothesis. However, this result depends strongly on the assumptions, especially that of the differential entry costs between the CBD and the SEC. What are the policy implications of this model? As in the model of Section 4.4, improvements in the efficiency of the matching function (better information, better market-structure organization) and/or in the transportation infrastructure will yield a lower level of unemployment. Another helpful policy would be to reduce the differential in the fixed entry cost in order to partially alleviate the spatial mismatch, such as by subsidizing the entry of firms into the CBD. This is typically what the French government has done recently by instituting tax-free districts ("zones franches") in which firms can set up without paying the social charges for their workers (this is similar to the enterprise zone programs in the United States). The aim of the policy is to induce firms to locate in areas where the "entry cost" is very high because of undesirable conditions in those neighborhoods.

Observe that in this model the interactions between land and labor markets are quite shallow, because the focus is more on the labor market, and therefore there is asymmetry between the two markets. In other words, the land market is not explicitly modeled; there are only two employment locations (Assumption 4.1) in which workers and firms can operate.

In this model, urban unemployment is mainly due to frictions in the labor market, as in the model in the preceding section. What would be interesting would be to show that the combination of housing discrimination and job suburbanization leads to unemployment. As pointed out by Arnott (1998), we need to understand why the combination of these two factors generates an increase in unemployment, rather than simply a decrease in the wage. A straightforward way to answer this question might be to use the job-search model of Wasmer and Zenou (1999) and apply it in the context of the spatial-mismatch hypothesis. Imagine that there are two employment centers: a CBD and an SEC located in the suburbs. Job suburbanization implies that there are more jobs in the SEC than in the CBD, and housing discrimination implies that (black) downtown residents cannot live in the suburbs. Because one of the main hypotheses of the model is that $a'(x) < 0$ (i.e., the probability of obtaining a job decreases with increasing distance to the employment center), unemployment will rise, and wages will not fall. The explanation is the following: The frictions in the labor market are more important for (black) downtown residents, for two reasons: The difficulty of obtaining information on suburban jobs is greater than for suburban residents, and the probability of finding jobs in the CBD for downtown residents is lower than the probability in the SEC for suburban residents. These two elements together imply that, all other things being equal, the probability of getting jobs for downtown residents is lower than for suburban residents, and thus the level of unemployment is greater. This argument works with a fixed exogenous wage as well as with an endogenous wage.

5 Conclusion

In this chapter we have tried to synthesize the theoretical literature on urban unemployment. The first part has been devoted to the locations of all workers in the city. By developing distinct urban models, we have shown that different urban configurations can emerge. Furthermore, the labor-market equilibrium has been analyzed, as well as its interaction with the land market. We have shown that some feedbacks exist between these two markets that yield interesting results.

However, a lot of work remains to be done. First, in order to have a better understanding of urban segregation, one must incorporate neighborhood or peer effects and local externalities, such as in the studies by Bound and Coulson (1989), Montgomery (1991), Benabou (1993), Mortensen and Vishwanath (1994), Borjas (1995), and Glaeser et al. (1996). In this framework, the probability of finding a job will depend on the worker's social network; individuals with very poor networks will have difficulty in finding jobs.

Second, it would be interesting to find a correspondence among individuals' social distance (Akerlof, 1997), their urban segregation, and unemployment (Brueckner et al., 1999b). In this context, the explanation for ghettos stems from two dimensions that correspond to two spaces: the social space, in which some workers (blacks, for example) are very distant from employers, so that they have a very low probability of finding jobs; the geographical space, in which some workers are located far away from jobs, which leads to poor information about jobs and thus a low probability of getting jobs. The combination of these two dimensions "distances" workers from jobs and thus makes it unlikely that they will ever leave the ghetto.

More generally, a complete theory of urban unemployment will require a much better understanding of the complex interactions between land and labor markets. We have described some models showing that equilibrium in one market depends crucially on the equilibrium in the other market, and vice versa. This must be continued if one wants to better understand the various aspects of urban unemployment.

References

Ades, A. F., and Glaeser, E. L. (1995). Trade and circuses: explaining urban giants. *Quarterly Journal of Economics* 110:195–227.

Akerlof, G. (1997). Social distance and social decisions. *Econometrica* 65:1005–27.

Arnott, R. (1998). Economic theory and the spatial mismatch hypothesis. *Urban Studies* 35:1171–86.

Benabou, R. (1993). Workings of a city: location, education, and production. *Quarterly Journal of Economics* 108:619–52.

Blanchflower, D. G., and Oswald, A. J. (1994). *The Wage Curve.* Cambridge, MA: MIT Press.

Blondel, S., and Marchand, O. (1997). Pourquoi les rendements locatifs parisiens augmentent-ils avec le chômage? *Revue d'Economie Régionale et Urbaine* 5:737–52.

Borjas, G. J. (1995). Ethnicity, neighborhoods, and human-capital externalities. *American Economic Review* 85:365–90.

Bound, E. W., and Coulson, E. N. (1989). Externalities, filtering, and neighborhood change. *Journal of Urban Economics* 26:231–49.

Brueckner, J. K. (1987). The structure of urban equilibria: a unified treatment of the Muth-Mills model. In: E. S. Mills (ed.), *Handbook of Regional and Urban Economics*, pp. 821–45. Amsterdam: North Holland.

Brueckner, J. K., and Martin, R. W. (1997). Spatial mismatch: an equilibrium analysis. *Regional Science and Urban Economics* 27:693–714.

Brueckner, J. K., Thisse, J.-F., and Zenou, Y. (1999a). Why is central Paris rich and downtown Detroit poor? An amenity-based theory. *European Economic Review* 43:91–107.

388 Yves Zenou

Brueckner, J. K., Thisse, J.-F., and Zenou, Y. (1999b). Local labor markets, job matching and urban location. CEPR Discussion Paper, London. CORE, Université Catholique de Louvain.

Coulson, E. N., Laing, D., and Wang, P. (1997). Spatial mismatch in search equilibrium. Working paper, Pennsylvania State University.

DeSalvo, J. S., and Eeckhoudt, L. R. (1982). Household behavior under income uncertainty in a monocentric urban area. *Journal of Urban Economics* 11:98–111.

Drèze, J., and Modigliani, F. (1972). Consumption decisions under uncertainty. *Journal of Economic Theory* 5:308–35.

Fujita, M. (1989). *Urban Economic Theory*. Cambridge University Press.

Gannon, F., and Zenou, Y. (1997). Segregation and labor discrimination in cities. *Annales d'Economie et de Statistiques* 45:233–49.

Garreau, J. (1991). *Edge City: Life on the New Frontier*. New York: Doubleday.

Glaeser, E. L., Sacerdote, B., and Scheinkman, J. A. (1996). Crime and social interactions. *Quarterly Journal of Economics* 111:507–48.

Gordon, I. R. (1987). *Unemployment, the Regions and Labour Markets: Reactions to Recession*. London: Pion.

Hartwick, J., Schweizer, U., and Varaiya, P. (1976). Comparative statics of a residential economy with several classes. *Journal of Economic Theory* 13:396–413.

Hasluck, C. (1987). *Urban Unemployment*. London: Longman.

Holzer, H. J. (1989). *Unemployment, Vacancies and Local Labor Markets*. Kalamazoo: W. E. Upjohn Institute for Employment Research.

Holzer, H. (1991). The spatial mismatch hypothesis: What has the evidence shown? *Urban Studies* 28:105–22.

Ihlanfeldt, K. R. (1997). Information on the spatial distribution of job opportunities within metropolitan areas. *Journal of Urban Economics* 41:218–42.

Ihlanfeldt, K. R., and Sjöquist, D. L. (1990). Job accessibility and racial differences in youth employment rates. *American Economic Review* 80:267–76.

Isserman, A., Taylor, C., Gerking, S., and Schubert, U. (1986). Regional labor market analysis. In: P. Nijkamp and E. S. Mills (eds.), *Handbook of Regional and Urban Economics*, vol. 1, pp. 543–80. Amsterdam: North Holland.

Jayet, H. (1990a). Spatial search processes and spatial interaction: 1. Sequential search, intervening opportunities, and spatial search equilibrium. *Environment and Planning A* 22:583–99.

Jayet, H. (1990b). Spatial search processes and spatial interaction: 2. Polarization, concentration, and spatial search equilibrium. *Environment and Planning A* 22:719–32.

Kain, J. F. (1968). Housing segregation, Negro employment, and metropolitan decentralization. *Quarterly Journal of Economics* 82:32–59.

Marston, S. T. (1985). Two views of the geographic distribution of unemployment. *Quarterly Journal of Economics* 100:57–79.

Montgomery, J. D. (1991). Social networks and labor-market outcomes. *American Economic Review* 81:1408–18.

Mortensen, D. T., and Vishwanath, T. (1994). Personal contacts and earnings. It is who you know! *Labour Economics* 1:187–201.

Pissarides, C. (1990). *Equilibrium Unemployment Theory*. Oxford: Blackwell.

Rogers, C. L. (1997). Job search and unemployment duration: implications for the spatial mismatch hypothesis. *Journal of Urban Economics* 42:109–32.

Simpson, W. (1992). *Urban Structure and the Labour Market. Worker Mobility, Commuting, and Underemployment in Cities*. Oxford: Clarendon Press.

Smith, T. E., and Zenou, Y. (1997). Dual labor markets, urban unemployment, and multicentric cities. *Journal of Economic Theory* 76:185–214.

Wasmer, E., and Zenou, Y. (1999). Does space affect search? A theory of local unemployment. CEPR Discussion Paper 2157, London.

Zax, J. S., and Kain, J. F. (1996). Moving to the suburbs: Do relocating companies leave their black employees behind? *Journal of Labor Economics* 14:472–93.

Zenou, Y., and Eeckhoudt, L. R. (1997). Bid rents under unemployment risk: delayed versus timeless uncertainty. *Journal of Urban Economics* 42:42–63.

Zenou, Y., and Smith, T. E. (1995). Efficiency wages, involuntary unemployment and urban spatial structure. *Regional Science and Urban Economics* 25:547–73.

CHAPTER 11

Rural versus Urban Location: The Spatial Division of Labor

Hubert Jayet

1 Introduction

Theories about the spatial division of labor were proposed by radical economists as long as two decades ago, in particular, by Aydalot (1976, 1985) and Massey (1984). This chapter's reformulation of the center–periphery model places emphasis upon two main ideas. First, various ways of life are spatially differentiated and may not fit with the latest production technologies. The main form of differentiation among locations concerns the differences between locations in which people follow a traditional lifestyle and locations in which people adopt the latest modern standards. In the traditional locations, workers have lower wage demands and a weaker position for wage bargaining with firms.

Second, wage bargains are fundamentally asymmetric, and space plays an important role in this asymmetry. Firms embrace larger spaces than do their employees and have more possibilities in choosing their locations. According to Aydalot (1985), "while agents are [stuck in] their initial environment and do not accept moving out, they must accept the decisions of large firms able to choose among several locations." Firms take advantage of this asymmetry and of workers' spatially differentiated ways of living. In traditional areas, they tend to develop unskilled production processes that are profitable because there they can find people willing to work for lower wages.

In France, many observers of the economic decentralization during the period 1960–1970 have confirmed the existence of such a spatial division of labor (Mary and Turpin, 1980; Hannoun and Sicherman, 1983). However, neoclassical analyses continue to ignore the main phenomenon analyzed by those theorists. Of course, the theoretical context in which the spatial division of labor was formulated differed considerably from the neoclassical paradigm. But that

Earlier versions of this study were presented at the 1995 ASRDLF meeting in Toulouse and at the 1996 ERSAI conference in Zurich, and this presentation has benefited from the comments of participants in those conferences. I particularly wish to acknowledge the advice and comments of Gilles Duranton, Jacques Thisse, and Yves Zenou. The usual disclaimers apply.

is not a sufficient reason to ignore a phenomenon confirmed by observations. Moreover, observations have shown that labor markets play an active role in polarization. The fact that firms have the opportunity to take advantage of low labor costs in peripheral areas implies quantitative limits to polarization. At the same time, the fact that decentralized jobs are low-skill jobs reinforces the qualitative components of polarization.

Even in the face of this evidence, few neoclassical theories of polarization and urban growth have allowed an active role for labor markets. In a study by Henderson (1985), the main limits to polarization were internal to the city; they came from the growth of infrastructure and commuting costs. There was nothing similar to consideration of the possibility of decentralizing in low-wage peripheral areas. In studies stemming from the work of Krugman (1991), the main polarizing force has been said to operate on goods markets. There is "a circular causality in the spatial agglomeration of firms and workers through a *forward linkage* (where the availability of a greater variety of consumption goods increases the real income of workers there) and a *backward linkage* (where a greater number of consumers supports a greater number of specialized firms)" (Fujita and Krugman, 1995).

In all of those models, the labor force was homogeneous, and labor markets adapted passively. In this chapter, we take the opposite approach. As in the study by Abdel-Rahman and Wang (1995), we focus on the role of heterogeneous labor markets. We consider a spatial system of small rural labor markets and a large metropolitan area with its own urban labor market. In all labor markets, workers are vertically differentiated with respect to their skills, higher skills being more productive. Contrary to the approach of Abdel-Rahman and Wang (1995), there is a continuum of skill levels, and skilled workers are not horizontally differentiated. Firms are differentiated with respect to their technological levels. Firms with higher technological levels are more sensitive to skill: For the same skill difference, the productivity difference is higher.

In this spatial system, the driving force for the spatial division of labor is the asymmetry between an oligopsonistically competitive metropolitan labor market and monopsonistic rural markets. In the large urban labor market, the coexistence of many vertically differentiated firms competing to hire vertically differentiated workers results in an oligopsonistically competitive equilibrium. This equilibrium is characterized by market segmentation: Each firm employs workers whose skill levels are close matches with its technological level. Wages increase with skill levels, because the higher the skill level, the higher the productivity in all firms, and the higher the wage that competitors will accept to pay. Therefore, firms employing more skilled workers must pay higher wages to outbid competitors.

Conversely, rural labor markets are small enough, and their number is large enough, for at most one firm to be present in each market. This monopsony position allows rural firms to pay workers only their opportunity wage, which is equal to the revenue they can earn in a traditional sector (e.g., agriculture or craft self-employment). Because one's skill level does not matter in the traditional sector, the opportunity cost of labor is constant, and all rural workers are paid the same wage.

This asymmetry between the oligopsonistically competitive metropolitan labor market and the monopsonistic rural markets has several consequences. Let us first note that rural wages do not depend on skills, whereas urban wages increase with skills. Hence, if worker migrations are allowed at some cost, the most skilled workers will move from rural areas to the metropolis. Only the unskilled workers will remain in rural areas. At the same time, in the urban area the competitive pressure will drive profits to zero and induce firms to relocate to rural areas where they can benefit from a monopsonistic position. However, because those with the highest skills in the rural areas will have migrated to the metropolis, high-technology firms cannot decentralize, because in rural areas they can no longer find the high skill levels they need. Only less technological firms will tend to move to rural areas, where they can employ the unskilled workers who have not moved out.

We thus have two simultaneous movements: skilled workers migrating to the metropolis, where they can benefit from higher wages, and less technological firms decentralizing to rural areas, where they can benefit from a monopsonistic position. This process is similar to a particular form of spatial division of labor.

The second section of this chapter presents the model. The third section analyzes monopsonistic competition in the metropolitan labor market. In the fourth section, we examine the behavior of rural labor markets, and, comparing them with the metropolis, we determine under which conditions and how decentralization will operate. The last section draws some conclusions.

2 An Urban–Rural System

2.1 The Spatial Structure

Let us consider a system of $N + 1$ local labor markets indexed by $n = 0, \ldots, N$. Labor market 0 is located in a large metropolitan area. Labor markets 1 to N are located in the small rural areas surrounding the metropolis. Without any migration, the size of the labor force located in area n is P_n. The metropolitan area being much larger than any rural area, we have $P_n / P_0 \approx 0$ for all $n > 0$. Two main production sectors can employ workers in both geographic areas: industrial firms and a traditional production sector. All firms produce the same composite good, which is sold on national and international competitive markets at unit price.

Workers can move from rural areas to the metropolis. However, migration is costly. The rural areas are sorted by increasing distance to the metropolis, so that the migration cost c_n is increasing in n. Therefore, for migration to be profitable for a rural worker, the difference between the wage he can receive in the urban area and his gain in his original rural area n must be higher than c_n. Note that the distance between the metropolis and the rural area n need not be interpreted as a physical distance only. It is probably more a social and psychological distance between the urban and rural ways of life. In a far-remote rural area, traditional ways of life will have changed only slightly. People still live in small communities, immersed in a natural environment. Social relationships and networks are inherited from past history, and people seldom meet outsiders. Custom everywhere plays a major role. Most workers are self-employed.

Migrants to the metropolis must adapt to the modern urban way of life. They will have to adapt and find their way about in large social networks in which initially they will know few people. In cities, social mobility is high. Employment is mainly wage employment. The urban environment is far from being natural. The migration cost c_n mainly reflects these adaptation costs. The less remote rural areas will have had more contact with the metropolis, and there some of the influence of the metropolis will already have been felt, so that the way of life in less remote areas will already have moved closer to the modern urban lifestyle. The adaptation costs for migrants from those less remote areas will be lower.[1]

2.2 The Structure of the Labor Markets

All labor markets have the same basic structure. Workers inelastically supply one unit of labor and are perfect substitutes for every industrial firm. However, workers are differentiated with respect to their skills, and firms with respect to their technologies. These two parallel differentiations also appeared in the work of Thisse and Zenou (1995), who adapted the Salop (1979) model. However, contrary to the study of Thisse and Zenou, who analyzed horizontal differentiation, here the skill differentiation between workers is vertical.[2] The skill levels and technological levels are continuously distributed on the interval $[q^-, q^+]$. In area n, the number of workers with skill levels below q equals $P_n L_n(q)$, where $L_n(q)$ is a cumulative distribution function with density $l_n(q)$. Because there are likely to be fewer workers with high skill levels, $l_n(q)$ is nonincreasing. Prior to any migration, the more rural the labor market, the lower the proportion

---

[1] We ignore migration between rural areas. The main reason behind this choice will appear later on: In every rural labor market, the worker's earnings are the same. Thus, with costly migration, no worker will be induced to move between rural areas.

[2] This choice is easy to understand. Vertical differentiation is central in the analysis of the spatial division of labor.

of skilled workers. Thus, if $m < n$, L_m stochastically dominates L_n at the first order: $L_m(q) < L_n(q)$ for all q.

The higher the skill level, the more efficient the worker. One labor unit supplied by a worker of skill level q working in firm i is equivalent to $h_i(q) = \alpha_i q + \beta_i$ standardized units of labor used in production, α_i being a positive coefficient. The marginal productivity of standardized labor units is constant and normalized to unity. The function h_i reflects the sensitivity of firm i to skill levels. The two coefficients α_i and β_i characterize the technology used by firm i. We assume that each firm can freely choose its technology from the same technological set $\mathcal{A}$: For all i, $(\alpha_i, \beta_i) \in \mathcal{A} \subset \mathbb{R}^+ \times \mathbb{R}$, $\mathcal{A}$ being compact.[3] Therefore, for all q, there is a finite upper limit $\varphi(q)$ to marginal productivity, defined as

$$\varphi(q) = \max_{(\alpha,\beta) \in \mathcal{A}} (\alpha q + \beta)$$

The function $\varphi(q)$ is the upper envelope of the sensitivity functions $\alpha q + \beta$. It can be interpreted as a technological frontier: The highest productivity attainable by a q-skill worker is $\varphi(q)$. Being defined as the upper envelope of increasing affine functions, the function φ is increasing and convex.[4]

Let us define an efficient technology as a technology reaching the technological frontier: For some θ, $\alpha\theta + \beta = \varphi(\theta)$. If φ has a first-order derivative, the properties of envelopes imply that $h(q) = \alpha q + \beta$ is the only line tangent to φ for $q = \theta$. Therefore, for all θ, there exists a unique efficient technology such that $\alpha\theta + \beta = \varphi(\theta)$, and it makes sense to say that this technology is the efficient technology of level θ. Moreover, the fact that $\alpha\theta + \beta$ is tangent to φ implies that $\alpha = \varphi'(\theta)$ and $\beta = \varphi(\theta) - \theta\varphi'(\theta)$. Writing $h(q, \theta)$ for the sensitivity of the level-θ efficient technology to skill levels, we have

$$h(q, \theta) = \alpha(\theta)q + \beta(\theta) = \varphi(\theta) + (q - \theta)\varphi'(\theta)$$

It is straightforward that if a firm can freely choose its technology in $\mathcal{A}$, it will pick up only an efficient technology. Therefore, from here on, we assume that all firms use efficient technologies.

An example of the curves $\varphi(\theta)$ and $h(q, \theta)$ is shown in Figure 11.1. Now, the maximum number of standardized labor units that a q-skill worker can supply is obtained by a firm using the technology $\theta = q$. This structure implies a one-to-one correspondence between skill levels and technological levels, which can be measured using the same scale: q is both a skill level and the technological level for which this skill level is the most productive. Similarly, θ is both a technological level and the skill level whose productivity is maximum when

---

[3] The compactness of $\mathcal{A}$ is a natural assumption. It implies that for every skill level, marginal productivity is bounded from above and that the upper bound is attainable.

[4] We also implicitly assume that φ is differentiable at all relevant orders.

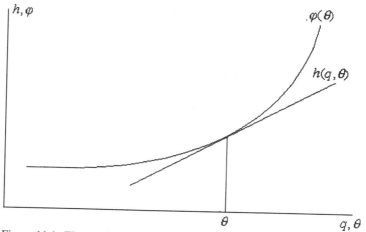

Figure 11.1. The sensitivity curve and the technological frontier.

using this technology. Working for a firm using the technology $\theta \neq q$ (hence $\Delta = q - \theta \neq 0$) implies a productivity loss:

$$T(\Delta, q) = \varphi(\theta) - h(\theta + \Delta, \theta) = \varphi(\theta + \Delta) - \varphi(\theta) - \Delta\varphi'(\theta)$$
$$= \Delta^2\varphi''(\theta)/2 + O(\Delta^3)$$

We can use this common scale to express simultaneously skill levels and technological levels. This scale is similar to a Hotelling linear space within which workers are vertically differentiated and firms are horizontally differentiated. The productivity loss $T(\Delta, \theta)$ is formally equivalent to a transport-cost function.

The first-order derivative of φ, $\varphi'(\theta) = \alpha(\theta)$, measures the sensitivity of technology θ to the skill level: The higher is θ, the higher is $\varphi'(\theta)$, and the more sensitive is the firm to differences in skill levels. As will be seen later on, the second-order derivative $\varphi''(\theta)$ is inversely related to the degree of differentiation between the firm using technology θ and its neighboring competitors. Everything else remaining equal, the higher is $\varphi''(\theta)$, the higher is the difference between the productivity of an employee of skill θ working for the firm using technology θ and his productivity when he works for its competitors, and then the lower is the competitors' ability to bid for the worker. For every skill level q, there exists at least one firm for which a q-skill worker is more productive than in the traditional sector, so that $\varphi(q) \geq \omega$ for all q.

Let us consider firm i using technology θ_i. The firm's labor pool can be represented by a function $e_i(q)$ such that $e_i(q)\,dq$ is the number of employed workers with skill levels between q and $q + dq$. Thus, the volume of standardized work units supplied to the firm by its labor pool, E_i, is

$$E_i = \int_{q^-}^{q^+} e_i(q)h(q, \theta_i)\, dq$$

The sensitivity to skill levels apart, all firms have access to the same production function, $F(E) = E - f_{n(i)}(\theta_i)$, where $f_{n(i)}(\theta_i)$ stands for fixed costs in the area $n(i)$, where firm i is located, measured in labor units (see Krugman, 1991, for a similar assumption).

When not employed by any firm, members of the labor force can work in the traditional sector. Because skill levels are linked to industrial technology only, the revenue ω earned in the traditional sector is the same for all workers. This extreme assumption simplifies the analytical treatment without modifying the main results. These results hold as long as industrial productivity is more sensitive to skill levels than to productivity in the traditional sector.

3 Monopsonistic Competition in the Urban Labor Market

3.1 A Segmented Labor Market

Assume first that industrial firms are established in the metropolis. We analyze the metropolitan labor market. There are I firms located in the metropolis, firm i using the technology θ_i. As is usual in spatial-competition models (Gabszewicz and Thisse, 1992), in this oligopsonistic labor market there are two stages. Before competing for workers, firms decide to enter or not enter the market, and they choose their technologies. This is a location stage. Its outcome is a vector of technologies, $(\theta_1, \ldots, \theta_I)$.

After entry, firms determine at what wage to bid for workers, and they hire all the workers willing to work for that wage. Firms know the skill level of each worker. They are thus able to discriminate perfectly among workers and to pay skill-specific wages $w(q)$. Therefore, in the second stage, the strategy of firm i is characterized by the function $w_i(q)$, where $w_i(q)$ is the wage proposed by the firm to q-skill workers. The corresponding employment level is $e_i(q)$. In this two-stage process, the market equilibrium concept is subgame perfect equilibrium.

As usual, let us first analyze second-stage competition. As noted by Gabszewicz and Thisse (1992), the wages proposed for different skills are *strategically independent*, and there is a separate Bertrand game at each skill level. To hire a q-skill worker, firm i must be the highest bidder, offering a wage $w_i(q)$ that is higher than the highest bid its competitors can make. Because the marginal productivity of standardized work units is unity, and a q-skill worker supplies $h(q, \theta_i)$ standardized work units to firm i, the worker has a marginal productivity of $h(q, \theta_i)$ when employed by firm i. But the maximum bid a firm can make equals the worker's marginal productivity. Therefore, firm i will be the highest bidder for a q-skill worker if it maximizes the worker's productivity $h(q, \theta_j)$ among all other existing firms. The wage $w_i(q)$ proposed by firm i will be marginally higher than the maximum second bid, $w_i(q) = \max_{j \neq i} w_j(q)$, or than ω if no other firm has a productivity higher than ω. The worker's productivity being constant and positive, all workers of skill q are hired, so that $e_i(q) = P_0 l_0(q)$.

The outcome of this bidding process is that the whole interval $[q^-, q^+]$ is divided into at most $I + 1$ segments $\mathcal{S}_0, \ldots, \mathcal{S}_I$. Segment $\mathcal{S}_i = [\gamma_{i-1,i}, \gamma_{i,i+1}]$ is the set of all workers hired by firm i, where, by convention, firm 0 stands for the traditional sector.[5] For all i and j,

$$\gamma_{i,j} = \gamma(\theta_i, \theta_j) = [\beta(\theta_i) - \beta(\theta_j)]/[\alpha(\theta_j) - \alpha(\theta_i)]$$

is the skill level such that the worker's productivity is the same in firms i and j. The function $\gamma(\theta_i, \theta_j)$ is increasing in both its argument, and if $\theta_i < \theta_j$, then $\theta_i = \gamma(\theta_i, \theta_i) < \gamma(\theta_i, \theta_j) < \gamma(\theta_j, \theta_j) = \theta_j$. Thus, for all i, $\theta_i \in \mathcal{S}_i$, and each firm occupies a segment located close to the skill level corresponding to its technological level. As noted earlier, it is for $q = \theta_i$ that an agent's productivity is maximized by firm i. No firm can outbid firm i for skill levels close to θ_i.

Thus, the higher the worker's skill level, the higher the technological level of the firm he is working in. This outcome of competition between firms is similar to the self-selection process analyzed in an interregional context by Borjas et al. (1992). Those authors showed that the more sensitive the regional wage was to skill levels, the greater was the ability of the region to attract skilled workers. Here, the greater the firm's sensitivity to skill levels, the higher the skill levels of the workers it can employ.

An example of this market structure is displayed in Figure 11.2. Within the interval $\mathcal{S}_i$, firm $i - 1$ is the second-highest bidder for $q < \gamma_{i-1,i+1}$; firm $i + 1$ is the second-highest bidder for $q > \gamma_{i-1,i+1}$. This property allows us to derive the wage curve. Let us define $\mathcal{S}_i^- = [\gamma_{i-1,i}, \gamma_{i-1,i+1}]$ and $\mathcal{S}_i^+ = [\gamma_{i-1,i+1}, \gamma_{i,i+1}]$. If $q \in \mathcal{S}_i^-$, then $w(q) = w_i(q) = h(q, \theta_{i-1})$. If $q \in \mathcal{S}_i^+$, then $w(q) = w_i(q) = h(q, \theta_{i+1})$. This wage curve is piecewise linear and increasing. Moreover, if I is large, firms are close to one another, and the wage bids by two neighboring firms are similar. This implies that $w(q)$ is close to $\varphi(q)$.

3.2 The Equilibrium Market Structure

In the first stage, firm i chooses its own technology so as to maximize its profits $\Pi_i = \Pi(\theta_{i-1}, \theta_i, \theta_{i+1})$,

$$\Pi_i = \int_{\gamma(\theta_{i-1}, \theta_i)}^{\gamma(\theta_i, \theta_{i+1})} \{h(q, \theta_i) - \max[h(q, \theta_{i-1}), h(q, \theta_{i+1})]\}\, dq \qquad (11.1)$$

---

[5] Consequently, we have $\alpha(\theta_0) = 0$ and $\beta(\theta_0) = \omega$.

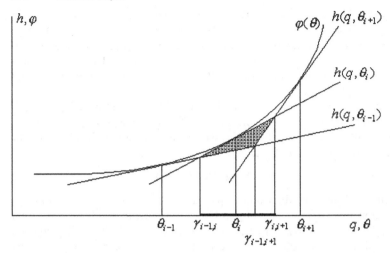

Figure 11.2. Competition among vertically differentiated firms.

When the labor-force density is constant, profit is proportional to the shaded area in Figure 11.2. More generally, let us note that when the length $\gamma_{i,i+1} - \gamma_{i-1,i}$ is small enough, a Taylor approximation of Π_i is

$$\Pi_i = \frac{l(\theta)\varphi''(\theta)}{32}(\gamma_{i,i+1} - \gamma_{i-1,i})^3 + O[(\gamma_{i,i+1} - \gamma_{i-1,i})^4]$$

Thus, for a given length of the market segment, profits are proportional to the local labor-force density $l(\theta)$ and to the local degree of differentiation between technologies, $\varphi''(\theta)$. The quantity $l(\theta)\varphi''(\theta)$ measures the local profitability conditions faced by a firm using technology θ.

The metropolitan labor market is in equilibrium when each firm makes its best reply. A noteworthy special case occurs when the labor-force density, $l(q)$, and the degree of differentiation, $\varphi''(\theta)$, are constant. The latter implies the same quadratic efficiency loss function for all technological levels, $T(\Delta, \theta) = T(\Delta) = a\Delta^2$. We are led back to a classical Hotelling model with discriminating prices analyzed by Lederer and Hurter (1986). Each firm locates at the center of its market segment, and the separating point between any two consecutive market segments, $\gamma_{i,i+1}$, is the midpoint between the two firms' locations, θ_i and θ_{i+1}: $\theta_i = (\gamma_{i-1,i} + \gamma_{i,i+1})/2$ and $\gamma_{i,i+1} = (\theta_i + \theta_{i+1})/2$.

Starting from this special case, we can analyze the respective effects of a varying labor-force density and of a varying intensity of competition. Let us first examine the latter. The following property is the main result.

Proposition 1. *When only the degree of differentiation varies, at market equilibrium each firm will remain at the center of its labor-market segment. Inside every interval where the degree of differentiation, $\varphi''(\theta)$, increases with respect to θ, the midpoint between any two market segments will be higher than the midpoint between the two firms' locations: $\gamma_{i,i+1} > (\theta_i + \theta_{i+1})/2$. The length of market segments, $\gamma(\theta_i, \theta_{i+1}) - \gamma(\theta_{i-1}, \theta_i)$, will decrease as the technological level increases. The opposite will hold inside every interval where the degree of differentiation decreases.*

Proof. See the Appendix.

Thus, the firms facing higher degrees of differentiation enjoy smaller market segments. When only the labor-force density varies, the following property will hold.

Proposition 2. *When only the labor-force density varies, the separating point between any two consecutive market segments will remain at the midpoint between the two firms' locations. At market equilibrium, for all i, $\theta_i - (\theta_{i-1} + \theta_{i+1})/2$ will have the same sign as $l'(\theta_i)$, and each firm will locate closer to the neighboring competitor with the highest labor-force density. Then, in every interval where $l(\theta)$ is increasing (respectively decreasing), the length of market segments will decrease (respectively increase).*

Proof. See the Appendix.

When both the labor-force density and the degree of differentiation vary, a general result can no longer be obtained. However, Jayet (1996) has proved the following property, which is a good approximation when, I being large enough, the interval separating any two firms is small enough.

Proposition 3. *Let $e_i = (\theta_i - \theta_{i-1})$ be the difference between the technological levels of firms $i - 1$ and i. At market equilibrium, the technological level of firm $i + 1$ will be $\theta_{i+1} = \psi(\theta_i, e_i)$, where a Taylor approximation of $\psi(\theta_i, e_i)$ is*

$$\theta_{i+1} = \psi(\theta_i, e_i) = \theta_i + e_i - \frac{\lambda(\theta_i) + \zeta(\theta_i)}{3} e_i^2 + O(e_i^3)$$

$$\gamma_{i-1,i} = \gamma(\theta_i - e_i) = \theta_i - \frac{1}{2} e_i + \frac{\zeta(\theta_i)}{12} e_i^2 + O(e_i^3)$$

$$\frac{\gamma_{i-1,i} + \gamma_{i,i+1}}{2} = \frac{\gamma(\theta_i - e_i, \theta_i) + \gamma[\theta_i, \psi(\theta_i, e_i)]}{2} = \theta_i - \frac{\lambda(\theta_i)}{12} e_i^2 + O(e_i^3)$$

where $\lambda(\theta) = d \log(\theta)/d\theta$ and $\zeta(\theta) = d \log \varphi''(\theta)/d\theta$.

The first equality of Proposition 3 shows that when $\lambda(\theta_i) + \zeta(\theta_i)$ is positive (respectively negative), $\theta_{i+1} - \theta_i$ is shorter (respectively longer) than $\theta_i - \theta_{i-1}$.

But $\lambda(\theta_i) + \zeta(\theta_i)$ is the log-derivative of the measure of local profitability, $l(\theta_i)\varphi''(\theta_i)$. Thus, firm i tends to locate closer to the neighboring competitor facing the best local profitability. For the general case, we confirm the results observed in the two special cases. Moreover, let us note that $\theta_i - e_i/2 = (\theta_i + \theta_{i-1})/2$. Then the second equality of Proposition 3 confirms that the location of the separating point between two adjacent market segments is governed by the evolution of the degree of differentiation. The separating point tends to move toward the firm facing the highest degree of differentiation. The third equality confirms that a firm's location within its market segment is governed by the evolution of the labor-force density. A firm tends to move closer to its frontier with the firm facing the highest labor-force density.

Therefore, in every case, firms facing good local conditions, that is, a high $l(\theta)\varphi''(\theta)$, because the labor-force density is high or the degree of differentiation is high, will tend to have smaller market segments. The local profitability conditions and the size of labor-market segments will influence profits in opposite directions. With good local conditions, a firm will make high profits if the length of its market segment is unchanged. However, a smaller size of the market segment will have a downward effect on profits. The final outcome of these two opposite forces is not clear.

Because the metropolis is large and its labor market is occupied by many firms, we can rely on asymptotic approximations once again. With enough firms for their distribution to be correctly approximated by a continuous density $n(\theta)$, the interval between any two firms is asymptotically approximated by $e(\theta) = n^{-1}(\theta)$. Thus, because firm $i+1$ uses technology $\theta_i = \psi[\theta_i, e(\theta_i)]$, we have $e[\theta_i + e(\theta_i)] = \psi[\theta_i, e(\theta_i)] - \theta_i$. Hence, after the first equality of Proposition 3,

$$\frac{\psi[\theta_i, e(\theta_i)] - \theta_i - e(\theta_i)}{e(\theta_i)} = \frac{e[\theta_i + e(\theta_i)] - e(\theta_i)}{e(\theta_i)}$$

$$\simeq e'(\theta_i) \simeq \frac{\lambda(\theta_i) + \zeta(\theta_i)}{3} e(\theta_i)$$

which leads to the following differential equation:

$$\frac{e'(\theta_i)}{e(\theta_i)} = -\frac{\lambda(\theta_i) + \zeta(\theta_i)}{3}$$

Then a first-order approximation for the density of firms is $n(\theta_i) = e(\theta_i)^{-1} = K\psi(\theta_i)^{1/3}$, where K is a constant determining the number of firms. Introducing this expression into the first-order approximation to equation (11.1), we find that $\Pi(\theta_i) \simeq 1/4K^3 - f$ and thus does not depend on the firms' technologies.

Therefore, in a large metropolis, at market equilibrium, competition roughly offsets the differences in local profitability conditions. All firms will reach approximately the same profit level.

3.3 Metropolitan Centralization

Assume, for the moment, that industrial firms in the metropolis cannot move to the rural areas.[6] All industrial firms are located in the metropolis, and only the traditional activities are carried out in rural areas. This situation of *metropolitan centralization* may result from the impossibility of transferring urban technologies outside the metropolitan area (either because urban entrepreneurs refuse to move their firms or because access to markets is fundamental), or it may be because the metropolis generates strong externalities.

When there is metropolitan centralization, then because all rural workers work in the traditional sector, they receive ω. At the same time, q-skill urban workers receive $w(q) \geq \omega$. As noted earlier, competition among a large number of firms implies that $w(q) \simeq \varphi(q)$, an approximation we shall accept from now on. Let us now examine rural labor market n. Because the metropolitan wage is higher than ω, no urban worker will be willing to relocate to a rural area. Similarly, because the productivity of the traditional sector is the same everywhere, there would be no gain in moving between rural areas.

We are led to consider rural-to-urban migrations only. For a q-skill rural worker to consider migration to the metropolis, the difference $w(q) - \omega \simeq \varphi(q) - \omega$ must cover the migration cost c_n. There will be migration when $\varphi(q) > \omega + c_n$. Because the wage curve is increasing, there exists a unique skill level $q_n^+ \leq q^+$ such that

$$\varphi(q) > \omega + c_n \iff q > q_n^+$$

Thus the rural area loses its most skilled workers, who migrate to the metropolis, where competition among urban firms enables them to earn higher wages. The rural labor market of area n is reduced to a subsegment $[q^-, q_n^+]$. Let us note that even when ω increases with q, the rural area still will lose its most skilled workers as long as ω increases more slowly than φ. That situation is quite likely when skill level is linked to the ability to fill jobs in the industrial sector.

Remember that because rural areas 1 to N are at increasing distances from the metropolis, the sequence $\{c_n, n = 1, \ldots, N\}$ is increasing with respect to n. Consequently, $\{q_n^+, n = 1, \ldots, N\}$ increases with respect to n. Rural labor markets closest to the metropolis lose more workers, because more skilled workers are attracted by the metropolis. This attraction of the metropolis and the resulting depressing effect on the hinterland has often been observed (Mary and Turpin, 1980). Because migration costs are higher for workers coming from remote rural areas, those areas are better able to retain their skilled workers.

Let us now define the function $\nu(\cdot)$ by the equivalence

$$\nu(q) = n \iff n = \max\{m \mid q_m^+ < q\}$$

---

[6] This assumption will be relaxed later on.

where $v(q)$ is the rank of the most distant area[7] that loses q-skill workers to the metropolis. It is an increasing function of q. After migrations have been completed, the labor-force density in area n is zero for skill levels higher than q_n^+, and the population of the area is reduced to $P_n L_n(q_n^+)$.

Conversely, in the metropolis, the higher the skill level, the greater the number of workers who have come from rural areas. Migrations increase the metropolitan population, the density of which becomes

$$\bar{P}_0(q) = \sum_{n < v(q)} P_n l_n(q)$$

Let us illustrate these observations with the case of a quadratic production frontier. Without loss of generality, we can assume that $q^- = 0$, $q^+ = 1$, and $\omega = 0$. The technological frontier is quadratic, with $\varphi(\theta) = \alpha(q + \mu)^2$, and $h(q, \theta) = \alpha(\theta + \mu)(2q - \theta + \mu)$, where μ is a non-negative shift parameter. We also assume that in every rural area the native labor force is uniformly distributed in the interval $[0, q_n^*]$, which implies that $l_n(q) = 1/q_n^*$ for $q \leq q_n^*$, and $l_n(q) = 0$ for $q > q_n^*$. Of course, the general assumption that the more remote rural areas will have less highly skilled native labor forces implies that q_n^* is a decreasing function of n. We also assume that q_1^* is close to 1 and that q_N^* is close to zero.[8]

In area n, the maximal skill level after migration is $q_n^x = \min(q_n^*, q_n^+)$, where q_n^* is the maximal skill level of the native labor force, and q_n^+, as defined earlier, is the minimal skill level such that out-migration will be profitable. We know that $\varphi(q_n^+) = \omega + c_n$; hence $\alpha(q_n^+ + \mu)^2 = c_n$ when $q_n^+ > 0$, and then $q_n^+ = \max(0, \mu + \sqrt{c_n/\alpha})$. We also know that the migration cost, c_n, increases with respect to n. If the migration cost is low for areas close to the metropolis, and very high for areas very far from the metropolis, c_1 is close to zero, and c_N is close to infinity. Therefore, there exists a unique n^* such that $q_n^x = q_n^+$ for $n < n^*$, and $q_n^x = q_n^*$ for $n > n^*$.

The outcome of this migration process is represented in Figure 11.3. The skill levels remaining in rural areas correspond to the shaded area. The maximal skill level in all rural areas is $q_{n*}^* \simeq q_{n*}^+$, which may be quite low if transport costs, c_n, decrease slowly with respect to n, or if the maximal native skill level, q_n^*, decreases rapidly. Moreover, if $n < n^*$ (on the left-hand side in Figure 11.3), the maximal local skill level is the maximal skill level for the remaining rural workers, q_n^+. Labor markets closer to the metropolis are strongly under the influence of migrations. Those labor markets are depressed by the metropolitan attraction. Conversely, if $n > n^*$ (right-hand side in Figure 11.3), there is no

---

[7] Remember that the distance is more a socioeconomic restraint than a physical impediment.
[8] This is only a simplifying assumption, without loss of generality when the scale for measuring q is appropriately chosen.

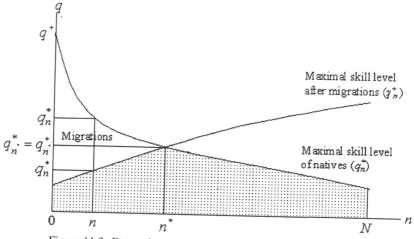

Figure 11.3. Determinants of the highest local skill level.

out-migration, and the maximal local skill level is the maximal skill level of native workers, q_n^*. Labor markets far from the metropolis suffer primarily from their inability to train skilled workers.

4 The Forces for Decentralization

4.1 Monopsonistic Firms in Rural Labor Markets

At the very start of industrial decentralization, the number of rural areas was large, and most of the rural areas were small. Thus, each decentralizing firm had the opportunity to choose an area that had not previously been entered by a decentralizing competitor. Moreover, in those small rural areas, a second decentralizing firm would be discouraged from setting up to compete there. And most decentralizing firms were large, able to employ the whole rural labor force in those areas into which they moved their new plants. Those firms did not need the support of regional production networks, whereas the small pioneer firms analyzed by Rauch (1993) and Hanson (1996) did need such networks.

If the decentralization process starts after workers' migrations, and if the firm using technology θ remains monopsonistic on labor market n, its profit will be

$$\Pi_n(\theta) = P_n \int_{g(\theta)}^{q_n^+} [h(q, \theta) - \omega] l_n(q) \, dq - f_n(\theta) \tag{11.2}$$

Comparison of (11.1) and (11.2) shows that for a firm, the decision to decentralize depends upon two main factors. On the one hand, a firm moving to a

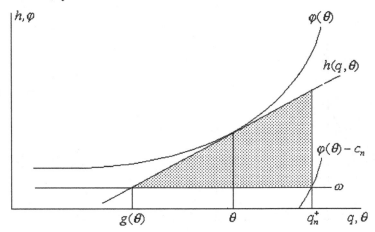

Figure 11.4. The monopsonistic firm.

rural labor market will change its status from monopsonistically competitive to purely monopsonistic. Its labor-market segment will no longer be limited by the presence of neighboring competitors. Moreover, because workers who decide to remain in the rural labor market have only one choice – that between a job with the industrial firm and a job in the traditional sector – the firm can pay all its employees the minimal wage ω, regardless of their skills. As seen in Figure 11.4, the contribution of a q-skill worker to the firm's profit is $h(q, \theta_i) - \omega$. On the urban labor market, the presence of close competitors would limit that contribution to $h(q, \theta_i) - \max[h(q, \theta_{i-1}), h(q, \theta_{i+1})]$, which would be smaller.

On the other hand, we know that rural labor markets have already lost their most skilled workers, who migrated to the metropolis where they could earn higher wages. In labor market n, the maximal skill level is q_n^+. This outmigration of the most highly skilled workers has an important impact on profit: Because all workers are paid the same wage, a worker's contribution to the firm's profit is larger the higher his skill level. Moreover, if firm i moves to rural area n, it no longer benefits from the urban externalities generated by the metropolis. Its rural fixed costs $f_n(\theta_i)$ are likely to be higher than were its metropolitan fixed costs $f_0(\theta_i)$.

Thus, when choosing between a metropolitan site and a rural location, a firm must arbitrate primarily between local monopsony rents extracted from rural workers, on one hand, and, on the other hand, urban externalities and a high labor-force density. A similar arbitration was discussed by Fujita, Thisse, and Zenou (1997) in an intra-urban context. The main difference between our model and theirs is that their labor force was homogeneous. To determine which firms will have the greatest incentive to decentralize, let us examine the derivative of Π_n with respect to θ, which can be written, after some manipulation,

$$\frac{\partial \Pi_n}{\partial \theta} = \varphi''(\theta) P_n \{L_n(q_n^+) - L_n[g(\theta)]\}\{E_n[g(\theta), q_n^+] - \theta\} - \frac{\partial f_n}{\partial \theta}$$

where $E_n[g(\theta), q_n^+] = \{L_n(q_n^+) - L_n[g(\theta)]\}^{-1} \int_{g(\theta)}^{q_n^+} q l(q) \, dq$ is the mean skill level for the labor force employed by the firm. It is straightforward that $E_n[g(\theta), q_n^+] > q^-$ and that for all $q > q_n^+$, $E_n[g(\theta), q_n^+] \leq q_n^+ < q$.

Let us first examine what happens when all firms have the same fixed costs, hence $\partial f_n/\partial \theta = 0$. For the less technological firms, θ being close to q_n^-, the skill level q for most workers will be higher than θ, and $h(q, \theta)$ will be increasing in θ. A slightly higher θ implies higher productivity for almost every worker and thus greater profit. Conversely, for the most technological firms, θ being higher than q_n^+, the skill level for all workers will be lower than θ, and $h(q, \theta)$ will be decreasing in θ. A slightly higher θ now implies lower productivity for every worker and thus lower profit. By continuity, there exists an optimal technological level $\theta^m(q_n^+)$. Characterized by the equality $\theta^m(q_n^+) = E_n\{g[\theta^m(q_n^+)], q_n^+\}$, the optimal technological level is lower than q_n^+. Moreover, because the mean skill level $E_n[g(\theta), q_n^+]$ is an increasing function of q_n^+, the optimal technological level will be lower when q_n^+ is lower (i.e, when more workers have migrated to the metropolis).

The fact that the optimal technology, $\theta^m(q_n^+)$, equals the mean skill level of the labor force employed by the firm, $E_n\{g[\theta^m(q_n^+)], q_n^+\}$, does not imply that the optimal technology is a medium-level technology. Recall that technological levels higher than q_n^+ cannot make the highest profits in area n. This is a consequence of the fact that the higher the technological level, the higher the productivity differential between high skill levels and low skill levels, and the more sensitive the firm will be to the departure of the highest-skill workers. Therefore, when q_n^+ is low, which is the case for rural areas close to the metropolis, θ^m is low.

Of course, higher migration costs from more distant rural areas imply higher maximal skill levels and thus higher optimal technological levels. Together with area n, let us consider a more remote rural area, say m, with $m > n$. Workers in area m will have higher migration costs to the metropolis: $c_m > c_n$. These higher migration costs imply a greater ability to retain the most skilled workers. The highest skill level will be lower the closer the area is to the metropolis: $q_m^+ > q_n^+$. When the labor force is identically distributed in both areas [for all q, $L_m(q) = L_n(q)$], the mean skill level will be lower in labor market n,

$$E_m[g(\theta), q_m^+] > E_n[g(\theta), q_n^+]$$

This has two consequences. First, without differences in fixed costs [$f_m(\theta) =$

$f_n(\theta)$ for all θ] or sizes ($P_m = P_n$) between areas, profit will be higher in the most remote rural area, for all technological levels: $\Pi_m(\theta) > \Pi_n(\theta)$. Second, if all technological levels have the same fixed costs [$\partial f_n(\theta)/\partial\theta = 0$ for all n], the firm making the highest profit will have a higher technological level in the most remote rural area: $\theta^m(q_m^+) > \theta^n(q_n^+)$. As long as these assumptions hold, the basic movement will be by medium-technology firms moving to the most distant rural areas. Those areas will be the most profitable. They entail the highest migration costs, which implies that even high-skill workers will not have out-migrated. Therefore, in those areas, medium technological levels are the most competitive.

However, the most likely assumption about the skill distribution is that highly rural societies will be unable to train a labor force well adapted to fill the jobs in the modern sector. Thus, the more rural an area, the lower the proportion of high skill levels in the native labor force: L_m stochastically dominates L_n at the first order. Without migration, for all n, $q_n^+ = q^+$, and a straightforward calculation leads to:

$$\Pi_n(\theta) = P_n \left[\int_{g(\theta)}^{q^+} h(q,\theta)l_n(q)\,dq - \omega(L\{q^+ - L[g(\theta)]\}) \right] - f_n(\theta)$$

and

$$E_m[g(\theta), q^+] < E_n[g(\theta), q^+]$$

A straightforward consequence of stochastic dominance is that the value of the integral is higher in area m than in area n. Therefore, for $\Pi_n(\theta)$ to be higher than $\Pi_m(\theta)$, $f_n(\theta)$ must be lower than $f_m(\theta)$, or P_n must be higher than P_m. The most rural labor markets must have lower fixed costs and/or larger populations. Both assumptions being unlikely, $\Pi_n(\theta) < \Pi_m(\theta)$, and more rural labor markets will be less profitable. Moreover, in less rural labor markets, the most profitable firms will have lower technological levels.

To summarize, whether a firm's profitability will increase or decrease when it moves from a less rural area to a more rural area will depend upon the balance involving four effects. The first is a size effect, with a smaller population implying lower profit. The second is a skill-distribution effect, with profit being lower when the proportion of low-skill workers is higher. The third is a fixed-cost effect, with high fixed costs having a negative effect on profit. The fourth is a migration effect, with more migrations implying more severe losses of high-skill workers and lower profit. The first three effects imply lower profit in more remote rural areas. The fourth effect implies lower profit for less remote rural areas, those closer to the metropolis.

Moreover, whatever the balance among these effects, each rural area will have a labor force with few high-skill workers, which implies that the incentive to decentralize is likely to be stronger for firms producing at lower techno-logical levels. Medium- and high-technology firms will have little incentive to decentralize to areas close to the metropolis. In those areas, labor markets will have been depressed by out-migration of high-skill workers to the metropolis. The same firms will have no incentive to decentralize to areas far from the metropolis, for those areas are not able to train skilled workers. Moreover, the variation in fixed costs, $\partial f_n / \partial \theta$ being positive, adds a negative term to $\partial \Pi_n / \partial \theta$. Therefore, in order to compensate for the increase in fixed costs, the mean skill level now will have to be higher than the optimal technological level. Then the optimal technological level will be lower when fixed costs increase with the technological level than when fixed costs are the same for all firms. The incentive to decentralize will be lower for high- and medium-technology firms.

4.2 Metropolitan Centralization versus Rural Decentralization

When should firms in the modern sector remain centralized in the metropolis, and when will economic forces prompt them to decentralize toward rural areas? The answer combines findings from analyses of both the metropolitan and rural labor markets. For each technological level θ, we are able to find the equilibrium profit level in the metropolis, $\Pi_0(\theta)$, and the maximal monopsonistic profit in a rural area, $\Pi_r(\theta) = \max_{n>1} \Pi_n(\theta)$. Metropolitan centralization will continue as long as the rural profit curve, $\Pi_r(\theta)$, lies everywhere below the metropolitan profit curve, $\Pi_0(\theta)$. Decentralization will start when, at least for some tech-nological levels, $\Pi_r(\theta)$ becomes higher than $\Pi_0(\theta)$. The larger the (positive) difference $\Pi_r(\theta) - \Pi_0(\theta)$, the stronger the incentive toward decentralization. For which technological levels is this incentive likely to be the strongest?

We know from Section 3.2 that because the metropolitan labor market is large, with many firms, all firms will have approximately the same profit level, regardless of the shape of the technological frontier and the distribution of the labor force across skill levels. Moreover, if the metropolitan labor market is oligopsonistically competitive, then at the long-term equilibrium all firms will have profits close to zero. Therefore, $\Pi_0(\theta)$ will be quite flat and close to zero, and the forces determining decentralization will come more from the rural labor markets than from the metropolitan market.

This does not imply that classical polarization forces, particularly urban externalities, play no role. When urban externalities increase, implying lower fixed costs f_0 in the metropolis, new urban firms will enter the metropolitan labor market until the marginal firm earns zero profit. With more firms in the metropolis, the polarization of the spatial system will be higher. However, profits in the metropolis at that new equilibrium will be unchanged, because they depend only on the shape of ψ. The decentralization incentives will thus remain unchanged, at least over the long run.

Because the urban profit curve, $\Pi_0(\theta)$, is quite flat and close to zero, we can approximate the decentralization condition, $\Pi_r(\theta) > \Pi_0(\theta)$, by the condition $\Pi_r(\theta) > 0$. Then

$$\Pi_n(\theta) = P_n \int_{g(\theta)}^{q_n^+} [h(q,\theta) - \omega] l_n(q)\, dq - f_n(\theta) > 0$$

for at least some $n > 0$ and some θ. Four parameters appear in this formula: the local population P_n, the maximal skill level q_n^+ (which is determined by the migration cost c_n), the reservation wage ω, and the fixed costs $f_n(\theta)$. It is straightforward that the effects of these parameters on profits are given by the partial derivatives $\partial \Pi_n / \partial P_n > 0$ and $\partial \Pi_n / \partial q_n^+ > 0$, and then $\partial \Pi_n / \partial c_n > 0$, $\partial \Pi_n / \partial \omega < 0$, and $\partial \Pi_n / \partial f$.

Three factors might then prevent decentralization. First, rural labor markets might be too small: For each n, the size of the rural labor force, $P_n L_n(q_n^+)$, would be too low. Second, the socioeconomic difference between rural areas and the metropolis might be small. Hence, the reservation wage ω would be close to the marginal productivity in industrial production, and the monopsonistic rent earned from employing a skill-q worker, $h(q, \theta) - \omega$, would be too low. Moreover, a small socioeconomic difference implies easier migration. Thus, for all n, c_n would be low, labor markets would more easily lose their most skilled workers, and the maximal skill levels, q_n^+, would be low. Hence, migration would contribute to the small size of the local labor force. Last, most new industrial technologies are highly sensitive to urban externalities, and fixed costs in rural areas, $f_n(\theta)$, might be high compared with fixed costs in the metropolis.

As long as these conditions prevail, there will be no decentralization. Decentralization can occur if one or more of the three barriers disappear. Demographic growth, agglomeration phenomena, and lower costs of daily transport will progressively enlarge rural labor markets: P_n will increase. With larger labor forces, rural areas will become more profitable. The enlarging socioeconomic gap will induce higher migration costs, c_n. Then q_n^+ will increase, and rural areas will be better able to retain their local labor forces and, within those labour forces, higher skill levels, which are the most profitable for firms. Moreover, the standardization of industrial technologies will make them less sensitive to urban externalities: $f_n(\theta)$ will decrease, at least for the lowest technological levels. All these changes will have similar effects on rural profits. They imply larger profits $\Pi_n(\theta)$ in rural areas. At the same time, as noted earlier, monopsonistic competition on the metropolitan labor market will maintain profits close to zero for all urban firms. Therefore, as soon as $\Pi_n(\theta)$ becomes significantly positive for at least some n and some θ, decentralization can start.

However, associated with the larger socioeconomic gap between rural and metropolitan areas, technical progress can have ambiguous effects. Localized primarily in the industrial sector, it increases the efficiency of firms, and the technological frontier, $\varphi(\theta)$, will move upward, whereas the reservation wage, ω, will be stable or even decrease with the crisis of the traditional sector. The monopsonistic rents, $h(q, \theta) - \omega$, will become larger. But at the same time, an upward move of the technological frontier will induce a similar upward move of the metropolitan wage curve, $w(q)$, and thus further rural migrations. The maximal skill level in rural areas, q_n^+, will decrease, which may offset the increase in monopsonistic rents.

These ambiguous effects of technological progress can be clearly seen in the case of the quadratic technological frontier introduced in Section 4.1, $\varphi(q) = \alpha(q + \mu)^2$. Technological progress moves the technological frontier φ upward through an increase in the shift parameter μ. One can easily show that if $\mu < q_n^x/2$, the optimal technology in area n will be $\theta^m = (2q_n^x - \mu)/3$, used by a firm employing only workers whose skill level is higher than $(q_n^x - 2\mu)/3$. Its profit will be

$$\Pi_n = -f_n + \alpha P_n \frac{q_n^x}{q_n^*} \left(q_n^x + \mu\right)^2$$

If $\mu > q_n^x/2$, the optimal technology in area n will be $\theta^m = q_n^x/2$, in a firm employing the entire local labor force. Its profit will be

$$\Pi_n = -f_n + \frac{8\alpha P_n}{27q_n^*} \left(q_n^x + \mu\right)^3$$

In both cases,

$$\frac{d\Pi_n}{d\mu} = \frac{\partial \Pi_n}{\partial \mu} + \frac{\partial \Pi_n}{\partial q_n^x} \frac{\partial q_n^x}{\partial \mu}$$

The direct effect of technical progress, $\partial \Pi_n/\partial \mu$, is positive. It corresponds to larger monopsonistic rents. However, because $q_n^x = \min(q_n^*, \sqrt{c_n/\alpha} - \mu)$ is a nonincreasing function of μ, the indirect effect, induced by migrations, $(\partial \Pi_n/\partial q_n^x)/(\partial q_n^x/\partial \mu)$, will be negative.

In the most remote rural areas, where n is close to N, then as long as μ is not too high, there will be no migrations, and $q_n^x = q_n^*$. There is no indirect effect, and technical progress benefits the firm. Conversely, in rural areas close to the metropolis, workers with the highest native skill levels will migrate to the metropolis, and $q_n^x = \sqrt{c_n/\alpha} - \mu$. If $\mu < (2/3)\sqrt{c_n/\alpha}$, the profit of the firm will be

$$\Pi_n = -f_n + \frac{\alpha P_n}{4q_n^*} \left(\frac{c_n}{\alpha} - \mu^2\right) \left(\sqrt{\frac{c_n}{\alpha}} + \mu\right)$$

That profit will increase for $\mu < \sqrt{c_n/\alpha}/(1 + \sqrt{3})$ and decrease thereafter. Conversely, if $\mu > (2/3)\sqrt{c_n/\alpha}$, the profit of the firm will be

$$\Pi_n = -f_n + \frac{8P_n}{27q_n^*}c_n^{3/2}\alpha^{-1/2}$$

and will no longer depend on μ. The direct and indirect effects exactly offset each other.

Therefore, technical progress does not appear as a factor for industrial decentralization. Only the most rural areas with low levels of out-migration would become more attractive. But those areas are also likely to be the less heavily populated areas, with the lowest skills and the highest fixed costs. In areas closer to the metropolis, technical progress will induce further out-migration by workers who seek to benefit from the higher metropolitan wages. The greatest impulses toward decentralization are not likely to come from technical progress. They result from demographic growth, agglomeration phenomena, and a lower sensitivity to urban externalities.

Which technologies will be able to decentralize first, and where? In Section 4.1, we saw that the optimal technological level in rural labor market n, $\theta^m(q_n^+)$, is strictly higher than q^- and strictly lower than q_n^+. A straightforward implication of this result is that the most advanced technological firms, which are the firms most sensitive to variations in the level of technology, cannot be the firms making the highest profits in rural areas. Hence they are not likely to be the first to decentralize. Moreover, decentralization is most likely for those firms operating at low technological levels. In areas close to the metropolis, because migration costs are low there, the best workers will be attracted to the metropolis. Because the highest skill level among the remaining rural workers, q_n^+, will be low, so will the optimal technological level, $\theta^m(q_n^+)$. In more remote rural areas, migration costs are higher, and thus q_n^+ will be higher. All other things being equal, the optimal technological level would be higher. But, as noted earlier, all other things are not equal, and there is a greater proportion of low-skill workers remaining in the rural workforce, and thus the optimal technological level is moved downward. In a period of large socioeconomic differences, this downward effect is likely to be strong, implying a low optimal technological level in each rural area.

However, the dynamics of this decentralization process will lead to its exhaustion. For its profit in a rural area to remain high, a decentralizing firm must continue to enjoy a monopsonistic position. As soon as a second firm sets up for business in the same area, the main advantages of the rural labor market disappear. The two firms will have to share the same labor force. Moreover, without collusion, each competitor must now bid for workers, offering a wage at least sufficient for it to match the productivity of its competitor. The monopsonistic rent, $h(q, \theta) - \omega$, disappears. Therefore, for a duopsony to be possible, the rural population, P_n, or the maximal skill level, q_n^+, must be much larger than that for a monopsonistic firm; or else the fixed costs, $f_n(\theta)$, must be lower.

The fact that duopsonistic profits largely fall short of monopsonistic profit contributes to the ability of a decentralized firm to maintain its local monopsony, at least in the early stages of the decentralization process. If P_n is large enough for a monopsony to be profitable, but is too low for duopsonistic firms to make positive profits, then the rural labor market is a natural monopsony. But as decentralization progresses, there will be fewer and fewer rural labor markets in which a newly decentralizing firm can enjoy a monopsonistic position, and the most profitable markets will be progressively occupied. More importantly, if rural labor markets continue to enlarge, their native populations will become sufficiently large that they will be able to attract more than one firm. Of course, as long as there are unexploited rural areas where setting up a monopsony is possible, decentralizing firms will continue to move to those areas. But as soon as there are no more untapped rural labor markets, firms will begin to move to occupied markets, progressively destroying the monopsonistic rents of their competitors.

Moreover, industrialization of rural labor markets induces transformations of rural ways of life, and then the socioeconomic gap between urban and rural areas narrows. All these factors imply lower rents for rural firms and lower incentives to decentralize. Hence, the decentralization process cannot continue forever. It is only a transition process from the state of highly concentrated industrial activity located in the metropolis to a more decentralized structure that will reach a point of stability, without further decentralization.

5 Conclusion: Do We Have Spatial Division of Labor?

We are now able to provide an abstract description of the process of decentralization. The emergence of decentralization results from the set of changes described earlier. The growth of rural agglomerations and decreases in transport costs enlarge rural labor markets. The standardization of industrial technologies makes them less sensitive to metropolitan externalities. Technological progress and its impact on the socioeconomic gap between urban and rural areas increase monopsonistic rents. But, at the same time, new rural workers are attracted by the metropolis.

What is likely to happen when socioeconomic conditions allow for decentralization? In Section 4 we have shown that the most highly technological firms are not likely to decentralize to rural areas. In those labor markets they cannot compete with the less highly technological firms that are less sensitive to the scarcity of high-skill workers. Therefore, metropolitan areas will continue to host the most highly technological firms. Moreover, even if migration flows are reduced, workers with the highest skill levels still will migrate to metropolitan areas. These areas will continue to concentrate the high-technology firms and the high-skill workers, and competitive pressure will oblige firms to pay every worker a wage close to his marginal productivity.

Decentralization involves primarily low and medium levels of technology. Decentralizing firms tend to expand into rural areas where the mean skill level is low, at least at the time decentralization begins, and wages remain close to the reservation wage. The outcome of the decentralization process is *spatial division of labor*. However, decentralization appears as a transition process, the dynamics of which will lead to its exhaustion: The most profitable rural labor markets will be progressively occupied. The labor force in a rural labor market will become large enough for duopsony to be possible, destroying the monopsony rent.

Although decentralization appears as a transition phase, that transition phase may have long-term consequences. If the ability of a rural area to train its labor force is linked to the mean technological level of the industries it hosts, then the mean skill level in that area will remain low. It will thus be able to attract only those firms whose production involves low technological levels. Spatial division of labor continues.

Appendix

Proof of Proposition 1

If only the degree of differentiation varies, the labor-force density remains fixed, $l(\theta) = l$. Differentiating (11.1), we find that

$$\frac{\partial \Pi_i}{\partial \theta_i} = l\varphi''(\theta_i) \int_{\gamma_{i-1,i}}^{\gamma_{i,i+1}} (q - \theta_i)\,dq = \frac{l\varphi''(\theta_i)}{2}$$
$$\times (\gamma_{i,i+1} - \gamma_{i-1,i})(\gamma_{i,i+1} + \gamma_{i-1,i} - 2\theta_i)$$

Because φ is convex and $\varphi''(\theta_i) > 0$ and $\gamma_{i,i+1} > \gamma_{i-1,i}$, for $\theta_i \in [\gamma_{i-1,i}, \gamma_{i,i+1}]$, Π_i has a unique maximum when $\theta_i = (\gamma_{i,i+1} + \gamma_{i-1,i})/2$, that is, when θ_i is the middle of the segment $[\gamma_{i-1,i}, \gamma_{i,i+1}]$.

Then the difference between any two consecutive market segments is

$$(\gamma_{i+1,i+2} - \gamma_{i,i+1}) - (\gamma_{i,i+1} - \gamma_{i-1,i}) = 2(\theta_{i+1} - \gamma_{i,i+1}) - 2(\gamma_{i,i+1} - \theta_i)$$

and, after straightforward calculations,

$$(\theta_{i+1} - \gamma_{i,i+1}) \gtreqless (\gamma_{i,i+1} - \theta_i) \Leftrightarrow \varphi(\theta_{i+1}) - \varphi(\theta_i) \gtreqless (\theta_{i+1} - \theta_i)$$
$$\times \frac{\varphi'(\theta_{i+1}) + \varphi'(\theta_i)}{2}$$

Moreover, when φ'' increases with respect to θ, we have the following inequality (which is reversed when φ'' decreases):

$$\varphi(\theta_{i+1}) - \varphi(\theta_i) \le (\theta_{i+1} - \theta_i)\frac{\varphi'(\theta_{i+1}) + \varphi'(\theta_i)}{2}$$

The last two inequalities imply $(\theta_{i+1} - \gamma_{i,i+1}) \le (\gamma_{i,i+1} - \theta_i)$, and then $\gamma_{i,i+1} \ge (\theta_{i+1} + \theta_i)/2$ and $(\gamma_{i+1,i+2} - \gamma_{i,i+1}) \le (\gamma_{i,i+1} - \gamma_{i-1,i})$. The opposite holds when φ'' decreases. ∎

Proof of Proposition 2

When only the labor-force density varies, the degree of differentiation, $\varphi''(\theta)$, is a constant, and $\varphi(\theta)$ is quadratic. Thus, $\varphi(\theta) = \varphi_2\theta^2 + \varphi_1\theta + \varphi_0$, $\alpha(\theta) = \varphi'(\theta) = 2\varphi_2\theta + \varphi_1$, $\beta(\theta) = \varphi(\theta) - \theta\varphi'(\theta) = \varphi_0 - \varphi_2\theta^2$, and

$$\gamma_{i,j} = \frac{\beta(\theta_i) - \beta(\theta_j)}{\alpha(\theta_j) - \alpha(\theta_i)} = \frac{\varphi_2(\theta_j^2 - \theta_i^2)}{2\varphi_2(\theta_j - \theta_i)} = \frac{\theta_i + \theta_j}{2}$$

which, applied to $j = i + 1$, gives $\gamma_{i,i+1} = (\theta_i + \theta_{i+1})/2$, and the separating point between the two consecutive market segments is the midpoint between the two firms' locations.

Now, differentiating formula (11.1), we find that

$$\frac{\partial \Pi_i}{\partial \theta_i} = 2\varphi_2 \int_{(\theta_{i-1} - \theta_i)/2}^{(\theta_{i+1} - \theta_i)/2} ql(q + \theta_i)\,dq$$

Let us assume that $l'(\theta) > 0$. If $\theta_i \le (\theta_{i-1} + \theta_{i+1})/2$, then $\theta_i - \theta_{i-1} \le \theta_{i+1} - \theta_i$, and

$$\frac{\partial \Pi_i}{\partial \theta_i} = 2\varphi_2 \int_0^{(\theta_i - \theta_{i-1})/2} ql[l(\theta_i + q) - l(\theta_i - q)]\,dq$$
$$+ 2\varphi_2 \int_{(\theta_i - \theta_{i-1})/2}^{(\theta_{i+1} - \theta_i)/2} ql(q + \theta_i)\,dq > 0$$

Thus, Π_i can reach its maximum for $\theta_i > (\theta_{i-1} + \theta_{i+1})/2$ only. A similar proof leads to the conclusion that when $l'(\theta) < 0$, Π_i can reach its maximum for $\theta_i < (\theta_{i-1} + \theta_{i+1})/2$ only. Summarizing,

$$l'(\theta) \gtrless 0 \Leftrightarrow \theta_i \gtrless \frac{\theta_{i-1} + \theta_{i+1}}{2} \Leftrightarrow \theta_i - \frac{\theta_{i-1} + \theta_{i+1}}{2} \gtrless 0$$

Then, on every interval where l is monotonically increasing,

$$\theta_i - \theta_{i-1} > \theta_{i+1} - \theta_i > \theta_{i+2} - \theta_{i+1}$$

which implies that

$$\gamma_{i,i+1} - \gamma_{i-1,i} = \frac{\theta_{i+1} - \theta_{i-1}}{2} > \frac{\theta_{i+2} - \theta_i}{2} = \gamma_{i+1,i+2} - \gamma_{i,i+1}$$

and the market segment of firm i is larger than the market segment of firm $i + 1$. A similar proof shows that the opposite holds when l is monotonically decreasing. ∎

References

Abdel-Rahman, H., and Wang, P. (1995). Toward a general equilibrium theory of a core–periphery system of cities. *Regional Science and Urban Economics* 25:529–46.

Aydalot, P. (1976). *Dynamique spatiale et développement inégal.* Paris: Economica.

Aydalot, P. (1985). *Economie Régionale et Urbaine.* Paris: Economica.

Borjas, G. J., Bronars, S. G., and Trejo, S. J. (1992). Self-selection and internal migration in the United States. NBER working paper 4002.

Fujita, M., and Krugman, P. (1995). When is the economy monocentric? von Thünen and Chamberlin unified. *Regional Science and Urban Economics* 25:505–28.

Fujita, M., Thisse, J.-F., and Zenou, Y. (1997). On the endogenous formation of secondary employment centers in a city. *Journal of Urban Economics* 41:337–57.

Gabszewicz, J., and Thisse, J.-F. (1992). Location. In: R. Auman and O. Hart (eds.), *Handbook of Game Theory with Economic Applications,* pp. 281–304. Amsterdam: North Holland.

Hannoun, M., and Sicherman, G. (1983). Résorption des disparités régionales et nouveaux clivages. *Economie et Statistique* 153:59–74.

Hanson, G. H. (1996). Agglomeration, dispersion and the pioneer firm. *Journal of Urban Economics* 39:255–81.

Henderson, J. V. (1985). *Economic Theory and the Cities.* London: Academic Press.

Jayet, H. (1996). Segmentation in a labour market with vertical differentiation. Mimeograph CESURE, Lille.

Krugman, P. (1991). *Geography and Trade.* Cambridge, MA: MIT Press.

Lederer, P. J., and Hurter, A. P. (1986). Competition of firms: discriminatory pricing and location. *Econometrica* 54:623–40.

Mary, S., and Turpin, E. (1980). *Panorama économique des régions françaises.* Paris: INSEE.

Massey, D. (1984). *Spatial Division of Labor: Social Structures and the Organisation of Production.* London: Macmillan.

Rauch, J. (1993). Does history matter when it matters a little? The case of city-industry location. *Quarterly Journal of Economics* 108:843–67.

Salop, S. (1979). Monopolistic competition with outside goods. *Bell Journal of Economics* 10:141–56.

Thisse, J., and Zenou, Y. (1995). Appariement et concurrence spatiale sur le marché du travail. *Revue Economique* 46:615–24.

CHAPTER 12

Cities and the Geography of Financial Centers
Thomas Gehrig

1 Introduction

When thinking about financial centers, the names of major cities immediately come to mind. Larger centers tend to be associated with cities that are also known for their cultural or political prominence, such as New York City, Tokyo, Hong Kong, Singapore, Paris, Frankfurt, Zurich, Amsterdam, Milan, and Toronto. The Corporation of London (the City of London) is London's financial center around Threadneedle Street and the Bank of England. Is it true that financial activity is so totally concentrated in cities? And if so, why? Moreover, are there systematic differences in the amounts of economic and financial activity across those cities? Should we expect to see even greater concentrations in fewer centers because of the ongoing integration of world capital markets, or will the established centers remain viable in international competition?

The recent creation of new offshore centers in the Bahamas, the Channel Islands, and the Cayman Islands suggests that there will be increases in the number of financial centers. Moreover, trends toward a delocalization of financial activity can also be observed. There are numerous examples in which financial activity does not seem to be concentrated in narrowly defined geographical locations. For example, currency trading nowadays takes place via worldwide computer networks. Any intermediary with access to the network can trade foreign currency from almost any location. Likewise, computer networks, such as the Arizona exchange, compete with established stock exchanges for trading volume in securities. Furthermore, financial intermediaries increasingly relegate substantial activities into suburban regions. Do these developments herald the decline of financial centers? Will computer networks and improvements in

Financial support from the Schweizerischer Nationalfonds is gratefully acknowledged. Without implicating them, I am grateful for the comments of Jean-Marie Huriot, Thilo Kaufmann, Monika Merz, Jacques Thisse, Carl-Christian von Weizsäcker, and Nobuyoshi Yamori. This study has also benefited from discussions with members of the New York Stock Exchange and seminar participants at the universities of Cologne and Nagoya. Katrin Eckert and Teja Flotho provided able research assistance.

communication technologies lead to a more even distribution of financial activity across space? Will geography even become irrelevant, as forcefully argued by O'Brien (1992)?

The answers to those questions will be particularly important for the development and survival of cities, as well as for regional distributions of employment and income. Accordingly, policy implications will affect city councils, city planners, and other regional interest groups. According to *The Economist* (1995a), it was mainly tourism and the growth of financial markets that halted the decline of Western cities. Indeed, financial centers tend to benefit disproportionately in terms of employment and tax revenues (Tschoegl, 1989). Consequently, those who determine the foreign and domestic policies of any nation should also be concerned about the determinants of the stability of financial centers.

But what precisely is a financial center? According to Kindleberger (1974, p. 6), "financial centers are needed not only to balance through time the savings and investments of individual entrepreneurs and to transfer financial capital from savers to investors, but also to effect payments and to transfer savings between places. Banking and financial centers perform a medium of exchange function and an inter-spatial store-of-value function. . . . [T]he specialized functions of international payments and foreign lending or borrowing are typically best performed at one central place that is also (in most instances) the specialized center for domestic interregional payments." Interestingly, Kindleberger defines financial centers by the functions they perform. He does not mention geographical criteria. For him, it seems obvious that a center consists of an agglomeration of banks and highly specialized intermediaries. For example, in his view, an international financial center provides "the highly specialized functions of lending abroad and serving as a clearinghouse for payments among countries. Banks, brokers, security dealers, and the like establish branches in such centers" (Kindleberger, 1974, p. 57). Surprisingly, Kindleberger does not account for the possibility that computer networks could provide precisely those functions and therefore also qualify as financial centers according to his definition.

Based largely on the work of Kindleberger, the recent empirical literature defines financial centers as geographical locations with agglomerations of branches or subsidiaries of banks and other financial intermediaries in narrowly defined regions. According to this definition, financial centers are typically located in cities, with the notable exceptions of some offshore centers.

There also seems to be wide agreement in the literature about the existence of a hierarchical structure of financial centers. Johnson (1976), for example, distinguishes international financial centers, such as New York City and London, from regional financial centers. In his view,

regional financial centers, such as Hong Kong, Singapore and Panama, derive their role primarily from a combination of geographical proximity to the countries in which customers operate and the safety and ease of operations of subsidiaries, branches, and agencies of foreign banks whose head office lies in the international financial centers, rather than in generating customers in other parts of the region through their own national size and international power and the competence of their own national banks in international financial business. They are largely hosts to foreign financial institutions that find it convenient to locate offices there, rather than magnets of financial power in their own right, attracting foreign financial enterprises to establish subsidiaries in order to obtain a piece of the action. (Johnson, 1976, p. 261)

Many authors distinguish even more layers of hierarchy in the order of financial centers. It seems that there is little disagreement about the existence of scale economies and agglomerative forces that favor concentration of international financial activity in a few international financial centers. On the other hand, diseconomies or deglomerative forces are viewed as providing the raison d'être for lower-order financial centers.[1]

Kindleberger suggests that scale economies in the organization of financial markets are major centripetal forces in financial markets. He views localized information, different time zones, and discriminatory practices in business relations as the major centrifugal forces. To the extent that local information can be transmitted readily through computer networks, according to this view, one might predict the decline of lower-order financial centers as information technology improves. This prediction is in line with observations of increasing concentrations of financial activity in fewer places in most national markets. But how does this prediction fit with the observation of growing lower-order financial centers in Asia and the emergence of new financial centers in Eastern Europe and the Near East? Should we expect a reversion of this trend or even a complete annihilation of lower-order financial centers? More generally, how do technological improvements affect the overall structure of financial centers?

This chapter explores the possible role of market frictions in providing answers to these questions and argues that a more detailed analysis of the current developments in financial markets worldwide is required. Empirical observations suggest the presence of apparently countervailing movements of increasing geographical concentration of certain activities and increasing delocalization of other activities. In order to try to understand these seemingly paradoxical observations, this study will argue that it is particularly useful to classify financial activities according to their informational content. *Trade in informationally sensitive securities is likely to be geographically concentrated at those locations where information about those securities is aggregated and communicated.* These (national) informational centers often happen to be (national) financial centers. In contrast, *trade in standardized securities is more*

---

[1] This finding mirrors central place theory (Christaller, 1933). According to Fujita and Thisse (Chapter 1, this volume), an explanation for the robust empirical regularity of a rank-size rule among cities remains a major challenge for economists.

likely to be footloose, reacting more sensitively to (regulatory) cost differentials. Moreover, reductions in transactions costs may reinforce these geographical patterns, in that they may increase the concentration of informationally sensitive activities in few locations and may lead to increased dispersion of informationally insensitive activities.

To the extent that financial centers are the locations where complex information about the prospects of a region's investment projects is produced and aggregated, they are attractive sites for multinational banks. Accordingly, technological improvements and reductions in barriers to trade support the development and growth of national financial centers. These centers tend to host primarily information-sensitive activities, whereas information-insensitive activities tend to be relocated to low-cost suburban areas or low-cost communication media such as computerized networks. As regions are becoming informationally more homogeneous, however, a decline of lower-order financial centers is rather likely. Ultimately, therefore, the questions about the future development of cities as financial centers are empirical issues, and their answers will depend on the relative importance and magnitude of centrifugal and centripetal forces in international financial markets.

This chapter is organized as follows. Section 2 provides an account of recent developments concerning financial centers worldwide. Sections 3 and 4 survey the main agglomerative forces and deglomerative forces, respectively, in financial markets. Section 5 discusses the relevance of centrifugal and centripetal forces for securities of different informational complexities. Section 6 provides an analysis of the different geographical implications of technological progress in information and communication technologies for different securities. Section 7 concludes the discussion.

2 The Changing Nature of Financial Centers

The recent experiences of financial centers have been rather mixed. Using Kindleberger's definition of a financial center as a geographical agglomeration of financial intermediaries, we can find centers that have experienced spectacular growth in employment and financial transactions – these are the cities selectively portrayed by *The Economist* (1995a) – and centers that have suffered rapid decline, or even a complete loss, of certain financial activities.

For example, the first report of the U.S. Stock Exchange Commission (SEC) reported 22 exchanges in 1935, whereas its report for 1985 covered only 7 regional exchanges (Table 12.1), plus the 3 national exchanges: the New York Stock Exchange (NYSE), the American Stock Exchange (AMEX), and the National Association of Securities Dealers (NASD) in the United States (Smith, 1991). Similarly, in Germany there existed 21 stock exchanges under the Weimar Republic, as compared with only 8 today (Gehrke and Rasch, 1993).

Table 12.1. *U.S. stock exchanges*

1935	1985
Baltimore Stock Exchange	
Boston Stock Exchange	Boston Stock Exchange
Buffalo Stock Exchange	Intermountain Stock Exchange
Chicago Board of Trade	
Chicago Stock Exchange	
Cincinatti Stock Exchange	Midwest Stock Exchange
Cleveland Stock Exchange	
Denver Stock Exchange	
Detroit Stock Exchange	
	Honolulu Stock Exchange
Los Angeles Stock Exchange	Pacific Stock Exchange
New Orleans Stock Exchange	
New York Curb Exchange	AMEX
New York Produce Exchange	
New York Real Estate Securities Exchange	
New York Stock Exchange	NYSE
Philadelphia Stock Exchange	Philadelphia-Baltimore-Washington SE
Pittsburgh Stock Exchange	
St. Louis Stock Exchange	
Salt Lake City Stock Exchange	
San Francisco Stock Exchange	
San Francisco Curb Exchange	
	Spokane Stock Exchange
Washington Stock Exchange	
	National Market (NASDAQ)

Source: Smith (1991).

On a more systematic basis, Reed (1980, 1981) analyzed the evolution of financial centers. Stock trading is just one activity performed in a financial center, albeit an important one, as we shall see later. Reed attempted to classify financial centers according to objective criteria. In a first stage he employed hierarchical cluster analysis to group a given set of financial centers, and in a second stage he performed stepwise multiple-discriminant analysis to test the group structure and identify the factors that produced the group structure.

In his analysis of 17 Asian financial centers from 1900 to 1975, Reed (1980) used (1) banking variables, such as the numbers of local bank headquarters, the numbers of links to other international financial centers, the numbers of private banks, the numbers of foreign-bank offices, and the links of foreign banks to other international financial centers, and (2) financial variables, such as the amounts of foreign financial assets and the amounts of foreign financial liabilities. According to those criteria, he identified a hierarchical structure of the Asian financial centers. Interestingly, he found decreases in the depths of the hierarchies from 5 levels in 1955 to 4 levels in 1965 and 3 levels in 1975 (Table 12.2).

From a long-run perspective, his analysis documented the relentless rise of Tokyo to the status of a dominant financial center. With a few further exceptions (Yokohama), however, his analysis also revealed little variation in the relative importance of the Asian financial centers. The number of banks headquartered in a given center and the links to other centers contributed significantly (in a statistical sense) to the determination of the estimated group structure. Foreign financial assets and liabilities also seemed relevant, but to a lesser extent.

Later, in a broader study with the larger sample of 80 international financial centers, Reed (1981) identified a strong hierarchical group structure. In 1980, London appeared as the top center, with New York City and Tokyo sharing level two. Amsterdam, Chicago, Frankfurt, Hamburg, Hong Kong, Paris, San Francisco, and Zurich were grouped on level three. Another 30 banks occupied level 4, and the remaining 39 banks were grouped on the lowest level, level five. Again, the numbers of headquartered intermediaries and the links to other financial centers appeared as significant predictors of the group rankings.

Choi et al. (1986, 1996) attempted a more highly structured approach to determining the factors of importance for a financial center. In particular, they tried to identify the sources for the attractiveness of financial centers. Using a sample of the 300 largest multinational banks, they analyzed the banks' location choices for headquarters and branches among 14 international financial centers: London, New York City, Tokyo, Amsterdam, Brussels, Frankfurt–Hamburg, Hong Kong, Los Angeles–San Francisco, Panama City, Paris, Rome–Milan, Singapore, Toronto–Montreal, and Zurich–Geneva. Their analysis for the years 1970 and 1980 has been extended to 1989 by Jeger et al. (1992).

In these analyses, the numbers of banks headquartered in city i that maintain branches in city j are recorded in a matrix (y_{ij}) (Table 12.3). When $y_{ij} > 0$, a one-way link between centers i and j exists, and when, additionally, $y_{ji} > 0$, the link is said to be a two-way link. A one-way link can be interpreted as a direction of influence from center i to center j in the sense that (large) banks from center i maintain internal communication channels to center j. A two-way link suggests an interest in internal communication links from both centers.

Apart from providing information about the direction of influence between two centers, these links allow the definition and measurement of the degrees of connectedness to other financial centers. Both studies mentioned earlier found clear evidence of a tendency toward increasing interconnectedness across financial centers. Absolute and relative numbers (as percentages of all possible

Table 12.2. *Organizational structure and rank of Asian international financial centers*

Organizational Structure

1955 (5 Groups)	1965 (4 Groups)	1975 (3 Groups)
Gp. 1 Hong Kong 2 Tokyo, Osaka 3 Singapore, Bombay, Calcutta 4 Bangkok, Rangoon, Manila, Kobe, Yokohama, Shanghai, Jakarta, Kuala Lumpur	Gp. 1 Tokyo 2 Hong Kong, Osaka Kobe, Singapore, Bombay, Yokohama, Kuala Lumpur, Manila, Calcutta, Bangkok	Gp. 1 Tokyo 2 Osaka, Hong Kong Singapore

Rank Score

1955		1965		1975	
Center	Score	Center	Score	Center	Score
Hong Kong	100	Tokyo	100	Tokyo	100
Tokyo	99	Hong Kong	90	Osaka	84
Osaka	93	Osaka	81	Hong Kong	81
				Singapore	81

Source: Kindleberger (1974).

Table 12.3. *Head offices of major banks and their representation in other centers, 1970, 1980, and 1990*

To: From:	LO	NY	TO	HK	SI	FH	PA	ZG	MR	LS	TM	BR	AM	PN	Sum
LO	14	9	4	1	1	4	8	1	2	2	0	2	7	0	55
	8	8	8	7	4	5	6	3	2	4	4	4	3	1	67
	9	4	5	4	3	2	5	4	2	1	3	3	3	0	48
NY	10	13	8	6	3	7	8	3	5	0	1	4	5	2	75
	9	9	8	8	9	8	8	5	7	7	4	4	3	4	94
	8	8	8	8	8	7	6	8	7	0	6	3	3	2	82
TO	8	8	17	2	2	2	2	1	1	6	1	1	1	0	52
	14	15	23	8	11	10	7	4	1	11	6	3	2	2	117
	17	18	20	14	14	13	10	6	7	13	9	7	3	5	158
HK	1	1	1	1	1	1	1	0	0	1	0	0	0	0	8
	1	1	1	1	1	1	1	1	0	1	1	0	1	0	11
	1	1	1	1	1	1	0	0	0	0	0	0	0	1	7
SI	0	0	0	1	1	0	0	0	0	0	0	0	0	0	2
	1	1	1	1	1	0	0	0	0	0	0	0	0	0	5
	3	3	3	3	3	0	0	0	0	3	0	0	0	0	18
FH	3	2	1	0	1	12	1	0	0	0	0	0	0	0	20
	3	6	4	5	3	12	2	0	1	1	2	1	0	1	42
	8	6	5	5	5	12	3	5	2	5	3	2	2	0	63
PA	5	3	3	1	1	3	7	1	4	1	0	3	4	1	37
	11	13	9	9	6	8	14	2	8	4	2	3	5	3	97
	8	8	7	7	7	5	12	6	8	4	4	5	2	3	86
ZG	1	1	1	1	1	0	1	3	0	1	1	0	1	0	12
	3	3	3	3	2	0	2	5	0	3	2	0	1	0	27
	2	3	3	3	2	0	1	4	1	2	2	0	1	1	25
MR	4	5	0	0	1	5	4	2	12	1	1	3	0	0	38
	7	7	5	3	4	6	4	0	10	4	3	4	0	0	57
	7	7	4	7	3	7	5	2	11	4	3	4	2	0	66
LS	5	4	5	5	1	2	1	1	1	8	0	2	1	1	37
	4	4	4	4	4	4	3	1	2	4	2	1	1	1	39
	3	2	3	3	3	2	2	2	1	4	1	1	1	1	29
TM	5	5	4	4	0	2	2	1	1	4	7	2	1	0	38
	5	5	5	5	4	4	4	1	2	5	5	1	1	2	49
	7	6	6	5	6	4	4	3	2	4	7	0	1	1	56
BR	0	1	0	0	0	1	0	0	0	0	0	3	0	0	5
	3	3	3	2	3	1	1	2	2	0	0	7	0	0	27
	4	4	3	3	1	0	1	2	2	1	0	6	0	0	27
AM	2	2	1	2	0	0	0	0	0	1	0	0	3	0	11
	2	3	2	2	2	0	0	0	1	2	0	1	4	1	20
	2	2	2	2	2	1	2	2	2	1	1	2	2	1	24
PN	0	0	0	0	0	0	0	0	0	0	0	0	0	1	1
	0	1	0	0	0	0	0	0	0	0	0	0	0	1	2
	0	1	0	0	0	0	0	0	0	0	0	0	0	1	2
Sum	58	54	35	39	45	13	24	25	13	23	20	5	26	11	391
	72	80	52	59	76	54	58	46	24	21	29	16	36	31	654
	79	73	70	65	58	54	51	46	45	42	39	33	20	16	691
Rank	1	2	5	4	3	11	8	7	11	9	10	14	6	13	
	3	1	7	4	2	6	5	8	12	13	11	14	9	10	
	1	2	3	4	5	6	7	8	9	10	11	12	13	14	

Notes: From top to bottom in each box: 1970, 1980, 1990. Sum of main diagonal: 102 in 1970, 105 in 1980, and 100 in 1990.
Source: Choi et al. (1996); *The Banker* (1971, 1981, 1991); *The Bankers' Almanac and Yearbook* (1970–71, 1980–81, 1990–91).

Table 12.4. *Degrees of interconnectedness*

Number of links	a) total	b) one-way	c) two-way	
1970	109	71	54	
1980	140	83	58	
1990	144	85	59	

Percentages of links	a) total	b) one-way	c) two-way	d) Cohen's Kappa
1970	60	78	59	0.82
1980	77	91	64	0.92
1990	79	93	65	0.93

links) of total links, one-way links and two-way links, have increased over time (Table 12.4), suggesting closer ties of multinational banks across financial centers. For example, the percentage of total links in terms of potential links (i.e., $14^2 - 14 = 182$) increased from 60% in 1970 to 77% in 1980 and 79% in 1989. Furthermore, the intensity of links (i.e., the number of direct banking connections) has increased over time. Accordingly, despite the technological advances in communication technology, multinational banks have invested in larger networks of offices across international financial centers.

The marginal row $y_{.j} = \sum_i y_{ij}$ can be interpreted as an absolute measure of the attractiveness of center j. Interestingly, the relative attractiveness of centers, as measured by the number of branches, does vary over time. London lost its number-1 position of 1970 (58 branches) in 1980 (72 branches), only to reclaim the top position in 1989 (79 branches). More spectacular is the growth of Singapore, from rank 11 in 1970 to rank 6 in 1989, as well as the decline of Amsterdam from rank 9 (1970) to rank 13 (1989). Also, Zurich improved its rank from number 11 (1970) to number 9 (1989). Single-city centers, such as New York City (NY), Tokyo (TO), London (LO), and Singapore (SI), tend to obtain higher rankings than the more fragmented two-city pairs, such as Frankfurt–Hamburg (FH), Los Angeles–San Francisco (LS), Rome-Milan (MR), and Toronto–Montreal (TM).

More importantly, both studies identified the same sources of attractiveness. The likelihood of attracting a branch of a multinational bank is strongly related to (1) the size of the local economy, (2) the number of banks already there, and (3) the stock-market turnover. Moreover, (4) bilateral trade flows and foreign-investment variables, as well as (5) a dummy variable for banking secrecy, are highly significant. Contrary to Kindleberger's suggestion, time zones do not exert a significant influence; see also Park and Essayyad (1989) and Porteus (1996).

Jeger et al. (1992) also found that the probability of establishing a branch in a given financial center is strongly affected by the trade flows to that center that originate in the bank's home financial center. Those authors interpreted that finding as strong evidence for banks following their customers. It seems that financial services follow real activity. The branch networks of multinational banks seem to reflect the trade flows from the bank's home market. In particular, these networks are not symmetric. For example, there are more Italian banks active in Frankfurt (4 in 1970 and 5 in 1980) than vice versa (0 and 1, respectively). Moreover, even at the end of the 1980s, global financial markets appeared rather fragmented.

In addition to the need to follow domestic clientele, Goldberg and Grosse (1994) and Yamori (1998) have found evidence for a leading role by banks. It appears that the location choices of foreign banks within the United States are also significantly affected by the banking opportunities there. Banks seem to value the (potential) presence of other banks.

Accordingly, the attractiveness of a financial center for multinational banks is closely related to the amount of real economic activity in the region surrounding the center, as well as to the presence of other multinational banks and liquid stock markets. At first sight, that finding may seem surprising, because one would expect that the presence of rival banks would reduce the location's attractiveness to other banks. However, there appear to be certain agglomeration advantages strong enough to overcompensate for the pressure on margins due to competition, but these agglomeration advantages are not strong enough to cause even greater degrees of concentration among the international financial centers. The majority of multinational banks have actually incurred substantial sunk costs in enlarging their branch networks across those centers.

3 Centripetal Forces in Financial Markets

The observations in Section 2 lead us to the question of the nature of the agglomeration advantages in financial markets. What precisely are the sources of such agglomeration advantages? What are their limits, and what are the potentially countervailing forces?

Interestingly, the financial literature has largely built on the paradigm of frictionless markets. In that view, the question of the locations of financial activity essentially reduces to issues of cross-border transactions and the different regulatory or tax treatments of financial transactions in different countries (Grabbe, 1996; Porteus, 1996). The roles of trading frictions and transactions costs typically are treated as subjects of minor relevance in that literature.

Within that traditional view, however, there is no role for spatial financial activity within a given nation. Implicitly, all national financial activity takes place within a single perfect market.[2] There are reasonable justifications for such a view, especially because, as we shall see, there are strong centripetal forces within homogeneous markets. However, within that traditional view it is difficult to explain the observed amount of fragmentation of financial activity. I shall argue later that it is precisely those frictions neglected by the traditional international-finance literature that compose a major force for geographical dispersion of financial activity. Accordingly, we shall next proceed with an account of the centripetal forces that contribute to concentrated markets. The centrifugal forces that cause geographical dispersion of financial activity will be discussed in Section 4.

3.1 Economies of Scale in the Payment Mechanism

Economies of scale constitute a major centripetal force. Such economies arise in the payment system and accordingly in the settlement of transactions. For example, Kindleberger (1974) argued that for a given number n of financial centers, the most efficient settlement system would involve a centralization of all payments in one single center. Thus, only $n - 1$ communication channels would be required, as opposed to the $n(n-1)/2$ in the case of bilateral settlement of payments. Moreover, these costs of the payment mechanism could perhaps be reduced by centralizing the overall activity in the center.

Economies of scale are important sources of concentration of certain activities, but they do not require that several activities be performed within a specific financial center. The payment systems, for example, are operated completely within electronic networks. All payments are executed at central computers, but the site of those computers is completely irrelevant for the participants. The major payment systems are run by SWIFT (Society for Worldwide Interbank Financial Communications), with 3,049 member banks in 84 countries (in 1990) and operating centers in Brussels, Amsterdam, and Culpepper (Virginia, USA), CHIPS (Clearing House Interbank Payment System), with 122 participants in the United States (1991), and Fedwire, with about 11,000 institutions in 1991 (for more details, see Grabbe, 1996). In the early 1990s, SWIFT executed about 1,100,000 messages per day, and CHIPS and Fedwire operated at daily averages of about 150,000 and 285,000 transfers, with average daily volumes of $866 billion and $766 billion, respectively.

Also, currency trading takes place within computer networks such as Reuter, EBS (Electronic Banking System), and Telerate. Any trader with access to a

---

[2] This is the basis for O'Brien's (1992) view. In the absence of trading frictions, geography becomes irrelevant for financial activities. The challenge for financial theory, however, is to explain the role of geography as a function of economic data such as trading frictions.

trading network can access the market from any location worldwide. Trading in currency is concentrated in time, and most of the trading occurs when the markets in New York City, Tokyo, and London are active. However, there is no need for a physical presence within those centers for trading purposes.

Eurocurrency markets provide a further example of markets with economies of scale in the transactions technology. These markets cover deposits in foreign currencies as well as payments from and transfers to such deposits. The management of straight deposits is a rather unsophisticated activity and can be operated at virtually any place worldwide. In this respect, the Eurodollar market, for example, is highly integrated and closely resembles the foreign-exchange markets.

The foregoing examples characterize markets in which cost considerations dominate the location of trading activity, such as rents, wages, and regulatory taxes. In these markets, the agglomeration of traders seems important because of economies in the transactions technology. The agglomeration, however, takes place within electronic communication networks. Essentially, these markets are integrated worldwide, and the particular location of activity is immaterial, except possibly for regulatory reasons. The situation is different in the presence of external economies, however. When financial agents can benefit from the presence of other agents at a given site, this site may become a financial center precisely because it is advantageous for market participants to be close to other market participants. Next we shall discuss two such external economies: information spillovers and the liquidity externality.

3.2 Information Spillovers

To the extent that the physical presence of other financial intermediaries stimulates communication among agents, more information can be exchanged among agents and correspondingly exploited. Communication can help to generate new ideas (see Section 5), but it also allows agents to benefit from information gleaned from others. Such information is particularly important for securities with more complex payoff structures, such a stocks and their derivatives.[3] Investors and traders in informationally complex securities are more inclined to take advantage of rumors about payoff-relevant factors when they are present at the market site.

For example, at the opening of trading at the NYSE, brokers gather around the specialists' trading pit in order to acquire information about the opening price, which they can usefully exploit in further rounds of trading with their own clients. Moreover, specialists tend to share information about the order book with other floor brokers quite frequently. This information is not available

---

3 Stocks are informationally complex, because payoffs vary delicately with states of nature. In contrast, bonds require information only about nonperforming states and coupon payments.

to brokers at other locations who observe the specialist's price quotes only on computer screens. In this case, the presence at the trading floor generates useful information, or at least advantages of timing. Although it may be true that fundamental information is eventually revealed in prices, securities traders can benefit from this information only so long as they enjoy a temporary informational advantage with respect to other traders (Hellwig, 1980). Physical proximity can be useful to generate this type of temporary informational advantage. Of course, this argument seems less relevant for securities, which are less informationally sensitive, less sophisticated. It also seems less relevant for very liquid and competitive markets in which informational advantages decay within minutes or even seconds, relative to less competitive markets. Accordingly, the need to trade close to information outlets seems greater for stocks than for fixed-income securities or even foreign exchange or currencies.

3.3 Liquidity and Thick Market Externalities

Presumably the most important centripetal force derives from market liquidity. A market is said to be liquid when individual transactions cause only minor price reactions. In illiquid markets, even small orders may significantly affect price changes. Risk-averse investors prefer to trade in liquid markets, because there the risk of price changes due to liquidity shocks caused by the moves of individual traders is lower. Accordingly, liquid markets attract more trading volume.

Pagano (1989) has demonstrated the centripetal force of liquidity for an exchange economy in which individual traders incur idiosyncratic endowment shocks. Sudden and unforeseen payment obligations or windfall gains (inheritances) may cause investors to adjust their asset portfolios by selling or buying securities. Pagano's model considers a finite two-period stock-market economy with n risk-averse investors. Investors $i = 1,...,n$ hold random endowments $K_i = K_0 + e_i$ of a risky security that are independently distributed with mean K_0 and variance σ_e^2. The security is traded in period 1 at price p, and in period 2 it pays an uncertain dividend d, with mean μ and variance σ. There is an alternative safe investment that pays R in period 2 with certainty. Each investor maximizes his expected mean-variance utility of terminal wealth $E(U_i) = E(w_i) - (b/2)\text{Var}(w_i)$, where $w_i = dx_i + R(K_i - x_i)$, by a judicious choice of his portfolio x_i of the security.

Pagano has shown that the expected utility of risk-averse investors increases when there are more traders in the market, provided that the idiosyncratic liquidity shocks are not perfectly correlated. In particular, when N investors enter a given market, their (gross) indirect utility from entry is

$$E[u^i(\cdot)] = \frac{b\sigma^2}{2\left[K_0^2 + (N-2)\sigma_e^2/(N-1)N - 2e_i^2/N\right]} + \text{constant}$$

Accordingly, indirect utility is affected by N in two ways. There is a positive contribution proportional to endowment volatility σ_e^2. Volatility raises one's chances to buy low and sell high. This term therefore can be considered as a speculative value of market participation. The second term, $-2e_i^2/N$, captures the price impact of large endowment shocks and captures the liquidity value of the market. As the number of traders grows, the elasticity of the market price with respect to individual transactions, the so-called price impact of an individual transaction, declines. Furthermore, the impact of liquidity shocks of other traders is reduced to the extent that these shocks are uncorrelated. Hence, a liquid market provides insurance against idiosyncratic endowment shocks.

A related centripetal force that is regularly attributed to the agglomeration of financial activity is seen in the labor market for highly specialized financial services. A large labor market is attractive for financial specialists because it provides better expected job matches (Kim, 1990). In this sense, the larger center offers more protection against mismatches in case of idiosyncratic employment shocks. The larger centers offer a more liquid labor market to specialists. In order to attract highly specialized workers, financial firms may be forced to offer jobs in centers with liquid labor markets. Otherwise, they would need to compensate by paying (even) higher wages.

4 Centrifugal Forces in Financial Markets

Explaining a geographical role for financial markets is much more difficult, because it requires the introduction of frictions into a financial economy. Especially in the absence of government-induced distortions or restrictions, it is necessary to understand the microstructure of financial activity on a rather basic level. For example, why is it that some investors trade a given asset in New York and not in London, and others in London and not New York, despite the presence of arbitrageurs in both (sub-) markets? The literature essentially offers two different answers: market access costs and local information.

4.1 Market Access Costs and Coordination

In the absence of further frictions, investors always prefer to trade in the most liquid market, and consequently trading should be concentrated in a single location. In the real world, however, trading is fragmented. IBM shares can be traded in New York, London, or Frankfurt. In order to explain the fragmentation of trading of homogeneous securities, Pagano (1989) analyzed market access costs as a particularly relevant form of transactions costs.[4] He found that

---

[4] Market access costs comprise transportation costs (Economides and Siow, 1988; Gehrig, 1998) as well as transactions costs that do not depend on distance (Pagano, 1989).

market access costs may cause coordination problems giving rise to multiple equilibria, with fragmented trading and with concentrated trading. With costly market access, investors, prior to trading, need to decide which market to enter and to compare expected utilities of market participation net of respective access costs accordingly. Because of the liquidity externality, the expected gain from trading depends on the market participation of other traders. In particular, large traders prefer to trade in markets with many other large traders. Otherwise their buy and sell orders might have significant price impacts. Pagano found that with symmetric market access costs there will always be concentration in one market because of the liquidity externality. When market access costs are different across markets, however, fragmented equilibria can also exist, where large traders (i.e., investors who expect to trade large quantities) select the market with higher access costs, and small traders select the market with lower access costs. In this equilibrium, large traders enjoy better insurance against price fluctuations in the high-cost market, and given that they rationally expect other large traders to enter the high-cost market as well, they cannot benefit from deviations to the low-cost market. This equilibrium relies on the self-fulfilling conjectures of large traders about their respective market choices.

In the case of heterogeneous market access costs, there can also be a Pareto-dominant symmetric equilibrium, with concentration of trading in one market. Coordination problems may prevent the efficient market choice. Market access costs, therefore, can be identified as an important centrifugal force in financial markets.

Economides and Siow (1988) explicitly analyzed the trade-off between liquidity and market access costs in a spatial context. In their model of an exchange economy, investors are distributed along a circular city. Because of asymmetric endowment shocks, they want to trade with one another. They need to select a market before the endowment shocks have occurred. Because of liquidity considerations, investors would prefer to trade in a single location. However, market access costs increase with the distance to the marketplace. Investors must be compensated for their transportation costs, because otherwise they would prefer not to trade at all. Accordingly, liquid markets with many traders attract investors from a wider range than do thinner markets with only few traders. Nevertheless, when liquid markets are very distant, investors may prefer to trade in less liquid markets in order to reduce transportation costs or even stay at home. This fundamental trade-off between liquidity and transportation costs causes investors to enter different markets.

Again, because of coordination problems, multiple equilibria exist. Economides and Siow have shown, however, that generally several market-places will be established (i.e., there will be several locations where traders choose to meet). Accordingly, the centripetal force of liquidity generates agglomerations of traders at distinct locations, the marketplaces, whereas the centrifugal force of transportation costs (market access costs) causes trading activity to spread over several markets.

In the presence of multiple agglomerations of financial activity, one may wonder about the likely effects of technological progress and economic growth on the structure of financial centers. Can such developments upset a given structure of trading places, or will the structure of trading be largely unaffected? In an analysis of that question (Gehrig, 1998), it has been found that new entry of a financial center between existing centers is quite costly in the presence of thick market externalities. In other words, a new center is likely to succeed only if it can attract sufficiently many market participants. Moreover, in a price-setting framework, the barrier to entry grows as the intensity of competition increases in the financial sector. Therefore, in the presence of agglomeration economies, one might expect strong evidence of path dependence. The empirical work of Reed (1980, 1981) seems to support this result. It appears that abrupt changes in the roles of financial centers, as in the cases of Berlin–Frankfurt and Yokohama–Tokyo, can be explained by idiosyncratic political and historical developments. The relative roles of financial centers seem to change rather slowly.

4.2 Rent-seeking and Political Intervention

Because of the agglomeration advantages of financial centers, interested third parties feel tempted to participate in the income generated in such centers. Fiscal authorities may attempt to tax transactions, and unions may try to secure higher wages. The stamp duty in Switzerland and the *Börsenumsatzsteuer* in Germany are recent examples of fiscal interventions. There is also concern about the wages of bank employees and the competitiveness of Swiss banks (Blattner, 1992). Naturally, those rent-seeking activities can reduce, or even annihilate, the attractiveness of financial centers and increase the chances of fragmentation. As argued earlier, the success of the Cayman Islands in the Eurocurrency markets is intimately related to unfavorable tax treatment in London, the historical center for Eurocurrency transactions.

In an analysis of the competition between different financial centers in an economy with differential market access costs (Gehrig, 1998) it has been shown that interested third parties will engage in indirect competition when competition between financial intermediaries is globalized, and the equilibrium levels for taxes, wages, and intervention costs will depend sensitively on the intensity of competition in the underlying financial sector. On the basis of those results, the recent wave of deregulation of national financial markets (Pagano and Roell, 1990) finds an explanation as an equilibrium response of third parties to increasing international competition. In this sense, the centrifugal force stemming from local rent-seeking activities is contained by the intensity of competition in global financial markets.

4.3 Localized Information

The second major centrifugal force for financial activity is localization of information. The geographical distribution of real activity across space also implies that information about real activity, production, tastes, and policy is generated locally across space.

Although much of this information can be collected and transmitted, it is difficult to imagine that all information relevant for investors and firms' management could be aggregated and communicated to any other location at no cost. But that is precisely the traditional international-finance view. The widespread observations of a pronounced preference of investors for domestic stocks (Cooper and Kaplanis, 1994; Tesar and Werner, 1995) seem paradoxical according to that view. The empirical size of the home bias can hardly be explained by exchange-rate risk, transactions costs, and regulatory and tax considerations alone. However, this "anomaly" can readily be explained by informational frictions. When investors, on average, enjoy superior information about domestic stocks, and when asset prices are not sufficient statistics of payoff-relevant information, a domestic bias emerges naturally, even in a capital-market equilibrium with rational expectations (Gehrig, 1993; Kang and Stulz, 1997). Whereas the argument is easily understood for irrational investors, it also holds under conditions of optimal learning from prices. The mere fact that prices reveal information to uninformed investors is an indication of the important role of security exchanges in aggregating and disseminating information. Furthermore, when prices aggregate information only imperfectly, privileged information is valuable (Grossman and Stiglitz, 1980), and traders may have incentives to observe the process of price formation rather closely in order to benefit from earlier access to information. Accordingly, investors with an active interest in a given security might wish to enter the markets where this security is traded.

Because the domestic bias is more pronounced for information-sensitive securities like stocks, relative to government bonds (Gehrig, 1993), the informational explanation seems rather attractive. Moreover, informational models can explain why the observed portfolio turnover for foreign stocks is larger than that for domestic stocks (Brennan and Cao, 1997). Investors tend to react more sensitively to information on assets whose details they know less precisely.

Local information alone, however, cannot explain a role for geography. In the absence of further transactions costs, all securities could be traded in New York, London, or at any other location, and investors could enjoy ready access to those marketplaces. Again, market access costs compose an important factor for generating a nondegenerate geographical distribution of financial activity. Gehrig et al. (1994) have analyzed the location choices of firms and risk-averse investors when market access is costly and investors have local information about the firms' returns. Firms decide where to list their securities. They can list their securities at several locations, but each listing involves a fixed cost, which can be thought of as a listing fee and the cost of producing a listing prospectus. Investors also can enter several markets. Each market entry requires a fixed access cost that can usefully be thought of as a terminal that connects the investor with the respective market (or exchange).

Again there are strong centripetal forces: Investors prefer to diversify their portfolios, and firms prefer large markets with a high demand for their securities. Nevertheless, Gehrig et al. (1994) have demonstrated that a concentrated equilibrium, in which all firms and investors enter the same market, may not necessarily exist, even though it does exist in "many" cases. The centrifugal forces arise jointly from market access costs and local information. If the informational asymmetry is large enough, (completely) fragmented equilibria will exist, in which local firms will seek local listings, and local investors will invest only in local securities. As in the work described earlier, multiple equilibria can arise because of coordination problems. They are endemic when market access is costly.

To the extent that informational differences vanish or market access costs decline, a unique concentrated equilibrium arises in that model (Gehrig et al., 1994). This result raises the question whether or not improvements in communication technology can actually reduce informational differences such that a fragmented structure becomes infeasible and concentration of trading becomes inevitable.

Next we present a more rigorous discussion of reasons that caution predictions about the imminent concentration of financial activity within a single integrated market, even when the communication of information is increasingly facilitated. In order to discuss the consequences of improved communication technology, it is necessary to discuss the nature of information in more detail.

5 Informational Complexity and the Geographic Distribution of Financial Activity

The classification of centripetal and centrifugal forces is quite useful for analysis of the geographical distribution of financial activity. Because (geographical) market access costs probably are rather similar for different financial products, the major structural difference among them is their informational content.

In order to value securities, an assessment of the returns at maturity, or redemption, is required for each state of nature. Accordingly, investors would like to obtain estimates as precise as possible regarding the likelihood of occurrence of the different states of nature. Because financial securities differ quite substantially in the amount of information required for valuation, it is useful to measure this informational complexity of a security for a number of states for which the security pays different returns. More formally, the complexity of a security can be defined by a measure of the coarseness of the coarsest partition required to measure the payoffs of a security.[5] Money deposits, for example, pay a constant interest in non-default states. Because default probabilities in the money market typically are small, relatively little information is required to value these securities. Presumably, more information is required for government bonds, and even more for private bonds, because default probabilities contain increasingly larger idiosyncratic factors. All these securities, however, are informationally quite economical as far as non-default states are concerned. Investors do not need to know by how wide a margin insolvency is avoided. Pure equity, in the other extreme, requires information about each single state of nature. It constitutes a security with high (maximal) informational complexity.

The classification of Sections 3 and 4 suggests increasing relevance of local information for securities that are increasingly informationally complex. Accordingly, centripetal forces may be expected to dominate in markets for informationally unsophisticated securities, such as money deposits. On the other hand, centrifugal forces should be particularly relevant in the markets for informationally complex securities, such as stocks and their derivatives. This implies a rather footloose geographical structure for informationally insensitive securities and a geographically fragmented structure for informationally demanding securities. Of course, centripetal forces also imply a tendency toward concentration of trading in regional stocks as well, but because of the value of local information, trading will concentrate on the sources where local information is aggregated. Hence, there may coexist different trading places for (different) regional stocks.

The classification of securities according to their informational content also allows us to predict the market reactions on regional regulatory policies. Transactions taxes, for example, would tend to reduce a region's attractiveness for informationally insensitive products to a larger extent than for informationally complex securities (Gehrig, 1998).

Indeed, the empirical observations seem to accord well with this classification scheme. In the Eurocurrency markets, for example, the Cayman Islands and the Bahamas have only recently grown into major offshore Eurocurrency centers. Also Bahrain, London, and Singapore are clearly known as centers for Eurocurrency transactions. It is important to note, however, that the specific location of Eurocurrency transactions is largely motivated by regulatory arbitrage for activities that are essentially footloose. Eurocurrency transactions are rather unsophisticated transactions similar to payments. Because they particularly comprise the management of short-term deposits, stability of the political and legal environment, as well as the tax treatment of interest income and the

---

[5] When the number of states of nature $n > 1$ is finite, for example, the complexity of a security can be measured by the number of different state-contingent payoffs. In this example, a safe bond has complexity 1 and pays a constant return, and a common stock has complexity n.

ready accessibility of funds, are important criteria for the location choice of market participants. In this regard, the success of the Cayman Islands, which attracted shell branches from 500–600 banks and trust companies, can be easily explained by the absence of a profit tax in the Cayman Islands and a favorable regulatory environment. In the traditional center for Eurodollar transactions, in London, traders have to pay significant transactions taxes. The example of the Cayman Islands demonstrates that regulatory (cost) considerations may significantly affect the location of footloose financial activity. In fact, the very name of Eurocurrencies refers to the circumvention activities of local regulations. The Eurodollar market was created during the sterling crisis in 1956–7 when British authorities banned the use of sterling to finance trade between non-sterling countries, as a market in dollars outside the geographical and legal borders of the United States.

On the other hand, the Eurobond markets exhibit a substantial amount of fragmentation. Eurobonds are bonds that are issued by corporations and international organizations in foreign currencies outside the domestic market. Whereas dollar-denominated bonds were issued as early as 1963, floating-rate notes of private corporations denominated in German marks and Japanese yen have developed since 1985. Despite the fact that Eurobonds are less informationally sensitive than straight stocks, and despite improvements in communication technologies, they seem to be very closely related to the corporations' domestic markets. In contrast to foreign-exchange or Eurocurrency markets, "trading in international bonds is more usefully considered as taking place in a set of loosely connected individual markets. Each of these individual markets is usually [more] closely tied to a corresponding domestic bond market than to another one of the international bond markets" (Grabbe, 1996, p. 267). This example of fragmentation among the newly established Eurobond markets accords well with the informational explanation of Gehrig et al. (1994) and seems to suggest that the centrifugal forces emanating from informational frictions and market access costs still are substantial enough to fragment bond markets of internationally active firms at the end of the twentieth century.

6 Information Technology and the Future of Financial Centers

How will technological advances affect the geography of finance? According to the preceding discussion, the nature of informational frictions constitutes the major determinant of the location of financial activity. Technological advances typically will reduce physical market access costs and the technical costs of collecting, communicating, and disseminating information. To the extent that informational frictions and technological transactions costs become obsolete, geography in finance will no longer matter. If, however, transactions costs remain small but positive, geography still will matter, and questions about the geographical structure will remain challenging. For example, the introduction of the telephone significantly reduced the role of space for securities markets and led to major structural changes in securities markets toward less fragmented structures. However, it did not abolish the role of geography in financial markets. Similarly, one may ask the same questions nowadays and conjecture a vanishing role for geography (O'Brien, 1992). However, as long as transactions costs exist, such conjectures are not well founded, as will be argued later.

According to the findings of Choi et al. (1986) and Jeger et al. (1992), the dramatic expansion of networks of international representations requires explanation. This finding is in apparent contrast to the hypothesis of a decreasing relevance of financial centers because of declining transactions costs. Investment in expensive networks of offices for local representative has been a popular strategy of internationally active intermediaries in recent years. In order to understand the incentives of multinational intermediaries to invest in international branch networks, a rather stylized model of information procession will be analyzed later. The example will show that a decline in communication costs may actually enhance intermediaries' incentives to invest in local branches, because investors will become more inclined to access foreign or less well known markets.

The following model is rather stylized and aims at identifying a basic mechanism that reinforces intermediaries' geographical interests. This mechanism rests on the assumptions that (1) on-site information is valuable but costly and (2) information cannot be communicated perfectly. Agents observe noisy signals that are affected by several factors, including idiosyncratic observation errors. In the model, agents can truthfully communicate the signals they observe. However, they cannot identify the various signal components. Whereas communication with many agents allows the separation of fundamental factors from idiosyncratic noise, certain local factors cannot be identified without a local presence in the market.

This example is meant to capture the idea that experts may easily communicate balance-sheet data and their expectations about the different items. However, they cannot easily communicate information that is essential for an interpretation of that information by the receiver. For example, a receiver in the United States or Europe may not be well versed in Indonesian accounting principles and therefore may not understand implied insolvency or market risks. Because the sender himself does not necessarily know in any detail the structural differences in accounting conventions, he cannot even warn the receiver about potential misunderstandings in any meaningful sense. In the terminology of the subsequent model, such information problems can be reduced only by fixed investments that are interpreted as local access.

For concreteness, consider a large economy with a large group of finance experts i. Furthermore, consider a risky asset with payoff $\tilde{x}$. Each expert observes a signal $\tilde{s}_i = \tilde{f} + \tilde{l} + \tilde{\varepsilon}_i$, consisting of a fundamental factor $\tilde{f}$, a local factor $\tilde{l}$, and an idiosyncratic observation error $\tilde{\varepsilon}_i$. The fundamental factor is an essential factor driving the returns $\tilde{x}$ [i.e., $\mathrm{cov}(\tilde{x}, \tilde{f}) \neq 0$]. The local factor will also affect the fundamental asset returns, and the idiosyncratic factors $\tilde{\varepsilon}_i$ are completely unrelated to the security returns. Let $E(\tilde{l}) = E(\tilde{\varepsilon}_i) = 0$ and $\mathrm{Var}(\varepsilon) = \mathrm{Var}(\varepsilon)$. This simplifying assumption implies the irrelevance of an expert's identity. It is only the number of experts that matters.

Assume that the local factor is observable only within informational centers. As argued earlier, the local factor consists of information that is difficult to describe, such as the general market sentiment or mood. Experts cannot separate this factor from any other fundamental information they may have access to. Assume further that experts can communicate only the signals they observe, and assume that they communicate their information truthfully. This assumption deliberately excludes incentive problems as one major source of imperfections in the communication process. Because communication costs inhibit market access, as argued earlier, this assumption favors delocalization of financial activity. Nevertheless, it will be shown that concentrated structure can emerge.

Intermediaries, or simply investors, can acquire information about the given security. In addition to their private signals, they may acquire information about the local component $\tilde{l}$, and by communicating with other experts they may have access to further signals $\tilde{s}_j$, $j \neq i$. They choose the number of signals to acquire. Access to the local information requires a fixed set-up cost $T > 0$, and communication with another financial intermediary requires communication costs $t > 0$ per communication link. T may be thought of as the cost of traveling to the given location or as the cost of establishing a subsidiary or representative office at the location where local information about security x is aggregated. The communication cost t may be interpreted as a telephone cost.

Intermediaries resell their information to clients. For example, they manage clients' portfolios or provide investment advice. When investors are risk-averse, they prefer precise information, and hence intermediaries have incentives to provide information that is as precise as is economical. Denote by $S(N) = (1/N) \sum_j \tilde{s}_j$ the average signal an intermediary acquires when talking to N other intermediaries. For any number of communication links, the expected signal value is $\mathrm{Var}(f)$. However, the precision of the average signal depends on the number of links and the mode of market access.

When intermediaries access a foreign market without establishing a branch, they can control the informational precision only by the number of communication lines N_R they establish. The associated communication costs are $N_R t$, and the variance of the average signal is

$$\mathrm{Var}[S_R(N_R)] = \mathrm{Var}(f) + \mathrm{Var}(l) + \frac{1}{N_R}\mathrm{Var}(\varepsilon)$$

Accordingly, the precision of remote market access is bounded by $[\text{Var}(f) + \text{Var}(l)]^{-1}$.

When intermediaries access the foreign market by establishing a foreign presence, they can observe the local component l and additionally adjust the number N_L of communication links. The associated costs are $T + N_L t$, and the variance of the average signal is

$$\text{Var}[S_L(N_L)] = \text{Var}(f) + \frac{1}{N_L}\text{Var}(\varepsilon)$$

In this case, the asymptotic precision is $\text{Var}^{-1}(f)$.

Now consider the cost functions of a typical intermediary. What are the costs of providing the information service at a given precision or, equivalently, at an average signal variance? Define the cost functions as follows:

$$C_R(v) = \min\left[N_R t \mid \text{Var}(f) + \text{Var}(l) + \frac{1}{N_R}\text{Var}(\varepsilon) \geq v\right]$$

$$C_L(v) = \min\left[T + N_L t \mid \text{Var}(f) + \frac{1}{N_L}\text{Var}(\varepsilon) \geq v\right]$$

These functions can be rewritten as

$$C_R(v) = \frac{\text{Var}(\varepsilon)}{v - \text{Var}(f) - \text{Var}(l)} t$$

$$C_L(v) = T + \frac{\text{Var}(\varepsilon)}{v - \text{Var}(f)} t$$

Figure 12.1 shows the cost functions. As can easily be seen, depending on the parameters of the economy, an intermediary may prefer remote access when risk concerns are not too dominant. When intermediaries need to offer high precision, however, they may prefer local presentations in order to get access to the local informational component.

The optimal organizational mode is determined by demand parameters. Depending on the importance that clients attach to precision, the given intermediary will select remote or local access. How will the intermediary's choice depend on the transactions costs t? As can be easily seen, when this technological parameter does not affect demand, the intersection of $C_R(v)$ and $C_L(v)$ will occur at a critical value of the average variance $\bar{v}(t/T)$, which negatively depends on the ratio of communication costs to local access costs t/T. As communication costs decline, or as the costs of establishing a local presence increase, the intermediary is more likely to select remote access. This scenario accords well with the view of an increasing delocalization of financial centers as communication costs increase. However, there is always room for intermediaries that offer more precise information than $\bar{v}(t/T)$. In this sense, and in the absence of

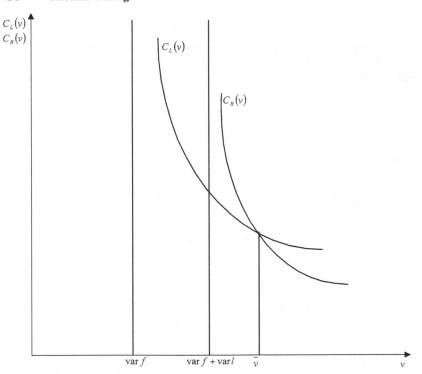

Figure 12.1. Cost functions.

further regulatory or agency issues, conservative regulation may actually help to fragment markets and force intermediaries into the local-access mode.

So far, the analysis has concentrated on technological aspects as summarized in intermediaries' cost functions. Will similar results remain valid when technological conditions interact with demand? To this end, the intermediary's decision problem has to be modeled in more detail. In particular, revenues need to be modeled as functions $R(v, t)$ of the precision of information v^{-1}, or its inverse, and communication costs t. Let this function be well-behaved and sufficiently differentiable. Intermediaries maximize $R(v, t) - C(v, t)$, where $C(v, t) := \min\{C_L(v), C_R(v)\}$ for given communication costs t. Profit-oriented intermediaries will collect information with precision $\hat{v}^{-1}$ such that $R_v(\hat{v}, t) = C_v(\hat{v}, t)$.

How does the optimal precision $\hat{v}^{-1}$ vary with changes in the communication costs t? In the example presented in this section, the answer is particularly simple when $R_{vv} < 0$, because this assumption implies the following relation for marginal technological improvements (and interior solutions $\hat{v}$):[6]

$$\text{sign}\left(\frac{d\,\hat{v}}{dt}\right) = \text{sign}[R_{vt}(\hat{v}, t)]$$

Accordingly, as before, $R_{vt}(\cdot, \cdot) > 0$ implies an increasing tendency to remote market access as communication costs decline. In this case, lower communication costs reduce the sensitivity of revenues with respect to the quality of information. To a certain degree, communication costs and the precision of local information are substitutes.

On the other hand, $R_{vt}(\cdot, \cdot) < 0$ implies an increasing preference toward local market access. In this case, reduced communication costs will increase clients' sensitivity with respect to asset risk. Accordingly, intermediaries will benefit disproportionately from offering information of higher quality. As the returns from improved information increase, intermediaries will increasingly be inclined to invest resources in local market access and hence increase their information networks. Here general public information measured by communication costs and local information are complements.

Especially on international stock markets, the possibility of complementary types of information seems plausible. General country information about foreign stock may induce investors to invest in foreign markets and to react increasingly sensitively to information generated locally in those foreign markets. Accordingly, intermediaries face increasing demands for local information and may therefore be increasingly tempted to establish overseas representations. In fact, the empirical analyses of Brennan and Cao (1997) have documented a high degree of sensitivity of portfolio flows in foreign stocks. Even in domestic markets, Coval and Moskowitz (1996) have found geographical preferences of U.S. mutual funds toward the home of these funds, suggesting considerable value of local information even in regions with similar business cultures, legal institutions, and languages. Furthermore, consistent with the local information hypothesis, Shuckla and van Inwegen (1995) have reported better performance by mutual funds managed within the United States relative to mutual funds managed abroad.

These simple results suggest a classification scheme of greater generality for analyzing the impacts of information technologies on the geographical structure of financial activity. In asset markets where complex local information and straightforward generally available information are substitutes, technological improvements tend to fragment and delocalize financial activity. In markets for information-sensitive assets, however, complex local information and straightforward public information could behave like complements, in which case

---

[6] Comparative-statics calculation of the optimal choice v yields $dv/dt = (C_{vt} - R_{vt})/(R_{vv} - C_{vv})$. In this example, $C_{vt} = 0$, $C_{vv} > 0$.

incentives to form information networks would be reinforced by technological improvements.

This classification of information parallels the classification of Gaspar and Glaeser (1996) according to the degree of its complexity. According to their classification, straightforward information can be easily communicated via computer networks or other means of modern information technology. Complex information, however, requires face-to-face communication, especially when interpretation of the information is highly contingent on many variables or when information can easily be manipulated. In such situations, typically, effective communication requires checks and reassurances. The difference between the two categories of information is the fact that straightforward information can be easily read and interpreted, whereas complex information may involve interventions, clarifications, and the reactions of all the communicating partners to one another, in order to prevent misinterpretations or to guarantee a certain degree of confidentiality. Gaspar and Glaeser have provided a microfoundation for the different qualities of information. They argue that the probability of a misunderstanding is a key force toward interactive communication. The more complex is the situation, the more likely are costly errors, and the more important are iterations of communication to check that the message has been correctly understood. Especially, information that conditions on specific knowledge of either communication partner can be misunderstood. When the likelihood of misunderstanding is small, however, fewer rounds of iteration are necessary, and less face-to-face communication is required.

Both classification schemes would seem to generate similar predictions. For example, physical improvements in information technology will primarily facilitate the collection, transmission, and interpretation of information-insensitive and straightforward information. Therefore, standardized financial activities can increasingly be relocated to low-cost locations. Indeed, certain financial services are prime examples of the increasing trend toward the suburbanization of jobs (Ota and Fujita, 1993). Many (standardized) back-office activities, such as order settlement or producing investor reports and recommendations, can be economically performed at (suburban) sites where office rents are lower.

Only activities that produce complex and sensitive information in interaction with other market participants may have to be performed in city front offices, close to the communication partners within the financial center. Typically, stock trading is an activity that produces sophisticated information. As long as the trading floor is located in Manhattan, the major financial intermediaries in New York are likely to maintain Manhattan offices in order to have immediate access to market information. Mechanical arbitrage activities, automated buy and sell orders, and portfolio insurance strategies, on the other hand, can easily be executed from back offices. Accordingly, technological improvements in communication technology would suggest a development toward a separation of tasks according to their informational role and complexity. Activities that generate information spillovers would be performed within the financial centers, and activities with negligible spillovers would be relegated to other sites, such as suburban back offices.

Intermediaries' main economic role consists in reducing market frictions. Because technological improvements contribute to reductions in market frictions, disintermediation may occur. However, when public information and local information are complements, there may be a role for intermediaries in investing in geographical-information networks across financial centers and in providing information about the credibility of trading partners, merger candidates, or takeover targets, as well as local financing and market conditions. Such information is particularly useful for internationally active firms that do not plan for a long-term physical presence in a given country. Multinational banks basically perform an information brokerage function for these firms, and in the presence of switching costs, network size serves as a strategic variable for the banks (Gehrig, 1996). As communication and real trading costs decline, the value of information brokerage increases, and banks' incentives to extend their branch networks rise. Moreover, by offering lower-cost information services, banks also tend to reduce the costs of trading real commodities and thus contribute to a chain of cumulative causation. In the limit, for low communication costs and mature markets, it has been found (Gehrig, 1996) that only few banks will maintain rather large, or even global, networks, and many other banks will specialize on information brokerage in niche markets. This explanation accords well with the empirical findings of Jeger et al. (1992) and Yamori (1998), who have demonstrated that the probability of establishing a new branch is positively related to trade flows to a given region (Section 2) and the bank's size as measured in the amount of financial liabilities.

Decreases in trading and communication costs, therefore, will stimulate international trade and the corresponding incentives of multinational banks to expand their informational networks across existing financial centers. As financial activity increases in a given center, the need for back-office tasks will increase, and communication between front and back offices will multiply. In this sense, face-to-face communication within a financial center and telecommunication are complements and tend to support each other (Gaspar and Glaeser, 1996).

7 Concluding Remarks

This chapter has developed the idea that the role of cities as financial centers and the nature of financial activity within these centers are largely determined by the degree of complementarity between the management of the payment system and the role of a financial center in aggregating information about local investment possibilities. Because the management of the payment system requires only unsophisticated straightforward transactions, the corresponding activities, such as foreign exchange transactions and Eurocurrency trading, are rather footloose. The trading of fixed-income securities and even more sophisticated instruments, however, requires additional issuer-specific information that is rather more tied to the particular geographic range of operations of the issuing firm. Accordingly, trading in these sophisticated securities is fragmented and localized. The localization of trading is particularly relevant to the extent that complex information cannot be communicated readily by means of standardized communication facilities. Accordingly, markets for bonds, stocks, and their derivatives are more geographically fragmented than markets for currencies. Of course, to the extent that trading in sophisticated instruments remains localized in specific financial centers, a substantial portion of payment transactions will be concentrated in those centers. Arbitrage-related payment operations, on the other hand, are footloose and can be performed at any cost-efficient site.

Consequently, the structure of financial centers depends decisively on their informational hinterland. This hinterland is likely to change in range and character, as evidenced by the steady consolidation of the national structures of trading places. Harmonization of regulatory systems and increasing mobility of firms tend to enlarge the range of established centers, thus causing an exit of redundant lower-order centers. On this basis, one might predict an even further consolidation of the system of European exchanges toward single national exchanges, such as Amsterdam, Brussels, Frankfurt, Paris, Rome, Zurich, and London, as an international European center.

Furthermore, we have argued in this chapter that improvements in communication and information technology are unlikely to completely upset the role of financial centers as sites of local information aggregation. To the extent that financial centers aggregate complex and rather sophisticated information, face-to-face communication can hardly be displaced by on-line communication. In such situations, intermediaries may prefer the geographical neighborhood of other intermediaries and may cluster within a financial center. Furthermore, technological advances are likely to foster such agglomerations when the value of such information for the intermediary, and ultimately its client, increases. As international portfolio investment increases, local information may become profitable, and intermediaries will be more inclined to set up new branches in other financial centers. The observations of Choi et al. (1986) offer some empirical evidence of increasing interest among multinational banks to expand their branch networks. At the same time, technological advances reduce the concentration of intra-firm activities. As communication costs shrink, office rents can be reduced, and front-office and back-office activities can be separated. Back-office activities typically are activities that use simple and standardized information that can be readily communicated and will not generate important information spillovers.

The analysis of market frictions and the technological debate about their size, however, should warn city planners. The attractiveness of cities to internationally active intermediaries crucially depends on their capacity to attract information-sensitive business and specialist human capital. This includes the capacity to attract the associated spectrum of accounting services, consultancy, and legal services. In order to compete successfully with the largely unregulated electronic markets, an attractive regulatory market environment seems a basic requirement.

References

Bessembinder, H., and Kaufmann, H. (1997). A cross-exchange comparison of execution costs and information flow for NYSE-listed stocks. *Journal of Financial Economics* 46:293–319.

Blattner, N. (1992). Competitiveness in banking: selected recent contributions and research priorities. In: N. Blattner, H. Genberg, and A. Swoboda (eds.), *Competitiveness in Banking*. Heidelberg: Physica-Verlag.

Brennan, M., and Cao, H. H. (1997). International portfolio investment flows. *Journal of Finance* 52:S.1851–80.

Choi, S.-R., Park, D., and Tschoegl, A. E. (1996). Banks and the world's major banking centers, 1990. *Weltwirtschaftliches Archiv* 132:774–93.

Choi, S.-R., Tschoegl, A. E., and Yu, C.-M. (1986). Banks and the world's major financial centers, 1970–1980. *Weltwirtschaftliches Archiv* 122:48–64.

Christaller, W. (1933). *Die zentralen Orte in Süddeutschland*. Jena: Gustav Fischer Verlag.

Cooper, I., and Kaplanis, E. (1994). What explains the home bias in portfolio investment? *Review of Financial Studies* 7:45–60.

Coval, J., and Moskowitz, T. (1996). Home bias at home: local equity preference in domestic portfolios. Mimeograph, UCLA, Los Angeles.

Economides, N., and Siow, A. (1988). The division of markets is limited by the extent of liquidity (spatial competition with externalities). *American Economic Review* 78:108–21.

Gaspar, J., and Glaeser, E. L. (1996). Information technology and the future of cities. NBER working paper 5562.

Gehrig, T. (1993). An information based explanation of the domestic bias in international equity investment. *Scandinavian Journal of Economics* 95:97–109.

Gehrig, T. (1996). Natural oligopoly in intermediated markets. *International Journal of Industrial Organization* 14:101–18.

Gehrig, T. (1998). Competing markets. *European Economic Review* 42:277–310.

Gehrig, T., Stahl, K., and Vives, X. (1994). Competing exchanges. In: *The Location of Economic Activity*, pp. 549–81. London: CEPR, Vigo.

Gehrke, W., and Rasch, S. (1993). Europas Wertpapierbörsen im Umbruch. *ZEW Wirtschaftsanalysen* 4:306–36.

444 References

Goldberg, L., and Grosse, R. (1994). Location choice of foreign banks in the United States. *Journal of Economics and Business* 46:367–79.

Grabbe, O. (1996). *International Financial Markets*. Englewood Cliffs, NJ: Prentice-Hall.

Grilli, V. (1989). Financial markets. *Economic Policy* 4:387–421.

Grossman, S., and Stiglitz, J. (1980). On the impossibility of informationally efficient markets. *American Economic Review* 70:393–408.

Hellwig, M. (1980). On the aggregation of information in competitive markets. *Journal of Economic Theory* 22:477–98.

Jeger, M., Haegler, U., and Theiss, R. (1992). On the attractiveness of financial centers. In: N. Blattner, H. Genberg, and Swoboda, A. (eds.), *Competitiveness in Banking*. Heidelberg: Physica-Verlag.

Johnson, H. G. (1976). Panama as a regional financial center. *Economic Development and Cultural Change* 261.

Kang, J.-K., and Stulz, R. (1997). Why is there a home bias? An analysis of foreign portfolio equity ownership in Japan. *Journal of Financial Economics* 46:3–28.

Kim, S. (1990). Labour heterogeneity, wage bargaining, and agglomeration economics. *Journal of Urban Economics* 28:160–77.

Kindleberger, C. P. (1974). *The Formation of Financial Centers: A Study of Comparative Economic History*. Princeton University Press.

O'Brien, R. (1992). *Global Financial Integration: The End of Geography*. London: Royal Institute of International Affairs, Chatham House.

Ota, M., and Fujita, M. (1993). Communication technologies and spatial organization of multi-unit firms in metropolitan areas. *Regional Science and Urban Economics* 23:695–729.

Pagano, M. (1989). Trading volume and asset liquidity. *Quarterly Journal of Economics* 104:255–74.

Pagano, M., and Roell, A. (1990). Trading systems in European stock exchanges: current performance and policy options. *Economic Policy* 10:63–115.

Park, Y. S., and Essayyad, M. (1989). *International Banking and Financial Centers*. Boston: Kluwer.

Porteus, D. (1996). *The Geography of Finance*. Aldershot: Brookfield.

Reed, H. C. (1980). The ascent of Tokyo as an international financial center. *Journal of International Business Studies* 11:3 19–35.

Reed, H. C. (1981). *The Preeminence of International Financial Centers*. New York: Praeger.

Shuckla, R., and van Inwegen, G. (1995). Do locals perform better than foreigners? *Journal of Economics and Business* 47: 241–54.

Smith, C. (1991). Globalization of financial markets. In: A. Meltzer and C. Plosser (eds.), *Carnegie Rochester Series on Public Policy*, pp. 19–33. Amsterdam: North Holland.

Tesar, L., and Werner, I. (1995). Home bias and high turnover. *Journal of International Money and Finance* 14:467–92

The Economist (1995a). Turn up the lights: a survey of cities. 29 July 1995.

The Economist (1995b). Multinationals. 24 June 1995.

Tschoegl, A. E. (1989). The benefits and costs of hosting financial centers. In: Y. S. Park and M. Essayyad (eds.), *International Banking and Financial Centers*. Boston: Kluwer.

Yamori, N. (1998). A note on the location of multinational banks: the case of Japanese financial institutions. *Journal of Banking and Finance* 22:109–20.

Yamori, N., and Baba, T. (1997). Japanese management views on overseas exchange listings. Mimeograph, Nagoya University.

Index